This sixth edition was researched and written by Henry Stedman. His work built upon that of Alexander Stewart who wrote the previous two editions of this book.

Born in Chatham, Kent, **HENRY STEDMAN** (top, on the Salkantay trek) has been writing guidebooks for 20 years now and is the author of Trailblazer's guides to *Kilimanjaro, Coast to Coast Path, Hadrian's Wall Path, Dales Way* and the co-author of their three titles to the *South West Coast Path*.

An inveterate traveller, **ALEXANDER STEWART** (left, on the Santa Teresa trek) has walked, trekked and tramped in more than 30 countries around the world. Over the last decade he has written guidebooks for several publishers including for Trailblazer: *New Zealand – The Great Walks, The Walker's Haute Route* and *Peddars Way and Norfolk Coast Path*.

Below: A young traveller dwarfed by the massive stones of Sacsayhuaman.

Authors

The Inca Trail, Cusco & Machu Picchu

First edition: 1999; this sixth edition Sep 2017

Publisher Trailblazer Publications 🖳 www.trailblazer-guides.com
The Old Manse, Tower Rd, Hindhead, Surrey, GU26 6SU, UK

British Library Cataloguing in Publication Data
A catalogue record for this book is available from the British Library

ISBN 978-1-905864-88-1

© **Trailblazer** 2011, 2013, 2017: Text and maps (unless otherwise credited)
© **Hugh Thomson**: Text on pp90-102, and pp198-9

Editor: Neil Pike **Cartography**: Nick Hill **Layout**: Anna Jacomb-Hood
Proof-reading: Jane Thomas **Index**: Anna Jacomb-Hood
Photographs (flora): C1: top left and bottom right © Bryn Thomas
C2 top: middle and right © Bryn Thomas; all others © Alexander Stewart
Photographs (other): © Bryn Thomas unless otherwise credited

Acknowledgements

First of all, thank you Zoe for all your hard work and patience over three months and four
countries; thank you, too, for looking after our boy so beautifully – and making the return
home from each trek such a joy. And of course thanks to Henry Jr – you may not remember this trip in years to come, but you've given both of us memories that will last forever.

Thanks, too, to guides Nico (Salkantay) and Seb (Ausangate); Dr Jacob Smith for your
company on the Ausangate and Lares treks; Hazel Correa, Philip Morrow and Flavia
McMateo for their chats on the Inca Trail; and to Meagan Hom, Omri Shaffer, Jacob, Kelly
Abrams, Nathalia La Rotta, Julie Takagi, Josemir Sales and Mirella Nestor for the laughs
on the Salkantay Trek. Thanks also to Matt Waugh at the SAE for all his help and advice;
and Juan Carlos the archaeologist from Trujillo at the Dirección Regional de Cultura.

At Trailblazer, thanks as ever to Bryn Thomas for keeping me in trekking boots, to Neil
Pike for diligent editing and working so hard to ensure that everything came together, to
Anna Jacomb-Hood for layout, Jane Thomas for proof-reading, to Nick Hill for drawing the
maps and archaeological site plans and to Anna Jacomb-Hood for the index.

A request

The authors and publisher have tried to ensure that this guide is as accurate and up to date
as possible. Nevertheless, things change. If you notice any changes or omissions that should
be included in the next edition of this book, please write to Trailblazer (address above) or
email us at 🖳 info@trailblazer-guides.com. A free copy of the next edition will be sent to
persons making a significant contribution.

Warning: mountain walking can be dangerous

Please read the notes on when to go (pp10-12), safety (p34, pp88-9 & p339) and on health
and safety in the mountains (pp119-21). Every effort has been made by the author and publisher to ensure that the information contained herein is as accurate and up to date as possible. However, they are unable to accept responsibility for any inconvenience, loss or
injury sustained by anyone as a result of the advice and information given in this guide.

Updated information will be available on: 🖳 www.trailblazer-guides.com

Photos – Front cover: Machu Picchu **Overleaf**: Condor soaring above the Apurímac valley at the start of the Choquequiao trek **This page**: Machu Picchu (All © Henry Stedman)

Printed in China; print production by D'Print (☎ +65-6581 3832), Singapore

THE
Inca Trail
CUSCO & MACHU PICCHU

ALEXANDER STEWART
& HENRY STEDMAN

With additional material by
HUGH THOMSON
ALISON ROBERTS, SOPHIE CAMPBELL & BRYN THOMAS

TRAILBLAZER PUBLICATIONS

Contents

Contents

INTRODUCTION

The mystery of the deep valleys which lie in the quadrant north to north-east of Mount Salcantay have long demanded attention. Separated from Ollantaytambo and Amaybamba by the Grand Canyon of the Urubamba, protected from Cuzco by the gigantic barrier of Salcantay, isolated from Vitcos by deep valleys and inhospitable, high windswept bleak regions called punas, they seem to have been unknown to the Spanish Conquerors and unsuspected by the historians… it appears to have been a terra incognita.
Hiram Bingham, *Lost City of the Incas*

In July 1911 the American explorer Hiram Bingham stumbled across the Inca ruins at Machu Picchu, the archetypal Lost City. The discovery was the realisation of many people's dreams and it has since proved to be the inspiration for innumerable adventure tales; none of the world's other great ruins can compare with Machu Picchu's location on a knife-like ridge, amid thick forest, high above a tumultuous river

> **None of the world's other great ruins can compare with Machu Picchu's location on a knife-like ridge**

and frequently cloaked in swirling cloud, with the horn of Huayna Picchu punching through the mist and snow-capped mountains glittering on the horizon.

These days, Bingham's first encounter with Machu Picchu is described as a 'scientific discovery', for the approximate whereabouts of the ruins was already common knowledge amongst several local farmers. Indeed, Bingham was directed to the region by these farmers. As Bingham describes it, after

Impressive Inca stonework on the semicircular Temple at Machu Picchu.

hacking through the forest for several hours, all at once they 'were confronted with an unexpected sight, a great flight of beautifully constructed stone-faced terraces, perhaps a hundred of them, each hundreds of feet long and ten feet high'. Pushing on, 'without any warning', Bingham happened upon a cave carved into a stunningly sculpted structure whose 'flowing lines… symmetrical arrangement

---

(**Opposite**): Following the water channel towards Soray Pampa on the first day of the Salkantay trek and High Inca Trail, with the glaciated twin peaks of Humantay (5917m/19,412ft) rising ahead.

Huinay Huayna (see p230), the last major ruins on the Inca Trail before you reach Machu Picchu and the most spectacular up to this point.

of ashlars, and gradual gradation of the courses combined to produce a wonderful effect... It seemed like an unbelievable dream. Dimly, I began to realise that this wall and its adjoining semicircular Temple over the cave were as fine as the finest stonework in the world. It fairly took my breath away...'

This was not Bingham's first discovery in the region, 'scientific' or otherwise. Prior to the revelation of Machu Picchu, Bingham had explored and uncovered the ruins at Choquequirao. He was also responsible for discovering two other Inca sites of great importance, Vitcos and Vilcabamba. Countless other expeditions have subsequently explored the region and numerous discoveries have been made, though none as significant as those unearthed by Bingham. In addition to this, a network of Inca roads crisscrossing the mountains and landscapes have been found; these led to the creation of trekking routes for modern-day pilgrims and adventurers to follow. The **Inca Trail** is just one such route, which penetrates the forest and crosses high passes to reach its goal, the ruins at Machu Picchu.

Heavily promoted and justifiably popular, the celebrated four-day Inca Trail almost became a victim of its own success, as a result of which strict rules were brought in that limit the number of people allowed each day on both this trek and the shortened two-day version.

In the wake of these stringent regulations, alternative options to reach Machu Picchu have been established and treks to the other Inca sites have developed as genuine alternatives to the crowded classic trek. In particular, the **Salkantay Trek** (see photo p6) starting from the village of Mollepata, which climbs over the 4635m/15,206ft Salkantay Pass and avoids many of the regulations associated with the Inca Trail – yet still gets you to Machu Picchu.

The **Lares region** (see p266) provides tough but rewarding treks with high mountain passes and remote villages such as Cancha Cancha (above).

In this edition we have also included a trek of the little explored **Lares region**, a picturesque rural area of deep valleys connected by lofty mountain passes. This trek starts and ends at the Sacred Valley, from where it's easy to catch transport to the popular Inca towns of Pisac and Ollantaytambo. The railway station at Ollantaytambo is on the main line between Cusco and Aguas Calientes, from where it's a quick bus trip up to Machu Picchu.

Alternatively, you may prefer to visit Inca ruins which, while almost as extensive as Machu Picchu, and which can be found in a location arguably even more dramatic, receive far fewer visitors. The **Choquequirao Trek** is a tough three- to five-day trek overlooking the roaring Río Apurímac. Or you can steer clear of Inca ruins altogether and head instead to the divine **Ausangate** region. In this book we describe a hike around the mountain after which the region is named, a four-day trek through exquisite high-altitude scenery replete with lakes, glaciers and isolated settlements that many trekkers agree is pretty close to perfection.

All the above are described in extensive detail in this guide. We also look at the **Vilcabamba Trail** (see p339) which explores puna, pampa, pasture, cloud forest and rainforest to lead you to Espíritu Pampa, the last refuge of the Incas. It was these ruins that Hiram Bingham was actually looking for when he stumbled upon Machu Picchu. The largely unrestored ruins of Vilcabamba are mostly still camouflaged and concealed by the forest.

But the charms of this region are not confined solely to walking. In particular there's **Cusco**, the Inca capital and a contemporary world-class city, which wears its celebrity lightly and remains true to its past. The Incas built temples, palaces, aqueducts and roads worthy of an empire that stretched

Inca doorway at **Choquequirao** (see p281). The ruins straddle a ridge surrounded by forest, with terraces clinging to the sheer slopes.

The **Ausangate** trek (see p297) is a gorgeous but remote trail and you'll need to be self-sufficient. Alternatively, you can hire an *arriero* and they'll provide food and mules to carry your luggage.

Cusco – Plaza des Armas and La Compañía Jesuits' church with its impressive facade.

(All photos on these pages © Henry Stedman).

from Colombia to Chile. The Spanish conquistadors under Pizarro then used the precisely cut stones as the foundations for their opulent churches and monasteries. It's a fascinating place to visit with well-designed museums to fire the imagination, including the Casa de Concha that houses the artefacts taken from Machu Picchu by Bingham and recently returned from Yale University.

Despite the pressures of mass tourism and the popularity of the better-known sites, it is still possible to explore the Cusco region free from crowds. Just take up the challenge and follow in the footsteps of the pioneers.

When to go

The trekking season in Peru typically runs during the dry season from April to October when there is likely to be the most sunshine and least rain on the trails. During this period the trails get particularly busy between June and July and it can be hard to

The trekking season runs during the dry season from April to October

Below: On the Inca Trail, the ruins of Intipata (see p228) enjoy some of the best views down the Urubamba valley. © Henry Stedman.

secure permits for some of the most popular treks, such as the classic Inca Trail, without planning a long way in advance. To maximise your enjoyment and escape the worst of the crowds target April-May or September-October for your trip.

At other times of year it is still possible to tackle most of the trails but be aware that in the wet they can become very much trickier propositions than in the dry, and the changeable and occasion-

A rail service operates between Cusco (Poroy) and Aguas Calientes below Machu Picchu.

INTRODUCTION

ally awful weather means that some of the treks are a washout. The Vilcabamba Trail is particularly affected by heavy rain and during continued wet periods you may struggle to find an agency willing to make the trip. If considering trekking independently, you should be an experienced trekker before setting off on some of the more arduous, out-of-the-way routes at this time of

For route options see p27

year. Remember that although Machu Picchu itself is open year-round and can be an enchanting, mysterious place when shrouded in cloud and clear of crowds, **the classic Inca Trail is closed completely in February**.

FOR HOW LONG?

The popularity of the Cusco region with trekkers is entirely understandable. Amongst some exceptionally dramatic scenery are hidden ruins and lost cities to rival anywhere else in the world. The treks described in this book take between two and five days to complete. When calculating how long your trip needs to be, remember to allow a day each way to travel between Cusco and Lima (more if you decide to travel overland rather than fly) and a couple of days in Cusco at the beginning to aid acclimatisation. This last factor is very important and will improve your chances of enjoying and succeeding on your trek and reduce the likelihood of you suffering from altitude sickness and inadvertently endangering your life. Since this is South America you may also want to build in a contingency day in case there are problems with the flights in either direction.

If you haven't pre-booked your trek and are arriving in Cusco hoping to put something together on spec, remember that it is impossible, except perhaps in the middle of the rainy season, to secure a permit on the classic Inca Trail this quickly because of the restricted numbers permitted to start the trek each day (see p14). You should be able to put together a trek on one of the other routes within a couple of days, though.

LIMA – CLIMATE CHARTS

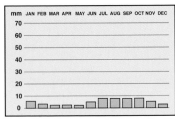

Max/min rainfall (mm)

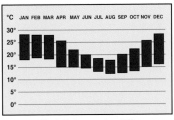

Max/min temperature (°C)

CUSCO – CLIMATE CHARTS

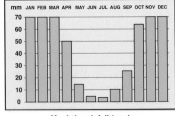

Max/min rainfall (mm)

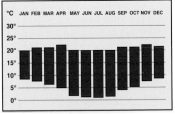

Max/min temperature (°C)

PLANNING YOUR TRIP

1

This section is designed to help you plan your trip: to make travel arrangements, calculate how much the trip will cost, and decide both when to go and which trek to take. It also sets out some simple rules to maximise your safety and outlines what to do in an emergency. There is a well-established trekking culture and infrastructure around Cusco. With the use of this book, an internet connection and just a little Spanish it's entirely feasible to organise your entire trip yourself.

Ultimately, though, how you approach your trip is a matter of personal choice and there's no substitute for practical experience when it comes to trekking. That said, the more you plan and prepare, the better equipped you are to deal with events on the ground, allowing you to make the most of the trip.

With a tour group or on your own?

In 2001 the Peruvian authorities outlawed independent trekking in the Machu Picchu Historical Sanctuary and brought in a series of strict regulations as to who could trek the trails to Machu Picchu and how they could tackle them. For a full breakdown of the regulations see box pp212-13 but, essentially, **you can only tackle the classic Inca Trail by signing up with a tour company or taking an accredited, licensed guide**. When the laws were first introduced, it was still possible to sneak onto the trail without paying. Since then the authorities have tightened up security and clamped down on people not abiding by the rules. Don't attempt the classic Inca Trail without a guide or without paying the proper fees. It's highly unlikely that you'll get away with it. Yes, it is a little expensive to trek the Inca Trail (see box p14) but the costs of maintaining the route are high and the regulations prevent overcrowding, excessive damage and erosion and help to reduce littering. Besides, almost whatever price you pay, it's still worth it.

For those who don't want to be constrained by the regulations, however, there are plenty of options. If you still want to trek to Machu Picchu take the Salkantay Trek (see p31) which is as yet largely free from regulations. Or take a hike in the Lares region (see p33) which finishes in the Sacred Valley, from where a combination of bus and train (do pre-book the latter) can convey you to the town of Aguas Calientes, from where you can catch a bus or hike up to Machu Picchu. Alternatively, head to the far less-visited ruins at Choquequirao (see pp32-3) or Vilcabamba (see box p34). Those whose interest in ruins is minimal, but who wish to see some of the most spectacular high-altitude scenery in South America, should take a bus over to Ausangate to tackle the 4-day hike around one of the region's most picturesque mountains (see pp33-4).

HOW TO BOOK

With the advent of tight restrictions on the number of people able to start the Inca Trail each day, your first priority on deciding to tackle the trek is to **book as far in advance as possible**. Long gone are the days of being able to turn up in Cusco and put together a trek there and then. Only 500 people in total are allowed on the Inca Trail each day, including guides and porters. This means that only around 200 tourists per day are able to begin the walk to Machu Picchu and each of these must have a permit that has been secured and paid for well in advance. The permits for the year used to be released in January, however, as we go to press it has just been announced that they will now be **released in October** for the following year. For the busy months they sell out within a few days.

Ultimately you should try and make a reservation as soon as you know your travel dates; during the peak season from June to August you ought to have

---

❏ Why is it so expensive?

The price of the classic 4-day Inca Trail may seem high but in comparison to other, equivalent treks worldwide it represents good value and has ensured a decent standard of general service, fair treatment of porters and increased revenue for a developing country. The flip side is that trekking on a budget is now nigh on impossible and as a result some less well-off individuals, including many Peruvians, are unable to tackle the trek.

The main issue is that there are some **fixed costs** that companies have to absorb whether you are taking a group service trek or a private service trek. Over recent years the cost of the classic Inca Trail has risen steeply as the government introduced minimum standards and started to enforce regulations. As a start point, the trek fee has to cover the accompanying crew's wages, food and transport. Then there's the entrance fee to the Inca Trail, s/292 (US$90) per person at the time of research; porters have to pay an entrance fee as well but at the reduced rate of s/42. Then there's food and fuel for your meals, the cost of camping kit and first-aid equipment, a bus from Machu Picchu to Aguas Calientes (currently US$12), a train ride from Aguas Calientes to Ollantaytambo (around US$78) and a private bus from Ollantaytambo to Cusco. Plus office costs and bank fees for holding the trek deposit. And, there's also the sales tax at 18%. The tax authorities have tightened up this aspect and you can now expect to pay around US$80 per person in sales tax, which is incorporated into the price of the trek. This all needs to be accounted for before the company running the expedition tries to make a profit.

The result is a minimum spend for every company operating an Inca Trail trek, although other costs vary considerably from company to company and are dependent on group size. If you choose a company with a smaller group size, expect the trip price to be higher.

things in place around six months ahead of your proposed trek departure date. Bear in mind that the departure dates aren't flexible and you are not allowed to change the name or passport details on the permit. Also, although Machu Picchu is open year-round, the classic Inca Trail is closed throughout February.

Do note that the above only refers to the classic four-day Inca Trail and the High Inca Trail. **If you want to tackle only the shortened, two-day version, there are usually plenty of permits available year-round for this and you should be able to pick one up at very short notice**.

Your second priority ought to be **choosing an agency**. Take time over this as it is an important decision: they are, after all, the ones who will arrange everything, supply the equipment and assign you a guide. Only licensed Peruvian agencies are entitled to sell **permits**, so you will have to make a reservation either directly with one of them, or through a separate tour company. By booking direct over the internet or by phone with the Peruvian agency you will potentially save yourself money by cutting out the middleman. You will also be dealing directly with the people who will be running and arranging your trip. You can take some satisfaction from the knowledge that whilst the money probably isn't going to the most destitute Peruvians, the money you spend on your trek will at least be going to support the local economy rather than into the pockets of a company outside Peru. For a list of the more-established, respected agencies in Cusco with secure online facilities see pp177-82. Alternatively, for the sake of convenience, you may wish to sign up with a foreign tour operator who will make all the arrangements on your behalf, for a fee. They will rarely offer you just a trek and nothing else. Airport transfers and accommodation in Cusco will nearly always be included in the package. For a bit extra they'll probably even organise your international flights, meaning that you can save yourself a considerable amount of time and hassle. For a selection of those who offer the Inca Trail amongst their activities see pp17-20.

If you fall foul of the regulations and are unable to organise a permit for the dates that you targeted, don't worry, simply check out the alternative route options that are outlined on pp30-4 and covered in detail later in this book. Whatever you do, do not be tempted to purchase tours or treks from sales people working in the airports or bus stations. Reputable companies do not operate like this. Always make a final reservation and conduct all payments in an agency office, making sure to ask for a written receipt and contract.

GROUP SERVICE OR PRIVATE SERVICE TREK

There are two main types of trek: 'group service' and 'private service'. The standard **group service** is the more popular and cheaper way of doing the trek. It involves joining a group of trekkers, so it can be a very social way of walking. However, you can end up with people of very mixed abilities and interests, meaning you may have to walk at a different pace than you'd like. The maximum group size is 16 people, though typically there will be 12-14 on the trail. If the group is larger than eight people, the regulations state that there must be two guides. That said, the trend is for smaller groups as it becomes harder for

❑ **On the trail with a trekking group**
Typically a day on any of the trails in the company of an agency-guided trek starts
with an early wake-up call and cup of tea in your tent. The porters will then bring a
bowl of warm water for you to wash in, whilst breakfast is prepared. The first meal
of the day usually consists of a hearty combination of fruit, porridge, bread and sometimes eggs. Following this, the day's walk will begin.

During the trek you are required to carry only a day pack containing wet- and
warm-weather clothing, adequate water, and supplies such as a camera and important
documents as the porters or *arrieros* (muleteers/donkey men) will shoulder the bulk
of the luggage. In the course of the morning the porters will catch up and overtake
you and then will race ahead to prepare lunch at a designated stop. After a brief break
in which to eat, the trek continues at a leisurely pace until you arrive at the next
evening's campsite, usually well before sunset. This gives you enough time to relax,
reflect and unwind before supper and a well-deserved early night.

agencies to secure permits as group size increases. Typically, travelling in a
group of 12-14, a trek costs US$500-600; the actual amount depends on the
agency and level of service provided. The basic maths ought to prove it's not feasible to run a quality trek for less than US$500; see box p14. At the other end of
the scale, prices can be double this if you book with a foreign tour operator.

The other option is to take a **private service** trek, which is laid on for just
you and your friends. Inevitably, if there are only a few of you this is a much
more expensive option as the cost of the guide, cook and porters has to be split
between just a handful of trekkers. Two people on a private service trek might
expect to pay around US$1700 each; with four this would fall to US$1050; and
with six people, expect to cough up US$850 each. Groups of 8-14 people
should anticipate spending US$620-750. The maximum group size is still 16 on
a private service trek, for which each person would pay around US$600. Prices
can again vary widely from company to company depending on the sort of service offered. In addition to smaller groups, you will also receive more attention,
probably be treated better and enjoy greater comforts than the group service can
offer. By booking a private service you are also more likely to get the departure
dates you want as the agency can close the booking as soon as you sign up; with
a group service they can't confirm the permits until they are ready to book the
entire group, so whilst waiting for the last spaces to be filled it is possible they
miss the boat and all the permits are bought by others. If that's the case, the trek
will be cancelled or they will attempt to offer you alternative dates. Ultimately,
you get what you pay for.

VISITING MACHU PICCHU WITHOUT DOING A TREK

It is, of course, entirely possible to visit the ruins at Machu Picchu without
undertaking any of the treks described here. Most of the companies listed in
Cusco and abroad offer basic tours of the ruins and will arrange to shuttle you
from Cusco to Aguas Calientes and from there up to the site itself.

It is equally easy, and potentially cheaper, to get to the ruins simply by using public transport. There is a train service from Cusco to Aguas Calientes and a bus service from there to Machu Picchu. For those on a really low budget there is a more arduous and time-consuming but usually cheaper way of accessing Aguas Calientes by bus followed by a short section of easy walking (see p183).

TOUR OPERATORS AND TREKKING AGENCIES

Booking with an agent in Peru (see pp177-82) is the cheapest way to organise your trek and most now have a website through which you can do this. Booking with a company in your home country, though, can provide additional peace of mind and get you a package that includes flights and transfers, albeit at a price. Most of the operators listed below operate treks on all the routes described in this book.

Agencies in the UK and Ireland

● **Amazonas Explorer** (🖥 www.amazonas-explorer.com), based in Peru (Cusco; see p177) but owned by British/Swiss expats, offer the Inca Trail, Choquequirao Trek and are one of the leading experts on the Lares region, a trek that culminates in the short Inca trail trek from Km104.

● **Andes** (☎ 01556 503929, 🖥 www.andes.org.uk) specialise in climbing expeditions but also tailor-make an Inca Mountain trek that is run on request.

● **Andean Trails** (☎ 0131 467 7086, 🖥 www.andeantrails.co.uk) organise treks for small groups including the Inca Trail, Lares, Ausangate (including a lodge-based Ausangate trek) and Choquequirao treks as well as tailor-made itineraries.

● **Audley Travel** (☎ 01993 838620, 🖥 www.audleytravel.com) offer a 14-day tour including the Inca Trail, and will also tailor-make a holiday round any of the treks in the region.

● **Charity Challenge** (☎ 020 8346 0500, 🖥 www.charitychallenge.com) arranges treks in the Lares region culminating in a visit to Machu Picchu, all for a number of charities.

● **Discover Adventure** (☎ 01722 718444, 🖥 www.discoveradventure.com) organise ordinary treks on the Inca Trail as well as treks for charity.

● **Exodus** (☎ 0845 863 9616, 🖥 www.exodus.co.uk) arrange a variety of treks and tours and are one of the few companies to offer the Salkantay Trek that links with the Inca Trail, which they call the High Inca Trail – a name we have adopted in this book too; see p31.

● **Explore** (☎ 01252 883726, 🖥 www.explore.co.uk) is a large company doing the Inca Trail and Salkantay Trek to Machu Picchu as well as several other Peruvian tours.

● **G Adventures** (formerly Gap Adventures; ☎ 0344 272 2060, 🖥 www.gadventures.com) A well-run international organisation offering many tours on the Inca Trail and the Salkantay Trek.

● **HF Holidays** (☎ 0345 470 8558, 🖥 www.hfholidays.co.uk) offer a couple of tours to Peru which include Machu Picchu and the Inca Trail.

● **High Places** (☎ 0114 352 0060, 🖥 www.highplaces.co.uk) operate an 18-day tour including Ausangate and Inca Trail treks.

● **Imaginative Traveller** (☎ 01728 862230, 💻 www.imaginative-traveller.com) offer several trips including the Inca Trail.

● **Intrepid Travel** (☎ 0808 274 5111, 💻 www.intrepidtravel.com) offer a variety of treks including the Inca Trail.

● **Journey Latin America** (☎ 020 3131 5186, 💻 www.journeylatinamerica.co.uk) are a well-established company for tours to South America; they arrange Inca Trail, Salkantay (both walking and horse-riding!), Lares, Ausangate and Choquequirao treks and can also tailor-make holidays.

● **KE Adventure Travel** (☎ 01768 773966, 💻 www.keadventure.com) arrange the Inca Trail, the Salkantay and Choquequirao treks as well as an intriguing extended trek from Ollantaytambo via Chilca, Paucarcancha and the Inca Trail to Machu Picchu.

● **Last Frontiers** (☎ 01296 653000, 💻 www.lastfrontiers.com) tailor-make holidays including the Inca Trail, High Inca Trail, Choquequirao, Lares and Salkantay treks (the last two on behalf of Mountain Lodges of Peru; see p181).

● **Llama Travel** (☎ 020 7263 3000, 💻 www.llamatravel.com) specialise in good-value trekking trips to Peru, including the Inca Trail as well as tours to Machu Picchu. Recommended.

● **Mountain Kingdoms** (☎ 01453 844400, 💻 www.mountainkingdoms.com) offer a variety of tailor-made treks including the Inca Trail, Salkantay Trek with Mountain Lodges of Peru (see p181) and a trip to Choquequirao.

● **Naturetrek** (☎ 01962 733051, 💻 www.naturetrek.co.uk) organise a Macaws and Machu Picchu trek, which includes the Inca Trail.

● **Peregrine** (☎ 020 7408 9021, 💻 www.peregrineadventures.com), an Australian outfit, offer a variety of holidays in the region which include the Inca Trail.

● **Pura Aventura** (☎ 01273 676712, 💻 www.pura-aventura.com) arrange Inca Trail treks as part of larger tours of Peru.

● **Rainbow Tours** (☎ 020 3131 6675, 💻 www.rainbowtours.co.uk) tailor-make tours to Peru and can include the Inca Trail, a Lares adventure, and a five-day trek in the Ausangate region to the celebrated Rainbow Mountain; they also operate the Salkantay Trek staying in Mountain Lodges of Peru lodges (see p181).

● **Red Spokes** (☎ 020 7502 7252, 💻 www.redspokes.co.uk) organise cycling trips in Peru as well as the Inca Trail trek, on foot.

● **Tucan Travel** (☎ 0800 8048435, 💻 www.tucantravel.com) is one of the largest tour operators in the area and organise everything from 7- to 65-day trips to Peru including the Inca Trail and a Lares trek. They have an operations office in Cusco (Av El Sol 616, Office 202).

● **Walks Worldwide** (☎ 01962 737565, 💻 www.walksworldwide.com) offer Inca Trail, Lares and Salkantay treks.

● **World Expeditions** (☎ 020 8875 5060, 💻 www.worldexpeditions.co.uk) arrange Inca Trail, Salkantay, and Choquequirao to Machu Picchu treks as well as tours which include the Inca Trail. They also arrange charity challenges.

Agencies in Continental Europe
- **Austria** El Mundo Reiseburo (☎ 0316 810698, 💻 www.elmundo.at).
- **Belgium** Allibert Trekking (☎ 02 318 32 02, 💻 www.allibert-trekking .com); **Joker** (💻 www.joker.be); **Divantoura** (☎ 09 223 00 69, 💻 www.divan toura.be).
- **Denmark** Inter-Travel (☎ 33 15 00 77, 💻 www.inter-travel.dk) Agents for Explore, see p17.
- **France** Allibert Trekking (☎ 04 76 45 50 50, 💻 www.allibert-trekking .com) Has branches in Paris, Chamonix, Nice, Chapareillan and Toulouse as well as in Belgium and Switzerland; **Huwans Club Aventure** (☎ 04 96 15 10 20, 💻 www.huwans-clubaventure.fr).
- **Germany** Chamäleon (☎ 030 347996-0, 💻 www.chamaeleon-reisen.de).
- **Netherlands** Kilroy (☎ 20 5245 100, 💻 www.kilroyworld.nl)
- **Switzerland** Allibert Trekking (☎ 022 519 03 23, 💻 www.allibert-trek king.com).

Agencies in the USA
- **Adventure Life** (☎ 1-406-541-2677, 💻 www.adventure-life.com) Arrange a variety of tours and treks in the region.
- **Andean Treks** (☎ 1-800-683-8148 or ☎ 617-924-1974, 💻 www.andeantreks .com) have many years of experience arranging tours and treks throughout Peru.
- **Explore** (☎ 1-800-715-1746, 💻 www.exploreworldwide.com) See p17.
- **G Adventures** (☎ 1-888-800-4100, 💻 www.gadventures.com) See also p17.
- **Holbrook Travel** (☎ 1-800-451-7111, 💻 www.holbrooktravel.com) No Inca Trail treks as standard but they offer several different Peru tours and can tailor-make your itinerary.
- **Tucan Travel** (New York & San Francisco ☎ 1-855-444-9110, 💻 www.tucan travel.com) See opposite.
- **Wilderness Travel** (☎ 510-558-2488, toll-free ☎ 1-800-368 2794, 💻 www .wildernesstravel.com) A company with a fine reputation; specialises in cultur-al, wildlife and trekking tours including a hike in the Sacred Valley, the Inca Trail and a Choquequirao trek; also offers a Salkantay trek staying in the Mountain Lodges of Peru, see p181.
- **Wildland Adventures** (☎ 1-800-345-4453, 💻 www.wildland.com) are a leading eco-tourism operator offering a variety of itineraries including the Inca Trail, Lares and a Mountain Lodges Salkantay trek, see p181.
- **World Expeditions** (☎ 1-613-241-2700, 💻 www.worldexpeditions.com); see opposite.

Agencies in Canada
- **Charity Challenge** (☎ 1-519-866-3362, 💻 www.charitychallenge.ca) See p17.
- **Explore** (☎ 1-888-216-3401, 💻 www.exploreworldwide.ca) See p17.
- **G Adventures** (☎ 1-416 260 0999, 💻 www.gadventures.com) See p17.
- **Tucan Travel** (Toronto; ☎ 1-855-566-8660, 💻 www.tucantravel.com) See opposite.

PLANNING YOUR TRIP

● **World Expeditions** (🖥 www.worldexpeditions.com/ca) has a branch in Ottawa (☎ 613-241-2700) as well as in Montreal (Expéditions Monde; ☎ 514-844-6364, toll-free ☎ 1-866-606-1721, 🖥 www.expeditionsmonde.com). See p18.

Agencies in Peru
See Cusco, pp177-82.

Agencies in South Africa
● **Exciting Destinations** (☎ 43-735 0983) Agent for Inca Tours, see below.
● **Tucan Travel** (☎ (+27) 0800 983999, 🖥 www.tucantravel.com); see p18.

Agencies in Australia
● **Adventure Associates** (☎ 02-6355 2022, 🖥 www.adventureassociates.com)
● **Adventure World** (☎ 1300 295 049, 🖥 www.adventureworld.com.au) Operate their own tours and are agents for some tours by other agencies.
● **Explore** (☎ 1300 439 756, 🖥 www.exploreworldwide.com.au) See p17.
● **G Adventures** (☎ 1300 853 325, 🖥 www.gadventures.com) See p17.
● **Inca Tours** (☎ 02-4351 2133 or toll-free ☎ 1-800 024 955, 🖥 www.incatours.net) Operates a variety of tours and treks.
● **Intrepid Travel** (☎ 03-86014422, 🖥 www.intrepidtravel.com) See p18. Intrepid has branches all over Australia; see their website for details.
● **Peregrine** (☎ 1300-854445, 🖥 www.peregrineadventures.com) See p18.
● **Tucan Travel** (☎ 02-9326 6633, ☎ 1-300 769249, 🖥 www.tucantravel.com) See p18.
● **World Expeditions** (toll free ☎ 1300 720 000, 🖥 www.worldexpeditions.com.au) has branches in: Sydney, Melbourne, Brisbane, Adelaide and Perth; see p18.

Agencies in New Zealand
● **Adventure World** (toll-free ☎ 0800 238368, 🖥 www.adventureworld.co.nz).
● **Explore** (☎ 0800 269 263, 🖥 www.exploreworldwide.co.nz) See p17.
● **High Places** (☎ 03 540 3208, 🖥 www.highplaces.co.nz) See p17.
● **Tucan Travel** (☎ 0800 005 100, 🖥 www.tucantravel.com) See p18.
● **World Expeditions** (☎ 09 368 4161, ☎ 0800-350354, 🖥 www.worldexpeditions.co.nz) See p18.

PORTERS, ARRIEROS AND GUIDES

In most instances you are likely to tackle the treks described here with an agency or tour company from Cusco, indeed in some cases this is the only way of undertaking the treks. The agency will supply you with guides, porters or mules. However, at the time of writing, **all the treks in this book apart from those covered by Inca Trail regulations (see pp212-13) can be done independently**, or with *arrieros* (muleteers) and mules that you have hired yourself.

Hiring arrieros and porters
Arrieros can be hired in Cusco. However, the best deal, and the best way of supporting the local economy, is to hire your team of muleteers from the start of the

❏ **The life of a porter**
The film *Mi Chacra* (🖳 www.michacrafilm.com), meaning 'My Land', is an award-winning documentary by Jason Burlage that chronicles the life of a porter. Framed by the seasons, the film was shot in 2007 and 2008 and follows a Peruvian farmer and his family from planting to harvest and through a season as a porter on the Inca Trail. The film was shot on the Inca Trail and in the family's village of Mullacas, in the mountains above the Sacred Valley. It showcases the natural beauty of the Sacred Valley but also provides a window into the lives of the Andean people, whilst painting a vivid portrait of the complexities of rural life and the reality of the conditions for porters working the trek to Machu Picchu.

trek or town closest to the trailhead. For the Salkantay Trek look for arrieros in Mollepata (see box p240); for the Choquequirao Trek try Cachora (pp287-8) or Colmena (p288). For the Lares Trek, your best bet would not be Huaran, where the trail starts, but Cancha Cancha, meaning that you'll have to trek for the first few hours uphill without one. For the Ausangate region arrieros usually meet tourists off the bus at the trailhead at Tinke, so you should have no trouble finding one there. Finally, for the Vilcabamba Trail try Huancacalle (see p341).

At the time of hiring, negotiate a fair price for a fair service. Don't exploit the local populace and don't haggle ridiculously hard for the sake of a few *soles* (see p117). **Note, too, that in addition to *his* service you'll also pay a daily rate for each mule that you use**. The arriero may insist on taking a second mule. This is not a con trick to get you to part with more money, it is an insurance factor should one mule go lame or get injured, or should you need to ride at any point due to exhaustion. At the time make sure you agree exactly what is expected of the arriero. Also agree where he will sleep and who will feed him; you may be required to provide shelter and meals for the duration of the trek. Bear in mind that you will need to factor in a sum for the time it takes the arrieros to return home after the trek, and you should allow for a tip too if they provide particularly good service.

For an arriero, the rate is around s/30-50 per day, plus a similar daily amount per mule. A tip in the order of 5-10% of the total fee is reasonable, but consider how hard the guy worked on your behalf and give generously. A porter will expect a similar amount to an arriero per day. See also box pp22-3.

Getting to Peru

BY AIR

Getting to Peru by air is relatively straightforward and by far the most common means of accessing the country. All international flights from Europe and North America use Lima's Jorge Chávez International Airport (🖳 www.lap.com.pe), a smart, modern airport voted the Best in South America in 2012.

Airlines with routes to and from Peru (Lima) include Aerolíneas Argentinas, AeroMéxico, Air Canada, Air France, Alitalia, American Airlines, Avianca, British Airways, Copa Airlines, Delta Airlines, Iberia, KLM, LATAM, LC Perú,

❏ PORTER WELFARE

Roughly 7000 porters now service the needs of the tens of thousands of tourists who walk the Inca Trail each year. These people have often been exploited in the past and frequently worked with inadequate, inappropriate clothing and gear for derisory wages. While this situation has changed there are still improvements to be made and unscrupulous agencies to be weeded out. There are now several organisations dedicated to the issue of porter welfare who are campaigning for better working conditions and reasonable rates of pay.

As an individual trekking to Machu Picchu, or any of the other sites in the area, there are several things you can do to improve the plight of those making your trek possible. **Let the agency in charge of your trek know that the welfare of porters is important to you**. Make sure they understand that you consider it an important factor when it comes to selecting an agency to run your trek. Porters need fair wages, decent meals and warm, dry overnight accommodation. There is still room for improvement with all of the agencies, but some are markedly better than others. Some of the cheaper agencies won't have the porters' best interests at heart or be paying them adequately (see box p14).

The Peruvian government has introduced laws to try to establish a minimum wage on the trail of s/43 per day. Food rations and transport to the trailhead should also be provided by their agency. Unfortunately, many operators have found it easy to bypass these regulations and typically pay around s/30 per day; some of the most unscrupulous agencies also expect their porters to pay for their own transport and even food.

The law also states that **porters should not carry in excess of 25kg**, a figure that includes a 5kg personal allowance for items such as blankets and clothes. Although strictly enforced, some companies make great efforts to get round this particular regulation. Don't stand for such sharp practice and say something if you see an abuse being perpetrated. Also enquire about the standard of equipment used by the porters; do they have waterproof clothing? Do they all sleep in tents with integral floors and have access to sleeping bags and mats? Showing you care about such things will encourage all operators and agencies to treat their porters fairly.

On the trek, **try to interact with your porters**. Take time to talk to them and learn something about their lives. Many have low self esteem so be bold and initiate the process, share some coca leaves (see box p84) and pick up a few words of Quechua (*Allillanchu?* means 'How are you?' whilst *Añáy* means 'Thank you'); see also pp345-9. The porters often have colourful stories to tell and can offer you a real insight into Andean traditions and culture.

At the end of the trek **make sure you tip your porters** and that they get the money that is intended for them. Tipping directly to each individual member of the team ensures they receive a fair share. Show them you appreciate the work they have done on your behalf by thanking them verbally and individually.

Report unscrupulous trekking agencies

If you witness porter abuse or neglect, or encounter unscrupulous agencies taking advantage of their porters, bring it to the attention of the guide. Upon your return to Cusco, make an official complaint at the agency office, ideally in front of other

Lufthansa, Peruvian Airlines, Star Peru, TACA, United Airlines and Varig. Fares vary according to the airline, the time of year and the route you take but are generally quite costly. The two high seasons and thus the most expensive fares are

potential clients, and if sufficiently bad, submit a report to the International Porter Protection Group. Equally, do let us know if you've had either a particularly good or poor experience on your trek. Your observations will mean that agencies are forced to face the fact that the issue is important and that in order to continue to do business they must respect those porters working for them and look after them properly.

Of course, if you are trekking independently and hiring guides, arrieros or porters directly, you personally need to take responsibility for the welfare of the team you hire, and again abide by the basic guidelines set out above.

International Porter Protection Group (IPPG)
The IPPG (⌨ ippg.net) is a volunteer organisation that is dedicated to improving the conditions of mountain porters in the tourism industry worldwide. Unfortunately the Inka Porter Project (Porteadores Inka Ñan) is no more and the IPPG website no longer carries any specific advice about trekking in Peru. Nevertheless, the IPPG's website carries plenty of useful advice and outlines a number of measures that you can take to ensure you have a positive effect on your porters and their welfare. In particular, the IPPG recommends you ask the following when booking the Inca Trail:

● Does the company follow the **IPPG's five guidelines on porter safety**? These are:
  1. Adequate clothing for protection from bad weather and high altitude should be provided to porters. This may mean windproof jackets and trousers, suitable footwear, socks, hats and gloves.
  2. Porters should have access to shelter, either in a room, lodge or tent (the trekkers' dining tent is not acceptable as it rarely has an integral floor and is not usually available until late evening, meaning that the porters potentially have to wait in inclement weather without shelter), sleeping bags and mats as well as cooking equipment.
  3. Porters should have the same access to medical care as tourists and also be covered by some form of insurance.
  4. Porters should not be paid off because of illness/injury without the guide or the trekkers assessing their condition carefully. The person in charge of the porters (sirdar) must let their trek leader or the trekkers know if a sick porter is about to be paid off. Failure to do this has resulted in many deaths. Sick/injured porters should never be sent down alone, but with someone who speaks their language and understands their problem, along with a letter describing their complaint. Sufficient funds should be provided to cover cost of rescue and treatment.
  5. Porters should carry no more than 25kg according to Peruvian law. Weight limits might need to be adjusted taking into consideration altitude, weather conditions and the state of the path. Child porters should never be employed.
● What is the company's policy on equipment and health care for porters?
● What does the company do to ensure its staff are properly trained to look after porters' welfare?
● Does the company ask about the treatment of porters in its post-trek questionnaire?
● If booking the trek from outside Peru, or through a middleman or agent who hires another agency to run the trek itself, you should also ask about that company's policy on training and monitoring porter care by its ground operator in Peru.

PLANNING YOUR TRIP

from mid December to mid January and July to mid August. The majority of the agencies listed on pp17-20 will be able to organise tickets on your behalf; otherwise check out their respective websites to see if you can secure a discount by booking online. International air fares are expensive in Peru as a result of high taxes so you are better off buying an open return if you don't know when you'll be coming back rather than trying to purchase a one-way ticket home once in Peru. (For details of the controversy surrounding the new International airport near Cusco, see box p195.)

From Europe

British Airways now operate a 14-hour service from the UK to Peru (Lima) – the only airline currently offering a direct flight from the UK. Otherwise, you'll have to fly via other European hubs such as Madrid or Amsterdam; via cities in the USA; or possibly via another Latin American country. Flight times are 16-22 hours depending on the route. Fares from the UK start at around £600 but rise very quickly.

For the best deals look at websites such as: ⌨ www.travelup.com, ⌨ www.ebookers.com, ⌨ www.expedia.co.uk or ⌨ www.cheapflights.com. Or visit ⌨ www.skyscanner.net, which surveys the offers from all the above websites – and several more – to find the cheapest fares.

UK-based travel agents to consider include: Flight Centre (☎ 0844 800 8660, ⌨ www.flightcentre.co.uk); STA Travel (☎ 0871 230 0040, ⌨ www.statravel.co.uk) which specialises in fares for students; Trailfinders (☎ 020 7368 1200, ⌨ www.trailfinders.com); Travel Bag (☎ 0871 703 4698, ⌨ www.travelbag.co.uk).

From the USA and Canada

Direct flights to Lima operate out of Atlanta, Dallas, Houston and Los Angeles although the major gateways are Miami and New York. Air Canada can book you all the way through from Toronto, and operate connecting flights from most Canadian cities including Montreal, Edmonton, Vancouver and Calgary to Toronto.

For good deals try: Exito Travel (USA ☎ 1 800 655 4053, Canada ☎ 800 670 2605, ⌨ www.exitotravel.com), who specialise in flights to South America; Cheap Flights (⌨ www.cheapflights.ca); STA Travel (☎ 1 800 781 4040, ⌨ www.statravel.com); Travel CUTS/Voyages Campus (☎ 1 800 667 2887, ⌨ www.travelcuts.com).

From Australia and New Zealand

There are no direct flights from either Australia or New Zealand to Peru. Flights are generally via the USA or a South American gateway. For good deals visit ⌨ www.cheapflights.com.au or ⌨ www.cheapflights.co.nz; alternatively, both Flight Centre (⌨ www.flightcentre.com.au or ⌨ www.flightcentre.co.nz) and STA Travel (⌨ www.statravel.com.au or ⌨ www.statravel.co.nz) have offices throughout Australia and New Zealand.

OVERLAND

The Darien Gap separating Panama and Colombia is uncrossed by either roads or railways. This missing chunk of the Pan American Highway effectively prevents all but the most adventurous from travelling overland to Peru. There are routes to Peru from neighbouring South American countries, though. This isn't quite as straightforward as it might appear, but it is possible to access Peru from Bolivia, Brazil, Chile, Colombia and Ecuador.

From **Bolivia** buses from La Paz cross overland into Southern Peru. It is also possible to cross the border on Lake Titicaca and then access Cusco from Puno. Overland travel from **Brazil** to Peru is possible via Iñapari or through the jungle to Puerto Maldonado, which is a long bus ride from Cusco. Alternatively, catch a ferry from Manaus to Iquitos, a thrilling journey that takes around 10 days and from where you can fly to Cusco.

The Pan American Highway crosses from **Chile** to Peru between Arica and Tacna in Peru's south. Buses from Tacna then go to Arequipa or Puno from where you can connect with others going on to Cusco.

The route into Peru from **Colombia** is hardly ever used but is feasible, crossing from one country to the other at Leticia and then pushing upriver to Iquitos. From **Ecuador** there are several road options into Northern Peru.

Budgeting

If you are planning on trekking with an organised group the major expense on a trekking trip to Peru will be the trek itself. For an outing on the four-day classic Inca Trail, set aside at least US$500 for a basic trek, more if you use a better agency with a well-established reputation or want to trek in a private group. Once on the Inca Trail though you won't have to pay for anything other than the occasional soft drink or snack from one of the locals' stands along the way. However, on any of the other routes which are not subject to the Inca Trail regulations you can trek independently and make all the arrangements yourself; carry your own bag and cook your own food and you'll find that the days that you spend trekking are the cheapest of your entire trip.

Away from the trails and the mountains, Cusco can cost virtually as little or as much as you like. In the main, transport, food and accommodation, the biggest three expenses in most people's travels, are reasonable and good value. You can of course treat yourself to a first-class train ride, a posh meal and de luxe accommodation, all of which are readily available in both Lima and Cusco.

As a guide, budget travellers can probably get by on less than US$20 per day, whilst up to US$50 buys you a better meal and the odd taxi ride as well as a private hot shower in more salubrious accommodation. More than US$100 should mean that you enjoy a comfortable stay and eat very well. A fully guided tour run by an international agency will almost certainly cost you far more though.

ACCOMMODATION

As with most things, you get what you pay for, and cheap, non-tourist accommodation is often available in rather grubby, sleazy parts of town. Basic tourist accommodation starts at around US$5-15 per night for a dorm, and a comfortable double room in a budget hotel should cost you US$25-50. A mid-range hotel might set you back US$50-100 per night. At the other end of the spectrum, rooms in five-star international chain hotels can easily cost US$300 whilst for luxury accommodation the sky's the limit.

The seasons impact heavily on prices, and in Cusco during the height of the season (June to August), you may find prices increase by up to 25%. The same thing happens around a major celebration or fiesta (see pp86-7).

Accommodation on the trek is almost always camping unless you use one of the trekking companies that have built lodges on the trail (ie Mountain Lodges, Salkantay Trekking or the budget Refugios Salkantay chain); the cost of your trek will increase considerably (less so with Refugios Salkantay), but so does the quality of your overnight stay.

FOOD

By roughing it in the countryside, eating locally sourced produce bought at market or from villagers, you can get by on very little. Even in major towns food can be dirt cheap if you stick to the street vendors who ply their wares at all hours of day and night or take advantage of the good set menu deals available in local restaurants, although hygiene standards are not always of the highest.

You will be able to find a good meal in a decent, clean restaurant for less than US$10. Top-end venues with superb reputations and food to match, of which there are plenty in Peru, will naturally set you back rather more.

TRANSPORT

Public transport costs are usually very reasonable in Peru, even for long-distance journeys. You are, of course, at the mercy of cramped, dilapidated buses and dozy drivers, but this is the reality of public transport here. Then again, rates are so reasonable it seems churlish to complain. Additional comfort and safety comes at only a slightly higher price if you opt to travel by private, luxury bus.

The exception to the good-value rule is the train from Cusco or Ollantaytambo to Aguas Calientes (see pp352-5), which has far higher rates than you might expect, as it is a monopoly and caters to a captive audience of eager tourists.

❏ **Other activities**
The Cusco region offers far more than simply trekking. Unless your schedule is tight, you should consider some of the other world-class activities, such as mountain-biking, white-water rafting, ballooning, sky-diving and trips to the rainforest – all available on the city's doorstep.

Route options

[**See Route Options map pp28-9**]. The treks described in this book include a selection of routes to Machu Picchu which take various lengths of time and cater for people of varying abilities and interest levels.

The legendary Inca Trail has become a 'must do' for many travellers. However, the popularity of the trek has meant that the trail and the ruins along it have had to deal with an increasing number of visitors. To counter the detrimental effects of this influx, the Peruvian government has imposed a strict limit on the number of people able to start the trek at any one time. The result has been that many people have fallen foul of the regulations and been unable to tackle the trek. Indeed, these days the most difficult part of the classic Inca Trail is trying to book it in the first place; if you achieve that, you'll find the actual trek itself is relatively straightforward in comparison.

The good news, though, is that there are a couple of alternative treks to Machu Picchu that aren't (currently) subject to the same restrictions but which nevertheless deliver you to the door of the ruins. Most famously and popularly, the Salkantay Trek offers delightful scenery and a 4635m pass on its way to the ruins. The Lares region, to the east of Machu Picchu, also offers spectacular scenery and trekkers can finish a Lares trek in the Sacred Valley, from where a combination of bus and train can take you to Aguas Calientes, in the valley below the Machu Picchu ruins. Alternatively you can ignore Machu Picchu altogether, opting instead for the trail to the less well-known but similarly stunning site of Choquequirao; a route and ruin that are more appealing in some respects as you don't have to share them with hundreds of other people. Or you can forget about ruins altogether and instead head to Ausangate, a wonderful place for trekking with views and scenery to take the breath away.

THE CLASSIC INCA TRAIL   [3-4 days, see pp215-31]

This is the trek that most people think of when picturing Peru: it has become synonymous with the country. Beginning at Km88 on the railway line to Aguas Calientes, the trek follows an original Inca path uncovered in 1911 by Hiram Bingham and developed in 1944 by Dr Paul Fejos, past the restored ruins at Patallacta, Runcu Raccay, Sayac Marca, Phuyu Pata Marca, Intipata and Huinay Huayna to arrive eventually at Machu Picchu.

The **33km (20½-mile) trek** is reasonably straightforward although the second day is fairly tough as it involves two steep passes, the highest at 4235m/ 13,894ft. The rewards are ample, for not only are there the ruins themselves but some of the trek is through exquisite cloud forest and rich subtropical jungle and bleak, damp puna.   (cont'd on p30)

PLANNING YOUR TRIP

Route options

Lares Trek
From Huaran to Yanahuara. A tough four-day yomp through the little-visited Lares Region, crossing numerous mountain passes and encountering several isolated mountain villages.

Classic Inca Trail
The classic route to Machu Picchu takes 3-4 days and begins at Km88. Other tours start at Km82 or Km77.

Machu Picchu
Santa Teresa
Aguas Calientes
La Hidroeléctrica
Lucmabamba
Km88
Km82
Km77
Ollantaytambo
Lares
Cancha Cancha
Ccolpapampa
Yanama
Chaullay
Salkantay △
Huayllabamba
Yanahuara
Urubamba
Huaran
Choquequirao
Soray
Pampa Cahuana
Marcoccasa
Mollepata
Huarocondo
Huarocondo
Pisac
Izcuchaca
Poroy
Limatambo
Cachora
Cusco
Abancay

Choquequirao Trek
From Cachora to Choquequirao and back takes 4-5 days, descending into then climbing out of the breathtakingly sheer Apurímac Valley.

Salkantay Trek
Currently permit free, this 3- to 4-day trek starts in Mollepata. It follows the forested Santa Teresa valley to La Hidroeléctrica at the foot of Machu Picchu Mountain.

High Inca Trail
From Mollepata to Huayllabamba and onwards. From Soray Pampa the trail climbs to the 4948m Abra Inka Chiriasqa before uniting with the Classic Trail at Huayllabamba.

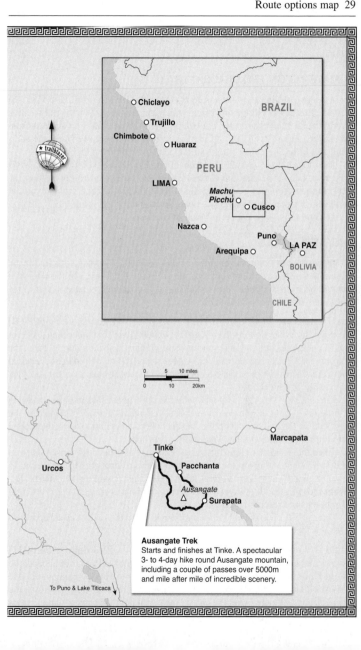

O Chiclayo

O Trujillo

Chimbote O

O Huaraz

BRAZIL

PERU

LIMA O

Machu Picchu O Cusco

Nazca O

Puno
O

Arequipa O

LA PAZ
O

BOLIVIA

CHILE

0   5   10 miles

0   10   20km

O Marcapata

Tinke
O

O Pacchanta

Ausangate
△

O Surapata

Urcos
O

To Puno & Lake Titicaca ↓

Ausangate Trek
Starts and finishes at Tinke. A spectacular
3- to 4-day hike round Ausangate mountain,
including a couple of passes over 5000m
and mile after mile of incredible scenery.

PLANNING YOUR TRIP

(cont'd from p27) This trail is subject to the Inca Trail regulations and permits must be secured well in advance of departure. It is closed completely during February.

VARIATIONS ON THE CLASSIC TRAIL

There are two straightforward variations to the classic Inca Trail. The first (see p231) **begins at the village of Chilca**, which stands at Km77 on the railway line before tracking alongside the Urubamba River to join the classic trail from Km88. Dry and dusty, it isn't all that interesting and not really worth the additional day of hiking unless your tour happens to begin from there.

The other option (see p232) is to **begin at Km82**, which offers half a day's more riverside stroll than the Km88 option, but is less monotonous than the Km77 stretch. You also get to visit the ruins at Huillca Raccay, which overlook Patallacta. Trekkers on both these routes are at the mercy of the Inca Trail regulations and must secure a permit well in advance.

SHORTER TRAILS

For those pushed for time or not inclined to mount a 4-day trek to Machu Picchu, there are several options that allow you to get a sense of the approach route to the ruins and then explore the site itself without having to resort to the shuttle bus from Aguas Calientes.

Km104 and the Purification Trail   [2 days; see pp234-6]

There are two route options from Km104 on the railway, both of which take two days to complete, although only one of these is actually spent trekking. From the Inca ruins at Chachabamba you can scale a steep hillside on a narrow, exposed path to reach Huinay Huayna and then join the classic Inca Trail for the final approach to Machu Picchu.

Alternatively you can head down the river to Choquesuysuy before tackling an arduous 3-hour climb to Huinay Huayna along a route nicknamed the 'Purification Trail'. The first option has the better scenery and views, the second option has more ruins but the walk itself is inferior.

Since the Trekkers' Hotel at Huinay Huayna has long since closed and you can't stay at the campsite there, you must descend through Machu Picchu to stay in Aguas Calientes overnight before returning to explore the site the following morning. Both options are subject to the Inca Trail regulations and trek permits must be reserved well in advance.

The route is open during February though, when the main, classic approach to Machu Picchu is shut.

Km88 Riverside Trail   [2-3 days; see p237]

From Km88 on the railway line it is possible to follow the Río Urubamba all the way to Km104, from where you are able to ascend to Huinay Huayna via one of two routes (see the Purification Trail, above). The scenic stroll avoids the tough climbs associated with the classic Inca Trail but it also avoids all the ruins that you would otherwise encounter along the route, making it a less-attractive option. That said, it's a very peaceful route – the chances are that from Km88 to Km104 you won't see anyone! This trek is subject to the Inca Trail regulations and should be arranged well in advance.

OTHER TREKS TO MACHU PICCHU

There are two other methods of trekking to Machu Picchu. One is an extended hike that begins with a genuine wilderness experience and a chance to explore the slopes of Nevado Salkantay, the sacred mountain of the Incas, before joining the classic Inca Trail for its final three days; the other is an excellent alternative to the classic trail that is currently unregulated and therefore is very popular.

The High Inca Trail   [6-7 days; see pp238-48]
Most agencies offer this trek though they may also, rather confusingly, refer to it as the Salkantay Trek. Indeed the High Inca Trail and the Salkantay Trek we describe below do share the same path for the first day and a bit, going their separate ways only at Salkantay Pampa. There, the Salkantay Trek heads over the western shoulder of Nevado Salkantay, while the High Inca Trail tackles its eastern shoulder, reaching a lofty 4948m/16,234ft before descending into the valley of the Urubamba via an impressive Inca-built canal.

In essence, this trek is a dramatic extension of the classic Inca Trail, for once it reaches Huayllabamba it continues along the traditional route to reach Machu Picchu. As a result, it is subject to the usual Inca Trail regulations and requires you to have a permit, secured well in advance.

The Salkantay Trek   [3-4 days; see pp249-65]
The name Salkantay derives from the Quechua word *salka*, meaning 'wild', 'savage' or 'invincible'. It is an apt name for the mountain under which this trek lies. This route to Machu Picchu, via the 'backdoor', has become increasingly popular, to the point where rumours are now abounding that it, too, will be subject to restrictions similar to the Inca Trail. This trek is the only route where some agents offer the option to stay in lodges (see Mountain Lodges of Peru, p181) rather than simply camp.

The 3- to 4-day trek begins from Mollepata and climbs over a pass (4635m/15,206ft) on the western shoulder of Nevado Salkantay before descending into the very attractive, forested Santa Teresa Valley. From here it clambers over a ridge into the Aobamba Valley and then joins the Urubamba Valley, finishing at the foot of Machu Picchu Mountain. Although there are hardly any Inca ruins along the trek, it is a very scenic walk through some of the region's most picturesque landscapes. The sprawling, partially uncovered yet highly significant site at Llactapata (the major Inca site on the trail) and the fact that the trek finishes on the doorstep of one of the finest archaeological sites in the Americas are some compensation though.

At present this route remains free from regulations and you are able to trek it independently and arrange your own guide and porters. The only compulsory fee is the entrance charge for Machu Picchu.

THE LARES TREK   [4-5 days; see pp266-80]

A reasonably popular alternative to the classic Inca Trail and its associated routes is the Lares Valley, which lies to the north of Urubamba and is renowned for its traditional Quechua communities and strong weaving culture.

It's important to note that there is no *single* official Lares route; instead, there are many that explore their way through this fascinating region. The one we describe in detail in this book is one of the more popular, although, if truth be told, none of the routes are especially popular, and even in the high season you may well find yourself alone on the trail for much of the time. While some may be put off by this isolation, it does allow you to fully appreciate a slice of rural life whilst revelling in the dramatic landscapes of this mountainous territory.

Many agencies often portray their Lares trek as an alternative to the Inca Trail so it needs to be emphasised that none of them take you to the ruins themselves. Instead, most treks finish (and indeed start) at some point along the main road running through the Sacred Valley. As such, it is typical for walkers on an organised tour to be met at the trek's end and taken by bus to Ollantaytambo, from where they can catch a train to Aguas Calientes and bus to Machu Picchu.

Permits are not required for any Lares trek and they can all be tackled independently. Remember, however, that if you want to tack on a visit to Machu

---

❏ Combining routes

It is possible to trek between the three main Inca sites of Choquequirao, Machu Picchu and Vilcabamba, and until recently these treks were reasonably popular amongst the more adventurous members of the trekking community. However, the putative building of a highway to the north of Choquequirao means that much of the charm and challenge of these trails will be rather lost. Still, none of these trails is regulated at present and they can be trekked independently with a team you have hired yourself.

The trek from **Choquequirao to Machu Picchu** usually takes 8 to 9 days and links two of the most spectacular Inca ruins by way of a stretch of stunning countryside. To begin with you spend the first couple of days walking from Cachora to the ruins at Choquequirao (a trek described on pp288-96), perched precariously high above the Apurímac valley. More ruins await at Pinchu Unuyoc before the trail tumbles down one hillside and clambers steeply up another. Having completed a crossing of the Abra San Juan, you then descend to Yanama, which is now connected to Ccolpapampa by a rough road. From here you can reach Machu Picchu via the 'back door' (see p256). Not for the faint-hearted, the route represents quite an undertaking but it does provide you with two exceptional archaeological sites and leads you though a wide range of Peru's vegetation zones so that you'll experience a huge variety of native flora.

If, instead of heading east from Yanama to Ccolpapampa, you headed north to cross the high pass at Choquetecarpo, you can complete the 8- to 9-day yomp from **Cachora to Huancacalle**, visiting the archeological sites at Ñusta España and Vitcos on the way. From here there is the opportunity to then push on to Espíritu Pampa and the ruins of Vilcabamba – the last refuge of the Inca – thereby completing a spectacular traverse that would probably take about a fortnight. Tough and occasionally tricky to follow, this route is a real challenge. The rewards, though, are spectacular and you will spend much of the walk free from crowds.

Picchu you'll need to secure both the entrance ticket to the ruins *and* your train tickets between Ollantaytambo and Aguas Calientes before you set off on the trek. Given that you usually need to secure both of these at least a few days beforehand, it's probably worth arranging everything *at least* a week in advance, and a fortnight in advance in the high season. If using the services of an agency, expect to pay upwards of US$450 if you include a visit to Machu Picchu after your Lares trek, though it's possible to get a trek for less than US$300 if you are returning to Cusco after the trek.

THE CHOQUEQUIRAO TREK [4-5 days; see pp280-97]

This trek travels from Cachora to the ruins at Choquequirao, the first major Inca site uncovered outside Cusco and one that is still to be fully explored. Having reached the ruins at the end of the second day you then retrace your steps and walk out along the same trail. With a day at the ruins to explore this extensive site you should reasonably expect the trek to take 4-5 days.

The trek is quite demanding physically as it requires you to descend 1475m/4839ft from the Capuliyoc Pass into the sheer Apurímac Valley in order to cross the Apurímac River (see box p290), then to climb 1565m/5135ft up the similarly steep opposite cliff to access the ruins perched on a ridge far above. It's hot and dry, and there are few points at which to collect water along the route so you must be prepared to carry additional supplies for much of the trek (having said that, we found that most campsites these days provide food – though you should check with other trekkers that this is still the case before setting off, just to be sure!). The vertiginous valley is spectacular and the ruins themselves, which resemble Machu Picchu in many respects, are fascinating, meaning that the trek is set to replace the classic Inca Trail as the serious hikers' alternative.

This trek isn't currently covered by any regulations and there are no permits required (you just need to buy a ticket for the ruins themselves which is available from a kiosk just before you enter the site), although this may well change as its popularity grows.

THE AUSANGATE TREK [4-5 days; see pp297-309]

The 4- to 5-day Ausangate Trek is quite unlike any of the others in this book. No Inca ruins, no cloud forest – it's not even in the same region as the other treks, being located around 100km east of Cusco in Quispicanchi Province. Yet anybody who has walked in this mountainous region will tell you that it would be verging on the criminal not to include it; and given that most trekkers who attempt an Ausangate trek originally set out from Cusco, we feel more than justified in writing about it.

The trek described in this book is a circumnavigation of Nevado Ausangate on a trail that encompasses some of the most spectacular scenery you'll find anywhere, with glaciers, variegated lakes, windswept mountain passes and isolated farming communities abounding. You will need to be self-sufficient on the

❏ **The Vilcabamba Trail**

This remote, rarely tackled trek (6- to 9-day trip with 4 days of walking; see pp339-45) follows the low-level route the Incas took as they fled from the conquistadors deep into the jungle, where they built the last capital of Vilcabamba. The trek itself takes roughly four days but because the path is rarely used it's sometimes overgrown, often muddy in places and prone to damage by landslips, it's worth factoring in additional time. You will also need to take into account the time it takes to get to the out-of-the-way trailheads at Huancacalle and Chaunquiri too, and might want to include additional days in Quillabamba or Huancacalle. It's best to set aside 6-9 days for the entire expedition.

The ruins at Espíritu Pampa, thought to be the site of Vilcabamba, are less immediately spectacular than those at Machu Picchu or Choquequirao, because they lie buried in the thick jungle and haven't been particularly cleared or restored. Instead they have a different type of appeal; much of the magic and reward comes from the jungle that you pass through and the varied flora you are able to see. Since the route isn't subject to any regulations you may trek it independently or arrange your own guides and arrieros to help shoulder the burden.

In the past there have been reports of narco-traffickers operating in the region, and at times it's been dangerous to attempt this walk. Things seem to have calmed down now but do check on the current situation before finalising your travel plans by talking to established, responsible agencies with experience of trekking in this region.

tour as there are no restaurants or hotels on the way. This probably means you'll need an arriero to carry all your baggage, camping equipment and food for the duration of the trip. They'll also make sure you don't lose your way. Agencies in Cusco can arrange an arriero for you beginning at US$190 for a 5-day trek, or you can arrange one yourself at Tinke, the starting point for the trail, for considerably less.

What to take

Walking in the Andes should not be taken lightly regardless of which trek you choose. An ill-fitting boot or a rucksack that won't adjust properly can cause discomfort and potentially spoil your trip. Try to travel light but strike a compromise between weight and what is really essential, making sure that you have sufficient appropriate clothing to be safe and comfortable. A lot of people make the mistake of overpacking. Given the quality and advances in modern gear, there's no reason to take enormous amounts of equipment or clothing with you. Don't forget that you can always pick up additional things in Peru.

Weight is a vital consideration on treks where you are responsible for carrying your own bags. On those trips where either porters or mules will be carrying most of your luggage, don't use this as an excuse to take unnecessary things just because someone else will be shouldering the load.

FOOTWEAR

Your top priority whilst trekking ought to be the condition of your feet. This will have the single biggest impact on your enjoyment of the trek and your ability to tackle some of the longer, more arduous stages.

Some people manage in a pair of stout trainers but these will not protect your ankles, are not waterproof and could result in you having bruised and sore feet after some of the more gruelling days spent crossing rocky or uneven terrain. Sections of the treks are rough and bumpy and you will definitely have to negotiate stretches of scree, scramble over loose boulders, cross wet, smooth rocks, wade through small streams and possibly trudge through patches of snow. Therefore you will need footwear that is supportive without being too restrictive or rigid, is waterproof, has sewn in tongues, and soles that can grip even in wet conditions. Ideally you should have a pair of sturdy **boots**. Get a pair that has a little room at the toe end to assist circulation and prevent your toes getting crushed or bruised in the course of prolonged periods of descent. Whatever you buy, make sure that your shoes are properly broken in well ahead of the start of your trek; otherwise you may end up with blisters.

Sandals or **flip flops** are a good idea to give your feet a bit of respite at the end of the day. They might also come in useful when crossing small streams.

Some people choose to wear **gaiters** on some of the tougher sections of track to help keep water, mud and other debris out of their boots. They will also stop your shins from getting scratched by the undergrowth.

Telescopic **walking poles** (particularly those containing shock-absorbing springs) are also a good idea, particularly for steep downhill sections, as they can give much-needed support to your knees; however, see p39 and p121. Whether you use one or two poles is down to personal preference.

CLOTHES

Since the treks described in this book take you across a range of landscapes and altitudes you will need to carry clothes that are appropriate for a range of temperatures and conditions. Adopt the simple but effective technique of **layering**. The base layer should keep the skin comfortable and dry. The second, insulation layer should trap and retain body heat in order to provide extra warmth, whilst the outer layer must protect you against the wind, rain, snow and even sun.

It is vital that the **base layer** dries easily and helps to conduct sweat away from the body. T-shirts made of synthetic materials do the best job of 'wicking' moisture away from the skin. Wool, silk or cotton are less useful for this layer.

Fleece is the most desirable material for the **insulation layer** since it is light, wind-resistant and quick drying. Wool is also a good insulator but dries very slowly and can become very heavy when wet. Try to ensure that, since you'll be bending and stretching as you work your way across uneven terrain, your lower back is adequately covered.

Your legs need to have as much freedom of movement as possible. Shorts offer the most flexibility. Lightweight, tough trousers are also essential and

PLANNING YOUR TRIP

ideally should be made of rip-stop fabric. In general avoid thick, heavy trousers, especially denim jeans as they restrict movement and can be very difficult to get dry.

The Andes get a lot of rainfall so good **waterproofs** are essential, even in summer. The weather can be highly unpredictable in the mountains and rain can occur pretty much year-round. Modern raincoats made from lightweight, waterproof, highly breathable fabric allow water vapour to pass through the jacket from the inside to the outside but stop water from leaking in. In this way condensation is prevented from forming on the inside of the coat, which would quickly drain away body heat. The arms of the jacket should be long enough to fit over warm under-layers and the coat should have a long-enough tail that your lower back isn't exposed when bending or stretching forward. The coat also ought to have a roomy hood that can be drawn tight but that still provides you with peripheral vision. A variety of pockets in which to store maps, snacks, etc is also useful.

A **hat** provides vital protection against the elements. A wide-brimmed version is a good idea to shield your eyes from the harsh mountain sun. A woolly hat can be useful for keeping your head warm in the evenings or when the temperature drops. Take a pair of **gloves** to keep your hands warm and your fingers flexible at higher altitudes or in less-than-perfect conditions.

EQUIPMENT

Rucksack
If you'll be carrying your own rucksack make sure it fits comfortably; this is vital when choosing a rucksack for a multi-day trek. Get an experienced shop-assistant to fit you with the right-sized pack before buying one. The **hip belt** ought to support about a third of the weight of the pack, with the rest being carried on your shoulders. Make sure that the **straps** are adjustable so that you can alter them to suit the terrain: when climbing it is better to take the weight on your shoulders, whilst when descending it is often more comfortable to release the shoulder straps slightly and tighten the hip belt.

Try not to buy a pack that is too large, otherwise the temptation is to try and fill it. The pack should have easily accessible **compartments** for the items you want most often, such as water bottles, guidebook, maps and snacks. Straps and buckles on the outside of the pack can also be useful for securing trekking poles or other bits of temporarily unnecessary kit. All materials should be robust and long lasting. Stitching on the pack must be high quality and any zips should be resilient and smooth running.

In very heavy rain even the most waterproof of packs can leak. As a precaution you should use a **heavy-duty waterproof inner liner** to protect your gear and a pack cover to sluice off the majority of the rain. For further protection put your things into plastic shopping bags or waterproof 'stuff sacks', which ought to guarantee that everything stays dry.

Sleeping bags and mats

A **sleeping bag** is essential since you will be camping on the trek. Some agencies will hire out or provide sleeping bags as part of the package that they offer. However, if you prefer to use your own bag, a lightweight, compact sleeping bag offering three-season comfort in temperatures of -5°C ought to be sufficient unless you are particularly susceptible to the cold in which case a four-season bag may be more appropriate.

Equally useful and certainly worth taking is a **sheet sleeping-bag** – essentially a sheet folded and sewn along two sides – to use as an inner liner for your main bag, since they offer an extra layer of warmth, are easy to wash and keep the inside of the main sleeping bag cleaner. **Sleeping mats** are also a good idea and can immeasurably improve sleep quality by cushioning you and insulating you from the cold ground. Old-fashioned foam mats are OK but you are better off with an inflatable Therm-a-Rest. These can puncture so take a repair kit with you, too.

Tent

All agencies are obliged to provide tents for the treks you undertake with them. These ought to be of serviceable quality and completely sufficient for your trip. If you are considering trekking independently, make sure you have a lightweight, robust tent that packs up compactly. You need to seal the seams to stop rain getting in. If you decide to travel independently once in Peru, it is possible to hire tents from several agencies and equipment stores in Cusco; single-person tents are more difficult to find but you should find a couple of agencies in Cusco that stock them.

Stoves, pans and crockery

On an organised trek the agency is also obliged to provide all the **cooking equipment** and enough crockery and cutlery for the entire group. However, should you want to trek independently, you will need to take your own. **Gas stoves** with screw-top cylinders are perfectly adequate – you may want to buy cylinders containing a butane-propane mix that will work more effectively at altitude. These are readily available in Cusco. Take light aluminium **pans** that can be stored one inside the other. Plates aren't necessary as long as you don't mind eating from the pan. Do take **cups** and **cutlery** though, as well as some sort of **wire scrubber** to clean the dirty dishes. All of this can be bought or hired in Cusco.

FOOD

There's no need to bring much from home as there are lots of opportunities to buy food in Cusco. Agencies will provide all the main meals for organised treks and probably produce fruit and sweets at opportune moments as well.

If you are setting out alone, take food that doesn't weigh too much but which delivers large amounts of carbohydrate. Potatoes (though these are heavy), *quinoa* (an Andean grain) and polenta are all good sources, as are pasta and dried noodles. Dried sausage or tinned meat is also useful (though tins are

PLANNING YOUR TRIP

also heavy). Herbs and spices as well as salt and pepper can help add flavour to otherwise uninspiring suppers. Soups or porridge are great for getting additional hot food and liquid into your body whilst nuts, chocolate and boiled sweets are a good way of raising your spirits, getting a quick energy boost or winning friends.

TOILETRIES

Take only those toiletries you think you'll actually need. If you can, try to estimate how much shower gel, shampoo etc you'll use on your trek, then decant that amount into a smaller bottle. It's surprising how much you'll trim off the total weight of your luggage by doing this. Whilst Cusco has several chemists, you are unlikely to find one in the smaller towns at the trailheads for each trek and you almost certainly won't come across any once the trek has begun.

A checklist should include: **a bar of soap** (keep it in a bag or container; liquid soap for washing clothes); **towel** (most outdoor shops now sell low-bulk, highly absorbent microfibre towels); **toothbrush** and **toothpaste** (take only as much toothpaste as you'll need – buy a small tube or take a part-used one to save space and weight**); toilet paper**; **pre-moistened tissues** (for example 'Wet-Wipes'; useful in a number of situations); **earplugs** (may help if sharing a campsite with a crowd of snorers); **lip balm** (essential on higher sections of the trek where the track is exposed to full sun); **tampons**; **contraceptives**.

MEDICAL KIT

Your medical kit should cover most eventualities though hopefully you won't have to use any of it. However, most people find they need to dip into their supplies sooner or later to sort out everyday ailments, such as blisters, caused by trekking. Perhaps most importantly, do not forget to take an adequate supply of any **prescription drugs** that you might need.

A basic medical kit should comprise **hydrocolloid blister pads** and **zinc oxide tape** with a strong adhesive for securing dressings or bandages. **Plasters** are good for covering and protecting minor cuts and injuries. **Sterilised gauze** is useful should you need to soak up blood or pus from a cut or graze. It is also useful in keeping a cut clean and free from infection. **Antiseptic cream** or spray will prevent minor infections from developing.

Anti-inflammatory painkillers such as Paracetamol are helpful in easing the discomfort of bruises or sprains. **Hydrocortisone cream** is a good aid if you suffer from heat rash. **Deep heat spray** will ease minor sprains and help to loosen or warm-up sore muscles. **Hypodermic needles** are essential tools for piercing blisters; use a sterilised needle to dig out a splinter that doesn't have a head/end proud of the skin for a tweezer to grip; **tweezers**, though, can be helpful for less-delicate work. A pair of small, sharp **scissors** is also a good idea. **Bandages** may be needed to cover more substantial wounds or to support damaged joints. An **elasticated knee support** is helpful for weak knees and useful on the long pounding descents.

High-factor **sun-cream** is vital, as the sun at altitude can be very harmful. **Aloe vera** is also useful in the wake of sunburn and to ease the discomfort of windburn, rashes or grazes. Although not strictly necessary, you may wish to take **multivitamin tablets** to supplement your diet in the course of the trek.

MISCELLANEOUS ITEMS

As well as the essential items you may also want to bring a few other bits and pieces. A **watch** is very useful for gauging how far and fast you have travelled as well as keeping track of time. **Sunglasses** help to cut out the sun's glare and will protect you from reflected light.

A **penknife** with all its various blades and tools is invaluable as is a **water bottle/pouch**, preferably with two-litre capacity. The modern Platypus or Camelbak system, whereby a pouch is connected to a tube so you can drink while you walk, is a good idea as it encourages you to drink more. **Water-purifying tablets** or iodine drops are useful if you haven't time to boil the water before drinking it. Many trekkers use a SteriPEN these days, which purifies water using ultraviolet light. They are quick and simple to use and don't flavour the water either. Sawyer mini filters are another effective alternative.

A reliable, compact waterproof **torch/flashlight** is a good idea, as are extra **batteries** for it. A **head torch** is even better as it means that your hands are still free. **Matches** and/or a **lighter** are necessary to ignite cooking gear. A **whistle** may prove to be a vital survival aid should you get lost or injured and need to attract attention. **String** has several uses – to fasten things to the outside of your pack, for example, or to act as an impromptu washing line. A **compass** or **GPS unit** (see p214) may be useful if you're trekking independently and could become essential in bad weather as the tracks are poorly defined in places.

Of course, a **mobile phone**, particularly a smartphone, will do the job of several of the items mentioned above (eg watch, GPS, torch) and can also be a lifesaver if you get in serious trouble and need to call for help. However, do remember that their battery life is limited, and the more tasks you want it to do the more limited that battery life will probably be; so be judicious as to when you use it, or bring some sort of external battery pack to make sure it doesn't fail you when you need it most. Remember, too, that the remote nature of all of these treks mean that mobile reception is likely to be minimal or, more probably, non-existent.

Walking poles (see also p35 and p121) are acceptable only if the tip is covered by a rubber bung so that the environment isn't damaged.

Finally, you must remember to take degradable **rubbish bags** since it is important that you pack any rubbish out of the mountains and get rid of it responsibly in a town.

PHOTOGRAPHIC EQUIPMENT

Mountains and landscapes are notoriously difficult to photograph well. The results often don't capture the scale or grandeur of the Andes and the powerful sweep and subtle colours of the hillsides quite often don't translate well to prints.

Good-quality, **compact digital cameras** are light, tough and take adequate photographs. **Digital SLR** cameras and a couple of lenses offer more scope for creativity and increase your chance of capturing the delicate light and effects found in the mountains. Don't forget your **battery charger** but also **spare batteries**. A **zoom lens** will afford you a greater degree of compositional flexibility without adding too much weight to your bag. A **lens hood** will reduce the glare from the sun, whilst a **UV filter** will cut through the high-altitude haze. A **polariser** will also cut through the haze and deepen the blue of the sky as well as adding colour and depth to lakes and coasts. For self-timer or longer exposure shots a small, lightweight, sturdy **tripod** is a good idea and a remote **shutter-release cable** is a good investment too.

A **carrying case** that can be attached to your belt or waist strap is useful since it means that your equipment will be readily accessible yet still be well protected. If you have to stop, drop your pack and rummage about for your camera you may be less inclined to use it. Make sure your camera bag is waterproof since there is quite a high likelihood that you'll get rained on.

MAPS

Good-quality, trekking-scale maps of Peru are not all that easy to come by. The **IGN (Instituto Geográfico Nacional)** in Lima produces a series of 1:100,000 scale topographic maps of the country that have contours at 50m intervals as well as spot heights. The legend includes all standard information such as settlements and roads plus a great deal of terrain and vegetation detail. Their weakness is the actual trails themselves, which are often crudely drawn on (and sometimes missing altogether). Some specialised map shops outside Peru also sell IGN maps such as Stanfords in the UK (12-14 Long Acre, London WC2E, and 29 Corn St, Bristol BS1) and online at ⌨ www.stanfords.co.uk.

The IGN maps you need for the classic Inca Trail are 2444 (27-r) and 2344 (27-q). However, for this trek we prefer the version by local publisher Lima 2000, available from Stanfords and elsewhere. The Lares Trek is also covered by 2444 (27-r).

For the trek to and from Choquequirao as well as the Salkantay Trek and High Inca Trail search out IGN maps 2343 (28-q) and 2344 (27-q). Be aware that old editions of 27-q do not show Mollepata, the start point for both the Salkantay Trek and High Inca Trail; the hamlet is featured on the newer version of the map. The Ausangate Trek featured in this book is covered wholly by map 28-t. For the Vilcabamba Trail you will also need the north-western section of 2344 (27-q) as well as 2244 (27-p) and 2245 (26-p). There is also a more general 1:200,000 scale map available of the region to the north of Cusco. Although this scale is inadequate for trekking, it does help to put the area into context.

ITMB Publishing (⌨ www.itmb.ca) also produces a detailed road map of *Cusco and South Peru*, updated in 2009. As well as the main map featuring neighbouring towns such as Pisac, Calca and Urubamba, there is a detailed town plan of Cusco at 1:11,000 scale and an inset of the Inca Trail at 1:50,000 scale, in addition to an annotated plan of the ruins at Machu Picchu.

Cusco **town plans** are also available from Editorial Lima 2000, whilst ITMB produces a decent street map of Lima.

RECOMMENDED READING

For a good introduction to Peru's history and culture, see *The Peru Reader: History, Culture, Politics* (Duke University Press). It's a fascinating anthology covering a wide range of subjects.

Guidebooks

Each of the major travel publishers has a guidebook to Peru. The best of these are the *Footprint Guide to Peru* and the *Rough Guide to Peru*. Lonely Planet also produce a very comprehensive *Peru* guide and a briefer guide, *Discover Peru*, which details the highlights in the country for people travelling on an organised tour or who have less time available. Their *Trekking in the Central Andes* highlights selected treks in Peru, Bolivia and Ecuador. Bradt Travel Guides also produce a comprehensive overview of the country, *Peru Highlights*, which contains itinerary suggestions along with all the country's essential must-see sites. Charles Brod's *Apus and Incas* (Inca Expeditions) guide to trekking in the Cusco region is available in Cusco, where you can also find Peter Frost's *Exploring Cusco*.

For a phrasebook, Lonely Planet's *Quechua Phrasebook* is recommended.

Expedition reports and travelogues

Lost City of the Incas by Hiram Bingham (Phoenix) is a reprint of the classic account of the rediscovery of Machu Picchu. It's a rip-roaring adventure story, although bear in mind that many of his theories about the site have not stood the test of time (see pp314-16).

For more on Hiram Bingham, his rediscovery of the site and the controversy surrounding the artefacts shipped home, see Chris Heaney's *Cradle of Gold: The Story of Hiram Bingham, A Real Life Indiana Jones, and his Search for Machu Picchu* (Palgrave MacMillan).

Earlier trip reports and accounts of expeditions include *Peregrinations of a Pariah* by Flora Tristan and *Peru, Travel and Exploration in the Land of the Incas* by E George Squier (Macmillan).

Turn Right at Machu Picchu (Plume) by Mark Adams is, in our opinion, the best of the books we've listed here, a well-written and fact-packed account of one middle-aged man's attempt to follow in the footsteps of Hiram Bingham. Funny, informative and erudite, this is a thoroughly enjoyable read.

Hugh Thomson's *The White Rock: An Exploration of the Inca Heartland* is a fascinating account of a modern explorer and archaeologist at work as the author and colleague Gary Ziegler search for and rediscover the Inca site at Coca Cota in the Vilcabamba region. There's good information on the Incas in general and on past explorers, whilst his book *Cochineal Red* (both published by Phoenix) is a thorough investigation of earlier civilisations, in which

Thomson investigates the Moche, Chavin, Nazca and other ancient civilisations of Peru and contains an interesting description of the recent archaeological work at the Inca site of Llactapata, near Machu Picchu. This book is also available as *A Sacred Landscape: The Search for Ancient Peru* (Overlook).

Classic travelogues include those by Ronald Wright, *Cut Stones and Crossroads* (Modern Classics), Christopher Isherwood, *The Condor and the Cows* (Vintage Classics) and Matthew Parris, *Inca Kola* (Weidenfeld and Nicholson).

Three Letters from the Andes by Patrick Leigh Fermor (John Murray) is an enthralling, typically lyrical account of the author's trip to Machu Picchu that perfectly captures the landscape and people he encounters.

Eight Feet in the Andes: Travels with a Mule in Unknown Peru (John Murray), describing a journey made in 1983, is Dervla Murphy at her best.

The Incas

There are countless books on the Incas, with titles aimed at everyone from children to academics.

The definitive text is John Hemming's *The Conquest of the Incas* (Pan), which ranks as one of the great pieces of historical writing. Hemming's book *Monuments of the Incas*, featuring stunning black and white photography by Edward Ranney, was updated in 2010 and reissued by Thames and Hudson.

The Last Days of the Incas (Little, Brown), by filmmaker and journalist Kim MacQuarrie, reads like a riveting novel and covers not only the Conquest but also the exploits of more modern adventurers rediscovering Machu Picchu and Vilcabamba.

Although the Incas had no form of writing there are some fascinating near-contemporary Spanish accounts. The most thorough is by Pedro de Cieza de Léon, a soldier who arrived in Peru in 1548 and recorded the Conquest in *The Discovery and Conquest of Peru* (Duke University Press). Garcilaso Inca de la Vega, the son of an Inca princess and a Spanish conquistador, wrote *The Royal Commentaries of the Inca* (abridged version by Hackett Publishing), originally published in 1609. It's most interesting for its description of Inca customs and culture, and of Peruvian flora and fauna. The version readily available in Peru is illustrated with some of the naïve drawings by Felipe Huamán Poma de Ayala originally published in his *Nueva Corónica y Buen Gobierno*.

Michael Moseley's illustrated archaeological survey, *The Incas and their Ancestors* (Thames and Hudson) is excellent.

Maria Rostworowski de Diez Canseco's *History of the Inca Realm* (Cambridge University Press) provides a Peruvian perspective on the Incas that is scholarly yet accessible.

Art in the Andes, from Chavin to Inca (Thames and Hudson) by Rebecca Stone-Miller is authoritative and well illustrated.

Machu Picchu and other Inca sites

Machu Picchu by John Hemming (Readers' Digest Wonders of Man Series) is a fine book on **Machu Picchu** and its position in Peru's history.

The Machu Picchu Guidebook: A Self-Guided Tour by Ruth Wright and Alfredo Zegarra (Johnson Books) is a good contemporary guide to the site and its features.

Machu Picchu, Unveiling the Mystery of the Incas (Yale), edited by Yale archaeologists Richard Burger and Lucy Salazar, was published to coincide with the Machu Picchu exhibition at the Museum of Natural History at Yale University. Apart from the excellent photographs and the catalogue of 120 objects from the site, the book is also interesting in that it includes Hiram Bingham's original 1913 report of the rediscovery and a scholarly modern overview of Machu Picchu and its significance.

Johan Reinhard refines the theory of Machu Picchu as a cosmological, hydrological and sacred geographical centre in the fourth edition of *Machu Picchu, Exploring an Ancient Sacred Center* (Cotsen Institute of Archaeology Press).

The Machu Picchu Historical Sanctuary by Jim Bartle and Peter Frost (Nuevas Imágenes) is an attractive illustrated look at the region.

Realm of the Incas by Max Milligan (Idlewild) includes a more sumptuous selection of photographs covering far more than just Machu Picchu.

Stone Offerings, Machu Picchu's Terraces of Enlightenment (Lightpoint Press) is an award-winning photographic book by architectural photographer Mike Torrey. The beautiful photos were taken over a few days during the summer and winter solstices. Though quite expensive it would make a perfect souvenir.

In comparison with Machu Picchu, however, there is precious little written about **Vilcabamba**. Vincent Lee's *Forgotten Vilcabamba – Final Stronghold of the Incas* (Sixpac Manco Publications) is by far the most comprehensive book on the site and its history and also contains a number of detailed diagrams of the ruins. Lee also produced an earlier guide, *Sixpac Manco – Travels amongst the Incas*, which contains some of the same information. Gene Savoy described his explorations of the region in *Antisuyu* (Simon and Schuster). John Hemming dedicated a number of chapters in *The Conquest of the Incas* to Vilcabamba and Hugh Thomson also provides good historical information and descriptions of the ruins in *The White Rock*.

Field guides

There aren't many readily available, good-quality, compact field guides for Peru's flora or fauna.

If you don't mind carrying fairly bulky books, John Dunning's *South American Birds*, the comprehensive *Birds of the High Andes* by Jon Fjeldsa and Niels Krabbe, or the *Field Guide to the Birds of Peru* by James Clements and Noam Shany are worth tracking down.

Most useful, though, is the *Field Guide to the Birds of Machu Picchu* by the ornithologist and Cusco resident Barry Walker. Although it's tricky to come by, you should be able to find a copy at the airports in Lima or Cusco, in bookshops in Cusco and (expensively) on Amazon.

If you're after more than just birds, *The Travellers' Wildlife Guide to Peru* by David Pearson and Les Beletsky contains superb illustrations of more than 500 of Peru's most common insects, amphibians, reptiles, birds and mammals.

❑ SOURCES OF FURTHER INFORMATION

Peru
A great place to start is perusing the comprehensive visitor information listed on **Andean Travel Web** (💻 www.andeantravelweb.com/peru), which focuses on Cusco but also provides good-quality information on Lima, Arequipa, Huaraz, Trujillo, Lake Titicaca, Paracas and the Amazon.

Otherwise, **for general information**, try: 💻 www.peru.info, the website of the official government tourism agency. Do bear in mind that many 'official' sites are nothing of the sort, just agencies looking to advertise treks and tours.
● 💻 **www.traficoperu.com** Detailed information on topics as diverse as flights, accommodation, places to eat and car hire.
● 💻 **www.livinginperu.com** Expat guide to local news and events.

Cusco
💻 www.cuscoperu.com is a listings site for Cusco with recommendations and links in English; 💻 www.cuscoonline.com is also worth a look.

Machu Picchu and the Inca Trail
For information on Machu Picchu and the Inca Trail try the Andean Travel Web site (see above); 💻 projects.exeter.ac.uk/RDavies/inca also has details and many links; Hugh Thomson's website (💻 www.thewhiterock.co.uk) is also worth a look.

Bradt's *Peruvian Wildlife: A Visitor's Guide to the High Andes*, by Gerard Cheshire, Barry Walker and Huw Lloyd, covers fauna and focuses on Cusco and the Sacred Valley. There's also a good section on orchids and birds in Peter Frost's and Jim Bartle's *Machu Picchu Historical Sanctuary*, to which Barry Walker has also contributed.

Other books
The Heights of Machu Picchu (Farrar, Straus & Giroux Inc) is Chilean poet Pablo Neruda's epic, inspired by the ruins. It's been called the single most-important piece of South American poetry, with comparisons to TS Eliot's *The Waste Land*.

The Royal Hunt of the Sun (Penguin Classic) is Peter Shaffer's gripping play about the fall of the last Inca, Atahualpa. *To the Last City* (Vintage) by Colin Thubron is a fictional account of a journey to Vilcabamba that perfectly captures the atmosphere of the place and the trek.

For children, try *The Angry Aztecs and the Incredible Incas* (Scholastic Hippo) by Terry Deary, in the Horrible Histories series, which has history mixed in with thrilling tales.

Health precautions, inoculations & insurance

Any form of outdoor physical activity carries with it the possibility of accidents and trekking in the Andes is no exception. However, there are certain golden rules to follow on the trail that will help to minimise the risk of accidents or getting lost. To avoid unpleasant or unwanted surprises, always plan each day's walk carefully, study a map and familiarise yourself with the route, the type of terrain to be covered and the length of time you expect to be trekking. There are also a few pre-trek preparations that you can take to further ensure that your walk is trouble-free, as described below.

FITNESS

Whilst a reasonable level of fitness is a good idea, there's no need to go overboard on training for trekking the Inca Trail. You will, however, enjoy the treks a lot more if you are fitter.

Pre-departure fitness preparation

If you lead a largely sedentary existence it is wise to do some pre-departure exercise before trekking. Any type of exercise is better than none at all just to confirm that you can walk for more than a couple of hours at a time, and for more than one day in a row.

The most efficient way to get fit for the trek is to walk up and down hills, preferably carrying at least a partially loaded pack. Climbing a staircase repeatedly will have a similar effect. Jogging helps to build up stamina and endurance. By walking regularly your body is becoming attuned to the rhythms and rigours of life on the trail.

HEALTH

Hopefully the worst complaint you'll have to endure is **sunburn**. The high Andean slopes are exposed and, as a result of the thin atmosphere and the reflection of sun off snow, ice or water, you will find that you burn very easily, even on an apparently overcast day. Wear a hat and use high-factor sun-cream to avoid getting burnt. Sun can do just as much damage to your eyes so protect them by wearing sunglasses.

The cold can be just as hazardous when trekking. The weather in the mountains is highly changeable and you should be prepared for sudden drops in temperature. Cold, wet and windy conditions can sometimes be the cause of **hypothermia**. General awareness, being properly equipped and the ability to react to the symptoms promptly should prevent a serious incident.

Blisters are the bane of trekkers and their most common complaint. Friction between the boot and the foot causes a protective layer of liquid to develop beneath the skin. This can take four or five days to heal properly. As with so many things, prevention is far better than cure.

By taking the necessary precautions in advance you ought to be able to avoid blisters altogether. Firstly, make sure that you break in all footwear well in advance of the trek. Wear proper walking socks. Never trek with wet feet as this is a sure-fire way of getting blisters. If your boots get soaked, wear plastic bags over dry socks in order to prevent them from becoming wet too. Change into dry socks when you take a break on the trail. Most importantly, never ignore the feeling that your boots may be rubbing; cover the sore area with zinc-oxide tape, a plaster or a specialised blister pad. This will act as an additional layer of skin and should stop the chafing. Vaseline, or at a push lip salve, when rubbed onto a sore toe or heel, can also stop abrasion and delay the onset of a blister.

There are minor adjustments that you can make to your boots depending on the terrain that will help to stave off blisters. Whilst going uphill tighten the upper section of your boot and loosen the laces slightly across the foot. Conversely, when descending, loosen the upper part a little and tighten the laces across the foot.

Should you develop blisters use a clean hypodermic needle to burst them. Allow the blister to dry out and then apply antiseptic cream and a dressing to keep it covered and free from infection.

Inoculations

Before travelling to Peru make sure you have had the following inoculations: **tetanus**, **polio**, **diphtheria**, **tuberculosis**, **hepatitis A** and **typhoid**. If it was a while since your original shot check whether you require a booster. If you are going to the jungle (below 2000m) or intend to tackle either the Vilcabamba or Choquequirao routes you should also take a course of anti-**malaria** tablets and consider having a **yellow fever** jab. Some doctors will also suggest you have a **rabies** inoculation if you are intending to tackle one of the longer treks as you may be several days' walk from the nearest transport or the closest hospital. However, the inoculation won't actually stop you getting the disease, it'll simply buy you more time to get to a hospital.

For a full list of the requirements or recommended jabs look at the US Center for Disease Control and Prevention website (🖥 www.cdc.gov), ask a doctor or visit a travel clinic.

In the UK you can get the latest advice and vaccinations from: Nomad Travellers Store & Medical Centre (clinics in London, Bath, Birmingham, Bristol, Cardiff, Manchester; see 🖥 www.nomadtravel.co.uk for address details) or from Trailfinders (🖥 www.trailfinders.com/travel-clinic, 194 Kensington High St, London) and Masta (🖥 www.masta-travel-health.com), which has clinics in some Boots stores as well as other places around the country. Travel clinics will, of course, charge for any inoculations they give.

HIGH-ALTITUDE TRAVEL

One of the most common complaints on the various treks described here is **Acute Mountain Sickness (AMS)/altitude sickness**. Cusco stands at 3360m/11,000ft above sea level and the highest pass described on one of the routes is 5000m/16,400ft. At these altitudes the air pressure is substantially lower than at sea level, having dropped by about one tenth for every 1000m/3300ft of altitude gained. Altitude sickness is caused by the body's inability to get enough oxygen at higher elevations. Since all your vital organs need oxygen to function, this can be a serious condition and, if ignored or left untreated, it can be fatal. However, it is also very common (some of the top hotels in Cusco even have supplementary oxygen in the rooms) and entirely preventable. For a full run-down on the causes, symptoms and treatments of altitude sickness read the section on p120 carefully.

Before you go, if you suffer from heart or lung problems, high blood pressure or are pregnant, you must visit your doctor to get advice on the wisdom of trekking through the Andes.

Acclimatisation

The safest way to avoid any problems with altitude is to acclimatise properly (see p120). The worst thing that you can do is fly in from Lima, which is at sea level, try to start a trek the following day and expect your body to be able to cope with the change in altitude. At the very least take a couple of days out to relax in Cusco and allow your body to adjust to the higher elevation. After this you'll find moving about much easier and after two weeks you'll barely notice the altitude at this level at all.

INSURANCE

Before setting off make sure you have travel insurance, or are covered by your domestic policies. When choosing travel insurance make sure the policy covers you for trekking the trails described in this book. Most policies will but some might not, so read the small print carefully. For complete peace of mind, take out insurance tailored for trekkers or mountaineers. The British Mountaineering Council (☎ 0161 445 6111, 🖳 www.thebmc.co.uk) offers this for its members though note that their regular 'Trek' insurance does not cover you for treks over 5000m – OK if you're just going on the classic Inca Trail but not suitable or valid if you're walking on the Salkantay/Ausangate treks. In this case you'll need to look at their other insurance policies to see which one is for you.

2

PERU

Facts about the country

Peru! There it was: vast, mysterious, grey-green, dirt poor, infinite, wealthy, ancient, reticent.   **Mario Vargas Llosa**

There are few countries on earth that can rival Peru for diversity. The stories and legends associated with it have fired people's imaginations for centuries, luring visitors to its shores since the Spanish came looking for treasure in the 16th century. Frequently portrayed as the land of unimaginable riches, the bloodiest conquest, the most heart-wrenching ballads and the most merciless revolutionaries, this country of superlatives also boasts one of the highest mountain ranges in the world, some of the driest deserts, part of the world's largest jungle and endless empty beaches within its borders. Despite these rugged, inhospitable extremes, Peru also ranks as one of the great centres of ancient civilisation; the Incas are just one in a long line of highly developed cultures to have evolved and thrived here.

The country has had a chequered recent past coloured by a brutal ruling regime and terrorism. However, it has emerged from these troubled times and is now battling to entrench democracy and to achieve economic progress and growth. The signs are currently positive and although the country is still finding its feet as a modern nation (unemployment remains rife and the lack of real opportunities is a major concern), as confidence in the country grows, so the likelihood of stability becomes more real.

Despite apparent advances and a willingness to embrace the influences of a wider world, the country remains firmly rooted in its indigenous traditions and celebrates its ethnic origins and sense of self. Peruvians are rightly proud of their heritage and the cultural riches their country has to offer.

GEOGRAPHICAL BACKGROUND

Peru is the third-largest country in South America. Covering an area of 1,285,000 square kilometres, it is approximately eight times smaller than the USA but five times the size of the UK.

Geographical regions

Uniquely in South America, there are three distinct geographical regions: *costa* (coast), *sierra* (highlands) and *selva* (jungle).

South America started life conjoined with other continents before splitting away. Mountains were forced up by the collision of two tectonic plates, with the fault line where the two plates pushed together lying offshore and running parallel with the coast. This fault line is the cause of Peru's frequent earthquakes. The formation of the Andes, the longest continuous mountain chain in the world, produced a temperate climate at higher altitudes, whilst the lowlands became dominated by tropical and semi-tropical conditions. The mountains are studded with volcanoes, many of which are extinct but a few occasionally still grumble to themselves.

In cross section, from east to west, the Andes of southern Peru have a distinctive profile. In effect, following the coastal desert there are two parallel mountain ranges separated by a high-altitude plain or steppe, which gives way to the jungle.

Coast Peru's coast, all 2500 kilometres (1500 miles) of it, is dry, barren and at the mercy of the **Humboldt (or Peru) Current** and the unique conditions that creates. This current is an ocean stream that flows in the direction of the Equator and can extend up to 1000 kilometres offshore. The nutrient-rich water supports an extraordinary abundance of marine life, even though it is very cold. In fact, the water is sufficiently cold to generate a mass of chill air above it. This cold coastal air blocks the warm moist winds blowing in from the Pacific, ensuring that hardly any rain falls on the coast, although clouds and fog are produced. This gloomy **mist**, which lies heavily over Lima for some of the year, is known as *garúa*. The current is largely responsible for the aridity that prevails along Peru's coast and for creating a long thin strip of desert, the Atacama, behind the barrier, which now stretches from Peru into Chile and extends 20-100km (12-60 miles) inland.

Highlands The *sierra*, Peru's central highland regions, which are synonymous with the country, are dominated by the **Cordillera de los Andes**. The word *sierra* comes from the Latin *serra* and literally means 'saw'. There are several branches of the Andes in Peru, including the **Cordillera Blanca** (White Range) that fronts the Amazon, the **Cordillera Negra** (Black Range) that fronts the coast and the smaller but no less dramatic **Cordillera Huayhuash**. Some of the Andes' highest peaks, including Huascarán (6746m/22,133ft) and Yerupajá (6617m/21,709ft) can be found amongst these ranges. The mountain slopes to the east have been heavily eroded by water, which has left them jagged and precipitous with sharp ridges rising between steep valleys. The slopes to the west have suffered comparatively little owing to the scarcity of water so are more even and rolling. Further south the ranges extend into the ridges of Vilcabamba and Vilcanota, which include Nevado Salkantay (6271m/20,574ft).

Characteristics of this rugged region include steep, deep valleys and high plateaus known as the *altiplano steppe*, or **alpine zone**. These enormous enclosed plains, trapped by the ranges to either side of them, are in turn distinguished by barren **grasslands**, *puna*, where coarse grasses clump together for survival in the cold air and poor soil. Almost half of Peru's population lives

PERU

scattered across the sierra despite the brutally inhospitable terrain and thin, freezing air.

Jungle *La selva* is the isolated rainforest region in the eastern part of Peru between the foothills of the Andes and the Amazon basin. Largely unexplored, it contains some of the finest, untouched **rainforest** in the world, including the Manu National Park, considered to be the world's most bio-diverse rainforest. The region where the forest begins on the foothills of the mountains is poetically described by locals as *Las cejas de la selva* or 'eyebrows of the jungle'. This subtropical region is where much of Peru's coffee is grown.

Climate

Temperatures on the **coast** fluctuate but it is almost always dry. During the summer months, from December to April, temperatures reach 25°C to 30°C. Winter is from May to November when typically the cooler temperatures reach 10°C. Winter is characterised by cloud, fog and what little rain that does fall, falls at

❏ **El Niño**

Peru is at the mercy of a weather condition known as El Niño. This is an important fluctuation in the surface temperature of the Eastern Pacific Ocean, which can have profound effects on the west coast of South America. The name *El Niño*, from the Spanish for 'little boy', refers to Jesus because the phenomenon is usually noticed around Christmas. There is an opposite effect, called *La Niña*, meaning 'little girl'. The condition is very difficult to predict but historically has occurred at irregular intervals of two to seven years and has usually lasted one or two years.

Essentially, El Niño is a change in the weather that is caused by an alteration in the currents of the Pacific Ocean. A rise in air pressure over the Indian Ocean coupled with a fall in air pressure over the Eastern Pacific means that trade winds in the south Pacific head east. Warm air rises near Peru and warm water spreads from the West Pacific to the East Pacific taking rain with it. The cold Humboldt Current is replaced by El Niño's warm tropical waters, meaning that the damp sea winds are able to roll over the desert, causing torrential rain. An El Niño is most often associated with very wet summers (December to February) when heavy downpours result in serious flooding and can cause enormous devastation. Usually many people die or are made homeless as a result. Other parts of the world are also affected, with drier than usual conditions experienced in South-East Asia and northern Australia, increasing bush fires, worsening haze and dramatically reducing air quality.

In addition to the climatic effects, El Niño reduces the upwelling of cold nutrient-rich ocean waters and diverts the Humboldt Current that supports so much of Peru's marine life. At this point, all the fish swim south to colder waters. The local fishing industry can therefore suffer terribly during a prolonged El Niño event.

Although the mechanics of the phenomenon are understood, no-one knows what triggers it, so it is very difficult to predict. Without any means of preparing for it, there is no way to counter the effects. During the last major event, 900 people died and an estimated US$90 billion damage was caused across the world. Worse has happened though and it has been suggested that a strong El Niño led to the demise of the great Moche and Tiahuanaco civilisations, and that the destruction of the fertile farm lands of the Chimú in a similar event led to them having to expand and conquer their neighbours.

this time. Temperatures in the **central highlands** are more consistent, rising to 20°C during the day and falling to below freezing during the night. However, the quantity of rainfall varies, with most falling during the wet season from November to March. During these months the evenings tend to be warmer as a result of the cloud cover. June to September tends to be relatively dry. The **jungle** has similar wet and dry seasons to the sierra, being driest from April to October and wettest from November to March. It's hot and humid almost all year though. (For information on when to go see pp10-12).

HISTORICAL OUTLINE

With the Incas taking centre stage in this book it's easy to forget that their time in Peru's long and complex history was relatively short. Their empire, the pinnacle of a series of other notable Pre-Columbian civilisations in South America, was little more than a century old before it was spectacularly brought down in the incredible clash of cultures with the Spanish *conquistadors* in 1532.

Peru – beginnings and the first cities in the Americas

Man first crossed the Bering Strait from Asia over 15,000 years ago and gradually moved south through the Americas. The first traces of human existence in Peru can be dated back to at least 9000BC and the first cultures emerged along the coast where food was abundant in the form of fish. Notable amongst these coastal peoples are the **Chinchorro** who appear to have been the first people in the world to practise mummification. Unlike for the Incas, Chinchorro mummification was for the masses; many have been found, with the earliest mummy radiocarbon-dated back to 5500BC.

These coastal groups gradually developed a farming culture, growing corn and cotton in the pastures of the valleys near the coast and domesticating the llama, alpaca and guinea pig. The settlements grew, in particular along the Supe River north of Lima, and by 3000BC a civilisation known as the **Norte Chico** had emerged that was contemporary with the civilisations developing in Egypt and Mesopotamia. The earliest cities in the Americas were in Peru, including **Caral**, which was the capital of a group of 18 city-states. The ruins of Caral near Barranca can be visited and include six stepped pyramids, raised ceremonial platforms and amphitheatres, dated to around 2500BC. Evidence of cassava (yuca) and sweet potatoes show that there were links with the Amazon and that some kind of trade must have been going on from around this time.

One of the striking things about these early South American civilisations is how sophisticated they became without discovering things like pottery making. Currently the oldest ceramic sample found was in the valley of Viru, near Trujillo; it dates back to 1800BC.

The Chavín – Early Horizon period (1000-200BC)

Until the dating of the city of Caral (see above) to around 2500BC, archaeologists believed the site at **Chavín de Huantar**, in the Cordillera Blanca highlands north-east of Caral, to be the earliest example of an urban culture. Chavín culture arose here around 900BC and thrived for about 700 years. This was dur-

PERU

ing what is known as the Early Horizon period, 'horizon' because it's the time when a number of artistic, architectural and religious styles from several different cultures appear to have come together. Shared artistic styles also suggest common belief systems. Metallurgy developed during this period: gold, silver and copper ornaments found near Chiclayo show Chavín-style motifs.

It's been suggested that there may have been some cultural contact between the Olmecs of Central America and the Chavín as both worshipped a fearsome fanged jaguar-man god – a stylised symbol that is a feature of Chavín art. The Chavín religious cult was widespread in Peru, eventually stretching two-thirds of the way along the coast and inland to the central highlands. The religion appears to have involved the use of psychotropic drugs, probably made from the San Pedro cactus, which is often shown in carvings. A shaman would take the drug to aid his transformation from human to animal.

The Chavín dominated Peruvian culture in this Early Horizon period yet since there do not appear to have been wars involving them it seems that this was achieved without force on their part. However, it's been suggested that the powerful **Sechín**, a contemporaneous culture centred on Casma, 380km north of Lima, may have ensured the spread of the cult having adopted it themselves.

Nazca and Moche – Early Intermediate period (200BC-600AD)

As the influence of the Chavín waned, in what is known as the Early Intermediate period, regional cultures began to dominate: in the north, the Moche, and in the south, the Nazca.

Paracas-Necropolis, named after the cemetery 260km south of Lima, was the first phase of Nazca culture and lasted from 300BC to 200AD. It's characterised by exquisite textiles of wool and cotton embroidered with hundreds of detailed figures, wrappings for some of the mummies found in this cemetery. The **Nazca** are famous today for the Nazca Lines, giant patterns and pictures etched into the desert plain that can best be appreciated from the air. This has led to some far-fetched theories about their creation. Eric von Daniken in *Chariots of the Gods* suggested that they were laid out by alien visitors as runways for their spacecraft. Maria Reiche, who made a life's work of their study, believed that this was an enormous observatory. More recent studies suggest that they may have been processional routes linking shrines and water sources. Nazca pottery, colourful and striking in design, is also significant.

In the north of Peru, the warlike **Moche** rose to power, creating an empire that extended along the coast from Piura to Casma and lasted from 100AD to 800AD. It's unlikely, however, that this 'empire' was anything more than a large group of autonomous states linked by a shared culture, but you can clearly see how it paved the way for the Incas. Organisational skills involved in building monumental structures were honed in the creation of the massive Temple of the Sun at their capital near Trujillo.

Again, as with the late development of pottery in South America, it seems incredible that a culture could develop to this level without the invention of writing. For record keeping, though, it's likely that the Moche used *quipus* (see box p73), strings of coloured threads each with a number of knots as counters.

It's a system that was later adopted by the Incas. Moche culture was sophisticated and their fine colourful pottery features scenes from daily life: religious ceremonies, battles, hunting and fishing. There are pots with amazingly lifelike human faces as well as the wide range of pornographic ceramics for which they've become known.

The demise of the Moche may have been the result of a prolonged drought and then flooding caused by an El Niño in the 6th century AD.

Huari-Tiahuanaco (600-1000AD)

As in the Early Horizon period with the association between the Chavín and their religious cult and the militaristic Sechín who helped spread it, there appears to have been a similar interaction between the cult practised at Tiahuanaco and the Huari (Wari) from around 600AD. However, the people of Tiahuanaco also sought to actively expand their empire so that by the end of the first millennium a large part of Peru was under the control of these two cultures.

The site at **Tiahuanaco**, by Lake Titicaca and now in Bolivia, was the capital of that civilisation and amongst the impressive ruins you can still see the Gateway of the Sun, the monumental doorway carved with the Gateway God, Viracocha. Although this area had been inhabited since 1500BC it was not until after it had developed as a cultural and religious centre (300BC to 300AD) that it

---

❏ The Lord of the Huari (Wari)

The entire timeline of Peru as we know and understand it has been rather thrown into turmoil recently by the discovery at Espíritu Pampa (see p342 & p344) of a Huari leader's tomb amidst the Inca ruins. In 2010 a team of Cusco archaeologists, led by Javier Fonseca, uncovered 16 tombs in total within a 450 sq metre area, half of which have subsequently been excavated. The discovery was remarkably surprising given that the Huari, a pre-Inca culture, were never thought to have reached the jungle and will require historians to re-examine the extent of Huari expansion and their possible relationship with the Incas.

The Huari thrived from 600AD to 1100AD, and according to preliminary studies, the tomb dates from around 1000AD, towards the time the civilisation would have been at its height. Typically, Huari tombs were associated with extended funerary rights and have been found within a larger complex; excavations over time may reveal such a centre at Espíritu Pampa. Due to the humidity of the jungle, the tombs contained little evidence of bones or textile other than fragments. The high-ranking noble though, dubbed the Lord of the Huari and sometimes referred to as the Lord of Vilca, was found with a silver death mask, large Y-shaped silver breastplate, two gold arm cuffs embossed with anthropomorphic feline figures, two wooden staffs sheathed in silver, several hundred large sequin-like silver pieces and necklaces decorated with lapis lazuli, turquoise and other stones. Pottery discovered includes Nazca designs, which hint at contact with coastal civilisations. Revised theories suggest that the Huari had a far larger empire than previously thought and a presence at Espíritu Pampa, which the Inca knew about. When it came to retreating from the conquistadors, the Inca established themselves on the site of this habitation and built their own structures. What is clear though is that this discovery complicates our understanding of how Peru's civilisations spread and how subsequent cultures repurposed existing settlements.

began to expand, creating an empire that eventually encompassed the northern third of Chile, part of western Bolivia and an area of Peru that included Arequipa.

The **Huari** were originally based in the central highlands, with their capital near Ayacucho. They were powerful empire builders, dominating the coast and central highlands of Peru from south of Nazca and Cusco almost to the border with modern Ecuador. Their legacy for the Incas was in their urban and agricultural infrastructure: terraces for the efficient cultivation of mountain slopes, drains and canals to control water, and roads to link all parts of their empire. See also box p53.

Chimú and other regional cultures (1000-1450AD)

The repressive Huari were not popular and the unity imposed on much of the country by them began to disintegrate at the start of the second millennium. Regional states, including that of the **Chachapoyas** at Kuélap in the northern highlands, the **Chanca** north of Lima and the **Chimú** near Trujillo, began to replace them. The Chimú built Chan Chan; covering more than 20 sq km this is the world's largest adobe city and was the largest pre-Hispanic city in the Americas. The Chimú were conquered in 1450.

Incas (1200-1542AD)   [see Inca History, pp90-102]

The **first eight Incas** (strictly speaking the term refers to the ruler though it has come to mean the people) cover the period from about 1200 to the early 15th century, a time when their power and influence was limited to the Cusco area. It was not until 1438 under **Pachacutec** (see pp94-6) that they began to create an empire that was soon to become the largest in pre-Columbian America, stretching north as far as Colombia, south into Chile and Argentina and east into Bolivia.

Pizarro and Almagro set sail.

FELIPE HUAMÁN POMA DE AYALA, FROM HIS *NUEVE CRÓNICA Y BUEN GOBIERNO* (c1600)

The Spanish and the conquest of the Incas   [also see pp98-100]

It's likely that the Spanish unknowingly unleashed an advance attack on the peoples of South America in the form of smallpox, which swept south across the continent from Colombia. Some, however, believe it may have been a local sand-fly disease. Whichever it was, it claimed the Inca emperor **Huayna Capac** in 1527 and it's estimated that by 1550 it had decimated between 50% and 75% of the population. On his deathbed Huayna Capac further weakened his empire by dividing it between his sons, **Atahualpa** and **Huascar**, pitting them against each other in a civil war.

The Spanish advance on the Americas was rapid after the voyages of Columbus between 1492 and 1503 to the Bahamas, the Caribbean islands, Central America and Colombia. In 1502, **Francisco Pizarro** sailed from Spain with 2500 other colonists in 30 ships. By 1519 he had risen to become mayor and magistrate of Panama City. No doubt inspired by the rumours of gold and silver in the lands to the south he organised his own expedition with Diego de Almagro. He made some preliminary voyages between 1524 and 1528 before returning to Spain to organise funds for a full-scale expedition and to crave the indulgence of the Spanish crown.

Granted the title of Governor of Peru, Pizarro landed near Tumbes in northern Peru in 1532 and marched south with a force of 106 foot-soldiers and 62 horsemen. Having defeated his brother Huascar, Atahualpa was also in the north, at Cajamarca with his army of 80,000 men. That meeting which sealed the fate of the continent is described on p90. In the resulting **Battle of Cajamarca**, on 16 November 1532, Pizarro famously trapped Atahualpa and greedily held him ransom for enough gold and silver to fill three rooms. Even though the ransom was fulfilled Pizarro realised that he could not keep the Inca emperor alive and, after a mock trial, convicted him of treason and of killing his brother. He had him executed in July 1533. Peter Shaffer's play, *The Royal Hunt of the Sun*, is a moving recreation of these final events.

Pizarro nominated a puppet ruler, **Túpac Huallpa**, brother of Atahualpa and Huascar, and marched south to take Cusco. Túpac died on the march so Pizarro replaced him with another brother, **Manco Inca Yupanqui**, who had come from the capital to meet them. Cusco fell in 1534 and the following year Pizarro founded Lima. Manco Inca attempted to retake Cusco, laying siege to the city in 1536 before retreating into the jungle around Vilcabamba. It was not until 1573 that the Incas were finally subdued.

Viceroyalty of Peru (1542-1826)

With Peru conquered and a handful of seditious conquistadors crushed in 1542, Spain sought to consolidate its hold on the country. In due course the Viceroyalty of Peru, as the colony was known, became the most prized asset in Spain's South American empire. Lima, which had been founded in 1535, became increasingly important, with traders all along the coast using its port to send goods out of the country. Over the next 200 years the capital developed into the main political, social and commercial centre for all of the surrounding countries. By contrast, Cusco became a relative backwater.

The *encomienda* system of rule The rulers of the new colony were the Spanish-born viceroys appointed by the Spanish crown. Immigrants from Spain were given most of the prestigious positions and power was contained by these individuals, who installed a feudal system of rule.

A theoretically fair system of rule, the *encomienda* system was authorised by the Spanish crown. The premise was that the crown governed and owned everything. This meant that the conquistadors could extract tribute for the crown and personal services for themselves in exchange for converting indigenous people to Christianity. In return for the salvation of their souls, the Indians were forced to give up their bodies and work for the Spanish. In theory, the

Spaniards could benefit from the labours of the Indians who lived on the land that they oversaw for the Spanish crown, but neither they nor the Indians could own the land, and the Indians were not to be treated as slaves. Nor could the Spaniards live on this land or pass it on to family or next of kin. Crown agents, *corregidors*, were appointed to supervise and enforce these rules.

Of course, in practice the system failed. The royal administrators found themselves in constant conflict with the *encomenderos*, who had no intention of fully emancipating the Indians or of treating them as equals. Fundamentally the colony was too far from the crown to be properly supervised. Greed inevitably surfaced and those Spaniards holding land were set on making as much money as they could, regardless of the conditions their labour force endured. As governor of Peru, Pizarro gave large groups of Indians to his allies and friends, effectively creating the basic colonial land tenure structure that the crown had set out to avoid. Much of Imperial Spain's wealth was subsequently built from the maltreatment of the descendants of the Incas.

Some of the stories, which became known as *La Leyenda Negra* (the **Black Legend**), and which tell of the violence and brutality meted out by the conquistadors on their new colony and its inhabitants, were no doubt true but they do not tell the whole story. The Incas are often portrayed as a harmonious people who endured countless atrocities and abuse at the hands of the Spanish, but they were a warlike, vicious society themselves: if the shoe had been on the other foot, Atahualpa acknowledged that he would have had no qualms about brutally incarcerating the Spanish if he had captured them. Nonetheless, the atrocities endured after the Conquest need to be recounted and recorded as this period was full of terrible violence.

The most horrific incidents related to the giant silver mines at Potosí (now in Bolivia), which were discovered in 1545. Forced off their land and conscripted into working in the mines, convoys of pressed Indian labour were driven from their homes to work themselves to death. Hundreds of thousands of Indians died as a result whilst Spanish coffers were filled with the necessary cash to finance wars across Europe.

Spain loses control The Spanish empire struggled to fully assert itself over its colonies and the crown's laws were frequently flouted. Coupled with this, locally born Spaniards (*Creoles*) became resentful of the fact that they were not entitled to any of the perks or positions of power that the immigrant Spanish enjoyed in Peru. It wasn't until the transition from the Hapsburgs to the Bourbon kings at the start of the 18th century that the empire was able to re-establish control. They did this by imposing dramatic changes to the way that Peru was governed: control was centralised, laws preventing Creoles from taking up positions of power were tightened and the Jesuits – who were seen as being too autonomous, and too tightly allied with the papacy – were driven out entirely. Spain's South American territories were also divided up.

The creation of Viceroyalties to the north, east and south of Peru meant that the area to be governed by the Viceroy of Peru was decreased so became more manageable. Trade regulations were also revamped and Lima lost its protected status as the country's main docks. Existing taxes were increased and additional levies implemented.

Uprisings in the 18th century These changes and the tightening of control inevitably resulted in resentment. Over the next hundred years a series of protests and rebellions on various scales broke out. In 1740 **Juan Santos Atahualpa** roused a group of forest Indians to revolt and successfully repelled attacks on his stronghold in the high jungle. He never succeeded in extending his power, though, nor gained any additional control before he died in 1756. A more important insurgence, drawing on the existing unrest, broke out in 1780. The *mestizo* José Gabriel Condorcanqui symbolically adopted the nickname **Túpac Amaru II**, and whipped up anti-Spanish feeling. Initially just a demonstration against the high charges and duties demanded as well as the harsh employment laws, his rebellion took on a more significant note when he imprisoned a corregidor, massacred a group of 600 Royalist soldiers and attempted to instigate Inca rule.

The empire's response was rapid and brutal, with troops from Lima despatched to quell the uprising. Within a year, following a decisive battle at Checacupe, Túpac Amaru was taken into prison, tortured and beheaded, although the uprising he inspired staggered on until 1783. (Incidentally, move forward a couple of hundred years and the Black Panther Afeni Shakur named her son after this inspirational revolutionary – a man who would later find fame in the world of rap music: Tupac Amaru Shakur.)

Although ultimately unsuccessful, Túpac Amaru II had demonstrated that there were deficiencies in Spanish rule and that a high level of popular unrest existed. Historians now consider his rebellion an important precursor to Peruvian independence.

Towards independence The late 18th century saw profound changes across the world. The North American colonies gained independence from Britain and France suffered a revolution. Liberal ideas spread across the globe; South America took notice, recognising that the potential to throw off the shackles of colonialism now existed. Inflammatory articles and newspapers began to appear in Lima; discontent became rife. Peruvian nationalism gained momentum and began to take shape as the philosophy of the Enlightenment pervaded the whole of the country.

The Peninsula War for control of Europe's Iberian Peninsula saw Napoleon cross Spain to attack Portugal before turning on his erstwhile Spanish allies in 1808. The beleaguered Spanish crown called for assistance from its colonies. In return for aid, the colonies demanded a relaxation in the regulations preventing Creoles from holding responsible positions of power and an increased recognition of their general rights, a step that meant that Peru tasted the early stages of independence.

By the time Ferdinand returned to the Spanish throne in 1814 much of South America was in upheaval and Royalist troops were struggling to maintain control. **San Martín** first liberated Argentina then, in 1817, Chile. At the same time

Simon Bolívar had ejected the Spanish from Venezuela and Colombia. By this stage it was just a matter of time before one of these great liberators reached Peru.

Independent Peru

San Martín, anxious to protect his territories and deprive the Spanish of the prized silver mines at Potosí, arrived first from the south, in 1818. Having persuaded an English naval officer, Lord Cochrane, to attack Lima, San Martín landed in Pisco and marched on the capital. Battling north he reached Lima in time to witness the Viceroy escape with the few Royalist troops he still had. Entering the city without a struggle, he proclaimed independence on 28 July 1821.

San Martín assumed political control as 'Protector of Peru' and initiated some immediate changes, declaring freedom for slaves' children, abolishing Indian service and actually outlawing the term Indian. However, with the Royalists still controlling chunks of the north of the country his changes were largely superficial.

Travelling north, San Martín tried to enlist the aid of Bolívar in routing the remnants of the occupiers. Bolívar, a man predisposed to megalomania, turned down the advance, intent on securing his own fame by achieving victory alone. Relenting, San Martín handed the initiative to his opposite number, who mopped up the last patches of resistance to independence in 1824.

Bolívar absorbed Peru into his vast Andean Confederation, which included Colombia, Venezuela, Ecuador and Bolivia. However, a year after his withdrawal from the country to return to Colombia, the Peruvians abandoned his constitution and in 1826 installed **General La Mar** as president. There quickly followed a series of *caudillos* (military leaders) who assumed power. Plots, counterplots and coups ensued, with **General Gamarra** seizing power in 1829, a move that set the tone for the rest of the country's history. Voted out of office four years later, Gamarra staged another coup in a bid to regain power, but was overwhelmed and exiled. Nonetheless, the military seized control.

In 1835-36 **Santa Cruz** invaded Peru from Bolivia and installed himself as Protector with the ambition of uniting the two countries. Chile and Argentina, in alliance with Gamarra, intervened and at the battle of Yungay in 1839 reinstated Peru's independence. Gamarra was installed as president once again and promptly attacked Bolivia. In 1841 he was slain at the Battle of Ingavi. Peru went on to have six presidents in the course of the next four years.

Finally, in 1845, **Ramón Castilla** came to office. Riding a wave of enthusiasm and prosperity heralded by the export of *guano* (bird excrement) fertiliser, Castilla oversaw a period of prosperity and real growth. By the early 1860s more than three-quarters of the Peruvian government's revenues were derived from the export of guano. Money was invested in the rail network and a programme of schooling and teaching the indigenous people went a long way to emancipating the slaves.

A second term in office saw him develop sugar and cotton as export commodities as the rich guano reserves ran out and cheaper alternatives were discovered. Sadly his successor, **Balta**, couldn't sustain the growth and enormous, ill-conceived expenditure on railways and other engineering works left Peru on the brink of economic collapse. On the back of the 1872 elections the military staged another coup, which was overthrown by a civilian mob and led to the country's first civilian president, **Manuel Pardo**, coming to power.

Despite the proclamation of independence, Spain refused to officially relinquish control of Peru. In 1864 a company of soldiers captured the Chincha Islands, which were responsible for much of the guano that fuelled Peru's early wealth. In alliance with Chile, Ecuador and Bolivia, Pardo went to **war with Spain**. Although the Spanish shelled Lima they never made land and eventually retreated. In 1871 a ceasefire was agreed, but it wasn't until 1879 that Spain formally recognised its former colony's status as an independent country.

The War of the Pacific

Peace and stability didn't last long. As Peru's economy collapsed under the weight of foreign debt, deteriorating relations with Chile and a squabble over nitrate-rich deposits located in Bolivia exacerbated the country's problems. When hostilities between Bolivia and Chile boiled over into war in 1879, Peru offered to act as a go-between, having made a secret pact with Bolivia to support each other.

In retaliation, Chile declared war on Peru. Early Peruvian victories at Iquique and the sinking of the Chilean corvette *Esmeralda* were offset by the loss of the ironclad frigate *Independencia*, followed by the loss of Tacna and Arica. Further victories on land and at sea saw Chilean forces occupy Lima at the start of 1881.

The treaty of Ancón in 1883 ended the dispute but saw Peru cede control of its southern provinces to Chile for 10 years. However, it wasn't until 1929 that an agreement was reached under the terms of which Tacna was returned to Peru, while Chile kept control of Arica and the rich nitrate deposits found there.

British bailout

Following the War of the Pacific, Peru was virtually bankrupt. With the loss of the nitrate rich territories the country's coffers soon ran dry and by 1890 Peru was unable to pay its foreign debts. An international plan to bail out Peru saw the creation of the Peruvian Corporation in London, which assumed the enormous debt in return for control of the economy. Foreign companies assumed control of the rail network and valuable guano production, and were given free access to the country's main ports. Despite the indignity of being bailed out, Peru did stabilise and a semblance of peace returned. The development of copper production buoyed the economy and reforms including direct suffrage, public education and municipal elections helped to ease the plight of the ordinary peasant.

In 1908 one of the big businessmen, **Augusto Leguía**, was elected president. During his tenure foreign investment increased and the capital was modernised, yet he made few concessions to support the poor and resentment swelled. Minor rebellions followed and in 1931, a year into his fourth term, he was ousted by a military coup.

PERU

APRA and the army

During the years Leguía had been in power, the Labour movement had steadily been growing in strength. The worldwide Depression in the early 1930s hit Peru hard as demand for its main exports declined drastically. At this time an originally Marxist movement, the **APRA** (Alianza Popular Revolucionaria Americana), stepped up its activity and resistance to what it saw as the financial hegemony of the United States. The group's founder, **Víctor Raúl Haya de la Torre**, stood for election in 1931 calling for state control of the economy and nationalisation of key industries, but was defeated. APRA, convinced that the group had been robbed, instigated disturbances in Trujillo targeting the sugar barons there. Fifty military prisoners, including ten officers, were killed in the violent uprising and the brutal retaliation by the army saw almost 5000 people massacred in the desert. In revenge, APRA assassinated the president in 1933.

The organisation was promptly banned, but went underground, operating secretly and becoming one of the largest and best-organised political parties in Peru. Legalised again in time for the 1945 election, APRA nominated **José Bustamente** who was a more neutral candidate than the contentious Haya de la Torre. Bustamente went on to win a majority in both the Senate and the Chamber of Deputies. No sooner was he in office than he announced his independence from APRA but, unable to control inflation, he increasingly relied on the army to consolidate his position until inevitably a military coup removed him from office. APRA was banned once more and its former members restricted in what they were allowed to do, so they couldn't continue to work, even clandestinely.

Agrarian reform and military rule

By the time of the 1956 elections a new political threat had emerged. The **National Youth Front** demanded radical reform. Only with the support of an unholy marriage of convenience between a weakened APRA and their traditional enemy, the army, was the then president **Manuel Prado** able to defeat the group's leader **Fernando Belaúnde Terry**. Strikes and disturbances persisted, particularly in the remoter parts of the country, and a bloody revolt led by **Hugo Blanco** broke out in the Cusco region. Peasants seized control of land and began to work their own plots. Landowners were forced to bribe the peasants to come back to work or risk going bankrupt. Although arrested in 1963, Blanco had laid the foundations for agrarian reform.

Following the deadlocked 1962 elections where Haya de la Torre, Belaúnde and General Odría all polled approximately a third of the votes, the army predictably took control. Fresh elections were called in 1963, by which time neither APRA nor the National Youth Front posed a serious threat to society, and Belaúnde swept to power. In order to appease the increasingly agitated campesinos he set about a series of radical agrarian reforms and distributed 500,000 acres of land to the people who were finally entitled to work it for themselves rather than for an absent landlord.

In 1968 the military once again intervened and seized control. Belaúnde was deported and a military regime installed. Relationships with the then Soviet Union and Eastern European countries were developed and various land reform initiatives were launched. The regime took control of industry and handed more land out to the campesinos. Large estates were taken over and reorganised as cooperatives. In 1973 the educational system was overhauled, rural schools were built and the equality of women was recognised. However, the fishing crisis of the 1970s, when stocks dwindled, coupled with the decline in the world price of copper and sugar resulted in increased national debt. Ultimately the army handed back control voluntarily by calling a democratic election in 1978.

Rise of terrorist groups

A new constitution was sketched out and Haya de la Torre eventually became president. His tenure was short-lived though and he was replaced in 1980 by Belaúnde, who set about reorganising the economy along free-market lines. However, his policy to further develop the Amazon and exploit the wealth there failed to stem the rise in inflation, which reached 100% in 1983-84. At the same time, two terrorist groups, the Maoist-inspired **Sendero Luminoso** and the Marxist **MRTA**, began to make their presence felt (see box p62). Inflation ran riot as the value of the sol collapsed.

In 1985 APRA swept to power and **Alan García** was elected president. An ambitious economic programme to cut taxes, reduce interest rates, freeze prices and devalue the currency was intended to solve many of Peru's deep-rooted economic and social problems. The short-term boom this produced led to far worse problems in the long-term and García's resolution to pay off only a tenth of Peru's foreign debt simply led to international banks suspending future loans. The situation rapidly deteriorated, with terrorists and the military, including a right-wing death squad comprising disaffected army personnel and police officers and known as the *Rodrigo Franco Commando*, engaged in a bloody, violent battle that inevitably harmed the campesinos caught in the crossfire more than it did either group actually involved in the struggle. García's abortive attempt to nationalise the banks only plunged Peru further into disarray and ensured that by the time he eventually went into exile, hounded by allegations of corruption, the country was bankrupt.

1990s – the reign of Fujimori

The 1990 election became one of Peru's most pivotal. In the run-up there were four main candidates: the popular and internationally renowned author **Mario Vargas Llosa** with his right-wing coalition; **Luís Alva Castro**, general secretary of APRA; **Alfonso Barrantes** in charge of a left-wing group; and **Henry Pease** of the United Left. The left were severely split and after five disastrous years in power APRA stood little chance of regaining the presidency, leaving Vargas Llosa the clear favourite. In the event, a brand new, unknown political party, Cambio 90 (Change 90), led by a young college professor of Japanese descent, **Alberto Fujimori**, proved the stiffest challenge. In a notable upset, the unfancied Fujimori defeated the favourite Vargas Llosa.

Once in power, Fujimori reneged on his promises, assumed complete control and rewrote the Peruvian constitution, declaring that he needed a freer hand to introduce market reforms and combat terrorism. He also adopted most of

Vargas Llosa's policies. Ever since it has been known as the **President's Coup**, since that is essentially what it amounted to: a bloodless coup d'état.

Fujimori's successes Fujimori embarked on a series of economic reforms designed to turn the country around. Although the prices of many staples such as flour and fuel trebled, he did manage to get hold of the economy and restore

---

❑ **Terrorism – the Shining Path and the MRTA**

Over the years, Peru has been menaced by two main terrorist movements: the **Sendero Luminoso** (Shining Path, also known as the Partido Comunista del Perú, Communist Party of Peru) and the MRTA (Movimiento Revolucionario Túpac Amaru, Túpac Amaru Revolutionary Movement). Founded in 1970 along the lines of the Chinese Gang of Four by Abimael Guzmán (aka Comrade or Presidente Gonzalo), Sendero Luminoso are Maoists opposed to global capitalism who have abandoned the possibility of democratic change. In 1976 the group adopted armed struggle as the only means of achieving its ends and bringing about revolution in Peru. Support for the group comes from the large number of disaffected campesinos in the country, especially farmers and families scratching a living in the group's traditional heartland, the highlands around Ayacucho.

Ruthless and savage, the Sendero persecuted anyone not allied with them or who didn't actively agree with their philosophy. The revolution was proclaimed through 'teachings' and by terrorising rural communities into acquiescing, whilst funding came from the cocaine trade and protection rackets. At their height during the 1980s and '90s, members numbered in their thousands and carried out attacks on business interests, local officials, police stations and anything deemed to be interfering with or oppressing the peasantry. Members met secretly and would simply melt back into the obscurity of their villages when put under pressure. Guzmán himself lived mainly underground, rarely seen even by members of his own organisation, until his capture in 1992; he still languishes in jail to this day. The events leading up to his capture in his Lima hideout were made into a book, *The Dancer Upstairs* by Nicholas Shakespeare, which subsequently became a film staring Javier Bardem. In 2003 a ruling that the anonymous trial by military personnel that convicted Guzmán was unconstitutional led to him being retried and again convicted to life in prison. However, other rulings delivered by military panels during the Fujimori years have been either overturned or annulled.

The urban-based, Marxist **MRTA** first found support in the shanty towns around Lima. Although more moderate than the Sendero, they have never been as well supported and indeed their capacity and confidence was rocked by an army ambush in 1988 that saw 62 militants killed. They first came to the world's attention on 17 December 1996 when they successfully infiltrated the Japanese ambassador's residence disguised as waiters. They held the building under siege for 126 days, with over 300 hostages including Fujimori's brother and a number of Peru's highest-ranked officials, whilst calling for the release of hundreds of jailed comrades. Four months into the siege, Fujimori authorised Peruvian forces to storm the building. All but one of the hostages were rescued alive, whilst all the terrorists were killed. Later, in 2003, the soldiers involved in the resolution of the stand-off were tried for massacring the terrorists in cold blood, but were acquitted on the basis that they had been involved in a military confrontation. Regardless, the MRTA remains a broken entity today and their former leader, Victor Polay, currently shares the same maximum-security prison as Guzmán.

international faith in Peru. His greatest success, and the turning point that enabled him to stand for a second term, was the capture of Sendero Luminoso leader Abimael Guzmán in September 1992. Even though Fujimori was unaware of the operation by the secret anti-terrorist police to grab Guzmán at his Lima hideout, he milked the success, publicly displaying the captured terrorist in a giant cage, dressed in a cartoonish prison outfit, and successfully convincing the international media that Peru was no longer a country where terrorists were set to take over.

The Peruvian people responded to his successes and Fujimori secured almost two-thirds of the votes in the 1995 election, when he defeated the former head of the United Nations **Javier Pérez de Cuéllar**. Continued economic success followed as inflation dipped from a record rate of 2777% in 1989 to 10% in 1996. A peace treaty with Ecuador, following skirmishes in 1995, 1997 and 1998 over ownership of oilfields on what the Peruvians claim is their side of the border, was also signed, but at considerable cost to human rights. Despite international aid agencies confirming widespread poverty and unemployment in Peru and the devastating effects of El Niño in 1998, the economy remained buoyant in the run-up to the 2000 elections.

Fujimori loses control Here Fujimori pushed his luck by once more rewriting the constitution in order to permit himself an unprecedented third term in office. Despite a stranglehold on the media Fujimori encountered strong opposition from **Alejandro Toledo**, who represented the interests of Andean communities and cities. Following a hotly contested election full of untruths and deceit, in which a smear campaign accusing Toledo of abandoning an illegitimate daughter and being financially unreliable surfaced amidst allegations of vote rigging and fraud, Fujimori claimed 49.87% of the vote, missing outright victory by 14,000 votes. Toledo withdrew from the contest in protest and Fujimori embarked on an historic third term.

No sooner had he settled back into office than he was forced to resign. Video tapes were leaked to the press of Fujimori's sinister chief assistant, **Vladimiro Montesinos**, head of the state intelligence agency SIN (**Servicio de Inteligencia Nacional**), bribing congressmen. In total around 2700 so-called 'Vladivideos' came to light, revealing the extent to which Montesinos had exerted control over the army, the intelligence service and the cocaine mafia through bribes, extortion, intimidation and threats of violence. Montesinos fled to Panama just as it was revealed that he had squirreled away more than US$50 million of what is thought to be drug money in foreign bank accounts. He successfully evaded capture until 2001 when he was held in Venezuela and returned to Peru to stand trial (see box p64).

Fujimori clung to power for a further two months. On a routine tour he stopped in Japan and in November 2000 sent his resignation as President of Peru to Congress. He then revealed that he had been a Japanese national throughout his time as president, a disclosure that meant he had illegally spent 10 years at the top since by law the Peruvian president must be a Peruvian national.

Peru in the 21st century

Fresh elections were called in 2001, with the centrist **Toledo** narrowly defeating Alan García, the man who had so badly damaged Peru's economy in the late 1980s. Toledo stood on a manifesto promising the creation of a million new jobs and a strong, stable economy. Carefully exploiting his Andean ancestry he adopted the nickname Pachacutec after the great Inca emperor. Sadly he was unable to live up to his namesake.

Having inherited a sceptical, pessimistic populace, a damaged domestic setup with slow growth and worsening social conditions, Toledo found his popularity rapidly falling. His pledge to create a million jobs remained unfulfilled, unemployment remained a serious problem, taxes increased, pledges to increase

❏ **Truth and reconciliation**

In 2003 Peru formally petitioned Japan for Fujimori's extradition to face multiple counts of bribery, corruption and being an illegal president. The same year, the Truth and Reconciliation Committee reported into the civil war of the 1980s to '90s stating that almost 70,000 Peruvians had been killed. There were also accusations Fujimori had made a US$15 million pay-off to Montesinos (see below) when he lost his job; established a programme of forced sterilisation of campesino women; and was linked to the Grupo Colina death-squad, who were responsible for a number of assassinations and kidnappings in the early 1990s. Since Peru has no formal extradition treaty with Japan there was no way of removing Fujimori, a Japanese national, and bringing him to trial to face charges. That is until he voluntarily left the country to mount a campaign to be elected president of Peru in 2006, claiming that he would be fully exonerated.

Upon entering Chile he was arrested on an extradition warrant and returned to Peru, the first time a court anywhere in the world had ordered the extradition of a former leader to be tried in his home country for human rights' violations. Following trial in 2007 Fujimori was sentenced to six years in jail for abuse of authority stemming from an illegal search of an apartment belonging to Montesinos' wife, which he ordered without a warrant. He was also fined the equivalent of US$135,000. In a separate trial for human rights' abuses, the charge being that he ordered the murder of 25 people at the hands of military death-squads, he was found guilty and sentenced to 25 years. In 2009 Fujimori was convicted of embezzling and sentenced to a further 7½ years in prison, having admitted to paying Montesinos US$15 million in government funds illegally. It is thought that he admitted the charge to avoid a protracted trial that might have harmed his daughter's candidacy for the 2011 presidential elections (see p66). Although she lost in a close-fought run-off, Keiko Fujimori went on to request a pardon for her father in October 2012 on humanitarian grounds, based on her father's deteriorating health and multiple (surgical) operations for oral cancer.

Montesinos fared little better. Having been traced to Venezuela, captured there and returned to Peru in 2001, he was convicted in 2003 of embezzlement (on relatively minor counts) and sentenced to nine years' imprisonment; he has since received tariffs of five and eight years on additional counts of bribery and abuse of power, as well as a further 15 years for corruption and conspiracy. Further trials convicted him of involvement in the Death Squad killings and awarded him a 20-year prison term for direct involvement in an arms deal to provide thousands of assault weapons to the Colombian rebel group, the FARC.

salaries fell through and the benefits of what few economic changes he did make failed to filter down to the populace at large.

Crippling strikes, violent street demonstrations and a series of major confrontations in 2002 and 2003 prompted him to call a state of emergency, whilst a series of scandals forced him to reshuffle his cabinet and relaunch his administration. Toledo's approval rating slumped to less than 10%, the lowest of any South American leader and lower even than the disgraced Fujimori (31%), who continued to broadcast a radio show on Radio Miraflores from his home in Japan, despite an international arrest warrant for his involvement with the death squad Grupo Colina.

Return of García in 2006 elections Sensing an opportunity, **Fujimori** returned from Japan in 2005 to stand for President in the 2006 elections. He was arrested in Chile (see box opposite) but was extradited back to Peru where he is now serving a 25-year jail sentence in Lima.

With Fujimori constitutionally banned from appearing on the ballot, the 2006 election became a stand off between the populist **Ollanta Humala**, an indigenous Andean ex-army officer who had served under Fujimori and was backed by the then Venezuelan President, Hugo Chávez, and the ex-president **Alan García** who pledged to rein in public spending and not fritter away the benefits of a positively expanding economy.

Voters, suspicious of Chavez's influence, clearly forgave García for putting Peru on the road to ruin in the 1980s and elected him back into office, much to the chagrin of Chávez who had championed Humala as part of his vision for South American socialist solidarity. Relations between Peru and Venezuela further soured after the election result, when Chávez refused ties with the García administration and accused him of being an American lapdog. In contrast, foreign investors and external observers reacted positively to the result. García's cabinet included APRA members and independents as well as six women. García, styling himself as a mature pragmatist, delivered a degree of stability and prosperity and on the back of economic growth, low inflation and a sensible spending policy, business leaders predicted an Andean renaissance.

However, he made little impact on the crippling poverty affecting so many Peruvians. Inevitably the huge numbers of people living on less than a dollar a day began to lose patience with empty promises and the president's approval rating fell. Demonstrations, strikes and street protests in the run up to the first anniversary of García's return to power soured what had appeared to be one of South America's great political comebacks.

The forced resignation of his entire cabinet in 2008 on the back of allegations of bribery and corruption further tarnished his reputation. An ill-advised law to allow foreign companies to exploit natural resources in the Amazon, passed in 2008, was revoked in 2009 following protests, roadblocks and confrontations between police and Amazon tribes, one of which left more than 30 people dead and 150 hurt near the town of Bagua. García accused the tribes of impeding progress; the tribes claimed they were seeing little benefit from the push to develop Peru's rich natural reserves. Subsequently García also rejected

PERU

a law that would give indigenous people more power to stop oil and mining projects on their lands. The law was passed by Congress but sent back by García, saying it went too far and that he couldn't let indigenous communities stop development that would benefit all Peruvians. The controversy and outcry continues, causing social friction and endangering the country's stability and prosperity.

García was unable to contest the 2011 election, which began as a fight between two right-wing political parties: Solidaridad Nacional led by a former mayor of Lima, Luis Castañeda Lossio, and Fuerza 2011, led by Keiko Fujimori, daughter of ex-president Alberto. Later in the campaign, APRA and Perú Posible, under the leadership of former president Alejandro Toledo, entered the race, along with Ollanta Humala, supported by Alianza Gana Perú (including the Nationalist, Socialist and Communist parties). Fujimori and Humala soon established themselves as front-runners. Fujimori ran on support of the status quo free-market policies but was seen as hindered by her relationship to her disgraced father, whom people feared she might pardon; Humala softened his anti-capitalist stance to look more moderate and talked extensively about making concessions to unite Peru. In one of the tightest and most bitter election races of recent years, neither of the top two candidates achieved the requisite 50% of votes after the first round. A second round run-off saw Humala triumph with just over 51% of the vote.

Other countries, business communities and the world financial markets responded favourably when he announced a moderate cabinet of experienced politicians, allaying fears of radical change. At his inauguration, Humala also promised social inclusion, an increase in the minimum monthly wage and a pension for those over 65. However, his first year in charge was marred by disputes and conflict, particularly in relation to key gold mining projects, and his approval rating fell from a high of more than 70% to just over 40%. Despite Peru's impressive economic boom throughout his tenure, Humala failed in his campaign to be re-elected in 2016 after being implicated in a bribery scandal (see p68). In his stead Pedro Pablo Kuczynski, a former prime minister in the government of Toledo, prevailed in an incredibly tight election. His main task now will be to find a way to continue the economic boom of the past few years, while simultaneously finding an alternative to the current economic model, which has failed to lift millions of Peruvians out of poverty.

THE PEOPLE

PERU

The vast majority (almost three-quarters) of Peru's 30.5 million inhabitants live in cosmopolitan modern cities. Nonetheless, the society is deeply rooted in the past and just under half the population is **Quechua**. The Quechua living in rural areas prefer to be known as *campesinos* (rural labourers) rather than *indios* (Indians), a term that is considered derogatory. Around a third of the population are *mestizo*, with mixed Spanish and Amerindian heritage and parentage.

Other groups include the **Aymara** living around Lake Titicaca and the **indigenous** tribes living in the Amazon, who number around 250,000.

There is also a small black **Afro-Peruvian** population, mostly living on the coast south of Lima and descended from those unfortunate enough to be brought to Peru as slaves, and a small **Asian** community made up of Chinese and Japanese immigrants. Descendants of the first Spanish families and other European immigrants constitute a small **Caucasian** population.

Life expectancy is currently 74½ years.

Education and literacy

About 20% of adult Peruvians living in the countryside are illiterate compared with 4% of urban dwellers. Education is now free and compulsory for both sexes up to the age of 16 – a boon for the 30% or so of Peru's population under the age of 14. This is understandably difficult to enforce in remote rural areas. Nonetheless, the government estimates that most of the country's children have access to primary education, two-thirds go to secondary school and around a quarter go on to tertiary education. Publicly funded schools don't have a great reputation and resources are very scarce, so those who can afford it tend to send their children to private schools.

Language

Spanish is the official language of Peru and spoken in all but the most remote areas (for a list of useful words and phrases see pp345-9). However, for a large percentage of the population this is a second language, and **Quechua** (or *Runasimi*, 'the people's mouth'), the official language of the Incas, whom it actually predates, is the indigenous first language. Most of the people who still speak Quechua are concentrated around Cusco and elsewhere in southern Peru. In the countryside surrounding Lake Titicaca a handful of people still speak Aymara, an ancient language dating to before the Incas.

There was no written version of Quechua until the 16th century so no standard way of transcribing it exists. Even now it is only fitfully being introduced into schools. As a result you will see the same words written differently. For instance, Inca can be spelt Inka, Cusco is sometimes written as Cuzco or Q'osqo and Sacsayhuaman sometimes shown as Saq'saywaman. The spellings in this book are consistent, if not the only versions of these names.

In and around Cusco, Lima and the other major tourist destinations such as Arequipa, English is also understood by some people.

Religion

From the 16th century onwards the Inca religion was displaced by Roman Catholicism as the conquistadors steadily converted the local population. Nowadays, around 82% of Peru considers itself **Roman Catholic**. The Peruvian church is also the cradle of 'Liberation Theory', a Socialist interpretation of Christianity designed to support the poor.

Although the vast majority of the population ostensibly claim to be Catholic, the reality is that few attend regular church services and a large proportion of this figure practise a form of **Pagan Catholicism**, whereby Catholicism is fused with a series of indigenous, animist beliefs such as the worship of deities from the natural world, including mountains, animals and plants. Viracocha (the creator) is often thought of as the Christian God, whilst Pachamama (the earth mother) is represented by the Virgin Mary and seemingly Catholic services generally have many layers of meaning.

An increasing number of the population now state that they are **Protestant** and the greatest threat to Catholicism in Peru comes from the predatory evangelical Protestant groups throughout the country. Around 12% of the population now consider themselves affiliated to these churches, some of which are American imports whilst others are homegrown organisations, such as the IEP (Evangelical Church of Peru), which has been active for more than a hundred years.

POLITICS AND ECONOMICS

Politics

Every five years presidential elections are held and at the same time the 120 Congressmen are selected. The president is then responsible for choosing his ministers. Peru is split into 25 departments, each governed by prefects that are also chosen by the president. Departments are further subdivided into provinces, which are further broken up into districts that are run by mayors elected every five years.

Current politics On July 28, 2016 Pedro Pablo Kuczynski took office after the closest general election ever experienced by the nation. In a run-off he defeated Keiko Fujimori by just 39,000 out of almost 18 million votes – a margin of just 0.2% – thereby inflicting a second narrow defeat on the daughter of the former president. Ollanta Humala, the previous president, failed in his bid to be re-elected following accusations of receiving payments from the Brazilian conglomerate Odebrecht in exchange for assigning them public works. Though President Humala rejected the accusations, his decision to avoid speaking to the media on the matter backfired during the elections, which instead became a two-horse race between Kuczynski and Fujimori.

Oxford-educated Kuczynski, better known by his initials of PPK, (the same initials as the party he had founded the previous year, Peruanos Por el Kambio, or Peruvians for Change), is of Polish, German and Swiss descent and, at 77, is also the oldest man to be elected president of Peru. He campaigned on a platform of greater equality for the people of Peru and a promise to fight inequality. He also promised to raise teachers' salaries and invest in schools in order to raise the country's education standards, improve access to drinking water for all Peruvians, and attempt to forge better relations with neighbouring Chile.

While few could, in public at least, voice any opposition to these ambitions, his party currently holds only 13 seats in the 130-seat Congress, thereby making it difficult – if not impossible – for them to push their policies through the legislature. Some of the country's more left-wing parties, which supported Kuczynski's campaign simply to prevent Fujimori being elected, have also stated that they won't support his liberal economic policies. It is against this hostile backdrop that Kuczynski attempts to impose his ambitious social program, which he hopes will be paid for by liberating the business environment, boosting foreign investment and increasing public spending. After a decade of the Peruvian Miracle, Kuczynski aims to drag the sluggish economy back to the 5% GDP growth mark by 2018.

Human rights During the hostilities between Sendero Luminoso and the army, countless campesinos were caught up in the ensuing violence. On the one hand the terrorists used force to cajole and bully the inhabitants of villages to comply with their message and on the other the military massacred anyone suspected of collaborating with the enemy. At the height of the conflict, there are thought to have been 10,000-15,000 secret Sendero members, against whom were ranged more than 6000 troops and anti-terrorist police. During the struggle, thousands of innocent people 'vanished' or were murdered. In 2002 the Truth and Reconciliation Commission, which was set up by the then president Toledo to examine atrocities committed in the 1980s and 1990s by the Sendero Luminoso, MRTA and the Peruvian army, began reporting on the horrific incidents. At the inauguration of the Commission a spokesman summed up the task ahead saying, 'What is absolute, what is definitive is that people were unjustly killed and human rights were violated. We are not trying to open Pandora's Box, we are trying to air things that have been forgotten and stink.'

In 2003 the commission reported back, its chairman remarking that, 'The report we hand in contains a double outrage: that of massive murder, disappearance and torture; and that of indolence, incompetence and indifference of those who could have stopped this human catastrophe but didn't.' In all, 69,280 Peruvians had been killed or disappeared during the conflict, more than doubling the number used in the past to catalogue the violence and making it one of Latin America's most brutal wars. Ayacucho, the Sendero heartland, bore the brunt of the losses, with campesinos accounting for three-quarters of the victims. Both the terrorists and the army were blamed for the loss of life. For more on this look out for *State of Fear*, a powerful documentary based on the findings of the Commission that tells the story of Peru's war on terror.

An ongoing lawsuit against the government concerns the issue of forced sterilisation. As part of a family planning policy introduced by Fujimori's government during the civil war, up to 300,000 sterilisations were performed without the consent of the women. The case has been shelved and reopened several times over the last decade and in 2015 a national registry of forced sterilisations was introduced. Fujimori's daughter was asked about the programme during her unsuccessful 2016 election campaign but blamed it upon the actions of several 'rogue' doctors – an accusation that the medical profession in Peru denies, saying that many doctors were forced against their will to carry out these procedures.

The economy

Peru's economy reflects its varied geography. The country has bountiful mineral deposits and a range of climates that allows the production of a wide range of produce. Poor economic guidance, political instability and crippling inflation have in the past brought the country virtually to its knees, though. Currently things are much healthier and the economy is thriving. Nonetheless, the gulf

❏ Coca and cocaine

Coca leaf (*Erythroxylum coca*) has been part of Andean life for thousands of years and is deeply intertwined into the practical and spiritual fabric of Peruvian society. Illustrations of people using coca can be found on the portrait pots of the Nazca and tools associated with its use date from the Moche culture. In Inca times it was so prized that only the nobility were allowed to use it, but since the arrival of the Spanish, who first tried to ban the practice before realising the value of allowing the indigenous population to chew coca, it has filtered down into common usage.

When a quid of leaves is chewed with a mixture of lime or quinoa and potash called *llipta*, it acts as a stimulant to help suppress hunger, thirst and fatigue. It also eases the effects of altitude, helps to calm nausea and fortify the body. What's more, it provides the recommended daily dose of iron, calcium, vitamin A and phosphorus so it's hardly surprising that local people still believe that it's a universal panacea.

Coca farming Until 1996 Peru was the world's largest coca-leaf producer. Overtaken and now a distant second to Colombia, the country still cultivates 34,000 hectares of coca per year. Easily purchased in Andean markets, it is used by people in all walks of life for many different purposes. The leaves contain 14 alkaloids, one of which is the narcotic cocaine. It has been said though that coca leaf has as much to do with cocaine as an elephant does to ivory – it is the base ingredient from which the final product comes, nothing more.

The leaf in its original, unprocessed form is perfectly legal in Peru and widely used by farmers and labourers involved in back-breaking work, as treatment for everything from toothache to childbirth, in religious ceremonies and as offerings to the Apus and as innocuously as in a cup of tea (Mate de coca, see box p84). This is not true of the cocaine that can be derived from it.

Discovery of cocaine First isolated in the 19th century by a scientist called Gaedeke, the cocaine alkaloid was initially received as a great scientific discovery and heralded as a pain-killing drug of great potency. Coca wine and other coca-containing preparations were sold as medicines and tonics, with claims of a wide range of health benefits. The original version of Coca-Cola was among these.

Cocaine trafficking After the addictive nature of the drug was realised these products became illegal. Unfortunately its abuse and restriction has created a monster. The main problem in Peru is the enormous wealth that production of the drug can bring. Production is generally run by organised, largely Colombian, gangs of narco-terrorists, whose lawless, brutal practices hold sway over some of the remoter sections of Peru. Much of the cocaine base is shipped to neighbouring Colombia for processing into cocaine, while finished cocaine is shipped out from Pacific ports to the international drug market. Increasing amounts are also making their way across the border into Brazil and Bolivia for distribution in Europe.

Since the 1980s the USA's Drug Enforcement Agency (DEA) has put political and economic pressure on Andean countries in a bid to eradicate the problem of cocaine trafficking and abuse by wiping out coca production in the Andes. This broad strategy overlooks the traditional value of the coca leaf to the Andean communities and ignores the poverty that drives campesinos without a viable alternative source of income to try growing it: coca is five or six times more valuable per kilo than coffee.

The internal perception in Peru is that cocaine is a problem of the urban Western world, where the demand is generated. The suspicion is that the war on drugs is cynically fought in the highlands of the Andes, largely out of sight and unreported, rather than in the West itself, because there are no voters or people to upset.

PERU

between those who have and those who have not is still vast, and there are still a lot of desperately poor Peruvians with few or no prospects.

Fujimori privatised large chunks of state-owned industry and overhauled the tax system. Toledo also followed a pro-market policy. Following the early reforms and a shift to a free market economy the growth rate for real GDP soared to 13% before stabilising around 7% by 1997. The worst El Niño of the 20th century and the Asian economic crisis in 1998 halved this figure, but since 2001 Peru's economy has been one of the fastest growing in South America. Aided by market-orientated economic reforms and a series of privatisations along with higher world prices for minerals, the increase in GDP grew from 5% in 2004 to 10% in 2008 before a dramatic fall in 2009 to 1%. Since then the Peruvian economy has continued to grow at an average of 3-9% per year, with a stable exchange rate and low inflation, due partly to a leap in private investment.

Recent economic expansion has been driven by construction, mining, export growth, investment and a swell in domestic demand. The country's chief exports are minerals and metals; Peru is the world's third-largest producer of silver and also mines a significant amount of gold, copper, zinc and lead. Mineral exports have consistently accounted for 50% of the country's export revenue, though this overdependence on minerals and metals inevitably exposes Peru to global price fluctuations. Other important exports include fishmeal, petroleum, pharmaceuticals, textiles and coffee.

Continuing economic problems Despite the apparently rosy outlook, there are still deep-rooted problems in Peru. The country's wealth is concentrated in the hands of a few and the vast majority of people still have very little. Unemployment is consistently around 7% and over a fifth of the population lives below the poverty line.

THE ENVIRONMENT

Just like anywhere else, Peru is struggling to reconcile the need to embrace a developing economy and the need to conserve ecologically sensitive parts of the country. The major issue confronting the country is the **ongoing oil programme** that is devastating chunks of the Peruvian rainforest. Sections of the rainforest have been cut down since the time of the Incas, but never at this rate or over such a large area, and never at such cost. Conservationists and eco-tourism operators are battling to prevent the programmes and associated problems of **deforestation** and environmental degradation, but they are up against substantial adversaries.

In 2003 the government granted oil companies greater access to indigenous lands throughout much of the Andes. Since then, the rainforest and jungle has come under intense pressure, particularly the area to the north of Quillabamba. There are 300 billion cubic metres of oil and gas buried beneath the jungle, but it is an area rich in bio-diversity and inhabited by native tribes, many of which have had little or no contact with the rest of the world. International pressure and outcry scared off a number of investors, including Shell, but a gas-production consortium took over what became known as the Camisea Project.

Two 800km gas pipes opened up the forest to migrants, loggers and developers; pipelines from the Camisea fields known as Block 88 in the lower Urubamba region cut through the Vilcabamba range and carry oil and gas to an export terminal on the coast, at Paracas. Planned for many years, the project finally got the green light from ex-president Alejandro Toledo in the belief that it would bring great economic benefits to Peru. Since then the government has quietly issued a decree entitling the project to commence oil and gas development in previously protected reserves. Allegedly tribes in these areas have been forcibly removed from ancestral lands, and the common problems associated with deforestation have become apparent, with landslips and increased erosion threatening the hillsides. Communities and farmers in the area have also been hit by outbreaks of infectious diseases. Nonetheless, extensive pressure from gas companies to open up adjacent areas succeeded and the neighbouring Block 56, located on the tribal lands of the Machiguenga indigenous communities, was opened up for a project known as Camisea 2. This was in spite of opposition from local groups and indigenous tribes who pointed to a report in 2006 that explained how the original pipeline running from Block 88 was poorly constructed by unskilled labourers, using old, corroded pipes, which meant that in the first 18 months after becoming operational, the pipeline ruptured four times. Campaigners also report a decline in the number of fish and animal populations in the region since the start of the project.

Ignoring this opposition, in 2008 García opened the Amazon to foreign prospectors, a move that caused more than two months of protests and road blocks which culminated in casualties on both indigenous and police sides of the stand-off, before the ill-advised law was revoked.

Issues have also arisen over **gold mining**, especially in the rich mineral deposits around Cajamarca where American outfit Newmont Mining planned to open the country's largest open-pit gold and copper mine.

Other problems include the melting of Peru's numerous tropical glaciers. **Global warming** is likely to be the main reason why the glaciers are shrinking – they are melting faster in the dry season than they are being replenished in the wet. The glaciers feed many of Peru's major waterways. If the glaciers disappear there is a very real danger that rivers will dry up and the land and people dependent on them will suffer. Desertification is a serious threat and the consequences are dire.

CULTURE

Literature

Although Peru has a powerful literary tradition, very few Peruvian writers ever make it into English. To track down some of the harder-to-find titles you may have to look in bookshops in Lima (see p136) or Cusco (see p161).

Many of the classic records of the Conquest are written by the conquistadors, but there are also Peruvian accounts offering a different perspective. **Garcilaso Inca de la Vega** and **Felipe Huamán Poma de Ayala** (see p42) are the two best examples.

❑ Quipus

The Incas never created a written version of their language. Nonetheless, they were able to communicate complex ideas and record enormous amounts of information by using quipus.

Quipus, which were used by early Andean societies and adopted by the Incas, are essentially a series of different coloured strings with knots tied in them. The colour, position and number of knots in the string could then be read by trained, skilled interpreters. Quipus may have just a few strands, but some have as many as 2000. A group known as Quipucamayocs, the accountants of the Inca society, created and deciphered the knots. They were capable of simple mathematics as well as recording information such as keeping track of *mit'a*, a form of taxation. The system was also used to record the census and to keep track of the calendar.

Today there aren't many quipus left in existence, as the Spanish suppressed the use of them and destroyed a large number. Historians are still attempting to decipher the knots and their messages. Most people maintain that the quipus only recorded numbers, but there is some evidence to support the theory that actually they contain far more information and were effectively written records or books.

Record keeper with his quipu.

FELIPE HUAMÁN POMA DE AYALA, FROM HIS *NUEVE CRÓNICA Y BUEN GOBIERNO* (c1600)

The best-known contemporary Peruvian writer is **Mario Vargas Llosa**, whose novels and commentaries stand comparison with those of other great South American literary figures. Essentially a novelist, Vargas Llosa has also written about Peruvian society and culture. The best examples of his complex, meandering narratives are the rather disturbing *Death in the Andes* (Faber and Faber) which deals with the Sendero Luminoso and Peruvian politics, *Aunt Julia and the Scriptwriter* (Picador), a comic novel about a Bolivian scriptwriter who arrives in Lima to write radio plays, which is full of insights into Miraflores society, and *A Fish in the Water* (Farrar, Straus and Giroux) which describes Vargas Llosa's unsuccessful attempt to run for presidency. Vargas Llosa was awarded the Nobel Prize for literature in 2010 in recognition of his writing.

Daniel Alarcón is a Peruvian-American author whose work has been featured in the New Yorker magazine. His collection of short stories, *War by Candlelight* (Harper Perennial), touches on a number of aspects of life in Lima, whilst his novel *Lost City Radio* (Fourth Estate) is a thinly veiled look at the disappearances and turmoil associated with the Sendero Luminoso.

José María Arguedas is an indigenous author who writes about native Andean people in his novels *Los Ríos Profundos* (*Deep Rivers* – Pergamon Press) and *Yawar Fiesta* (Quartet Books). **Ciro Alegría** also carefully depicts Andean communities in *El Mundo es Ancho y Ajeno* (*Broad and Alien is the World* – Merlin Press). **César Vallejo** is one of South America's great poets and one of the

PERU

most innovative Spanish-language poets in the world. His romantic imagery and unusual use of language make his poems both beautiful and powerful.

Visual arts

During the late 16th, 17th and 18th centuries a form of painting known as the **Cusco School** flourished in Peru. Formal European subjects and themes such as religion were reinterpreted by indigenous artists who had been taught by Spanish masters such as Juan Iñigo de Loyola, who arrived in 1545. These largely anonymous local artists drew on Spanish Mannerism to create paintings of unique and extraordinary beauty that mixed religious and native Andean imagery. The best examples include sumptuously dressed holy figures and archangels armed as soldiers of heaven. The hallmark of Cusco painting is the lack of perspective in the dramatic images, the predominance of red, yellow and earth colours and the application of gold to imitate the appearance of embroidered designs. The best examples can be seen in Cusco Cathedral. In the San Blas district of Cusco you can buy paintings in this style.

Martín Chambi is the best-known Peruvian photographer. His images of Cusco, surrounding villages and communities and the first iconic photographs of Machu Picchu taken in 1920 are internationally renowned. Described by Mario Vargas Llosa as 'a true inventor, a veritable force of invention, a recreator of life', Chambi was a prolific portrait photographer but also captured landscapes exquisitely. These he sold mainly in the form of postcards, a format he pioneered in Peru. In 1990 the Smithsonian Institution published a collection of his pictures, *Martín Chambi – Photographs 1920-1950*. Phaidon also published a collection of his photographs in 2002.

Peruvian cinema suffered as a result of a decision by the then prime minister Fujimori to overturn a law promoting domestic films. Ever since the industry has remained underfunded.

Music and dance

Music and dance are big parts of Peruvian life. Traditional music is a fusion of intercontinental styles using a mix of instruments to produce a generally soulful sound. Key instruments include the *quena*, bamboo flutes of varying lengths; *zampoñas*, double-rowed pan pipes; *charangos*, ten-stringed mandolins with a box made of armadillo shell, as well as drums, guitars, harps and brass instruments.

In the Andes, *huayno* is the staple musical form. This traditional, infectious rhythm relies on wind instruments and lyrics that fuse joy and sorrow. A Spanish version of huayno known as *música folklórica* also uses string instruments such as mandolins and harps. The traditional huayno tune *El Condor Pasa*, originally written in the 18th century to mark the death of the rebel Túpac Amaru II, achieved international fame when covered by Simon and Garfunkel and still endures today. However, the style has also fused with other sounds such as rock and Colombian *cumbia* to evolve into *chicha*, a form popular in the working-class districts of cities or in the shanty towns and Andean villages. Lyrics focus on love in all its forms but also the harshness of Andean life, drawing on themes such as displacement, exploitation and hardship for its power. The best-known chicha bands include Belem and Los Shapis.

From the coast rises up the sound of *criolla*, which has its roots in both Spain and Africa. The most famous criolla style is the *vals peruano* (the Peruvian Waltz), which is faster than its European equivalent and full of complex guitar melodies, making it ideal for dancing. The best exponents of this form are Chabuca Granda, Susana Baca, Eva Ayllón and the band Perú Negro. Both Baca and Ayllón are also excellent exponents of *landó*, a bluesier style of criolla. Ideally both these styles should be heard live in order to capture the full energy and passion within the music. The bars, clubs and *peñas* in Lima are the best places to catch a performance.

The national dance is the *marinera*. Performed to criolla it is a flirtatious courtship between a man and a woman who circle each other. Other routines include the closely related *zamacueca* and the rather simpler *zapateo*, which translates literally as foot-stomping.

Media

The most-established daily **newspapers** are *El Comercio* (🖥 elcomercio.pe), *Expreso* (🖥 www.expreso.com.pe) and *La República* (🖥 larepublica.pe) but they are only published in Spanish. There are also a multitude of tabloid-style papers whose staple material is sex and sport with gruesome accidents or horrific murders thrown in for good measure. Slightly out-of-date US and English newspapers can also be found in Lima. For travel journalism pick up the magazine *Rumbos* (🖥 www.rumbosdelperu.com).

There are several terrestrial **TV channels** in addition to a wide range of cable TV stations such as CNN and BBC World. The bulk of domestic television content is imported Spanish-language soap operas or locally made low-budget talk and news programmes.

Radio is a very popular form of entertainment and in the mountains is often the only way that people can keep abreast of the news. As well as the state run Radio Nacional there are three main national stations, all based in Lima.

Sport

Fútbol (soccer) is the most fanatically followed sport in the country, watched with an almost unparalleled zeal by hordes of spectators. The main teams, Alianza, Cristal and Universitario are from Lima (the classic local derby is Alianza versus Universitario), but Cusco giant killers Cienciano won the Recopa Sudamericana against Argentinean favourites Boca Juniors in 2004, sparking wild celebrations in the city. Unfortunately Peru hasn't qualified for the World Cup since 1982 and on two occasions has been squeezed out by local rivals Chile and Ecuador; however, the national team is currently enjoying a bit of a resurgence and came third at the 2015 Copa América. Although most Peruvian teams and players will be unknown to you, key international stars such as Claudio Pizarro have played in the UK.

Other sports struggle to compete for attention, but **bullfighting** and **surfing** have dedicated followings.

Practical information for the visitor

DOCUMENTS AND VISAS

Citizens of the EU, USA, Canada, South Africa, Australia and New Zealand do not need a visa to enter Peru and are entitled to remain in the country as tourists for up to 183 days. Check with your local Peruvian embassy before departure to ensure that this is still the case as the situation does change periodically.

Before entering the country you will have to complete a *Tarjeta de Embarque/Tarjeta Andina de Migración* (**embarkation card/TAM**) on the plane or at the border crossing. In theory you must have a return ticket before being given a card but in practice this is rarely checked. Keep the card and your passport with you at all times when moving about the country, particularly in remote areas. The law also states that you must carry these documents on the Inca Trail. If you lose the card you may be fined.

As you enter the country the immigration officer will stamp your passport to authorise a stay of 30, 60, 90 or 183 days; note **that this cannot be extended within Peru** so ensure you request up to the maximum period you might possibly stay.

If you need to **extend your stay**, you can cross one of Peru's borders and get a new tourist card when coming back in to the country.

MONEY

Currency

The **nuevo sol** (s/) is the currency of Peru and what you'll need for everyday transactions at local shops and restaurants, on transport and at places outside Cusco and Aguas Calientes. However the US dollar (US$) can be used for some tourist transactions such as buying flights or a trek, and at international restaurants and big hotels.

The Peruvian *nuevo sol* (plural: *soles*), usually called just the *sol*, is broken down into 100 *céntimos* (cents). During the 1980s and early '90s Peru suffered very high inflation, running at thousands of percent at one stage, and the currency was devalued twice, changing from the sol to the inti and then again to the nuevo sol. Some of the old notes may still be in circulation but they are worthless. Fortunately they look very different to the new notes, which have 'nuevo' clearly printed on them.

❏ **Rates of exchange**

	Peru Nuevo Sol (PEN)	US$
Au$1	s/2.60	$0.80
Ca$1	s/2.66	$0.82
€1	s/3.88	$1.19
NZ$1	s/2.37	$0.73
UK£1	s/4.41	$1.36
US$1	s/3.25	–

At the time of going to print the exchange rates were as above but these will fluctuate over time; for up-to-the-minute rates of exchange check 🖵 www.xe.com/ucc.

PERU

Notes in circulation are s/200, s/100, s/50, s/20 and s/10. Coins come in s/5, s/2, s/1, s/0.50, s/0.20 and s/0.10 denominations. Always ask for small bills when changing money or receiving local currency as the larger bills can be hard to break in remote communities or small towns. Make sure that all the notes are in good condition as some hotel owners or shopkeepers will refuse worn, torn or otherwise damaged currency.

Depending on who you bank with, you may get a better rate if you withdraw dollars at an ATM and change them into soles rather than withdrawing soles.

Banks and casas de cambio

Banks are usually open during weekdays (9am-noon and 4-6pm). Generally, try to get to the bank earlier in the day and avoid going on Friday afternoons. Most banks have 24-hour ATMs (cash machines) which accept foreign credit and debit cards. Be sure to retrieve your card since there is no warning sound to remind you to do so.

Casas de cambio are generally open all day. Changing money here is straightforward as long as you have your passport with you to prove your identity. **Money changers** often loiter outside banks or congregate on street corners where there are banks or ATMs. Some wear jackets or badges with logos sug-

---

❏ **Minimising ATM bank charges**
One of the biggest irritations when travelling in Peru (and indeed much of South America) is the charges levied every time you take money out of a cash machine using your bank card. It's not uncommon to be charged around US$10 for a single transaction – which, if you're travelling through the region for a month or more, can soon add up to quite a significant total. To try to minimise these charges, travellers will often look to withdraw as much as possible (thereby minimising the number of times they need to use an ATM and thus get charged). However, this just means you end up walking around with a lot of cash on your person, which isn't ideal.

Potentially the best solution of all is to sign up to the global money system Revolut (🖳 www.revolut.com). They claim to have eliminated bank fees altogether – and reviews from travellers have been very positive. With this ingenious app you can transfer money from your bank account to a Revolutcard, which can then be used in an ATM or to buy goods and services directly. They also claim to use the best available (ie the real one) exchange rate – and because it is an app you get updates about your balance on your phone instantly and keep up to date with what the exchange rate is. However, in 2016 they introduced a Fair Usage policy, limiting free ATM withdrawals to the equivalent of £500 per calendar month – there's a 2% charge for anything above that. To top up from a US$ bank account is subject to a 3% or 4% charge.

If you're unsure about using Revolut, another possible solution is to sign up for a **prepaid card**. Simply load up the card with credit before you go, then you can use it in cash machines abroad – or pay for things directly, like a credit card – with no fees attached. ICE, FairFX, Caxton FX, Travelex and Avios are five such cards. Do note that they are not entirely free: often there is a charge for redeeming your card when you have finished with it and other fees may be attached. If you think your card really is relatively fee-free then look at the exchange rate they are using – often it is inferior to other cards that do make a charge. Nevertheless, if you are in South America for more than just a brief visit they are certainly worth investigating.

gesting that they are official or regulated *cambistas* (money changers) licensed by the local municipality. However, they rarely offer better rates than those you can obtain from a bank and are far more likely to try and short-change you.

Using debit/credit cards

There are lots of ATMs in Lima and Cusco where it is possible to withdraw money on your Visa or MasterCard. Using your **debit card** through an ATM that has Cirrus, Maestro or Plus system logos on it ought to give you access to your bank account. Cash withdrawals can usually be made in either US dollars or nuevo soles. Some banks charge for using this service so, before leaving home, check if this is the case with your bank. **Credit cards** are also widely accepted in moderate to expensive hotels, shops and restaurants in larger towns and cities although you should not rely on this means of payment once outside of the towns and cities. Visa is the most commonly accepted card.

GETTING AROUND

Travelling between cities

By air There are regular **flights** between Lima and Cusco as well as other major towns such as Arequipa, Iquitos, Puerto Maldonado and Trujillo. The domestic airline network is frequently in turmoil though and service providers often spring up and then fail. The most-established, reliable operators include: **LATAM Airlines** (🖳 www.latam.com) which flies to the most touristy destinations; **Avianca** (🖳 www.avianca.com) which has a regular service between Lima and Cusco; **Star Perú** (🖳 www.starperu.com) which has flights to Cusco and a handful of less obvious cities as well; and **Peruvian Airlines** (🖳 www.peruvian.pe) who operate between major centres and cities including Piura and Pucallpa. There's also a small quirky operator, **LC Perú** (🖳 www.lcperu.pe), which began life as a cargo transportation company but evolved into a passenger service, with a handful of scheduled flights to Andahuaylas, Ayacucho, Cajamarca and Huaraz as well as half a dozen flights daily each way between Cusco and Lima, aboard small 19-seat planes.

> **❏ Airport tax**
> For pretty much everyone this should now be included on their ticket but if not you may have to pay cash at the airport to cover an **international departure tax** of US$31 or the equivalent in local currency. On internal flights, such as the flight from Lima to Cusco, there is a **domestic departure tax** of US$7.40 – again, usually included in the price of the ticket. Be very suspicious – and ask for a second opinion – if someone asks you to pay any airport tax in cash at the airport.

Overland A popular alternative to flying is to travel overland by **bus**, the norm for most Peruvians. Services are regular and reasonably reliable although the buses can vary immensely in terms of quality from luxury coaches to scruffy ex-US school buses. There are scores of competing companies with the biggest names operating the most frequent long-distance routes. The largest company is probably **Cruz del Sur** (🖳 www.cruzdelsur.com.pe). Slowly Peruvian cities are adjusting to having a single bus terminal and centralising the arrival and departure of the numerous operators, but these may still be clustered around a square. It is also possible that the departure point is in an entirely different place to the ticket office so make sure you check from where the bus is leaving. Arrival and departure times are loosely timetabled so take the journey times quoted with a pinch of salt.

Since the privatisation of the railways in the late 1990s **train** services have ceased to be the cost-effective means of travel they once were. **PeruRail** (🖥 www.perurail.com) has daily services between Cusco (Poroy), Urubamba, Ollantaytambo and Aguas Calientes (below Machu Picchu) and between Cusco and Puno. The extension from Puno to Arequipa has been suspended but still occasionally runs as a charter service. Competition on the popular Ollantaytambo to Aguas Calientes route comes from **Inca Rail** (🖥 www.inca rail.com; see p353 & p355). There is also a seasonal service operated by **Ferrocarril Central Andino** (🖥 www.ferrocarrilcentral.com.pe) from Lima to Huancayo in the central highlands. This only runs once a month in each direction from mid April to the end of October but climbs to 4781m (15,685ft) in the course of the trip.

As a last measure it's possible to **hitch** a ride, although this isn't the safest way to travel and shouldn't be attempted alone. However, trucks often charge for giving a lift in rural areas, so hitching is not necessarily cheaper than any other form of travelling.

Local transport
Walking is usually a safe and practical way of exploring a city. Alternatively jump in a **taxi**. Taxis don't usually have meters and will try to charge whatever they think they can get away with. Always ask what the fare is in advance and fix a price for the journey. If it seems outrageous don't be afraid to haggle: offer to pay half to three-quarters of the fare. In Cusco, most journeys are around s/5, though to and from the airport may well be a couple of *soles* more. Tipping is neither the norm nor expected. Official, regulated cabs called by telephone are usually more expensive than the private cars with a taxi sticker in the window flagged down in the street, but are generally more reliable.

People travelling alone, especially women, should always use a regulated taxi. Shared taxis for longer trips often wait by main junctions or roundabouts to collect multiple fares.

Local **buses** are almost always beaten-up old bangers, but they are astonishingly cheap. *Micros* or *combis* (which may also be referred to as *colectivos*, even though strictly these are shared taxis that ply set routes) are minibuses or minivans that hustle for business on the streets of most towns. Stickers on the outside identify the route and the destination; although the system appears chaotic, they cover almost everywhere in a city. A conductor leans out of the door calling for business and once on board you must squeeze into place or risk standing for the entire journey. Fares are collected once you're on the move. Safety and personal health aren't usually top of the driver's priorities and you will often endure a pretty hair-raising ride.

Hiring a car

Driving in Peru is not for the faint hearted. It's a long way from place to place, traffic jams in Lima are horrendous, pollution is a real problem, the roads aren't especially good and other road users are often aggressive and bad-tempered. There are major car-hire firm offices in Lima and a handful of larger cities, including Cusco. A driver's licence from your own country is usually sufficient unless you want to hire the vehicle for more than a month, in which case you will require an International Driving Licence. You will also need a credit card and usually have to be aged 25 or older.

Rates vary considerably from company to company and fuel is extra. For sound advice on motoring in Peru contact the Touring y Automóvil Club del Perú (🖳 www.touringperu.com.pe); however, the website is in Spanish.

ACCOMMODATION

Rates

Rates in this book are split into three categories: **budget**, **mid-range** and **expensive**. Hotel rates are particularly changeable and may well vary in comparison to those quoted here. Nonetheless you will be able to make comparisons between the relative price brackets.

Rates are quoted for single/double/triple rooms (**sgl/dbl/tpl**); the description includes relevant information about whether bathrooms are attached (**att**) or shared/communal (**com**), other facilities and the availability of breakfast.

Budget rooms cost US$5-35 for a room. Mid-range options are from US$35 to US$100. There has been a real explosion in this price bracket reflecting the growth in domestic and international tourism. Expensive hotels are defined as those charging more than US$100 per night and again there has been a raft of top-end, luxury hotel openings with rates to match. These hotels may also add 10% for service and 18% for tax.

If you're travelling in the low season you may be able to negotiate a cheaper rate. Try asking '*¿Tiene algo un poco más económico?*' ('Have you got anything a bit cheaper?'). Paying cash might also get you a discount.

Standards

Peru boasts the standard range of South American accommodation options, from five-star top-end hotels to basic rooms and shared dorms in hostels. A Peruvian hotel is entitled to call itself *residencial*, *hostal*, *hotel*, *pensión* or *hospedaje* and must identify itself with a plaque posted outside indicating the type of establishment, even though this makes no difference to the standard of accommodation. There is no universal standard of grading accommodation in Peru. When booking a budget place you might find yourself in a filthy, basic bolthole in a dangerous part of town overseen by an intimidating hotelier, or you could end up in a charming, atmospheric colonial mansion. Your best bet, therefore, is to actually look at a room to see whether it suits you before handing over your money.

Camping is often possible and is usually free except in formal campsites. It is also possible to stay with local families on a **homestay** (see p163 & p181).

FOOD

Peru has the most extensive menu on the continent and some of the world's top chefs, who are finally getting international recognition and are encouraging the spread of Peruvian food worldwide with restaurant openings across the Americas, Spain and in London. Yet mention Peruvian food to most people and the few that have heard of it might think of guinea pig. The country's cuisine is about so much more than that, though. Lima is now one of the top gastronomic capitals of the continent with some world-class restaurants serving the *Novoandina* cuisine pioneered by the chef and restaurateur Gastón Acurio that blends indigenous, Spanish and Asian influences to mouth-watering effect. Other gastronomic centres include Arequipa, Chiclayo, Cusco and Trujillo.

Even in smaller regional restaurants Peruvian cooking can be very appealing; there's nothing finer than sitting in a darkened *picantería* (a traditional local restaurant often serving spicy food) with a steaming plate of *chicharrones* (fried pork and pork skin), and a mug of *chicha de jora*, the country's famous fermented maize beer. And *cuy* (guinea pig), be it fried, baked or barbecued, is actually very tasty.

Fish

Peru has excellent fish that includes *congrio* (conger eel), *corvina* (sea bass), *lenguado* (sole) and shellfish. Try the Peruvian version of fish & chips, *jalea* (fried whitebait) which is served with fried *yuca* (cassava or manioc), fried yellow peppers and a dollop of spicy *ají* sauce, *chupe de camarones* (traditional creamy prawn chowder), and that famous Peruvian dish, *ceviche* (see box below).

Meat

Meat dishes are numerous and varied. Most common are *lomo cordon bleu* (beef loin steak stuffed with cheese and ham), *lomo milanesa* (beaten into a thin

---

❑ Ceviche

Ceviche (cebiche) – fresh, raw white fish, marinated in lime juice, chillies and red onions and often served with two types of maize and sweet potato – is usually a lunch dish and is deliciously light and tasty. Many countries in South America lay claim to ceviche, but to suggest that it is anything but a Peruvian creation whilst in Lima or elsewhere along the coast is likely to get you into serious trouble.

How to make ceviche

- 1kg fresh raw white fish (lemon sole or halibut, alternatively mix half fish and half shellfish)
- 2 large red onions, sliced
- 1 or 2 chillies, chopped
- juice of 6 limes
- 1 tbsp olive oil
- 4 tbsp fresh coriander
- Seasoning to taste

Method: Wash and cut the fish into bite-sized pieces. Place in a dish with the onions, chilli and coriander. Mix up a marinade (known as *leche de tigre*, or tiger's milk) using the lime juice and olive oil and season to taste. Pour over the fish and store in a cool spot or refrigerator. How long you leave it for is a matter of taste. Some restaurants serve it after less than ten minutes, sashimi style; to 'cook' it through thoroughly will take about an hour. Serve with boiled sweet potatoes and corn on the cob.

PERU

> ❏ **Health warning**
> You should always be conscious of where your **food** has come from and how it has
> been prepared otherwise you run the risk of contracting food poisoning. Beware of
> **tap water** unless you are absolutely confident of the source, and if necessary boil or
> purify it before drinking. To be on the safe side, buy bottled water. Don't then get
> caught out by using ice that could have been made from contaminated water.
>
> All food that can't be peeled or shelled should be washed in purified water. Be
> wary of salads as they may have been washed in tap water. Ice-cream from a rep-
> utable brand ought to be okay, unless the vendor has allowed it to melt and refreeze.
> Freshly, fully cooked food is generally safest, and try to stay clear of reheated dish-
> es. That said *ceviche*, which isn't technically 'cooked' but marinated in lime, is per-
> fectly safe if served fresh in a reputable restaurant.

steak and fried in breadcrumbs), and *lomo a lo pobre* (fried with an egg on top).
Chicken is also often served like this or simply roasted. *Parilladas* (a mixed
grill and a restaurant that sells grilled meat) are generally very good.

More interesting dishes include *lomo saltado* (strips of beef stir-fried with
onions, spicy orange peppers, tomatoes and soy sauce, served with rice and
fried potatoes), *anticucho* (beef-heart kebabs cooked on a skewer over hot coals
and served with a range of spicy sauces), *causa rellena* (a lightly spiced potato
cake mixed with tuna or chicken), *ají de gallina* (shredded chicken stewed in a
rich, gently spiced cream sauce) and the coronary-inducing *chicharrones* (deep-
fried chunks of pork or pork skin; the original hot pork scratchings).

Most unusual for many foreigners is the tradition of eating *cuy*, that popular childhood pet, the guinea pig. Considered a delicacy, it's usually fried or
baked, prepared with *huacatay* (an aromatic Andean herb), cumin and garlic
and tastes a little like duck but with a unique gamey flavour. It is generally
served whole, head, paws and all, as if it has just been run over in the traffic and
peeled off a car wheel, and can be quite fiddly to eat.

Once scorned by the middle classes as being fit only for the poor peasant
farmers, alpaca steak is now a staple on many *Novoandina* menus.

Other dishes

It was Viracocha's sons who discovered the **potato**, having been sent to Lake
Titicaca by their Creator father to bring back the plants that grew there. So goes
the Inca myth. It's not far from the truth, though, as research shows that this is
where the earliest potatoes evolved. Hunter-gatherers learnt to farm the tubers that
grew there about 7000 years ago. Some 200 species of wild potato are found in
South America and an astounding 5000 varieties are now cultivated in the Andes.

Popular dishes include: *causa*, made with yellow potatoes, lemons, hard-
boiled eggs, olives, sweet corn, sweet potato and cheese and served with an
onion sauce; *papas a la Huancaína*, a cold appetiser of potatoes in a thick, spicy
cheese sauce; and *papa rellena*, where a potato is baked then fried before being
stuffed with meat, olives, onions, boiled egg and raisins.

You should also try *chuño*, freeze-dried potato. It was the Incas who developed freeze-drying as a way of preserving potatoes, which were then stored as

a reserve if other crops failed. They freeze-dried them by leaving them out on winter nights in sub-zero temperatures. You may still see this process happening on some of the mountain trails in this guide.

Quinoa used to be highly important within Andean civilisations, second only to the potato. In contemporary times its value is again being recognised because of its high nutritional and protein content, making it an unusually complete foodstuff. In markets you'll see **maize (corn)** in an amazing variety of colours and sizes. Unlike the puny corn found elsewhere, Peruvian corn comprises giant white kernels bursting with flavour and juice. Corn has been planted in Peru for over 3000 years. The ancient farmers achieved a degree of sophistication in the selection and creation of new varieties that adapted to varying terrains and climates. Corn is cooked in a number of ways; on the cob, *choclo* or *choclo con queso* (with a piece of cheese), boiled, ground with a pestle and mortar, toasted or fermented into *chicha* (see p84). You'll find cornmash pastries (*tamales* and *humitas*), savoury or sweet and in a wide range of colours.

Soups are often hearty and filling. Try *yacu-chupe*, a green soup made from potatoes, cheese, garlic, coriander, peppers, eggs and onions, or the pleasantly spiced *sopa a la criolla*, made with thin noodles, beef hearts and bits of egg and vegetables.

As well as the wide range of Peruvian dishes you'll find excellent approximations of other cuisines: **pasta** is often freshly made and **Chinese food** (*Chifa*) is usually good.

Dessert

There's a wide range of options available for the sweet tooth, and the Peruvian tooth can be very sweet indeed. The most common puddings are *picarones* (light fried doughnuts with honey) and the jelly-like *mazamorra morada* (a sweet-tasting dish made from purple maize). When in Lima make sure you try *Suspiro de Limeña* (see p142), a classic dessert from the city.

In addition to all the standard citrus fruits and recognisable fruits such as bananas, guavas, pineapples, papayas, mangoes and passionfruits there are also four unusual varieties; the custard-ish *chirimoya* (custard apple), *guanabana* (soursop), the gloopy *granadilla* (similar to passionfruit) and the native powdery, peachy *lúcuma* (eggfruit).

Taxes and tipping

Expensive restaurants will add 18% tax to the bill. They may also add a 10% service charge, which is meant to go to the waiter meaning that tipping is unnecessary. However, the money often doesn't reach the people who've earned or deserve it so you might want to consider leaving a cash tip as well. In budget or moderate restaurants tipping is normal although not obligatory.

DRINK

Non-alcoholic

Tea is widely drunk. It is usually served without milk but with sugar and lemon. Herbal teas are also popular. *Mate de coca* (see box p84), made from coca leaves,

> ❏ **Mate de coca**
> This herbal tea is made by submerging the leaves of the coca plant in hot water or by using a pre-prepared tea bag. The tea is greenish yellow and has a slightly bitter flavour. Although legal in Peru, most countries do not distinguish between the coca leaf and any other substance containing cocaine, so the possession of coca leaf, even as a tea bag, is prohibited. If you try to take some home you run the risk of arrest and a possible prison sentence.

is readily available in the cafés and restaurants in Cusco and helps to alleviate the symptoms of altitude sickness. **Coffee**, surprisingly for a coffee-producing country, is pretty poor and is either served as coffee essence, to which you add hot water, or instant coffee. Milk is again served separately. However, there are also plenty of places in Cusco that now serve a cappuccino or espresso.

Bottled water is sold widely and should be drunk when you aren't confident of the water source or haven't had a chance to purify or boil the water yourself (see box p82). The usual range of **soft drinks** is available, with the addition of chicha morada, made from purple maize, and the ubiquitous, home-grown, iridescent Inca Kola, which outsells the imported American equivalent in Peru. Try it just once to appreciate the sickly sweet, bubblegum flavour.

Alcoholic

Peruvian **lager** is pretty drinkable. There are numerous bottled brands including Arequipeña, Cristal, Cusqueña and Pilsen Callao that are all brewed to about 5% alcohol content and all taste quite similar. For a change try the sweetish dark ale Cusqueña Malta.

Peruvian **wine** is yet to reach the same heights as its South American neighbours, and the lack of infrastructure and poor marketing probably mean international sales are a way off; you're better off sticking to Chilean or Argentinean wine instead. If you are feeling adventurous try the Tacama, Ocucaje or Vista Alegre red or white wines from Ica.

Chicha is a maize wine that dates back to the time of the Incas but is still drunk today in the rural Andes. Nicknamed 'the champagne of the Incas', and made from a specific type of yellow maize called *jora*, it actually tastes like a type of cloudy pale cider. The name derives from the Spanish *chichal*, meaning 'saliva' or 'to spit', which refers to the Andean people's early methods of production: for centuries they found saliva an effective means of converting starches in the maize grains into fermentable sugars. Nowadays sugar is used to kick-start the process. Houses that brew and sell chicha can be identified by the red plastic bags hung outside on the end of

> ❏ **Pisco Sour**
> 60ml pisco
> Half a lemon or one lime
> 1 egg white, whisked
> 1 tablespoon of sugar
>
> Beat the egg white and sugar together. Add the pisco and lemon juice and blend. Serve the cocktail over crushed ice and garnish with a dash of angostura bitters.

PERU

long poles, not unlike pub signs. **Pisco** is a potent clear spirit distilled from grapes. Usually drunk as part of a Pisco Sour cocktail, it can be deceptively strong. Chileans also consider it their national drink and there is plenty of friction between the two countries over the origin of the drink.

POST AND COMMUNICATIONS

Telephone
You can make **international phone calls** from public phones in the street operated by Telefónica-Peru, but these days it's much cheaper to use the internet and call using Skype. If you have an unlocked mobile you may be able to get a SIM card on arrival to use in your phone, though this is probably worth it only if you're going to be in the country for a while and plan on making a lot of phone calls whilst there. Movistar and Claro are the two main network providers.

> ❏ **Phone codes and numbers**
> To call Peru from abroad dial your international access code and then ☎ 51. Add ☎ 1 for Lima or ☎ 84 for Cusco.
>
> To make an international call from Peru dial 00 and then add your country code, STD and the number.
>
> | | |
> |---|---|
> | Operator | ☎ 100 |
> | Directory enquiries | ☎ 103 |
> | Emergency services | ☎ 105 |
> | International operator | ☎ 108 |
>
> To call a Peruvian mobile whilst in Peru, simply dial the nine-digit number (that always begins with 9).

Internet access
Although internet cafés open and close with alarming rapidity, there are usually lots to choose from in large towns and even in smaller places; many hotels and hostels and tourist restaurants now also offer wifi.

Post
Post in Peru is slow but generally reliable. Letters to Peru take 7-14 days whilst letters to Europe or the USA from Peru take 10-21 days. **Stamps** (*estampillas*) are usually available in the same places that sell postcards. Post offices are called *correos* in Spanish.

ELECTRICITY

220V, 60Hz AC. Power cuts and surges still happen so it's worth bringing a surge protector for any valuable equipment such as laptops. Plugs usually have two flat pins side by side (as is common in the USA) or two round pins (common in Europe).

TIME

Peru is five hours behind GMT (UK winter time), in line with Eastern Standard Time in the USA. Peruvians are notoriously late a lot of the time – according to one statistic, Peruvians are on average 107 hours late in total for appointments per year. There has even been a government drive to eradicate this habitual tardiness, and though things have improved, don't expect meetings to necessarily start on time. In Mark Adam's *Turn Right at Machu Picchu* (see p41) he recounts how one

PERU

of his Peruvian friends had to tell his own mother that he was getting married at noon, when in reality the service wasn't until 4pm, in the hope that she'd be on time; even then she only made it to the service with ten minutes to spare!

HOLIDAYS AND FESTIVALS

Festivals are an intrinsic part of Peruvian life and take place with alarming regularity. The fiestas themselves are almost all vibrant, lively affairs that make for a great spectacle. Hard partying, dancing and drinking disguise the fact that the reason for the frenetic festival is usually a practical one, be it a plea for favourable harvests or the health of livestock. The carousing, eating and drinking are considered to be ways of showing thanks for and celebrating the sun and the rain, which give rise to all life. Try to remember this when you awake after several days celebrating feeling rather the worse for wear.

January
● **1st   New Year's Day** (all Peru but major fiesta in Huancayo)
● **6th   Fiesta de Ollantaytambo** (Cusco)
● **14th Feria de Pampamarca Agricultural fair** (Cusco)
● **18th Celebration of the founding of Lima** (Lima)
● **20th Procession of saints** (San Sebastián district of Cusco).

February/March
● Cusco hosts a wild and debauched **carnival**, with food and water fights in the streets and vast amounts of *chicha* drunk (Cusco).

March/April
● **Semana Santa**, Holy Week – the week before Easter is a series of colourful, frequently raucous celebrations and processions; and Easter (all Peru).
● **Easter Monday** The blackened crucifix El Señor de los Temblores (Lord of the Earthquakes) is paraded around Cusco, starting and finishing in Plaza de Armas where thousands of people gather to celebrate and make merry (Cusco).

May
● **1st Labour Day** (all Peru)
● **2nd/3rd** The **Vigil of the Cross** is held on any mountain top with a cross on the summit (Cusco).

June
● **7th-9th** The festival and pilgrimage of **Qoyllur Rit'i** led by the ukuku bear dancers (see box p300).
● **Ninth Thursday after Easter Corpus Christi**: all the statues of saints from Cusco's many churches are paraded through the city and brought to the Cathedral, which is packed with revellers (all Peru, but Cusco in particular).
● **24th Inti Raymi** (the Resurrection of the Sun) is the ancient Inca festival of the winter solstice. Re-enacted at Sacsayhuaman, the lavish festival actually begins at the Coricancha, from where a procession makes its way through Cusco and up to the ruins above the city. The entire spectacle lasts all day and is a great family day out for locals (Cusco).

● **29th   San Pedro y San Pablo** Festival of St Peter and St Paul (all Peru).

July

● **15th-18th   Fiesta de la Virgen del Carmen** is held in Paucartambo, about 100km north-east of Cusco, during the Quechua month of Earthly purification. The statue of the Virgin is paraded through the town amidst boisterous dancing, drinking and re-enactments of battles between mythical figures during which good triumphs over evil for another year (Paucartambo, but also in Pisac and Pucara).

● **28th-29th   Independence Day** In Lima this is marked with fireworks, live music and a lot of drinking in Plaza de Armas (all Peru).

August

● **Last Sunday** The Inca manhood rite of passage **Huarachicoy** is re-enacted at Sacsayhuaman (Cusco).

● **30th   Fiesta de Santa Rosa de Lima** (Saint's day of Santa Rosa) (Lima).

September

● **8th** The **Day of the Virgin** is marked by parades and masked dancers performing in Plaza de San Francisco (Cusco).

● **Mid Sep   La Mistura**, a giant gastronomy fair and celebration of Peruvian food with workshops and demonstrations by the leading local chefs (Lima).

October

● **4th   Fiesta de la Virgen del Rosario** (Lima and Cusco).

● **18th-19th   El Señor de los Milagros** (Our Lord of the Miracles): a venerated copy of this painting is paraded through Lima on an enormous silver litter weighing almost a ton (Lima).

November

● **1st   Todos Santos**, All Saints' Day (all Peru).

● **2nd Dia de los Muertos**; day when Peruvians remember their dead (all Peru).

● **5th** Birth of the first Inca, Manco Capac; week-long festival centred on this date (Puno).

December

● **8th   Immaculate Conception** Processions in honour of the Virgin Mary (all Peru).

● **8th** Everywhere shuts down around noon on **Cusco's national day** (Cusco).

● **24th   Santurantikuy** This literally means 'saints for sale'. In Cusco this was originally a market where figurines for nativity scenes were sold, it is now a general market; elsewhere the day is a pre-Christmas holiday (Cusco).

● **25th   Christmas** (all Peru).

SHOPPING

Fabrics

The Andean people have always placed great store by intricately woven textiles and fabrics have a long history amongst indigenous culture. Rugs, ponchos, clothes and wall-hangings are all readily available from markets such as those at Chinchero, Pisac and Ollantaytambo.

Alpaca wool is widely used and most shopkeepers will proudly tell you that the fabric you're holding comes from 'baby alpaca'. The quality varies enormously. Modern dyes are less subtle than traditionally applied ones. If you singe a couple of fibres and it smells like burning plastic, the material is acrylic. If it smells very bad when wet, it's probably llama as alpaca is odourless whether wet or dry. The finest wool is from **vicuña**. The national animal of Peru was once hunted almost to extinction; in 1974 only 6000 remained but conservation has led to them being taken off the endangered list and there are now more than 350,000. Their wool is expensive because they can be shorn only every three years.

Arts and crafts

Andean crafts and folk art, ceramics, wood carvings, hand-tooled leather, gold and silver jewellery and *arpilleras* (appliqué pictures of Peruvian life) are all good buys and can be picked up at many of the markets or shops in larger towns. Never buy the framed insects seen for sale in Cusco, though. They are often endangered species and the trade in them depletes the resources of the Amazon. If you are tempted, remember that if they are restricted or protected species customs will confiscate them from you. Genuine 'Inca' artefacts are often nothing more than cheap knock-offs; any actual relics you find must not be taken out of the country – it's illegal to export them.

Bargaining

Haggling and bargaining are often part of the ritual when shopping at markets and fairs. Foreigners, including those with backpacks, are seen as rich; in comparison to the many Peruvians who live below the poverty line, they really are. Prices can therefore sometimes be inflated. However, the vast majority of Peruvians are not out to take advantage of you. When buying hand-crafted goods remember that the seller has probably toiled to produce the exquisite textile or carving, and recognise the craftsmanship, skill and time that have gone into producing your souvenir. The tiny saving you might make by aggressive haggling could actually represent rather more to the person you are bargaining with. The seller may even be forced to sell their goods at any price in order to survive. Do not take advantage of this; only bargain when you feel that the price really is too high. Pay the fairest price, not necessarily the lowest price.

SAFETY

Pickpockets and opportunist thefts are the biggest problem for travellers. Usually thieves work in teams and target anyone who looks to have money. One of them will distract you using any number of ingenious techniques to get your attention. Most frequently, someone will trip or fall into you, an old lady might collapse in front of you or someone may spit or stick chewing gum to your clothes. Whilst you are distracted an accomplice relieves you of your wallet, by opening your bag with a razor or simply grabbing it and running. Muggings and assaults do happen too but are less common.

❏ **Tourist Protection Service**
There is a special police force, **Policía de Turismo (POLTUR)**, just for tourist and tourism matters. Theft, loss of passports, assaults and, most commonly, contract violations and general rip-offs are all part of their remit. See p137 for details of the police service in Lima and p161 for the service in Cusco.

By not flaunting your valuables and staying alert in crowded or busy areas, such as markets, bus depots or railway stations, you can reduce the risk to yourself. Be careful when travelling at night and if necessary take a taxi rather than walk. A moneybelt is a good way of concealing your cash. Alternatively, make sure that you carry your cash in several different places in order to minimise the risk of losing it all.

Be on your guard when seemingly confronted by a policeman. Always ask to see identification and at no point simply hand over your passport or documents. If you can help it, avoid getting into a police car and instead insist on walking to the police station.

Should the worst happen, try to stay calm, remember that they are just after your money, and hand it over. It's not worth getting killed for. If you are a victim of crime, or do get ripped off, report it to the tourist police (see box above); they generally speak English and are usually helpful. Make sure that you get a police report for your insurance claim. Bearing all of this in mind, most people still have no problems when visiting Peru. Take care and you will probably be fine.

On the Inca Trail
A lot of agencies and guidebooks imply that the Trail is rife with opportunistic criminals and tent slashers waiting to steal your possessions. These tend to be exaggerated claims and theft itself is now uncommon on the Inca Trail, as long as you take a series of basic precautions. Don't take unnecessary valuables with you. Make sure not to take jewellery or large quantities of cash along (do remember to take your passport though as it must be shown at checkpoints). Carry any valuables that you do take in a safe pouch and make sure that you keep your camera in sight at all times, especially at meal times. When camping, remove temptation by ensuring that all your belongings are stored inside the tent, not outside or around it.

DRUGS
The possession of drugs in Peru, essentially marijuana or cocaine (see box p70), is considered a very serious offence and usually leads to draconian penalties. There is no bail for serious charges and you may be imprisoned for some time before coming to trial. If you are suspected or convicted of trafficking in drugs the sentence can be up to 15 years in prison. Avoid having any casual conversations with someone who offers you drugs, as the person you are speaking to may be a police informant or plainclothes officer.

3 THE INCAS

Hugh Thomson

The Imperial Landscape
A Reading of Inca History in the Sacred Valley

When the Inca emperor Atahualpa first met the Spanish conquistadors, he offered them a drink from a *qeros*, a drinking flask, in the traditional ceremony of reciprocal toasting that had always been practised in the Andes. The Spaniards refused, showing him a Bible instead – which Atahualpa, insulted by their refusal to drink with him, spurned. What was this 'writing' anyway, these scribbles on a piece of paper? Nor had the Spaniards arrived with the traditional gifts, so the Inca emperor sent them an insulting present of ducks gutted and filled with straw. This, went the inference, was what he could do to the conquistadors whenever he wanted. The Spaniards, in their turn, were outraged at Atahualpa's insult to the Bible.

A more telling instance of the clash and mutual misunderstanding of civilisations could not be imagined.

But before we become too self-congratulatory and assume that we understand such things in ways the brutal Spaniards did not, it is as well to remember that an encounter with Inca civilisation is still almost the nearest we can find to experiencing an entirely alien mind-set – and as a result we can misunderstand them just as easily.

Ancient Peru is one of the oldest civilisations on earth; yet it is also one of the most isolated. Until the relatively late arrival of the Spaniards in 1532, the Incas and the many cultures that preceded them had a unique way of looking at the world – one that excluded writing, the wheel and many other necessities of the so-called 'Old World', but managed to build magnificent monuments and a stable society in a terrifyingly unstable landscape.

Conqvista en los banos estava Atagvalga Inga. Conquistadors (Sebastián de Benalcázar and Hernando Pizarro) confront Atahualpa Inca at the royal baths, (Cajamarca).

FELIPE HUAMÁN POMA DE AYALA, FROM HIS *NUEVE CRÓNICA Y BUEN GOBIERNO* (C1600)

And their relationship to that landscape is consequently very different. When you travel down the Sacred Valley and on towards Machu Picchu, you are passing through a region of extraordinarily stratified history. The eminent Andeanist Susan Niles has said that, given they were unable to record their history in writing, 'in many ways, the Incas sought to make history visible'; that is, the buildings they left behind were to remind their successors of their achievements. This is true of course of many monuments around the world, from the Pyramids to Les Invalides, but for the Inca Emperors it had the added urgency of being the only way they would be remembered: they carry no inscriptions.

Thus the so-called 'Sacred Valley' – the term was not used by the Incas themselves, as is often assumed, but was a marketing invention of 1950, designed to promote a driving rally held in the valley that year – could just as much be described as the Imperial Valley. From Huchuy Cusco, with its first essay at the architecture of the Inca 'royal estate', the moya, to the greatest example of all, Machu Picchu, the Urubamba valley is studded with calculated reminders of the imperial presence, and not just in the buildings but in the way the terraces and actual river have been landscaped and controlled; 'terraformed', as the archaeologists like to say.

Amojonadores deste reino,
vna Cavcho Inga,
Cona Raqvi Inga.
Surveyors of this kingdom:
Una Caucho Inca and Cona
Raqvi Inca.

<small>FELIPE HUAMÁN POMA DE AYALA,
(c1600)</small>

Take Machu Picchu for instance: while almost certainly built by the emperor Pachacutec, probably as a winter retreat for the court from the rigours of more upland Cusco, it was also a reminder to new subjects he had conquered in the surrounding valleys that the Incas were here to stay; not only that, but as an additional humiliation those same new subjects were doubtless forced to build this new symbol of occupation by the Inca – and on a site that must have posed extreme engineering problems, as we know from the depths of the foundations and the bulwark terracing needed to support the spectacular city on a mountaintop.

Their labourers built with extraordinary facility and speed. When the Spaniards appointed a 'puppet Inca Emperor', having murdered his predecessor Atahualpa, they were astonished when a palace was constructed for him in what seemed to them little less than a day. But then the Incas were always a tribe in a hurry, and to understand them fully one needs to appreciate their historical imperative.

The Incas were prodigious builders, accomplished engineers and skilled architects. Without the art of writing, they left their history in stone. They were able, however, to keep records of accounts and taxes using quipus, coloured knotted strings (see box p73).

BIRTH OF THE INCA EMPIRE

It was only after 1400AD that the Incas began to expand out of their heartland around Cusco, so their empire lasted for little more than a century before being brutally cut short by the Spaniards. The Incas were the last in a whole series of cultures pre-dating the Spanish Conquest that stretched back to around 3000BC. The world has taken a while to appreciate the achievements of these more shadowy, earlier Peruvian civilisations, not least because the Incas downplayed the achievements of preceding civilisations and in some cases ignored them completely.

The Spanish chronicler Pedro de Cieza de León quoted his Inca sources as telling him that 'before them, there were only naked savages and that these natives were stupid and brutish beyond belief. They say they were like animals, and that many ate human flesh, and others took their daughters and mothers to wife and committed other even graver sins.'

This manipulative distortion of history was so successful – the same myth was repeated by other chroniclers like Garcilaso de la Vega in the early 17th century – that the truth has emerged comparatively recently.

Far from imposing order on an unruly bunch of savages, the Incas were the latest dominant tribe (and a short-lived one at that) in a series of Andean civilisations that had flourished over the preceding 4000 years: the Moche in the north of Peru, with their magnificent pottery, the Huari of the central states and the Tiahuanaco culture near Lake Titicaca were just a few of the cultures who had attained a high level and on whose achievements the Incas had often built.

The Incas were just one of a number of competing tribes in the area around Cusco, before beginning to build up their substantial empire under a series of dynamic and capable emperors. At its height Tahuantinsuyo, 'the land of four quarters' as their empire was called, spanned the Andean spine of the continent from Colombia to Chile.

To call it 'an empire' is strictly speaking misleading, if familiar – it was in some ways more like an extensive trading association controlled by the Incas. Nor were all Inca conquests military: Tahuantinsuyo can be compared to an aggressive modern corporation offering overwhelmingly compelling reasons to each client tribe why they should join – consumer benefits. The Incas also made it clear to any opponent that they would win whatever happened, because they always did. Cieza reported one Inca Emperor as saying to a prospective new tribe, 'these lands will soon be ours, like those we already possess.' Given the

---

(**Opposite**) Unable to record their history in writing, the Incas sought to make it visible in the form of beautiful and dramatic buildings and stonework full of symbolism.

Top: Vast concentric rings and agricultural terraces created by the Incas as an experimental farm at Moray (see p200). They were able to construct terraces for cultivation on even the steepest slopes, demonstrating their supreme engineering skills. (Photo © Henry Stedman).

Bottom: The Incas showed mastery over their medium in their use of stones, sometimes of enormous size, dressed to fit perfectly together without the use of mortar. This wall is in Ollantaytambo (see p201). (Photo © Zoe Ashdown).

Indians' often fatalistic turn of mind, this proved effective diplomacy and many tribes capitulated without a fight. The Inca use of history to legitimise their leadership and facilitate such conquests was adroit.

Nowhere is this more evident than in their 'creation myths': one of these claims that the original Adam and Eve of the Inca line, Manco Capac and his sister, Mama Ocllo, had emerged from the Island of the Sun (now in Bolivia) on distant Lake Titicaca. This island, revered as the birthplace of the sun, had been a place of pilgrimage for the earlier Tiahuanaco civilisation whose buildings were still so admired on the *altiplano*. By claiming that they too had come from the Island of the Sun, the Incas were harnessing the cultural power of an earlier mighty civilisation, from the stones of whose great ruins, they implied, they somehow drew some of their own strength.

A SACRED LANDSCAPE

Stone was far more than just a building material for the Incas: they worshipped some of the great naturally occurring boulders in the region – like Chuquipalta, the 'White Rock' near Vitcos, or Q'enko – making them into *huacas* (shrines) with elaborate carvings. Such stone monuments were a reminder to themselves and others of their mountain origins and dynastic power.

In another Inca creation myth, Lord Viracocha formed the first man out of stone. Later, when the greatest of all Inca emperors, Pachacutec, successfully defeated the rival Chanca at the birth of his imperial Inca dynasty, he was said to have summoned 'the very boulders around Cusco' to rise up and fight with him in a desperate defence of the capital against the invaders.

There is an idea in the West that stone must imply some notion of permanence, but this is not necessarily true in the Andes, which is not a static landscape. In an area of volcanic activity and landslides, with recurring and violent El Niño activity over the millennia, the landscape has always been changing. For the Incas, stone was a much more volatile, organic medium. This sense of stone as a life-force is crucial to understanding the Inca architectural and sculptural aesthetic. That old, tired phrase about 'the living stones' of some great site suddenly becomes a powerful, resurrected cliché when we look at Inca sites.

The sheer primacy given to monumental stonework by the Incas is remarkable. In doing so, they again claimed descent – and legitimacy – from the great Tiahuanaco civilisation whose ruined city with its monoliths was still so admired across the Andes. Pachacutec even brought Colla stone masons all the

---

(Opposite) Top: The impressive terraces and citadel at Pisac were built during the reign of Pachacutec, perhaps the greatest Inca, who is believed to have been responsible for the building of Machu Picchu. (Photo © Zoe Ashdown).

Bottom: The Coricancha in Cusco (see pp151-2) was the Incas' Temple of the Sun, the grandest building in the entire world. After the Conquest the Dominicans built their monastery, Santo Domingo, right on top of it in a symbolic show of dominance of their religion. The superiority of the fine Inca masonry is obvious and it was also shown to be more technically advanced in the earthquake of 1950 when the monastery collapsed but the Inca stonework remained unharmed.

THE INCAS

Coreon major i menor.
Hatvn Chasqvi, Chvrv Mvllo
Chasqvi, Cvraca.
Couriers of greater and lesser
rank: Hatun Chasqui (chief
courier), Churu Mullu
Chasqui (the courier who
carries the conch shell),
Curaca (local chasqui).
FELIPE HUAMÀN POMA DE AYALA,
(c1600)

The vast size of the Inca
empire meant that it required
efficient communications to
maintain control. The Incas
built a network of paved
roads covering more than
14,000 miles (22,500km) and
stretching from north of Quito
in modern Ecuador to south
of Santiago in Chile. Since
there was no knowledge of
the wheel or any horses,
transportation was by porter
or by using llamas as pack
animals. Communications
were provided by teams of
chasquis (couriers). They
would run in relays between
tambos (way stations) and it
is said that they moved so
quickly that they could bring
fresh fish from the sea up to
Cusco without it spoiling.

way from Lake Titicaca to try to replicate the
look of Tiahuanaco at some of the ambitious sites
he built, like Ollantaytambo; we know because
the masons rebelled against the harsh working
conditions.

GROWTH OF THE INCA EMPIRE

The phenomenal growth of the Inca Empire is
attributed by many chroniclers to the achievements of this one man: Pachacutec, who according
to these accounts, deserves to be as well known as
Alexander the Great or Napoleon.

Originally known as Inca Yupanqui,
Pachacutec was a younger son of the Emperor
Viracocha. During Viracocha's reign, in around
1438, the Chanca, a rival tribe to the north of
Cusco, attacked the Incas with such ferocity that
Viracocha and his designated heir, Inca Urcon,
fled the capital – some believe to the site of
Huchuy Cusco, the fascinating early estate built on
the hills above Calca, one of the least visited and
most evocative of the sites along the Sacred Valley.
Only a small band of captains led by Inca
Yupanqui remained to give a last-ditch defence.

It was now, according to the myth he later
assiduously propagated, that Pachacutec called 'on
the very stones of Cusco' to fight alongside them.
Not only were the Chanca sent packing, but Inca
Yupanqui (who then adopted the soubriquet
Pachacutec, 'Transformer of the Earth', and took
the throne from his disgraced father and brother)
embarked on an ambitious programme of conquest
that initiated the imperial phase of Inca culture.
Within a generation the Incas had grown from an
anonymous small tribe of the Cusco valley to
become the dominant force of the Andes.

During his long reign from c1438 to 1471,
Pachacutec's achievements seem almost to beggar
geographical comprehension: he led the first wave
of conquests over to Bolivia and Lake Titicaca; his
son Topa Inca, working under his direction, followed with further expansion north up to Ecuador,
until the empire stretched to an area the size of
Continental Europe.

Pachacutec was also acutely conscious of the need to create his own myth and legitimise his new dynasty. In the words of the chronicler Juan de Betanzos, 'he decreed the remembrance of history'. After his victory over the Chanca, he gathered the stones that were supposed to have helped him in his fight and set them up as carved rocks, or huacas, in places where they could be worshipped. He enthused the Incas with the idea that they were a people of power, of destiny, and created an elaborate hierarchy devolving down from his own position as the 'Sapa Inca', the emperor. The nobility became a separate tier in this hierarchy and were allowed to wear ear-plugs as a distinguishing feature. Tribes living close to Cusco were accommodated within this concept by being made *Incas de Privilegio*, 'Honorary Incas'.

He also ensured that impressive monuments were erected – from stone of course – to this idea of an imperial destiny. Inca leaders had always been expected to build (one of the slurs perpetuated about the disgraced Inca Urcon, the brother that Pachacutec had usurped, was that he was too weak to leave a building to his name). But Pachacutec took this principle to new, grandiose extremes. He ordered the construction of Sacsayhuaman, of the temple-fortress at Ollantaytambo and, it seems probable, of Machu Picchu and Pisac. Any one of these sites would be a substantial monument; cumulatively they represent a quite exceptional achievement.

Pachacutec was said, according to later Inca accounts, to have laid down all the basic framework for the institutions of state over his long reign of approximately thirty years – institutions which his successors were ritualistically to preserve in his name. For the first time, the peoples of the coast and the mountains were given a unified administration that allowed peaceful trading and co-operation, with Quechua as the *lingua franca*. Where there had previously been darkness, so this story went, the Inca Empire brought order.

This account of Pachacutec, however, needs to be treated with some care. It is a seductive idea – an empire carved out by the sheer will-power of

El noveno Inga, Pachacvti Inga Ivpanqvi.
The ninth Inca, Pachacutec.
FELIPE HUAMÁN POMA DE AYALA, (c1600)

Astrólogo Pveta Q save del sol y de la luna...
Astrologer and Shaman who studies the sun and the moon and the stars in order to know when to plant the fields. (Note that he carries a quipu, marking his astrological calculations with knots on the strings).
FELIPE HUAMÁN POMA DE AYALA, (c1600)

THE INCAS

***Travaxa: Zara, Papa
Hallmai Mita.***
Work in January.
Maize, time of rain and
digging. Month of the
biggest feast.
FELIPE HUAMÁN POMA DE AYALA,
(c1600)

***Travaxa: Zara, Papa
Apaicvi Aimoray.***
Work in July.
Maize and potatoes. Month
of the harvest and
distribution of the lands.
FELIPE HUAMÁN POMA DE AYALA,
(c1600)

one individual, single-handedly turning the tide of a nation's destiny – and as such appealing to Spanish chroniclers reared on just such chivalric exploits themselves.

Pachacutec was undoubtedly a dynamic and capable leader. But what has come down to us is very much the 'official version' of the history, carefully propagated by his own descendants; a usurping family, they had an interest in denigrating the achievements of their predecessors, who consequently may have received short shrift (just as the Incas were prone to ignore the influence of preceding civilisations). As the old English saying goes: 'Treason shall never prosper, for if it prosper it is no longer treason.'

While Pachacutec initially concentrated on the southern Andes and Bolivia, his son Topa Inca began the expansion into the northern ranges and Ecuador that was to have such a profound consequence for 'the land of the four quarters'.

The Incas had a prolonged love-affair with the warm climate of Ecuador: fertile land, the trade in exotic desirables like seashells and the attractions of the local girls combined to make it irresistible to the aesthetes from the highlands. Successive emperors spent more and more time campaigning there.

The rhythm of such campaigns allowed plenty of time to enjoy the place: the normal, very civilised practice of pre-Columbian peoples was for fighting to pause during harvest-time to allow both sides to gather in crops (when the Spaniards arrived, they disconcerted the natives by ignoring this convention). Cieza de León also reports that the Incas often found it too hot to fight in the summer.

Topa Inca, like his father, was a formidable builder: it is likely that he was responsible for Choquequirao, the spectacular site high above the Apurímac which emulates, or competes with, Machu Picchu; he also built an estate at Chincheros, the great walls of which support the later church plaza built by the Spaniards.

In Ecuador he founded the city of Tumipampa (modern-day Cuenca), where his son Huayna Capac, the future emperor, was born. When Huayna succeeded to the throne, Ecuador clearly appealed to him more than the harsher climate of the Inca heartland. He chose to stay for many years in his birthplace of Tumipampa, and was said to have preferred it to Cusco as a capital.

This did not stop him from ensuring that a substantial country palace, Quispiquanca, was built for him in what is now the town of Urubamba, beside the modern road ascending to the Chicón glacier; the site has recently been restored and is impressive if little visited, despite the nearby location of the best restaurant in the valley, El Huacatay (see p198).

By Inca standards Huayna seems to have been a bit of a *bon viveur*, perhaps because of his Ecuadorian upbringing: he was said to be able to drink three times as much as any of his subjects. When asked how it was that he never became intoxicated, he replied that 'he drank for the poor, of whom he supported many.'

Yet the push up into Ecuador by the Incas can with hindsight be seen as an expansion too far. In just three generations, under first Pachacutec, then his son Topa Inca and finally his grandson Huayna Capac, the Inca empire had grown from an enclave around Cusco to one that stretched right along the Andes. In the process it had become fatally distended.

The endless campaigns that Huayna waged in Ecuador had created a permanent standing army in the north, with powerful generals, a disruption to the normal Inca convention that armies were temporary and centred on Cusco; he had also fathered several sons there, which had serious dynastic implications.

In around 1527 came disaster: a fatal epidemic (opinions vary as to whether it was European smallpox that had swept down the South American coast from the north, or a local sand-fly disease, bartonellosis) killed as much as half the population of 25 million, including Huayna Capac himself.

The cracks in the Incas' new empire quickly started to show. Huayna had been away in the north for over ten years. His legitimate successor and son, Huascar, was based back in Cusco. Now a contingent of Incas in Quito led by his son

Andas del Inga. Pillco Randa.
The Inca's red litter, used in war. Here Huayna Capac is shown going to war with the Cañari in northern Ecuador.
FELIPE HUAMÁN POMA DE AYALA, (c1600)

Fiesta de los Ingas. Varicza, Aravi del Inga. Canta con sv pvca llama.
Fiesta of the Incas. Dance, song of the Inca. He sings with his red llama.
FELIPE HUAMÁN POMA DE AYALA, (c1600)

Conqvista preso Atagvalpa Inga.
Atahualpa in prison, Cajamarca.

FELIPE HUAMÁN POMA DE AYALA, (c1600)

'Do you eat gold?' asks the Inca. 'I eat gold', replies the Conquistador.

FELIPE HUAMÁN POMA DE AYALA, (c1600)

Atahualpa (who may well have had an Ecuadorian mother) decided that they were far enough away both from Cusco and Huascar to declare independence.

The resulting civil war between the Ecuadorian and Peruvian sides of the Empire was devastating. It was the turning point in Inca fortunes, much more so than the Spanish Conquest of 1532, which simply exploited the wreckage it caused. The two sides were evenly matched: as the legitimate contender, Huascar had all the resources of the Cusco state behind him; Atahualpa was the more experienced soldier, with a strong Ecuadorian power-base and a ruthless streak – indeed far from being the passive and noble Indian sometimes portrayed, Atahualpa was one of the most brutal of all Inca emperors. Atahualpa eventually defeated Huascar and had him killed, but not before the country had been laid waste. Despite the civil war, Huascar still ensured that a country palace was built for him at Calca.

The epidemic and then the great Inca civil war so weakened Tahuantinsuyo that by 1532, when the Spaniards arrived, they could simply walk in and take it. The conquistadors, as so often, were incredibly lucky. After landing on the coast, at Tumbes, they travelled south down the Royal Road towards the Inca capital, moving through a civilisation which had been fatally weakened by first disease and then internal divisions.

After the famous meeting with Atahualpa, in which the *barbudos*, the bearded ones, and the emperor so signally failed to understand one another, it was not long before Francisco Pizarro and his men kidnapped Atahualpa in the main square at Cajamarca; after extorting a huge ransom of gold and silver from the Inca, they executed him regardless and marched on Cusco to claim the Empire for themselves.

THE POWER OF THE MUMMY

The astonishing expansion of the Incas across a few generations before the arrival of the Spaniards can only partly be explained by dynamic leadership. Other factors contributed to their success: a facility for trade, their opportunism and an occasionally overlooked factor – the curious Inca laws of dynastic inheritance. When each Inca emperor died, his estate (or *panaca*) continued to maintain his household as if he were still alive – he remained 'resident' in his old palace as a mummy, to be brought out on feast days or for the coronation of his successors, and each of those successors would therefore have to build themselves a new palace. When a new emperor was crowned, the mummies of the whole previous dynasty of dead Inca emperors were carried in procession alongside him, along with their fingernail and hair trimmings, which had been scrupulously preserved while they were alive. The sense of a 'living' dynastic succession must have been overwhelming.

Entiero de Chinchaisvios.
Chinchaysuyu burial.

FELIPE HUAMÁN POMA DE AYALA,
(c1600)

Here a Chinchaysuyu mummy is being carried to its burial chamber. The Inca region of Chinchaysuyu was the northernmost part of the empire, in north Equador and southern Colombia. Atahualpa's mother was from this area.

At the time of the Spanish Conquest there were 12 such *panacas* in existence. Each mummy would have its own litter, bearers and attendants from that *panaca*, and a pavilion would be erected for them on the main square where the coronation took place. In a ceremony that built on the traditional consumption of vast quantities of alcohol by the Inca's new subjects, the incoming emperor, the 'Sapa Inca', would also exchange toasts with each of his dead ancestors, with the mummy's attendants drinking on behalf of the corpse.

It is clear that the 'mummy lobby' had grown very powerful towards the end of the Inca Empire and precipitated a bitter divide in Cusco. Huascar Inca, who had a reforming agenda during his brief tenure as emperor, tried to limit what he saw as the abuses that had grown up.

According to the chronicler Bernabé Cobo, 'So many nobles were involved in serving these dead bodies, and their lives were so licentious, that one day Huascar Inca became angry with them and he said that there should be an order to have all the dead bodies buried and to take all their riches away from them. He went on to say that the dead should not be a part of his court, only the living, because the dead had taken over the best of everything in his kingdom.'

It must have been particularly galling for each new emperor that the mummy of his predecessor got to keep all his land, wealth and particularly palaces, so that the incoming Inca would have to build a new one.

The main square of Cusco when the conquistadors arrived was witness to this: each side was lined with the palaces of past Incas, still inhabited by their mummies. Indeed there had been no space left for Huascar on the square itself and he had been forced, to his fury, to build a new palace on the hill above; he caused outrage at one point by threatening to confiscate one of the palaces of his dead forebears instead, according to Pedro Pizarro, one of the liveliest of Spanish chroniclers.

Much the same applied to the country palaces. One probable reason why Machu Picchu seems to have been abandoned by the time of the Spanish Conquest is that after the death of Pachacutec, it reverted to his panaca, not the incoming new Emperor, and therefore went into a gentle decline, without the imperial resources to maintain such a grandiose site.

And therein lies a powerful engine for continual Inca expansion: the fact that the mummy of a departed Inca and his panaca continued to own his palaces and land even after his death was a powerful incentive for every new emperor to go out and conquer new lands, since he would not simply be inheriting them.

THE GUERRILLA CAMPAIGN AFTER THE SPANISH CONQUEST

The Incas did not just roll over and die after the arrival of the Spaniards in 1532, despite the initial success of the conquistadors. After Atahualpa's death, the Spaniards decided to install a puppet emperor on the throne, a brother of his called Manco; this proved to be a costly error. After a few years of obedience, Manco revolted, calling troops up from all over Tahuantinsuyo for one last blowing up of the fire from the dying embers.

Conqvista. Milagro del Señor Santiago major, apóstol de Jesu Cristo.
St James the Great, Apostle of Jesus Christ.
(St James comes to the aid of the Conquistadors and saves Cusco).

FELIPE HUAMÁN POMA DE AYALA, (c1600)

Pedro de Cieza de León described the conquistadors' dismay at suddenly seeing the strength of Manco's forces camped around Cusco: 'So numerous were the [Indian] troops who came here that they covered the fields, and by day it looked as if a black cloth had been spread over the ground for half a league.' Many of Pizarro's comrades had gone to Chile on an expedition, while others were in the newly founded city of Lima. The remaining Spaniards were taken by surprise and trapped in the streets of the town, while the Incas gathered outside the walls and in the great fortress above at Sacsayhuaman.

By setting fire to the roofs of Cusco and keeping up a punishing siege, the Incas came close to defeating the Spaniards. There were fewer than two hundred of the conquistadors, and of these, as Pedro candidly admits, only the cavalrymen really mattered, as the Spaniards on foot were no match for the agile Indians: 'the Indians hold the infantrymen in slight account'.

It was the European horses which were the Spaniards' only hope if they were to hold over 100,000 Inca soldiers at bay. On open ground, an armoured Spanish horseman with steel weapons against a native infantryman was like a tank against an archer. But in the cramped streets of Cusco, the horses were no longer so agile or effective. The Indians built palisades to contain them, and used slings to hurl burning cloth at the buildings where the Spaniards were sheltering. The defenders realised they were in an impossible position.

They mounted a despairing charge and rode up to take Sacsayhuaman, before Manco could assemble even more native troops for the siege. However much one might dislike the motives or morals of the conquistadors, this was a bold and brave move given how few of them there were and the overwhelming superiority of the Incas.

The Incas under Manco were forced to retreat. He led his men into the wild Vilcabamba area to the west of Cusco from where he and his successors remarkably managed to hold out against the Spanish for another forty years, waging intermittent guerrilla attacks.

It is in this area that some of the most deliberately inaccessible Inca ruins can still be found, like the settlement at Espíritu Pampa which more intrepid trekkers reach in a descent from Vitcos, a site originally built by Pachacutec but later reoccupied by Manco as a symbol that he was continuing in his ancestor's great tradition, however straitened his circumstances.

Manco used the emotive power of the mummies during his exile, carrying the surviving bodies of previous Inca emperors with him into the Vilcabamba, as well as the Punchao, the sunshield. Even though the mummies were captured by the Spaniards and brought back to Cusco, they passed back into native hands and continued to be used by the underground resistance movement for the next 20 years.

In some ways, Manco Inca is the forgotten hero of Inca history. His predecessor Atahualpa is remembered as the emperor whom Pizarro and his men first seized and ransomed for rooms full of gold and silver before executing, while the name of Túpac Amaru, the very last Inca, lives on for its symbolic value and has been sporadically revived as the focus for later resistance groups.

La Preción de Topa Amao Ynga.
Túpac Amaru is led into Cusco.

FELIPE HUAMÁN POMA DE AYALA, (c1600)

But Manco was a more admirable character than either of them. When he was placed as a puppet on the throne by the Spaniards, he had already survived both a brutal civil war and the Spanish Conquest, which along with the epidemic had managed to lay waste one of the world's great empires in less than ten years. The world he had known had crumbled around him. Out of the ashes, and with some consummate political manoeuvring, he somehow managed to rally a rebellion which, if not ultimately successful, at least gave heart to his people.

MODERN PERU AND THE INCA LEGACY

The sense of landscape and buildings as important repositories of history still runs deep in the Peruvian psyche. When President Toledo – the first Peruvian president of Indian origin – was inaugurated, he chose to do so at Machu Picchu rather than as previously in Lima, a very deliberate nod to the Inca tradition.

Certain aspects of the Inca world-view – the belief in cooperative labour by communities, their superb agriculture and husbanding of shared resources, a spirituality rooted in stone and maize and the mountains, and in a sacred landscape – are still part of the Quechua inheritance, despite the intervening imposition of 300 years of Spanish rule.

Now the *indigenismo* movement of the early 20th century and recent political initiatives have sought again to place the Inca empire and its beliefs at the heart of Peru's sense of national identity, with a great national pride in their pre-Columbian achievements.

This has had one desirable outcome, in that the conservation and promotion of archaeological monuments has proceeded apace: from Choquequirao to Vitcos and even the formidably jungle-covered site of Espíritu Pampa, the visitor will see evidence of sustained reconstruction, if sometimes perhaps a little too over-enthusiastic. Only a few historic sites, like Huchuy Cusco, are still neglected, although these have the virtue of an atmospheric, overgrown setting as a result.

The recent work of historians and archaeologists such as John Howland Rowe, Susan Niles, Brian Bauer and Richard Burger has given us more of an insight into the historical events that shaped the spectacular Inca architecture of their heartland around the Sacred Valley. But we still know less about the Incas and their predecessors than we do of other ancient civilisations, partly because of their illiteracy but also because we have come to a true study of their culture surprisingly late.

It would therefore be a mistake to underestimate the difference in outlook between the Incas and ourselves, and the difficulties in bridging that divide that still remain. When offered a cup by the Inca world, as the conquistadors were by Atahualpa, we should choose to drink deeply if we want to understand them.

Elements of the above article are drawn from Hugh Thomson's books on Peru: *The White Rock: An Exploration of the Inca Heartland* and *Cochineal Red: Travels through Ancient Peru* (both Phoenix).

In addition to writing the above books, Hugh Thomson has led several research expeditions to the area around Cusco and made the first reports of some previously unknown Inca sites. For more information see ⌨ www.thewhiterock .co.uk.

FLORA & FAUNA

4

The Machu Picchu Historical Sanctuary is a **UNESCO World Heritage Site** and, unusually, it's a World Heritage Site for both architecture and wildlife. The Sanctuary covers some 325 sq km in an area of wilderness banded to the north by the watershed of the Nevado Veronica massif, in the east and west by the Cusichaca and Aobamba valleys, and in the south by the ridgeline of the Salkantay massif.

The area represents one of the world's most biologically diverse regions: 10% of Peru's entire **biodiversity** is represented within the confines of the Sanctuary alone. This includes around 200 species of orchid, more than 700 species of butterfly and over 400 species of bird. Of the 9000 or so registered bird species in the world, those found in Europe and North America account for around 1400. Peru accounts for almost 1800 on its own, of which 120 are endemic to Peru. The Sanctuary plays host to almost 5% of the world's known bird species.

❏ The Peruvian paso

The Spanish conquistadors were responsible for introducing the horse to South America. Initially used to intimidate the Inca troops who hadn't encountered horses in battle before, they were then used for transportation and breeding. Breeds included the jennet, an ideal light riding horse, the barb, which had great stamina and the Andalusian, an elegant, strongly built breed favoured as a warhorse. Horses with good endurance and a smooth gait were particularly prized; characteristics that led to the selective breeding of the Peruvian paso, noted for its good temperament and comfortable ride. Instead of a trot, the Peruvian paso performs an amble somewhere between a walk and a canter. The four-beat lateral gait – right hind, right front, left hind, left front – accounts for the smooth ride since it causes none of the vertical bounce associated with trotting. The gait, which is natural and doesn't require training, also makes the horse very stable as there are always two and sometimes three hooves on the ground. The horses have great stamina and spirit, known locally as 'brio', and are able to cover great distances without tiring, travelling at a comfortable canter over uneven terrain. They are also willing to work and very biddable, making them an incredibly useful steed.

The past 30 years have seen a resurgence in the Peruvian paso's fortunes. Indeed, the annual National Show just outside Lima that attempts to find the most elegant and beautiful horse in the country has developed into a major event in Peruvian cultural life.

The reason for this is the great variety of **ecosystems** generated by the wide range of altitudes found within the Sanctuary. The mouth of the Aobamba River lies at 1725m/5658ft, whilst a mere 20km away the peak of Nevado Salkantay grazes 6271m/20,574ft. The high mountain ridges generate microclimates that are particularly favourable to the evolution of certain species. The 4546m/14,916ft altitude span results in a broad scope of temperatures being available for different species to dwell in whilst regular rainfall and frequent cloud and mist mean that the region is also humid for much of the year.

The Sanctuary is classified into ten distinct 'Life Zones', which range from the permanent snows of the high peaks through two types of high-altitude grass-land to seven zones of forest. The best-known and most-recognised zones are the treeless, mountain grassland environment known as puna and the cloud for-est, which harbours four Life Zones and is most commonly characterised by a dense and varied mass of trees, smothered in lichens, bromeliads and orchids, surrounded by tree ferns and bamboo. The Sanctuary is also home to some of the few remaining native Andean *Polylepis* forests, which are found on steep slopes and cliffs at higher altitudes; the classic Inca Trail passes through one such section during the ascent to Dead Woman's Pass (see pp220-1).

See pp43-4 for details of field guides to the region.

FLORA

In the Andes flowers and plants from the valleys and highland plains grow alongside each other as a result of the variations in altitude and climate found there. Consequently the region boasts a wide range of habitats and microhabi-tats, and features a huge diversity of wild species.

Trees

There are several beautiful trees found throughout the cloud forest. **Aliso** (*Alnus jorullensis*) grows up to 20m tall and is frequently found on the banks of rivers and streams between 2500m and 3800m. The Incas and the Spanish used its large trunks as beams and lintels in buildings. Today, doors, windows and fruit crates are made from its pale yellow wood.

The smaller **chacpa** (*Oreocallis grandiflora*) ranges in height from two to six metres. It has a host of pink flowered heads that can readily be seen in the Cusichaca Valley on the early stages of the Inca Trail. Baskets are made from the small, flexible branches and locals chew the leaves in order to prevent tooth decay.

The thorny **tara tree** (*Caesalpinia spinosa*) is very common in the Cusichaca Valley. It is unusual in that it bears fruit year-round. These fruits con-tain tannin, used for tanning leather. They are also used to ease throat pain. The tara is most easily recognised by the characteristic orange/red seedpods it pro-duces that resemble tough-skinned broad beans.

The **chamana** (*Dodonaea viscosa*) is also found in the Cusichaca Valley. It is a smaller shrub that grows to 2m and is covered in abundant foliage. It is the perfect plant for binding the soil along the steep mountainsides. The wood burns well even when fresh as it contains an oily substance that is flammable. The similar-sized **llaulli** (*Barnadesia horrida*) is a thorny bush that can be found in the ravines adjacent to the Urubamba Valley between 2900m and 3800m. The local farmers cultivate it as a hedge and use it to make a lattice on the roofs of their adobe huts upon which tiles are laid. The pink, daisy-like flowers are good for alleviating respiratory problems and bronchitis.

The town of Chilca, in the Urubamba Valley, gets its name from the **chilca bush** (*Baccharis latifolia*), which is abundant throughout the valley between 2500m and 3400m. Balls of white flowers form at the end of the branches in clusters. The leaves and flowers are used to make a yellow/green dye for wool. A ball of ash and calcium, called llipta, which locals chew with coca leaves, is made from its ashes.

The town Mollepata on the other hand, the start point for the treks round Nevado Salkantay, is so called because the Incas cultivated molle trees in the region. The name literally translates as 'The place of the molles'. The **molle** (*Schinus molle*) tree can grow to 10m and is attractive enough to be used as an ornamental plant. The Incas used resin collected from it to embalm their mummified dead. Today, the tree's wood is used in carpentry and its ashes used for tanning and in the production of soap. Oil extracted from its leaves is used in perfumes and by the toothpaste industry. Honey, vinegar, tincture and condiments are all made from the small red fruits that the tree produces.

Other attractive ornamental trees include the **rata rata** (*Abutilon sylvaticum*), the pink and white conical flowers of which are used to decorate city plazas and gardens but is found wild in the Cusichaca Valley around Huayllabamba, and the **unca** (*Myrcanthes oreophyl*), which grows up to 15m tall and has very pretty, large white flowers with many filaments. The Incas used to make *qeros*, ceremonial drinking flasks, from its heavy, white wood, whilst today it's used in furniture making.

The bright red splashes of colour visible around the towns of Pisac, Calca and Urubamba in the Sacred Valley are likely to be flowering **pisonay** (*Erythrina edulis*). This giant, leafy, 15m tall tree is native to the high jungle but the Incas acclimatised it to the highlands and considered it to be sacred. However, the real giant of the forest is likely to be the **eucalyptus** (*Eucalyptus globulus*). This imported tree grows up to 30m tall and is the most industrialised, commercialised and useful tree to the Andean people as it grows very quickly in comparison to Andean trees. Its wood is used in the building and mining industries and to make furniture, posts and railway sleepers. Its leaves are used to cure colds and to produce menthol on behalf of the drug and food industries.

Finally, keep your eyes peeled for the **kantu** (*Cantua buxifolia*), known locally as *Flor del Inca*, Peru's national flower. This red and yellow tubular flower, which opens out like a trumpet, grows on a shrub that stands up to 4m tall and grows between 2300m and 3800m. The Incas dedicated this plant to the Sun God and used the pattern of its flower on their pottery, textiles and ceremonial vases. Kantu are often grown as ornamental plants in town plazas, such as in Cusco and are a common sight throughout the Sacred Valley.

FLORA & FAUNA

Orchids

The Machu Picchu Historical Sanctuary is famous for the quantities of orchids that flourish there. Over 70 genera and around 250 species thrive in the moist, humid confines of the Sanctuary. However, much of the region remains unexplored and there are undoubtedly more to be discovered, possibly for the very first time.

Although orchids abound, numbers around the Inca trail and in particular at Machu Picchu itself have dwindled significantly over recent years as a direct consequence of illegal collection by visitors. The biggest threats though are from deforestation and forest fires, which destroy valuable orchid gene banks and prime habitat as well as altering and annihilating entire ecosystems. A particular case in point is the unsympathetic and extensive clearing that occurred around Intipata (see box p228) on the Inca Trail, which resulted in the loss of unique habitat for the rare orchid *Telipogon papilio*, which now faces extinction in the Sanctuary. Conserving these orchids is everyone's responsibility.

The observant or interested trekker should spot orchids at any time of year. We found the greatest concentration of them on the high path running between Km104 and Huinay Huayna, though the most-likely places to come across these exquisite flowers are off the beaten track, especially in the cloud forest between 1800m and 3000m. Most flower during the rainy season, from October to March. The diversity of species on show is stunning.

The most widespread and populous genus is *Epidendrum*, of which there are around 30 species in the Sanctuary. The most common is *Epidendrum secundum*, known locally as **huinay huayna**, meaning 'forever young', a reference to the fact that this diminutive, striking orchid flowers almost all year. The small splashes of vibrant colour are most readily spotted around the ruins of Huinay Huayna on the Inca Trail, which is named after the plant. Its abundant flowers are red, pink, yellow or violet.

Other species include the delicate and fragrant *Epidendrum ciliare*, which grows on trees and rocks at the lower elevations of the Sanctuary, and *Epidendrum coronatum*, which grows in open areas amidst other plants at altitudes between 2800m and 3200m.

Also commonly seen on the forest border and on open slopes are the *Odontoglossum sp*, whose bright yellow flowers are distinctively shaped and protected by brown or purple sepals.

Once widespread, *Masdevallia veitchiana*, known locally as **huakanki**, which means 'you'll cry', has been collected almost to extinction. One of the most striking orchids, its purple and orange flowers with three slight pointed petals are very distinctive and still sought after. The orchid requires open sunny areas and can still be seen at Huinay Huayna on the Inca Trail, where it clings to rocky outcrops carpeted in moss. It flowers from May to July.

The bamboo orchid, *Sobralia dichotoma*, also known as the **Inca orchid** or *Flor del Paraíso*, is visible around Machu Picchu by virtue of the fact that it grows so tall (up to 5m) and has large, showy, 8cm-diameter purple flowers that bloom from July to September and can easily be seen above the surrounding foliage. At the other end of the scale is one of the world's smallest orchids, a *Stelis* whose flower is barely 2mm wide.

Bromeliads, cacti and grasses
Bromeliads, relatives of the pineapple, can be seen throughout the Sanctuary. Several types of cacti are also common. The **agave cactus** (*Agave americana*) is a broad plant with bluish spiked succulent leaves that grows on the dry mountainsides. The Incas made ropes and knitted suspension bridges from the leaf fibres. They also made sandals from it. Local people now use it to form an impenetrable hedge and in the production of products such as soap. The **prickly pear cactus** is cultivated in order to obtain carmine, a natural red colourant used in food, and pharmaceutical and cosmetic industries. Carmine is obtained from the cochineal, a parasitic insect found in the cactus. The fruits of the cactus are delicious and are sold in many of the towns in the Sacred Valley.

There are two types of common **grasses**. *Stipa ichu*, the golden or brown stems of which grow in tussocks on the puna from 3000m to 4500m, is a tough, ubiquitous grass used to make roofs on huts, insulate beds and tents and as animal feed. The other is *Cortaderia nitida*, which stands much taller and looks like a fox tail. A type of succulent grass, *Plantago rigida*, grows in round, rigid cushions; its inflexible leaves grow in star shapes in high swampy areas between 4500m and 4800m. Trekkers often use these cushions as stepping-stones across boggy areas. The Quechua name, *qachqa oku*, refers to the plant's texture (*qachqa* means 'rough') and habitat (*oku* means 'wet'). This plant is the favoured foodstuff of alpacas.

Shrubs and flowers
Familiar plants frequently seen whilst out walking in the UK, Europe and the US can be spotted in the Sanctuary, too. **Broom** (*Spartium junceum*), a member of the sweet pea family, was introduced from Spain in 1580. This yellow flowering shrub grows well in grasslands up to 3500m. The plant is cultivated in order to produce dye, firewood and for use as decoration. Its bright flowers are used medicinally to treat rheumatism, oedema, liver diseases and abscesses. They also serve as makeshift confetti in parades.

Lupins (*Lupinus sp*) are another common shrub found throughout the grasslands in the area. Its blueish, lavender flowers are shaped like pea flowers and have bright yellow centres. The leaves, flowers and stems are used for a cream- or green-coloured dye.

Ladies' slipper (*Calceolaria engleriana*) is a member of the snapdragon family. The flowers of this 2m tall shrub resemble tiny 2cm slippers – the Latin name is derived from *calceolus*, meaning 'slipper'. In Quechua the plant is called *pucllu*, which means 'bag' or 'sack' and again refers to the shape of the flowers. Its Spanish nickname is *globitus*, meaning 'little balloons', because you can pop the flowers between your fingers. Various species are used by local people in tea as a cure for uterine problems or as a diuretic. Also readily identifiable are the flowers of the **wild potato** (*Solanaceae sp*). This erect, clambering herb has violet flowers with five points and protruding yellow anthers.

There are some 135 species of this genus in Peru alone, growing in rocky or wooded areas.

A type of **lily**, *Bomarea dulcis*, grows around boulders in grassy areas. The plant produces between two and five dangling 5cm flowers that resemble tubular bells. The sepals of these are reddish pink but have darker edges. The Quechua name for this plant is *milli milli*, meaning 'twins' and describes the two flowers often seen hanging together. The equally distinctive, purple-violet dangling flowers of *Brachyotum grisebachi* can be readily seen on the edges of the cloud forest near to water. This 2.5m shrub has many branches and produces masses of the distinctive flowers, which are occasionally worn by local people as ear decorations. **Begonias** (*Begonia bracteosa*) flourish within the Sanctuary and the red, white or pink flowers of various species can be seen on numerous dry, sunny, stepped slopes. **Bomareas** can be seen in two colours. The showy orange bracts of *Bomarea aurantiaca* and the deep red bracts of *Bomarea coccinea* are particularly visible in the humid cloud forest around Phuyu Pata Marca on the Inca Trail and in the jungle surrounding the Santa Teresa Valley.

Daisies, **fuchsias**, **elders** and **buttercups** are also prevalent. More unusual is the **datura** (**moonflower**), *Brugmansia arborea*; there are two types, which have white and red/green flowers respectively. Both are hallucinogenic and toxic if consumed.

FAUNA

Mammals

Although you may have heard of the **Andean (or spectacled) bear** (*Tremarctos ornatus*), the only member of its family found in South America, it is very shy and consequently difficult to see. Measuring 1.5-2m from head to tail, this black bear which gets its nickname from its creamy face markings and dark eye rings, is classified as 'vulnerable' because its territory has been reduced by deforestation, farming and other human activity. The bear survives in this hostile situation by being willing to eat anything, a policy that occasionally gets it into trouble when it raids maize crops at the edge of cloud forests. Typically though, these harmless animals feed on cacti, orchid bulbs, fallen fruit and assorted leaves, though they also prey on small animals such as rabbits, mice and nesting birds. However, the bear's favourite food is bromeliads; it will construct rudimentary platforms in order to clamber up trees, like Paddington reaching for marmalade, to be able to get at these plants. Having feasted, and without any natural predator (except man), the bear often just falls asleep. See also box p300.

Even more enigmatic and tricky to spot are **puma** (*Felis concolor*). These powerful, tawny cats are usually solitary animals that prefer habitats with dense underbrush and rocky areas perfect for stalking and ambushing prey. Once revered by the Incas as a symbol of power and elegance, their numbers have declined due to hunting and the loss of habitat and they are now rare in this region. The **culpeo fox**, known locally as *zorro*, is more common. This bold, versatile scavenger preys on rodents including Andean **skunks** and **weasels**,

Moonflower
Brugmansia arborea

Tailed Phragmipedium orchid
Phragmipedium caudatum

Ulluypiña
Eustephia coccinea

Begonia
Begonia bracteosa

*Odontoglossum
mystacinum* (Orchid)

Kantu/Cantuta
Cantua buxifolia

Bromeliad
Bromeliaceae

Huinay Huayna orchid
('Forever young')
Epidendrum secundum

Huakanki orchid
('You'll cry')
Masdevallia veitchiana

Llama llama
('Flames')
Oreocallis grandiflora

Flor del Paraíso
(Inca orchid)
Sobralia dichotoma

Lupin
(Tarwi, Chocho)
Lupinus sp.

Ladies' slipper
(Zaptitos: 'Little shoes')
Calceolaria engleriana

Wild potato
Solanum aloysifolium

Red datura/moonflower
Datura sanguinea

Broom (Retama)
Spartium junceum

rabbits and birds, although it will also make do with carrion. There are two types of high-altitude grassland deer, the endangered **north Andean huemul**, or *taruka* as it is called in Quechua, and the rather more common **white-tailed deer**. The Sanctuary is also home to **pudu** (*sachacabra* in Quechua), secretive pygmy deer that are nocturnal and consequently rarely seen during the day.

Mountain **viscachas** (*Lagidium peruanum*) look a lot like rabbits but are in fact close relatives of the chinchilla. These bushy-tailed rodents with long furry ears are widespread, but blend easily into the background, their grey and brown fur perfect camouflage against the rocks that they like to sun themselves on. There are also large colonies living amongst the ruins at Machu Picchu.

Llamas (*Lama glama*) and **alpacas** (*Lama pacos*) are the most regularly seen animals in the Sanctuary. Relatives of the Old World camel, both species were domesticated many thousands of years ago by pre-Columbian Andean tribes who recognised these hardy creatures could carry substantial loads as pack animals and also represented a useful source of food and warm wool. Llamas are the most common and strongest of the Andean camelids. They stand around 2m tall and can carry up to 60kg. The alpaca, known as *pacocha* in Quechua, with its smaller and more-rounded silhouette, resembles a cross between a llama and a teddy bear. In general, alpacas have more and better-quality wool than llamas, the most desirable being from baby alpaca, which is soft and fine. Alpaca meat is also being promoted and many of the restaurants in Cusco serve it.

These two camelids have two wild relatives: the **guanaco** (*Lama guanicoe*), which stands just over a metre tall at the shoulder and has a grey face, short ears and a white belly, and the **vicuña** (*Vicugna vicugna*) which is a smaller, grace-ful-looking creature with inquisitive eyes, tawny brown fur on their upper parts and longer white fur on the throat and underside, reputed to be the finest animal wool in the world. Both of these are rarely seen in the Machu Picchu Sanctuary having been shot and trapped extensively by hunters and poachers, but are for-tunately more common in the south; those attempting the Ausangate trek have a good chance of encountering them on the trail (though it will probably be a long-distance encounter). They are now protected species in Peru and although still vulnerable, their numbers have started to increase again.

Insects

Peru is justifiably famous for its **butterflies**: a fifth of the world's butterfly species is found here. Some 1300 species have been recorded in the communi-ty of Pakitza, in Manu National Park and over 1200 species have been noted at a community 235km away on the Tambopata River. Incredibly, only 60% of these species overlapped. Scientists estimate that there must be more than 4000 species in the country, only about 3600 of which have currently been registered. Considering that North America boasts 679 species and Europe a mere 441 species, this is an astounding number.

The Andean highlands above 5000m/16,400ft are home to relatively few species. Those that do survive here are specially adapted to the rigorous environment. Tropical forests are the preferred habitat of most butterfly species. Trekkers on the Vilcabamba Trail are likely to see the most diverse array of butterflies, often encountering huge swarms congregating together.

Unfortunately, you are also likely to become very well acquainted with the **midges** that can be encountered throughout the Sanctuary, but most especially in the Santa Teresa Valley. They also plague the approach to Choquequirao.

Reptiles and amphibians

Few reptiles are known about, as the forest tends to be so dense and inaccessible. Keep a look out for snakes; coral **snakes**, bushmasters and the rare velvet fer-de-lance are endemic to the Sanctuary. They are all poisonous and should not be approached if encountered. Fortunately most snakes found in the Andes are non-venomous. Most frequently encountered are harmless whipsnakes: slender green snakes with yellow underbellies.

Frogs of the genus *Atelopus* also live in the forest above 2000m.

Birds

The Incas believed that birds were the messengers of the *apus*, the gods who lived on the summits of mountains. The condor, being the most impressive bird, was associated with the highest peaks whilst less-remarkable birds were considered to carry the thoughts and words of spirits residing on lower mountains.

The Sanctuary has an impressive array of avifauna for such a compact area. Many birds have relatively small altitudinal ranges, meaning that each of the Sanctuary's ten habitats is home to species that are found in no other zone. More than 400 species are known to exist in the Sanctuary and more than 200 of these can be readily observed along the Inca Trail or on the Salkantay, Lares, Ausangate and Choquequirao treks.

The *Polylepis* woodland contains some of the rarest birds, including titspinetails and high-altitude hummingbirds, but the cloud forest is home to the greatest diversity and here you can expect to see tinamous, guans, parakeets, hummingbirds, wrens, jays, swallows, quetzals, woodpeckers, flycatchers and tanagers.

The best way to spot these birds is to look for them at the correct time of day. Although you can see birds at any time, your best chance is first thing in the morning or at dusk, when they are singing and most active. Be quiet as you walk through the forest and stop periodically to look around carefully. To improve your chances further, bring binoculars on your trip.

● **Andean condor** The emblematic Andean condor (*Vultur gryphus*) is actually an enormous vulture, boasting the largest wing span of any land bird. Some individuals have spans in excess of 3m/10ft and measure well over a metre from their bill to the tip of their tail. They can weigh up to 11kg. The adult plumage is uniformly black, with the exception of a white ruff

ANDEAN CONDOR

surrounding the base of the neck. The head and neck are blackish red and bald, an adaptation for hygiene given that the bird primarily feeds on carrion and rotting meat. When in flight, it can be identified by its sheer size and characteristic silhouette: the finger feathers at the tips of its wings point forward. Condors prefer relatively open areas that allow them to spot carrion from the air and favour rocky cliffs and outcrops on which to nest. Although considered a mountain bird, it is more common on the coast.

The Andean condor is a national symbol of Peru and plays an important role in indigenous folklore and mythology. More recently it has endured a swathe of negative press, and stories abound of birds harrying travellers, killing livestock and even snatching small children whilst shepherds tended to their llama flocks. Writers including Bruce Chatwin (*In Patagonia*) and E. George Squier (*Peru – Incidents of Travel and Exploration in the Land of the Incas*, 1877) documented instances where they came under attack from condors.

Hiram Bingham recounted in *Lost City of the Incas* that local shepherds had to wage a constant battle with condors that had no difficulty in carrying off a sheep. Even today some of the less-discerning newspapers occasionally run stories about condors snatching away unguarded infants. If you come across a condor in captivity or happen to see a stuffed specimen, a quick look at their ineffective, talon-free feet, akin to those of an enormous domestic chicken, which have been adapted for walking rather than holding or carrying objects, will debunk the notion that they could carry off anything substantial, let alone a small child or sheep wriggling to be free.

● **Birds of prey** The bigger birds in the high Andes are usually raptors or birds of prey. Look out for the **American kestrel** (*Falco sparverius*), a pair of **Aplomado falcons** (*Falco femoralis*) or a **mountain caracara** (*Phalcoboenus megalopterus*). The kestrel, colloquially known as a sparrow hawk, is a small raptor, averaging around 20cm from beak to tail, with blue-grey wings, a white head with blue-grey cap, white cheeks and a pair of vertical black face markings. Its breast and tail are a brownish, rust-colour. The medium-sized falcon is 10-20cm longer but very slim. It has a dark blue-grey head, long, light brown pointed wings, a tapering tail with narrow white or grey bars and a paler breast. The caracara is larger still, measuring up to 50cm from beak to tail. It has characteristic black, white and grey wings, a black and white tail and the bare skin of its face is an orangey colour. A highly opportunistic scavenger, it can often be seen walking on the ground in search of carrion and can often be found near human habitation.

MOUNTAIN CARACARA

Other species to spot include a number of types of **hawk**, most common of which is the **red-backed hawk** (*Buteo polyosoma*), and the **black-chested buzzard eagle** (*Geranoaetus melanoleucus*). The latter is a big, bulky, power-

BLACK-CHESTED BUZZARD EAGLE

FLORA & FAUNA

ful-looking bird measuring up to 80cm from beak to tail. Its plumage is predominantly a blue-hued grey colour, with black edges to its wings and a black neck and head. It is identifiable in flight by the short, wedge-shaped tail that scarcely protrudes from its broad wings.

● **Guans** These large pheasant-like birds can be seen, or more frequently heard, crashing about in the trees of the humid montane forests. The most common is the **Andean guan** (*Penelope montagnii*). This turkey-sized bird, with orange-brown plumage and a red wattle, lives in the trees and feeds on fruit, seeds and other vegetable matter, rarely descending to the ground.

● **Motmots** These beautifully coloured birds are related to kingfishers. They occur in all types of forest as well as on open areas of grassland. Colourful, long and slender, they are medium-sized birds with long, broad bills that are somewhat curved down at the end. The most distinctive feature though is their tail.

In most motmots, two central feather shafts grow much longer than the others. The **Highland motmot** (*Momotus aequatorialis*) grows up to 50cm and has a turquoise-blue forecrown and green underparts. It can be seen all along the Urubamba Valley, often perched on riverside boulders, and around Aguas Calientes. Similar, but slightly smaller and with brown underparts, is the **blue crowned motmot** (*Momotus coeruliceps*).

● **Tanagers** Amongst the forests' most common and visible birds, tanagers often congregate in small flocks near human habitation to feed in fruit trees. They are noted for their colourful plumage and few other species can compete with the broad spectrum of colours found on their feathers.

There are 135 species recorded in Peru, 60 of which can be seen around Machu Picchu; those most commonly spotted along the Inca Trail are the **blue-and-yellow tanager**, the **blue-grey tanager**, the **saffron-crowned tanager**, the **fawn-breasted tanager** and the **silver-beaked tanager**.

● **Trogons** Although less well known than other gaudy birds, trogons are often considered to be the most visually impressive. The largest of the species, the quetzals, are the most dazzling. Males are consistently more colourful than the females and have metallic or glittering green, blue or violet heads, backs and chests. Their breasts and undersides are contrasting bright red, yellow or orange. The females usually have darker brown or grey backs and heads, but they share the brightly coloured chests of the males. The long characteristic tail is squared off and striped black and white on the underside. Look out for the green-headed **collared trogon** (*Trogon collaris*) and the similar **masked trogon** (*Trogon personatus*), which can be distinguished by the thicker bars on its tail feathers.

● **Wrens** These are small, brownish birds that tend to skulk in thick undergrowth. The Latin name of the genus, *Troglodytes*, refers to a cave dweller, a reference to the wren's predilection for nesting in holes and crevices. They are very vocal and have attractive singing voices. The typical sound heard at Machu

Picchu is the song of the **Inca wren** (*Thryothorus eisenmanni*), which is native to Peru and whose distinctive spotted breast marks it out from other types of wren.

● **Hummingbirds**   Almost everyone can identify hummingbirds, which evolved in the Andes. They are mostly tiny birds, usually clad in iridescent metallic greens, reds, violets and blues. These tiny, nectar-drinking birds rely entirely on their wings for locomotion since their feet and legs are too weak for anything but perching. There are more than 130 species of hummingbird in Peru, the majority of which are found in the Andes.

The most commonly spotted hummingbird along the Inca Trail or in Cusco gardens is the **sparkling violetear** (*Colibri coruscans*), which has a violet-blue chest and violet ear that extends to its chin. It is a tireless singer.

The slightly larger **green-and-white hummingbird** (*Leucippus viridicauda*) is regularly recorded around Machu Picchu, where it can be identified by its white chest.

The world's largest hummingbird is the surprisingly muted (at least in comparison to its relatives) **giant hummingbird** (*Patagona gigas*), which can measure more than 20cm from the tip of its long bill to the end of its tail.

You will also come across **sunangels**, **sapphirewings**, **coquettes**, **golden-throats**, **sunbeams** and **coronets**, each of which is as beautiful as its name promises.

● **Waterfowl**   In mountain streams as well as along the Urubamba River, you can find **torrent ducks** (*Merganetta armata*). Uniquely adapted to swimming, diving and feeding in the fast rushing waters that cascade off the mountains, the ducks rarely stray far from the streams and even nest in crevices between boulders on the water's edge. Male torrent ducks have striking black and white striped heads and red beaks, and females have orange underparts, grey backs and a yellow bill.

Andean gulls (*Larus serranus*), the only gulls to be found in the high Andes, also live along the Urubamba or can be found on the higher elevation tarns. You can also see the **Andean (or ruddy) duck**, which is rust-red with a spiky black tail, and has a white face with a black cap and wide blue bill, and the **crested duck**, a sleek grey with a touch of red on the wings.

The heavily built **Andean geese** (*Chloephaga melanoptera*), with white plumage and small pink bills, prefer being on land to swimming so that they can graze, whilst black and white **giant coots** are common on the water.

Elegant **puna ibis** (*Plegadis ridgwayi*), which have dark purplish-brown feathers and a chestnut face, can often be seen on the Ausangate and Lares trails and along the first stages of the railway trip to Machu Picchu, foraging slowly and probing the shallow waters and mud with their distinctive long, curved bills. You may also come across the **black-faced ibis** (*Theristicus melanopis*), rarer than the above though they can be encountered occasionally in the Sacred Valley, on the Salkantay Trek and the higher trails.

FLORA & FAUNA

● **Other birds**   The magnificent **cock of the rock** (*Rupicola peruviana*), with its prominent fan-shaped headdress of bright orange or scarlet feathers, is Peru's national bird. The female of the species is significantly darker and browner. Frequently seen along the railway tracks around Machu Picchu, it is also common in the forests surrounding Espíritu Pampa, where gatherings of males compete for breeding females by displaying their gaudy plumage, bobbing and making a series of calls.

Other stunning, noisy birds often spotted are **parakeets**, which can often be seen and heard around Aguas Calientes or in the forests along the trails.

On the ground you can see furtive **tinamous**, a type of partridge. Prior to the introduction of the chicken by the Spanish, the Incas domesticated tinamous for their meat and eggs. At one stage these birds were so common that they gave their name to the town in the Sacred Valley: Pisac means 'partridge'.

Swifts and **swallows**, with their distinctive swept-back wings and pointed tails, have easily identifiable silhouettes as they flash overhead.

Woodpeckers, such as the **bar-bellied woodpecker** (*Veniliornis nigriceps*) and **crimson-mantled woodpecker** (*Piculus rivolii*) are recognisable due to their shape and habit of drilling in tree trunks.

The attractive **Andean flicker** (*Colaptes rupicola*), a fairly common, largish woodpecker (30cm from beak to tail) with a light brown head and black cap, grey and dark brown feathers and a yellow breast, lives in puna and scrubland where, rather unusually, it nests in earth banks and old adobe buildings.

MINIMUM IMPACT & OUTDOOR SAFETY

5

Minimum impact trekking

Tourism is a vital source of income for Peru and, directly or indirectly, a great many Peruvians benefit from the increasing numbers of trekkers and tourists flocking to the country. However, there are undoubtedly problems along the Inca Trail and the other trekking routes in the region that are caused by the arrival of hordes of visitors. Litter, erosion, pollution and the destruction of the landscape and the Inca archaeological sites are all sadly the realities of large numbers of people visiting these areas.

The Peruvian authorities do nominally try to keep the place clean, but unfortunately their actions aren't all that effective. Whilst it's easy to blame the authorities for the decline of the pristine wilderness, trekkers are equally at fault. People on the trails also have to take responsibility for their own litter and actions; each individual should remember that their thoughtlessness and selfishness potentially has consequences for everyone else.

ENVIRONMENTAL IMPACT

Damaged vegetation, litter, polluted waterways, deteriorating facilities and an increase in erosion are all indications that trekkers have had a negative impact on the landscape. Fortunately, most people are now much more conscious of the potential impact that they have on the environment and are more likely to adopt a considerate, responsible attitude whilst trekking or otherwise enjoying the landscape. It's important that we all maintain this new-found responsibility.

Pack it in, pack it out

All waste must be carried off the mountain. Human detritus is one of the most significant threats to the natural environment. Unsightly and unhealthy, accumulated rubbish is a hazard for people and wildlife alike. If you are with an official group, in theory all you have to do is hand the litter to a staff member who will then ensure that it is removed from the trail. Unfortunately this isn't always the case and more unscrupulous guides or porters may dump or drop rubbish along the route.

Keep an eye on your team and make sure they understand that it is important to you that they adhere to this rule. In addition, don't give them batteries to dispose of; keep hold of them and take them back home where there are proper facilities for getting rid of them. If you are trekking independently, take rubbish bags with you to carry all your waste and be conscious of the amount of litter you are likely to generate when preparing to trek. If you come across litter along the trail you should pick it up and remove it, if at all possible, in order to set a good example.

Bury your excrement

Where possible, always use the purpose-built toilet blocks along the trails or at the campsites. If you are trekking on one of the routes that doesn't have facilities, or are caught short on the trail, stick to the following rules: make sure you're at least 20m away from both the path and any water source or stream; take a trowel with you so that you can dig a small hole to squat over and cover the hole with plenty of soil once you're done; dispose of your toilet paper properly either by carefully burning it or burying it deeply in the same hole. Better still pack it out along with everything else, having taken the precaution of double-bagging (preferably in a zip-lock bag) the offending article.

Don't pollute water

The Andean waterways and lakes are fragile ecosystems. Contamination can easily lead to deterioration in water quality. Equally, no-one wants to bathe in other people's bathwater. Or cook with it, do their laundry in it or indeed drink it. Yet this is the consequence for the local people if you wash your hair or body or clothes in the mountain streams, no matter how romantic an image this might conjure up. Your guide will almost certainly provide you with a bowl of warm water at the start and end of the day with which you can wash. Dispose of this carefully, at least 20m away from any other water source or stream, and wait until you finish the trek to have a proper wash.

Erosion

In general, the Inca trails are clearly marked and easy to follow. Try to stay on these paths wherever possible. The continued use of shortcuts, particularly on some of the steeper sections of trail, erodes the slopes. From the various passes it is very tempting to descend quickly and directly, and you may see people, especially guides, doing just that. Faster and possibly more fun, the shortcuts nonetheless destroy the fabric of the hillside and cause irreparable damage. Tedious as it may sound, stick to the marked paths.

Camping

When camping, try to have as little impact as possible on the countryside. Ask permission if near to a farm or small-holding. Confine yourself to as small a space as is realistic and do not spread yourself out unduly. Don't litter the area and when you strike camp make sure you tidy everything up and leave the site as you found it, undisturbed.

Campfires

Whilst a campfire sounds very appealing and the stuff of true camping expeditions, the reality of an out-of-control fire means that it just isn't worth the risk.

There's absolutely no need to light a fire on any of the treks described here: for cooking you or your guides ought to use a portable stove, whilst for heat you should simply put on another jumper or layer of clothes.

Don't camp in the ruins
The ancient stones have been badly damaged by trekkers in the past who liked the idea of spending a night amongst the Inca sites. Litter and human waste are not the only problems of this selfish action. Campfires damage the walls and clumsy campers dislodge and remove the stones themselves. Camping at the sites along the Inca Trail or at Choquequirao itself is banned and trekkers must adhere to these rules.

Don't pick flowers or disturb fauna
Leave the flora and fauna alone. The Cusco region, a dedicated UNESCO natural World Heritage Site, is full of stunning flowers and some extraordinary bird and animal life. It is illegal to remove anything from the trails or the sanctuary, so leave it all where it belongs for others to enjoy as well.

ECONOMIC IMPACT

The economic importance of tourism for Peru is undeniable. However, not everyone benefits equally. If you book an organised trek through a foreign operator, the bulk of your money stays outside the country. Book a trek through an agency in Cusco, and a far greater proportion of the money remains in the city. The porters and trek team may not be from the city, although they will benefit from the opportunity to work. If you trek independently where possible, you will contribute far more to the local economy. Employ a local porter or *arriero*. Some independent trekkers feel that being burdened by their pack is part of the experience, but it is far more useful to the region if you hire help, and if arranged whilst there, can be a surprisingly simple, cheap way of putting something back and making your trip more enjoyable.

Pay a fair price for a fair service
Recognise the worth of a service to you and pay a reasonable rate for it. Do not attempt to bargain porters or arrieros right down and do not haggle overly aggressively. They are paid poorly for back-breaking work, yet are worth every sol to the success of a trek (see Porter welfare, box pp22-3). However, do not believe the market traders and touts who tell you that goods have a fixed price!

CULTURAL IMPACT

The places that you are visiting are of great spiritual, historical and cultural importance. Show these places the respect that they deserve. To fully appreciate and understand the cultural history and value of the place that you are visiting you ought to spend some time learning about its people and history (see pp51-66).

Whilst you are trekking be considerate to other visitors and users of the countryside. Try to keep noise to a minimum. As a general rule, be selfless and remember that you are only visiting.

Encourage local pride

Encourage local pride by giving Peruvians a balanced view of life in your home country. In answer to queries about how much you earn, reply honestly but put the figures into context by comparing how much it costs to rent a flat or buy certain types of goods. Tell them what you think is good about their lifestyle – the extraordinary surroundings, the lack of real crime, the clean air – and comment on what appeals to you about their lifestyle. If you particularly enjoyed your stay or trek be sure to let them know.

To give or not to give?

Giving to beggars can perpetrate an attitude of dependency. Don't load up with sweets or other gifts to answer the children's begging requests. Although handing things out might make you feel good in the short term, it can lead to a detrimental effect on the recipient, resulting in low self-esteem and an associated idea that the West and tourists hold the answer rather than their own culture. Additionally, there are no dentists in the rural communities and giving sweets to children here is not helpful.

If someone has done something helpful, consider rewarding them, but be careful as to how you do it. Requests for pens and other school equipment are harder to refuse, but donations should really be made to a school rather than an individual to ensure equal distribution.

You should also be wary of handing out medicines along the trails. Strong or prescription medicines may be taken incorrectly and do more harm than good. If you have additional or left over medicines, donate them to an agency or organisation that can distribute them to a hospital instead.

Ask permission before taking a person's photograph

Respect their privacy and if they aren't comfortable or happy with the situation then leave them alone. Ideally you should not pay people for posing. If you offer to send someone a copy of the photo you've taken, make sure you get the address and follow through your promise.

Don't flaunt your wealth

Your wealth, however poor you may be by the standards of your home country, is far in excess of that of most Peruvians, so don't make a big issue of it and certainly don't flaunt it. Take care of valuables and put them away so as to remove temptation. When camping make sure that all your equipment is out of sight inside the tent, especially at night.

Don't lose your temper

Peruvians rarely lose their rag, and you should work hard to control your temper as well, even when things aren't working out as you might have hoped they would. Be polite and the chances are the courtesy will be returned.

Health and safety in the mountains

SAFETY

Although there are hazards in the mountains, a properly prepared expedition with the right equipment and a bit of common sense should not be troubled by them.

Weather
The weather in the Andes is very changeable. You should expect rain whatever the season and ought to carry warm clothing at all times, even if it seems to be a sunny day, since temperatures can plummet and conditions change very quickly. As a general guide, check the weather forecast with your agency or online before setting out and keep an eye on the weather as you walk. For more information about the climate, see p10-12.

Keeping on course
Although the majority of trails in the Cusco region are well trodden, there are also plenty of areas where you will come across very few people and where the path has disappeared, particularly on the Vilcabamba Trail. Bad weather can also mean that a path previously simple to follow becomes obscured and much harder to trace. In thick cloud or fog do not leave the path.

An accurate topographic map and a compass are helpful, as long as you know how to use them. Similarly, a handheld GPS can help you to find your way. See the box p214 for further details about how to keep to the trail.

Tell someone where you're going
If you are planning on trekking independently, before you set off on your trek, tell someone responsible, at your hotel or hostel for example, where you are going and when you expect to return. They should be aware of what to do if you don't come back, and how long they should wait before raising the alarm.

Beware of the dog
Rural dogs can be dangerous, some may even carry rabies, but are more often just a nuisance. If confronted by an angry, barking dog often just bending down as if to pick up a stone is enough to cause them to turn tail – this is what the locals do and the dogs are used to being pelted.

HEALTH IN THE MOUNTAINS

Trekkers often revel in the horror stories about the diseases encountered on treks and trips to the developing world. Whilst Peru does have a handful of serious health problems, you are very unlikely to be affected by them and if you follow simple guidelines you'll minimise the risk to yourself.

Acute mountain sickness (AMS)

It is recommended for all members of your group to have some knowledge of symptoms and treatment of AMS. See ▣ www.altitude.org or the Mountain Medicine section at the International Climbing and Mountaineering Federation website (▣ www.theuiaa.org) for detailed and up to date information.

AMS (also known as **altitude sickness**) is a potentially fatal condition which generally occurs above 3000m (10,000ft) and must not be underestimated. At the altitudes covered by this book, it can be prevented with adequate acclimatisation. However, there is no hard and fast rule as to how long it takes to acclimatise to increases in altitude, as individuals are affected differently.

AMS and High Altitude Pulmonary Oedema (HAPE) and High Altitude Cerebral Oedema (HACE), the serious, life-threatening conditions that can occur as a result of it, are entirely preventable, if certain precautions are taken:

● Don't exceed the recommended rate of ascent (above 2500-3000m the next night should not be planned more than 300-500m higher than the previous one)
● Keep hydrated by drinking plenty of liquid and avoiding alcohol
● Avoid overexertion by climbing slowly and steadily
● Look out for early symptoms of AMS and react to them.

Mild symptoms are uncomfortable, but not dangerous, and will pass in a couple of days. They include a headache and nausea on top of breathlessness and an irritating dry cough. In more serious conditions vomiting begins to occur. Increasing tiredness, confusion and a reduction in coordination are more severe symptoms.

With light to moderate symptoms you should remain at the same altitude, avoiding workloads, until symptoms disappear. Treat nausea with antiemetics and headaches with paracetamol or ibuprofen (if these fail, consider taking acetazolamide), and try and drink enough to avoid dehydration. Descend if symptoms don't improve, or worsen.

If symptoms become severe you must descend (with company) at once, even during the night, to the last camp where you felt well. Dropping even small vertical amounts can have a beneficial effect. See p47 for more on AMS.

Hypothermia

Also known as exposure, hypothermia develops as a result of someone being extremely cold. If they are hypothermic, they'll stumble, be confused, slur their speech, act oddly and be very cold to the touch. They may be oblivious to the fact that they are in danger. To try to prevent the onset of the condition or the deterioration of the casualty, try to warm them up, most usually by getting them out of wet clothing or by sharing bodily warmth.

Sunburn and sun-stroke

The strong Andean sun burns quickly. Protect against sunburn by wearing a hat, sunglasses and a shirt with a collar. You'll also need sunscreen as the sun is strong, and even an apparently cloudy day is no guarantee that you won't get burnt. Occasionally, if a person's temperature is driven dangerously high, they can develop sun-stroke. A victim of this will be delirious and confused, whilst their pulse will be racing and their breathing fast and erratic. Try to reduce their temperature gradually by fanning, sponging them with a damp cloth and shading them. If they lose consciousness you must try to get them to a doctor as quickly as possible because sun-stroke can be life-threatening.

Care of feet, ankles and knees
Whilst trekking, your feet are your most valuable tools. A twisted ankle, sore knee or septic blister can severely spoil your trek so take precautions to prevent them. Wear comfortable boots with good ankle support. Don't carry too much or over-stress your joints. Avoid walking in the dark. Wash and dry your feet thoroughly and change your socks regularly. If you do feel a blister developing, act immediately to prevent it from getting worse.

● **Blisters** Prevention is far better than cure when it comes to blisters. If you feel a tingling sensation or 'hot spot' developing stop at once and cover the irritated area with a piece of moleskin or Second Skin. If a blister does form either burst it with a sterilised needle and apply a dressing or build a moleskin dressing around the unburst blister to protect it.

● **Sprains** Reduce the risk of a sprain by wearing boots with good support. Mind your step as you walk over rough or uneven terrain too. If you do sprain an ankle, soak it in cold water and keep it bandaged. Aspirin is good for reducing swelling and easing the pain.

● **Knee problems** Sustained sections of steep downhill trail can result in sore, strained knees. When descending this type of trail take small steps and tread carefully to lessen the impact and jarring on the joints. Knee supports can give some assistance, and walking (trekking) poles (see p39) can also help for long descents, particularly if you have a previous history of knee problems.

Chapped skin and lips
Carry moisturiser or Vaseline to apply to chapped skin. Use lip balm to soothe cracked or dry lips.

Food
To improve your chances of not getting sick when eating, maintain a high standard of hygiene. Essentially, if you can't cook it, peel it or wash it in clean, purified water you should be wary of it.

Water purification
Always boil, filter or purify your drinking water. This will help to reduce the risk of picking up a water-borne illness such as giardia, but will also reduce the number of non-returnable, non-reusable, non-biodegradable and very environmentally unfriendly plastic mineral water bottles found occasionally on every route. Iodine tablets or iodine drops are ideal for treating water; simply follow the instructions on the packet or bottle. SteriPENs, which purify water using ultra-violet light, and Sawyer MINI Water Filters are also good solutions. If you treat your water yourself you reduce the risk of it simply being warmed up in a kettle and can be absolutely sure that it has been purified.

LIMA

At the centre of the city lies the decaying hulk of a great colonial shipwreck. In flaking baroque these relics gaze, stained and weary, over the tin and concrete and electric wires. **Matthew Parris**, *Inca Kola*, 1990

Matthew Parris's words above were certainly true in 1990 but Lima has undergone massive changes over the last 25 years.

The city lies below a shroud of sea cloud for many months of the year and can look a little uninviting and uniform. It has also been subject to decades of negative press, with reports of how the city had become shabby and unsafe, or simply boring. Consequently it became just a stepping-stone for people travelling to the Andes or Amazon, an overnight stop to endure rather than enjoy. Yet the former Spanish capital of South America, originally christened Ciudad de los Reyes (City of Kings), was once one of the continent's most alluring and impressive cities. These days, a resurgent local middle class are taking pride in their city again and pioneering a renaissance to ensure Lima's reputation is restored.

Lima is a wonderful introduction to what you'll see and find elsewhere. Archaeological sites stand amidst residential neighbourhoods whose architecture spans styles from the last 500 years. There are good museums, world-class restaurants and a burgeoning food scene, lively night spots and an irresistible energy and edge borne out of the multicultural mix found here.

HISTORY

There's evidence of life and habitation in and around Lima dating back 7000 years. The earliest residents of the mouth of the Rio Rímac were settlers who came to the region to fish. They were followed by more sophisticated cultures who left their mark in the form of temples and pyramids. These adobe structures, dating from around 3000BC, still stand although they have been assimilated into Lima's urban sprawl and now appear amidst residential districts.

Around 500AD the local oracle, Pachacámac, was established, meaning that it was ancient even before the Incas arrived in the 15th century. The Incas adopted the site into their society and developed a chain of temples along the coast, supported by peaceful communities. They never placed excessive emphasis on the region though, as the centre of their Empire lay east, in Cusco.

In contrast, the conquistadors recognised the need for a coastal capital, a link to the outside world and to Spain in particular. Having subdued Cusco, Francisco Pizarro established Lima in 1535, picking a site with a good natural harbour and reliable water supply to set up his capital. Almost immediately Lima came under threat as rebel Incas, led by Manco Inca, sought to cut off the Spanish supply line and link to the motherland by sacking the city. Although they staged a substantial siege, the Incas were broken by the Spanish cavalry, who easily dominated the Inca infantry on flat ground. With this defeat and failure to break the line of supply and communication, the rebellion was undone before it really got going.

Under the rule of the Spanish, Lima became a thriving and important city. The viceroy of South America was based here and surrounded himself with the trappings of power associated with his position; there are documented reports of the celebrations that followed the arrival of a new viceroy that illustrate the wealth that was on show, with tapestries hung in the streets and individuals dressed in fine fabrics to attend bullfights and banquets. Other prominent institutions also established themselves here; the University of San Marcos, the oldest in South America, was opened in 1551, whilst the Spanish Inquisition also made Lima the centre of their operations in 1569. However, other, less-welcome visitors were also lured to Lima by the promise of riches; privateers including Sir Francis Drake raided the city in 1579, whilst other pirate attacks followed. In response, the city rebuilt its defensive walls. The

Civdad La Villa de Callav.
City of Callao,
Gateway to Lima.
FELIPE HUAMÁN POMA DE AYALA,
(c1600)

walls couldn't withstand a massive earthquake in 1746 though, which levelled many of the colonial buildings; 16,000 people died from the quake and the diseases that followed in its aftermath.

Such was the wealth and richness the city enjoyed under the Spanish that it resisted attempts to be liberated by San Martín. He in turn allowed the Limeños to continue as they were until they realised that there was no support forthcoming from Spain, at which point the viceroy fled into the mountains with a band of supporters and the city's residents switched allegiance to San Martín.

Unfortunately, Lima declined in post-independence Peru. What was once a spectacular city became shabby and untended, with streets unpaved and littered with filth that was picked over by vultures. Charles Darwin recorded in *The Voyage of the Beagle* in 1830 that 'Lima, the City of the Kings, must formerly have been a splendid town.' He declared though that at the time of his visit, it was, 'in a filthy state of decay.'

Nonetheless the city continued to grow and to such an extent that the outer walls were torn down to make space for new housing. This proved to be a costly mistake since without its defensive structures the Chileans easily overran the city in 1881, during the War of the Pacific. This latest batch of invaders didn't leave for two years.

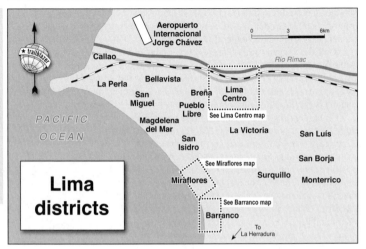

Lima saw spectacular growth during the early years of the 1920s, when large numbers of unskilled labourers arrived looking for work. Despite attempts to accommodate them and provide sewerage and open spaces, the city struggled under the weight of numbers, which increased to 170,000. Over-crowding has been a problem ever since; there are now more than 10 million inhabitants in Lima, around a quarter of the total population of Peru lives here. Many of these are poor and live in *pueblos jóvenes* (shanty towns), where unemployment is rife.

The city does have another side to it though and many districts display the wealth and opulence of successful Limeños. First among these are San Isidro and Miraflores, where the middle class make their homes. In 1991 the historic centre was recognised by UNESCO as a World Heritage site and by the end of the decade restoration work was underway on buildings, parks had been planted, streets cleaned, the police presence increased and even street vendors moved on. Run-down areas are being regenerated, infrastructure is being modernised and heritage sites are being preserved. There are still plenty of problems, as there are in all world capitals, of poverty, race and class, but the multicultural mix of indigenous and Spanish influences, grime and glamour makes the city endlessly interesting.

WHAT TO SEE AND DO

Lima Centro   [see map pp128-9]
At the heart of the city is **Plaza de Armas**, also known as Plaza Mayor. A bronze fountain from 1650 stands at the centre of the square, which was established on the site of an Inca market and meeting place. It was here that Pizarro founded the city in 1535. The northern end of the plaza is dominated by the

imposing, gated **Palacio de Gobierno** (Government Palace; only open for occasional public events), which fills the entire length of one side; at noon it's possible to watch **the changing of the guard** ceremony.

On the western side stands the grand **Palacio Arzobispal**, built in 1924 as the seat of the Archbishop of Lima, with intricately carved wooden balconies. The mildly interesting interior can be viewed by visiting the **museum** (Mon-Fri 9am-5pm, Sat 9am-1pm; entrance s/20). Adjacent to this is the **Cathedral** (Mon-Fri 9am-5pm, Sat 10am-1pm; entrance s/10, s/2 students). A cathedral has stood on this site since 1535 but as a result of numerous earthquakes has had to be rebuilt several times; the massive quake in 1746 completely levelled it. The current building dates from 1758 and contains some elaborately carved choir stalls as well as a coffin that is reputed to hold the remains of Francisco Pizarro, who laid the first stone for the cathedral foundations and who was later assassinated in the plaza. There's an impressive **statue of Pizarro** astride his horse in the square although, allegedly, he was a fairly mediocre rider.

Colonial architecture There are numerous examples of fine colonial architecture throughout Lima that have survived earthquakes, expansion and being damaged by the sea air; start by investigating the smart colonial buildings that surround Plaza de Armas and Plaza San Martín. Elsewhere, walk along Calle Ucayali, Conde de Superunda, Huancavelica or Jirón de la Union where you can see attractive *casonas* (large houses/mansions).

In particular, look out for **Palacio Torre Tagle**, Jr Ucayali 363, an 18th-century mansion considered one of the finest in the city, which is now home to the Foreign Ministry. Although a government building, it is possible to poke your head round the entrance in order to catch a glimpse of the delicate carvings and attractive Moorish balconies within. Across the street is **Casa Goyeneche**, Jr Ucayali 358, an impressive 18th-century mansion which has a distinctive European influence and characteristic carved balconies and ornate doors.

Iglesia de la Merced La Merced (cnr Jirón de la Unión and Jr Miró Quesada; Mon-Sat 8am-12.30pm & 4-7pm, Sun 7am-1pm & 4-7pm; free) stands on the site of the first Catholic mass in Lima, held in 1534. Built in 1541 but subsequently remodelled, it's one of the city's most important religious buildings.

Santo Domingo church and convent The Santo Domingo church and convent (🖳 www.conventosantodomingo.pe; Jirón Camaná; Mon-Sat 9am-12.30pm & 3-6pm, Sun 9am-1pm; church free, convent s/7) is one of Lima's most striking religious buildings. It was established by the friar Vicente de Valverde, who accompanied Pizarro and the conquistadors; it was Valverde who had a hand in persuading Pizarro to execute Atahualpa. The pink façade is eye-catching and there are several attractive chapels and peaceful courtyards with beautiful tilework to explore and the skulls of two of the city's most venerated saints, Santa Rosa and San Martín de Porres, to discover, encased in glass in a shrine adjacent to the main altar. The saints' tombs are in the convent, surrounded by Baroque paintings and Spanish tile work.

It's well worth climbing the **bell tower** for superb views of the city.

❏ **Walking routes for central Lima and Miraflores**
Although essentially Lima isn't a walker's city, within each district and especially in
the centre, Miraflores or Barranco (see box p132), it's possible to enjoy exploring on
foot, taking in the sights and atmosphere of the city and pausing *en route* to try out
the cafés and restaurants you come across.

● **Lima Centro** (see map pp128-9) With a full day of exploration ahead why not
start with a **buffet breakfast** at the **Sheraton Lima Hotel** (see p138).
     When you are ready to start turn left out of the hotel and head straight up **Jirón
Belén** (there's a pistachio-coloured building on the corner). After a block, look left to
spot **Iglesia La Recoleta**, a blue church with a giant snowflake window, which stands
in **Plaza Francia**. Continue straight ahead until you reach **Plaza San Martín** which
is ringed with white wedding-cake mansions and one pink one. In the centre of the
plaza is a **statue of General San Martín** on a horse. The plaza is particularly delightful in October/November when the jacaranda trees are in bloom.
     Keep to the left side of the plaza, passing **Teatro Colón** (once a luxurious and
respected theatre, it became a cinema in the 1950s and closed in 2003) and **Gran
Hotel Bolívar** (see p137-8) on Plaza San Martín then head up Jirón de la Unión past
Iglesia de la Merced (see p125).
     At Plaza de Armas turn left for one block then right onto Jirón Camaná to come
to **Santo Domingo** (see p125). Head directly away from the church to re-join Jirón
de la Unión, turn right and return to Plaza de Armas, turning left to walk along one
side before turning left onto Jirón Carabaya to pass **Palacio de Gobierno** (see p125).
A quick diversion to the route could be made to the **cathedral** (see p125).
     At the junction with Jirón Ancash turn right by *El Cordano* and visit the **church
of San Francisco** (see opposite) before walking another block and turning right onto
Av Abancay. Pass Plaza Bolívar, there's the **Museo de la Inquisición** (see opposite)
then turn right onto Jirón Junin for a block before a sharp right onto Jirón Ayacucho,
which brings you to **Mercado Central**, a bustling market that occupies a whole block
and sells just about everything. It is close to Bario Chino (Chinatown) so consider
carrying on east for a block before turning right onto Jr Paruro where you'll find *Wa
Lok* (see p143) which makes an ideal lunch stop. After lunch retrace your steps and
head away from the market past a row of impressive colonial buildings including
strawberry-pink **Palacio Torre Tagle**; look out for Toby jug faces peering down from
an exquisite wooden balcony. Finally, turn left onto Jr Carabaya and continue to Plaza
San Martín, which you can cut across to reward yourself with a Pisco Sour in Hotel
Gran Bolívar. Allow a full day to take in everything along the route.

● **Miraflores** (see map p130) A gentle stroll taking several hours through
Miraflores will allow you to enjoy this neighbourhood. Start by sampling **ceviche
and seafood** at either Pescados Capitales (see p142) or La Mar (see p142) before
making your way to the coast path and setting off south along the length of the clifftop path, **Malecón de la Marina**, admiring the views and drama of the waves breaking on the beaches below.
     As you walk off your lunch, enjoy the parks and public spaces you wander
through and take advantage of lots of opportunities for people-watching, along with
the chance to see (or join) paragliders jumping from the high points. Pass a **lighthouse** and come to the picturesque **Parque del Amor** with its pretty mosaics before
finishing at **Larcomar mall**, where you can sit and relax on one of the café terraces
here; Mangos has the best vantage point.
                                                    (Thanks to **Alison Roberts** for route planning)

San Francisco church and monastery The sizeable church of San Francisco (🖥 www.museocatacumbas.com; cnr Lampa and Ancash; daily 7-11am & 4-8pm; entrance s/10) was consecrated in 1673 and has endured despite the earthquakes. Although this Baroque building is attractive in its own right, with pretty yellow and white paintwork and a dramatic stone façade, the main attractions here include some spectacular artworks, pretty tile work and a vast 17th-century library containing 25,000 texts. The cavernous **catacombs** (9.30am-5.30pm) contain the bones of some 70,000 of the city's former residents; these are creatively if gruesomely arranged. Admission includes a guided tour (30 mins); tours leave when there are enough people.

Museo de la Inquisición (🖥 www.congreso.gob.pe/museo.htm; Plaza Bolívar, Calle Junin 548; daily 9am-5pm; free) Recently closed for renovation, the museum should now have reopened. This colonial mansion was the one time headquarters of the Spanish Inquisition in South America, which operated from 1584 to 1820. The main tribunal room is wonderfully ornate and has a carved wooden ceiling, completely at odds with the dungeons elsewhere that have illustrations of the terrible types of torture conducted here in the name of eliminating heresy and blasphemy in the New World.

Museo de Arte de Lima (🖥 www.mali.pe; Paseo de Colón 125; Tue-Sun 10am-8pm, Sat to 5pm; entrance s/30 but free on Thur from 3pm) MALI, as it's sometimes referred to, contains everything from 3000-year-old pre-Columbian ceramics to post-conquistador paintings by the Cusco School and contemporary indigenous art. The eclectic collection, housed in a building designed by Alexandre Eiffel, is fascinating and the permanent exhibits provide an excellent overview of Peruvian art from all the important periods of the country's history.

Parks and cliffs In the centre, **Parque de la Cultura** stages live music performances. One kilometre south of here, in **Parque de la Reserva**, is the **Circuito Mágico del Agua** (Magic Water Circuit; 🖥 www.circuitomagicode lagua.com.pe; daily 3-10pm, shows at 7.15pm, 8.15pm and 9.30pm; s/4). This remarkable series of fountains backed by a light and music show is said to be the largest fountain complex in the world, including one 80m high jet.

Miraflores   **[see walking route box opposite, map p130]**
Huaca Pucllana (Cnr General Borgoño and Tarapacá; Wed-Mon 9am-4.30pm; night tours 7-10pm; s/12) In the midst of a Miraflores residential area stands this large adobe pre-Columbian complex, centred on a pyramid and constructed some time in the 6th century. A ceremonial and administrative centre in its day, it has been quite heavily eroded by the elements but is still striking; the pyramid, which would have stood 23m high, is a powerful contrast to the contemporary buildings that sit immediately adjacent to the site. Excavations are ongoing but guided tours, mainly in Spanish, highlight the main features here.

Beside the site, *Restaurant Huaca Pucllana* (see p143), one of Lima's top restaurants, affords diners spectacular views of the illuminated ruins at night.

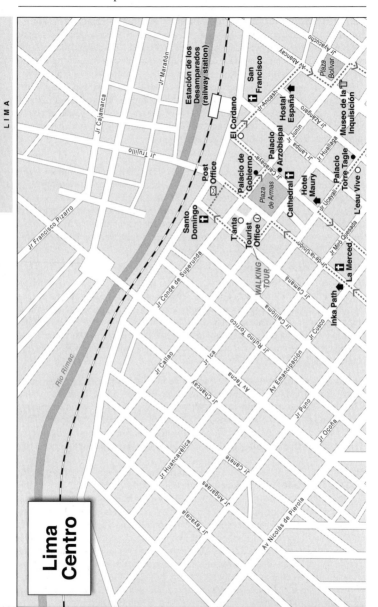

LIMA

Lima
Centro

Rio Rimac

Jr Francisco Pizarro
Jr Cajamarca
Jr Marañón
Jr Trujillo

Estación de los Desamparados (railway station)

Post Office

Santo Domingo

Jr Conde de Superunda

T'anta
Tourist Office ①

WALKING TOUR

Jr Callao
Jr Rufino Torrico
Jr Caylloma
Jr Camaná
Jr de la Unión

Jr Ica
Av Tacna
Jr Chancay

Av Emancipación
Jr Cusco

Jr Huancavélica
Jr Cañete
Jr Angaraes
Jr Tayacaja

Av Nicolás de Piérola

Jr Puno
Jr Ocoña

San Francisco
El Cordano
Palacio de Gobierno
Palacio Arzobispal
Jr Carabaya
Plaza de Armas
Cathedral
Hotel Maury
Jr Ucayali
Palacio Torre Tagle
L'eau Vive
La Merced
Inka Path
Jr Miró Quesada

Jr Ancash
Hostal España
Jr Junín
Jr Lampa
Jr Huallaga
Jr Azángaro
Jr Ayacucho
Av Abancay

Plaza Bolívar
Museo de la Inquisición

LIMA

Jr Andahuaylas
Jr Paruro
Barrio Chino
Jr Cusco
Mercado Central
Jr Ayacucho
Wa Lok
Jr Ucayali
San Pedro
Jr Miro Quesada
Jr Abancay
Av Nicolás de Piérola
Av Grau
Casa Goyeneche
Jr Cusco
Jr Puno
Jr Azángaro
Jr Lampa
Parque Universitario
Jr Leticia
Jr Montevideo
Jr Carabaya
Av Roosevelt
Jr Pachila
Jr Carabamba
Av Grau
Miguel
To Miraflores,
Parque de la Reserva (1km)
& Circuito Mágico del Agua
Plaza San Martín
Estadio Fútbol Bar
Gran Hotel Bolívar
FINISH WALKING TOUR
Jr de la Unión
Jr Ocoña
Av Nicolás de Piérola
Teatro Colón
Iglesia La Recoleta
Jr Belén
WALKING TOUR
Paseo de la República
Plaza Grau
Museo de Arte de Lima
Parque de la Cultura
Plaza Francia
Sheraton Lima
START WALKING TOUR
(Paseo Colón)
Av Wilson
Av Garcilaso de la Vega
Jr Quilca
Av Washington
Jr Lisson
Jr Dávalos
Av Uruguay
Av Bolivia
Av España
Av 9 de Diciembre
1900 Backpackers
Alfonso Ugarte
Jr Portugal
Jr Iquique
Hostal Iquique
Plaza Bolognesi
Las Brisas de Titicaca

0   100   200   300m

LIMA

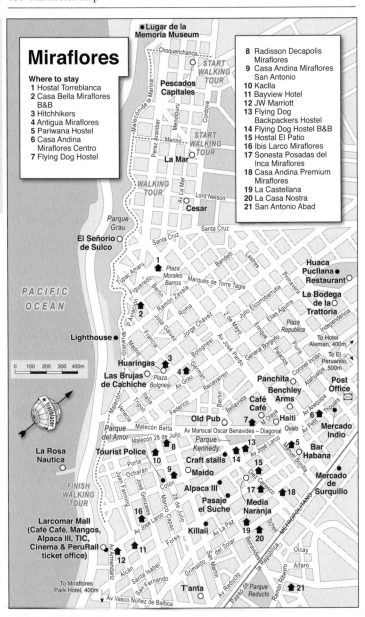

Miraflores

Where to stay
1 Hostal Torreblanca
2 Casa Bella Miraflores B&B
3 Hitchhikers
4 Antigua Miraflores
5 Pariwana Hostel
6 Casa Andina Miraflores Centro
7 Flying Dog Hostel

8 Radisson Decapolis Miraflores
9 Casa Andina Miraflores San Antonio
10 Kaclla
11 Bayview Hotel
12 JW Marriott
13 Flying Dog Backpackers Hostel
14 Flying Dog Hostel B&B
15 Hostal El Patio
16 Ibis Larco Miraflores
17 Sonesta Posadas del Inca Miraflores
18 Casa Andina Premium Miraflores
19 La Castellana
20 La Casa Nostra
21 San Antonio Abad

Lugar de la Memoria Museum

Choquenchanca

START WALKING TOUR

Pescados Capitales

START WALKING TOUR

La Mar

WALKING TOUR

Cesar

Parque Grau

El Señorío de Sulco

Huaca Pucllana Restaurant

La Bodega de la Trattoria

PACIFIC OCEAN

Lighthouse

Plaza Morales Barros

Plaza Republica

To Hotel Aleman, 400m
To El Peruanito, 500m

Huaringas

Las Brujas de Cachiche

Plaza Bolognesi

Panchita

Benchley Arms

Café Café

Old Pub

Haiti

Post Office

Mercado Indio

Parque del Amor

La Rosa Nautica

Tourist Police

Parque Kennedy

Craft stalls

Maido

Bar Habana

Mercado de Surquillo

FINISH WALKING TOUR

Alpaca III

Pasaje el Suche

Media Naranja

Larcomar Mall (Café Café, Mangos, Alpaca III, TIC, Cinema & PeruRail ticket office)

Killaii

To Miraflores Park Hotel, 400m

T'anta

0 100 200 300 400m

trailblazer

MAC
(Modern Art
Museum)

Av-El-Sol-Oeste

Paul-Harris

Tacna

La 73

Av Miguel Grau

L I M A

Barranco

Where to stay
1 La Puerte Verde
2 Cozy Wasi
3 Hotel B
4 The Point
5 Second Home Peru
6 Kaminu
7 Barranco's Backpackers

WALKING
TOUR

Centenario

Sofa

La Cuadra de
Salvador

2

Av Pierola

To Del Carajo

1

Perez Roca

Av-San-Martin

Launderette

Miraflores

Seafront
Restaurants
& Bars

3

Bakery

Cala

Paseo Sáenz Peña

Dédalo

Malecón-Pazos

Tacna

Av Miguel Grau

Martinez

San Antonio

Santa Rosa

Circuito De Playas

Cavero

Colina

**Metro
Supermarket**

Posada
del Angel

Canta Rana

Bank

Cajamarca

Ayahuasca

4

METROPOLITANO

Av Bolognesi

Junin

Domeyer

Union

**La
Noche**

5

Statue of
Chabuca Granda

La Bajado
de Baños

Bank

Sanchez
Carrion

Juan Pazos

La Victoria

Ermita
Church

El-Libertador

Bank

La
Candelaría

Bars and
sunset
viewpoint

6

Paseo
Chabuca
Granda

Parque
Municipal

Puente de
los Suspiros

7

Mariscal Castilla

Museo de la
Electricidad

28 de Julio

Posada
del Angel

Av-San-Pedro-de-Osma

BLU
Gelato

Panama

trailblazer

To Museo Pedro
de Osma, 350m
& MATE

Herrera

Estación
Estadio Unión

❑ Barranco walking route   [See map p131]

Barranco was originally a seaside resort for Lima's wealthiest families wishing to escape the stifling summer heat downtown. Neglected for many years, its magnificent mansions fell into neglect in the latter part of the last century. However, many are now being restored and it's rapidly becoming the very fashionable neighbourhood it once was.

This **half-day walk** starts at **Parque Muncipal**. Walk south down **Av San Pedro de Osma** passing **Museo de la Electricidad** (🖳 museodelaelectricidad.blogspot .co.uk; 9am-5pm daily, free) on the left; in front of which is a tram which used to run between Barranco, Miraflores and Lima Centro. You can continue walking for a couple of blocks, to reach **MATE Museo Mario Testino** (Tue-Sun, 10am-7pm, s/10), founded by the photographer to promote local artists. Further along, at No 423 is **Museo Pedro de Osma** (see opposite). Retrace your steps and take a right up 28 de Julio and another left to bring you back to Parque Muncipal. Pop your head into *Juanito's* (Av Grau 274; p144) to see a traditional *bodega* (bar that also serves snacks) and try one of their sandwiches. Cross the park, stopping to admire the red biblioteca on your left, the equally red church on your right, the pool with Romanesque statue and fountain and locals promenading in the purple shadow of the jacaranda trees.

Follow pedestrianised **Paseo Chabuca Granda** straight ahead (passing the bodega on your left which has a display of plastic cocktails outside) and then take the steps down (don't cross the bridge). Follow cobbled **Bajada de Baños** (see opposite) towards the sea. This shady walkway is flanked by what were once grand houses and boughs of bougainvillea. It makes for an enjoyable stroll but if you're alone turn back before reaching the end as this area has a reputation for crime.

Climb back up the steps and cross the wooden **Puente de los Suspiros** (see opposite). Turn left and pass the mustard-coloured, almost roofless, **Ermita Church**. Another legend suggests that fishermen, lost at sea in thick fog, had their prayers answered when a luminous cross appeared on the cliff top and guided them safely home. The church was later built on the very same spot. There are a number of bars here with great ocean views, perfect for admiring the sunset so maybe you'd prefer to end the walk here and wait for the show.

Back at the bridge there is a **Statue of Chabuca Granda**, a Peruvian singer and composer. One of the bars at the *mirador* is named after her best-known song *La Flor de la Canela*. Follow the steps up, cross the road and walk down **Junín** for a couple of blocks until you see the ocean. Follow the palm trees and strip of parkland along the cliff top. Ahead you can see Miraflores and its skyscrapers. Below are the beaches and surfers. Shortly you will see a blue and red tiled staircase on your right which leads to **Av Sáenz Peña**, a wide boulevard of some of Barranco's finest buildings. Usually the *D'Anafria* ice-cream men are here on their yellow tricycles, blowing their duck whistles in case you hadn't noticed them. It's a nice spot to sit or have a look around the craft gallery **Dédalo** (see p144) which has a garden *café*.

You can either return to Parque Muncipal along **Av San Martín** (the second right off Av Sáenz Peña), or continue along the cliff top, weaving through the park and listening to the crashing waves below until you reach **Av El Sol Oeste**. Walk up the street for two blocks and stop for a snack at *La 73* (see p143) or *Sofa* nearby (see p142).

If you're alone don't walk down to or back from the beach road at night.
                                                                    Alison Roberts

Lugar de la Memoria Museum (🖥 www.lum.cultura.pe; Bajada San Martin 151; Tues-Sun 10am-6pm; free) Recently opened, in a modern building built into the cliff, this museum commemorates the victims of Peru's armed conflict with the Shining Path and MRTA from 1980 to 2000. There are no English captions yet but even if you can't understand much Spanish the pictures tell much of the story and it's a moving experience to visit.

Parks and cliffs Stroll through **Parque del Amor**, which has elements of Gaudi's Parque Güell in Barcelona but was designed by Victor Delfín. Pick your way past amorous couples to find benches decorated with mosaics and covered in hearts and romantic writings along with a giant statue of two people caught in a clinch. There are good views from the tall cliffs, too.

Barranco   [see walking route box opposite, map p131]
Puente de los Suspiros When walking around Barranco, look out for the attractive wooden footbridge known as Puente de los Suspiros (Bridge of Sighs), so named for the sounds of sighs that could be heard by people passing by the house of a noble's daughter who fell in love with a road sweeper but couldn't act upon it so would watch him from her window.

The bridge connects to a small cobbled passageway, **La Bajada de Baños** (The Bathing Path), which leads to a good sea view. There are steps down to the beach here but you shouldn't stray too far as this section of the beach isn't safe.

Museo Pedro de Osma (🖥 www.museopedrodeosma.org, Av Pedro de Osma 423; Tue-Sun 10am-6pm; s/20) Inside the ornate Palacio de Osma, the former beaux arts residence of the Osma family, is a private museum full of paintings by the Cusco School, colonial art, furniture and sculpture as well as silver pieces from the 16th to 19th centuries.

Pueblo Libre
Museo Nacional de Arqueología, Antropología e História del Peru
(Plaza Bolívar, Pueblo Libre; Mon-Sat 8.45am-4pm, Sun 8.45am-3.30pm; entrance s/10) This excellent museum, in an attractive colonial mansion, gives a very good overview of Peruvian history.

Some of the most impressive pieces are from the Chavín de Huantar site close to Huaraz, including the Raimondi Stela, an elaborately carved statue that can be viewed both up and down to see a different image, and the Tello Obelisk, a carefully sculpted pair of caimans. There are rooms dedicated to individual pre-Hispanic cultures along with mummies from the Paracas region, ceramics, metalwork, textiles and models of Inca archaeological sites.

Next door stands **Quinta de los Liberatores**, once home to both the liberators San Martín (1821-2) and Bolívar (1823-6) and now a restaurant. There are several good places to eat here, perhaps the best being the traditional *La Sucursal de Quierolo*, (🖥 www.lasucursaldequeirolo.com) next door.

Museo Larco (🖥 www.museolarco.org; Av Bolívar 1515; daily 9am-10pm, to 6pm on public holidays; s/30) Within a privately-owned colonial mansion that once belonged to the viceroy, itself built on top of the remains of a 7th-century pyramid, is this scholarly museum. Founded by Rafael Larco Hoyle in 1926, it houses his obsessively-collected pre-Columbian trove, very professionally displayed. Many of the pieces were created by the Moche, Chimu and Chancay cultures, demonstrating that Peru's history is about more than just the Incas. There are hundreds of gold and silver exhibits along with textiles and an amazing array of pottery; there are thought to be more than 50,000 pots on display. More pieces are stored in a warehouse. A separate gallery is given over to erotic-themed artefacts and earthenware that illustrate all manner of sexual activity. There's an upmarket *restaurant* (🖥 www.cafedelmuseo.com).

Elsewhere

Museo de Oro (🖥 www.museoroperu.com.pe, Calle Alonso de Molina 1100, Monterrico; daily 10.30am-6pm; s/33) The Gold Museum is a vast private collection of pre-Hispanic gold. Unfortunately it has been tarnished by the discovery that a huge percentage of the items are fakes or copies; the museum maintains that what is now on display is authentic though. Take what you see with a pinch of salt – some of the exhibits are labelled as 'reproductions'. There's a large collection of weaponry as well as textiles and ceramics. There's little information available on the displays, though.

Huaca Huallamarca Within a residential section of San Isidro stands this temple (Calle Nicholás de Rivera and Av Rosario; Tue-Sun 9am-5pm; s/10), built by the Lima Culture around 200AD. The main adobe pyramid has been restored and a small site museum explains the huaca's history and contains a mummy found by archaeologists here.

Museo de la Nación (Av Javier Prado Este 2465, San Borja; Tue-Sun 9am-5pm) This was once Lima's leading historical museum but it closed in 2016 for major renovations. Only a few galleries have so far reopened and it's unclear

---

❏ Pachacámac

To the south of Lima, 31km away near the coast, stands the site of the ancient oracle and shrine to Pachacámac (🖥 pachacamac.cultura.pe; Tues-Sat 9am-5pm, Sun 9am-4pm; s/15), which operated at its height under the Huari culture in the 10th century. It was later assimilated into the Inca Empire and became a place of pilgrimage for them as well; they added the Temple of the Sun to the main citadel. Most of the pyramid structures here are heavily eroded and take some imagination to visualise at their height. However, there is some reconstruction to give you an impression of how significant a site this was before it was pillaged by the conquistadors and allowed to fall into disrepair. An excellent **museum** opened here in 2015 and there's now also a *café*. This is a great day out from Lima.

Getting there Bus tours (🖥 www.turibusperu.com) cost $25 from Parque Kennedy and there are pricey organised mountainbiking excursions (🖥 www.perubike.com, US$100) but you can easily get here on local buses. From Miraflores get to the bridge, called the Puente Primavera, over the Via Panamericana. Go down to the highway and this is where the buses pull over to pick up passengers. Look for a bus with signs on the front or side for Pachacamac/Lurín (30-40 mins, s/3.50), if possible a *directo* or you'll make many stops. Ask to be dropped near the *ruinas*.

when – or even if – the rest of it will reopen in its original form, charting the history of Peru in fascinating detail. The photographic display, *Yuyanapaq* (free entry), covering the Shining Path and Peru's dark days from 1980 to 2000 is open now and worth seeing but coverage is similar to the new Lugar de la Memoria Museum (see p133) more conveniently located in Miraflores.

PRACTICAL INFORMATION
Arrival
All flights arrive at the modern **Aeropuerto Internacional Jorge Chávez** (🖥 www .lima-airport.com/eng), in Callao 16km north-west of the city centre. Inside the arrivals hall there are exchange bureaux and ATMs; the exchange rates are better in town though. There are also car-hire desks, fixed rate taxi companies – Taxi Green (🖥 www.taxigreen.com.pe) is good, and an iPerú information desk.

Taxis run from outside the arrivals hall; it's quickest, easiest and safest if you've just arrived in Peru to use one of the fixed-rate companies (above). Fares are around s/40-60 depending on whether you go to the centre, San Isidro, Miraflores or Barranco. Cheaper, unlicensed cars can be hailed outside opposite the terminal although you'll have to haggle hard and it's probably safer not to use them if you're alone.

Orientation
Lima is built on a flat plain above a large arc of a bay. A sprawling city, it has many different neighbourhoods and districts (see map p124), the distances between which are often too big to walk. Within each district though there are some very attractive walking routes that you can follow to check off the main sites.

Lima Centro is the old heart of the city, several miles inland from the coast, on the banks of the Río Rimac. Plaza de Armas is the main focal point although other squares include Plaza Bolívar and Plaza San Martín. Amidst the chaotic, often snarled, centre there are a host of sights, museums and excellent restaurants. To the south-east is the industrial-commercial area of **La Victoria** and the suburbs of **San Luis** and **San Borja**. Further out is wealthy **Monterrico**.

To the south-west in **Breña** are more residential streets. West of the centre is

Bellavista, the coast and the port of **Callao**, overlooked by a fort. South of Callao, along the coast lie **San Miguel**, **Magdalena del Mar** and more affluent, smarter **San Isidro**, where many of the international embassies are.

Beyond this is the well-to-do residential neighbourhood and shopping area of **Miraflores**, set above some vertiginous cliffs, and then the more bohemian district of **Barranco**, a one-time coastal retreat that has been absorbed into the city but which boasts hip hotels and bars, a lively night scene and several art galleries.

Getting around
Taxis There are countless cabs plying their trade on the streets of Lima. Not all of these are registered, let alone regulated. For the safest ride and fairest fare, hail a yellow cab with a number painted on the door. Always agree the fare before you set off.

From Miraflores to the city centre is about s/20 and to Barranco around s/10.

Metropolitano, combis, collectivos
The modern electric bus, **Metropolitano** (🖥 www.metropolitano.com.pe) that runs north-south along a dedicated road across the city is efficient. Buy a card (*tarjeta inteligente*, s/5) from a machine at any of the stops and load it with at least s/5.

Lima's bus network of **combis** and **collectivos**, identified by their size, looks confusing to the uninitiated. However, it's actually pretty efficient, far-reaching and surprisingly cheap. Destinations are written in the window; you can flag them down or ask them to stop anywhere along this route. Beware though, buses can be crowded and are often targeted by pickpockets.

Tours
A large number of agencies offer organised, guided tours of Lima; these are ideal if you

LIMA

find the sprawling city confusing or difficult to get around. Don't buy tours from touts at the airport or taxi drivers.

Lima Vision (🖥 www.limavision .com, ☎ 447 7710) in Miraflores offers half-day tours of contemporary and colonial Lima, as does **Turibus** (🖥 www .turibusperu.com ☎ 234 0249) which departs from Larcomar in Miraflores.

To travel under your own steam, join a **bike tour** of Lima (🖥 www.biketoursof lima .com, ☎ 445 3172, Calle Bolívar 150); it is an ideal way to spend a day exploring the city. There are several guided routes to choose from costing s/110 or you can just rent a bike for a day for s/60.

Car rental
Many of the major international car-hire chains have offices in Lima and branches at the airport but it's probably best to organise this before you arrive. Expect to pay around US$50 per day for a compact car, more if you want a bigger vehicle or an SUV.

Services
Tourist information There's an **iPerú office** at the airport (☎ 574 8000) that's open 24 hours. In town, if you need directions or want a straightforward answer to a question, visit the iPerú office in Larcomar (see map p130; ☎ 445 9400; daily 11am-9pm).

There is a more substantial **Municipal tourist office** on Pasaje Ribera el Viejo in Lima Centro (see map pp128) and half a dozen or so **information kiosks** dotted around Miraflores.

Sadly the **South American Explorers' Club** has now closed.

Books & newspapers
One of Lima's leading **bookshops** (*librerías*), El Virrey (🖥 www.elvirrey.com; Calle Bolognesi 510), has a range of speciality titles on subjects such as science and history. There are smaller branches in San Isidro (Miguel Dasso 141) and at Larcomar in Miraflores. SBS (🖥 www.sbs.com.pe; Av Angamos Oeste 301) has a good collection of guidebooks and several branches in Lima.

Maps **City plans** and **street maps** can be picked up in hotels or bought from tourist shops and kiosks.

If you're looking for **hiking maps**, head to Instituto Geográfico Nacional (🖥 www.ign.gob.pe, ☎ 475 9960) on Av A Aramburú 1198, Surquillo, which sells road maps of the entire country at 1:2,000,000 and hiking maps that cover the treks described in this book at 1:100,000.

Banks & casas de cambio
There are 24-hour **ATMs** throughout Lima as well as at the airport in the international arrivals hall. Several **banks** also have branches all across the city, with most represented on Av Larco at least.

Although the banks exchange currency, **casas de cambio** give a better rate. *Cambistas (*street changers) offer an even better rate but beware that these people, identified by the green or blue bibs they wear and the wads of notes they clutch, can be less scrupulous and there are plenty of scams associated with changing money this way.

Laundry Many hotels offer a laundry service. If this isn't available, *lavandería* (launderettes) are easy to find throughout the city. They charge about s/5 per kilo.

Communications
Internet Most hotels and some cafés offer free internet access. There are internet cafés all across Lima if you need one.

Telephone The code for calling Lima when outside the city is 01. You can make calls using coin-operated Telefónica phone booths. Alternatively buy a pre-paid telephone card from a kiosk or shop; scratch off the silver colouring to reveal a code, dial the number and follow the instructions to make your call.

Post The main post office (*correo;* Mon-Sat 8am-9pm) is at Jirón Camaná 195, just off Plaza de Armas.

In Miraflores there's a post office (Mon-Sat 8am-8pm, Sun 9am-1pm) at Petit Thouars 5201, Angamos Oeste.

Emergencies

Police Since 2012 there's been an increase in the numbers of tourist police on the streets. They speak English and are easily recognisable in their white shirts, should you need them. If you lose something and require a report for insurance purposes you'll need to visit their headquarters: **Policía de Turismo** (☎ 225-8699, 437-8171) at the Museo de la Nacion, Javier Prado Este 2465, 5th floor.

Embassies and consulates

Australia (🖳 www.embassy.gov.au/peru, ☎ 630 0500, Av. La Paz 1049, Piso 10, Miraflores); **Canada** (🖳 www.canadainternational.gc .ca/peru-perou, ☎ 319 3200, Bolognesi 228, Miraflores); **New Zealand** (🖳 cblume@ cbconsultperu.com, ☎ 627 7778, Leonidas Yerovi 106, Oficina 42, San Isidro); **UK** (🖳 www.gov.uk/government/world/peru, ☎ 617 3000, 22nd Floor, Torre Parque Mar, Av José Larco 1301, Miraflores); **USA** (🖳 pe.usembassy.gov, ☎ 618 2000, Av La Encalada 17, Surco).

Medical

Pharmacies such as Inka Farma are open 24 hours and are usually well stocked. Look for them along Av Larco, Jirón de la Unión and Av Grau. In many cases you won't need a prescription to buy medicines. If you need **medical help**, try Clínica Anglo Americano (🖳 www.anglo americana.com.pe, ☎ 616 8900) at Av Salazar or Clínica Internacional (🖳 www.clinicainternacional.com.pe, ☎ 619 6161) at Av. Guardia Civil 421, San Borja.

WHERE TO STAY

In conjunction with the hotel price information below, it's worth checking the prices on hotel-booking websites such as 🖳 **www.booking.com** and **www.hotels.com**.

Airport

Budget *Pay Purix Backpackers* (🖳 www.paypurix.com, ☎ 484 9118, Av Japno 16138, Callao) is a 15-minute walk from the airport but at night for safety you should take a taxi – the hostel will organise it. Dorm beds are from s/40 and rooms are s/130/160/240 (sgl/dbl/tpl).

Lima Centro [see map pp128-9]

Budget *1900 Backpackers* (🖳 www .1900hostel.com, ☎ 424 3358, Ave Garcilaso de la Vega 1588) is a very popular place in a renovated building said to have been designed by Gustav Eiffel. A bed costs from US$9 in an 18-bedded dorm to US$14 in a 4-bed and there are also rooms for US$24/34 (sgl/dbl com) or $49 (dbl att). Not your average backpacker dive.

Hostal Iquique (🖳 www.hostaliquique.com, ☎ 433 4724, Jirón Iquique 758) is a straightforward, conveniently located hostel set in a safe street that has an attractively tiled lobby, clean, functional rooms, a small garden, free wi-fi and a helpful attitude. There's also table football and pool on a rooftop-type terrace. The rooms with private bathrooms cost US$25/36/44 (sgl/dbl/tpl); those with shared facilities are US$18/30/36 (sgl/dbl/tpl). For quiet, ask for a room on the upper floors, at the back.

The *Hostal España* (🖳 www.hotel espanaperu.com, ☎ 428 5546, Jr Azangaro 105) stands close to the San Francisco church in a fine colonial building filled with statues and plants. There's a garden on the roof that's a great space to relax in. The rooms within the rambling house are basic but more than adequate. Rooms with private facilities cost US$25/27/35/45 (sgl/dbl/tpl/qd). There are also some cheaper rooms without attached bathrooms.

Mid-range *Inka Path* (🖳 www.hotelinkapath .com, ☎ 426 1919, Jirón de la Unión 654) is a couple of blocks from Plaza de Armas and represents good value; the rooms are clean and cost US$58/68/87 (sgl/dbl/tpl).

Hotel Maury (🖳 www.hotelmaury .hoteles, ☎ 428 8188, Jirón Ucayali 201) is close to Plaza de Armas and the centre's main attractions. The communal areas are full of Victorian-style furniture whilst the bar boasts that it helped to invent the Pisco Sour in the 1930s, though there's plenty of competition for that honour. The rooms are spacious but a little tired; rates start at US$57/69/80 (tw/dbl/tpl att).

Gran Hotel Bolívar (🖳 www.gran hotelbolivar.com.pe, ☎ 619 7171, Jirón de la Unión 958), on Plaza San Martín, is an institution in the city. A national monument dating from 1924, it has a wealth of interesting architectural features that include marble columns, high roofs and lamps imported from France that create an air of luxury despite the fact that the hotel is a little ragged round the edges.

The rooms are similarly opulent, whilst the bar is a popular place for a Pisco Sour. It's possible to get surprisingly good deals on rooms here, sometimes as little as US$60 for an economy double or US$80 for a larger double.

Expensive *Sheraton Lima* (🖥 www.she raton.com, ☎ 315 5000, Av Paseo de la Republica 170) is an imposing concrete structure dominating downtown that offers everything you might expect from a top-class hotel. There's also a casino, tennis court, health club and outdoor pool. Room rates vary widely depending on style and season but range from around US$120 to about US$350.

Miraflores [see map p130]
Budget *Pariwana* (🖥 pariwana-hostel.com, ☎ 242 4350, Av Larco 189) is popular and gets rave reviews. It's clean and welcoming with comfortable beds. Dorms are from s/39 whilst twin or double rooms cost s/132/152 (com/att). There's free continental breakfast, internet access and use of the communal kitchen. It's very centrally located, so a pair of ear-plugs may be useful for rooms above the main road.

Hitchhikers (🖥 www.hhikersperu .com, ☎ 242 3008, Calle Bolognesi 400) stands in a pleasant residential area and has a fully equipped kitchen and BBQ area. Dorms cost s/30 whilst rooms are s/75/75/113 (sgl/dbl/tpl, com) for shared bathrooms and s/90/90/135 (sgl/dbl/tpl) for private bathrooms. There are free bikes to use and there's also plenty of parking if you're driving or motorbiking in Peru.

Flying Dog Hostel (🖥 www.flyingdog peru.com) has branches at: Diez Canseco 117 (**backpackers hostel**; ☎ 242 7145); Calle Lima 457 (**hostel and B&B**; ☎ 444 5753); and Martir Olaya 280 (**hostel**; ☎ 447 0673). Dorms cost from s/35 and double rooms are s/110/130 (com/att). The latter is the largest and has more private rooms.

Continuing with the canine theme, *Kaclla – The Healing Dog* (🖥 www.kaclla hostel.com, ☎ 241 8977, Calle Porta 461) is in a quieter location. Dorm beds cost from US$12 and there are dbl/tw/tpl/qd rooms for US$34/34/48/62 (com), all with breakfast.

Mid-range There's masses of choice in this category and some good deals to be had due to the competition.

La Casa Nostra (🖥 www.lacasanostra peru.com, ☎ 241 1718, Grimaldo del Solar 265), in a colonial complex, is a smart and well-turned-out place to stay with everything you might need in a cosy, albeit pretty generic environment. The rooms cost s/90/180/270 (sgl/dbl/tpl) and all have en suite bathrooms and include breakfast.

Conversely, *Hostal El Patio* (🖥 www .hostalelpatio.net, ☎ 444 2107, Diez Canseco 341a) is full of character. Comfortable, friendly and only a few minutes' walk from central Miraflores, there's also a plant-filled patio that's great for relaxing in and free wi-fi throughout.

The rooms cost from US$45/55 (sgl/dbl) and include private bathrooms, cable TV and filtered water. Mini suites (US$70) have a small kitchenette and mini-bar whilst mini suites (US$80) boast a separate bedroom and living room along with a fully equipped kitchen.

Hotel Alemán (off map to north; 🖥 www.hotelaleman.com.pe, ☎ 445 6999, Av Arequipa 4704) is a surprisingly quiet place to stay given that it's on a busy main street. There's a secure garage if you're driving and a café where guests can take advantage of the buffet breakfast. The spacious rooms

---

Note: Abbreviations used: **sgl/tw/dbl/tpl/qd** = single/twin/double/triple/quad room, **att** = room with attached bathroom, **com** = room with common (shared) bathroom.

are decked out in traditional textiles and cost US$70/80/90/100 (sgl/dbl/tpl/qd).

Hostal Torreblanca (🖥 www.torre blancaperu.com, ☎ 447 0142, Av José Pardo 1453) is a large terracotta-coloured building peacefully located on the edge of a park near the sea. Rooms are comfortable and rates are US$65/75/95 (sgl/dbl/tpl).

San Antonio Abad (🖥 www.hotelsan antonioabad.com, ☎ 447 6766, Av Ramón Ribeyro 301) is a large, justifiably popular, yellow corner building close to parks and attractions that lays on a free airport pick-up if you reserve in advance. Run by friendly, helpful staff; rooms cost US$60/65/75 (sgl/dbl/tpl).

Bayview Hotel (🖥 www.bayviewho tel.com.pe, ☎ 519 0770, Las Dalias 276) is a colonial-style house in a quiet location that has a shady garden, bar and a good restaurant. The rooms are comfortable and well equipped; rate are around US$65/75/88 (sgl/dbl/tpl).

Ibis Larco Miraflores (🖥 www.ibis.com, ☎ 634 8888, Larco 1140) is well located, part of the international chain and exactly as you'd expect – clean, comfortable and characterless. You could be in any modern city in the world if you stay here. Doubles are around US$75.

La Castellana Hotel (🖥 www.castel lanahotel.com, ☎ 444 3530, Grimaldo del Solar 222) stands in an impressive hundred-year-old manor house. The interior décor is somewhat dark and colonial but there's lots of space and a decent restaurant. The rooms cost US$75/80/105 (sgl/dbl/tpl).

Antigua Miraflores (🖥 www.antigua miraflores.com, ☎ 201 2060, Av Grau 350) is a pretty, Republican-era house full of tasteful touches; the tiled floors, chandeliers and woodwork are all well preserved and give an impression of the house's history. Old fashioned, with the emphasis on friendliness, it's a well-located, welcoming place to stay. Traditional rooms cost US$90/105 (sgl/dbl) and Colonial rooms

are US$113/129 (sgl/dbl). Senorial rooms – junior suites with bigger beds, Jacuzzis and kitchenettes – are a little pricier.

The reliable **Casa Andina chain** (🖥 www.casa-andina.com, ☎ 391 6500) has several properties in Miraflores, two of which are in their Classic category and fall in this price bracket: *Miraflores San Antonio* (Av 28 de Julio 1088) and *Miraflores Centro* (Av Petit Thouars 5444). Both are smart, modern and professional places with all mod-cons. The former is slightly cheaper, with prices starting from US$75 (dbl) as opposed to US$105 (dbl) but rates vary depending on the month.

Expensive You're spoiled for choice when it comes to blowing the budget in Miraflores but you do get some great hotels for the money.

Radisson Decapolis Miraflores (🖥 www.radisson.com, ☎ 625 1200, 28 de Julio 151) is a modern, international-standard hotel often favoured by business travellers; it boasts a rooftop pool, fitness centre, massage rooms, a Martini bar and a sushi bar. Standard rooms are US$149, whilst superior ones start at US$174 and junior suites will set you back US$200.

Sonesta Posadas del Inca Miraflores (🖥 en.sonestapimiraflores.com, ☎ 241 7688, Alcanfores 329) is popular with tour groups who come for the comfortable rooms and personal service. The rooms cost from US$120/145 (sgl/dbl).

Casa Andina Premium Miraflores (🖥 www.casa-andina.com, ☎ 213 4300, Av La Paz 463) one of the top-end properties in the Casa Andina chain. Close to Parque Central it has contemporary rooms, many with good views of the coast. Facilities include a heated pool, gym and lobby bar. The rooms cost from US$175 but there are often internet deals which can bring this down as low as US$120.

Miraflores Park Hotel (off map to south-east; 🖥 www.miraflorespark.com, ☎

610 4000, Malecon de la Reserva 1035) is owned by Orient Express and as you'd expect from them, this place is opulent, with first-rate facilities and service. Set atop the Miraflores cliffs and amid some pretty gardens, it's a pleasant place to get your bearing and explore the city. The hotel also has an open-air, heated rooftop pool and spa and several excellent restaurants, making it a really attractive option in this price range. Suites are from US$350.

JW Marriott (🖳 www.marriott.com, ☎ 217 7000, Malecon de la Reserva 615) also trades on its location, standing on the cliffs just by Larcomar Mall; every room has sea views. Ultra modern and set up to indulge guests, it has an outdoor rooftop pool and tennis courts along with a really good restaurant. The rooms start at around US$300.

Barranco   [see map p131]
Budget *The Point* (🖳 thepointhostels .com/peru/lima.html, ☎ 247 7997, Malecón Junín 300) is a spacious, sea-front house with high ceilings and wide corridors that attracts backpackers and travellers with its laidback attitude and tendency to host impromptu parties that move onto Barranco's nightspots after. Always busy, it can get a little overwhelming. There's a big range of dorm beds (s/34-42), twin rooms (s/90 com) and doubles (s/110 att). Includes breakfast, wifi, cable TV, films and a weekly BBQ.

Barranco's Backpacker Inn (🖳 www .barrancobackpackersperu.com, ☎ 412 6918, Malecón Castilla 260) is a quieter proposition, even closer to the coast and with great ocean views. The rooms starting at US$35 for a twin (US$45 for a double) are cheery, as are the staff. Rooms have attached bathrooms. Dorm beds are US$11.

Compact and bijou, *Kaminu* (🖳 www .kaminu.com, ☎ 252 8680, Bajada de Baños 342) has a great location below Puente de los Suspiros. There's a roof terrace to relax on and a weekly BBQ. Bunk beds cost US$10-12 or beds in a tent for US$8. In a nearby apartment they have a range of rooms from US$16 (sgl) and US$27 (dbl).

Cozy Wasi (🖳 www.cozywasi.com, ☎ 984 108785, Nicolas de Pierola 229) is clean, cheap and friendly – sgl/dbl/tw rooms for US$15/20/25 and doubles with bath attached for US$30.

La Puerte Verde (🖳 www.lapuerte verde.pe, ☎ 964 610154, Jr Pérez Roca 232), behind the green gate is a great family-run B&B. There's a sun terrace, friendly helpful staff and free use of bicycles. There are dbl/tw/tpl rooms from around US$36/38/45 and dorms beds for US$14. You'll need to book early as this place is justifiably popular.

Mid-range *Second Home Peru* (🖳 www .secondhomeperu.com, ☎ 247 5522, Domeyer 366) is an impressive guesthouse with just five bedrooms, each incredibly comfortable, and equipped with luxurious linens and Louis XV tubs. Once the home of Peruvian sculptor Victor Delfin, it's tastefully and quirkily decorated with art and artefacts. It also has an outdoor pool, ocean and garden views. The rooms cost US$135/150 depending on the view, marking it out as great value as well.

Expensive *Hotel B* (🖳 hotelb.pe, ☎ 206 0800, Sáenz Peña 204) is a swanky boutique hotel and the top place to stay in Barranco. The luxurious rooms cost from around $300. If you can't afford to stay here it's worth visiting just for a drink in the bar or for dinner.

San Isidro
Budget *Malka Youth Hostel* (🖳 www .youthhostelperu.com, ☎ 442 0162, Av Javier Prado Este) is an affordable option in an often expensive part of town.

Run by a climber it's full of spectacular mountain photographs and has a small climbing wall in the garden along with all the usual facilities and add-ons such as cable TV, ping-pong tables and a café. Dorm beds with shared bathrooms cost s/35, whilst double rooms are s/112/128 with shared/private facilities.

Mid range *Casa Bella Peru* (🖳 www .casabellaperu.net/sanisidro, ☎ 421 7354,

Las Flores 459) is set in a renovated mansion from the 1930s just a block back from the golf course and Country Club. The rooms are simply decorated but come with the usual range of services including cable TV and wi-fi. They cost from US$69/75/119 (dbl/tw/tpl).

Libertador Lima (⌨ www.libertador .com.pe/en/libertador/lima, ☎ 518 6300, Los Eucaliptos 550), opposite the golf course, is part of this chain's portfolio of spa hotels. A fairly small hotel, its rooms are a good size and equipped with everything the business traveller might require. The rooms start at US$125 but rates rise quite quickly if you upgrade to a superior room or suite.

Expensive *Sonesta Hotel El Olivar* (⌨ en.sonestaelolivar.com, ☎ 712 6000, Pancho Fierro 194) overlooks Olive Grove Park. Large and comfortable, it can be excellent value, with rooms from US$150/165 (sgl/dbl).

Swissotel (⌨ www.swissotel.com/ho tels/lima, ☎ 421 4400, Via Central 150) is one of the smartest hotels in Lima. Luxurious and well thought out, the rooms are stylish and complemented by cutting-edge amenities. The cheapest rooms, Premier, are US$256 with larger rooms boasting more facilities correspondingly more expensive. Prices on the internet can be about 30% lower.

Country Club Lima (⌨ www.hotel country.com, ☎ 611 9000, Los Eucaliptos 590) is an exclusive, modern boutique hotel in a sprawling building held to be a national monument with lavish rooms, restaurants and a bar along with a garden. Communal areas are decorated with tiling, textiles and reproduction Cusco School paintings. There are five styles of room, which range from a Master room at US$207, to the Presidential suites at US$2370.

WHERE TO EAT

Whilst in Lima, make sure you discover the food scene; this is now arguably the food capital of South America. Local life revolves around food and it is a chance to sample an emerging world cuisine in its original loca-

tion. Countless eateries can rustle up versions of Peru's fusion food but look out in particular for ceviche, nutty stews, anticuchos and *causas*. See also pp81-3.

Eating here is surprisingly affordable but to really keep costs down and still enjoy a sensational meal, look for the daily *menús* that are often available at local restaurants.

Fast food

There are lots of cheap eateries around Lima Centro. These include rotisserie chicken joints and all the international chains, especially around Parque Kennedy, but you're better off trying local spots and discovering the traditional flavours of Peru.

Cafés

Miraflores area (see map p130) There are numerous café-bars in central Miraflores around Kennedy Park. Particularly good is *Haiti* (Diagonal 160) which is stuck in a time warp with retro décor and formal waiters but serves up tasty sandwiches and pastries in an ideal spot for people watching.

Similarly good for whiling away time and watching the world, *Café Café* (Martin Olaya 250) has a sprawling drinks menu that includes two dozen types of coffee and a range of inexpensive snacks, pizzas and sandwiches. There's also a **branch** in Larcomar mall.

However, if you are in the mall you should try *Mangos* (⌨ www.mangosperu .com; buffets: Mon-Sat 4.30-8pm, daily 12.30-4pm, Sat & Sun 7.30-11.30am, happy hour Mon-Thur 7-10pm), one of the best of the cafés in the mall, with a broad deck and good views over the ocean as well as some decent food and drink.

To see the humble potato transformed, eat at *Cesar* (Av La Mar 814), which boasts dozens of inventive hot and cold *causa* recipes, which combine potato with vegetables, meat and seafood to tantalising effect.

Lima centro (see map pp128-9) A bit more upmarket, *T'anta* (Pasaje de los Escribanos 142; Mon-Sat 9am-10pm, Sun 9am-6pm), is part of celebrity-chef Gastón Acurio's stable of restaurants . The food in this café-bistro is an interesting mix of plates from Peru, Italy and elsewhere but also features salads and sandwiches. Prices are fuelled by the big name attached to the business but by and large dishes are tasty and a little unusual, whilst the wine list and cocktails are definitely superior to other places.

There are also branches in **San Isidro** (Panchio Fierro 115) and **Miraflores** (Av 28 de Julio 888; see map p130).

Barranco (see map p131) *Sofa* (Av San Martin 480) is a great café, bar and restaurant that's open from 8am for breakfast and through the day until at least midnight.

One place you mustn't miss while in Barranco is *BLU Gelato* (🖳 www.blugelateria.com; 28 de Julio 202), probably the best place for ice-cream or sorbet anywhere in Lima.

Cevicheria and seafood
Peru's national dish, ceviche, has to be tried and Lima is one of the best places in the country to sample the original or innovative variations of this classic.

There are plenty of authentic neighbourhood *cevicherías* but also a number of more sophisticated joints where it is given the fine dining treatment. In line with cevichería tradition, most restaurants only open till about 5pm.

Miraflores area (see map p130) There was no way celebrated chef Gastón Acurio wasn't going to tackle a local speciality like ceviche; stylish *La Mar* (🖳 www.lamarcebicheria.com/lima/, Av La Mar 770; Mon-Thur noon-5pm, Fri-Sun to 5.30pm) is a high-end ceviche restaurant, popular with wealthy locals and visitors alike; many opt

for the tasting menu to avoid having to choose between the mouth-watering dishes on offer. You need to come early to get a table or be prepared for a long wait.

Also excellent is *Pescados Capitales* (🖳 www.pescadoscapitales.com, Av La Mar 1337; daily 12.30-5pm & 8-11pm) further north on the same street. The kitchen knocks up superb ceviche, served along with a wide range of South American wines in an airy restaurant.

La Rosa Nautica (🖳 www.larosanautica.com, Espigon 4, Costa Verde; daily noon-midnight) is superbly sited in a Victorian-style end-of-pier restaurant. Once *the* place for ceviche, the seafood is still good – but other restaurants in town have caught up. The location though is unparalleled but you should probably take a taxi here at night.

Barranco (see map p131) *Canta Rana* (Génova 101) has been in business for a quarter of a century despite the fact that it isn't properly signed and can be a little hard to find; look for the locals who flock to the Singing Frog to sample the 17 types of ceviche that the place is renowned for. Informal and simply decorated, it is in fact quite expensive but justifies it by being the epitome of the local *cevichería*.

Peruvian
San Isidro area (see map p130) *Astrid y Gastón* (🖳 www.astridygaston.com, Av Paz Soldan 290; Mon-Sat 12.30-3.30pm & 7-11pm) is where the Peruvian food renaissance began. Chef Gastón Acurio and his wife Astrid pioneered *novoandina* cuisine, fusing traditional foodstuffs with Asian, African and Spanish flavours to startling effect. The grand dame of the scene now

---

❏ Suspiro de Limeña (Lima Sigh)
This classic Peruvian dessert consists of a thick caramel bottom layer made from condensed milk, vanilla and egg yolks, topped with meringue combined with port syrup and a sprinkle of ground cinnamon as the finishing touch. Legend has it that it was named by the famous writer and poet Jose Galvez Amparo Ayarez, whose wife created it, because it was 'as sweet and soft as the sigh of a young woman from Lima.' First served in 1818, it epitomises the Peruvian love of sweet things. **Alison Roberts**

has plenty of competition but the colourful restaurant decked in modern art still packs a punch and creates innovative and unusual combinations that will tantalise and satisfy. As well as ceviche there are delicious lamb recipes and Peruvian curries of tubers, vegetables and grains.

Panchita (Av 2 de Mayo 298), one of Acurio's later projects, focuses on street food and captures authentic flavours such as flame-grilled anticuchos and *tamales*. It is not possible to book a table here so queues can be long.

Restaurant Huaca Pucllana (General Borgoño cuadra 8) is a smart restaurant alongside the Huaca Pucllana ruins (see p127); the views of the site are good especially in the evening from the covered terrace as the adobe ruins are illuminated. The food is contemporary Peruvian, a reinterpretation of *criollo* cuisine, well-cooked and artfully presented, with a range of dishes from typical chowders to *cuy* (guinea pig).

Las Brujas de Cachiche (🖥 www.bru jasdecachiche.com.pe, Jirón Bolognesi 472; Mon-Sat noon-midnight, Sun 12.30-4.30pm), the Witches of Cachiche, is a series of bars and dining rooms in an old mansion house. Elaborately and elegantly decorated, it's an exclusive albeit expensive place to try Peruvian and criollo dishes, especially if you tackle the lunchtime buffet. Ancient and pre-Columbian recipes are also reinvigorated with unusual accompaniments to great effect. They also host live criollo music shows.

El Señorio de Sulco (🖥 www.senorio desulco.com, Malecón Cisneros 1470; Mon-Sat 12.30-11.30pm, Sun 12.30-4.30pm) is a popular place, fêted for its Criollo dishes, especially the seafood. Expensive, it is worth the extra cost for the clifftop views and atmosphere.

San Isidro *Malabar* (🖥 www.malabar .com.pe, Camino Real 101) is a consistently well-rated restaurant in the heart of San Isidro. They source many of their vegetables from their own farm. The cuisine includes Amazonian ingredients and a seasonal menu that draws on these. Try catfish caviar, tiradito of sole, or carpaccio of pig's

trotter. There's also a devilishly good cocktail list.

Barranco (see map p131)   Also well established and reliable is *La 73* (Av El Sol Oeste 175, ☎ 247 0780; Mon-Sat noon-midnight, Sun and holidays to 10pm) where the cooking's imaginative and the menu's also in English. There's everything from wontons filled with mushrooms and tamarind sauce to lemon pie.

There are also several dedicated steak restaurants but they tend to be pricey. Try *La Cudra de Salvador* (Av Miguel Grau), or further north up the same street at 1502 and opposite MAC, *La Cabrera* (🖥 www.lacabreraperu.com) where top class steaks cost around s/120.

Down in the new development by the sea there are several upmarket bars and expensive restaurants including *Cala Restaurante* (🖥 www.calarestaurante.com; Playa Barranquito) which has an excellent reputation for its seafood and Peruvian dishes.

International
Lima centro (see map pp128-9) There are plenty of *chifa* (Chinese) restaurants but for something a little special, seek out *Wa Lok* (🖥 www.walok.com.pe; daily 9am-11pm; Jirón Paruro 864) in Barrio Chino (Chinatown); the Cantonese dim sum are especially delicious but the noodles and stir fries are also very good.

French-influenced food with a Peruvian twist is available at *L'Eau Vive* (Ucayali 370), opposite Torre Tagle Palace in an old building. It has a fixed-price lunch (three courses for s/19) served in a simple dining room along with a broader à la carte menu available in a grand salon. Run by an order of nuns, there's a rendition of *Ave Maria* every evening at 9pm. Proceeds are donated to charity by the nuns.

Miraflores area (see map p130)   *La Bodega de la Trattoria* (🖥 www.labodega delatrattoria.com, Av General Borgoño 784) serves good approximations of Italian cuisine, especially ravioli, and is part of a small reliable chain.

Maido (🖥 www.maido.pe; San Martin 399) is one of the world's best restaurants, in the lauded Top 50 list, but if you want to get in here you'll usually need to reserve well in advance to experience this amazing Japanese-Peruvian fusion cuisine.

BARS AND NIGHTLIFE
Lima has a more contemporary and happening nightlife than any other city in Peru. Barranco in particular has a lively atmosphere and a wide range of places in which to hang out.

Lima Centro
The many **bars** in the centre of Lima cater to all tastes. For old-world elegance head to the *Gran Hotel Bolívar* bar, on Plaza San Martin, to sip a Pisco Sour; for that essential sporting occasion try *Estadio Fútbol Bar* (Nicolás de Piérola 934).

The best **folklórica show** in Lima is at *Las Brisas del Titicaca* (🖥 www.brisasdel titicaca.com, Pasaje Walkuski 168), where folk and criolla are combined into an all-singing, all-dancing extravaganza.

Miraflores
Miraflores has a number of expat-style bars that are frequently full and boast a good atmosphere and range of international drinks. *Benchley Arms* (Atahualpa 174) and *Old Pub* (San Ramón 295) are two of the longest running. Alternatively, try *Bar Habana* (Manuel Bonilla 107), an artsy hangout run by a Cuban-Peruvian couple who combine each country's specialist cocktails.

There's also *Media Naranja* (Schell 130), which has a Brazilian vibe, and *Huaringas* (Bolognesi 460), a busy lounge bar with a huge range of cocktails and a DJ on most weekends.

For a night that doesn't involve drinking or dancing, there's a **cinema** in Larcomar mall (🖥 www.larcomar.com/cine .html), which shows both Spanish- and English-language films.

Barranco
The hip and unofficial centre of the city's nightlife, Barranco is the district to descend on if you're after a good night out or the chance to enjoy the eclectic music scene in Lima.

Start your evening in *Ayahuasca* (San Martín 130), a fashionable bar in an old three-storey mansion, *Juanito's* (Av Grau; see box p132), where a bohemian crowd congregates, or one of the branches of *Posada del Angel* (Pedro de Osma 164 & 218 and Av San Martín 157).

Afterwards, head to *tabernas* including *La Noche* (🖥 www.lanoche.com.pe) Bolognesi 307) in search of live Andean music, criolla or Latin jazz.

Finally, hit the *peñas* such as *Del Carajo* (San Ambrosio 328) and *La Candelaría* (Bolognesi 292).

SHOPPING
Lima boasts the widest range of shopping in Peru. The main precinct is **Jirón de la Unión**, which is full of boutique shops and big brands.

However, Miraflores has a wide variety of boutiques and brand-name shops so it is the best place to browse. On the clifftops at the end of Av Larco stands **Larcomar**, a large mall that's home to international brands as well as a varied food court. Interrupt your shopping for a coffee and a chance to look out over the ocean and watch the paragliders who jump off adjacent cliffs drift past. There are plenty of interesting outlets to discover selling handicrafts, clothes, bags and jewellery, although things are a little more expensive because of the location.

For an alternative experience, visit the **markets**, making sure to take your haggling skills with you. Gamarra in La Victoria is home to 20,000 stalls; **Mercado Indio** in Miraflores sells alpaca clothing and crafts and the **craft stalls** on Av Petit Thouars in Miraflores are good for art and souvenirs. Visit **Mercado de Surquillo** in Miraflores to see where Lima's restaurants source their produce.

For more expensive or bespoke pieces, head to **Dédalo** at Paseo Saenz Peña 295 in Barranco to pick up beautiful craft pieces and jewellery. **Killaii** on the corner of San Martín and Alcanfores, in Miraflores, also has a range of contemporary crafts, whilst **Agua y Tierra**, at Ernesto Diez Canseco 298, specialises in indigenous crafts from the Amazon. **Pasaje el Suche** is an interesting area to explore with a small number of souvenir shops to browse and a range of cafés and bars in which to relax.

The shops belonging to **Kuna by Alpacca III**, branches of which can be found at the airport, on Av Larco and in Larcomar mall amongst other venues, are ideal for woollen clothing in contemporary designs and colours.

MOVING ON

Lima is an effective gateway to the rest of Peru and it's possible to go to every corner of the country from the capital. To get to Cusco, you can either fly or take a bus.

Air

The flight from Lima to Cusco takes just less than an hour; flights depart in the morning because the weather is generally better. Sit on the left-hand side of the plane for particularly good views of Mt Salkantay shortly before landing in Cusco.

Note that you may find that flying into Cusco from sea level leaves you poorly acclimatised and struggling to move around freely, at least for the first couple of days.

Bus

Lima doesn't have a central bus terminal so each operator manages its own departure points. Some even have several depending on the final destination so check carefully where you need to be to meet your ride. If you're travelling a long way it's also worth checking that you've a comfy seat; buses marked 'bus cama' have more generous, reclining seats.

There are two **overland routes to Cusco**. The majority of bus companies work their way south along the coast, via Nazca to Arequipa, where you have to change and board a bus that loops inland and north to Cusco. The journey takes some 20 hours to complete.

The alternative is to travel through the highlands, via Ayacucho, a route that is more direct but more precipitous and adventurous to travel although it is no longer plagued by the terrorists that held sway in Ayacucho during the 1980s and early '90s.

Reliable companies include Cruz del Sur (🖳 www.cruzdelsur.com.pe, ☎ 311 5050), which has several daily services that depart from either Quilca 531 in Lima Centro (economy Imperial and Ideal services to Cusco and elsewhere), or Av Javier Prado Este 1109 in San Isidro (luxury Cruzero and Cruzero suite services to Cusco and beyond). Tickets one-way are from s/185; you can book online.

Tepsa (🖳 www.tepsa.com.pe, ☎ 617 9000) also travel to Cusco, departing from Paseo de la República 151-A in Lima Centro and Javier Prado Este 1091. Fares are a little cheaper at s/125. Also try Movil Tours (🖳 www.moviltours.com.pe; Av Javier Prado Este 1093). These companies also offer bus services to other parts of Peru.

❏ **Domestic airline offices in Lima**
- **LATAM** (🖳 www.latam.com, ☎ 213 8200), Av José Pardo 513, Miraflores
- **Star Perú** (🖳 www.starperu.com, ☎ 213 8813), Av Comandante Espinar 331, Miraflores
- **Avianca** (🖳 www.avianca.com, ☎ 511 8222), Av José Pardo 811, Miraflores
- **Peruvian** (🖳 www.peruvian.pe, ☎ 715 6122), Av José Pardo 495, Miraflores
- **LC Peru** (🖳 www.lcperu.pe, ☎ 204 1313), Av. José Pardo 269, Miraflores

CUSCO & AROUND

Cusco
(Qosqo, Cuzco)

In the whole of old Peru, there was undoubtably no place that was as deeply revered as the imperial city of Cuzco, which is where all the Inca kings held court and established the seat of government.
Garcilaso Inca de la Vega *The Royal Commentaries of the Incas* (1609)

The cultural and religious centre of the Inca world, Cusco was once a truly awesome city. The seat of the God-king, the Inca, it was built to reflect the might of the Empire. Yet despite its brutal sacking by the Spanish conquistadors – and a subsequent history dotted with siege and earthquake – Cusco remains an exciting and vibrant place, much more than just a tourist town. The capital of Cusco Department, it's also the undisputed archaeological capital of South America and a UNESCO World Heritage Site.

Spectacular colonial architecture stands astride monolithic ruined Inca palaces made of perfectly hewn stone, which line atmospheric, scorched cobbled plazas. White-washed alleys and terracotta-tiled roofs house a rich mix of history, lively nightlife and a vast array of museums, sights and scenery. Although it has embraced tourism and developed a sound infrastructure to support the influx of visitors, the city's magnificent historical past still has a powerful hold on its glorious present. The collision and fusion of indigenous Andean and imported colonial cultures is fascinating and always evident, even to those tourists who come to the city only as a staging post for the Inca Trail to Machu Picchu.

It would be a stretch to suggest that Cusco is anything but on the tourist trail these days, yet the city wears its celebrity lightly and retains an authenticity other must-see cities around the world lose. Although there are some tried and tested traveller haunts, and the cementing of the city's status has finally seen the arrival of global food chains and brands, there are also quirky finds, quiet corners and plenty of local eateries specialising in the country's indigenous flavours. Essentially, what was a backpacker Mecca has grown up. But it has done so in style as a rash of new boutique and top-end hotel openings demonstrate, which, coupled with the arrival of celebrity chefs from Lima, ensure that the city has a broader, more chic appeal than ever whilst the traditional reasons for visiting – the history, architecture, location and atmosphere – remain as relevant as ever. Much more than just a history lesson, Cusco now has a contemporary feel. To paraphrase the 17th-century chronicler of Inca life, Felipe Huamán Poma de Ayala, it's '*un espacio mágico*' (a magic space).

The city stands at 3360m (11,000ft) above sea level so the air is thinner here than you might be used to. Upon arrival spend a couple of days acclimatising before you attempt anything too strenuous. This is especially important if you're flying in from Lima as your body will take a while to adapt to going from sea level to altitude in an hour. Consider travelling down to the Sacred Valley (see p190), some 500m lower, to aid acclimatisation and to take in the superb sights here as well.

HISTORY

Origins and early history

Legend states that the city was founded around 1100AD when the original Inca Manco Capac, having descended from the sun and risen from Lake Titicaca, plunged a staff into the soil and declared it fertile enough to support a city, a city he called Cusco (popularly thought to mean 'navel of the earth').

With no written records, the history of Cusco before the arrival of the Spanish is unclear. There is, however, archaeological evidence to suggest that other tribes lived here long before the arrival of the Incas. The Killke were probably the first but they were subjugated by the powerful and successful Huari culture, which came to dominate the area, with the Sacred Valley forming part of their northern highland frontier. Eventually the Huari moved away and the Killke resumed control of the region and secured it with hilltop fortifications. However, they never built in the Cusco valley, leading archaeologists to believe that by the 12th century there were already stable, sizeable settlements there. These weren't strong enough to resist the Incas though, and by the 13th century most had been subdued by the new arrivals, although it wasn't until the early 15th century that Cusco enjoyed its great expansion and rise to prominence.

Inca capital

During its heyday, as the Inca capital, the city must have looked dazzling with gold, silver and precious stones adorning its fine buildings, truly awe-inspiring to the visitor. It was the centre of political power and the cultural and religious heart of the society. All roads led to Cusco: the main roads to each of the four corners of the empire led away from the main plaza, whilst sacred and religious lines from other spiritually significant sites convened on the Coricancha. Built to reflect the enormity of the Incas' achievements and visibly demonstrate their superiority, Cusco ranked alongside many of the great European cities when it came to elaborate architecture and sheer opulence.

The city was allegedly constructed on the orders of the Inca Pachacutec, who oversaw the destruction of the original simple structures found there after the conquest and demanded a city of stone be built in their place. Legend tells that Pachacutec went on to design the city in the shape of a puma, one of the

Incas' sacred animals: the river Tullumayo forms the spine, the river Huatanay the belly and Sacsayhuaman (see pp187-90) is laid out in the shape of the animal's head. The success of the city was down to Pachacutec's skills as a sophisticated urban planner. The city's superb infrastructure and a series of channels that diverted streams across the city provided fresh drinking water and ferried waste away, making it clean and hospitable.

Sadly the city was gutted in the wake of the Spanish conquest and now appears as a pale imitation of itself. The gold, silver and jewels that adorned the buildings were all looted, whilst the most significant and impressive buildings were all torn down. The infrastructure was damaged and the city allowed to become squalid and dirty. In a final desperate bid to oust the Spanish, the rebel Incas set fire to their own city and torched what was left of their once-magnificent capital.

Cusco after the conquest

Once the Spanish had definitively added Peru to the realms of Charles V, they realised that they needed a capital by the sea in order to support their new conquest. Since Cusco was set inland and moreover had strong associations with the past, it wasn't a suitable seat for government. With the transference of power to Lima, Cusco's influence inevitably waned.

The city was rebuilt, using stones pillaged from once-great Inca buildings to construct new colonial structures. Often these new buildings rose phoenix-like from the foundations of the Inca buildings, a not-so-subtle visual reminder of the dominance of the Spanish over their subjects. Unfortunately the colonial buildings were less robust than their predecessors and the occasional earthquakes that Peru experiences inevitably reduced them to rubble, leaving the remnants of the Inca architecture still standing.

Despite taking a back seat in determining the country's future and direction, Cusco still enjoyed moments in the headlines. During the 17th and 18th centuries the **Cusco School of painting** developed here and attracted a worldwide reputation. In 1780 it was the centre for the revolution staged by José Gabriel Condorcanqui, who took on the name Túpac Amaru II. In 1825 Bolívar arrived in the city and later the first royal oath of independence was sworn before the giant blackened crucifix nicknamed *El Señor de los Temblores*, now kept in the cathedral (see opposite).

More recently, with the uncovering and popularisation of Machu Picchu and other Inca ruins, the city has developed a role as Peru's most important tourist centre, a fact which has ensured its renaissance and re-emergence as one of the country's most vital, important cities.

WHAT TO SEE AND DO

Plaza de Armas   [see map pp156-7 & p164]

The main square has always been the city's focal point although during the time of the Incas it was twice as large. Once called Aucaypata ('the square of war or weeping'), it was a ceremonial site surrounded on three sides by huge Inca mansions. Along one side, in a stone ditch, ran the river Huatanay. On the far side of the river stood Cusipata ('the joyful square'), which is where modern-day Plaza Regocijo now stands. Cusipata was the setting for Inca celebrations and feasts. Nowadays, colonial arcades full of shops and restaurants line the square, and the balconies that overlook the original heart of the Inca capital are used by cafés and restaurants to provide exceptional views.

There are usually two flags flying in the square: the red-and-white-striped Peruvian national flag and the rainbow-striped Quechua flag, which bears a striking resemblance to the gay pride banner, and from which it can be distinguished by an additional blue line.

La Catedral   [see map pp156 & map p164]

(Daily 9am-6pm; entrance through Iglesia de Jesús María; free with CRA ticket, see box on p150); otherwise s/25, s/12.50 students) Built between 1556 and 1669 on the site of the Inca Viracocha's palace, the monolithic renaissance-style cathedral dominates one side of the plaza and acts as a significant statement of religious superiority, designed to awe the local population.

The cathedral stands between the church of Jesús María (to the left as you look at the cathedral) built in 1733, and Cusco's oldest church, El Triunfo (to the right), which dates from 1536 and is the resting place of the historian Garcilaso de la Vega. The main doors, which are discreetly marked with a carved puma head, are open first thing in the morning for genuine worshippers. This is an excellent time to slip in and see the cathedral, and to appreciate the stunning works of art in rather better light than the gloom that pervades once the doors are shut again.

Full of treasures, the cathedral is one of the city's best repositories of colonial art, particularly from the Cusco School, and has a sacristy full of portraits of priests from the past. There are also wonderful murals, gilded altars and a very finely carved choir representing 80 saints and dating from the 17th century by Martín Torres and Melchor Huamán, as well as a solid-silver high altar backed by a *retablo* that's considered a masterpiece of indigenous carving. Elsewhere, look for the blackened crucifix, *El Señor de los Temblores* (the Lord of the Earthquakes) that was paraded around Cusco in 1650 to stop a giant earthquake and which now stands in an alcove adjacent to the entrance to El Triunfo.

The parade worked, the earthquake stopped before the cathedral was destroyed, and the event has been commemorated in a giant canvas that stands facing the entrance of El Triunfo. The colouring of the cross is a result of decades of exposure to candle smoke. In the north-east corner of the cathedral there's also a very famous painting of the Last Supper by Marcos Zapata, painted with an Andean audience in mind, so with Christ and his disciples feasting on roast *cuy* (guinea pig) and drinking chicha. Some people hold that the face of Judas is actually a portrait of Pizarro.

The three buildings are periodically restored and worked on, meaning that sections may be shut off or various works of art covered or moved into storage.

La Compañía (Jesuits' Church)   [see map pp156-7]

(Daily 9am-11.30am & 1-5.30pm; s/10) This Jesuit church is the other massive building on Plaza de Armas. Built on the ruins of the palace of the Inca Huayna Capac, described by chronicler Pedro Sancho as the greatest Inca palace, it is a grand building complete with decorative baroque façade and a pair of impressive belfries.

Work began in 1578 but a giant earthquake in 1650 practically demolished the building and it wasn't finished until 1668. The Jesuits intended the church to outshine the neighbouring cathedral, but Pope Paul III intervened and declared it must not. Unfortunately by the time the message filtered back to Peru the work had already been completed. The two buildings are quite similar, although some believe that La Compañía eclipses its neighbour.

The interior is cool and dark, the shadows hiding interesting paintings of local weddings that show plenty of period detail, including a representation of

---

❑ **Boleto Turístico Único (BTU) – Visitor's Ticket**

Admission to many of Cusco's museums and archaeological sites can only be achieved by using the **Boleto Turístico Único** (BTU or Visitor's Ticket; 🖳 www.cos ituc.gob.pe), which costs s/130 (US$40) for adults and s/70 for students with a valid ISIC card; it is valid for 10 days and is sold at the **Oficina Ejecutiva del Comité (OFEC)** office at Av El Sol 103 (Mon-Sat 8am-6pm, Sun 8am-1pm).

It is also possible to buy a ticket at most of the sites featured although this is a gamble as they may have run out; ideally, buy the ticket from the office in advance of visiting the sites.

Sites covered within Cusco and the surrounding region are the Municipal Museum of Contemporary Art, Regional History Museum, Coricancha site museum, Pachacutec monument, Sacsayhuaman, Q'enko, Puca Pucara, Tambo Machay, Tipón, Pikillacta, Pisac, Ollantaytambo, Chinchero and Moray.

The ticket allows only one entrance to each of these sites; this is tiresome if you want to go back to any but if you paid entrance fees for all the sites separately it would cost much more than s/130. Note that the ticket does not cover the Coricancha-Santo Domingo complex (see opposite), merely the small museum in the grounds whose entrance is on Av El Sol. Nor does it include any religious sites (most of which are covered by a separate ticket – see below) or access to Machu Picchu.

Alternatively, there are three **partial boletos**, divided as circuits, which can be bought separately and which enable you to visit a selection of the sites. Each of these costs s/70. **Circuit 1** (valid for one day) combines Sacsayhuaman, Q'enko, Puca Pucara and Tambo Machay; **Circuit 2** (two days) combines the Museum of Contemporary Art, Museum of Regional History, Coricancha Museum, the Pachacutec monument, Tipón and Pikillacta; **Circuit 3** (two days) combines Pisac, Ollantaytambo, Chinchero and Moray.

Several of the major sites, including Ollantaytambo, Sacsayhuaman, Pisac and Chinchero, can only be accessed with a Boleto Turístico. Other, smaller sites such as Tipón and Moray can be seen by buying individual tickets at the site. Overall the best buy is the full Boleto Turístico as it offers the widest range of access.

If you want to go to any of the religious sites it is worth considering a **Circuito Religioso Arzobispal (CRA, Ticket of the Religious Circuit**; s/30) ticket. This secures entry to the cathedral, the churches of San Blas and San Cristóbal as well as Museo de Arte Religioso.

the marriage of Martín García de Loyola to the Inca princess Nusta Beatriz. The baroque style, gold-leaf-covered altar is vast and impressive and the catacombs beneath the church are worth exploring. Often illuminated at night, the church is visible from many of the hotels and hostels high on the surrounding slopes.

Inca walls   [see map p164]

The Inca walls that line the north-western side of Plaza de Armas are reputed to be part of Pachacutec's palace, whilst those in the northern corner belong to the palace of Sinchi Roca. There is also some fine Inca masonry (walls) on Calle Loreto; see map p153.

Coricancha (Temple of the Sun) and Santo Domingo   [map p157]

(Mon-Sat 8.30am-5.30pm; s/15, s/6 for students, not on the Visitor's Ticket)

> 'All the Incas enriched this city and, among its countless monuments, the Temple of the Sun remained the principal object of their attention. They vied with one another in ornamenting it with incredible wealth, each Inca seeking to surpass his predecessor.'   **Garcilaso Inca de la Vega** *The Royal Commentaries of the Incas* (1609)

To the south-east of Plaza de Armas, the Inca Sun Temple, Coricancha (also written as Koricancha or Qoricancha) is Quechua for 'Golden Enclosure' and it was the centre of the Inca religion, having previously been the site of a Huari sun temple. The building comprised four small sanctuaries set around a central courtyard and was once lavishly decorated with gold plates and precious stones. Writing 50 years after the conquest, the historian Garcilaso de la Vega described the awe-inspiring magnificence of the main sanctuary, dedicated to the Sun:

> 'The four walls were hung with plaques of gold, from top to bottom, and a likeness of the Sun topped the high altar. This likeness was made from a gold plaque twice as thick as those that paneled the walls, and was composed of a round face, prolonged by rays and flames, the way Spanish painters represent it; the whole thing was so immense that it occupied the entire back of the temple, from one wall to the other.'
> **Garcilaso Inca de la Vega**   *The Royal Commentaries of the Incas* (1609)

The Spanish conquistadors pillaged the site and stole the lot.

The other sanctuaries within the temple, which boast some of the most exceptional stonework and polished jointing in the city, were dedicated to various deities including the Moon (the bride of the Sun); Venus, the Pleiades and the stars; Thunder and the Rainbow. Garcilaso de la Vega noted that, 'They called the rainbow cuichu and revered it very specially. When it appeared, they immediately put their hands over their mouths through fear, they said, that it might make their teeth decay. I can't say why'.

The mummies of previous Incas were kept here, as were the kidnapped principal idols of tribes that the Incas defeated. 'They were', wrote Garcilaso, 'so well preserved that they seemed to be alive. They were seated on their golden thrones resting on plaques of this same metal, and they looked directly at the visitor.' He went on to describe the astonishing garden outside the temple:

> 'In the time of the Incas, this garden, in which today the convent brothers cultivate their vegetables, was entirely made of gold and silver; and there were similar gardens

CUSCO

about all the royal mansions. Here could be seen all sorts of plants, flowers, trees, animals, both small and large, wild and tame, tiny, crawling creatures such as snakes, lizards and snails, as well as butterflies and birds of every size... quinoa as well as other vegetables and fruit trees... very faithfully produced in gold and silver... and large statues of men and women and children made from the same materials.'

Garcilaso Inca de la Vega *The Royal Commentaries of the Incas* (1609)

The Spanish looted almost everything from here too.

Conquering Cusco, Juan Pizarro, the younger brother of Francisco, took control of the Coricancha. Fatally wounded at the siege of Sacsayhuaman, he bequeathed the temple to the Dominicans, who built the Monastery of Santo Domingo here. Constructing the monastery on the foundations of the Inca building was meant to demonstrate the superiority of Christianity over the indigenous beliefs. An earthquake in 1950 destroyed the monastery but left the Inca stonework, some of the finest masonry in Peru, undamaged.

The **Chapel of Santo Domingo** also merits a visit, with intricate carvings, the priests' fine clothing and other fabrics on display. The graves of the rebel Incas, Sayuri Túpac and Túpac Amaru, and of the conquistador Juan Pizarro are also here. Black and white photographs in the entrance to the complex catalogue the damage sustained by the chapel during the various earthquakes. Outside the temple is a set of grassy gardens with a pre-Inca spring and bath dating back to the Huari culture.

Coricancha Museum (Mon-Sat 9am-5pm, Sun 8am-2pm; Visitor's Ticket) is under the gardens and can be accessed by walking downhill from the complex on Av El Sol. Although small this archaeological museum boasts some interesting pieces including pre-Inca ceramics and stonework, Inca crafts and carvings, some found in the Coricancha, and a mummy.

West and south of Plaza de Armas [see map pp156-7]

This constitutes the area west of Plateros, behind Portales de Comercio and Confiturías.

● **La Merced** (Mon-Sat 8am-12.30pm & 2-5.30pm; s/10, s/5 students; not included in the CRA, see box p150) Originally built in 1534 this grand church, Cusco's third most important colonial church, was largely reconstructed after the 1650 earthquake in a combination of baroque and renaissance styles. Inside are riches to rival those contained in the cathedral, with the ornate white-stone cloisters and large collection of Cusco School religious art a special highlight.

The church's most prized possession – a metre-tall solid-gold *monstrance* (vessel) covered in precious stones, diamonds and pearls – is kept in a locked cloister. Because the church faces on to the market the priests were able to preach directly to the milling crowds of Indians and espouse their message to a large audience. Buried here are the conquistadors Gonzalo Pizarro and Diego de Almagro.

● **Museo y Convento de San Francisco** (Daily 9am-6pm; s/10 including a guided tour; not included in the CRA, see box p150) This forbidding building, dating from the mid 17th century, dominates Plaza San Francisco. Inside are: the oldest cloister in Cusco, a carefully crafted choir, suitably bloodthirsty decorations, paintings by local artists as well as a bone-filled crypt.

● **Iglesia de Santa Clara** (Irregular opening hours; free) This 16th-century church is only rarely open, but worth a visit if you are lucky enough to come upon it whilst a service is in progress. If you do go during a service, the nuns sometimes sing from behind a substantial metal grille. Inside the church are huge mirrors; originally intended to lure curious Indians into the building, they now multiply and reflect the candle-light magnificently.

● **Museo Histórico Regional y Casa Garcilaso** (Mon-Sat 8am-5pm; the only way of visiting is with a Visitor's Ticket) Originally inhabited by the historian Garcilaso de la Vega, the building was rebuilt by the famous Peruvian architect Víctor Pimentel after the 1986 earthquake reduced it almost to rubble.

The museum offers a basic but decent overview of Peruvian history and has a token collection of pre-Inca ceramics, pottery, arrow heads and other Inca weaponry, architectural tools and agricultural implements, a Nazca mummy and some gold jewellery found at Machu Picchu.

● **Mercado San Pedro** (Daily) An essential stop on any tour of the city, the central market is opposite San Pedro railway station. Everything is for sale, from fruit and veg to meats you recognise and some you won't. Noisy, busy, smelly and something of a sensory overload, it's a great place to people-watch. Keep an eye on your wallet and bag as pickpockets operate here. Half of the market is now given over to souvenirs so for a more authentic (and cheaper) shopping experience, head to the streets surrounding the market.

● **Santa Teresa** (Irregular opening hours; free) This is a rather nondescript building from the outside but it is set in an attractive square and the stone wall bordering Calle Saphi is a very good example of polygonal masonry.

East and south of Plaza de Armas [see map pp156-7]

These are the streets east of Av El Sol and south of Triunfo, which lie behind La Compañía.

● **Calle Loreto** The finely crafted stonework of this renowned Inca alley, which runs south-east alongside La Compañía, is well worth a look. The left-hand wall was part of the Acllahuasi, a convent of Inca nuns drawn from the most beautiful women throughout the empire.

● **Scotiabank** (Open during bank hours; free) The bank that now stands on Calle Maruri occupies the site of the palace of Túpac Inca Yupanqui. The elegantly cut and finely sculpted stone walls are still hugely impressive although somewhat at odds with the modern operation inside them. There is also a small museum inside that explains the history of the building. On the 1st floor is a fascinating permanent exhibition of black and white photographs by the Peruvian photographer Martín Chambi (s/10; see p74).

● **Museo de Arte Religioso y Palacio del Arzobispal** (Mon-Sat 8am-6pm; free with CRA, see box p150; otherwise s/10, s/5 students) Standing on the remains of an original Inca building, the colonial mansion that houses the museum and **Archbishop's Palace** is striking. Inside is a large collection of religious art from the Cusco School including paintings by Marcos Zapata and the Corpus Christi collection by an unknown artist.

The museum and palace is situated at one end of **Calle Hatun Rumiyoc**, the narrow alley that boasts the famous 12-sided stone that has become something of a symbol for Cusco and can be seen throughout the city. The original Inca wall in which the stone is set used to be part of the palace of Inca Roca. At the far end of the wall is a small side street that runs along what would have been the back of the palace. This, too, boasts beautifully moulded stones. These intricately worked blocks conceal the outline of a puma, which the locals sitting round it will happily point out to you, for a small fee, if you're struggling to make it out.

● **Monasterio de Santa Catalina de Sena** (Mon-Sat 8.30am-5.30pm; s/8) This small convent is a beautiful building but the contents of the museum, a handful of dioramas and a look at the day-to-day lives of the nuns who lived here, are relatively disappointing in comparison.

● **Museo de Casa Concha** (Mon-Sat 9am-6pm; s/20) This is perhaps the most fascinating museum in the city – and the most relevant for those about to embark on the Inca Trail. Covering two floors of a large colonial building, the 'Shell House' is now the repository for some of the 4000 artefacts removed from Machu Picchu by Hiram Bingham and shipped back to the USA. After years of high-profile petitioning to Yale University, many of these pieces were returned in 2012 and can now be seen in Peru for the first time.

A series of rooms around a large courtyard contain historical photographs and original documentation of early exploration and the approach to Machu Picchu, a giant-scale diorama of the site complete with narration, pottery and ceramics found there and a number of objects connected to daily life at Machu Picchu. There's also an examination of the practice of cranial deformation, an examination of the Incas' interest in archaeoastronomy and the way that they understood the seasons and skies, a fascinating quipu and a selection of pre-Inca musical instruments. Most of the exhibits are described in Spanish. In addition there's a very impressive interactive **3D tour of Machu Picchu** that you can control, bringing up photographs taken by Bingham and a commentary on what you're seeing.

● **Iglesia de San Blas** (Mon-Sat 8am-6pm, Sun 2-6pm; free with CRA ticket, see box p150; otherwise s/10, s/5 students) This simple adobe church contains a breathtakingly intricate carved cedar-wood pulpit dating from the 17th century, the detail of which includes an angel, a sun-disc, some faces and bunches of grapes. At the top is St Paul with his foot on a skull believed to be that of the craftsman responsible for the carving. The church also has a baroque gold-leafed altar. Don't forget to climb the stairs for the view over San Blas.

North of Plaza de Armas [see map pp156-7 & map p164]

● **Iglesia de San Cristóbal** (Mon-Sat 8am-6pm; Sun 2-6pm; free with CRA ticket, see box p150; otherwise s/10, s/5 students) Set high above Cusco, this church is thought to have been built on the site of the palace of Manco Capac, the first Inca. Surrounded by a massive Inca stone wall, the church was built by Paullu Inca as a means of demonstrating his new Christian faith.

● **Museo Inka** (Mon-Sat 8am-6.30pm; s/10) This impressive colonial house stands on Inca foundations, on the corner of Ataud and Tucumán. Inside is a massive stairway, guarded by sculptures of mythical creatures, and an attractive courtyard.

The building, originally belonging to Admiral Don Francisco Maldonado, was badly damaged by the 1650 earthquake but was rebuilt and is still a striking structure. Most importantly, the museum houses the finest collection of Inca artefacts in the city and the largest collection of Inca objects in the world. Metal- and gold-work, jewellery, pottery, ceramics, textiles and paintings are all on display and laid out in an easy-to-follow and informative fashion and although the English-language explanations are sometimes a little basic, and sometimes non-existent, this is nevertheless an excellent overview of the Incas' world. There is also a reconstructed burial chamber containing several mummies.

High-quality, expensive weavings are for sale in the courtyard of the house and you can often find craftsmen working here on the beautiful fabrics.

● **Palacio Nazarenas Hotel** This building, on Plazoleta de las Nazarenas, was formerly called **House of the Serpents** because of the snakes carved into the door lintels. The house is reputed to have once belonged to the man responsible for stealing the golden disc of the sun from the Coricancha. Garcilaso de la Vega describes how he lost it:

> 'When the Spaniards entered Cuzco, this likeness of the Sun, as the result of a division of property, fell into the hands of one of the early conquistadors, who was a man of noble birth by the name of Mancio Serra de Leguisamo, whom I knew very well before I came to Spain. He was a great gambler and he had no sooner acquired this treasure than he gambled and lost it in one night; and we might even say, echoing Father Acosta, that this is the origin of the expression "to gamble the Sun before it rises".' **Garcilaso Inca de la Vega** *The Royal Commentaries of the Incas* (1609)

These days, it has been converted into a luxurious hotel (Palacio Nazarenas; see p169). It's possible to step inside even if you aren't a guest, in order to admire the original features of this exceptional building. Through the imposing stone doorway is a tiled reception and a courtyard ringed by original frescoes that tell a series of stories and depict nuns, bullfights and daily life. Also ask to see the library and its stock of original books.

● **Museo de Arte Precolombino/Casa Cabrera** (Daily 8am-10pm; s/20, student s/10) This small yet fascinating museum is set within the grand, spacious confines of the Earl of Cabrera's colonial mansion. Cabrera was responsible for founding Ica on Peru's coast. *(cont'd on p158)*

CUSCO

CUSCO

Mercado
San Blas

Pumacaccha

San
Blas

Plazoleta
San Blás

Carmen B

Chihuampata

Kiskapata

Tandapata

Tandapata

Tullumayo

Choquechaca

Angelitos

Atocsaicuchi

Carmen Alto

Museo de Arte
Religioso y Palacio
del Arzobispal

Siete Angelitos

Sta Mónica

San Agustín

Museo de
Casa Concha

Pumacurco

Museo de Arte
Precolombino/
Casa Cabrera

Plazoleta
de las
Nazarenas

Hatun Rumiyoc

Palacio

Calle Herrajes

Santa
Catalina

Ese

Arco Iris

Purgatorio

Tucumán

Museo
del Pisco

Loreto

Arequipa

Waynapata

Ataud

Iglesia de
Jesús María

La Catedral
El Triunfo

La
Compañía

Museo
de Historia
Natural

San
Cristóbal

Suecia

Resbalosa

Procuradores

Triunfo

Plateros

Plaza
de Armas

See 'Plaza de
Armas area' map

Corcalle

Suecia

Tigre

Plaza
Regocijo

Espinar

Garcilaso

Heladeros

Mantas

iPerú office

To Sacsayhuaman
(see 'Around Cusco' map)

Tecsecocha

Town
Hall

DRC

To Sacsayhuaman
and other local Inca sites
(see 'Around Cusco' map)

Sta Teresa

S Juan de Dios

Siete Cuartones

Santa
Teresa

Teatro

Arones

Granada

Tordo

Saphi

Amargura

Museo Histórico
Regional y
Casa Garcilaso

Tandapata de Pôquen

Meloc

Museo y Convento
de San Francisco

Nueva Alta

Nueva Baja

Sta Ana

Arcopata

Calle Fierro

★ trailblazer

0   100   200m

Cusco

Colla Calle

Arcopunco

Av Garcilaso

Av Huascar

Pachacutec

95

Plaza Limacpampa

Tullumayo

90

Av Tullumayo

Buses for Sacred Valley (Pisac/Urubamba)

Huanchac station

To Terminal Terrestre & airport, 5km

Coricancha & Santo Domingo

Ahuacpinta

San Agustín

91

92

93

Coricancha Museum

Romeritos

89

Av el Sol

Post Office

Scotiabank

P Castillo

Arequipa

Matará

Av Pardo

Av Regional

Loreto

Marun

94

SBS Bookshop

Centenario

San Andrés

Cuichipunco

iPerú office & OFEC

Av el Sol

Colectivo Station

Camen Quicllo

Ayacucho

Buses for Sacred Valley (Chinchero/Urubamba)

La Merced

San Bernardo

Pavitos

Av Grau

Instituto Nacional de Cultura

Quera

Lechugal

Belén

Tecte

3 Cruces de Oro

Mesón de la Estrella

87

88

Cruz Verde

Pera

Concebidayoc

Calle Nueva

Plaza San Francisco

Sta Clara

Santa Clara

Mercado San Pedro

Ccascaparo

Molleistea

Desamparados

Tupac Amaru

San Pedro

San Pedro station

Trains no longer operate from here

Unión

Chaparro

CUSCO

(cont'd from p155) The museum covers the artistic achievements of the various ancient Peruvian cultures and houses a superb collection of artefacts from the Moche, Chimú, Paracas, Nazca and Inca cultures. Dating from 1250 to 1532, these archaeological treasures include carvings, ceramics, and gold- and silver-work, all of which are superbly lit and well presented with both English and Spanish text explaining what you are looking at.

● **Hotel Monasterio** This hotel (see p168), Cusco's finest, was converted from the elegant old **Seminary of San Antonio Abad**. Although a very upmarket establishment, it is possible to visit if you drop in for a beer at the bar. Once through the Inca-colonial doorway you look onto a spacious courtyard, which is only slightly spoiled by the glassed-in cloisters surrounding them.

PRACTICAL INFORMATION
Arrival
As a result of its position high in the Andes, **you will need to take a couple of days to acclimatise** once you have arrived in Cusco, especially if you arrive from Lima or other low-lying places. Do not attempt anything too strenuous whilst your body adjusts. Acclimatisation (see p120) is quicker if you do not eat or drink excessively.

By air Aeropuerto Alejandro Velasco Astete (information ☎ 222611) lies 5km from the main Plaza de Armas at Quispiquilla. A 10-minute taxi ride will cost about s/10-15 from the airport car park or about half that from the street outside as drivers here don't have to pay the waiting fee levied by the car park. *Colectivos* to the centre cost even less and can also be hailed from the street outside the airport. You could walk to the plaza in around an hour but it's a bit of a schlep and not to be advised after dark.

By rail Trains from Juliaca and Puno arrive at **Huanchac station**, at the south-eastern end of Av El Sol, about a 20-minute walk from Plaza de Armas. Taxis from outside the station cost s/5 to the centre of town.

Trains to and from Machu Picchu or Ollantaytambo operated by PeruRail arrive and depart from **Poroy**, over a hill from Cusco on the road to Urubamba, about a 30-minute drive from Plaza de Armas. Those run by Inca Rail start and finish at Ollantaytambo; see p203.

Sadly trains no longer operate from Cusco's historic San Pedro station.

By bus Long-distance buses arrive and depart from **Terminal Terrestre** on Av Vallejo Santoni, close to the giant statue of Pachacutec, south-east of the city centre. A taxi from here to Plaza de Armas costs around s/5 whilst a colectivo to the centre will charge s/1.

Orientation
Cusco is divided into five districts, each centred on a square or temple. At the heart of the city lies Plaza de Armas. The majority of sights are within easy walking distance of here. South of the Plaza, Av El Sol runs past Coricancha. Heading uphill and south-west from Av El Sol there are Plaza San Francisco, Mercado San Pedro and Iglesia de Santa Clara. One block west of Plaza de Armas is Plaza Regocijo which has Inca origins and contains some of the city's finest mansions and municipal palaces.

From the south-east corner of Plaza de Armas, Calle Triunfo climbs steeply through a stunning Inca-walled street to the artisan quarter of San Blas, centred on an attractive church. Uphill and north-west from Plaza de Armas, Calle Plateros climbs towards the Inca fortress Sacsayhuaman and the giant statue of Christ that overlooks the city.

Incidentally, don't be fooled by the road names. For example, everyone may know the name of the major thoroughfare heading south from near the Plaza de Armas as Av El Sol – but that's not the name that you'll find on the road-sign for at least part of its length, which is

CUSCO MAP KEY – see previous pages for map

Where to stay

1 El Balcón Inn
2 Loki Backpackers Hostel
3 Niños (Meloc)
4 Niños (Fierro)
5 Ecopackers
6 Hoteles Costa del Sol Ramada Cusco
7 Hotel Royal Inka II
8 Hotel Royal Inka I
12 Casa Andina Classic Cusco Plaza
13 WalkOn Inn
14 Hostal Corihuasi
16 Hostel Backpackers Felix
19 Sungate Hostels
22 Del Prado Inn
23 Hostal Suecia I
25 Hostal Resbalosa
26 Albergue Municipal
27 Inkaterra La Casona
28 Fallen Angel
30 Casa Cartagena
31 Hotel Arqueologo
32 Hostal Rumi Punku
33 Los Apus Hotel y Mirador
34 Palacio Nazarenas
37 Hostal El Grial
38 Casa de Campo Hostal
39 Hospedaje Familiar Kuntur Wasi
40 Sunset House Flashpackers
41 Pensión Alemana
43 Pisko & Soul Hostel
44 Quinta San Blas
47 Tierra Viva San Blas
48 Amazon Hostal
49 El Mirador del Inka
50 Illa Hotel
53 Casona los Pleiades
60 Antigua Casona San Blas
61 Casa Andina Classic Cusco San Blas
63 Boutique Hotel Casa San Blas
66 Amaru Hostal
72 Hotel Monasterio
77 Hostal Monasterio del Inka
79 Emperador Plaza Hotel
80 Casa Andina Classic Cusco Catedral
83 JW Marriott El Convento Cusco
84 Hotel Ruinas
85 Novotel Cusco
86 Albergue Casa Campesina
87 Pariwana Hostel
88 The Point
91 Casa Andina Classic Cusco Koricancha
92 Casa Andina Private Collection Cusco
93 Hotel Libertador Palacio del Inka
94 Maison de la Jeunesse

Where to eat and drink

9 Chicha
10 El Truco
11 Valeriana
15 Los Perros
17 La Chupitería
18 Indigo Bar
20 Qucharitas
21 Tapa Tapa y ¡Olé¡
24 Organika
28 Fallen Angel
29 MAP Café
35 Waykis & Punchay
36 Le Buffet Francés
42 Juanito's
45 La Boheme
46 La Casa Del Cheesecake
51 Cuse
52 Eusebio & Maniol
54 Korma Sutra
55 Tacomania
56 Yunsa
57 La Paccha
58 Meeting Place
59 Green Point
62 Pachapapa
64 El Buen Pastor
65 Macondo
67 Granja Heidi
68 Jack's
69 La Mariana
70 Cholos
71 Cocoliso
73 Inkazuela
74 Uchu Peruvian Steakhouse
75 Marcelo Batata
76 Cicciolina & A Mi Manera
78 La Bodega 138
81 Shaman Vegan Raw
82 El Encuentro
89 Le Soleil
90 Qosqo Maki
95 La Cusqueñita

Mut'uchaka; and this is not the only example. Ask people where Avenida (Av) El Sol is and everyone will know where you're talking about, whereas ask people where Mut'uchaka is and you'll probably get a blank look.

Getting around

The centre of Cusco is fairly compact and easy to explore on foot, though for trips after dark or longer journeys consider taking a **taxi**. These can be found throughout the city, particularly around Plaza de Armas. They ought to charge a flat fare of s/4-5, rising to s/5-6 after 9pm, for journeys in the city, but if they suspect you've just arrived or aren't on the ball they may try to charge extra. For longer journeys always agree a price in advance as the cabs don't have meters. In the past there have been reports of taxi drivers robbing people though we haven't heard of such incidents happening for a while now.

If you are uncomfortable flagging one down in the street, ask your hotel to arrange a taxi or call one of the licensed operators: Aló Cusco (☎ 222222) and Radio Taxi (☎ 222000) are both reliable and have good reputations. Alternatively, catch a communal **colectivo**, which will inevitably be cheaper but less comfortable, and which aren't allowed within two blocks of Plaza de Armas.

There is also a hop-on, hop-off tourist **tram** service, Tranvia (☎ 223840) which operates on a 90-minute city circuit (s/20) beginning and ending in Plaza de Armas; services depart around half-a-dozen times daily.

Those on a larger budget may choose to **hire a car**. Most agencies have an office at the airport although some, including

Hertz (☎ 445 5716; Av El Sol 808) can be found in the city centre.

Tourist information

There is a very helpful **iPerú** tourist information office (☎ 23 7364; 24hr helpline ☎ 01 574 8000, 🖳 www.peru.travel/en; Mon-Sat 6am-5pm) in the arrivals hall of the airport, which provides tourist information and assistance. Free maps are also available. In the city centre, **Dircetur** (Mon-Sat 8am-8pm, Sun 8am-1pm), which is more city-centric, is on Av Mantas.

Peru Travel Aid (☎ 94-526-0109, 🖳 perutravelaid.org) is a not-for-profit organisation started by travellers, for travellers, that can provide free assistance should something go wrong on your trip (altitude sickness, lost documents, etc).

OFEC (see box p150) is at Av El Sol 103.

Entrance tickets for Machu Picchu (see p318) are available from the **Dirección Regional de Cultura** (**DRC**; ☎ 582030; Mon-Sat 7am-8pm) office on Calle Garcilaso, west of Plaza de Armas.

Banks and cambios

There are many **banks** strung out along Av El Sol. These all have **ATMs** with 24hr access and security protection, from which you can withdraw US$ and soles. Queues are common and service can be slow. Banks typically shut 1-3pm.

In addition to the ATMs at the banks, there are some on Plaza de Armas, Av La Cultura and in the San Blas district. Be warned that the yellow Interbank/ GlobalNet ATMs that can be found in various popular hostels, shops and other places where tourists might need them charge commission above that which your bank

---

❏ **Word of warning**

Cusco once had a deservedly mixed reputation for robbery and while the situation has vastly improved since we first visited about 15 years ago, it pays to still be wary. The areas around the markets and the old San Pedro railway station were always the worst, particularly for pickpockets. It is still wise to take care when walking after dark, or to hail a licensed taxi. Similarly be streetwise if visiting out-of-the-way ruins, especially if going alone or late in the day.

will charge you; avoid them unless it's essential. Try to find a cashpoint that allows you to withdraw s/700 – such as the BCP cashpoints on Plaza de Armas – rather than the usual s/400, and over time you'll save yourself some money in withdrawal fees.

There are **cambios** all over Cusco, especially on the western side of Plaza de Armas, and it's difficult to pick out any one over the other. These tend to charge slightly higher commission than those on Av El Sol, the best of which is **LAC Dólar** at Av El Sol 150. **DHL/Western Union** (☎ 233214) is further down Av El Sol at No 608.

Try to save your small change and lower denomination bills as you will need these once outside Cusco, since there is usually a shortage of change in the smaller villages and people will not be able to break a large note for you.

Bookshops
Try **SBS Librería Internacional** (🖳 www.sbs.com.pe; Mon-Fri 9am-8.30pm, Sat 9.30am-1.30pm & 4-8pm), at Av El Sol 864, for a decent selection of material on Peru's history, local anthropology and archaeology – as well as a rack of English-language novels.

In San Blas, **Kuskan** on Plazoleta San Blas has a very good selection given its small size. On Plazoleta de las Nazarenas at 167B is **Hanan Pacha**, with a good selection of cookery books amongst the more ubiquitous tourist titles. Finally, where Santa Catalina Ancha bends eastwards you'll find **Librería Genesis** with a good selection of English-language books.

Communications
● **Telephone** There are public pay phones everywhere and it's easy to ring abroad with a Telefónica **phonecard** that can be bought from almost any of the small shops lining Plaza de Armas. Alternatively, you can get someone else to do it for you in one of the numerous internet cafés.
● **Post** For letters, the **correos** (post office; Mon-Sat 7.30am-8pm, Sun 8am-2pm) is on the west side of Av El Sol, No 800, on the fifth block downhill from Plaza de Armas at the junction with Av Garcilaso.

DHL/Western Union (☎ 233214) have an office at Av El Sol 608 if you want to send packages overseas.
● **Internet access** Internet cafés open and close around Cusco with alarming regularity but you're never far from one; there are a great many to choose from, the main difference being the speed of connection and other facilities on offer. The best places will also have scanners, webcams, CD burners and knowledgeable staff.

Festivals
See pp86-7 for details of the main festivals and events in Cusco.

Medical services
Hospitals: Regional (☎ 231131, 🖳 www .hospitalregionalcusco.gob.pe in emergencies), Av de la Cultura; Clinica Pardo (☎ 256976), Av de la Cultura 710; **Tourist Medical Assistance** (☎ 260101), Heladeros Street 157, offers emergency medical services, health information and legal assistance, **Pharmacies**: Boticas Arcangel, Calle Mantas 132, and Inka Farma (☎ 240167), Av El Sol 210.

Equipment rental
Equipment and trekking gear can be hired from the travel agencies along Procuradores or from a number of shops on Plateros. Make sure you check everything carefully in advance as it has been known for bits to be missing and the standard of stuff available can be pretty poor. Butane

C U S C O

❏ **Emergencies**
Fire: ☎ 103;   **Police**: ☎ 105;
Tourist Police Policía de Turismo (POLTUR; ☎ 84 235123), see box p89, have their main office on Plaza Túpac Amaru, about a 15-minute walk from Plaza de Armas. It's the first place to go if you are the victim of a crime; they are also very helpful if you lose your passport.

Few countries have a **consulate office** in Cusco; if necessary contact your embassy in Lima (see p137).

and other cooking stove fuel can also be bought from these places. To hire anything you will have to leave a deposit and maybe a copy of your passport too. **The Camping Shop** (☎ 248424), at Plateros 306, has a fair selection of equipment for sale or hire; there are a couple of other outlets on this strip too.

If you're looking to buy your kit rather than rent it, international-brand **North Face** has a couple of concessions, including one on Plaza de Armas at 194 Portal de Comercio, and another at Espinar 188; there's also **Rockford Outdoor Experience**, on the main square at Portal Carrizos 252, and **Piramide Outdoor** on Santa Catalina Ancha.

Tatoo, on Calle del Medio 130, has high-quality gear available at appropriately high prices. Big brand-name hiking, climbing and camping gear is on offer alongside the own-brand clothing.

Trekking provisions

Mercado San Pedro (San Pedro Market; see p153), opposite San Pedro station, is the best place to stock up on basic supplies.

Alternatively Orion supermarket has several branches that are convenient for Plaza de Armas, including one to the north of San Pedro market and one on Calle Meloc (opposite Niños Hotel). Alternatively try **Supermercado Gato**, next to Emperor Plaza at Santa Catalina Ancha 377.

Laundry

You won't have any trouble finding someone willing to take in your laundry for a small consideration; look out for the 'lavandería' signs in many doorways around town. The cheapest we found was opposite Loki Backpackers Hostel (s/2.5 per kg) but unless you're staying there it's a hell of an uphill walk. Most other places charge around s/3 per kg, though it can go up to s/6-10 per kilo if you hand your laundry to

your hotel reception for them to deal with it. Most places are open 7.30am-8pm.

Language courses

Peru has become an increasingly popular country in which to study Spanish. Most organisations run classes for 20 hours a week. It is cheaper to study for a longer period of time or in a group though. One-to-one sessions cost around US$10-20 whilst group classes cost US$5-10 per hour. Try **San Blas Spanish School** (🖳 www.spanish schoolperu.com), Carmen Bajo 224.

Massage

You won't need to look far to find a massage – indeed, they'll come and find you; touts advertising massages are particularly numerous on Triunfo and the main Plaza de Armas. Of these 'tourist' massages, the one with the best reputation at the time of writing is **Hampi Maki Spa**, near Piedra de los 12 Angulos at Hatun Rumiyoc 487 (the continuation of Triunfo as it heads towards San Blas, opposite the famous multi-angled stone). **Cusco Therapeutic Massage** (☎ 966145697, 🖳 www.cuscotherapeuticmas sage.com), near San Blas Market at Av Lucrepata F-21, 402, is run by expat Daniel Rowe and offers special post-trek massages that concentrate on the legs and shoulders (ie the bits that are likely to hurt!) for US$40 per hour.

WHERE TO STAY

[See map pp156-7; for the Plaza de Armas area see map p164] Cusco is extraordinarily well equipped for tourists and has an enormous number of places to stay that should suit all tastes and budgets. Whilst rates are proportionally more expensive than elsewhere in Peru, they still tend to represent remarkably good value for money.

Quoted rates also tend to be negotiable, as they are seasonally affected and driven by demand.

CUSCO

The city gets busiest during July and August and during the run-up to Inti Raymi (see p86), when rates rocket by as much as 20%, but outside of peak season you ought to be able to negotiate a good deal.

Plaza de Armas is understandably the focus for most people when looking for places to stay, but the hotels here tend to be those with the most inflated prices. Step away from the plaza, though, and there are good deals aplenty, particularly in the hilly streets that lead up to Sacsayhuaman or up towards the San Blas district.

Breakfast is not always a given so it is included in the description where it is available. It's a rare place that doesn't offer **wi-fi** now so we haven't included this in our descriptions – though if wi-fi is important to you it's always worth double-checking with the hotel before checking in, just in case.

Host Family Peru (☎ 741636, 💻 www.hostfamilyperu.com) has been set up to help people looking for accommodation with local families. **Peru Treks** (see p181) also operates an Andean homestay programme and arranges places to stay in the mountains surrounding Cusco.

Budget accommodation
There are two sorts of hostels in Cusco; the first category is more like a **'normal' hostel**, where you pay for a bed or private room; in other words it's fundamentally a place to sleep. The second sort of hostel, however, is quite a different animal. A place where you can organise tours and treks, buy bus tickets, play pool and table tennis, swap stories with your fellow trekkers while eating in the in-house café – then afterwards get drunk and dance the night away while a DJ thumps out the latest beats. In other words, these so-called **'party' hostels** can be places where sleep can be hard to come by.

Whether you stay at a party hostel or something more tranquil is, of course, entirely up to you. If you are travelling solo and want to make friends the party hostels

are great places to do so; and, indeed, some of the rooms at these places are still quiet. However, do note, too, that we know of more than one person who has missed their trek due to oversleeping as a direct result of over-indulging the night before!

'Party' hostels
● **Plaza de Armas area** A drunken stagger away from Plaza de Armas, at the top of Procuradores at Tecsecocha 171, are a couple of dirt cheap and excellent-value hostels which, despite the price, are not completely lacking in charm. The only problem is that they tend to be raucous, party-fuelled places with music blaring pretty much throughout the day in the central courtyard.

Standing opposite the top of Procuradores is *Hostel Backpackers Felix* (☎ 254327, 💻 www.cuscobackpackersfelix .com), a huge place built round a central courtyard furnished with table tennis, table football, a pool table, and a tour agency. All very good value – as long as you've got earplugs – with per person prices s/25 in a dorm, rising to s/35pp in a double with private bathroom. Breakfast is not included.

The smaller, newer and quieter of the two is *Sungate Hostels* (☎ 5956889, 💻 www.sungatehostels.com), with smart rooms with heaters and decent-sized lockers, bathrooms and a smart dining area, all built round a central courtyard. Other features include a book exchange and even oxygen. Rates start at s/33-40 for a bed in a dorm (the exact amount depending on the size of the dorm), with private double rooms s/100-120. Breakfast is not included.

The original party hostel is still going strong too. *The Point* (☎ 506698, 💻 www .thepointhostels.com), at Mesón de la Estrella 172, is part of a well-respected small chain that provides secure, clean, comfortable surroundings for backpackers at reasonable rates. The raucous home of Horny Llama Bar, this hostel revels in its reputation as one of the premier party places for backpackers. Dorms in the spacious

CUSCO

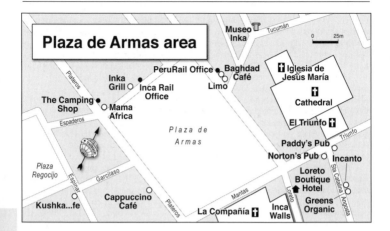

Plaza de Armas area

Museo Inka · Tucumán

0   25m

PeruRail Office · Baghdad Café

Inka Grill ○ · Inca Rail Office · Limo

The Camping Shop · ○ Mama Africa

Espaderos

Iglesia de Jesús María

Cathedral

El Triunfo

Plaza de Armas

Triunfo

Paddy's Pub
Norton's Pub · Incanto

Plaza Regocijo

Garcilaso

Espinar

Loreto Boutique Hotel

Kushka...fe · Cappuccino Café · Plateros · Mantas · Loreto

Inca Walls

Greens Organic

La Compañía

Sta Catalina Angosta

colonial house cost s/22-30 depending on the number of beds; just don't expect an early or especially quiet night.

It must be quite galling for The Point, however, to be usurped in the popularity stakes in this section, particularly by a hostel that lies less than 50m away at No 136. *Pariwana Hostel* (☎ 233571, 🖥 www.pariwana-hostel.com) boasts a really lovely courtyard and its own travel agency, arranging tours to local sights (though you can get cheaper prices elsewhere). Beds start at s/35 in a 12-bed dorm, with private rooms s/152/182 for twin/dbl rooms.

● **San Blas area** The top choice in San Blas for budget party hostels – indeed, perhaps the best of the lot – is the rather spectacular *El Mirador del Inka* (☎ 241804, 🖥 www.elmiradordelinka.com), owned and run by the ambitious Harry. Hidden behind a rather unremarkable wooden door on Tandapata is a huge hostel with very good-value rooms built around two courtyards (s/50/60 for sgl/dbl, com; s/60/80 for sgl/dbl, att; s/70/90 for rooms with a panoramic view). What really separates this place from its competitors, however, are the communal areas, with a TV & games room with pool table and dartboard, and above that the new glass-roofed Limbus Bar with perhaps the best view of all over the city.

Spectacular. Best of all, these communal areas are separated from the rooms themselves so there's a better chance of getting a good night's sleep.

● **Plaza Regocijo** To the west of the main plaza there are fewer options, but still some gems to be found. Our favourite is *Ecopackers* (☎ 231800, 🖥 www.ecopackersperu.com), Calle Santa Teresa 375. Less laid-back than some of the crusties' crash-pads in the city but with helpful staff, lots of facilities including a travel agency, and an excellent central location, it is housed in what was once one of the first colonial houses in the city. With hot power showers, lockers with chargers integrated within them (a great idea!), book exchange, satellite TV and a private cinema area, it really is a decent option. Rates (all including breakfast) are slightly more expensive than other hostels, with dorm beds US$15 in a 15-bed dorm, rising to US$23.50 to sleep in a 4-bed dorm. Private rooms are US$48.50 (dbl, com).

Loki Backpackers Hostel (☎ 243705, 🖥 www.lokihostel.com/en/cusco), Cuesta Santa Ana 601, is a historic viceroy's residence transformed into a hairy backpacker's hangout, with mixed and single-sex dorms, a shared kitchen, a bar sporting superb views over the city and a lively (at night) if laid-back (during the day) atmosphere. Surprisingly, despite its deserved reputation as the No 1 party place, it is actually extremely efficiently run, with guests wearing wristbands that are scanned everytime they purchase something and then presented with the total bill on departure. Rates are s/28 for a bed in a 12- or 14-bed dorm, s/32 in an 8-bed dorm, s/36 in a 6-bed dorm and s/42 for a bed in the en suite 6-bed dorm. Private rooms are s/100 (twin, com), s/115 (sgl/dbl, att), or it's s/160 for one with a panoramic view.

Regular hostels
● **Plaza de Armas area** A good budget bet in a central location is the hostel *Albergue Municipal* (☎ 252506, 🖳 albergue@municusco.gob.pe), at Kiskapata 240, which is spanking clean, has a café and good views from a sunny concrete balcony, though it's largely reserved for groups. The price can't be faulted at just s/15 per person in the 4- to 8-bed dorms, rising to s/40 for a double room.

Also highly recommended is *Hostal Resbalosa* (☎ 224839, 🖳 www.hostalresbalosa.com), Calle Resbalosa 494, which has a bright friendly courtyard, awesome 180° views over the town towards Nevado Ausangate, and costs just s/25/30/60 (dorm/sgl/dbl, com; inc breakfast). The rooms with private facilities are around s/20 more. Avoid the rooms around the entrance, which are older and noisier. It's a great place; indeed, the only fault we can find with this place is that it's been discovered by the tour operators, who often take over the whole hostel; that and the fact that taxis can only reach within about 100m of the hostel as it is set on a steep, cobbled, pedestrian-only street.

Other places worth looking at in this area include *Hostal Suecia I* (☎ 233282, 🖳 www.hostalsuecia1.com), at Calle Suecia 332. The plain rooms surrounding the courtyard cost s/32-42/43/51 (sgl/dbl/tpl, att) with breakfast included – which represents good value considering the location.

Further away from the square and the noise, at the top of the hill near San Cristóbal on a corner that catches the sun,

WalkOn Inn (☎ 235065, 🖳 www.walkoninn.com.pe), Calle Suecia 504, has great views, a family atmosphere and smart internal décor. Dorm beds are s/25 whilst private rooms cost s/70 (sgl/dbl, com) or s/90 (sgl/dbl, att). Breakfast is included – making this great value.

● **San Blas area** *Sunset House Cusco Flashpackers Hostel* (☎ 237370, 🖳 www.sunsethousehostel.com), at Tandapata No 353-B, is one of the few in San Blas with dormitory accommodation, with beds in an 8-bed dorm just s/30 (s/35 in a 4-bed dorm); their private rooms with attached bathroom are a tad overpriced at s/150.

If it's privacy you're after when it comes to choosing your room, you're better off looking up the road at *Hospedaje Familiar Kuntur Wasi* (☎ 227570), Tandapata 352A, which is run by a very considerate, friendly local family. Regular hot water, access to a decent kitchen and the great atmosphere make this a good choice; it will only set you back s/45 per person in a room with shared bathroom, or it's s/80/120 (sgl/dbl) for rooms with private bathrooms.

Another favourite in this area is *Pisko & Soul Hostel* (☎ 221998, 🖳 www.piskoandsoulhostel.com) at the top of Calle Carmen Alto at No 294. When researching this book we found it to be a favourite with solo travellers, particularly female travellers. We have no idea why but it's certainly a safe and friendly place with pleasant communal areas, wi-fi, towels and heaters in every room and an excellent central location near Plaza San Blas. Dorm rooms start at US$11 per bed, with singles US$23, twins US$35.

● **Elsewhere** *Maison de la Jeunesse* (☎ 235617, 🖳 hostellingcusco@hotmail.com) is down a small side street, 5 Pasaje Grace, off Av El Sol, opposite the Coricancha. Affiliated to Hostelling International (🖳 www.hihostels.com), this is a good-quality hostel with kitchen facilities, communal rooms and a balcony. Dorms cost US$9 whilst private rooms start from US$20/28 (sgl/dbl, att).

CUSCO

Mid-range accommodation

● **Plaza de Armas area** *Loreto Boutique Hotel* (see map p164; ☎ 226352, 🖥 www.loretoboutiquehotel.com; US$85/ 105/125 sgl/dbl/tpl, att), Calle Loreto 115, deserves a mention because some of the rather dark rooms have genuine Inca walls; it's also very conveniently located, right by the plaza, down an alley adjacent to La Compañía.

Much better value is *Hostal Corihuasi* (☎ 232233, 🖥 www.corihuasi.com), Calle Suecia 561, which charges US$56/68/80 (sgl/dbl/tpl, att, breakfast). This labyrinthine, larger hotel set on the slopes north of the plaza is favoured by some adventure-tour companies and can get fully booked easily. The good-sized rustic rooms are equipped with alpaca blankets and woven textiles. Try to get the room directly above reception (No 1), which has the best view. The rate includes complimentary pick up from the airport.

If you fancy something a little more central there's *Emperador Plaza Hotel* (☎ 261733, 🖥 www.emperadorplaza.com), Santa Catalina Ancha 377. It's clean, has cable TV in the rooms and costs from US$80/90/120 (sgl/dbl/tpl, att, breakfast); the balcony rooms are the best.

Another good option is *Del Prado Inn* (☎ 224442, 🖥 www.delpradoinn.com), Calle Suecia 310, a smart hotel charging US$75/110-130/135 (sgl/dbl/tpl, att) depending on whether the room has a balcony or not (the balcony rooms can be noisy though); the room with Jacuzzi is US$150. You can save 15% by booking online. Towards the top end of this price bracket, the superb central location can't be faulted and the dining room's original Inca walls are gobsmacking – but we found it a tad charmless otherwise.

● **San Blas area** There are numerous options in this bracket in this area.

Amaru Hostal (☎ 225933, 🖥 www .amaruhostal.com), Cuesta de San Blas 541, is an old house with a sociable green courtyard filled with geraniums in rusty cans. Some of the rooms off the courtyard boast original Inca walls. It also has a free book exchange, piano and oxygen. They charge US$50/60/80 (sgl/dbl/tpl, att).

On Carmen Bajo at No 243, amongst the vegan restaurants, language schools and yoga centres, is the brand spanking new *Antigua Casona San Blas* (☎ 200700, 🖥 www.antiguacusco.com) with some lovely carved wooden furniture and reasonable rates (US$98/113 sgl/dbl, att, with breakfast); until it gets a regular customer base you should be able to negotiate even better prices.

Tandapata is the main street for accommodation in San Blas, with some splendid places, many with excellent views. If you're after a pleasant little bed and breakfast joint try *Casona los Pleiades* (☎ 506430, 🖥 www.casona-pleiades.com), Calle Tandapata 116; it has compact, tidy rooms in a renovated colonial house overlooking the city and costing US$77 per room (att, breakfast), or US$82 if you want one with a view. The staff here are helpful, friendly and keen to offer advice.

At Calle Tandapata 660, *Amazon Hostal* (☎ 236770, 🖥 www.amazonhotel cusco.com) is a bright, friendly place run by Amazon Trails Peru (a trekking and tour agency, see p178). It offers reasonable rooms for s/99/136/186 (sgl/dbl/tpl, com, breakfast) and has a garden and terrace with panoramic views where you can unwind after your trek.

On Carmen Alto there are three very smart boutique hotels vying for your custom. Tasteful and replete with all mod-cons, they nevertheless lack the panoramic views of those further up the hill; those smug budget travellers on Tandapata must be snorting into their *mate de coca*. Newest among them is *Quinta San Blas* (central reservations ☎ 1-421 7790, 🖥 www.ananay hotels.com), where the rooms (all doubles or twins) are equipped with the finest linen bedsheets, radiators, organic body lotions in the attached bathrooms and cable TV, with a buffet breakfast thrown in as well. The price for all this is US$90-120, with no discount for single travellers.

Moving towards the square, *Tierra Viva Cusco San Blas* (☎ 233070, 🖥 www .tierravivahoteles.com) is actually one of no less than five hotels owned by the Tierra Viva chain in the city. Beyond the glass doors are 24 super-sumptuous rooms surrounding the courtyard of this old colonial residence, with all the facilities you'd expect. Prices hover at about the US$90-130 mark. Nearest the square, *Illa Hotel* (☎ 253396, 🖳 www.illahotel.com) stands apart as being the only one of the three that's not part of a chain, though in other respects it's similar to the other two, with lovely, facility-filled rooms surrounding the courtyard of what was once an old colonial residence. Rates are around US$99/129/169 (dbl/tpl/suite).

On the other side of the street, the rooms at *Hostal El Grial* (☎ 223012, 🖳 www.hostalelgrial.com), Carmen Alto 112, are modern and well-kept, as is the cosy lounge. Rates are US$37/57/77 (sgl/dbl/tpl, att, breakfast) in high season, with low season prices about US$7 lower.

Pensión Alemana (☎ 226861, 🖳 www.hotel-cuzco.com), Calle Tandapata 260, is a Swiss-German hostel whose clean, European décor looks as if it would be more at home in the Alps. Popular with European travellers, it is a comfortable, attractive place to stay with good heating, cable TV, safes for your valuables and oxygen for those who are really struggling with the altitude. What's more, at US$63/70 (sgl/dbl att) during the low season (add US$5 for rooms that take advantage of the panoramic view, and US$9 more during the high season) it shouldn't break the bank either.

Hotel Rumi Punku (☎ 221102, 🖳 www.rumipunku.com), Choquechaca 339, is instantly identifiable because of the giant Inca stonework around the main door. This stylish colonial house has good-quality rooms costing US$95-110/110-130/130-170 (sgl/dbl/tpl, att, breakfast) depending on the size of room and season. Suites cost US$200. There is also a rooftop terrace as well as attractive gardens and the staff are particularly helpful.

For those who want to get away from it all, *Casa de Campo Hostal* (☎ 244404, 🖳 www.hotelcasadecampo.com), at the very northern end of Calle Tandapata (No

298) in San Blas, is just delightful. Built on a slope overlooking the town, the rooms and terrace are simply gorgeous, the location peaceful, and they'll even throw in an airport pick up if you book in advance. The rooms start at US$60/70/100 (sgl/dbl/junior suite), though bargaining is distinctly possible.

● **Plaza Regocijo area** One of the most impressive hotels in this category is *El Balcón Inn* (☎ 236738, 🖳 www.balconcusco.com), Tambo de Montero 222, housed in a restored pre-colonial house dating back to 1630. All 16 rooms are en suite, many with magnificent views of the city, and the staff are incredibly friendly. It's a bit of a climb to get here, but it's worth every step: room rates are US$59 on the 1st floor, US$79 on the view-tastic 2nd floor (all att, with breakfast), with suites US$129-149; though prices can be lower on their website.

● **Elsewhere** If you're looking for somewhere south of the plaza consider tranquil *Albergue Casa Campesina* (☎ 233466), Av Tullumayo 274. It is a pleasant hostel with rooms costing s/110/145/160 (sgl/dbl/tpl, com). The money generated here goes to support the Casa Campesina organisation that in turn works to promote and help local campesino communities. The **Store of the Weavers** is on the same site.

North of the plaza two places worth looking at are run by **Niños Unidos Peruanos Foundation** (🖳 www.ninoshotel.com), which was established by a Dutch couple to support neglected and underprivileged street kids; the couple have adopted a dozen street children themselves. Both of their places are called *Niños Hotel* (☎ 231424); the first is at Calle Meloc 442, a 17th-century colonial house which has been converted into a stylish, spotless place to stay, with gorgeous rooms set around a pretty courtyard. Service is fabulous and the breakfast is sumptuous though it costs extra. The second, at Calle Fierro 476, a little further from the centre, follows a similar design. Rates in both are US$55 (sgl/dbl, att) and US$25/50 (sgl/dbl, com). The proceeds from both are used to fund the charity.

CUSCO

Hostal Monasterio del Inka (☎ 431397) behind Museo Arzobispal, is a smart and tidy little place in a quiet yet very centrally located passage, Calle Herrajes, Pasaje Inka Roca 116. The rooms, all en suite, come with the usual mod-cons including breakfast – but perhaps the best feature is not within the hotel at all, but rather its position opposite a prime piece of original Inca wall. All in all, fairly priced at US$40/50 (sgl/dbl, att).

Expensive accommodation
● Plaza de Armas area *Hotel Ruinas* (☎ 260644, 🖳 www.hotelruinas.com), Calle Ruinas 472, is a well-sited place popular with business travellers and tour groups that has little real character although the rooms are spacious and well presented. Those with outside views are the best. It is well run; rates are US$110/150 (sgl/dbl, att, breakfast), with bargaining for cheaper rates distinctly possible.

Nearby, *JW Marriott El Convento Cusco* (☎ 582200, 🖳 www.jwmarriottcus co.com), Esquina de la Calle Ruinas 432 y San Agustín, is a beautiful place built, as its name suggests, in a former convent, with exquisite décor that always feels livelier and more atmospheric than other places in a similar price bracket. Rooms are around US$180-290 for a double, though the cheaper places tend to be in low season only.

Hoteles Costa del Sol Ramada Cusco (Lima ☎ 252330, 🖳 www.costadelsolperu .com/cusco), Santa Teresa 344, was once the colonial home of the Marqués de Picoaga and remains a sumptuous place to stay. The large contemporary and colonial double rooms around the attractive, shady courtyard of this fine building cost upwards of US$199/219 (sgl/dbl att).

● San Blas *Hotel Arqueologo* (☎ 232522, 🖳 www.hotelarqueologo.com), Calle Pumacurco 408, is named after the Inca stonework in the street leading to the entrance. A favourite with the French, it's pleasant enough and the inner courtyard and fireplace lounge are great places to hang out; prices range from US$74 to US$139. Similarly priced but better value

is *Boutique Hotel Casa San Blas* (☎ 237900, 🖳 www.casasanblas.com), Tocuyeros 566; it was Cusco's first boutique hotel. Set in an 18th-century colonial mansion and centred round a courtyard are some spacious but simple rooms costing US$136 (sgl/dbl, att, breakfast), rising to US$198-240 for the suites. Service here is polished and personalised.

Also worth a look is *Los Apus Hotel y Mirador* (☎ 264243, 🖳 www.losapushotel .com), at Atocsaycuchi 515, an atmospheric if rather cramped Swiss-run establishment full of distinctive features, varnished wood and classy furnishings. The best views are from the breakfast lookout on the top floor. Prices start at around US$80 (sgl/dbl, att) in the low season.

Many of Cusco's finest hotels can be found in this area. *Novotel Cusco* (☎ 5810303, 🖳 www.novotel.com), Calle San Agustín 239, has evolved from the earthquake-damaged ruins of the home of the conquistador Miguel Sanchez Ponce and now includes elegant stone archways, a glass-roofed courtyard and a central fountain. The rates start from US$90 (sgl/dbl, att) if booked online, around US$145/155 (sgl/dbl, att, breakfast) otherwise.

Once the stand-out hotel in Cusco, *Hotel Monasterio* (☎ 604000, 🖳 www .monasteriohotel.com), Calle Palacio 140, Plazoleta de las Nazarenas, remains incredibly impressive but is no longer alone in this category. The hotel is a sensitive conversion of the old Seminary of San Antonio Abad (see p158) that retains a sense of its roots and original purpose. Along with everything you'd expect from an international five-star hotel it also has a gilded baroque chapel, peaceful courtyards, elegant cloisters and oxygen-enriched air in the rooms (additional US$30). Being one of Cusco's finest hotels it is not cheap – US$757-880 (dbl, att, breakfast, suites US$999-2657). You may be able to negotiate a better rate – but if you can afford these prices in the first place, would you need to?

While the Monastery used to be the best hotel in the city, these days it's not even the best on the plaza. Next door, at

Plazoleta de las Nazarenas 144, stands *Palacio Nazarenas* (☎ 458222, 🖥 www .palacionazarenas.com), which would provide some healthy competition to the Monasterio were it not for the fact that they're both now owned by the same chain, Belmond. History is superimposed on history in this luxurious hotel inside a converted colonial building (see p155). The original courtyard and many features remain, including a beautiful set of frescoes from the 18th century. Amidst the labyrinthine interior is a secret garden, spa, swimming pool and several herb gardens plus an 18th-century library complete with original books. The Palacio and Nazarenas suites are the finest, with stunning architectural elements, all mod-cons and good views. Prices start at around US$1000 and climb to around US$3500 for the Palacio suite.

A little more affordable is *Casa Cartagena* (☎ 224356, 🖥 www.casacartagena.com), at Pumacurco 336, on the street leading away from Plazoleta de las Nazarenas. Another sympathetically restored colonial mansion, it has original frescoes and balconies but also Italian design touches with pieces of sculpture that stand up to 2m high, a pool, spa and flagship Royal Suite that includes a giant imported Italian marble Jacuzzi. Rates start at about US$300 if booking online, rising to US$1810 for the Royal Suite. Additional oxygen is US$70 for 24 hours.

If it's cool you're after, try *Fallen Angel* (☎ 258184, 🖥 www.fallenangelincusco.com) in the corner of Plazoleta de las Nazarenas (No 221). Best known as a bar (see Bars and nightlife), the venue is also a guesthouse with four or five uniquely designed rooms, costing US$350-400, which have an eclectic, contemporary style; some will find this hotel achingly hip, others will think that it's just trying way, way too hard. We preferred *Inkaterra La Casona* (☎ 184234, 🖥 www.inkaterra.com), next door, said to be Cusco's first boutique hotel (though Boutique Hotel Casa San Blas, see opposite, makes the same boast). Set in a 16th-century manor house, its 11 rooms, all suites, have some beautiful touches (just look at the ornately carved

doors, for example) and, on the whole, it just feels a deal more classy than its neighbour. Rates start at about US$838 for the junior suites, rising to over US$1000.

● **Plaza Regocijo area** *Hotel Royal Inka I* (central reservations ☎ 263276, hotel ☎ 223876, 🖥 www.royalinkahotel .pe), Plaza Regocijo 299, is built on the foundations of Pachacutec's palace and has front rooms with colonial furnishings overlooking the plaza as well as a bar and restaurant. Rates (US$99/123 sgl/dbl, att, breakfast) depend on the season. It's slightly better than its similarly priced sister, *Hotel Royal Inka II* (hotel ☎ 222284), which is just up the road at Santa Teresa 335, and has a sauna and Jacuzzi – as well as an impressive mosaic in the central lobby.

Casa Andina (🖥 www.casa-andina .com) is part of an upmarket Peruvian chain. There are five hotels in Cusco: *Classic Cusco Catedral* (☎ 233661) at Santa Catalina Angosta 149, close to the cathedral; *Classic Cusco Plaza* (☎ 231733), Portal Espinar 142, between Plaza de Armas and Plaza Regocijo; *Classic Cusco Koricancha* (☎ 252633), San Agustín 371, near to the Coricancha; and *Classic Cusco San Blas* (☎ 263694), Chihuampata 278, in San Blas. The flagship branch, *Private Collection Cusco* (☎ 232610), Plazoleta Limacpampa Chico 473, is in a smart colonial mansion with four courtyards, a gourmet restaurant and a pisco bar. Service is exemplary at all Casa Andina's hotels and rates (including breakfast) for the modern, well-equipped rooms start from US$91; discounts are often available.

● **Elsewhere** *Hotel Libertador Palacio del Inka* (☎ 231961, 🖥 www.libertador .com.pe), Plazoleta Santo Domingo 259, is an enormous converted colonial building, once a palace called Casa de Los Cuatro Bustos. Every bit as luxurious as the other top-end hotels around here, this award-winning place offers the full five-star package, an excellent restaurant and is a little more welcoming to dirty trekkers. It costs upward of US$832 (dbl, att, breakfast) and suites start at US$902.

CUSCO

WHERE TO EAT

There's almost too much choice in Cusco when it comes to picking a place to eat. From cheap steaming *anticucho* barrows on the street to five-star, white-linen restaurants where you have to book in advance there's something for everyone and every budget. If you're just after a drink and a snack wander along Calle Procuradores or Calle Plateros and you'll inevitably stumble on somewhere that takes your fancy. Those staying in San Blas have a wealth of choice too, with a multitude of cafés and restaurants catering to all budgets. Many of the bars and clubs (see Bars, pp175-6) also offer food. Wi-fi, by the way, comes as standard in most of the eateries listed here.

If you regret coming to Cusco, are having a terrible time and wish you'd never set foot in the country, you can stick to the Western fast-food chains such as McDonald's, KFC, Starbucks and Subway – all of which can be found on or just off Plaza de Armas. If you choose to be even the tiniest bit adventurous, however, you won't be sorry.

Cheap eats

If you're after very cheap meals there are plenty of fixed menu places offering three courses for s/5 on Pampa del Castillo near the Coricancha or south of Plaza de Armas. One of the cheapest and most convenient places to eat is the covered **Mercado San Blas**, where sandwiches are s/1.50-6 (it's worth paying top price for 'Machu Picchu', a tower of egg, chicken, tomato, cheese and avocado; messy but oh so delicious), and you can wash it down with a pint or so of pure juice (s/3.50-6). Alternatively, you can also get a two-course meal (usually soup and a main course starting at about s/4.50) at the same place.

Mercado San Pedro (see map p157) is also a good bet, offering the finest, freshest juices squeezed in front of you, soups and main dishes in the heart of a traditional, boisterous setting. Beware though, your stomach should be attuned to local food before you go and some of the sights and smells in the market might just put you off your meal.

If this is too 'local' for you, tourist restaurants also offer a two-course lunch menu starting at around s/10-15.

Breakfast, coffee and snacks

Pretty much all the following places offer more substantial meals as well but we found that they were ideal places for a caffeine (and cake) hit. One of our favourite spots is actually a small distance from the main tourist heartland at Av Tullumayo 465. *Qosqo Maki* (⌨ www.qosqomaki.org; Mon-Sat 6.30am-9pm) is an authentic French-style bakery helping street children that boasts a fine selection of croissants, pan con chocolate, Danish pastries and other scrumptious snacks, with great juices and coffee with which to wash it all down. Note, however, that there are only four tables so get here early.

Oddly, it's not the only charitable bakery in town. On the road up to San Blas is *El Buen Pastor*, at 579 Cuesta San Blas, which has everything you could ask for from a bakery: great, great bread, good *empanadas* and fair prices. They also help to finance a home for girls from disadvantaged backgrounds.

Speaking of charities, a little way up the hill on the Plazoleta in San Blas, *Meeting Place* is a pleasant, charitable little stop where the staff are volunteers and the profits go towards various good causes. The waffle is the best in Cusco (s/8-13) and their burgers (s/15-21) are good too. You can also buy various souvenirs here including 'No soy turista' T-shirts – useful if you're fed up with being hassled by the massage touts.

Above it, on Tandapata, *La Paccha* is a popular place at lunchtime but we prefer to come here mid morning for their Salkantay-sized wedges of cake (from s/6), baked daily, and all washed down with a delicious freshly brewed coffee.

Still in San Blas, *Eusebio & Maniol*, just off the plazoleta at Calle Carmen Alto 116, is a typically tiny place on this street and offers little but tea and coffee accompanied by empanadas. But what it does, it does well, with a wide range of teas available, and coffee served in several different ways, including some laced with whisky (s/15). Further up the road, *La Boheme*, on Carmen Alto, describes itself as a 'Backpacker Creperia' and it's certainly reasonable value, with crêpes s/10-17. Very nearby, *La Casa del Cheesecake* is a typically small 'cubby-hole' of a place on Carmen Alto, with cheesecakes from s/6 a slice.

Moving back down the hill towards the main Plaza de Armas, if you don't fancy queuing at Jack's (see p174), just along the way is *La Mariana* at Calle Triunfo 370, with great coffee, superb French toast (s/14) and terrible muesli (s/14).

There are also two places on Choquechaca that share the same entrance at No 229 and the same traveller ethos too. *Punchay* is the first you come to, with good-value meals including breakfasts (s/8-12), and sandwiches (s/5-12), as well as some basic pasta dishes (s/16-17). The main reason people come here, however, is not the food but the events, such as their weekly movie (at the time of research Tuesday at 8pm), salsa lessons and Spanish classes. Behind them, *Waykiss* sells pretty standard travellers' fare (eg avocado sandwich plus a juice or coffee for s/7) in a small courtyard. Not exceptional, but popular and the pictures of pop-stars superimposed on local sights that adorn the walls is fun.

Continuing south, *Cocoliso*, on Palacio, is a nice place to take a breather and escape the hubbub, with the sun-trap courtyard a pleasant place to decompress for half an hour. The menu offers something different too, with croque monsieur (s/7), or quesadillas with guacamole (s/13), to accompany your caffeine.

At least once in your trip you should hang out at one of the 1st floor eateries on the main plaza. There are plenty of places to choose from but our favourite is *Cappuccino Café*, Portal de Comercio 141, which has three small balconies directly opposite the cathedral that overlooks Plaza de Armas. It has a relaxed atmosphere, good breakfasts and 30 different types of coffee. Larger meals are also available.

North of the square, *Qucharitas*, on Procuradores, is a colourful ice-cream, crêpe and waffle parlour (waffles s/8-14) where the ice-cream is made in front of your very eyes. Our only gripe is that it's so busy and cramped that it's not a very relaxed experience – though there is a reason for this popularity as the food is delicious.

Quite a bit further up the hill, on Resbalosa 410, *Organika* is a great spot, a lovely little place with most of the ingredients in their food sourced from their organic farm in the Sacred Valley. The food is imaginative (eg rustic pesto and chicken fettuccini s/18, shrimp salad s/15), beautifully presented, delicious and very reasonably priced.

Finally, moving further south, *Valeriana* is one of several places around Plaza Regocijo; most of the fare is unexceptional (sandwiches s/10-13, empanadas s/6-8) but it's all about sitting outside in the shade of the colonnade – and of all the eateries on this block, Valeriana is the most stylish.

Kushka...fe (🖥 www.kushkafe.pe), Calle Espinar 159, part of Plaza Regocijo, is a relaxed literary-style café where you can feel completely at ease as you enjoy a selection of pastries and a coffee, or come for the generous sandwiches, which include traditional *butifarra* (pork and sweet onion salsa sandwich), and smoked ham and chicharrón with sweet potato.

Vegetarian and vegan food

Most restaurants have some sort of vegetarian option on their menu. However, there are a couple of specialist veggie restaurants, including two on Las Ruinas. Our favourite is *El Encuentro* (🖥 www.restaurantelencuentro.blogspot.pe); it's a very popular joint and understandably so, with a wide range of good-value dishes (breakfast from s/9, soups s/9-12) and some decent veggie takes on some classic carnivore options (eg lomo saltado s/20, or a soya hamburger for s/21). If that's not hardcore enough for you, very close by, down a passage opposite Emperador Hotel, is *Shaman Vegan Raw* (Mon-Sat noon-9pm, Sun 4-8pm). This place is for those who like their food to be served straight from the ground with as little human interference as possible. Not to

CUSCO

everyone's taste, of course, though they do at least offer several dishes that you won't find anywhere else, including their 'power salad' (s/19), a combination of 19 different fruits, vegetables and nuts on one plate.

However, the vegan restaurant that draws the biggest crowds and has the most glowing reputation is *Green Point* (🖳 www .greenpointveganrestaurant.com), on Carmen Baja in San Blas. Indeed, this is one of only a handful of restaurants where you'll have to book beforehand or you may end up queueing (Jack's and Bodega 138 are two others). Their success is obvious, with a deli opened next door and a new place on Plaza San Francisco with a smaller and cheaper menu – and its own bakery. However, while there's no doubting the artistry involved in preparing the food, and some of the dishes are truly tasty (goulash s/25, mushroom risotto s/25), others are a little bland. Furthermore, the side order of smugness that comes with every dish leaves a bit of a sour taste in the mouth; make sure you don't read their mission statement on the front of their menu, or you may find yourself bringing your whole dinner back up.

Local cuisine

The following tend to be quite upmarket though you'll have no problem finding local food at local prices if you want – just head to the markets, or indeed anywhere away from the tourist heartland and you'll soon encounter lots of local restaurants.

La Cusqueñita, at Av Tullumayo 227, is a huge establishment and a great one to savour the flavours of Peru while watching one of their daily dance shows. The food is plentiful (try their guinea pig, cooked in the traditional way with head and feet all intact) and the dancing exuberant and lively. Classic Peruvian food can also be found at *Pachapapa* (🖳 www.cuscorestaurants .com), Plazoleta San Blas 120. Dishes range from commonplace but expensive roast cuy (guinea pig, s/72), to the more exotic marinated alpaca brochette with stuffed hot peppers (s/48); a very pleasant

evening can be had munching on the native wildlife. The outdoor seating around an open fire pit is a bonus too, though you may have to wait awhile for your food. If it's out of your price bracket, *Amaranto Anticuchos and Cafe*, up Carmen Alto, also offers exotic local fare, this time in kebab form (eg guinea pig kebab s/35).

Inkazuela, on swish Plazoleta de las Nazarenas, is a breath of fresh air. Given its location, they could probably charge a fortune and there would be enough people falling out of the nearby five-star hotels in blissful ignorance of the price of things who would pay it. But they don't; instead, they're a decent mid-range restaurant serving some fine and filling fare (eg home-made chilli with beef and pork for s/20) with a lovely fireplace and a good view over the square. Note it's closed on Sunday.

On Plaza de Armas, on Portal de Carnes, to the left of the cathedral as you look at it, are several 1st-floor restaurants; *Limo* (🖳 www.cuscorestaurants.com; at No 236) is a Peruvian cookery and pisco bar that rustles up a high standard Amazon fish stew (s/69). There's also a large number of pisco-based drinks to try.

Next door, *Baghdad Café* has a good balcony view over the plaza from which to enjoy baked *cuy* (s/44). It's also worth trying their pork chicharrón – pork fried in its own fat with golden potatoes and salad.

El Truco, Plaza Regocijo 261, is stylish and has good service although it is popular with tour groups who come for the generous buffet lunches and nightly folk music shows, so can be very busy. Their vegetarian jungle rice (coconut rice with tomatoes, pineapple, banana chips, cashews, ginger, coriander and chillies) is packed full of flavour. *Chicha*, on the 2nd floor here, is renowned chef Gastón Acurio's first Cusco restaurant and features his take on regional highland cooking. The results are full of bold flavours – try the river shrimp fried and served with yuca and salsa (s/40). The bar here also makes a mean pisco sour.

(Opposite) One of the many parades that take place in the Plaza de Armas, here passing in front of the impressive baroque façade of La Compañía. (Photo © Zoe Ashdown).

For traditional Peruvian fare or contemporary *Novoandina* dishes try **Inka Grill** (💻 www.cuscorestaurants.com), at Portal de Panes 115 on Plaza de Armas; it is a decent place in which to treat yourself. They try to give Peruvian dishes a contemporary twist, so you could have Novoandina dishes such as thin slices of smoked trout with capers, anchovies, white onion, olive oil, red vinegar and parmesan cheese, or a good chicken risotto with quinoa.

Around the corner at Palacio 135 is **Uchu Peruvian Steakhouse**, which serves delicious meat a myriad of ways in a fine dining surrounding. A mixed meat plate gives you a bit of beef, lamb and alpaca, although the stone-cooked alpaca tenderloin with a selection of sauces and chilli peanut mash is the standout (s/52). If you want something other than steak, there are also prawn kebabs and fish although vegetarians will have to console themselves with the extensive wine list. Further up Palacio is **Marcelo Batata** (see Bars and nightlife), which is run by the same people and has a range of contemporary Peruvian dishes, and a fine panoramic view from the roof terrace across the terracotta tiles of the city. They also run cooking classes.

For more unusual dishes try **Macondo**, at Cuesta San Blas 571, one of the coolest and campest restaurants in Cusco, and run by one of its most flamboyant citizens. The walls are decorated with regularly changing art exhibitions, sofas are made out of bedsteads and cushions are scattered on most of the surfaces. The food is contemporary Andean, Amazonian and international (eg alpaca mignon wrapped in bacon with Peruvian jacket potato, green salad and cherry tomatoes; s/38), based on local recipes that are given a twist. Desserts are first-rate and the cocktails dangerously good.

Equally good first thing in the morning is **Cicciolina**, Calle Triunfo 393. Set off the main street adjacent to a courtyard this two-storey building caters to different tastes: on the ground floor is a bakery doling out generous breakfasts and fresh, tasty pastries whilst upstairs is a highly rated sophisticated Spanish-themed restaurant that cleverly fuses Andean and Mediterranean food and styles of cooking (eg fillet of alpaca with a creamy pepper sauce with a crispy yuca soufflé and roasted tomatoes; s/49). As befits a bakery, the desserts are also excellent, and more than one expat reckons this is the finest restaurant in the city.

Next door provides some useful competition. **A Mi Manera** (💻 www.cuscorestaurant-amimanera.com) serves classy, simple dishes (eg grilled lake trout served with a smooth sweet potato purée and a Mediterranean-style tomato, caper and orange sauce, s/42) in a relaxed and friendly environment.

International food

● Burgers One of our favourite places in Cusco – and where we'd traditionally head to for a post-trek feed-up – is **Cuse** (☎ 437514) in San Blas at Calle Carmen Alto 120. The reason why is simple – the food is delicious and the portions huge! Try the 6-hour smoked rack of ribs (s/25) served with a rich homemade Jack Daniel's BBQ sauce, or one of their burgers (s/18-22) such as the smoked BBQ topped with cheddar cheese and a handful of pulled pork and you'll see what we mean. It's a relatively new place but already the queues are forming outside. If they're too lengthy but you're in the market for a burger, **Juanito's**, nearby at Siete Angelitos 243, advertises 31 varieties of burger, including alpaca (s/20).

● Italian *Bodega 138* is one of the more authentic Italian eateries in the city, spread over two floors south of Plaza de Armas at Calle Herrajes 138. If you don't want to queue come before 7pm – it's that popular. The popularity is deserved, with a good selection of local beers and great pizzas (s/35 for a medium). Portions of their other

C U S C O

(Opposite) Top left: Loved-up llamas posing for the tourist cameras at Machu Picchu. **Right**: Celebrating the Feast of Santa Ana, Plaza de Armas, Cusco. **Middle**: *Cuy* (guinea pig) is usually served whole, with its head and feet. (Photos above all © Henry Stedman). **Bottom**: Waiting for the National Day parade to start in Pisac. (Photo © Zoe Ashdown).

dishes (eg spam bolognaise, lasagne, both s/27) are a little on the light side, but still tasty. If the queue is too much, not far away, on the ground floor of Santa Catalina Angosta 135, just off Plaza de Armas, is *Incanto* (☎ 254753, 🖳 www.cuscorestaurants.com), a fine Italian-style restaurant known for its pastas.

Over in San Blas, *Yunsa*, at Tandapata 676, has a wood-fired oven for its pizzas (from s/24), which come with a choice of three bases, and a cosy upstairs eating area from which to view the square and the roofs of the city beyond.

● **French** *Le Buffet Francés*, on Carmen Alto 596, is a simple but pretty authentic French deli (it's run by an expat French woman) with cheeses, pâté, baguettes and croissants all available. Some of the cakes, too, including the brownies (s/6), are reason enough to return. Overall, a lovely, homely place. Rather more upmarket, *Le Soleil*, at Calle San Agustín 275, is a very smart place, with the service impeccable and the food approaching exquisite; often they're quite quiet, however, possibly due to the prices. Their five-course fixed-menu specials (s/152) include such typical French dishes as snails in butter and garlic sauce, duck foie gras and chicken terrine flambéed with brandy; or you can order à la carte including rabbit cooked with Dijon mustard, traditional purée and vegetables (s/83).

● **Spanish** *Tapa Tapa y ¡Olé!* at Calle Suecia 343c is a lively, grafitti-strewn Spanish eaterie, run by a couple from Valencia, with a nice line in paella – including their popular cuy paella – as well as scrumptious fideuá (noodles with seafood). Prices are usually s/28 for a main.

● **Indian** *Korma Sutra*, at Tandapata 909 overlooking Plazoleta San Blas, is Cusco's best (and possibly only) curry house. It is an odd mix: authentic Indian food cooked up at high altitude in the heart of South America – and all owned by a Brit. It's a fun place and deservedly busy, with some imaginative fusions (tandoori guinea pig, anyone?) and more traditional Indian favourites. Manage to eat one of their famously fiery phaals

(s/32) and you get a certificate and, more importantly, a free ice-cold beer.

● **Mexican** *Tacomania* is a colourful and fun little place above Plazoleta San Blas where you 'build' your own Mexican food – you choose whether to have tacos, enchiladas, which of four fillings to use, what rice to have and what sauce to pour over the top. The price depends on the filling (s/22-24). Not quite authentic, according to a Mexican friend, but probably the best you'll get in Cusco.

● **General** We must confess that before actually setting foot inside the place, we were quite inclined to dislike *Jack's*. Seeing the queues of tourists snaking along the pavement on the corner of Choquechaca and Cuesta San Blas, our initial reaction was to view them as little more than sheep, frightened to venture out and try the local cuisine. But as we soon discovered, what brings people here is not fear, it's the desire for some truly delicious, hearty and homely food. Dishes such as shepherd's pie (s/28.50), are bound to bring a smile to anyone who tries it, while their drinks (fresh lemonade, lime and bitters, s/8) are likewise scrumptious. And to be fair, the queue tends to move quite quickly so you shouldn't have too long to wait.

On Portal de Belen, which runs away from the south-east corner of the plaza, look for *Greens Organic* (🖳 www.cuscorestaurants.com), an atmospheric 1st floor restaurant at Santa Catalina Angosta 135, with an innovative chef and changing menu. Dishes are always fresh, organically grown and carefully sourced; look out for beer-battered trout (s/48), African curry (s/42) or slow-cooked lamb shank (s/58).

For somewhere truly unique, head to *Fallen Angel* (see Where to stay), in the corner of Plazoleta de las Nazarenas. Run by the same individual who owns Macondo (see p173), it uses aquariumesque Perspex-topped baths full of fish and coral as tables and is crammed full of glitter and kitsch. The food is sumptuous though (mains s/48-58), especially the steaks (eg in a blue Andean cheese with stir-fried vegetables), and the cocktails are devilishly good.

Another of Cusco's best restaurants is found next door. *MAP Café* (🖥 www.cusco restaurants.com), in Casa Cabrera, home to the Museum of Pre-Columbian Art, Plazoleta de las Nazarenas 231, is run by the same people as are in charge of several of Cusco's good-quality restaurants. Set in the beautiful courtyard of a restored colonial house, it serves a creative menu of excellent Peruvian cuisine including slow-cooked deboned *ossobuco* (veal shanks), or goat cheese and raisin-stuffed chicken breast and guinea pig confit with peanut-tossed potatoes. An excellent range of European and New World wines is available to wash your meal down with. Quality comes at a price though and it isn't cheap (main course s/57-77, desserts s/34-37).

During the day Swiss-run *Granja Heidi*, at Cuesta San Blas 525, offers freshly sourced and prepared food, yoghurt and delicious crêpes (from s/17). The contemporary Peruvian dishes, such as *ossobuco de res* (beef braised with vegetables in a white wine sauce with risotto, s/46) and *quiches* (s/10) are also well worth trying.

BARS AND NIGHTLIFE

Other than Lima, no Peruvian city can match Cusco for places to drink and dance. The city has a huge range of venues, to suit all tastes; you just need to listen out for the latest thing. Plaza de Armas is a hive of activity from early to late, though the trendiest hangouts usually emerge in the less obvious parts of the city.

Cholos, in a lovely courtyard down from Hotel Monasterio, at Palacio 110, is a great little hideaway with 12 beers on tap – ideal to wash down their burger and fries (s/15) or meatballs (s/20).

Norton's Pub, which previously revelled in the name Norton's Rat Tavern, overlooks Plaza de Armas; the entrance is on Santa Catalina Angosta 116. It's almost a North American biker bar and has TVs, darts and pool tables as well as a balcony from which to watch the world go by. The food is simple but filling and wholesome.

Paddy's Pub (formerly Paddy Flaherty's), at Triunfo 124, is a compact Irish bar complete with Guinness, that's usually absolutely heaving with travellers, although largely devoid of locals. There are TVs, games and a happy hour.

Museo del Pisco (🖥 www.museo delpisco.org), on Santa Catalina Ancha, takes Peru's national alcoholic drink rather seriously. The result is rather different, a lively and popular bar that everyone should visit at least once on their stay in Cusco, with pisco tastings, lessons in how to make the perfect Pisco sour, as well as hundreds of infusions and *chilcanos* (pisco cocktails). Good fun.

Los Perros, on Tecsecocha 238, is a very comfortable place to kick back and while away an afternoon or evening. One of Cusco's favourite watering holes, it is renowned for its magnificent salads, wontons (s/23) to die for, curries, stir fries and puddings such as sticky fig cake. There are also board games and the TV to keep you entertained. Nearby, *Indigo Bar*, on the 1st floor of Tecsecocha 415, has draught beers, a warming fireplace, free wi-fi, sport on the

❑ **Sapo**

This game of skill involves throwing a disc into a series of holes in the top of a box, worth different amounts of points, with a series of obstacles designed to make these targets more challenging. The most valuable hole is guarded by an ornate metal frog and to score the highest points you must throw the disc into the frog's mouth, at which point the player typically yells 'Sapo!'.

The game, similar in many ways to the British Pitch Penny, evolved from a game where the Incas would toss a gold coin into a lake in the hope that a frog, which was considered powerful, would take the piece in its mouth. If the frog (El Sapu) took the piece, the player was instantly granted a wish and the frog turned into solid gold. In reality the frog is rarely gold and the wishes made rarely come true, but it is still an exciting, entertaining way to pass the time over a couple of pisco sours.

telly, board games and a pleasant atmosphere; *La Chupitería*, at 418, is a shot bar, unwavering in its dedication to getting tourists sozzled with teapots of booze, cocktails, flaming shots, absinthe, and what they advertise as Cusco's biggest, boldest drinks list.

Marcelo Batata (see Where to eat), on the 3rd floor of Palacio 121, is a popular hangout with a great roof terrace that has unprecedented views across the roof of the cathedral and surrounding buildings. To go with the views are great pisco mixes including infused ginger, purple corn and lemongrass (s/21-22), shots of flavoured pisco and a range of classic cocktails. There are also tempting snacks and well-made mains complete with food and wine pairing suggestions.

Cult favourite *Fallen Angel* (see Where to stay & Where to eat), on Plazoleta de las Nazarenas, is popular with a hip crowd of discerning locals and adventurous visitors. It occasionally hosts outrageous parties but consistently serves decidedly devilish cocktails, as does its sister bar, *Macondo* (see p173), at Cuesta San Blas 571.

You will have no trouble finding a club in Cusco; the difficult part is trying to avoid them. Although clubs come and go and the names change, the venues and addresses usually remain the same. The longest-running venue is *Mama Africa*, Portal Harinas 191 (2nd floor), which plays something for everyone and is usually packed, particularly for its happy hour.

Other entertainment

There's a regular, nightly folk music and dance show at **Centro Qosqo de Arte Nativo** (Av El Sol 604), which was founded by a group of artists in 1924. Entrance to the energetic, authentic shows, which run from 7 to 8.30pm, is free with a Visitor's Ticket (see box p150).

Teatro Municipal, on Calle Mesón de la Estrella 149, is the main theatre in the city, regularly hosting plays and dance classes. **Teatro Kusikay**, on Unión 117, hosts a spectacular traditional dance show (Mon-Sat 7.30pm; s/110), which draws its inspiration from local festivals and costumes. **Teatro Intl Raymi**, at Saphi 605, has one of the

best live music shows, every evening from 6.45pm.

SHOPPING

Cusco has some of the finest craft markets and authentic souvenirs anywhere in Peru. Sadly in a bid to clean up Cusco, the authorities have moved on the artisans so often seen in the streets and plazas and relocated them to the giant **Centro Artesanal** at the end of Av El Sol. Not many tourists actually trek all the way down here, which is very bad for the local craftsmen but very good for those who do make the trip as they can expect a bargain if prepared to haggle. There are, however, a handful of much smaller **markets** dotted about and a number of weekend fairs.

San Blas is Cusco's traditional artisan district and several workshops here are worth visiting.

In addition there are the many souvenir shops that line the main streets and tend to feature similar produce, at similar prices.

General souvenirs

There are loads of places to choose from around Plaza de Armas. One of the better, more-discerning places is **Jatum Maqui**, just up from the plaza at Tecsecocha 432, which keeps prices down without compromising the quality of the goods. We also liked **Kukuli Souvenirs** at No 555 Cuesta San Blas, and **Makinchi's** at No 573.

There's a great little Fairtrade store on the outskirts of San Blas. **Awana Wasinchis**, at Chihuampata 515, is a friendly place owned by a mother and her son, with a great collection of leather goods, textiles, clothes, jewellery and other knick-knacks. It's not that cheap but the quality and style of the merchandise is unique.

Jewellery

Ilaria, at Calle del Medio 111, is part of a nationwide chain of high-quality jewellers. There are also branches in Hotel Monasterio, Hotel Libertador, outside JW Marriott Hotel on Calle Ruinas and at the airport.

For more unusual, unique designs in gold, silver or using semi-precious stones check out **Alpaca7** at Triunfo 120, and **Spondylus** on the Plazoleta San Blas 617.

Some of the best stuff can be found at **Andean Treasures** at Triunfo 375, and **Inka Treasure** at Portal de Panes 163, at Santa Catalina Ancha 177 and on Plazoleta de las Nazarenas 159.

Alpaca and llama woollens

For upmarket and stand-out clothing made from our South American camelid friends, try **Kuna** (💻 www.kuna.com.pe), with branches on Plaza de Armas at Portal de Panes 127 and Portal de Belen 115, at Plaza Regocijo 202, at the JW Marriott Hotel on Calle Ruinas and Hotel Libertador on Plazoleta Santo Domingo, and at Calle El Triunfo 366, has good-quality alpaca coats, scarves and other knitwear but note that there's a cheaper branch of the same shop in the departure lounge of the airport. **Alpacas Best**, Portal Confitura 221 and Plazoleta de las Nazarenas 197-199, have a selection of handmade sweaters, jackets, coats and accessories. Also on Nazarenas is Sol Alpaca at 167A, and Alpaca Golden at 165.

The **Center for Traditional Textiles of Cusco** (💻 www.textilescusco.org), Av El Sol 603A, is a non-profit organisation set up to aid the survival of the Incas' textile traditions and to provide support to those communities with a history of weaving. By researching and documenting complex styles and techniques the Center helps to ensure that 2000-year-old textile traditions will not be lost. Examples of the fine work are available for sale in the Center but work of this quality does not come cheap.

T-shirts, bags and shoes

For something a bit different from the common-or-garden Peruvian football shirt, the ubiquitous Cusqueña and Inca Kola shirts ('*La Bebida del Perú*') do check out **Cocoliso** on Palacio, opposite the café of the same name, which has some unusual T-shirt and bag designs that put one in mind of the work of Banksy, though with a Peruvian theme. Next-door is one of smartest bag shops, **Peruvian Q'eswa**.

Handmade leather shoes and boots are available from **Away** at Tecsecocha 426.

Textiles, ponchos, traditional clothing

The anonymous shop at Portal Comercio 173, on Plaza de Armas, has the widest range of antique and new ponchos in central Cusco. A little expensive but it's worth coming here to see some of the fabulous old blankets, *mantas* (shawls) and ponchos they have in the store even if you don't want to buy.

Tankar Gallery, upstairs in the Llama House, Calle Palacio 121, has a variety of tapestries produced by local artists that are representative of Andean traditions and customs. They also produce handmade ceramics.

If you want to dress like a local, there are a couple of shops on Plaza Limacpampa at the foot of Tullumayo. **Trajes Típicos Imperio**, at 553, is a fascinating place even if you aren't really inclined to buy anything; for hat collectors and lovers of beautifully embroidered traditional skirts and jackets it's great (though note that they charge if you just want to try things on and take photos). They also stock the more outlandish festival wear, including oversized sombreros and sequined suits.

Instruments, ceramics pottery

Anyone interested in Andean music should head to **Ayarachi's** at Hatun Rumiyoc 487. The knowledgeable owner runs a workshop and shop here producing and selling typical musical instruments.

TREKKING AGENCIES

Listed here are some of the better-established agencies with good reputations and a solid history of delivering services of a high standard, in line with the regulations and requirements to look after porters and crew. Inclusion in the list is no guarantee of quality, though; you should do your own research before settling on a group to guide you.

● **Amazonas Explorer** (☎ 252846, 💻 www.amazonas-explorer.com, Av Collasuyo 910, Miravalle) A specialist whitewater rafting and mountain-biking company owned by British and Swiss expats living in Cusco that is renowned for its adventure tours but which also runs decent, small-group, fixed-departure Inca Trail trips as well as treks on the Lares route. Has a good reputation for treating its porters and staff well and paying proper salaries.

CUSCO

● **Amazon Trails Peru** (☎ 437374, 🖵 www.amazontrailsperu.com, Calle Tandapata 660) German-Peruvian outfit that runs jungle trips (see box p180), has their own accommodation, Amazon Hostal, in Cusco (see p166) and organises a handful of trips and treks in the Cusco and Sacred Valley area including the Inca Trail, Salkantay and Choquequirao treks as well as a two-day jaunt around Yanacocha in the Sacred Valley.

● **Andina Travel** (☎ 251892, 🖵 www.andinatravel.com, Plazoleta Santa Catalina 219) Recommended American-Peruvian outfit committed to supporting local communities through sustainable development and which runs good-quality Inca Trail,

---

❏ TREK AGENCIES, LICENCES AND WHAT THEY REALLY REPRESENT

Background Over the last decade the Peruvian government has introduced a series of rules and regulations designed to control and regulate access to the Inca Trail and so reduce the environmental impact of thousands of trekkers descending on the trail every year. The rules are stringently adhered to, so you must be aware of them (see box pp212-13 for a comprehensive list of Inca Trail regulations).

One of the requirements is that **for any trek that uses the classic Inca Trail between Huayllabamba and Machu Picchu you must have a licensed guide and a trekking permit, both of which must come from a regulated agency**. Consequently this is also a requirement for the short Inca Trail from Km104, and for the latter part of the High Inca Trail. At the time of writing this wasn't a requirement for the Salkantay, Lares, Choquequirao, Vilcabamba or Ausangate treks, but the situation may change (particularly with the very popular Salkantay Trek) and there have been various whispers about proposed alterations to the regulations to include some or all of these routes.

Licence requirements In theory a licence means that the agency has satisfied a series of criteria and been deemed professional and responsible enough to organise treks. They should have good equipment, provide a reasonable standard of food and service and employ properly qualified guides. However, there are still a lot of frankly poor companies in Cusco who are allowed to operate. The cheaper deals they tend to offer aren't necessarily the best value and almost certainly mean a compromise in standards. These agencies have a reputation for: cutting corners; pairing up groups with others; being environmentally insensitive and not clearing up after themselves; and for failing to look after their porters. On top of this, the food could well be pretty grim, the equipment dodgy and there are usually hidden costs that make the whole unpleasant experience more expensive than it was first advertised. Essentially, you get what you pay for.

At the time of writing there are over 195 agencies licensed to operate Inca Trail treks and competing for business. The list is reviewed every year, with licences renewed or revoked, so before handing over any money make sure to check carefully that the agency you are considering is still allowed to operate and has the requisite paperwork. Be aware that **licences are issued only to Peruvian companies**, not to overseas outfits or foreign tour operators. Note, too, that if you've signed up with an agency to tackle the Inca Trail, but they're not on the list of approved agencies, you've either unknowingly signed up with a middleman who will just pass your details onto the agency that will actually run the tour, or you've been duped, no reservation has been made for you, and you won't be trekking the Inca Trail at all. Thankfully, this last situation is rare. If you're worried that you may fall into the latter category, ask the agency you've booked with to send you a copy of the permit which may help to allay your fears.

Lares, Ausangate and Choquequirao treks as well as both trails round Salkantay. They can also arrange jungle trips (see box p180) and bespoke treks. Prices are dependent on group size.

● **Apumayo** (☎ 246018, 🖳 www.apumayo .com, Jr Ricardo Palma Ñ-11, Santa Monica) Professional, high-quality white-water-rafting specialist with a strong environmental agenda. Also run trips and tours in the Sacred Valley region as well as Inca Trail, Salkantay, Lares, Ausangate and Choquequirao treks.

● **Big Foot** (☎ 233836, 🖳 www.bigfootcus co.com, Calle Triunfo 392) Tends to focus on tailor-made itineraries but does run

---

Better still, of course, is to sign up with a licensed agency in the first place – then you can rest assured your trek is booked and safe. For the most comprehensive, up-to-date list of licensed agencies check out 🖳 www.incatrailperu.com; while to check the availability of Inca Trail trek permits visit 🖳 www.machupicchu.gob.pe.

Costs There is a wide range of prices quoted for trekking the Inca Trail – from about US$500 to virtually whatever you're prepared to part with. Realistically a classic four-day trek will set you back US$500-600. Although there are deals out there for less than this, simple arithmetic combining all the individual food and transport costs, entrance fees, permits and equipment hire shows that it just isn't possible to run a good-quality trek for less than US$500 (see box p14). Don't allow agencies to fob you off with 'estimates' either, get a definite quote to prevent a nasty surprise later.

At the lower end of the scale are companies such as **Aventuras X-Treme Tourbulencia** where you can pick up a trek for US$500 if you're willing to carry your own luggage. They have a reputation for delivering an all-round good service without compromising standards, or porter welfare. Good-quality mid-range outfits selling treks from around US$600-700 but still offering a high-level of service and a responsible attitude towards their porters include **Peru Treks**, **SAS**, **Q'ente**, **Llama Path** and **United Mice**. At the upper end of the scale, charging upwards of US$800 are the exclusive agencies such as **Condor Travel**, **Explorandes**, **Inka Natura** and **Inca Explorers**.

When booking any trek in Cusco, always pay for it at the agency's office and demand a written receipt and contract. There have been various instances where people claiming to be representatives of big agencies have taken money for a place on a trek at a bus station or airport and simply disappeared with the cash.

Arriving in Cusco without a booking It hasn't been possible to pitch up in Cusco and arrange to walk a route subject to the Inca Trail regulations for some time now, but still people arrive expecting to do this. At the very slowest times of year (Dec-Jan) it might be possible to pull something together within a couple of weeks, but usually you have to book a place on an Inca Trail trek at least three months in advance of the departure date. During the high season (Jun-Aug) you should consider signing up five to six months in advance to guarantee availability, especially if you aren't able to be flexible about departure dates.

Should you arrive in Cusco without anything arranged though, don't despair. There are plenty of alternatives to the classic Inca Trail and it is possible to organise the Salkantay Trek (which actually finishes at Machu Picchu) at shorter notice. Other treks that are currently unregulated and so easier to arrange are the Vilcabamba and Choquequirao treks. You might also want to consider the Ausangate or Lares treks, or multi-day white-water rafting, mountain-biking or jungle trips.

adventure tours such as biking around the Maras and Moray regions and horse-riding around Cusco, in addition to the more standard Inca Trail, Salkantay, Lares, Choquequirao and Ausangate Circuit treks.

● **Ch'aska Tours** (☎ 240424, 🖥 www.chaskatours.com, Calle Garcilaso 265) Cultural and nature tours available but also good-value treks on the Inca Trail, Choquequirao, Lares and Salkantay paths.

● **Condor Travel** (☎ 615 3000, 🖥 www.condortravel.com) Expensive, top-end agency offering high-class tours and trips throughout Peru and South America. Slick and professional operation with regular departures on the Inca Trail as well as other treks in the Cusco area. Well-connected and the local representative for a number of international airlines if you are after plane tickets. The head office is at Armando Blondet 249, San Isidro, Lima.

● **Ecotrek Peru** (☎ 247286, 🖥 www.ecotrekperu.net, Urb Quispicanchi F-3) Decent, porter-friendly outfit specialising in jungle trips to the Pongo de Mainique but also arranges single and multi-day mountain-biking tours and cultural trips as well as treks in the Cusco region, including the Inca Trail, Salkantay, Lares and Ausangate.

● **Enigma** (☎ 222155, 🖥 www.enigmaperu.com, Calle Fortunato L Herrera 214) Smaller, quality operator based away from the city centre in a residential part of town offering reasonably priced mid-range treks supported with good equipment and some knowledgeable guides on the Inca Trail, Salkantay and Choquequirao treks as well as the Ausangate Circuit and cultural treks such as the Lares Valley hike.

● **Eric Adventures** (☎ 272862, 🖥 www.ericadventures.com, Urb Santa Maria A1-6) Offer a number of treks including variations on the Inca Trail, Salkantay and Choquequirao to Machu Picchu as well as, unusually, a ten-day jaunt to Espíritu Pampa. They also offer several activities.

● **Explorandes** (☎ 238380, 🖥 www.explorandes.com, Paseo Zarzuela Q-2 Huancaro) Well-established major tour operator at the top-end of the market, with correspondingly high prices, that offers a superb range of treks throughout Peru including the classic Inca Trail, Salkantay and Choquequirao treks in addition to an Ancascocha trek to Machu Picchu. Departures are flexible and group sizes are kept small. Also ecologically aware, committed to preserving the environment and conscious of the need for the

❏ **The Inca Jungle Trek**
You may come across an increasingly large number of agencies in Cusco offering another 'back door' route to Machu Picchu. The Inca Jungle Trek is an activity-filled approach to the ruins that avoids any regulations but which also offers little in the way of Inca history until you arrive at your final goal. The trip sees you initially driving from Cusco to Abra Málaga. You then travel by bike and on foot to Machu Picchu.

The first day involves a straightforward 4- to 5-hour 2-wheeled descent from the high pass at Abra Málaga (4350m) to Santa María. The following day is a 6- to 7-hour trek through the cloud forest from Santa María to Santa Teresa that is fairly taxing if a little unspectacular, although there is a section of authentic Inca trail along the way; some operators opt to drive you over this section. Having recuperated overnight in Santa Teresa and at the hot springs nearby, or gone in search of more thrills at the nearby zipline (see box p258), you spend six hours walking from Santa Teresa to Aguas Calientes, much of it along railway tracks.

The fourth and final day is spent exploring the ruins at Machu Picchu. The trip details vary considerably according to operator, with different levels of accommodation and equipment offered. Side-trips and excursions, such as white-water rafting from Santa Teresa, can also be added to the journey. Make sure to check what your trip price includes before you sign up but expect to pay upwards of US$200 for a decent tour, safety equipment, access to Machu Picchu and a return train fare and transfer back to Cusco.

further development of ecotourism.

● **Inka Natura** (Lima ☎ 203 5000, 💻 www.inkanatura.com, Manuel Bañon 461, San Isidro, Lima) Pricey, professional outfit that specialises in jungle trips (see box opposite), but also has various hikes including, uniquely, a four-day Inca Quarry trek; all treks are well supported and expensive.

● **Llama Path** (☎ 223448, 💻 www.llama path.com, Calle Cuychipunco 257) Midrange outfit operated by a Peruvian-Welsh partnership that has a wide range of treks, including the Inca Trail, Salkantay, Lares and Choquequirao treks, at reasonable rates. Inclined to try and keep group numbers small they have dependable, fixed departure dates and are committed to sustainable tourism.

● **Machete Tours** (☎ 224829, 💻 www .machetetours.com, Calle San Andres 477) Budget operator run by a Peruvian-Danish pair who run Inca Trail, Salkantay (including the lesser-used route that connects with the Inca Trail), Espíritu Pampa and Choquequirao outings.

● **Mayuc** (☎ 232666, 💻 www.mayuc.com, Portal Confiturías 211) White-water-rafting specialist but also runs private and group treks on the Inca Trail, Lares, Ausangate, Salkantay, Choquequirao and Vilcabamba trails.

● **Mountain Lodges of Peru** (☎ 262640, 💻 www.mountainlodgesofperu.com, Av El Sol 948, Of 403) This was the original agency offering lodge accommodation on the Salkantay Trek. Each lodge (Salkantay Lodge & Adventure Resort, Wayra Lodge, Colpa Lodge, Lucma Lodge) boasts friendly, attentive staff and excellent facilities. Rooms are double, twin or triple and all have en suite facilities, including hot showers. Saunas are available at no extra cost

too. Some of the lodges boast an outdoor Jacuzzi and a professional massage service is offered too. Should you feel the need, you can also communicate with the wider world via the satellite phone and internet access available at each lodge. They have similarly luxurious accommodation in the Lares area at Huacay and Huacahuasi (see p278) to serve their five- and seven-day itineraries. The prospect of an evening of relative comfort and good food is a great incentive when trekking. However, for the pleasure of not camping you'll have to pay a princely sum.

● **Peru Treks & Adventure** (☎ 222722, 💻 www.perutreks.com, Av Pardo 540) Peruvian-English trekking specialist that focuses on the Inca Trail and which has an excellent reputation for looking after their porters and crew. They are heavily involved with sustainable tourism, and plough much of their profit into schemes and projects set up to help local people and communities. They also run a **homestay** programme where you can stay with families in Chinchero (see p193 & p195) and experience their way of life and culture.

● **Q'ente** (☎ 222535, 💻 www.qente.com, Calle Choquechaca 229, 2nd Floor) Upmarket mid-range agency whose name is Quechua for 'hummingbird'. Their helpful and accommodating staff, knowledgeable guides and wide range of treks make them a good bet. Treks include the usual Inca Trail, Santa Teresa, Salkantay, Choquequirao, and Ausangate Circuit as well as more adventurous trips including a 17-day Choquequirao to Espíritu Pampa trip. They also boast numerous city and Sacred Valley tours.

● **Refugios Salkantay** (☎ 984372258, 💻 www.refugiossalkantay.com, Mollepata) Taking the Mountain Lodges of Peru blue-

CUSCO

❏ **Rainbow Mountain (Vinicunca)**
This is a popular day trip to the viewpoint for these amazing striped hills located south-west of Ausangate peak (see p298). The colours – greeny-blues, yellowy browns and purply reds – come from the different layers of rock that have been recently exposed across the ridges. You can pay anything from US$30 to over US$150 for the day trip but essentially it involves leaving Cusco around 4am for the three-hour drive to where you start the 3-4 hour walk climbing from 4200m (13,800ft) to 5200m (17,000ft). You need to be acclimatised (see p47) to do this.

print (see p181) and reworking it for those on smaller budgets, Refugios Salkantay have several inexpensive properties at Soray Pampa, Chaullay and Lucmabamba. Based in Mollepata at the start of the route, the company is really little more than a group of families who live along the trail, grew disillusioned after seeing how many of the travel agencies were 'trashing' the route, so got together to offer accommodation and treks themselves. It's true that the accommodation can be a bit too basic for some, but if you fancy the Salkantay Trek, don't want to camp, and are on a budget, this is a great choice.

● **Salkantay Trekking** (☎ 84 632307, ☐ www.salkantaytrekking.com, Triunfo 392) Another company in the mould of Mountain Lodges, though on a smaller scale with campsites rather than lodges for accommodation, and only two of these. Still, their Mountain Sky Huts at Soray Pampa are most eye-catching with their tinted glass roofs (excellent for star-gazing at night) and Inca doorways. Their other campsite on the trail, at Chaullay, is a more conventional affair with thatched roofs covering the tents. A decent company and one that concentrates solely on Salkantay, with prices around the US$400-500 mark for a four-day Salkantay Trek.

● **SAS Travel** (☎ 249194, ☐ www.sastrav elperu.com, Calle Garcilaso 270) Large, well-organised agency with plenty of staff and guides meaning that it is able to offer regular Inca Trail departures as well as treks to Choquequirao and the Lares Valley – and is one of the few to offer the Salkantay Trek that connects with the Inca Trail (see p31). Justifiably popular and a little more expensive because of it, especially if you want to travel in a small group. Also offers white-water rafting, mountain-biking and horse-riding expeditions.

● **United Mice** (☎ 221139, ☐ www.united mice.com, Av Pachacuteq 424) This outfit has the most memorable name. It offers a range of budget- to mid-range treks including some limited departures on the Inca Trail, Salkantay, Choquequirao and Choquequirao to Machu Picchu treks – and is another to offer the Salkantay Trek that links with the Inca Trail (see p31). A small

percentage of their profit is donated to a foundation supporting street kids in Cusco.
● **Wayki Trek** (☎ 224092, ☐ www.wayki trek.net, Quera 239) Small budget agency, whose name is Quechua for 'brother', with a reputation and popularity that belies their size. On offer are good-value Inca Trail treks but also Salkantay, Choquequirao, Lares and the Ausangate Circuit, all in groups around half the size of most other operators. Wayki also offer plenty of opportunities for clients to get out and experience what life is like in the local communities through various social projects that they run.
● **Xtreme Tourbulencia** (☎ 224362, ☐ www.x-tremetourbulencia.com, 364 Plateros, Cusco) Perhaps the biggest of the budget agencies to offer the classic Inca Trail (as well as the full roster of other trekking destinations in the region, including the rarely advertised Vilcabamba Trail). Perhaps surprisingly, given their reasonable prices, they also have some idea of responsible tourism, are reputed to treat their porters well and offer various 'cultural immersion' programmes.

MOVING ON
Air
The airport is a few kilometres south of Plaza de Armas – a five-minute taxi journey. From here you can fly to most major Peruvian towns. See box p78 for information about departure taxes.

Airline offices huddle together near the main post office on Av El Sol and include: **LATAM** (☎ ☐ www.latam.com), Av El Sol 627B; **Star Perú** (☎ 262768, ☐ www.starperu.com), Av El Sol 627; **Avianca** (☐ www.avianca.com), Av El Sol 602B; **Peruvian** (☎ 254890; ☐ www.peru vian.pe), Av El Sol 627-A.

There are plenty of flights daily to Lima (50 mins). The cheapest leaves early in the morning. Fares start at around US$60 but can easily rise to double or even treble this. There are spectacular views of Salkantay out of the right-hand side windows, about 10 minutes after take off. You should try and catch as early a flight as possible since there is a higher risk of flights being delayed or cancelled later in the day.

Buses and colectivos

For most destinations, particularly those in this book, travellers have a choice: bus or colectivo. **Buses** usually leave from the main **bus terminal** (Terminal Terrestre), 2km south of Plaza de Armas, near the airport. Agencies on Av El Sol and in Plaza de Armas sell tickets for a healthy commission; you will get far cheaper tickets at the terminal itself. It isn't necessary to book far in advance; if you arrange your tickets the day before you can usually choose your seat.

The alternative is a *colectivo*, which are often quicker, sometimes cheaper, and often depart Cusco from places more convenient for Plaza de Armas. The only drawback with them is that they don't operate to a set timetable but instead leave when full, so it's entirely possible you could end up waiting for several hours to leave. Your chances of leaving promptly are greatly enhanced if you try to leave early in the morning.

All international and long-distance buses use the main bus terminal. The most direct route to **Lima** is via Abancay and Nazca – it takes 20-22 hours and costs US$25-60. Alternative, longer routes go via Arequipa or Ayacucho. Other destinations include: **Nazca** (14hrs); **Abancay** (4-5hrs) – take this bus for **Cachora**, see pp287-8; **Juliaca** (5-6hrs); **Puno** (6-7hrs); and **Arequipa** (9-11hrs).

Buses to **Quillabamba** leave from Santiago bus terminal in the west of the city.

For the **Sacred Valley** you're much better off catching a colectivo. Services to **Pisac** (s/4-5; 45 mins) leave from Calle Puputi. These services often terminate at **Urubamba** but if this is your final destination you're better off catching a colectivo from the junction of Av Grau and Av Pavitos; these go via **Chinchero** (s/4; 45 mins), leave frequently throughout the day, and take less time (s/6; 2hrs) than those via Pisac. Occasionally colectivos from Av Grau will continue on to **Ollantaytambo** (s/10 and 2½hrs from Cusco), the furthest destination in the Sacred Valley; if they don't you will have to change at Urubamba and get an onward connection from there (s/2-3).

Finally, for those interested in the Ausangate trek, the bus to **Tinke** (s/10) leaves from Tomasa Titto Condemayta, by Coliseo Cerrado, about 3km south-east of Plaza de Armas, several times a day.

The cheap way to Machu Picchu

In the past you had no choice but to take the train to Aguas Calientes and were at the mercy of the expensive fares levied by the train operator. However, there is an alternative, cheaper route as a result of the bridge that was built across the Urubamba.

From Terminal Terrestre catch a bus or colectivo to Quillabamba (s/35) but ask to be dropped off at Santa María, from where you can pick up a minibus/colectivo to Santa Teresa (s/10), two hours away. The next step is to get a taxi (s/5) or hike the 10km to La Hidroeléctrica, crossing the Urubamba on the new bridge. Trains from La Hidroeléctrica to Aguas Calientes leave thrice daily at 7.54am, 3pm and 4.35pm (US$18). Alternatively, walk along the tracks and after 2-3 hours you will come to the town.

If all the transport changes outlined above sound a bit daunting, you can always catch a **tourist bus to La Hidroeléctrica** for s/50 (s/70 return), which departs from Cusco at 8am, arriving 2pm – thereby giving you enough time to walk to Aguas Calientes to visit Machu Picchu the next day.

Rail [see pp352-5]

Trains for Juliaca and Puno leave from **Estación Huanchac** on Av Pachacutec. Tickets must be bought at the station.

Trains for Aguas Calientes (for Machu Picchu) leave from **Poroy**, just outside Cusco, or from Ollantaytambo, depending on the train operator. Tickets for these routes must also be bought in advance (see below).

Pay close attention to timetables, opening hours and ticket prices as these change frequently.

To get to Machu Picchu as cheaply as possible see above.

Buying tickets

The main office for **PeruRail** can be contacted on Cusco ☎ 581 414 or via 🖳 www.perurail.com. They have an office on Plaza de Armas at Portal de Carnes 214 and a second at Plaza Regocijo

CUSCO

202; both are open daily 7am-10pm. Estación Huanchac is open for ticket sales (Mon-Fri 7am-5pm, Sat & Sun 7am-noon).

Rival company **Inca Rail** (💻 www.incarail.com), whose trains leave from Ollantaytambo for Aguas Calientes and Machu Picchu, also has an office (☎ 233 030; Mon-Fri 7am-9pm, Sat to 7pm, Sun to 2pm) on the Plaza, at Portal de Panes 105.

When buying tickets from either company make sure you have ID, preferably your passport. It is also possible to buy tickets in advance online with a credit card. This generates an e-voucher that is not valid for travel; it must be converted into a proper ticket at least an hour before departure.

Around Cusco

RUINS NEAR CUSCO (DAY HIKE)   [see map opposite]

The landscape around Cusco is dotted with small, interesting archaeological sites, many within easy walking, horse-riding or mountain-biking distance of the city. Five of the main sites can be visited in the course of a half-day's trek, which allows you plenty of time at each ruin. Note that between many of these sites you'll find other archaeology that is clearly Inca in origin – an altar here, a carved boulder there – which aren't marked on any map nor require any ticket to visit. What's more, this gentle stroll across the rolling grasslands is also an ideal way to acclimatise to the altitude here.

Access to four of the five main sites is with the Visitor's Ticket (BTU, see box p150). The fifth, Amaru Marka Wasi (also known as Salapunco or the Temple of the Moon), is free anyway. If you do not have a Visitor's Ticket it is possible to buy a separate ticket for just these four sites; the **Boleto** covering this 'circuit' is Circuit 1 (see box p150) which costs s/70.

The walk is almost exactly 6.3km (4 miles) long though this doesn't include any walking you do at the actual sites. The route detailed below gives access to Tambo Machay, Puca Pucara, Amaru Marka Wasi, Q'enko and Sacsayhuaman. The trek can be done in either direction but it is simpler to catch a taxi out to the furthest point and then walk back. This way each site builds in magnificence too, until you arrive at Sacsayhuaman, one of the most spectacular standing stone sites anywhere in the world. (That said, there is an argument to begin with Sacsayhuaman, before the crowds turn up and while you've still got the energy to fully appreciate it.) Taxis from Plaza de Armas to Tambo Machay cost around s/20 one way. Alternatively take a bus bound for Pisac and ask to be dropped off at Tambo Machay (about s/2).

In the past there have been robberies and muggings around the ruins close to Cusco, so keep your wits about you, leave all your valuables in your hotel and don't try to visit these places after dusk. It is always much safer to walk in small groups rather than on your own.

Tambo Machay

Tambo Machay (7am-5.30pm; only possible with Visitor's Ticket) sits near a bend in the main Cusco–Pisac road. The name Tambo Machay translates as 'Inn

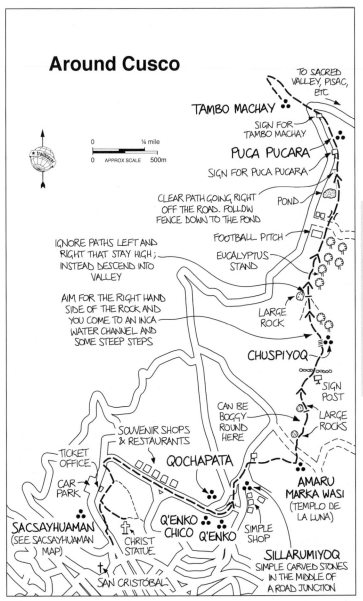

Around Cusco

TO SACRED VALLEY, PISAC, ETC

TAMBO MACHAY

SIGN FOR TAMBO MACHAY

PUCA PUCARA

SIGN FOR PUCA PUCARA

CLEAR PATH GOING RIGHT OFF THE ROAD. FOLLOW FENCE DOWN TO THE POND

POND

FOOTBALL PITCH

IGNORE PATHS LEFT AND RIGHT THAT STAY HIGH; INSTEAD DESCEND INTO VALLEY

EUCALYPTUS STAND

AIM FOR THE RIGHT HAND SIDE OF THE ROCK AND YOU COME TO AN INCA WATER CHANNEL AND SOME STEEP STEPS

LARGE ROCK

CHUSPIYOQ

SIGN POST

LARGE ROCKS

CAN BE BOGGY ROUND HERE

SOUVENIR SHOPS & RESTAURANTS

QOCHAPATA

TICKET OFFICE

CAR PARK

AMARU MARKA WASI (TEMPLO DE LA LUNA)

SACSAYHUAMAN (SEE SACSAYHUAMAN MAP)

CHRIST STATUE

Q'ENKO CHICO

Q'ENKO

SIMPLE SHOP

SAN CRISTÓBAL

SILLARUMIYOQ SIMPLE CARVED STONES IN THE MIDDLE OF A ROAD JUNCTION

0 ¼ mile
0 APPROX SCALE 500m

AROUND CUSCO

Cave', but is more frequently referred to as Los Baños del Inca ('The Inca's Baths'). The carefully cut stones frame and channel a fresh water spring which issues from high on the slope above the site and is channelled from one terrace to another, vanishes underground before re-emerging. As with most Inca sites the precise purpose of it is unknown but it is likely that it was used in the worship of water.

Returning to the main road you can see Puca Pucara, the next site on our tour, ahead on your right. Simply cross the road, head to the green road sign for Tambo Machay, and there you'll find the path taking you away from the road and straight to Puca Pucara.

Puca Pucara

This collection of stone buildings (7am-5.30pm; Visitor's Ticket) perched on a promontory overlooking a deep valley was probably a private hunting lodge connected to one of the Inca's private estates. It has also been suggested that it used to be a military fort or checkpoint along an Inca road, since the literal translation of the name means 'Red Watchtower' or 'Red Fort'.

● **Route to Amaru Marka Wasi** Beyond Puca Pucara walk along the road for 50m in the direction of Cusco; the path heads down the hill to the east (left) of the pond, village and football pitch. Beyond this, continue down the hill keeping the line of eucalyptus on your left to the large rock ahead. Just beyond, the path divides. Take the lowest path which sticks to the valley floor and descends amidst scrub and small trees. As you get lower, keep an eye out for Andean flickers (see p114), a type of woodpecker, which live in the surrounding area. At the point where the path and valley turn right is a large boulder in which is set a staircase alongside a water channel, while nearby stands an altar and other distinctively Inca masonry. This is **Chuspiyoq**, about which little is known. Continue down the valley and after the path bends left you'll come to several other rocks and boulders which also clearly show Inca workmanship. The most impressive outcrop of all, however, lies straight ahead.

Amaru Marka Wasi

Amaru Marka Wasi (always open; free), Templo de la Luna (Temple of the Moon), is a giant limestone boulder that is riddled with passages and carvings, many representing animals. Cut steps lead to the top of the rock, where there are polished surfaces and smoothed seats giving excellent views out over the surrounding countryside. The site is usually fairly deserted. Over the years there has been a fair amount of excavation here; archaeologists have discovered remnants of Inca walls and other structures buried beneath the site. In fact, it appears that there may be several metres of interesting features here below ground level, although nobody knows why this might be the case.

● **Route to Q'enko** If you stand on top of Amaru Marka Wasi and look toward Cusco (ie in the opposite direction from the way you've just come), you'll see a faint trail heading diagonally westwards (ie on your right) between a couple of farmers' fields towards the Cusco suburb of Villa San Blas. Follow this to the huddle of Inca rocks known as **Sillarumiyoq** at the top of Villa San Blas. Continue straight ahead on the same line, following the road down to the road junction; straight ahead is the site of **Qochapata** while on your left down the hill you'll see Q'enko.

Q'enko
Q'enko (7am-5.30pm; Visitor's Ticket) is yet another limestone outcrop, the name of which translates as 'zigzag' or 'labyrinth'. Smaller than Amaru Marka Wasi, it has far more designs cut into it, many of which are very detailed. The site is a huaca (sacred site) and many of the carvings have special significance. A llama, a condor and snakes have all been identified, although unfortunately most of these are on the upper surface of the rock and it is now forbidden to climb on the stone. Channels and rivulets have been cut into the stone and may have been used to course *chicha* during ceremonies.

At the front of the site, a standing stone enclosed by a finely sculpted niched wall has also been identified as casting a shadow shaped like a puma's head when the sun rises on the winter solstice (21st June). Inside the huaca is a tunnel that leads to what appears to be a beautifully sculpted altar.

● **Route to Sacsayhuaman** Rejoining the road that runs above Q'enko, turn left down the hill past **Q'enko Chico** (Little Q'enko) on your left, which is built above a stone wall that includes a fitted block with 21 angles, and a llama farm. At a sharp leftward bend in the road continue straight on to pass a straggle of souvenir shops before arriving at the ticket office for the most impressive site of them all, the awesome ruin of Sacsayhuaman.

Sacsayhuaman   [see map p189]
To avoid the worst of the crowds at Sacsayhuaman (7am-5.30pm; Visitor's Ticket) consider getting here early, before the tour buses arrive, or later in the afternoon once they have moved on.

The size of the stones here really is incredible and historian Garcilaso de la Vega was massively impressed but quite at a loss for an explanation as to the construction of Sacsayhuaman:

'A Spanish monk, who recently visited Peru, told me on his return, that he would never have believed what people tell him about this fortress if he hadn't seen it with his own eyes, because it is even more difficult to imagine than one can say; and that, in reality, it seemed hardly possible that such a project could have been successfully carried out without the help of the Evil One. Those were his very words. If we think, too, that this incredible work was accomplished without the help of a single machine, is it too much to say that it represents an even greater enigma than the seven wonders of the world?... One sees how the Egyptian pyramids were constructed, with the combined forces of time and countless workers... But how may we explain the fact that these Peruvian Indians were able to split, carve, lift, carry, hoist and lower such enormous blocks of stone, which are more like pieces of a mountain than building stones, without the help of a single machine or instrument. An enigma such as this one cannot be easily solved without seeking the help of magic, particularly when one recalls the great familiarity of these people with devils.'
Garcilaso Inca de la Vega *The Royal Commentaries of the Incas* (1609)

This prepared the way for theorists such as Eric von Daniken who was convinced that this was the work of visitors from outer space.

The Spanish nicknamed the site 'the Fortress'. However, recent research and the discovery of Inca tombs containing the bodies of priests in the area suggest that it was more likely to have been a temple. The layout of the site makes it likely that it was used as a sanctuary and place to worship the sun. Regardless of the original reason for its construction, the massive stone walls were used as a fort by the armies of Manco Inca as he fought to evict the Spanish from Cusco (see p100).

The site itself is one of the most impressive stone monuments left standing in the world and is awe-inspiring in its stature and form. Enormous stone blocks stand solemnly in three tiers of zigzag **walls** that stretch 360 metres. John Hemming calculated in *Conquest of the Incas* that the largest stone in the structure stands 8.5m high and weighs 361 tonnes. The massive blocks curve into one another as if squashed together like clay. For structural strength the largest stones are set at the apexes of the zigzags that form the wall. Unfortunately the site has been used as an unofficial quarry for cut stones over the years and many of the smaller stones have been pillaged by people for use in construction elsewhere. The structure used to be topped by three giant towers, called **Salla Marca**, **Paunca Marca** and **Muyu Marca**, which were razed to the ground following the defeat of Manco Inca. The foundations and concentric ringed outlines of these three giants are slowly being uncovered and renovated.

Across a broad, flat space known as the Esplanade, stands a giant mound called the **Inca Throne**, where an altar has been carved out of the rock. It is thought the Inca or other high-ranking individual oversaw ceremonies from here. Nearby are numbers of seats cut into the stone. Nowadays, however, the smooth grooves and polished slopes on the far side of the mound are used by children as a **slide**, giving the mound the nickname *el rodadero* (literally means rolling easily). Beyond the mound is a small amphitheatre and a section of hill riddled with **tunnels**. Some of these remain open, but you'll need a torch to make your way through them.

● **Returning to Cusco** Once you've finished with Sacsayhuaman, rejoin the cobbled path running downhill along its eastern side. Begin walking down the hill and you'll soon come to a path off to the left that leads to the **Christ Statue** (**Cristo Blanco**). Donated by Palestinian refugees to express their thanks in 1944, the statue is clearly visible from Cusco during the day and at night it is brilliantly illuminated. Returning to the cobbled path, it takes about 20-30 minutes to stroll gently downhill to Plaza de Armas.

At the bottom of the cobbles is a ticket office that checks Visitor Tickets for people walking up to the site. Join the road here and follow it carefully around a set of S-bends to reach the **church of San Cristóbal** (entry with CRA ticket, see box p150). This church was built by Cristóbal Paullu Inca and dedicated to his patron saint; it is open during the day. Inside the gloomy interior it is just about possible to make out the restored atrium. Lining the back wall of the terrace outside the church is an original Inca stone wall featuring 11 large, doorway-sized

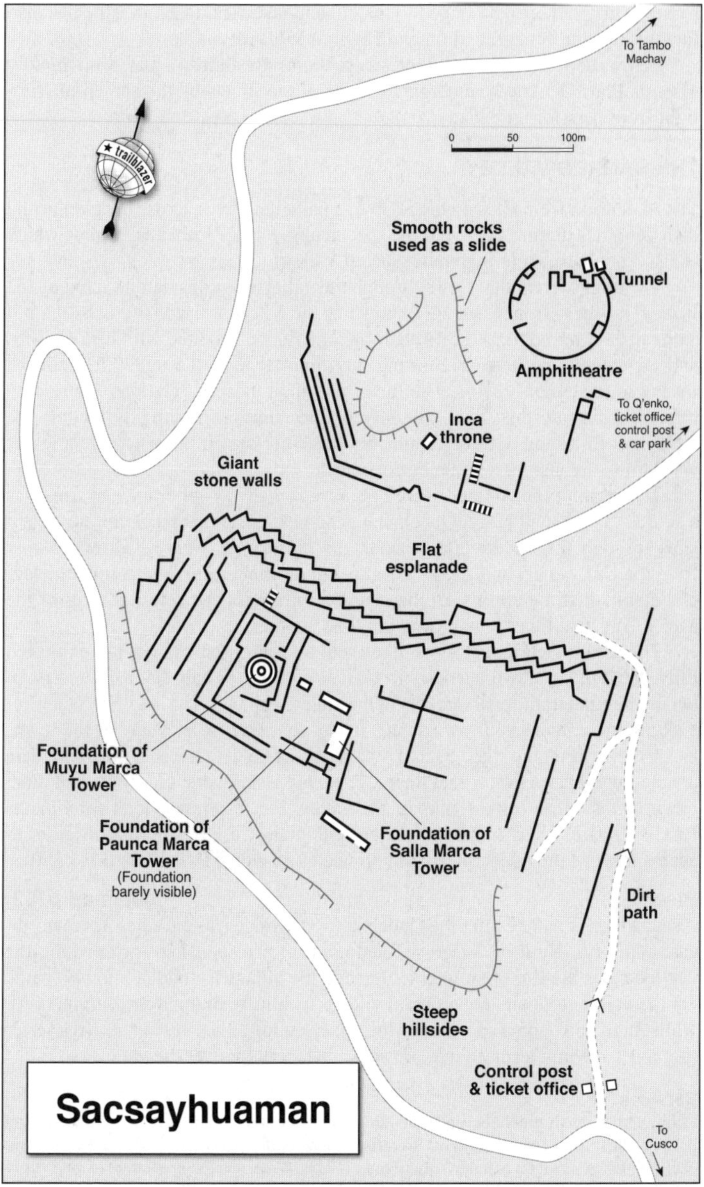

To Tambo
Machay

Trailblazer

0   50   100m

Smooth rocks
used as a slide

Tunnel

Amphitheatre

To Q'enko,
ticket office/
control post
& car park

Inca
throne

Giant
stone walls

Flat
esplanade

Foundation of
Muyu Marca
Tower

Foundation of
Paunca Marca
Tower
(Foundation
barely visible)

Foundation of
Salla Marca
Tower

Dirt
path

Steep
hillsides

Control post
& ticket office

To
Cusco

Sacsayhuaman

AROUND CUSCO

niches. This wall once belonged to the Palacio de Colcampata, in which Manco Inca lived prior to his rebellion and flight to Vilcabamba.

Below here there is a set of steep stairs (**Resbalosa**) that drop rapidly towards Plaza de Armas, emerging on one of the streets by the cathedral. Turn right from here for the plaza.

THE SACRED VALLEY

The road north from Cusco climbs up to a pass, undulates across the pampa and then descends dramatically into the spectacular, fertile Urubamba Valley, which is also known as **Valle Sagrado** (Sacred Valley).

The mighty river that flows through the valley was considered sacred by the Incas. Upstream from Pisac it is known as the Vilcanota, whilst downstream it tends to be referred to as the Urubamba. The region is dotted with historic sites and archaeological ruins, signifying the importance of the valley to both the Incas and the conquistadors. The Incas built their palaces, religious centres and retreats alongside this giant tributary of the Amazon: highlights include the citadels at Pisac and Ollantaytambo, but less well-known sites such as Salineras and Moray are also here to be discovered.

The region is considered sacred because of its vital importance to Cusco as a source of food and grain. Quechua legend also holds that when the sun sets it slips through the underworld beneath the Urubamba, where it draws deeply from the chill waters and rises the following morning refreshed. A separate legend claims that the earthly Urubamba is a mirror for the celestial river of the Milky Way, and that the two flow into one another.

The area is rich in history so it's worth allocating several days to explore it fully. Most of the travel agencies in Cusco offer day or half-day trips to a number of sites and traditional markets in the valley, although you are often better off tackling these under your own steam and at your own pace. Many of the towns and villages throughout the Sacred Valley are set up to receive visitors and there are plenty of places to stay and linger. There are also several Inca trails and more recent paths cut into the flanks of the valley. For inspiration look for Charles Brod's *Apus & Incas* in one of the bookshops in Cusco. Note that in order to access most of the major sites you will need a Visitor's Ticket (see box p150).

Pisac   [see map p192]
Pisac, which is named after the Quechua for partridge (*pisaca*), lies 32km northeast of Cusco. Built by Viceroy Toledo, the man responsible for crushing the last Incas, on the site of an Inca settlement, the village is divided into two parts. On the valley floor sits the colonial village with its traditional Andean markets, whilst high above on a spur stands the citadel, a lofty Inca site set above a series of giant sweeping terraces that presides magisterially over the valley.

Services
Lively, traditional **markets** in Pisac are held on Plaza de Armas. The most significant one takes place on Sunday, when you can see traditionally dressed locals buying and selling crops, foodstuffs and craftwork. This is an ideal opportunity to pick up a

The Sacred Valley

well-made souvenir; the ceramics and rugs here are particularly high quality though they're not the cheapest. Locals pack the plaza early on and the chaotic scene unfolds throughout the morning, before easing down around lunchtime. There is an **ATM** (cashpoint) on Plaza de Armas.

Where to stay
There are a few options if you are tempted to stay in Pisac. *Hospedaje Beho* (☎ 203001), 50m north of Plaza de Armas, on the path to the ruins, started out as a small shop with a few rooms at the back though the B&B side of things now dominates. It's a friendly place offering simple bed and breakfast (s/35 per person in an en suite room, s/20pp in one with shared facilities) in rooms overlooking a pleasant garden. *Hospedaje Familiar Semana Wasi* (☎ 203018), on the eastern edge of the plaza, has basic but clean rooms (s/50/80 sgl/dbl att, s/70 dbl with shared facilities); *Pisac Inn* (☎ 203062, 🖳 www.pisacinn.com), in the south-west corner of the square, has an attractive courtyard, a relaxed ambience and renovated rooms (s/147/183-210/237, sgl/dbl/tpl, att in low season, rising to s/185/230-265/295 in July & Aug).

A little further out are two superior places. *Paz y Luz* (☎ 216293, 🖳 www.pazy luzperu.com; s/160/250/310 sgl/dbl/tpl, suites for s/280, breakfast), is 1km east of the centre, close to the river, with a homely feel, a well-kept garden and impressive views of the surrounding hills. The expat owner also offers healing courses drawn from Andean and international traditions, meditation classes, Reiki and yoga sessions.

The second option stands a 10-minute walk west of town, or five minutes by one of the little moto-taxis that buzz around the town. *La Casa Del Conde* (☎ 787818, 🖳 www.cuscovalle.com; rates from US$45-60/60-100 sgl/dbl) is a lovely little place of just seven well-appointed rooms with balconies set in a peaceful, rural setting with carefully tended gardens.

Where to eat
Should you get hungry, there are a couple of eateries boasting giant **clay ovens**, on

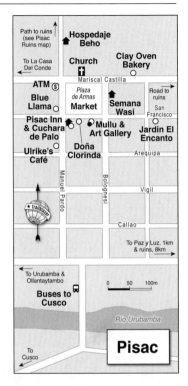

Mariscal Castilla, that are used to bake traditional flatbreads and empanadas or sometimes to roast guinea pig. Alternatively, there are several decent **cafés** adjacent to the plaza on which the market is held.

Laid-back **Mullu** stands on the 2nd floor of a house opposite the church and has a rickety balcony from which to watch the activity whilst enjoying a selection of juices and smoothies, sandwiches and other Novoandina cuisine snacks. There's also an **art gallery** downstairs.

Blue Llama is good for coffee, breakfast, juices and sandwiches which can be consumed on the 1st floor balcony overlooking the square; they also have a tasty range of vegetarian dishes. *Ulrike's Café* has a rooftop terrace, wi-fi and book exchange though the coffee and cakes are better reasons to visit. They too have a good selection of vegetarian food and a daily menu (s/25).

Cuchara de Palo, in Pisac Inn, is a very good restaurant; it serves more café staples than available elsewhere and specialises in Novoandina cuisine. If the Plaza is a little too hectic, however, there is no better retreat than *Jardín El Encanto*, where their floor-to-ceiling windows overlook the most beautiful botanical garden in which hummingbirds flit from plant to plant – all of which you'll have plenty of time to admire as you wait the interminably long time for your lunch. The food, when it does finally make its way to your table, is tasty, imaginative and well presented; try their three-coloured risotto quinoa or the crispy trout (s/25 each). We do recommend a visit – though not if you're in a hurry.

Transport
Buses to Cusco leave from the west side of the bridge; services leave when full, with the fare s/4-5.

Pisac ruins (see map p194) The **citadel** is open 7am-5.30pm and entry is possible only with a Visitor's Ticket (see box p150). The ruins at Pisac are enormous, as befits a site that was believed to have had military, religious and agricultural purposes. As such, you should allow at least a couple of hours to explore the terraces, water ducts, ruins and hidden chambers as well as to take in the superb views of the valley, the patchwork of patterned fields, sheer cliffs and jagged ridges.

The ruins were built during the reign of Pachacutec. Narrow paths edge above steep drops and you have to pass through **giant stone archways** and a short stretch of **tunnel** to reach the ceremonial centre of Pisac, at the heart of which stands a rare intact **Intihuatana** – a sacred sculpted rock or 'hitching post of the sun', the vast majority of which were decapitated by the conquistadors. A number of tombs have been uncovered in the cliff faces behind the site, on the far side of the Quitamayo Gorge; all have now been plundered and today they are closed to visitors.

The stiff climb up to the site from the valley floor takes 1-1½ hours. If you aren't already acclimatised to the altitude you will have to take it even more slowly. Note that the most direct path from the lower half of the site to its upper reaches was closed at the time of research and still may be when you are there so anyone hoping to travel between the bottom and top of the site will have to trek via the Intihuatana. From the market in the heart of the village pick up the path to the north of the square, which sets off west of the church. If you'd rather not walk uphill all that way, a 15-minute taxi ride from Pisac to the top of the ruins costs s/20.

Chinchero
This small town north-west of Cusco is set amidst the Anta plains, overlooking the Sacred Valley. The village mostly comprises adobe houses, but there is also a split-level plaza at the top of a steep winding street, with an impressive Inca wall inset with large trapezoidal niches separating the two sections. Beyond here there are also **Inca remains and terraces** (7am-5.30pm; Visitor's Ticket).

AROUND CUSCO

Cusco department area code: ☎ 84. If phoning from outside Peru dial ☎ +51-1.

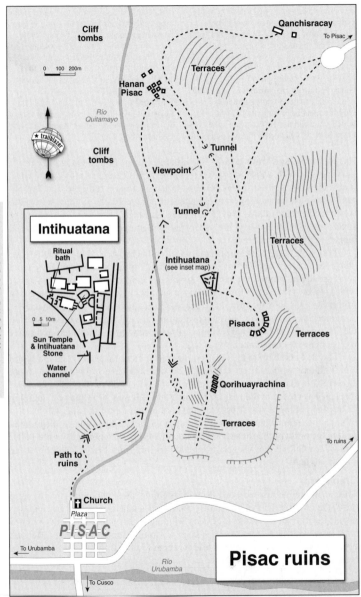

Pisac ruins

Qanchisracay

To Pisac

Cliff tombs

Terraces

0   100   200m

Hanan Pisac

Río Quitamayo

Cliff tombs

Tunnel

Viewpoint

Tunnel

Terraces

Intihuatana
(see inset map)

Intihuatana

Ritual bath

0   5   10m

Sun Temple & Intihuatana Stone

Water channel

Pisaca

Terraces

Qorihuayrachina

Terraces

Path to ruins

To ruins

Church

Plaza

PISAC

To Urubamba

Río Urubamba

To Cusco

AROUND CUSCO

Further down the valley there are also interesting examples of channels and stairs cut into the rocks. The attractive **colonial church**, built on the upper level of the plaza and dating from the early 17th century, was constructed on Inca foundations and has been unusually decorated inside with red and blue floral patterns. It also has paintings from the Cusco School. The colourful **Sunday market** (crafts as well as local produce) is worth coming for as it attracts fewer tourists than the Pisac markets and is considered to be more traditional.

Where to stay

There are very few places to stay in Chinchero. Your best bet, other than a handful of rather basic hospedajes, is *La Casa de Barro* (☎ 306031, 🖥 www.lacasa debarro.com; US$109 full board in a double room), a modern hotel with hot water, a bar and its own restaurant.

However, Peru Treks & Adventure (see p181), in partnership with Andean Travel Web (see box p44), have a well-established **homestay** programme, where you can stay with a local family (s/50 per person). Facilities at the house are generally very basic and the family only speak Quechua and Spanish, but you are able to gain an insight into their daily lives. Contact the agency to arrange a visit.

Transport

To return to Cusco catch the bus (about s/3; 30 mins) from the main road. Take any bus that crosses the high pampa rather than those that go to Cusco via Pisac.

❏ New Cusco Airport proposal

The project to relocate the main airport for Cusco from the city to the high plain adjacent to Chinchero, which was first mooted several years ago, is still rumbling on. The airport in Cusco is deemed to have served its purpose, largely because it can't accommodate international flights. The land it currently stands on is also prime real estate in a city that struggles for space because of the natural barriers to expansion all around it. Initially, few thought such a large-scale project, and all the environmental devastation that would accompany it, would be allowed to proceed. However, in 2012 it was announced that **Chinchero Cusco International Airport**, as it is called, would indeed go ahead and large amounts of money as compensation were paid to a handful of communities on whose farmland the airport will be constructed. Other inhabitants on the vast open area aren't scheduled to receive anything.

The impact on the region could be colossal; the wild, empty plain will be developed and the views over the Chincheros plain to Nevado Veronica past lakes and fields will be impacted not only by the airport itself but also all the ancillary buildings and developments that will inevitably follow. Whether the airport, which will be 400m higher than the current city airport, will work as an international destination remains to be seen. The pampa here is also often cold and obscured with cloud, conditions that hardly suit large aircraft, making the project and choice of location seem even riskier. Opponents have proposed using Pampa de Anta instead as it's several hundred metres lower, closer to Cusco and much less damaging to local communities. Currently the suggestion has fallen on deaf ears.

Early in 2016 it was announced that work would start imminently, with a scheduled completion date set for 2021. By July 2016, however, there had been no progress on the airport's construction and word got out that the project was stalling due to a lack of funding. Though it was promised that these problems would be sorted out by September, at the time of writing, work on building the airport had still yet to begin.

Urubamba

This sprawling transport hub at the junction of the roads from Pisac and Chinchero is often a necessary stepping stone to somewhere else in the Sacred Valley. Urubamba's not a particularly attractive town, although it has a palm-filled plaza and grand colonial church, but the setting is magnificent, beneath a set of fine snow-capped peaks.

Many of the **adventure activities** run by agencies in Cusco, such as white-water rafting, hot air-ballooning and horse riding, begin from Urubamba. It also hosts a local **market** one block west of the plaza and is home to a number of artisans including weavers, ceramicists, potters, sculptors and artists. It is quite possible to spend half a day wandering about the **studios and workshops** watching the workers create their wares.

The town has a small **tourist office** (on the colectivo side; Mon-Fri 8am-1pm & 2-4.30pm) in the bus station, several **ATMs**, and the garage on the junction of Av Ferrocarril and Av Mariscal Castilla serves as a **supermarket** too.

Where to stay

There are plenty of hotels in Urubamba but also some cheaper places to the north of the Plaza de Armas. The best hostel is *Misky Illary Wasi* (✉ miskyillarywasy@hotmail.com), two blocks north of the main square at Calle Belen, Cuadra 6, with clean and comfortable rooms, hot water, wi-fi and some good information on attractions in the local area – and how to get to them. Rates are s/30/50-65/90 (sgl/dbl/tpl, att) and include use of the kitchen. Slightly further north, *Hotel La Florida* (Jirón Zavala 438) is a simple yet fairly charming place set round a courtyard with en suite rooms (s/80-120, dbl, not including breakfast).

Many of the more **upmarket hotels** are lined up along the main road running along the south-western edge of the town. Most luxurious is *Tambo del Inka* (✆ 581777, ✉ www.libertador.com.pe; US$206/206-459, sgl/dbl, att), Av Ferrocarril, which has large colonial-style rooms in expansive grounds and a world-class spa. There's also a private railway station in the grounds where the PeruRail service to Machu Picchu stops. The grounds are spacious and attractive and service is exemplary.

Just west of town is the charming *Sol y Luna Lodge Spa* (✆ 608930, ✉ www.hotelsolyluna.com; US$350/350/425/525, sgl/dbl/tpl/quad, breakfast), now part of the Relais and Chateaux chain, boasting luxury

bungalows set in a pleasant garden full of eucalyptus and cypress trees, its own restaurant that hosts folk shows, tennis courts and a spa.

On the road to Ollantaytambo, 3km from Urubamba, is a handful of colourful, rustic cottages complete with small kitchen, terrace and balcony, to rent at *K'uychi Rumi* (✆ 201169, ✉ www.urubamba.com; US$120/140/180/230, sgl/dbl/tpl/quad); cottages that can sleep up to seven people cost US$350.

San Agustín Urubamba (✆ 201444, ✉ www.hotelessanagustin.com.pe) lies 1km east of town in spacious grounds and with a swimming pool, sauna and Jacuzzi. Rates start at US$61 if booked online.

On the outskirts of Urubamba at Jirón Recoleta and part of the same chain is *San Agustín Monasterio de la Recoleta* (✆ 201666, ✉ www.hotelessanagustin.com.pe; rates from US$83 if booked online). Set in a converted 15th-century monastery, this striking hotel offers standard rooms and more luxurious suites but also retains the chapel and cloistered courtyards of its original incarnation.

Best of all though is *Rio Sagrado Hotel* (✆ 201631, ✉ www.belmond.com; rates from US$295, sgl/dbl), owned by the Belmond chain and set just above the river with a tranquil garden and raft of facilities including a sauna, Jacuzzi and well-tended

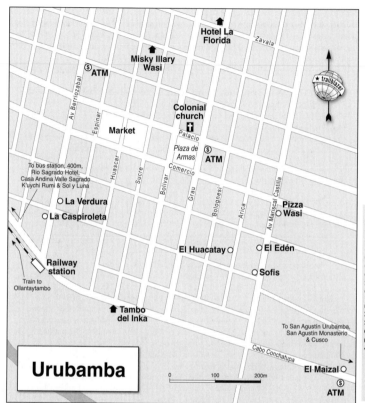

Urubamba

Map labels:
- Hotel La Florida
- Zavala
- Misky Illary Wasi
- ATM
- Av Berriozabal
- Espinar
- Colonial church
- Palacio
- Market
- Plaza de Armas
- ATM
- To bus station, 400m, Río Sagrado Hotel, Casa Andina Valle Sagrado K'uychi Rumi & Sol y Luna
- Huascar
- Sucre
- Bolivar
- Comercio
- Grau
- Bolognesi
- Arica
- Av Mariscal Castilla
- La Verdura
- La Caspiroleta
- Pizza Wasi
- El Huacatay
- El Edén
- Railway station
- Train to Ollantaytambo
- Sofis
- Tambo del Inka
- To San Agustín Urubamba, San Agustín Monasterio & Cusco
- Cabo Conchatupa
- El Maizal
- ATM
- 0   100   200m

AROUND CUSCO

bar and restaurant. The rooms are extravagant and elegant, with giant panoramic windows that look out over the garden and river below.

Not quite as decadent but a very good choice at the price is *Casa Andina Valle Sagrado* (☎ 765501, 🖳 www.casa-andina.com; rooms from US$115), which is further away but very quietly sited, set back from the main road in attractive, expansive grounds. Tiers of two-storey cottages feel homely and are kitted out in traditional textiles. There's a large restaurant and more intimate bar area along with a spa, gym and sauna.

Where to eat
If you're not eating in your hotel and want to head out for food, there's a *café* on the western side of the plaza.

There are several **pizza restaurants** and chicken roasters on Av Mariscal Castilla, the best of which is *Pizza Wasi*; it offers lasagne and ravioli in addition to the standard fare. Also on this strip, across the road and down a block or two, is *El Edén*, a lovely little spot where pretty much everything is homemade and they have a range of jams, teas and other locally produced goods for sale. They also bake up some delicious cakes as well as a delightful tiramisu (s/4.50) and several pasta dishes for those looking for something more substantial. A couple of doors down, *Sofis* is a good cheap place to get a coffee and a couple of croissants, which shouldn't set you back more than s/5.

Some of the best food is at *El Huacatay* (🖳 www.elhuacatay.com), Jirón Arica 620, a smart atmospheric place that serves great Novoandina staples with a contemporary flourish.

❏ **Hugh Thomson describes living in the small market town of Urubamba**
'While writing a book on Peru, I wanted to find a quiet base where I could live with my family. Cuzco itself does not have the healthiest climate for kids, as the high mountain bowl can trap the car pollution and they can find the altitude hard, whereas the town of Urubamba seemed more easy going and had a good school. I remembered the American traveller Ephraim George Squier's comments in the 19th century:

> *Although only 2500 feet lower than the Cuzco Basin, the Yucay [Urubamba] Valley, protected on all sides, enjoys a much more benign climate, similar to that of Nimes and other parts of the south of France. Both healthy and fertile, easily accessible from the capital, and with a vegetation unrivalled in the Sierra, this sweet and tranquil valley, surrounded by some of the highest mountains of the Continent, quickly became the favourite place of recreation for the Incas. The soil is rich and the climate, in spite of the fact that the Valley is enclosed by high snow-capped mountains, is soft and agreeable. A more beautiful place than this does not exist in all of the Andes...'*

We found a house on the outskirts of Urubamba, at a place called K'uychi Rumi which means 'rainbow stone' in Quechua: the houses shared a communal garden, a riot of hibiscus, abutilon, poinsettias and roses, with arum lilies growing alongside the small irrigation ditches that ran through the property; the owners, architect Carlos Rey and his wife, Claudia, had also introduced some pre-Columbian plants – *polylepis* trees and *quinoa*. A line of yellow broom led along paths to a large stand of eucalyptus at the far end of the property where the children would spend many happy hours swinging over the stream; immediately beyond rose the ravine up to Pumahuanca, one of the passes leading to the Amazon.

The rhythm of such small market towns had always appealed to me and I now quickly found it seductive: the Post Office that never seemed to open; the old men moving around the benches in the Plaza to keep getting the sun – I overheard one telling another: 'get it written down on paper because you know that words can be blown away by the wind'; a shoe shine boy playing his Gameboy while he waited for customers; the café on the corner of the square called, with the utmost simplicity, 'The Corner Café'.

But Urubamba was a mountain as well as a market town: like a settlement in the old West where the main drag is only a temporary slowing of a longer route through the wilderness, the high street past the gas station turned into a country lane which led directly up to the Chicón glacier.

We rode up there sometimes from the town, picking our way through the cobbled streets nervously as the odd mototaxi could shoot without warning from an alley and scare the horses, the drivers treating them as if they were errant pedestrians. By riding, we could get glimpses over the high patio walls of hidden courtyards, orchards and market gardens. The surrounding fields were a reminder too that Urubamba was organised not around its streets but around its water supply: there was a complicated series of irrigation canals, which could be diverted at different points during the day under a tightly regulated system. Woe betide the *campesino* who 'forgot' to divert a canal back to his neighbour at the appointed hour – or for

On the other side of town, Av Berriozabal plays host to a couple of decent places. *La Verdura* is a smart, relaxed new café with excellent wi-fi and a small but decent menu including a two-course set lunch for s/12, and mains such as Peruvian free-range chicken lasagne for s/25. Across the road, *La Caspiroleta* is named after a popular local drink made of hot milk, eggs, cinnamon, brandy, sugar and usually some

that matter the three-year-old boy like ours, Leo, who enjoyed damming or diverting them at 'inappropriate' moments.

Within a few weeks of arriving we were invited to a local wedding and realised that we already knew most of the congregation. The bride and groom emerged from the town hall registry office to a full band playing in the town square, a band in which the bridegroom usually played himself.

I had met Joyo several times at the Corner Café, eating empanadas with a saxophone slung over his shoulder. He was an architect who had travelled in France, been an active revolutionary during the 1968 Sorbonne uprising, and had since settled in Urubamba with Lola, his French girlfriend and now bride, to play music; they were getting married to regularise both their own nationalities and those of their adopted children. Unfortunately, as Joyo had told me, the Peruvian authorities had made a mistake and thought initially they wanted to get divorced, not married. Peruvian bureaucracy, once started, will move in only one direction: Joyo's protests that they could not get divorced because they weren't married had fallen on deaf ears; it had taken six months of bureaucratic confusion before their 'divorce' had come through and they could get 'remarried'.

Joyo unslung his sax and was leading his own wedding procession around the town square and up to their house for a wedding party that would last all day and all of the night. One of his band had played with the Grateful Dead. There were fond memories of the time Keith Richards had passed through with the Stones on one of their Peruvian adventures and busked in the Corner Café (it had been a country that had always appealed to Mick Jagger, not least because when in the Amazon to film *Fitzcarraldo*, no one had recognised him).

Indeed over the months that we lived there, I began to realise that there was a bohemian diaspora around Urubamba of pony-tailed hippies and Peace Corps veterans of a certain age, who had fetched up here in the cheap land and low regulations of the '70s, when dope could be grown in your back garden. The valley had changed considerably since then. In recent years the beginnings of the tourist boom engulfing Peru had spilled over from Cuzco and hotels were being built at an alarming rate, usually with our landlord Carlos Rey as architect. There were also many exiled Limeños, like Carlos, who had moved here for the good life. Some had put Jacuzzis into their haciendas. Even the taxi drivers now had mobile phones.

It intrigued me that the picture I had always had of Urubamba from afar – the small market town in the heart of the Sacred Valley, the grain basket of the Incas – should have such a touch of Laurel Canyon about it. Of course there were still plenty of local villagers still keeping horses, minding their small plots and threatening to shoot the neighbours if the irrigation canal wasn't turned over to them at the appointed hour. But just when you least expected it, with the wood-smoke drifting past the eucalyptus stands and the sun setting on the Chicón glacier, a four-wheel drive would flash past blaring out rap music'.

Hugh Thomson wrote, while based in Urubamba,
Cochineal Red: Travels through Ancient Peru

other ingredient too (s/10 if you want to try it). The place itself is large and welcoming and though the menu is small (sandwiches for s/7-10 and cakes being the mainstays), it's a pleasant place to get out of the heat and the hubbub.

On the main road you'll find the rustic *El Maizal* which also serves Novoandina dishes from an extensive buffet.

Transport

Urubamba **bus station** is just to the west of the town, on the main road.

On one side are the colectivos to the local area (including Maras, for the trip to Moray).

On the other (eastern) side are buses and colectivos to Cusco (s/6; 2hrs) and further afield. These leave throughout the day, going via Pisac or (quicker) via Chinchero.

There's also a tourist **train service** between Urubamba and Aguas Calientes (see p354).

Around Urubamba

An interesting day can be spent touring two local Inca sights in the hills to the south of Urubamba.

To begin your journey, catch a colectivo (s/2.5) from Urubamba's bus terminal to the former silver-mining town of Maras. If none appears to be leaving soon, you can catch a Cusco-bound bus and jump off at the junction with the road to Maras, where taxi drivers often wait for custom. From either the junction or the main square in **Maras** you can negotiate with the taxi drivers to take you to Moray (around s/25 return trip including an hour at the site from either place). Alternatively, it's a sweaty 9km (6-mile) walk from Maras.

Moray (dawn to dusk; entrance with the Visitor's Ticket only) is an unusual, and highly atmospheric site. Three large concentric depressions in the earth have been cut and shaped into circular terraces of varying sizes. Hidden from sight until you are virtually on top of them, these giant amphitheatres are very striking. If you clamber up the hill behind the deepest depression you get a view of all three amphitheatres and can see the entire site in context. Thought to be an Inca farm, this extraordinary place was used to test the effects of altitude on different plants. The deepest depression is around 30m from rim to floor and temperatures within the bowl can vary by up to 10°C. It is thought that the terraces, built over retaining walls filled with fertile earth and watered by complex irrigation systems, each had their own micro-climate enabling the Incas to grow more than 250 species of plants.

Having returned to Maras, for an extra s/5-10 you could ask the taxi driver to drop you down at **Salineras** (6am-5pm; s/10). (The alternative, to walk, takes about an hour: head north from Maras to the clearly signposted road junction, from where it's an hour's schlep north and downhill along the dusty road). Mineral-rich, salty water from a hot spring higher up the valley is channelled into thousands of large, flat, shallow pans and allowed to evaporate so that salt is produced. This is then collected intensively by hand, just as it has been for hundreds of years, and continues to provide work for the locals.

From the northern end of the Salineras (ie the end furthest from the ticket office), you can take the path that heads down to the Urubamba River. At the river turn right and cross the bridge to the excellent *Arco Iris Lodge* (dorms US$15; US$55-60 dbl, att with breakfast; try for one of the rooms upstairs, which are brighter), in the village of **Tarabamba**. From the main road here you can then hail a s/1 colectivo ride back to Urubamba.

Ollantaytambo   [see map p202 & p204]

The historic town of Ollantaytambo stands at the far end of the Urubamba Valley, 68km from Cusco. Here the fertile valley narrows and the river flows into a gorge. In this strategic spot the Inca Pachacutec built the fortress and religious complex of Ollantaytambo, having subjugated the valley's former residents. The massive ruins set above a compact town are some of the most striking and impressive in the whole of the Sacred Valley.

The town itself is a relaxing, easy-going alternative to Cusco and a good way of escaping some of the bustle associated with the larger city. However, since PeruRail started using Ollantaytambo as the start and end point for its train services to Machu Picchu, the town periodically becomes congested with lorries and buses that battle through the narrow streets; the latter are trying to meet the trains and the passengers they disgorge. The resulting queues can choke the access roads and main plaza – they were never designed to accommodate such large, or so many, vehicles – spoiling the relaxed Andean ambience here.

The town is compact and it's easy to walk everywhere. It is about 150 metres from the plaza to the ruins (see p203).

The old town The photogenic town set in the shadow of the illustrious ruins is one of the finest examples of Inca town planning. In most towns the original Inca streets and housing have been knocked down and built over, but in Ollantaytambo there are still plenty of original examples of each. The town is laid out in a grid and the corners of the main streets are marked by giant stone blocks. The Incas arranged their towns in communal blocks called *canchas*, which housed a number of families. The double-jamb doorways to these canchas indicate that the residents must have been part of the Inca elite. Simpler structures that would have belonged to poorer, less-important citizens employed to work for the Incas can be found in the northern part of the town.

El Museo CATCCO (☎ 204204; Tue-Sun 10am-1pm & 3-6pm; entrance by donation) is one block west of Plaza de Armas on Patacalle. Inside this well-kept museum dedicated to ethnography and regional history are superb displays of historical and cultural artefacts. Local artisans, weavers and ceramicists also work on the premises; their wares are for sale in the museum shop or in the Casa Ecológica shop next door to the restaurant Mayupata. Guides trained by the museum can be hired here and they can also arrange tours of the surrounding area. For a fascinating, detailed examination of the Inca stonework here, read *Inca Architecture and Construction at Ollantaytambo* by Jean-Pierre Protzen (1993).

AROUND CUSCO

The **market** consists of souvenir stalls for tourists and **Mercado Central** sells food and goods for the locals as well as trekking gear. There is a small **tourist information point** on the plaza and an ATM, though it is expensive to withdraw money here.

Where to stay

On Av Estudiante, *Camping/Hostel Ollantaytambo* (☎ 308499) is the cheapest place in town, with rooms for just s/15, or s/20 for those with private facilities. **Camping** is s/12. It's not bad but you do get what you paid for – ie, not much.

The best-value option in town is the lovely *Casa de Wow* (☎ 204010, 🖥 www.casadewow.com; s/55/70/90, sgl/dbl/tpl, com, s/85/120 sgl/dbl, att) a couple of minutes' walk away from the plaza on a quiet side street, Calle Patacalle. This very friendly place, run by a creative local, is decorated in traditional style and has beds built by the owner himself. There's free tea and coffee, use of the kitchen and wi-fi and a pretty roof terrace as well. It's a great place and the hosts are a mine of information. Back towards the plaza on the same

street, at No 722, is *Hostal Iskay* (☎ 434109, 🖥 www.hostaliskay.com; US$39/45-75 sgl/dbl), a smart and friendly enough place with some very pleasant rooms and a lovely terraced garden. Room rates are cheaper if booked through their website.

Hostal Munay Tika (☎ 204111, 🖥 www.munaytika.com), Av Ferrocarril 554, on the road to the station, is an attractive guesthouse with a bar and sauna as well as quiet, spacious rooms (US$110/150/190, sgl/dbl/tpl, breakfast) with access to the kitchen for guests.

Nearby, *Las Orquideas* (☎ 204032, 🖥 www.lasorquideasollantaytambo.com) is a reasonably priced hostel with basic rooms (US$30/45/55/60 sgl/dbl/tpl/quad, breakfast) and a pleasant courtyard in which to lounge.

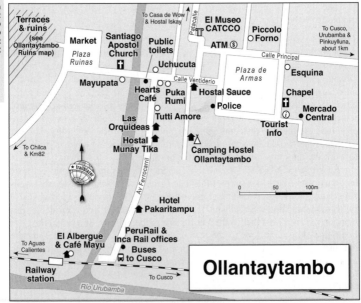

The excellent North American-owned *El Albergue* (☎ 204014, 🖳 www.elalbergue.com; US$99/109, dbl/tpl, att, breakfast, rooms with balcony US$199), Estacion de Tren, has 16 elegant rooms set around a courtyard with a shop by reception selling handicrafts, all situated at the railway station with entrance via the platform. Good discounts are available during the low season. Handy for the trains, it is some 800m to the town though.

The modern terracotta-coloured *Hotel Pakaritampu* (☎ 204020, 🖳 www.pakaritampu.com; US$183/191/244, sgl/dbl/tpl, att), on the road just up from the station, is comfortable and friendly, has a bar and restaurant as well as a TV room.

Hostal Sauce (☎ 204044, 🖳 www.hostalsauce.com.pe; s/312/390/546, sgl/dbl/tpl, att, breakfast) has the best location, overlooking the Inca ruins and close to the main plaza. The rooms are comfortable though service is sometimes brusque.

Where to eat
Our favourite spot is *Puka Rumi*, upstairs near the bridge. An extensive menu of hearty expertly cooked dishes, including excellent steaks and veggie burritos, are available in this unpretentious, friendly place. Next door, *Hearts Café* (🖳 www.heartscafe.org), on Av Ventiderio, opens early for breakfast and specialises in vegetarian and wholefood dishes cooked with a local twist but also has a range of international dishes. The profits are ploughed back into the community and go towards children's and women's projects in the Sacred Valley. Across the way, *Uchucuta* has some exquisite and imaginative Peruvian dishes, all beautifully presented, including rolled chicken and alpaca ravioli; mains are around the s/30 mark, which counts as great

value for what you get. Nearby, back towards the plaza, *Il Piccolo Forno* does some authentic Italian dishes including lasagne, calzones and very good pizzas. On Plaza de Armas is *Esquina*, which is the perfect spot for a plum brownie or a combo salad bowl, hot chocolate and a chance to watch the activity in the square.

The restaurant at *El Albergue* is the smartest place in town. The food, largely organic and displaying a mix of Western, Asian and Peruvian influences, is fairly simple but the quality top notch; try the alpaca burger (s/33), or lamb with chimichurri sauce (s/42). Their vegetarian options are refreshingly wide too. If that's too expensive, and you've got an hour free during the day, at least come to their *Cafe Mayu* for a coffee (roasted on site) and cake (baked on the premises); it's a lovely place to sit and watch all the action at the railway station. If the station is too far, stop on the way at *Tutti Amore* for delicious homemade ice-cream in a wide range of flavours.

Transport
From here there are **trains** to Aguas Calientes. Having caught the train back from Aguas Calientes it is very easy to pick up an onward bus to Cusco. See pp352-5 for details of the tourist train service from Cusco to Ollantaytambo. The station is about a 10-minute walk from Plaza de Armas.

Buses and **colectivos** depart for Urubamba (s/2-3), Chilca and Km82 from the main plaza and outside the station. Direct buses to Cusco (s/10) sometimes depart from outside the station, where they meet the incoming trains. To avoid the scrum you may be better taking a colectivo to Urubamba and catching a bus on to Cusco from there.

Ollantaytambo ruins [see map p204]

The daunting **fortress** was described by Pedro Pizarro as 'so well fortified that it was a thing of horror'. It was to this mighty castle that Manco Inca retreated following his uprising. Pursued by the Spanish, he holed up in the fortress high above the surrounding plain and faced the conquistadors. After two days of heavy fighting he forced the Spanish to retreat, the first time that the colonial army had been bested in combat by the Incas. Manco realised he wouldn't be

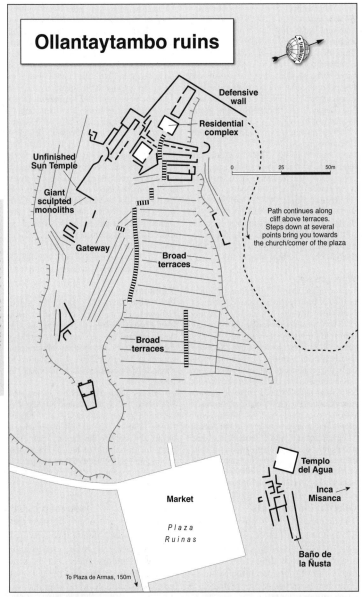

Ollantaytambo ruins

Defensive wall

Residential complex

Unfinished Sun Temple

Giant sculpted monoliths

Gateway

Broad terraces

Path continues along cliff above terraces. Steps down at several points bring you towards the church/corner of the plaza

0   25   50m

Broad terraces

Templo del Agua

Inca Misanca

Baño de la Ñusta

Market

Plaza Ruinas

To Plaza de Armas, 150m

AROUND CUSCO

Colour photos (© Henry Stedman, unless otherwise credited)
● **Top**: Looking down from the fortress to Ollantaytambo town, laid out in a grid by the Incas (photo © Bryn Thomas). Their street drainage system (**right,** © Zoe Ashdown) still operates. **Above left**: Salt pans – Salineras (see p200).
● **C2 (overleaf) Ausangate region – Left**: The gorgeous views over the chain of turquoise lakes are just one of the highlights of the path to Acosere on the Ausangate trail.
Top right: Collecting water from a glacial lake on the way to Abra Ausangate.
Middle: Alpaca are well suited to the tough conditions here, with even their faces protected by thick fur. **Bottom**: Staying in a farmer's hut before Pampacancha.
● **C3 Choquequirao – Top**: The Lower Plaza of Choquequirao with the Apurímac valley beyond. **Bottom left**: Mules carrying supplies on the steep, dry, dusty trail to Choquequirao.
Right: Uniquely, the Inca terraces here were decorated with the images of 24 llamas.

C2

able to maintain his superiority so close to Cusco and sadly abandoned the fortress to move over the mountains to Vilcabamba.

The fortress (7am-5.30pm; Visitor's Ticket) still looks much as it once did and it's easy to see how the Spanish would have been appalled at the prospect of throwing themselves against the 16 great walled terraces that hug the contours of the hills and bar the route up to the unassailable fortress.

More than 200 **steps** lead steeply through the terraces from the plaza below. Giant walls rise from the almost sheer cliff-faces preventing any attacker from flanking the site. At the top of the steps stands the **unfinished Sun Temple**, which is made up of six enormous, mortarless monoliths cut from pink porphyry and mottled with orange lichen. These upright stones have been carefully fitted together aligned east to west. Double-jambed archways on the approach to this point indicate that this was a very important centre.

From the top you can see the quarry Cachicata, 3.5km south-west of the site at the foot of Yana Urco (the Black Mountain), where a huge rockfall provided loose stones of huge size. From the top of the fortress you get a very good impression of the Herculean task required to haul the stones all the way from the quarry to the temple. In order to cross the Urubamba, it is thought that the Incas simply diverted the river around the blocks positioned on its banks.

A handful of giant blocks, known poetically as *piedras cansadas* ('tired stones'), litter the valley floor, lying where they were presumably abandoned whilst being transported from the quarry.

Work your way along the terraces north-east and descend again to a point just behind a church set on the side of the small plaza. There are a few smaller Inca ruins here including a small temple or observatory called **Inca Misanca**, and 200m below, the **Baño de la Ñusta**, a site associated with ritual bathing and the worship of water.

Opposite the main site, on the eastern edge of Ollantaytambo, is a steep cliff known as **Pinkuylluna** (off map p202). High on this cliff-face are the remnants of several *qolqas* (storehouses). There's a faint path that climbs to the storehouses but you need to be careful and should take a guide rather than set off alone.

Cusichaca Valley

Some 26km from Ollantaytambo is the Cusichaca Valley. This area has been at the heart of a series of excavations carried out by the archaeologist Ann Kendall over the last 30 years (🖳 www.cusichaca.org). The organisation also pioneers integrated rural development projects in tandem with local communities, promoting the use of local resources, traditional skills and appropriate modern techniques to benefit the communities involved.

The Inca Fort **Huillca Raccay** (see box p234) was uncovered in the late 1970s before work focused on the ruins at **Patallacta** (see box p218), at the start of the classic Inca Trail. Subsequent excavation has been done in the Patacancha Valley to the north-east of Ollantaytambo.

(Opposite) Looking down from the remote and lofty Huillquijasa Pass (4417m/14,491ft) on the Lares trek. (See p274; photo © Henry Stedman).

Aguas Calientes (Pueblo Machu Picchu)   [see map opposite]

Officially known as Pueblo Machu Picchu, this village is very much the end of the line now that the track that used to run on to Quillabamba has been destroyed. Really just a dormitory town for the ruins themselves, it's an ugly rash in the pristine forest of the Sanctuary and has in the past been described as the 'Armpit of Peru'. The town is, however, undergoing something of a renaissance and amidst all the development work there now stand several fine hotels and some very good eateries, too.

Information is available from the **iPerú branch** (Mon-Sat 9am-1pm & 2-6pm, Sun 9am-1pm) on Av Pachacutec, in the same building as the **Machu Picchu ticket office** that sells entrance tickets to the ruins. (Note that you should already have bought your ticket online if you're hoping to visit the ruins in the next day or two – **for information on buying tickets see p318**).

For several years now, regulation changes have meant that you can no longer buy entrance tickets for Machu Picchu at the site itself. Similarly, if you want to climb Huayna Picchu or Machu Picchu Mountain you must buy a ticket in advance – in the high season, months in advance – as these also can no longer be arranged at Machu Picchu. If you are travelling with a trekking agency or tour group they should ensure that you are provided with an entrance ticket and any additional tickets. Tickets are available from the Dirección Regional de Cultura in Aguas Calientes, in the same building as iPerú (see above). The office opens at 5am and payment can be in cash or card. Tickets are for a single entry to the site; if you want to return to Machu Picchu you will have to buy a second ticket. Tickets are also available in Cusco (see p160).

There are plenty of **internet cafés** and **cash machines** on Av Pachacutec, around the plaza and throughout the town. Trawl the **market** adjacent to the main station for textiles, T-shirts and other souvenirs.

The **hot springs** (daily 5.30am-7.30pm; s/20) after which the town is named comprise a series of rather pungent communal baths several minutes' walk north from town. If you are tempted, the pools are cleanest and most pleasant first thing in the morning.

On the road to Machu Picchu it's worth visiting **Museo de Sitio Manuel Chávez Ballón – Machu Picchu Museum** (Carretera Hiram Bingham; 10am-4pm; s/22) a small museum displaying a number of objects uncovered at Machu Picchu. There are interactive displays and a wealth of information on excavations, Inca building methods, cosmology and other cultural bits and pieces. There's also an interesting **botanical garden** here.

Where to stay

Cheapest of all is the *municipal campground* (s/15 per person; cold water shower) about 1km downhill from the centre of town towards Machu Picchu and adjacent to the bridge over the Urubamba. Take great care of your possessions here.

For more solid accommodation, the local railway station is a branch of the excellent hostel chain *EcoPackers* (☎ 211121, ✉ www.ecopackersperu.com). Like its sibling in Cusco, this is another facility-filled hostel with reasonable rates,

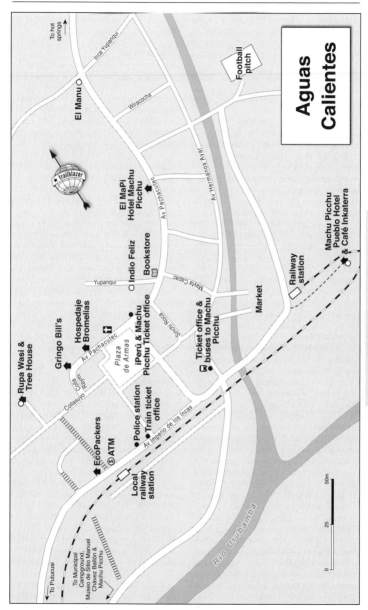

Aguas Calientes

To hot springs

Inca Yupanqui

Football pitch

Wiracocha

El Manu

Av Hermanos Ayar

Av Pachacutec

El MaPi Hotel Machu Picchu

Indio Feliz

Bookstore

Machu Picchu Pueblo Hotel & Café Inkaterra

Yupanqui

Railway station

Mayta Capac

Hospedaje Bromelias

Gringo Bill's

Market

Rupa Wasi & Tree House

Sinchi Roca

iPerú & Machu Picchu Ticket office

Ticket office & buses to Machu Picchu

Av Pachacutec

Plaza de Armas

Colla Raymi

Collasuyo

Police station

Train ticket office

EcoPackers

ATM

Local railway station

Av Imperio de los Incas

To Putucusi

To Municipal Campground, Museo de Sitio Manuel Chávez Ballón & Machu Picchu

Río Urubamba

AROUND CUSCO

0   25   50m

with a bed in a dorm US$14.50-18.50, the exact price depending on the number of beds in the room; a private double is US$60. Discounts are sometimes available from their website.

On the plaza just before Gringo Bill's, *Hospedaje Bromelias* (☎ 211145) is rough and ready but cheap as a result (s/60, sgl or dbl, att).

The bohemian *Rupa Wasi* (☎ 211101, 🖥 www.rupawasi.net; rooms start at US$60 dbl, breakfast) is a rustic eco-lodge hidden up Huanacaure, a small alley off Collasuyo. Ridiculously laid-back, it's a haven for those who just want to chill out, although cooking classes, birdwatching trips and other treks can be arranged by the knowledgeable, friendly owners as well.

Gringo Bill's (☎ 211046, 🖥 www .gringobills.com) is at Calle Colla Raymi 104, just off the plaza. The place is something of an institution in Aguas Calientes and still maintains its high standards, remaining friendly, easy-going and offering reasonable value at US$105/140 (dbl/tpl, att). There's a restaurant, a bar and a rooftop Terraza Lounge; the latter is a great space to relax in or catch up with other travellers.

El MaPi Hotel Machu Picchu (Lima office ☎ 01 422 6574, 🖥 www.elmapihotel .com), at Pachacutec 109, is a smart, stylish hotel full of restored and recycled materials that is part of Inkaterra's more affordable arm. It's all relative though and the rooms still cost upwards of US$220. For the money, the rooms, adorned with slogans on the walls are small but the general ambience is relaxed and the restaurant is good. The bar also makes a decent pisco sour.

The top hotel is *Machu Picchu Pueblo Hotel* (reservations in Lima ☎ 01 510 0400, 🖥 www.inkaterra.com), where beautiful colonial-style bungalows are set in 12 acres of exquisite, enclosing forest, five-minutes' walk east from the rest of town; to get here follow the basic path next to the railway line. It boasts a pool, sauna, spa and expensive restaurant. Room rates begin around US$500 and rise sharply depending on the style of room and the season; the Inkaterra Suite tops the bill at more than US$1100.

There's also an expensive *hotel* at the ruins themselves (see p319).

Where to eat

In a town with a growing reputation for fleecing tourists by providing average food and service at top-dollar prices, there are a couple of outstanding choices. *Tree House Restaurant* (Calle Huanacaure 180), opposite Rupa Wasi, is a lovely spot with a great menu of simple but imaginative, hearty and tasty fare. It's not cheap but nevertheless fair value; try the beef tenderloin steak in elderberry sauce (s/55). Perhaps even better than this is the outstanding French-run *Indio Feliz* (☎ 211090, 🖥 www.indiofeliz .com), Calle Lloque Yupanqui 103. It's a great spot, the walls festooned with notes, messages and memorabilia. Dishes here include Urubamba trout with garlic cream, chicken with mango from the jungle, beef skewers and a wide range of delicious desserts. The wine list is well chosen and prices are reasonable.

Café Inkaterra at Machu Picchu Pueblo Hotel (see Where to stay) is not a bad third option with high-class Peruvian fusion food and good views over the river. You can get decent veggie food at *El Manu*, which is one of the town's better-value eateries.

Transport

Aguas Calientes boasts two **railway stations**: the modern one, surrounded by wire fencing and policed by armed guards, serves the expensive tourist trains. The ticket office here is open 6.30am-5.30pm.

Local trains set off from the stretch of tracks running beneath the police station, to the south of the main square. There's no indication that this is a station, for it's little more than a rail track with pizza restaurants either side. All train tickets must be bought from the ticket office (8.30am-6pm) to the east of the police station. See pp352-5 for details and timetables of the train service. This is also where the train from La Hidroeléctrica, at the end of the Salkantay Trek, stops (see pp263-4).

The **buses for Machu Picchu** leave from the bus 'station'; it's just a patch of concrete where the train tracks pass over a small stream, The first buses leave at around 5.30am or half an hour before dawn and then depart every 10-20 minutes. The bus ticket office in Aguas Calientes opens 15 minutes before the first bus leaves.

See p319 for more information on transport from Aguas Calientes and Machu Picchu.

SOUTH AND EAST OF CUSCO

For many people the focus of a trip to Cusco is the Sacred Valley and Machu Picchu. However, there are also several fascinating ruins to see to the south and east of the city.

A paved road runs south-east from Cusco to **Sicuani**, following the upper reaches of the Río Urubamba. There are some ruins scattered across the altiplano here, indicating the spread of the Incas towards Lake Titicaca, where the road eventually arrives at Puno.

Just outside Cusco, making it virtually a suburb, stands **San Jerónimo**, which hosts an enormous fruit and veg market on Saturdays. South-east from here the valley narrows as you approach Oropesa, before which lie the ruins of Tipón and after which the ruins at Pikillacta.

Tipón (7.30am-4.30pm; s/20; free with Visitor's Ticket) is 25km from Cusco. About 2km before Oropesa, at Choquepata, you turn left and follow the road for 4km to the ruins. This turn off the main highway is signposted and it's opposite a bizarre larger than life statue of a woman holding a plate of *cuy* (guinea pig). She's advertising the fact that Oropesa and the surrounding area is one of the best places to try this Peruvian delicacy; there are *cuyerías* lining the roadside.

It'll take around an hour to walk from the main road up to Tipón, which is hidden at the head of a small valley beyond the remains of

This statue advertising *cuy* is a good marker for where to get off the bus for the side road up to Tipón.

the hacienda Quispicanchi. The extensive Inca ruins here include a series of agricultural terraces, ceremonial baths, fountains and stone-lined irrigation channels, many of which still carry water. Above the last terrace a trail leads to a temple complex built around a *huaca*. An enormous reservoir collected water from a spring, which was then distributed to the terraces along a series of channels. Behind and to the left of the main site a faint trail leads to a further series of ruins and well-preserved Inca terraces that are now in use by local people. So extensive are the terraces here that archaeologists have suggested the site may have been an experimental farm, much like Moray (see p200).

Historians counter that Tipón could have been a palace but the accounts left by chroniclers make it difficult to say whose it was. Garcilaso de la Vega believed that it was the royal house of Viracocha whose father, Yáhuar Huácac,

The extensive Inca waterways at Tipón still function.

was defeated by the Chancas. Viracocha stood up to and later defeated the Chancas, and was subsequently crowned Inca in place of his father. Garcilaso wrote that, 'It was determined that the son, as most of the court decided, would be the head of the kingdom; and to avoid riots and civil wars, they accepted everything the prince wanted. After it was agreed, they obtained a Royal House, between Muyna and Quepicancha, in a pleasant place with all the gifts, fields, gardens and other royal amusements for hunting and fishing.' Other chroniclers, such as Pedro Cieza de León and Juan de Betanzos, claim that it was actually Viracocha's son Pachacutec who defeated the Chancas after his father and older brother Inca Urcon had fled Cusco.

Further on from Tipón are the villages of **Oropesa** and **Huacarpay**; the latter stands on the shores of Laguna Huacarpay. Dotted around the lake are several pre-Columbian sites. Foremost of these is **Pikillacta** (7am-4.30pm; s/20, free with Visitor's Ticket), whose name translates rather unfortunately as 'City of Fleas'. The substantial site, 32km from Cusco and 7km from Oropesa, is the largest provincial outpost of the Ayacucho-based Huari (AD600-1000) and is the only major pre-Inca site around Cusco. The large complex, which is surrounded by a defensive wall, is thought to have been a storehouse or centre for collecting tributes and supplies. There were also adobe buildings and tambos here, many of them more than one storey tall, and many whose rough walls were treated with lime. Unusually the doors to these buildings appear to be on the first floor and in theory they must have been entered via ladders. Not much is known of the history of the site, but the small turquoise figurines in Museo Inka (see p155) were found here. The Incas subsequently modified the site and possibly built the aqueduct that links Pikillacta to Rumicolca.

Around 1km beyond Pikillacta stands the beautifully crafted, enormous Inca archway and defensive passage at **Rumicolca** (open all day; free). Built on top of an original Huari site, the Inca stonework is vastly superior to the cruder, original construction. The archway itself rears up from the altiplano in a series of four tiers and stands a full 12m/40ft above the plain. During Inca times all traffic on the road to and from Cusco had to pass through the giant, imposing archway, which acted as a checkpoint, regulating the passage of goods and people.

To get to any of these sites from Cusco catch a bus to Urcos, departing from Av de la Cultura. For Tipón ask to be dropped off by the statue (see p209), 2km before Oropesa. For Pikillacta or Rumicolca, both of which are on the main road, ask to be dropped by the entrance to the site. Alternatively, you can catch a taxi from Cusco, or take an organised tour run by one of the agencies in town (see pp177-82).

ROUTE GUIDE & MAPS

8

Using this guide

ROUTE DESCRIPTIONS

Directions in the following chapter are shown as an instruction to go left or right and as a compass point. For instance, if the instruction stated 'turn right (west)', it would indicate that west is to your right.

Direction

The trails described in this book are laid out as they are usually walked, from the traditional start point to the typical finish point. In a number of instances it is possible to walk the trail in either direction. The exceptions are that you are not allowed to start at Machu Picchu and hike the Inca Trail in reverse, meaning that you can't finish at Km104, Km88, Km82, Chilca (Km77) or Mollepata. The Choquequirao Trek is typically done as a there-and-back hike along the same route, although it is possible to connect it to other treks and complete a linear hike, finishing at Vilcabamba or even Machu Picchu.

ROUTE MAP NOTES [See pp28-9 for route planning map]

Scale and walking times

Most of the trekking maps in this guide are drawn at the same scale, roughly 1:50,000 (20mm = 1km; 1¼ inches = one mile). Many of the trails are uphill and downhill so the length of a trek is not an accurate reflection of the time it will take you to complete. The times included on the maps are there only as a guideline. They refer to **walking times only** and do not include any stops for breaks or food. To calculate the total time it will take to complete a section you will need to make allowances for these and add on a few minutes.

Overall you may find that you need to **add between 20% and 40%** depending on your walking speed and average length of time taken at each break.

Gradient arrows

There are gradient arrows marked on the trekking maps throughout the book. The arrows point uphill; two arrows close together mean that the hill is steep, one on its own means that it is a gentler gradient. If, for example, you are walking between A (at 3100m) and B (at 3300m) and the path between the two is short and steep, it would be illustrated as follows: A – – –>> – – – B.

Place names

The Quechua names for many of the ruins and archaeological sites along the various treks can be spelt in several ways as the original language had no alphabet or written guide. The more common Hispanic versions have been used here as they appear on most maps in this form. However, there has been a movement to reclaim a lot of colonial names for the indigenous language; this has caused confusion and ensured that in some cases there are now two or three versions of a name.

Where there's the potential for confusion all names are shown so, for instance, the ruins of Llactapata (see box pp260-1) on the Salkantay Trail are also referred to as Paltallacta or Patallacta (ie with no first 'l').

Just to further confuse the issue, some places may share the same name. For example, there are actually two ruins known as Llactapata! The first are those referred to above, which lie to the west of Machu Picchu. But there is also a

---

❑ Inca Trail regulations explained

The Inca Trail is governed by a series of complex and convoluted regulations, which are enforced stringently. They also change frequently and prices are hiked from time to time. Before booking check the latest information with Andean Travel Web (🖥 www.andeantravelweb.com/peru) and for **permit availability** go to 🖥 www.machu picchu.gob.pe then click 'Queries' along the top menu then 'Availability' (bottom menu, left) which will only then let you pull down the menu above to reveal 'Camino Inka' under the otherwise visible Machu Picchu tickets list.

● **Permit** The key elements to remember are that **you must have a permit before embarking on the trek to Machu Picchu**. A maximum of 500 people including guides, cooks and porters are allowed to start the trail each day. In reality this means that only around 200 tourists per day can begin the trek. For official purposes, the Inca Trail starts at Huayllabamba, so it doesn't matter whether you're starting at Km77, Km82, Km 88 or using the High Inca Trail (that joins the Inca Trail at Huayllabamba), you'll still be considered as one of the 500. The two shorter routes from Km104 are subject to their own limits of 250 per day in total, all for trekkers, though these seldom sell out.

The result is that there is fierce competition for the permits, and in order to secure a preferred departure date you must **book well in advance**. The permits used to be issued in January but are now issued at the start of October for the following year, so if you are looking to trek in the high season (Jun-Aug) you should try to secure your permit at this time; in our experience, the permits for June are 'sold out' pretty much immediately. If you have specific dates on which you need to trek, you should monitor the above websites closely and book your permit as soon as they become available. For the quieter months, however, you have a bit more time to play with.

To book a permit you must use a **licensed agency** based in Peru; they are not issued directly to tourists. In order to obtain a licence, the agency must prove that they provide professional, licensed guides, good-quality camping equipment, radio equipment and first-aid supplies including oxygen. Licences are reviewed annually in February. Agencies can only take groups of up to 16 people at any one time, and must provide two or more guides for groups of more than eight people (seven on the routes from Km104).

Llactapata to the east of Machu Picchu, ie the first major ruins you come to on the classic Inca Trail. To differentiate, we use the name Llactapata for the former, while referring to the latter as Patallacta.

How not to get lost

On the classic Inca Trail getting lost is not really an issue. Given that the rules insist that you are accompanied on your walk by a guide, you would probably have to deliberately try to get lost in order to do so, especially as the quality of the path is such that it's difficult to stray. However, on the other trails described in this guide the chances of getting lost are greater, though to varying extents. The **Salkantay** and **Choquequirao** routes are easy to follow. The former is very popular now and the path well-trodden, while the latter is clear because there's just a single route descending into and climbing out of a sheer valley. Should you find yourself erring from a path, the chances are a steep drop or a thick forest will deflect you back in the right direction.

See pp177-82 for information on arranging treks in Cusco and for a list of well-established companies with sound reputations. You will need to provide the agency with your name and passport details, and pay the entrance fee in advance. Permits are issued for an individual and are not transferable. Nor are they refundable. Once issued, it is also impossible to change the start date. Agencies have to make the booking for an entire group in one go and can't make alterations so they prefer to wait as long as possible to secure as many trekkers as they can before committing themselves to a set of permits.

Regulations have also been imposed to try and improve the plight of **porters** working on the Inca Trail, whose permits are paid for by the agency that employs them (see pp22-3).

● **Entrance fees** The fee for the **classic Inca Trail** is s/292 (about US$90) for adults and half price for children and students; see Notes below. The fee is payable by anyone trekking to Machu Picchu via Huayllabamba regardless of where their trek starts. The entrance fee for the shorter routes from Km104 is s/222/112 (US$68/34) for adults/students. Note the above fees include the s/152/77 (adult/children and students) (US$47/24) half-day entrance charge to Machu Picchu.

Notes: In all cases the dollar rate quoted is approximate as it depends on the exchange rate at the time. **Children** aged 8-17 and **students** under 28 who can present a valid International Student Identity Card (ISIC) at the time of booking pay half the rate; those who are under 8 when they visit the ruins can go in for free.

● **Documents** Whilst on the Inca Trail, trekkers must carry their actual **passport** with them; a photocopy is not sufficient. You will be required to present your passport at various checkpoints with your trek permit and, if relevant, your **ISIC card**.

● **Banned items** As part of an attempt to conserve the trail, the following are banned: **plastic bottles** (although evidence along the trail suggests that this isn't being enforced properly); **pets** and **pack animals** (although llamas are allowed as far as Huayllabamba); and **walking poles with a sharp tip** (they are OK if the tip is covered by a rubber bung as that will minimise damage to the Inca paths).

The **High Inca**, **Lares** and **Ausangate** trails are a little trickier, especially as they are more susceptible to snowfall which can obscure the path. These areas are pretty isolated, too, so there's a good chance there'll be no-one around to ask if you do lose the trail. Thankfully there are several ways of ensuring that you stick to the correct trail.

Perhaps the most reliable way of avoiding getting lost is to use a **GPS**, an inexpensive, well-established if non-essential navigational aid. In no time at all a GPS receiver with a clear view of the sky will establish your position and altitude. The maps in the route guide include numbered waypoints based around landmarks or objectives along the trail; these correlate to the list on pp356-8, which gives the latitude/longitude position in a decimal minute format as well as a description. You can download the complete list of these waypoints for free as a GPS-readable file (that doesn't include the text descriptions) from the Trailblazer website: 🖥 www.trailblazer-guides.com.

One must remember, however, two important things before setting off on the trail. The first is make sure you have enough batteries to last the trek; and second, know how to use your GPS unit correctly before you head off into the wilderness.

Of course, many people will be happy to set off with little more than **a compass and a map**; and if you are experienced at orienteering there is no reason why you can't navigate your way around the Peruvian Andes too. Indeed, we think it's possible to follow the correct path by using this book alone – though it's probably sensible to buy a second map as well, in case you want to deviate from the trails we describe in this guide. The IGN series (see p40) of maps have been the standard bearers for several years in Peru now, though we have found them to be of variable standard. In particular, the trails that they draw on their maps tend to be rather clumsily drawn and occasionally incomplete, so do take care.

Another way of keeping to the one true path is to use an **app** on your phone. MAPS.ME is one such app that we found people using successfully in Peru, particularly on the Ausangate and Lares trails. The advantage with this app is that the maps are available offline – very useful in the wilds of Peru where internet connections are non-existent. They also not only show you the path, but where you are on the map. Remember that the battery life is quite short on most smartphones – and apps such as these make it even shorter! Take a spare battery pack with you.

Of course, it is possible to **hire guides** for every trail in this book. Even if the guide doesn't speak English and your Spanish is non-existent, at least they will be able to make sure you keep to the correct trail. In place of an official guide, most people will instead hire an arriero, who provides the added advantage of carrying your luggage on his mule; pay him a little extra and he'll probably cook for you too. We have heard of some arrieros who, while happy to use their beasts to carry your luggage, are reluctant to act as a guide as well unless you pay a premium. Our advice, in this case, is to find yourself another arriero. If this is not possible and you agree to hire him, at least you can follow his path on the trail; and if he's too fast for you to keep pace with and you think you might have lost your way, at least you know that there is somebody who knows that you've gone astray, and can either return to find you or raise the alarm.

Note that all distances and altitudes are approximate.

Getting to the trailheads

For the Inca Trail you will be trekking with an agency, which means that you will be collected in Cusco and taken to the trailhead either by bus or by train. Many agencies use minibuses to transport trekkers to Km82, as they are quicker and can depart at any time whereas trains operate to a schedule. The **trains** to Aguas Calientes, which go via the trailheads at Km77, 82, 88 and 104, leave regularly each day though; most trekkers using the train start walking from Km88. See pp352-5 for details of times and prices.

Information on how to get to the starting points of the other trails can be found at the start of each trail description. So, for information on how to get to Mollepata for the **Salkantay Trek** and **High Inca Trail**, please see p240; for Cachora for the **Choquequirao Trek** see pp286-7; for Huaran Fondo at the start of the **Lares Trek**, visit pp268-9; while to get to Tinke, the starting point for the fabulous **Ausangate Trek**, go to p300.

The classic Inca Trail

This **33km (20½-mile)** trek is the undisputed draw for most people coming to Cusco and is the most popular and over-subscribed trek in the region. Given that you can get to Machu Picchu in four hours on a train, there has to be something intrinsically exciting and rewarding about the Inca Trail to merit spending four days walking to the same destination. And there is. For one thing, it is a beautiful trek, with exquisite scenery and breathtaking panoramas. But outstanding views and dramatic landscapes are pretty much a certainty in this part of the world. No, the best thing about the Inca Trail is the chance it offers to visit ruins that aren't otherwise accessible except on foot. As a result, this often means you'll have them either all to yourself or, if not, you'll be sharing them only with other like-minded individuals who were also prepared to spend the money and time to tackle this trail.

There's no doubt it's a spellbinding way to arrive at Machu Picchu and, as a result, makes it the stand-out trek in this region – for all the undoubted charms of the others around here.

Classic Inca Trail & Variant Routes Overview

KM88 (QORIHUAYRACHINA) TO HUAYLLABAMBA   [MAP 1, p219]

There are a couple of large and significant ruins on this **8.4km** first stage (**5¼ miles; 2hrs to 2hrs 25 mins**) of the classic Inca Trail – the first of which can be found at the very start of the walk. The train from Cusco only stops briefly at Km88, sometimes also referred to by its Quechua name Qorihuayrachina, so watch the kilometre markers after Km82 and be ready to disembark. Once off the train continue to walk west along the tracks, in the same direction as the train was heading. A path leads away from the tracks and down to the river, where there is a substantial **bridge and a warden's hut**. A guard here will check your permit and passport before letting you cross the river and begin the trail proper.

Once on the far side of the bridge you'll notice the considerable ruins of Qorihuayrachina on your right; your trail, however, takes you left (east) to climb gently through a stand of eucalyptus trees above the southern bank of the Urubamba.

About 30 minutes after setting off from the bridge you will come to the mouth of the Cusichaca Valley and the river of the same name. At the junction of the two valleys lie the sprawling ruins of **Patallacta** (see box p218). The trail bends along the edge of the lowest terraces of Patallacta, near the small round tower of **Pulpituyoc**, standing on a ridge by the river. On the far, southern, side of the terraces the path drops to a bridge over the Cusichaca leading to a couple of *campsites* on either side of the trail. Gently gaining height, the trail continues south to settle on the Cusichaca's eastern bank, heading upstream towards Huayllabamba.

The path climbs gently but steadily for an hour up the valley, passing first beneath cliffs covered in bromeliads and then through gentler terrain. It is possible to *camp* on this side opposite the houses on the western bank but most groups continue on the trail to the main bridge (**puente**), pausing occasionally to admire the good views back down the Cusichaca valley to Nevado Veronica, which is visible as a pyramid in the middle of the valley.

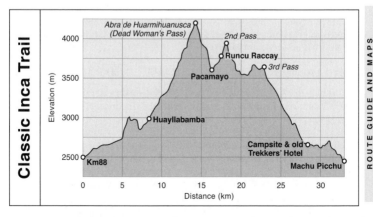

Classic Inca Trail

❏ **Patallacta and Pulpituyoc**
Although first uncovered by Hiram Bingham in 1911 and partially excavated by him in 1915, it wasn't until the late 1970s when Ann Kendall and the Cusichaca Trust extensively excavated the site that people realised just how substantial **Patallacta**, sometimes called Llactapata, was; it was one of the largest settlements in the region.

The site, on a crescent-shaped bluff where the Cusichaca joins the Urubamba, is laid out in a typical Inca fashion and dates from the mid 15th century. There are 116 buildings and five baths laid out in a regular pattern. A canal feeds the main baths but appears to have fallen into disuse shortly after the invasion of the Spanish conquistadors, implying that the site was abandoned around 1540.

Extensive terraces surround the buildings, suggesting that the site used to be primarily an agricultural station responsible for the production of crops such as maize that would have been used to supply other Inca sites in the region, and a distribution centre for those crops produced higher up the Cusichaca valley such as potatoes. Ann Kendall oversaw the excavation and restoration of around ten kilometres of Inca irrigation channels, which helped to transform the farming possibilities in the region. The site probably also had a strategic function as it sits at the junction of a number of Inca paths, and was ideally placed to regulate traffic and monitor who was moving where.

The round tower standing close to the main ruins, **Pulpituyoc**, whose name means 'containing a pulpit', was the religious centre for the site. Here there are eleven buildings, two baths and a carefully sculpted rock, reminiscent of the one close to Vitcos (see p341) and enclosed by a curved wall, which acted as a shrine. Although the exact purpose and use for the buildings isn't known, the fact that they have curved walls signifies that this was a place of great spiritual importance to the Incas.

Having crossed the Cusichaca you'll come to several small homesteads, each offering camping, toilet facilities (s/1) and soft drinks. The path continues on its riparian way, soon reaching **Huayllabamba**, an attractive, sprawling place of three dozen families built above Inca terraces. This is the largest village on the trail and the last place where you can buy basic food supplies. Across the Río Llulluchayoc, a tributary of the Cusichaca that bisects the village, you'll find a church, fish farm, and a couple of *campsites* with toilet blocks and cold running water; while at the top of the village is a **warden's office** where you must register and where porters have their loads checked and weighed before they can progress.

HUAYLLABAMBA TO PACAMAYO CAMP   [MAP 1; MAP 2, p220]

The path on this **7.8km (4¾ miles; 3hrs 50 mins to 4hrs 40 mins)** second stage begins by sticking to the Llulluchayoc's left-hand (south-west) bank, where you engage in an uphill slog for 45 minutes. The path eventually drops briefly to cross the Río Chaupihuayjo (also shown as the Río Huayruro on some maps), where you'll find the *Yunkachimpa* campsite, whereafter it gets a little steeper. Mercifully, *Ayapata campsite*, your probable destination at the end of the first day, is not far away. The campsite is set on several tiers with a large toilet block at its far (northern) end. You'll usually find an enterprising local hanging about the place selling soft drinks, beer and biscuits.

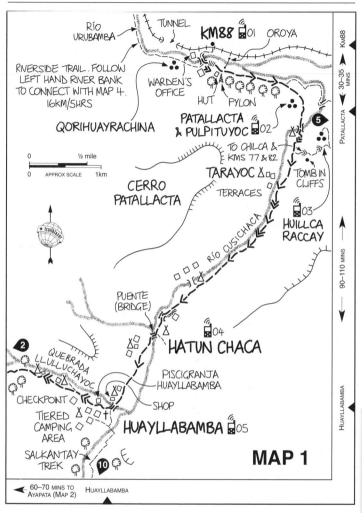

The trail now embarks on the toughest section of the entire trail. Hugging the left-hand (south-west) bank of Quebrada Llulluchayoc, the trail continues on its westerly way, with lupins and snapdragons lining the path. Soon you enter a beautiful cloud forest or *polylepis* woodland. The path climbs through the forest alongside the course of the river, occasionally close to the water and at other times high above it, on a series of steep steps.

ROUTE GUIDE AND MAPS

Just above the fringe of the forest is the ***Llulluchapampa Campsite***, an exposed campsite that can get very cold at night. Boasting running water and a toilet block, the camp's main attraction for most people are the exceptional views down the valley to Huayllabamba and up towards the pass, both of which are quite visible on a clear day.

The pass is **Abra de Huarmihuanusca (First Pass)**, sometimes spelled Warmiwañusqa but more commonly known as **Dead Woman's Pass**. It isn't known who the dead woman was or even if there was actually a dead woman at all, with many putting the name down to the fact that the pass resembles a woman lying on her back as if dead. (You'll see this more clearly on the other

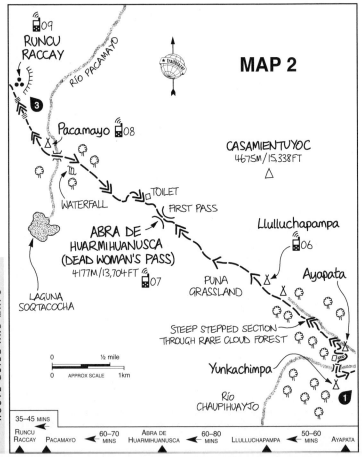

side of the pass from the ruins at Runcu Raccay.) The ascent to the pass looks deceptively simple but the gradual, steady climb is actually quite punishing, particularly as the ground underfoot is largely made up of stone steps or paving, placed here in 1998 to prevent erosion. The gradient also increases sharply as you near the top. For most of the way the trail runs parallel to the river, crossing a section of puna once it has reached the river's source. From Llulluchapampa it takes at least an hour to reach the high point (4177m/ 13,704ft). At the top, amidst all the photo-taking, backslapping and high-fiving from your fellow trekkers, the porters who share the path with you will silently take themselves off to a quiet corner with their onerous loads, doubtless steeling themselves for the next obstacle to come.

From the broad saddle that marks the pass, the path descends steeply and swiftly into the neighbouring valley, plummeting over 500m in the course of just over 2km. Remember to extend your walking poles for this dizzying descent along a very neat path that wouldn't look out of place in an English country garden; the vegetation, however, including the exotic Peruvian magic tree (*Cantua buxifolia*) with its red tubular flowers and the yellow *Calceolaria*, known locally as *zapatitos* or 'little shoes' because of the shape of the flowers, may well do. At the bottom is ***Pacamayo campsite***, a vast, sprawling place set amidst some scrubby trees that lies adjacent to the Río Pacamayo. It is popular with large tour groups and although the facilities here are reasonably good, with two toilet blocks, it is often noisy and crowded. Guides have to register at the **warden's hut** in the centre of the site.

PACAMAYO CAMP TO THE THIRD PASS   [MAP 2; MAP 3, p225]

This **6.7km (4¼ miles; 3hrs 20 mins to 4hrs 5 mins)** third stage starts by climbing very steeply from the Pacamayo camp up a series of steps, crossing two bridged sections over precipitous drops where the original trail has crumbled away. Take the opportunity during the climb to admire the viewpoints over the valley below whilst pausing for breath on the way up.

After about three-quarters of an hour you reach the Inca ruins of **Runcu Raccay** (see box p222). The site is best viewed from higher up the path and overlooking the site, where you can see both structures together as well as outstanding views back to Dead Woman's Pass.

The **second pass** (3962m/12,999ft), sometimes called Abra de Runcu Raccay, is at least another 35 minutes further up, beyond a series of false summits and at the top of a series of steep staircases. The birdcall you can hear on the way up is actually produced by a species of grasshopper that thrives in the damp conditions up here.

❏ **Important note – walking times**
Unless otherwise specified, **all times in this book refer only to the time spent walking**. You will need to add 20-40% to allow for rests, photography, checking the map, drinking water etc. When planning the day's hike count on 5-7 hours' actual walking.

❏ Runcu Raccay

The compact ruins at Runcu Raccay, perched precariously above a vertiginous chasm on a large terrace, were found by Hiram Bingham. Given its location on the Inca Trail and the fact that it had superlative views across the valley to Abra de Huarmihuanusca, Bingham decided that it must have been a fortress or watchtower. The archaeologist Dr Paul Fejos examined it in 1940 and concluded that it was a *tambo* for passing travellers or *chasquis*.

The site consists of two structures: a larger, round building with a double skin and walls indented with niches and a smaller, lower, rectangular structure. Both are completed in fairly basic, rustic style and the stonework is rough and ready in comparison to what the Incas could really do. The popular theory is that the site is a transitional building, taking travellers from the purely practical buildings in the Cusichaca Valley to the far more elaborate, significant structures closer to Machu Picchu. Its location would have been very deliberate though, with the Incas keen that people passing this way had the chance to venerate their surroundings.

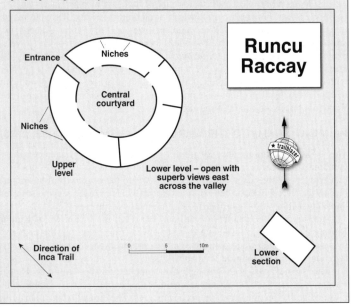

Just before the real pass, the path winds by a **lake** where Andean gulls sometimes gather. The ground around the lakes is boggy so don't stray from the dirt-gravel path as you risk damaging this very fragile ecosystem. By the tarns there's a sign saying 'Deer Area', but you'll be very lucky to see any, the deer themselves having probably decamped to some place where there aren't 500 people marching through daily. The second pass is another broad saddle and boasts exceptional views of Pumasillo (5991m/19,656ft) and the Vilcabamba range. Below it the path again falls away steeply into an adjoining valley.

Having descended through a **short tunnel** the trail begins a series of tight switchbacks, dropping height quickly until it reaches a small viewpoint atop a promontory. Beyond here the descent is more gradual, tranquil and lovely, the path curling and coiling across the left-hand (southern walls) of the valley, while on your right (north) broods a large, algae-covered lake. The path tumbles down a stretch of hillside towards a hairpin bend. Just before this dog-leg right is a staircase that branches left (south-west) and climbs 50m/150ft to the entrance of **Sayac Marca** (see box below and map p224).

Around the hairpin bend and sitting in the shadow of Sayac Marca is the small set of ruins at **Concha Marca**. Tucked in a little valley and perched atop a series of tall, rounded terraces, these ruins were only uncovered in the early 1980s. The small stream here is a good place to fill up with water as there isn't another water source until the third pass; though, as with any water collected from the trail, do make sure you purify it carefully.

❏ **Sayac Marca**   **[see map overleaf]**

The dramatically sited ruins of Sayac Marca are protected on three sides by sheer cliffs that fall away to the jungle far below. Hiram Bingham again first found the site, but it was Dr Paul Fejos who gave it the appropriate, descriptive moniker Sayac Marca, meaning 'Inaccessible Town', in the 1940s. The ruins, made up of a dozen chambers, passages and retaining walls, overlook the Aobamba Valley and stand at a fork in the original Inca road.

The classic Inca Trail continues on one branch of the fork whilst the other descends through the jungle to the river Aobamba that flows along the bottom of the valley, then climbs steeply up the other side of the valley to the ruins at Llactapata (see box pp260-1), before dropping off the far side of the next ridge and descending to the river Santa Teresa. Fifteen kilometres from Sayac Marca it clambers once more to the ruins at Ochopata before becoming completely subsumed by the jungle.

Bingham believed that the site was a fortress and an outpost for Machu Picchu. Fejos disagreed saying that it wasn't impressive enough to be a fortress. Neither is the stone work of sufficiently high quality for the site to be a religious centre although there are ceremonial water channels at the base of the outcrop. Nor are there enough terraces or agricultural land in the vicinity for it to have been a farming outpost. With the compact **Concha Marca** ruins just below, it is also unlikely to have simply been a tambo, meaning that no-one is actually sure what these superb ruins were original-ly used for.

The building appears to grow organically out of the rocky promontory on which it stands and the entire shape of the structure emphasises and exaggerates the natural features and shape of the prow that sticks out from the hillside. At the heart of the site is a large, unadorned outcrop of rock that juts up from the foundations. The stonework is more impressive than that at Runcu Raccay, marking the next stage on the pil-grimage to Machu Picchu, but is still quite rustic in appearance.

Bingham drew particular attention to the 'eye-bonders', holes drilled in corners of walls, which were used to fasten thatched roofs onto the stone structures. The elab-orate layout of the site and the way in which it incorporates the natural terrain has led archaeologists to date the ruins to the second half of the 15th century.

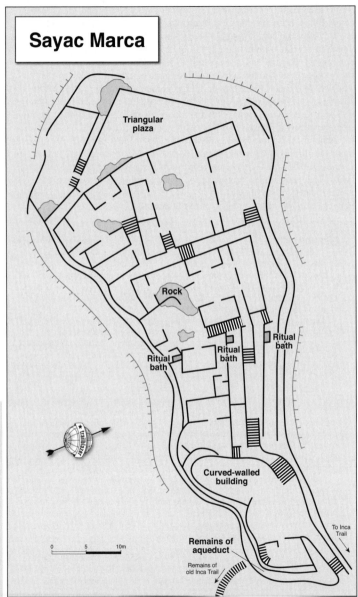

Sayac Marca

Triangular plaza

Rock

Ritual bath

Ritual bath

Ritual bath

Curved-walled building

Remains of aqueduct

To Inca Trail

Remains of old Inca Trail

0   5   10m

MAP 3

EXTENDED SERIES OF STEEP INCA STAIRS

PHUYU PATA MARCA 15

SMALL RUIN- 'TAMBILLO'

CAVE WITH NICHES-GOOD SHELTER

THIRD PASS
3665M
12,024FT

SERIES OF EXCELLENT VIEWPOINTS ALONG HERE

FROM THIRD PASS SUPERB VIEWS SOUTH OF MOUNT SALKANTAY & SURROUNDING PEAKS

INCA TUNNEL 14

Chaquicocha 13

BOGGY

CONCHA MARCA 12

SHORT TUNNEL

LAKES

VERY ATTRACTIVE CLOUD FOREST

SECOND PASS
3962M
12,999FT

LAKES

SAYAC MARCA 11

10

0   ½ mile
0   APPROX SCALE   1km

25-30 MINS
30-40 MINS FROM RUNCU RACCAY (MAP 2)

130-155 MINS TO OLD TREKKERS' HOTEL (MAP 4)   THIRD PASS   75-90 MINS   CHAQUICOCHA   SAYAC MARCA   35-40 MINS   SECOND PASS

Beyond the ruins lies a stretch of very attractive trail, the path skirting a series of precipices on stone slabs, most of which are of Inca origin, and contouring through some very beautiful cloud forest. If you find yourself tackling this stretch in cloud or mist you would do well to wait it out, itinerary and time allowing, in order to enjoy the drama and beauty around you. Twenty minutes' easy walk from Sayac Marca is an open section of hillside called **Chaquicocha**, a very popular *campsite*, particularly with midges which swarm here in their billions to take advantage of the damp conditions and the moving buffet of passing trekkers that come through every day.

From the campsite the path snakes steeply uphill for a few minutes but thereafter is rather straightforward and any inclines encountered are not severe. The trail passes a couple of **viewpoints** before rounding a spur and turning from north-west to north-east. A section of intricately laid Inca paving leads down to an **Inca tunnel**, a 16m-long corridor that exploits a fault in the seemingly sheer cliff blocking the way ahead. Emerging from the impressive tunnel the path climbs again towards the third pass, narrowing just before it reaches it; near the top, if the weather is good, walkers get the chance to see into both the Urubamba and Aobamba valleys simultaneously.

From the large *campsite* set around the **third pass** (3665m/12,024ft) there are also spectacular views. Looking south and left to right are the peaks of Palcay (c5600m/18,370ft) and Salkantay (6271m/20,574ft). Some 35km west lie the high, sharp summit of Pumasillo (5991m/19,656ft)) and a string of lesser peaks, whilst 15km north-east is Veronica (5682m/18,642ft).

THE THIRD PASS TO MACHU PICCHU [MAP 3, p225; MAP 4, p229]

Though you may now have reached the summit of the third and final pass on the Inca Trail, don't be misled into thinking that this **10.1km (6¼ miles; 3hrs 50 mins to 4hrs 35 mins)** stage is going to be any easier than the previous stages; indeed, those of a certain age whose joints are screaming will find the steep and relentless descent that follows excruciating.

From this stunning eyrie there are also excellent views of the impressive Inca site of **Phuyu Pata Marca** (see box opposite), just below the lip of the pass. This extensive site was first spotted by Hiram Bingham, who discovered the baths and the tops of a couple of walls protruding from the thick jungle. However, he failed to grasp the size or the importance of the site.

Paul Fejos did realise what lay below the jungle covering, but after several months' excavation had still managed to clear only a fraction of the site, uncovering two plazas, four groups of houses and a hidden house concealed in a terrace. He christened the site 'Cloud Level Town' and with the site often shrouded in swirling Wagnerian mists, it is an apt nickname. Despite this it still looks spectacular and potentially even more atmospheric; even the presence of the large campsite just above can't spoil it. What's more, when the cloud clears, the views from the Urubamba up towards Nevados Yanantin and Salkantay are spectacular.

From the lowest terrace of the ruins pick up the **flight of stairs** heading downhill. This is the most impressive set of steps on the entire Inca Trail. The Incas turned a 500m (1500ft) hillside into a staircase, etching each step out of the natural shape of the bedrock: one giant boulder has over 30 steps carved into it. The trail coils down into dense cloud forest, one of the most delightful wooded sections on the trek. It's a lovely walk though if your knees had faces, they'd be wincing at the prospect of such a steep descent. In fact, trekkers a few years ago had it a lot easier, because there used to be two trails from Phuyu Pata Marca. The old trail, which everyone took up until the dramatic Inca Staircase was discovered during the early 1980s, left Phuyu Pata Marca from the west and contoured around the valley side, hugging the lie of the land. Although a couple of kilometres longer it offered excellent views of the Urubamba valley and eventually wound its way to Intipata. This route has subsequently been closed and the majority of it allowed to become overgrown and virtually impassable.

Back on the current trail, pause for a while and you may be able to hear the horn of the train echoing up from the valley below – even if the mist or terrain does not allow you to see the train itself. It's further evidence that you are coming towards the end of your adventure. Around two hours from Phuyu Pata Marca the path passes to the left of a pylon set just off the trail. Just before the pylon, a narrow trail breaks away right (east) and descends to the hotel within

❏ Phuyu Pata Marca

The site is thought to date from the late 15th century and is attributed to Pachacutec or his successor, Topa Inca. It is built in an atypical style, unlike the more structured Inca sites elsewhere. However, the stone work is very good in parts, particularly on the upper terraces.

The ruins occupy a pyramid of seven terraces that hug the contours of a spur, linked by a fine stairway. The long, straight staircase descends between several tiers of buildings. To one side are six 'Inca baths' (five ceremonial baths and one principal one) that were probably not actually used to wash in, but are more likely to have been used in conjunction with the ritual worship of water.

The function of the site is again unclear and the handful of basic Inca ceramics found in the ruins give no clues as to its purpose. The most likely theory states that the site was connected with the ritual worship of water, but other suggestions range from a guard house to a private hunting lodge. Similar structures can be seen at Tambo Machay and further along the Inca Trail at Huinay Huayna and at Machu Picchu itself.

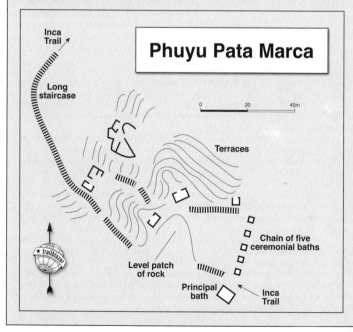

Phuyu Pata Marca

Inca Trail

Long staircase

0   20   40m

Terraces

Chain of five ceremonial baths

★ trailblazer

Level patch of rock

Principal bath

Inca Trail

half an hour, losing height rapidly through a series of short, tight switchbacks. However, the shortcut doesn't really save you all that much time and it is in fact far less scenic than the traditional route, which pushes on beneath the pylon cables towards **Intipata** (see box below).

As you approach the site you first glimpse it through the trees and can better gauge its enormous size. The path emerges on one of the upper terraces. Descend to the lowest terrace, from where a trail leads to the campsite and the **old Trekkers' Hotel**. Sadly the hotel is now closed and has been allowed to fall into disrepair. This is, though, the last place before Machu Picchu where you are allowed to *camp*. Because of this it is always full, meaning you are likely to have a crowded, noisy night.

From the campsite a short 10-minute trek takes you to the ruins of **Huinay Huayna** (see box p230), a stunning terraced complex, 500m and a world away from the modern mess you've just left. The name Huinay Huayna (sometimes written as Wiñay Wayna) belongs to an attractive orchid that grows in the region, and means 'forever young'. The site is little short of spectacular. Dating from the second half of the 15th century, the site shares a number of characteristics with Intipata: both comprise a series of fine, curving terraces spread across a hillside and both were used to grow crops. However, Huinay Huayna is a much more significant and important site; the stonework here is very impressive and of a much higher quality than at Intipata. Note: the ruins are locked every evening around dusk and you should be careful not to leave valuables lying about your tent whilst visiting.

❏ **Intipata**

The name Intipata literally means 'sunny slope' and is particularly apt for this massed range of terraces that seem to stretch on endlessly. Whilst clearing the huge steps over a period of four months during 1940, Dr Paul Fejos despairingly described in his diary terraces 'extending indefinitely to the south'. In total he cleared and mapped 48 terraces.

There are no plazas, ceremonial sites or fortifications to disturb the broad sweeping terraces suggesting that the site was used exclusively as an agricultural outpost. However, three houses are concealed in hollow terraces. Given the broad panoramic views down into the valley to the site of Choquesuysuy and across the mountains to the lookout platform on top of Cerro Machu Picchu, the site probably had some sort of strategic importance as well. By using Intipata as a mid point, messages could have been transmitted from the valley floor all the way to Machu Picchu. Though you arrive at the top of Intipata, it's best viewed from below the bottom terrace, from where the sheer scale and full majesty of the terraces can be best appreciated.

Despite cutting and removing 40,000 square metres of jungle, Dr Fejos was convinced that there was still more to be uncovered. Although historians are anxious to try and reveal as much as possible, naturalists are concerned that insensitive clearing and blunt restoration techniques have damaged prime habitat favoured by a particular breed of very rare orchid. In order to preserve the habitat and protect the flower, there are frequent rumours that the site will be closed and left uncleared, and that the jungle will simply be allowed to reclaim the ancient stones.

From Old Trekkers Hotel it takes about an hour to trek the 3km to Intipunku ('Gateway to the Sun'). Machu Picchu is another 40 minutes further on. Remember to have your torch handy as you'll be packing and starting to walk

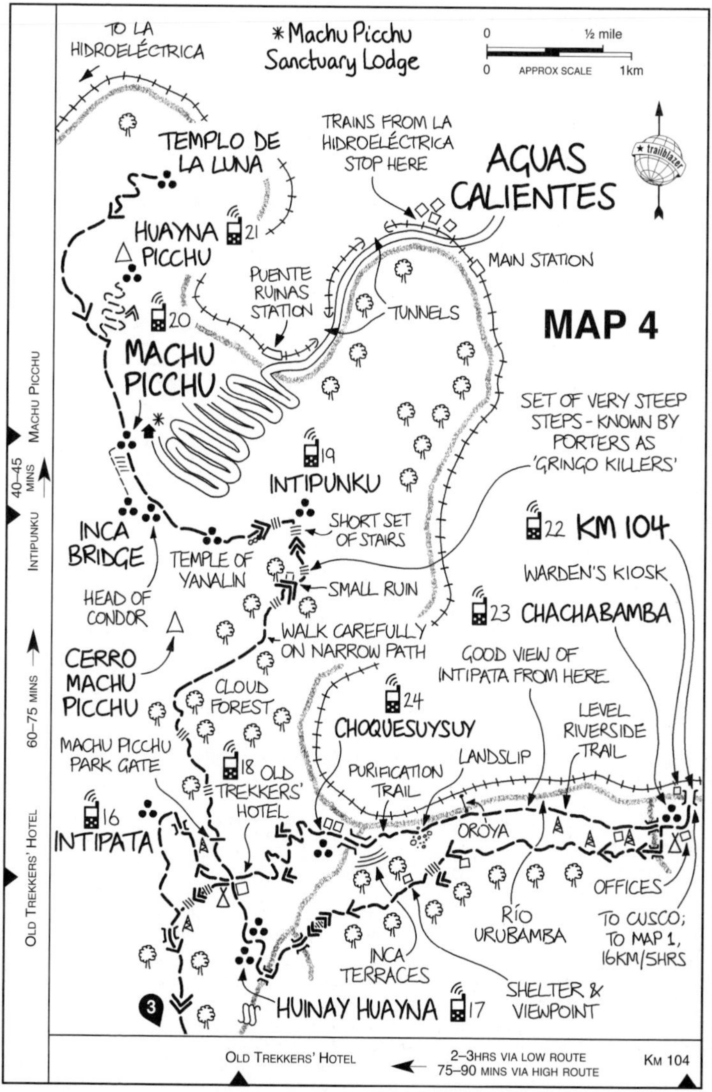
TO LA HIDROELÉCTRICA
* Machu Picchu Sanctuary Lodge
0 ½ mile
0 APPROX SCALE 1km
TEMPLO DE LA LUNA
TRAINS FROM LA HIDROELÉCTRICA STOP HERE
AGUAS CALIENTES
HUAYNA PICCHU
21
MAIN STATION
PUENTE RUINAS STATION
TUNNELS
20
MAP 4
MACHU PICCHU
SET OF VERY STEEP STEPS - KNOWN BY PORTERS AS 'GRINGO KILLERS'
19
INTIPUNKU
22 KM 104
INCA BRIDGE
SHORT SET OF STAIRS
TEMPLE OF YANALIN
WARDEN'S KIOSK
SMALL RUIN
HEAD OF CONDOR
23 CHACHABAMBA
WALK CAREFULLY ON NARROW PATH
CERRO MACHU PICCHU
GOOD VIEW OF INTIPATA FROM HERE
CLOUD FOREST
24
CHOQUESUYSUY
LEVEL RIVERSIDE TRAIL
MACHU PICCHU PARK GATE
LANDSLIP
18 OLD TREKKERS' HOTEL
PURIFICATION TRAIL
16
INTIPATA
OROYA
OFFICES
RÍO URUBAMBA
TO CUSCO; TO MAP 1, 16KM/5HRS
INCA TERRACES
SHELTER & VIEWPOINT
3
HUINAY HUAYNA
17
MACHU PICCHU
40–45 MINS
INTIPUNKU
60–75 MINS
OLD TREKKERS' HOTEL
OLD TREKKERS' HOTEL
2–3HRS VIA LOW ROUTE
75–90 MINS VIA HIGH ROUTE
KM 104

❏ Huinay Huayna (Wiñay Wayna)

This complex's sweeping terraces lead round to a series of buildings with high-quality masonry, a *double-jamb* doorway and a curved structure that looks out over Nevado Veronica. The finest examples of Inca stonework can be found in these buildings, which are constructed out of some of the largest and most perfectly fitted blocks along the Inca Trail. There are also lots of gables and exterior pegs used to secure thatched roofs. From this upper cluster a staircase descends to a second level, alongside a sequence of 10 stone baths, down which flows water from a spring that originates at Phuyu Pata Marca. The likelihood is that these were involved in the ritual worship of water and that the site had an important role as a ceremonial or religious centre.

From the last structure at the lowest level, there's a trapezoidal window that frames a nearby waterfall, reinforcing the idea that the site was connected with the veneration of water.

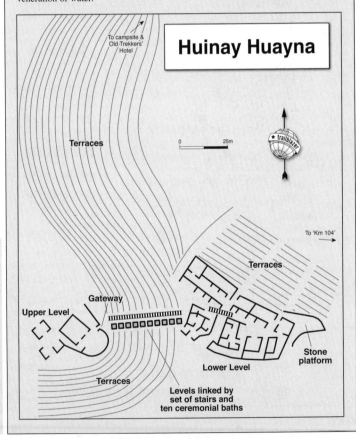

To campsite & Old Trekkers' Hotel

Huinay Huayna

Terraces

0   25m

★ trailblazer

To 'Km 104'

Terraces

Gateway

Upper Level

Terraces

Lower Level

Stone platform

Levels linked by set of stairs and ten ceremonial baths

in the dark. The gate out of the campsite opens at 5.30am and closes at 3.30pm. Most groups crowd by the gate in the dark, hoping to get the earliest start to Machu Picchu when it opens; if it's raining, it can get quite fraught as trekkers attempt to squeeze themselves under the inadequate tin-roof shelter. The result is a convoy of bobbing headlamps, rustling waterproofs and irate voices filling the air. While most will want to reach Intipunku by sunrise, you may consider delaying your departure from the campsite by 15-30 minutes to enjoy an emptier path, better light and the very attractive final section of the Inca Trail. After all, sunrise over Machu Picchu is often hazy or shrouded in light cloud, so the chances are you won't miss much by arriving a little later – you'll still get to enjoy the ruins before the tours and trainloads of day-trippers arrive.

The trail to Intipunku is straightforward to follow though those expecting it to be easy are in for a bit of a shock: undulating and steep in places, the trail ensures that you'll be pretty exhausted by the time you reach Intipunku. On the way the trail passes a couple of steep rock faces before climbing a collection of **very steep steps** to what you assume is the Gateway to the Sun. It's actually the remains of a watchtower commanding superb views south back to Intipata, Huinay Huayna, Phuyu Pata Marca and to Choquesuysuy at the start of the Purification Trail. Intipunku is, in fact, just around the corner, at the top of a short set of rather gentler stairs. This is an awe-inspiring approach, the architecture reinforcing your sense of anticipation. When you finally arrive at **Intipunku**, the view across the wide bend of the Urubamba explodes before you and you can at last see, sheltering under the sugar-loaf mountain of Huayna Picchu (see p321), your journey's end. There are several more ruins on the 40-minute walk down but, inevitably, most people will want to press on to **Machu Picchu** (see pp310-38) and the end of the trek.

Variations on the classic trail

These variations are up to four hours longer than the first day of the classic Inca trail and provide alternative start points. They are particularly popular with trekking agencies, which tend to begin all their trips from Km82. You won't gain much from starting at Chilca instead, although it is a scenic, simple stroll to the main trail that allows you to ease in to the trek proper.

FROM CHILCA (KM77)   [off MAP 5, p233]

The small hamlet of Chilca stands at Km77 on the railway. It is also readily accessible by road; indeed a couple of trekking agencies drive here to start their organised hikes. Although little more than a collection of adobe houses and shacks, Chilca is still more substantial than anything found at Km82 or Km88.

From the railway station the path heads south and winds through the houses towards the road and bridge across the Urubamba. Crossing the river here you then turn right (west) to follow the clearly defined dirt track along the southern bank of the river as it descends towards a stand of eucalyptus trees. Bromeliads, wild pepper trees and chilca bushes, from which the village gets its name, also line the path. Beyond the small copse the path bears north-west and undulates through a patch of dry scrub dotted with cacti, crossing the small Quebrada Runtumayo, to reach the village of **Rocabamba**, where there is a stream but no facilities.

Bearing west, the path crosses the stream and weaves through a further patch of scrub to arrive at the Km82 bridge, 1½ hours after leaving Chilca.

For the continuation of the route see below.

FROM KM82 [MAP 5]

This point, also known as Piscacucho, is the end of the road for tourist buses and the furthest point along the Urubamba Valley accessible by road. Most tour agencies pull into the car park to the north of the houses here and start the trek from this point. There are precious few amenities here, but a couple of enterprising individuals sell last-minute supplies and cold soft drinks. The famous sign at the start of the trail lies by the railway track; photos taken, drop down under the sign to the **warden's** kiosk, where you must present your passport and register.

From the kiosk, you cross the bridge to the south side of the Urubamba, from where the path turns right (west) – the fainter path left goes to Chilca. After an initial climb to a viewpoint over the river, the trail for the first hour to the village of Miskay is relatively straightforward, passing a few scattered houses, pylons and even a little settlement with its own cemetery and **football pitch**. Leaving the houses behind, look to your right across the river and on the opposite bank you'll see your first ruins visible from the trail. This simple stone-and-clay structure, sometimes called **Qanabamba** or **Ccallabamba**, was a *tambo* or resting place for travellers, in particular the *chasquis*, the foot messengers who carried communications throughout the empire. The ruins, including half a dozen *colcas* (simple circular buildings used by the Incas for storing their food) and a water channel, were uncovered by Hiram Bingham in 1911.

More spectacular – and nearer – ruins follow in short order, after the village of **Miskay**. At the far end of the village the path divides. Take the less-substantial left-hand fork (south) and head briefly towards a rocky cliff before veering right (west). Follow the path as it ducks into and scrambles out of a small gully, having crossed a stream. Just beyond here, commanding the mouth of the Cusichaca Valley, stands the Inca hillfort **Huillca Raccay** (see box p234).

Further west on the far side of the valley lies the sprawling site of Patallacta (see box p218) though it's unlikely, if you started your trek at Km82, that you'll descend to the ruins. Instead your guide will lead you round the back of Huillca Raccay to descend in a series of zigzags to the main Inca trail from Km88. Look up at the cliffs on your left-hand side to see the entrance of an Inca tomb. At the bottom of the descent turn left and head up the valley (south) towards the village of Huayllabamba on the broad, well-worn trail.

See p218 for the continuation of the route to Machu Picchu.

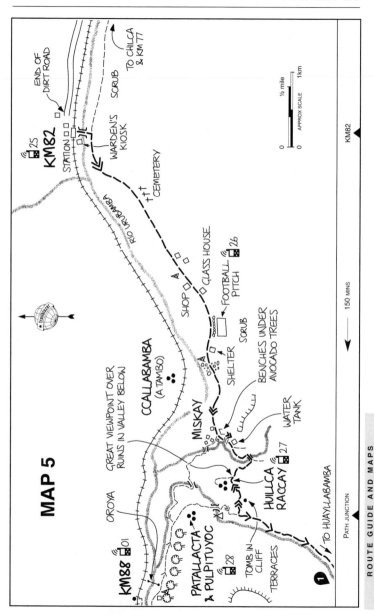

MAP 5

END OF DIRT ROAD

KM82 ☐ 25

STATION ☐ ☐

WARDEN'S KIOSK

TO CHILCA & KM77

SCRUB

RIO URUBAMBA

† † †
CEMETERY

GLASS HOUSE

FOOTBALL PITCH 26

SHOP

SHELTER

SCRUB

BENCHES UNDER AVOCADO TREES

CCALLABAMBA (A TAMBO)

GREAT VIEWPOINT OVER RUINS IN VALLEY BELOW

MISKAY

WATER TANK

HUILLCA RACCAY 27

OROYA

KM88 ☐ 01

PATALLACTA & PULPITUYOC

☐ 28

TOMB IN CLIFF

TERRACES

TO HUAYLLABAMBA

150 MINS

PATH JUNCTION

1

KM82 ◀

APPROX SCALE
0   ½ mile   1km
0

> ❏ **Huillca Raccay**
> It doesn't look like much but this fort is thought to be one of the earliest built in the region. Between 1978 and 1980 it was extensively excavated by Ann Kendall who discovered that people inhabited the area long before the Incas arrived. Once they had subdued the original residents of the valley, the Incas built the fort to maintain control and assert their dominance over the local tribes.
>
> The ruins comprise a complicated collection of gate-houses, lofts and what are thought to be barracks. In total there are 37 Inca buildings here and some 70 pre-Inca constructions scattered on the flatter land behind. From this vantage point the Incas commanded exceptional views up and down the Urubamba and managed access to the Cusichaca. Later, once Llactapata had been built, the fort protected and controlled the agrarian settlements further down the valley.

The shorter trails

For those people who don't have the time or inclination to tackle a four-day walk there are various alternatives. It's only a half-day hike uphill to Huinay Huayna (see p230) and the old Trekkers' Hotel from Km104 on the railway line (Map 4) and just an hour's gentle stroll along the classic Inca Trail from here to the first glimpse of Machu Picchu and the ruins themselves.

Alternatively, follow the southern bank of the Urubamba downstream from Km104 for a couple of hours to the ruins at Choquesuysuy and then climb more steeply towards Huinay Huayna, from where you join the Inca Trail for the final push to Machu Picchu. Both of these treks are open year-round – including February when the classic Inca Trail is shut.

KM104 TO HUINAY HUAYNA (PURIFICATION TRAIL) [MAP 4, p229]

The train takes 3½-4 hours to travel from Cusco to Km104, where it pauses briefly to let people disembark. Over the bridge across the Urubamba are several kiosks and offices where you must present your passport and register.

On the far side of the river turn right (west) and shortly come to the ruins at **Chachabamba** (see box opposite). Dating from the late 15th century, it is a sophisticated site set on an old Inca road. Uncovered in 1940 by Dr Paul Fejos, the site had lain undisturbed despite the construction of the railway on the opposite bank of the river some time earlier. Since then it has been cleared and a number of buildings uncovered.

From the ruins the path divides: the right-hand path, seldom used by trekkers these days, follows the river west towards **Choquesuysuy** (see box p236) before scrambling steeply up to the ruins at Huinay Huayna alongside the old Trekkers' Hotel. These days, however, nearly every trekker takes the higher route which, picking up on the perceived religious function of Huinay Huana, has been dubbed the Purification Trail. It takes 2-3 hours to climb from the valley floor to the site (see box p230), which you pass through on a staircase adjacent to a series of ceremonial baths. From here you pick up a path from the upper level of the site that undulates for a further 15 minutes to reach the abandoned Trekkers' Hotel, which is still used as the final **campsite** (see p228) on the classic Inca Trail.

Alternative route from Km104 to Huinay Huayna

A gentler and now more popular alternative to the riverside route and its steep vertical ascent to Huinay Huayna, is to take the left-hand fork just after Chachabamba.

This route is undoubtedly more picturesque and we prefer it, largely because of the lovely views it offers both up and down the valley and the gorgeous flowers that thrive on the slopes bisected by the path: species such as *Oreocallis grandiflora*, known as *llama llama* ('flames' in Spanish) after the tubular flowers that emerge from the tips of the stems, and the spectacular

❏ **Chachabamba**
Amongst the buildings on the site is a natural shrine and 14 ceremonial baths. This is more than almost anywhere else along the Inca Trail, suggesting that the site must have been an important religious centre and associated with water worship. It probably also fulfilled a function as a watchtower, controlling access to Machu Picchu.

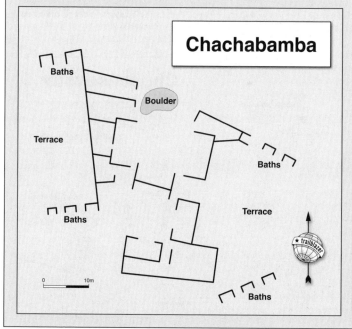

Chachabamba

Baths

Boulder

Terrace

Baths

Baths

Terrace

0   10m

★ trailblazer

Baths

purple orchid *Sobralia dichotoma*. However, you do miss out on the ruins at Choquesuysuy and the path can be narrow at times – with a sheer drop on one side a possible deterrent to those afraid of heights.

From the junction with the riverside route the path crosses the bridge over a stream, before climbing evenly across an increasingly exposed slope in a westerly direction. It's a good idea to make sure you're carrying two litres of water since the climb is exposed and exhausting in direct sunshine.

After about 20 minutes you gain your first glimpse of the campsite and the massed terraces of Intipata (see box p228) beyond it. A little after this, good views of Huinay Huayna come into focus.

The narrow path continues to climb up and across the mountainside, passing a couple of small shelters en route, before levelling and undulating briefly through some lusher terrain to an impressive waterfall, before you finally emerge at the foot of Huinay Huayna. Climb the staircase through the site and then up past the stone baths to the upper level. Turn right (north-west) and leave the site on a well-trodden trail that leads to the campsite (see p228) after 10 minutes.

❑ **Choquesuysuy**
Built on either side of a tributary of the Urubamba at Km107, Choquesuysuy comprises six groups of buildings, totalling 18 houses, a series of seven ceremonial baths and a number of well-crafted terraces and walls. The site is ideally placed to oversee traffic along the valley floor and commands the approach to Machu Picchu, although the hydroelectric power station now blocks the path. The quality of the stonework and the presence of the baths suggest it was also a religious centre.

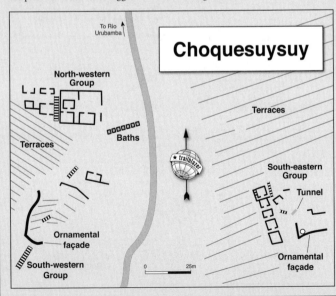

ROUTE GUIDE AND MAPS

KM88 TO KM104 (RIVERSIDE TRAIL)   [MAP 1, p219; MAP 4, p229]

Instead of following the classic Inca Trail, there is the option to escape the crowds and the majority of the stiff climbs by following the river as it flows downstream from Km88 to Km104 before ascending to Huinay Huayna and the campsite and old Trekkers' Hotel. Rarely done and consequently not nearly as well-worn as the classic trail, this gentle riverside stroll is an excellent way of accessing the major ruins at the end of the trek and allows you to explore some interesting sites along the way, including Machu Q'ente and Huayna Q'ente and the Inca compound Torontoy which boasts a 44-angle stone in one of its walls.

The trail typically takes **two days** to complete. You will need a **permit** for the trek though and because it overlaps with the final section of the classic Inca Trail the route is subject to the same regulations and restrictions.

Note: The start and end of the route are shown on Map 1 and Map 4 respectively. The intervening section is not mapped but is very easy as you simply follow the river bank.

Having registered at the **warden's kiosk** before the bridge at Km88, cross the Urubamba but instead of turning left for the classic Inca Trail, turn right and having headed south for 50m bear west along the southern bank of the river in the lee of several sheer cliffs. The 16km (10-mile) path is clear and reasonably well maintained, but as a result of the reduced traffic it receives can occasionally be overgrown.

Around 20 minutes after crossing the Urubamba you come to the rarely visited ruins of **Huayna Q'ente** and **Machu Q'ente** (see box below). These two sites stand on the Inca road to Chachabamba, although the road actually follows the river all the way to the Amazon.

There are *campsites* just two hours down from Km88 and at Chachabamba, five hours from Km88. From Chachabamba you have the option of ascending to Huinay Huayna via the standard route (see p228), or via Choquesuysuy and the Purification Trail (see pp234-6).

❏ **Huayna Q'ente and Machu Q'ente**
The exact purpose of these two sites isn't known, but they are thought to have multiple functions, including being resthouses or inns, religious sites and agricultural posts.

Huayna Q'ente is the more impressive structure. Dating from the second half of the 15th century, it is thought to have been built either during the reign of Pachacutec or that of his successor Topa Inca. It is an intricately constructed site with plenty of fine stonework on display, suggesting that it was used as a tambo (a type of inn) by people making pilgrimages to Machu Picchu. There are two stone baths connected with the worship of water and two sacred rocks thought to be huacas (sacred sites). Extensive terraces support the site and a clever canal system supplies the various levels of agricultural land with water.

In contrast, **Machu Q'ente** is plainer, suggesting that it had a primarily agricultural function, although there are also the remnants of a large building thought to have perhaps been a barracks. Close by is a large, peculiarly carved stone that looks similar to Ñusta España (see p341), the sculpted boulder close to Huancacalle.

The High Inca Trail

This is essentially an extension of the Inca Trail that allows you to experience a fantastic section of wilderness, free from most of the crowds, before committing to the final three days of the classic Inca Trail culminating at Machu Picchu. The **6- to 7-day trek (71km; 44 miles)** from the watershed of the Apurímac to the ruins overlooking the Urubamba is quite arduous, as you must cross a high pass at a shade under 5000m. The views of the Vilcabamba range and the proximity to the bulk of Nevado Salkantay more than compensate for the effort required.

That said, this trek is seldom walked these days thanks to the regulations that insist that you take a tour group along the Inca Trail – ie, along the last half of this trek. As such, the only people who are likely to use this trail today are either organised groups who can turn left at Huayllabamba and continue on the Inca Trail to Machu Picchu; or independent trekkers who have accepted that they can't go on the Inca Trail but instead will have to continue down the valley to the Urubamba. At the river, two options present themselves: head left (west) to Km88, from where it's possible to catch a train to Machu Picchu; or right (east) to Km82, where it's also possible to catch the train, or the bus back to Ollantaytambo.

This trek is advertised under various names, and you may see it listed as the **Mollepata Trek** or **Salkantay Trek**. To avoid confusion with the 'other', more popular Salkantay route – which we describe beginning on p249 – we have called it the **High Inca Trail**, the name used by the British company Exodus, the largest agency using this trail.

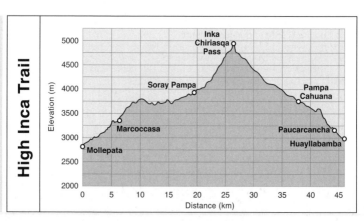

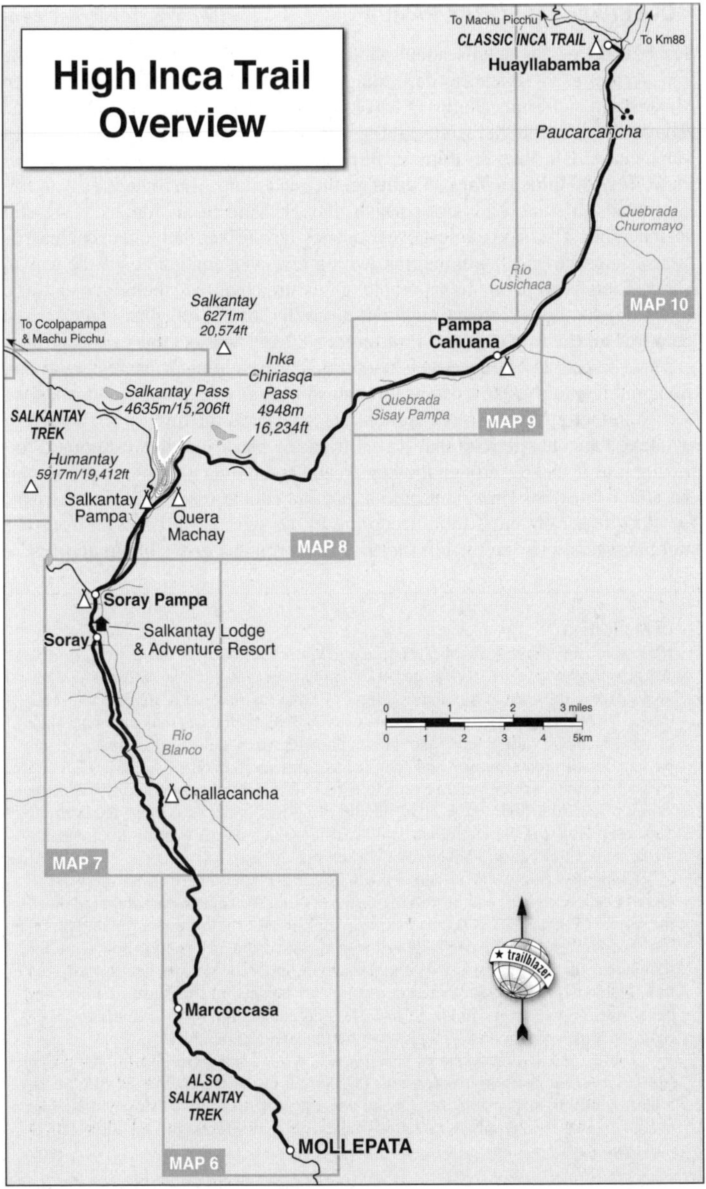

High Inca Trail Overview

To Machu Picchu
CLASSIC INCA TRAIL · To Km88
Huayllabamba

Paucarcancha

Quebrada Churomayo

Rio Cusichaca

MAP 10

To Ccolpapampa & Machu Picchu

Salkantay 6271m 20,574ft

Inka Chiriasqa Pass 4948m 16,234ft

Pampa Cahuana

Quebrada Sisay Pampa

MAP 9

Salkantay Pass 4635m/15,206ft

SALKANTAY TREK

Humantay 5917m/19,412ft

Salkantay Pampa

Quera Machay

MAP 8

Soray Pampa

Soray

Salkantay Lodge & Adventure Resort

Rio Blanco

Challacancha

0 1 2 3 miles
0 1 2 3 4 5km

MAP 7

Marcoccasa

ALSO SALKANTAY TREK

MOLLEPATA

MAP 6

trailblazer

MOLLEPATA TO SORAY PAMPA   [MAP 6; MAP 7, p243]

See box below for details about Mollepata. This **19.2-19.7km/12-12¼ mile** trail – the exact distance depending on which route you take between Marcoccasa and Soray Pampa – leaves from Mollepata's Plaza de Armas and follows the dirt road that winds all the way to Soray via the small settlement of Marcoccasa. It's **4hrs 35 mins to 5hrs 25 mins** on the upper water channel route; **4hrs 40 mins to 5hrs 35 mins** on the road route. The route is easy to follow thanks to some blue signs which, though battered and defaced, are still decipherable. That said, almost every agency now drives their clients at least as far as Marcoccasa to begin the trek, with a few even continuing all the way to Soray. There is no public transport along this stretch of road though you may be able to hitch a lift with one of the tour buses. Or, from Mollepata you can even get a **taxi all the way to Soray Pampa** for s/80 and miss out this first stage altogether. The path to Marcoccasa is not particularly exciting or interesting to trek along but it is fairly short, passes through some pretty farmland – and is a good way to limber up for the more arduous stages later in the trek.

Take the concrete road that leaves from the plaza's north-west corner, following it as it snakes through the houses and continuing until the concrete runs out at a T-junction. Turn right onto a dirt and cobble road, keeping left at the first fork (the right-hand fork, according to the sign, is for buses) to follow a trail that veers round to the left (north-west) through a **grove of eucalyptus**.

❏ Mollepata
Mollepata lies 60km west of Cusco, at the end of a track off the main Cusco to Abancay highway. This track is currently being upgraded – when the work is complete, expect the current bus-journey time of three hours to be nearer the two-hour mark. Described by E George Squier as 'a collection of wretched huts on a high shelf of the mountain with a tumbledown church, a drunken governor... a place unsurpassed in evil repute by any in Peru', it has fortunately evolved since 1877 into a pleasant mountain town perched on a hillside overlooking the deep citrus-producing valley of the Apurímac. This small huddle of houses is the start point for both the Salkantay Trek and the High Inca Trail, each of which passes beneath the imposing glaciated peak of Nevado Salkantay (6271m/20,574ft).

Colectivos from Cusco (from 6am; s/12-15; 2-3 hours) leave from the western end of Calle Arcopata, within walking distance of the Plaza de Armas, taking you all the way to Mollepata's main square. Try to catch an early morning one; by mid morning the number of passengers thins out and you could be waiting hours for the minibus to fill up – and you may end up arriving in Mollepata too late to start your trek. If this happens to you there are a couple of **hostels on the plaza**, the best one being *Apu Tilca*, situated in the north-eastern corner and run by the genial José, with rooms s/20 per person or s/25 for one with hot water and breakfast.

There are a few small stores where you can buy some basic last-minute provisions. There are also arrieros for hire. In addition to the wages and the hire of the mules, you are responsible for paying for the arrieros' return trip, which from Huayllabamba should only be one day, whilst from Santa Teresa or La Hidroeléctrica takes two days.

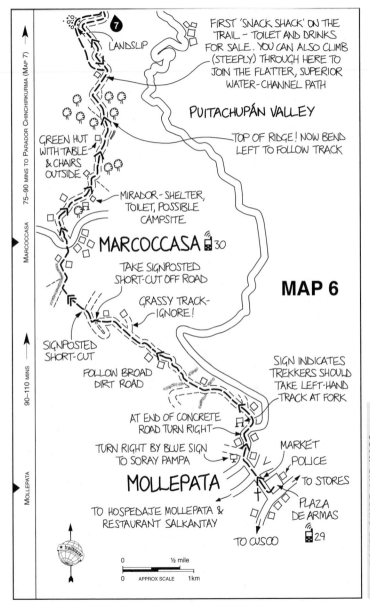

FIRST 'SNACK SHACK' ON THE TRAIL – TOILET AND DRINKS FOR SALE. YOU CAN ALSO CLIMB (STEEPLY) THROUGH HERE TO JOIN THE FLATTER, SUPERIOR WATER-CHANNEL PATH

LANDSLIP

PUITACHUPÁN VALLEY

TOP OF RIDGE! NOW BEND LEFT TO FOLLOW TRACK

GREEN HUT WITH TABLE & CHAIRS OUTSIDE

MIRADOR – SHELTER, TOILET, POSSIBLE CAMPSITE

MARCOCCASA 30

MAP 6

TAKE SIGNPOSTED SHORT-CUT OFF ROAD

GRASSY TRACK – IGNORE!

SIGN INDICATES TREKKERS SHOULD TAKE LEFT-HAND TRACK AT FORK

SIGNPOSTED SHORT-CUT

FOLLOW BROAD DIRT ROAD

AT END OF CONCRETE ROAD TURN RIGHT

MARKET

TURN RIGHT BY BLUE SIGN TO SORAY PAMPA

POLICE

TO STORES

MOLLEPATA

PLAZA DE ARMAS 29

TO HOSPEDAJE MOLLEPATA & RESTAURANT SALKANTAY

TO CUSCO

75–90 MINS TO PARADOR CHINCHIRKURMA (MAP 7)

MARCOCCASA

90–110 MINS

MOLLEPATA

Trailblazer

0   ½ mile
0   APPROX SCALE   1km

ROUTE GUIDE AND MAPS

The road from the village eases along the left (west) side of a valley that's heading roughly north-west. Continue to obey the blue signs and after about an hour you'll be cutting between the bends and switchbacks of the road on several steep short-cuts. A concrete **irrigation channel** carrying snowmelt from Salkantay lies at the top of the last one. Turn right to follow it and a few minutes later you'll find yourself emerging onto the dirt road at the micro-settlement of **Marcoccasa** (3341m/10,961ft). It takes 90 minutes minimum to reach this village from Mollepata. Fill up your water bottles at a spring behind some houses at the back of the cleared area (where the power lines lead to), because the streams are unreliable on the way to Soray. From Marcoccasa there are some superb, expansive views of the snow-capped Huarohuirani (to the north behind the hill), the village of Qurawasi away in the distance to the west, and Mollepata off to the south.

The signboard at Marcoccasa that shows the route of the trail also marks the start of the path to Soray. Take the small trail by the water channel which leads up towards a pleasant viewpoint with toilets and a shelter and a good place to camp for the night. The path climbs to a ridge overlooking a high valley feeding down to the Limatambo.

The trail now turns left, following the valley high on its western slope, before the trail passes the first of several shacks on this first day where you can **buy drinks** and use the toilet facilities (for a sol). Rather than following the regular trail, most trekkers these days climb steeply past the shelter here and continue up the slopes for a few minutes to a water channel.

Turning right, you can follow this channel all the way to Soray on a path that is pretty much flat the whole way. As such it's superior to the regular trail, which, at a viewpoint called **Parador Chinchirkurma**, drops steadily down to the valley floor and then spends most of its time climbing back up again to some high puna fields – **Soray Pampa**. By now you will have excellent views of the bulk of Nevado Humantay and to its right as you look at the sheer pyramid of Nevado Salkantay, whose name means 'Savage Mountain'.

The beginning of the pampa is latticed with small streams that you'll have to cross (though these disappear in dry years). Keep to the left (west) side of the pampa, close to the rock wall if you want to remain dry footed.

There are several lodges here. Near where the two paths to Soray meet is *Hospedaje Soray Pampa*, a small and informal place with very simple rooms. *Refugios Salkantay* (see pp181-2) is small but charming with its wooden balcony, hammocks and thatch-and-corrugated see-through-plastic roofs. Then there are the two more luxurious lodges reserved for the exclusive use of clients of two of the largest trekking operators. Right on the pampa is *Salkantay Lodge & Adventure Resort*, run by Mountain Lodges of Peru (see p181), which can only be used by people on the lodge-to-lodge trek to Santa Teresa. The second place is run by *Salkantay Trekking* (see p182) and features geodesic domes which look great when lit up at night and which have Inca-style entrances – it's all rather fabulous!

Beyond these two lodges are several *campsites*, most of which have shelters under which you can pitch your tent for extra protection. The last campsite in Soray is the biggest and has a pretty well-stocked **shop**.

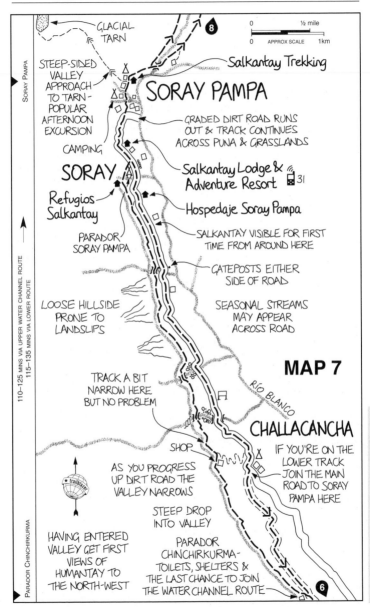

GLACIAL TARN

STEEP-SIDED VALLEY APPROACH TO TARN – POPULAR AFTERNOON EXCURSION

Salkantay Trekking

SORAY PAMPA

GRADED DIRT ROAD RUNS OUT & TRACK CONTINUES ACROSS PUNA & GRASSLANDS

CAMPING

SORAY

Salkantay Lodge & Adventure Resort 31

Refugios Salkantay

Hospedaje Soray Pampa

PARADOR SORAY PAMPA

SALKANTAY VISIBLE FOR FIRST TIME FROM AROUND HERE

GATEPOSTS EITHER SIDE OF ROAD

LOOSE HILLSIDE PRONE TO LANDSLIPS

SEASONAL STREAMS MAY APPEAR ACROSS ROAD

MAP 7

TRACK A BIT NARROW HERE BUT NO PROBLEM

RÍO BLANCO

CHALLACANCHA

SHOP

IF YOU'RE ON THE LOWER TRACK JOIN THE MAIN ROAD TO SORAY PAMPA HERE

AS YOU PROGRESS UP DIRT ROAD THE VALLEY NARROWS

STEEP DROP INTO VALLEY

HAVING ENTERED VALLEY GET FIRST VIEWS OF HUMANTAY TO THE NORTH-WEST

PARADOR CHINCHIRKURMA – TOILETS, SHELTERS & THE LAST CHANCE TO JOIN THE WATER CHANNEL ROUTE

½ mile

APPROX SCALE

1km

There's an interesting detour from here that climbs north-west away from the campsite to a pretty glacial, turquoise tarn below the slopes and shrinking glaciers of Nevado Humantay, which itself often has impressive cornices and overhanging snowy ridges. The ascent to the tarn takes around an hour whilst the return journey lasts half that time.

SORAY PAMPA TO HUAYLLABAMBA
[MAP 7, p243; MAP 8; MAP 9, p246; MAP 10, p247]

From Soray this **26.5km (16½ miles; 6hrs 50 mins to 8hrs 10 mins)** trail begins by heading up the valley to the north-east (right) directly towards Mount Salkantay. There are two paths, one each side of the **Río Salkantay** that runs down the valley's centre; the left-hand (northerly) path is lower and more undulating and thus slightly harder, though both are, in all honesty, simple. At **Salkantay Pampa** you finally bid farewell to the hordes of trekkers tackling the Salkantay Trek via the western side of the mountain, in order to follow a path that is much less travelled. Looking north from the pampa Nevado Salkantay, the sacred mountain of the Incas, is ahead of you. Before it, at the head of the valley, is a massive wall of scree – the **terminal moraine** (end debris) of a glacier. It is here that the path divides, the left-hand fork bearing north-west while your path takes the right-hand fork (north-east), crossing back over the stream, towards the pass at Inka Chiriasqa.

A series of steep switchbacks climbs sharply up the eastern shoulder of Nevado Salkantay. A short distance into the climb the path passes a flat patch of hillside called **Quera Machay** which makes for a decent *campsite*. Beyond here the path heads north and then east, continuing to climb all the while. Alternative trails branch off and descend to the lateral moraine of the glacier. Ignore these and keep the river between you and the glacier.

As you gain height and climb through **Pampa Japonés** the valley narrows dramatically. From a high point there are good views back over the wall of lateral moraine to a pair of lakes. At this point the ridge is visible ahead and the pass can be made out above a very steep slope. It is tempting to cut out the last climb and nip over the watershed by the glacier instead, but this is potentially very dangerous. **Inka Chiriasqa** (aka Chiriaska/ca/q'ua; 4948m/16,234ft), which translates as 'the place where the Inca cools down', is a narrow (barely a metre wide) knife-like pass.

From the pass there are stunning views of both the valley behind you and the one that lies ahead. The path drops quickly from the high point, descending swiftly into the adjoining valley. You can **camp** pretty much anywhere in this valley, though initially this upper part is rather bleak and unappealing. The path is reasonably clear and easy to make out – it simply follows the valley down. If in doubt which path to follow, see the instructions on the map opposite.

Initially the trail crosses puna heading south-east but soon bends north-east and steepens. A little further on, beyond the ridge, the path tracks across a patch of glacial outwash and **Quebrada Sisay Pampa** (Map 9), occasionally used as a *campsite*. Continue downstream as the path continues to descend whilst the

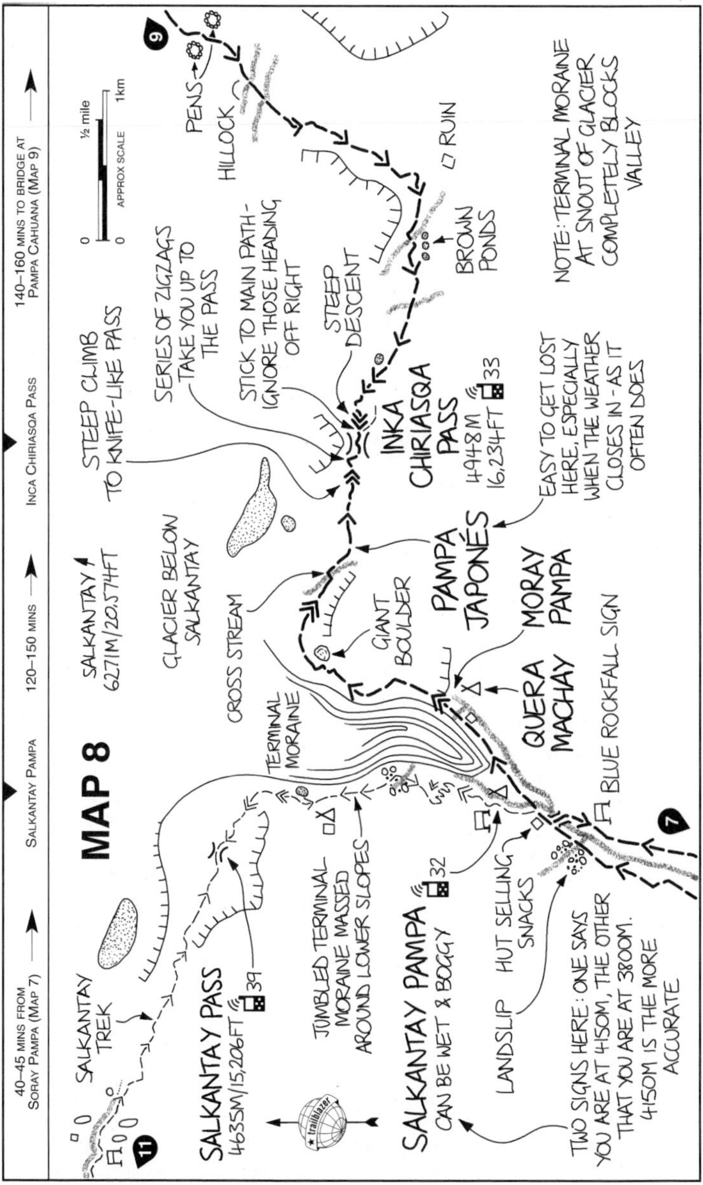
MAP 8
40–45 MINS FROM SORAY PAMPA (MAP 7)
SALKANTAY PAMPA
120–150 MINS
INCA CHIRIASQA PASS
140–160 MINS TO BRIDGE AT PAMPA CAHUANA (MAP 9)
½ mile
1km
APPROX SCALE
SALKANTAY TREK
SALKANTAY PASS
4635M/15,206FT
39
SALKANTAY 6271M/20,574FT
GLACIER BELOW SALKANTAY
TUMBLED TERMINAL MORAINE MASSED AROUND LOWER SLOPES
TERMINAL MORAINE
CROSS STREAM
SALKANTAY PAMPA
CAN BE WET & BOGGY
32
LANDSLIP
HUT SELLING SNACKS
TWO SIGNS HERE: ONE SAYS YOU ARE AT 4150M, THE OTHER THAT YOU ARE AT 3800M. 4150M IS THE MORE ACCURATE
BLUE ROCKFALL SIGN
QUERA MACHAY
MORAY PAMPA
GIANT BOULDER
PAMPA JAPONÉS
EASY TO GET LOST HERE, ESPECIALLY WHEN THE WEATHER CLOSES IN - AS IT OFTEN DOES
STEEP CLIMB TO KNIFE-LIKE PASS
SERIES OF ZIGZAGS TAKE YOU UP TO THE PASS
STICK TO MAIN PATH - IGNORE THOSE HEADING OFF RIGHT
STEEP DESCENT
INKA CHIRIASQA PASS
4948M 16,234FT
33
BROWN PONDS
RUIN
HILLOCK
PENS
NOTE: TERMINAL MORAINE AT SNOUT OF GLACIER COMPLETELY BLOCKS VALLEY
trailblazer

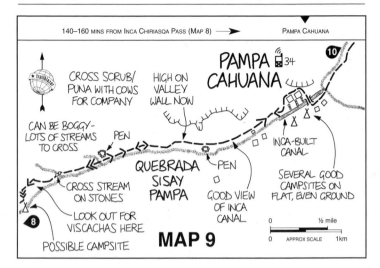

140–160 MINS FROM INCA CHIRIASQA PASS (MAP 8) ⟶

PAMPA CAHUANA

CROSS SCRUB/ PUNA WITH COWS FOR COMPANY

HIGH ON VALLEY WALL NOW

PAMPA CAHUANA 🔋34 ⑩

CAN BE BOGGY- LOTS OF STREAMS TO CROSS   PEN

QUEBRADA SISAY PAMPA   PEN

GOOD VIEW OF INCA CANAL

INCA-BUILT CANAL

SEVERAL GOOD CAMPSITES ON FLAT, EVEN GROUND

CROSS STREAM ON STONES

LOOK OUT FOR VISCACHAS HERE

⑧

POSSIBLE CAMPSITE

MAP 9

0   ½ mile
0   APPROX SCALE   1km

surrounding hillsides become increasingly steep. A broad river joins from the south. Almost immediately after this the valley turns north-east. From here you can make out an Inca canal below you. This area, around 2½ hours from the pass, is **Pampa Cahuana** (Map 10). The path meanders between a clutch of houses and farms before crossing a bridge to the eastern (right-hand) bank of the **Inca-built canal**. Constructed to drain the flat upper valley and prevent the river meandering lazily here, the well-engineered canal was used to irrigate this section of the basin and still carries melt water into the valley bottom. There are some good flat places to *camp* here.

At the far end of a narrow gorge the valley and canal, which develops into Río Cusichaca, turn north and continue to descend through changing vegetation until, around 1½ hours from the bridge, the path arrives at the small hamlet and ruins of **Paucarcancha** (see box p248).

Beyond the ruins and the small village continue the trek to Huayllabamba (30-45 mins; see p218). Once there you can join the classic Inca Trail, or walk down the Cusichaca Valley and either catch a train back to Cusco or onwards to Aguas Calientes from Km88; alternatively you can walk to the road at Km82, or even trek along the river to Machu Picchu.

❏ **Important note – walking times**
All times in this book refer only to the time spent walking. You will need to add 20-40% to allow for rests, photography, checking the map, drinking water etc.

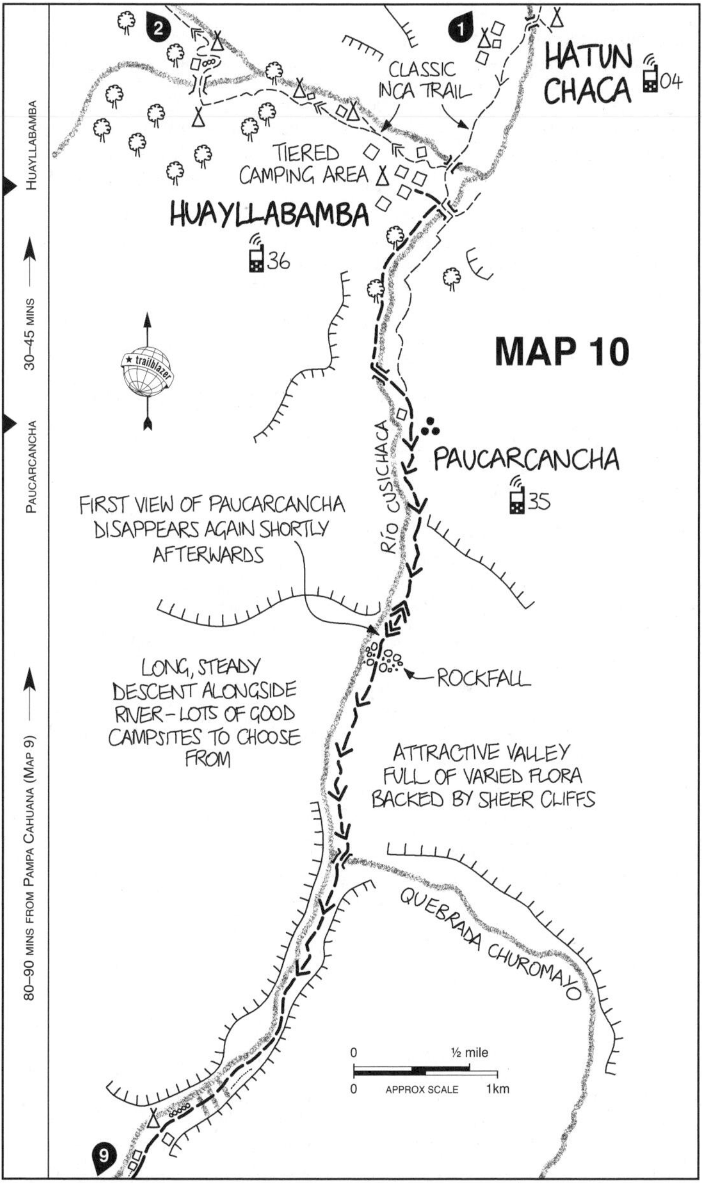
HUAYLLABAMBA
30–45 MINS
PAUCARCANCHA
80–90 MINS FROM PAMPA CAHUANA (MAP 9)
2
1
CLASSIC INCA TRAIL
HATUN CHACA
04
TIERED CAMPING AREA
HUAYLLABAMBA
36
MAP 10
trailblazer
PAUCARCANCHA
35
RÍO CUSICHACA
FIRST VIEW OF PAUCARCANCHA DISAPPEARS AGAIN SHORTLY AFTERWARDS
ROCKFALL
LONG, STEADY DESCENT ALONGSIDE RIVER – LOTS OF GOOD CAMPSITES TO CHOOSE FROM
ATTRACTIVE VALLEY FULL OF VARIED FLORA BACKED BY SHEER CLIFFS
QUEBRADA CHUROMAYO
0
½ mile
0
APPROX SCALE
1km
9

ROUTE GUIDE AND MAPS

❏ Paucarcancha

This partially renovated ruin, also sometimes referred to as **Incarajay**, stands guard over the Cusichaca river, dominating the valley and protecting an approach to Machu Picchu from the Apurímac to the south. The Incas were not native to this valley, but this imposing fort built following the submission of the indigenous tribes sometime in the second half of the 15th century, would have served as a potent reminder of the new rulers of the region. It would also have served as a strategically sited tambo.

The fort contains 16 buildings, some of which are thought to be barracks. Trapezoidal windows look out over the countryside and large sets of terraces adorn the surrounding hillsides, presumably providing crops and foodstuffs for the inhabitants.

To Huayllabamba & Inca Trail

Paucarcancha

Terraces

0   5   10m

Gabled house

Trapezoidal windows

Trapezoidal windows

Reconstructed section

★ trailblazer

Reconstructed section

Grassy area

Terraces

To Mollepata

The Salkantay Trek

This route is the nearest thing to a 'back door' approach to Machu Picchu (see overview map on p250). Closed for a number of years in the wake of the massive landslide in 1998 that wiped out the village of Santa Teresa (see box p258) and the nearby railway line, it was only re-opened by the authorities to ease the pressure on the Inca Trail and provide an alternative for those who are short of time or money – or were simply too late to book their Inca Trail trek.

All this means it is no longer the deserted, remote route it once was and since there are no regulations on the number of people beginning the route each day it can get very, very busy during the peak season. As such, there are rumours that the government will impose a set of rules in line with those already in place on the classic Inca Trail. Check with Andean Travel Web (see box p44) for the latest status. However, for the moment **you don't need any sort of permit to trek on this route**.

Although the routes finish at the same point, this **82.5-83km (51¼- to 51½-mile) trek** (if walking all the way from Mollepata to Aguas Calientes) is a very different type of trek to the classic Inca Trail. There are no Inca ruins until Llactapata, by which time you are in sight of Machu Picchu. However, the scenery is stunning and the varied range of landscapes that you pass through make the Salkantay Trek an excellent outing in its own right. You'll climb closer to the snowline and descend further into the subtropical forest than you would on the classic Inca Trail, meaning that you'll have a much better chance of seeing a wider range of birdlife and flora.

The best time to tackle the trek is during the dry season (May to September), as the high pass can be blocked by snow during the wet season. The

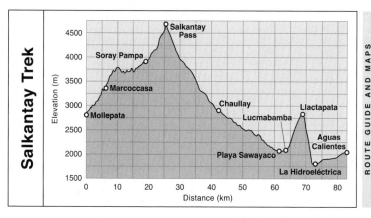

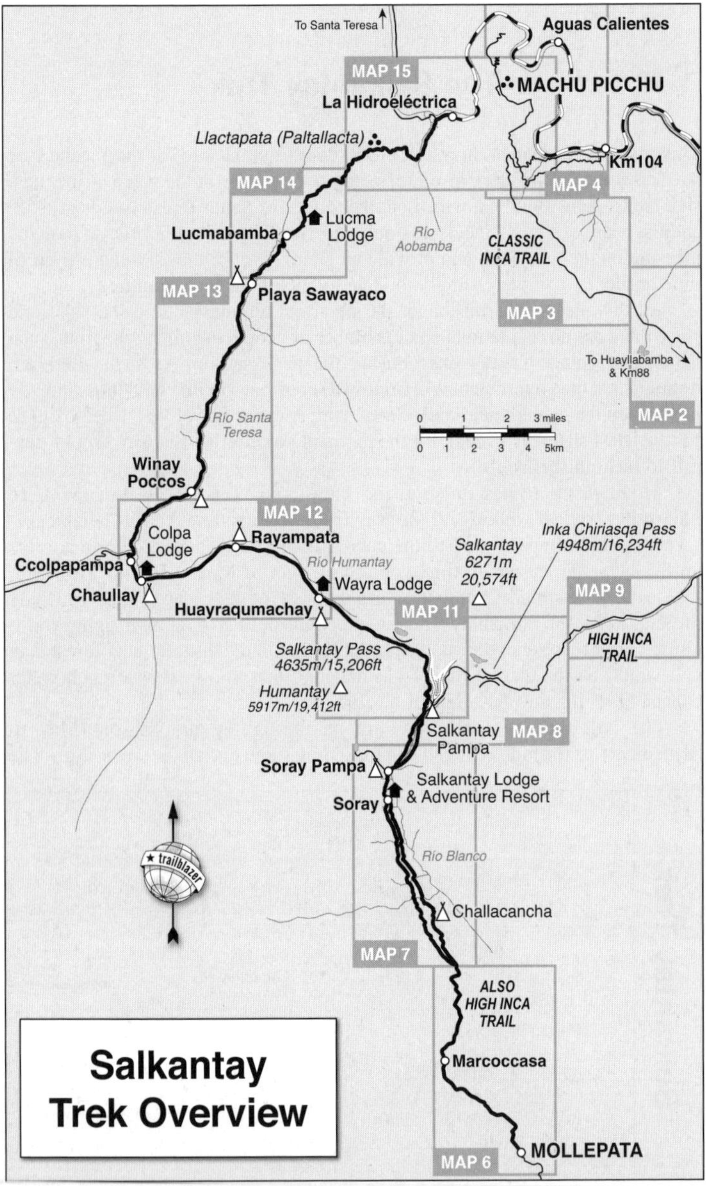

To Santa Teresa

Aguas Calientes

MAP 15

La Hidroeléctrica

Llactapata (Paltallacta) ∴

MACHU PICCHU

Km104

MAP 4

MAP 14

Rio Aobamba

Lucma Lodge

Lucmabamba

CLASSIC INCA TRAIL

MAP 3

MAP 13

Playa Sawayaco

To Huayllabamba & Km88

Rio Santa Teresa

MAP 2

0 1 2 3 miles

0 1 2 3 4 5km

Winay Poccos

MAP 12

Colpa Lodge

△ **Rayampata**

Rio Humantay

Salkantay 6271m 20,574ft △

Inka Chiriasqa Pass 4948m/16,234ft

Ccolpapampa

Chaullay

Wayra Lodge

MAP 9

Huayraqumachay △

MAP 11

HIGH INCA TRAIL

Salkantay Pass 4635m/15,206ft

Humantay 5917m/19,412ft △

Salkantay Pampa

MAP 8

Soray Pampa △

Salkantay Lodge & Adventure Resort

Soray

Rio Blanco

△ Challacancha

MAP 7

ALSO HIGH INCA TRAIL

★ trailblazer

Marcoccasa

MAP 6

MOLLEPATA

Salkantay Trek Overview

ROUTE GUIDE AND MAPS

trek begins from Mollepata and traditionally takes four days. You should factor in a fifth to explore Machu Picchu properly. Though most companies seem to offer much the same itinerary, in fact there is lots of variety. (Mountain Lodges – see p181 – for example, turns this essentially straightforward four-day trek into a seven-day extravaganza, incorporating excursions to many of the nearby lakes, glaciers and valley walls.) Remember the path is subject to the whims of nature, too, particularly landslips that are oh-so common in the area, and which may cause the path to be diverted – possibly permanently – and even closed for a while. Here we present the most typical route, while at the same time trying to point out the various options on the way.

This standard route is a little strenuous since it climbs from the watershed of the Apurímac (2800m/9185ft) to cross a 4635m/15,206ft pass below Nevado Salkantay, tumbles back down into the thickly forested Santa Teresa valley, breaches another pass at 2795m/9170ft and descends almost a thousand metres into the Aobamba valley before finishing at Aguas Calientes, at the foot of Machu Picchu Mountain.

Note that **if you signed up with an agency**, the chances are that you'll miss out on the last pass – and the Llactapata ruins – and instead on the third afternoon you'll be picked up from the trail and driven to Santa Teresa, there to sit in a thermal bath for the rest of the day. You'll also be given the option to go zip lining the next morning, before being returned to the trail at La Hidroeléctrica; see p256 for details of this itinerary. This does mean you'll miss out on the only Inca ruins on the trail itself before Machu Picchu – but it is a very popular diversion from the trail. If you want to go with an agency but would rather walk the whole way, make sure you negotiate with the agency beforehand and they should be able to arrange for you to walk the final stage too.

Note that, like the High Inca Trail, **this trek has several different names** including the Mollepata trek and Santa Teresa Trek (a name that we used in the last edition of this guide). We, however, have bowed to public opinion and have gone with the most popular moniker: The Salkantay Trek.

MOLLEPATA TO SORAY PAMPA   [MAP 6, p241; MAP 7, p243]

For information on getting to the trailhead at Mollepata see box p240. For details about this **19.2-19.7km** first stage of the trek (**12-12¼ miles** – the exact distance depending on what route you take between Marcoccasa and Soray Pampa; **4hrs 35 mins to 5hrs 25 mins** on the upper water channel route; **4 hrs 40 mins to 5hrs 35 mins** on the road route) follow the directions from Mollepata on the High Inca Trail (see pp240-4). Note that if you've signed up with an agency the chances are you'll be driven from Mollepata to Marcoccasa and thus have to walk only the last part of the first stage, from Marcoccasa to Soray Pampa (thereby deducting 6km from the above distances). Note, too, that if you aren't part of an organised tour and are beginning your walk in Mollepata, then Salkantay Pampa is too ambitious as a destination for the first day's walk; instead, aim to reach Soray Pampa – or, if you set off late from Mollepata, trim your ambition still further and spend the first night at Marcoccasa.

SORAY PAMPA TO CHAULLAY
[MAP 7, p243; MAP 8, p245, MAP 11; MAP 12, p255]

The chances are that if you are on a group tour, you'll be awoken before dawn today – 4am or soon after isn't unusual. If you're trekking independently then, of course, it's up to you when you rise, but it probably pays not to set off too much later than the groups – after all, you've got a lot of walking to do on this, the longest day of the trek (**23.2km, 14½ miles; 6½hrs to 7hrs 50 mins**), and the one where you reach the highest point as you cross the Salkantay Pass.

Some people dread the section leading up to the pass the most, and it's true that it can be quite exhausting hauling your carcass 707m from Soray Pampa up to the pass; but it's the descent afterwards that can drag, with a long stretch down to Huayraqumachay, the usual lunch-spot, followed by an even more taxing descent to **Chaullay**, where the tour groups tend to spend the night. If it all gets a bit much, just direct your mind to your happy place, think positive thoughts, and tell yourself that by the end of the day you'll be once more breathing the relatively oxygen-rich air of Chaullay – at 3435m, it's 1200m below the pass itself. And if that fails, you can always hire a horse to take you from Soray Pampa to Chaullay for s/100.

In addition to the altitude, you face a couple of other hazards today. The first is **horses** which were probably absent from yesterday's walk (the path by the water channel being too narrow for them), but of which you'll encounter plenty on today's hike, particularly on the descent. Remember to make sure that when they pass, you aren't precariously perched on the edge of some steep drop; try to get 'cliffside' of them if you can. The second potential hazard is the ground underfoot, where loose rocks and stones have caused many a twisted ankle in the past, and will doubtless do so again in the future. If you've got a pair of boots with good ankle support, use them today – the Salkantay Pass is not a place where you want to be injured, for medical help will be a loooong way away.

For the start of this stage from Soray Pampa, please see p244. At **Salkantay Pampa** (where there's a small shack selling snacks and where it's possible to **camp**), the trail divides. The High Inca Trail (see p244) branches right (north-east) around the moraine at the foot of Nevado Salkantay towards the Inka Chiriasqa pass and Huayllabamba. For your trail, however, you want to bear left (north-west) around the left-hand side of the moraine. The path begins to climb steeply up seven tight switchbacks, known as **Siete Culebras** (the Seven Serpents), and crests a small knoll after which it undulates north, parallel to the moraine, gradually gaining height.

Having scrambled through a boulder field, you snake across a level pampa and arrive at a small lake, **Laguna Soroy**, at its western end. **Soroyccocha** (3939m/12,923ft), the area of flat, clear ground just before the lake, makes for a good *campsite*; high and exposed it can get cold here but there's some protection from the nearby moraine ridge and the setting, backed by hills and looking directly onto the face of Nevado Salkantay, is superb.

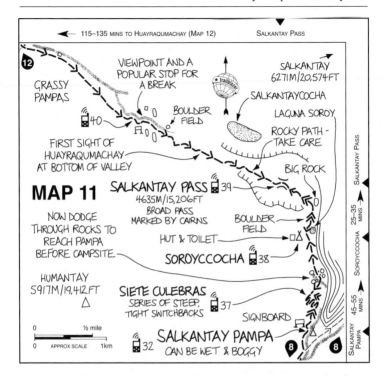

← 115–135 MINS TO HUAYRAQUMACHAY (MAP 12)   SALKANTAY PASS

VIEWPOINT AND A POPULAR STOP FOR A BREAK

SALKANTAY 6271M/20,574FT

GRASSY PAMPAS

SALKANTAYCOCHA

LAGUNA SOROY

BOULDER FIELD

📱40

ROCKY PATH - TAKE CARE

FIRST SIGHT OF HUAYRAQUMACHAY AT BOTTOM OF VALLEY

BIG ROCK

MAP 11

SALKANTAY PASS 📱39
4635M/15,206FT
BROAD PASS MARKED BY CAIRNS

NOW DODGE THROUGH ROCKS TO REACH PAMPA BEFORE CAMPSITE

BOULDER FIELD

HUT & TOILET

SOROYCCOCHA 📱38

HUMANTAY 5917M/19,412FT

SIETE CULEBRAS 📱37
SERIES OF STEEP, TIGHT SWITCHBACKS

SIGNBOARD

0   ½ mile
0   APPROX SCALE   1km

📱32 SALKANTAY PAMPA
CAN BE WET & BOGGY

8   8

SALKANTAY PASS (right side, vertical)
25–35 MINS
SOROYCCOCHA
45–55 MINS
SALKANTAY PAMPA

The track passes to the left (south) of the lake and climbs above it for a further 25-35 minutes, steep and tiring at this altitude though straightforward enough, to **Salkantay Pass** (4635m/15,206ft, occasionally known as the Humantay Pass or Apacheta Pass). It's usually busy up here with people celebrating their successful ascent in their own way: most trekkers will take a photo or two; a few of the more creative souls add to the collection of cairns (*apachetas*) that decorate the pass; while the more spiritual amongst us (or at least those who want to be seen to be) will take themselves off to a nearby rock to ostentatiously arrange themselves in the lotus position and meditate, like garden gnomes. While the more sensible will simply reapply their sunscreen, congratulate each other – and steel themselves for the big descent to come. It will have taken around two hours of walking to complete the six kilometres (four miles) to the pass from the Soray campsites – though by the time you've added in breaks etc, expect it to be nearer 3-4 hours from pampa to pass.

The pass is part of the shoulder of Salkantay, which rises to the north-east. If it is clear you should be able to see across the south face of the mountain to the high pass Inka Chiriasqa in the distance. To the south stands Tucarhuay whilst to the south-west lie the glaciated twin peaks of Humantay and to the west stands Pumasillo.

Beyond Salkantay Pass the path descends steadily west, dropping past a small tarn and through a **boulder field** that chokes the narrow valley. The bogs and streams eventually give rise to **Río Humantay**, which you follow on its left (west) bank, crossing small tributaries as you go.

About two hours from the pass on the left bank of the river, you'll reach **Huayraqumachay** or 'Eye of the Wind', an elongated farm settlement that dribbles on down the valley for almost a mile. There are several farm huts here and plenty of places for *camping*. **Wayra Lodge**, part of Mountain Lodges of Peru (see p181), is across the Humantay, enjoying spectacular views down the valley. No doubt there'll also be a confusion of trekkers struggling to find their group, and which hut they are supposed to be eating in.

After Huayraqumachay the path keeps to the left (west) of the river and remains fairly high in the valley. You'll pass a number of simple farm plots amidst some giant boulders. Below these the valley sides steepen and the puna gives way to scrub.

Just above the treeline is a large, well-prepared *campsite*. The path then descends into the cloud forest, which is draped with moss and lichen; there are also lots of bomaria and orchids to spot, as well as the distinctive *Brachyotum rostratum* with its bell-shaped purple flowers emerging from a red calyx. Look out, too, for parakeets and hummingbirds.

This track continues to descend steadily through the cloud forest and around 1¼-1½ hours after Huayraqumachay you'll pass the first buildings you've seen since the end of Huayraqumachay. This is **Rayampata** (Map 12), shown as Arayan Niyoc on some maps. Several huts are adjacent to the track and there are a few small terraces where you can *camp*. Water can be collected from the river below the huts. The families occasionally have soft drinks for sale. The views from the huts down the valley, of the snow-capped range ahead, are excellent.

From Rayampata you descend through thickly forested slopes, passing another small *campsite* that takes advantage of the flat ground on top of broad terraces for tent pitches. After an hour the path passes a pair of *collpas* (small earthen cliffs), clay licks used by parakeets, and in about 30 minutes you reach the village of Chaullay. Just prior to entering the village a small trail breaks right from the main path and quickly zigzags down a steep slope to reach the Río Humantay. On the far side a corresponding path ascends to *Colpa Lodge*, owned by Mountain Lodges of Peru (see p181). The lodge has an attractive front lawn that acts as a panoramic viewpoint overlooking Ccolpapampa and the valley ahead.

Chaullay is a smoky, ramshackle settlement at the junction of two valleys with a handful of rudimentary stores selling basic provisions. There are also several covered areas where you can eat and a basic shop advertising itself as a bar. Greener and cleaner than Rayampata, it has a pleasant *campsite* where you pitch your tent amongst the turkeys, dogs and other pets and livestock – as well as clouds of mosquitoes! There's even the chance to have a shower (s/10). **Refugios Salkantay** also have a place here offering basic rooms and food.

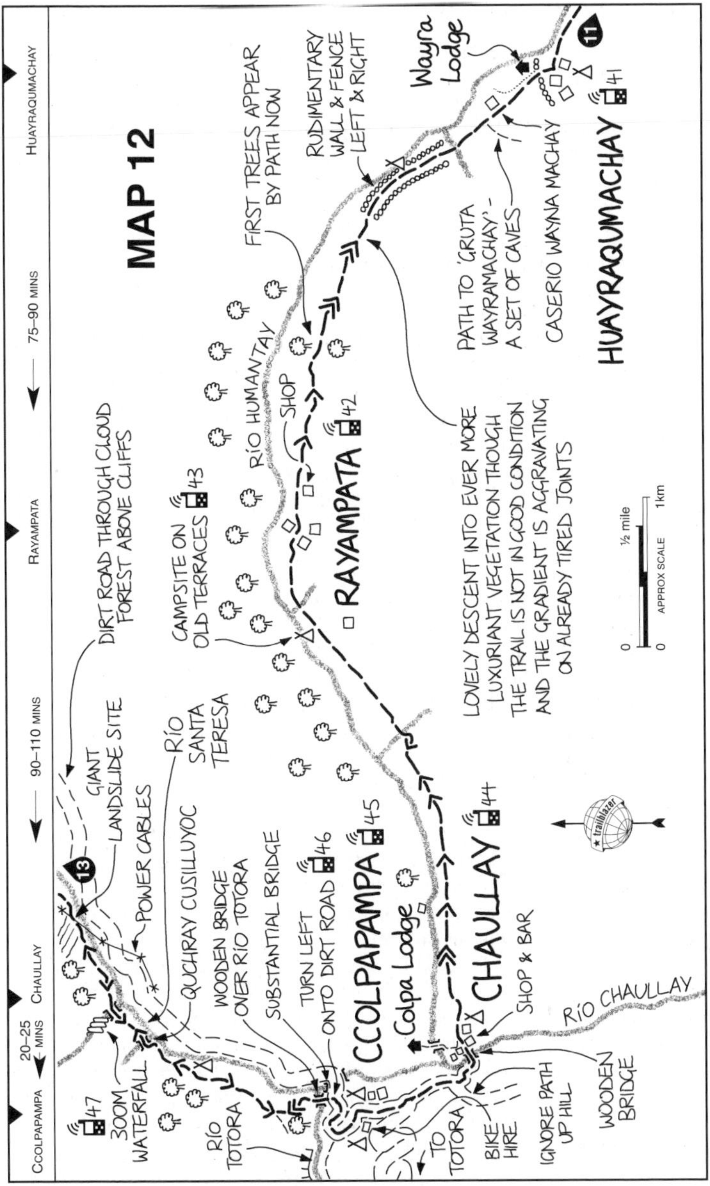

MAP 12

CCOLPAPAMPA ◀ 20-25 MINS CHAULLAY ▶ 90-110 MINS RAYAMPATA ▶ 75-90 MINS HUAYRAQUMACHAY ▶

DIRT ROAD THROUGH CLOUD FOREST ABOVE CLIFFS

GIANT LANDSLIDE SITE

POWER CABLES

RÍO SANTA TERESA

QUCHRAY CUSILLUYOC

WOODEN BRIDGE OVER RÍO TOTORA

SUBSTANTIAL BRIDGE

TURN LEFT ONTO DIRT ROAD 🏠46

CCOLPAPAMPA 🏕45
Colpa Lodge

RÍO TOTORA

300M WATERFALL 🏞47

CAMPSITE ON OLD TERRACES 🏕43

RÍO HUMANTAY

SHOP

RAYAMPATA 🏠42

FIRST TREES APPEAR BY PATH NOW

RUDIMENTARY WALL & FENCE LEFT & RIGHT

Wayra Lodge

PATH TO 'GRUTA WAYRAMACHAY' - A SET OF CAVES

CASERÍO WAYNA MACHAY

HUAYRAQUMACHAY

LONELY DESCENT INTO EVER MORE LUXURIANT VEGETATION THOUGH THE TRAIL IS NOT IN GOOD CONDITION AND THE GRADIENT IS AGGRAVATING ON ALREADY TIRED JOINTS

0   ½ mile
0   APPROX SCALE   1km

CHAULLAY 🏠44

SHOP & BAR

RÍO CHAULLAY

BIKE HIRE

TO TOTORA

IGNORE PATH UP HILL

WOODEN BRIDGE

TO TOTORA

CHAULLAY TO PLAYA SAWAYACO   [MAP 12, p255; MAP 13]

Once again if you're trekking as part of an organised group you'll probably be awoken before dawn, though this time it's not because you have a long day's walking ahead: instead, it's probably because you'll have a mere morning's stroll of **19km (11¾ miles; 3½ to 4¼hrs)** followed by an afternoon soak in the **Cocalmayo thermal baths** (s/10), to be followed in short order by dinner and a party.

The day begins with a crossing of the Río Chaullay on the wooden suspension bridge after the village, before turning right (north) on the far bank. Ignore the well-trodden trail that zigzags west up the side of the valley to pick up the broad, graded road from Santa Teresa, and instead follow the road downstream along the left (west) bank of the river to **Ccolpapampa**, a slightly larger community than Chaullay. There are several level pitches on which to *camp* here and even a place where you can **hire bikes**. Nowadays, Ccolpapampa is well connected to the outside world, with the road extension from Santa Teresa bringing trucks to the rough and ready collection of tin-roofed huts. There are also a couple of basic places to pick up a beer or soft drinks.

The road continues down the valley and soon bends left (west) into **Quebrada Totora**. Follow it down a sweeping bend, with an eye on the landslip scars that mark the steep slopes all around. A smaller path branches off left from the apex of the bend but ignore this, it actually leads to Choquequirao and is part of the route that links Choquequirao to Machu Picchu.

Before a substantial steel, wood and concrete bridge over the Río Chaullay, which joins Río Totora, the path divides and you have a choice. The first option is to simply continue across the main bridge on the road. The better option, however, is to take the small path before the bridge that leads steeply down to a makeshift wooden-and-turf bridge across the raging Totora. Once across, a path traverses the western side of the river, now the **Río Santa Teresa**, in a north-easterly direction through the thick vegetation of the cloud forest.

At one point the path crosses beneath the thundering course of a **300m waterfall**, which plunges from the cliff tops through the forest, crashing into the river below in six great bounds. About 2km (1¼ miles) further on, you'll have to scramble over a **landslide** that has devastated the path and scarred the hillside, although vegetation and scrub has begun to grow back.

Cross a second stream on stepping stones and pass through a **gate** before descending to **Winay Poccos**, a lovely, sun kissed *campsite* with passion fruit (s/1 for four) and avocados (s/1) for sale, as well as chocolate and soft drinks, all presided over by a couple of noisy but harmless dogs and a resident donkey that will eat anything – so be careful. Those who opted to take the road route can also enjoy this lovely little place by clambering down to cross the river.

The path continues down the valley, passing a second *campsite* (known by some as **Huascamayo**) with an *oroya*; nearby you'll also get your first brief glimpse of Machu Picchu Mountain before it is obscured by an intervening ridge as you continue to descend.

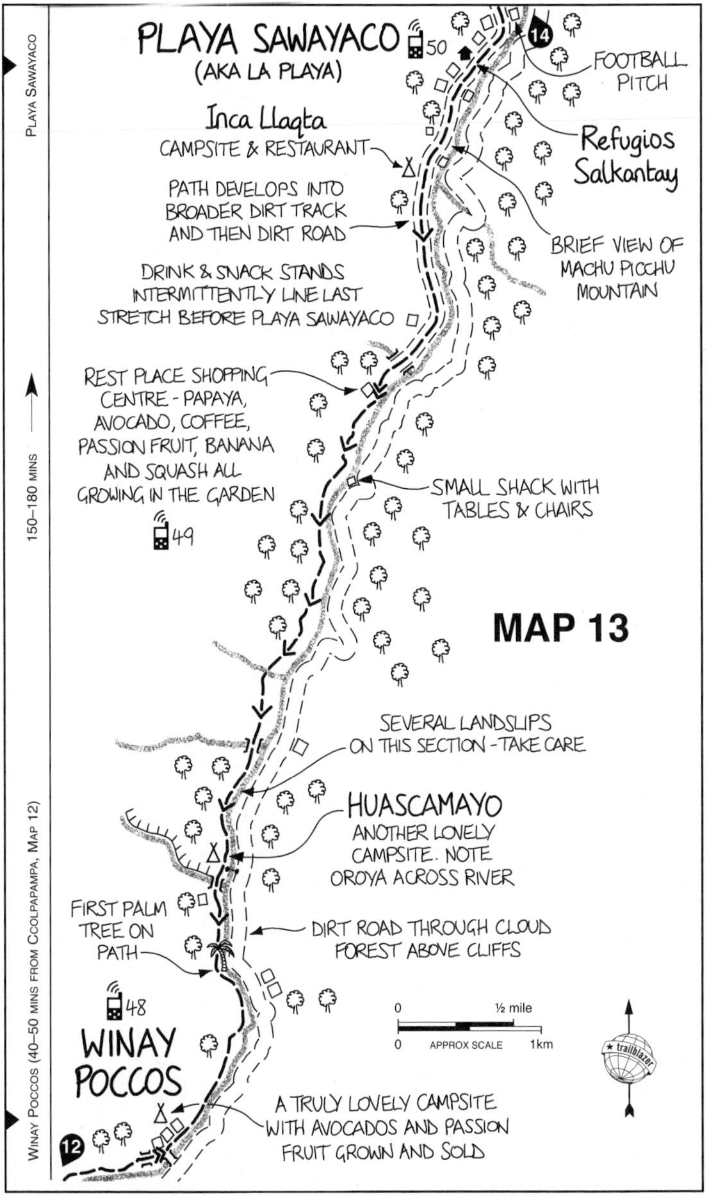

PLAYA SAWAYACO 📱50
(AKA LA PLAYA)

14

FOOTBALL PITCH

Refugios Salkantay

Inca Llaqta
CAMPSITE & RESTAURANT

PATH DEVELOPS INTO
BROADER DIRT TRACK
AND THEN DIRT ROAD

BRIEF VIEW OF
MACHU PICCHU
MOUNTAIN

DRINK & SNACK STANDS
INTERMITTENTLY LINE LAST
STRETCH BEFORE PLAYA SAWAYACO

REST PLACE SHOPPING
CENTRE - PAPAYA,
AVOCADO, COFFEE,
PASSION FRUIT, BANANA
AND SQUASH ALL
GROWING IN THE GARDEN
📱49

SMALL SHACK WITH
TABLES & CHAIRS

MAP 13

SEVERAL LANDSLIPS
ON THIS SECTION - TAKE CARE

HUASCAMAYO
ANOTHER LOVELY
CAMPSITE. NOTE
OROYA ACROSS RIVER

FIRST PALM
TREE ON
PATH

DIRT ROAD THROUGH CLOUD
FOREST ABOVE CLIFFS

0   ½ mile
0   1km
APPROX SCALE

📱48

WINAY
POCCOS

12

A TRULY LOVELY CAMPSITE
WITH AVOCADOS AND PASSION
FRUIT GROWN AND SOLD

PLAYA SAWAYACO

150-180 MINS

WINAY POCCOS (40-50 MINS FROM CCOLPAPAMPA, MAP 12)

ROUTE GUIDE AND MAPS

At least two hours after Winay Poccos the path develops into a dirt road and meanders into **Playa Sawayaco**, sometimes known more simply as La Playa, a relatively large community of farmers and arrieros that is embracing the numbers of trekkers now taking this route. With the increased number of visitors, the once makeshift bridge across the river that divides the town has been improved and the road extended, meaning that La Playa has been able to develop quite considerably. As you enter the village there's a series of shacks selling drinks and snacks but most people wait to cross the river where there are a couple of **bars/restaurants** that tend to cater to the tour groups but welcome independent trekkers too. The quietest place to **camp** is on the far side of the river that runs through the village; the campsite is on a slightly raised patch of ground adjacent to the old square, looking back across the village and up the valley. (That said, there are some even lovelier campsites just 15-20 minutes further along the trail at Lucmabamba – see p263.)

❏ **Santa Teresa**
Santa Teresa (also called Huadquina) used to be a small, subtropical village connected to Aguas Calientes – and therefore Machu Picchu – by a short train ride. The railway represented the main link between it and the outside world. In spring 1998 both the village and the railway line were destroyed by an enormous landslide that swept down from the surrounding mountains. Torrential El Niño rainstorms loosened the soil on the mountainside, releasing a colossal landslip into the Río Urubamba. Around 15 people died and over 350 families were affected. Almost 80% of the buildings in the old part of Santa Teresa were destroyed or partly damaged. The railway line was mangled beyond use and at the time of research still hadn't been repaired. The power station, La Hidroeléctrica, was also badly damaged.

The reconstruction and regeneration of Santa Teresa has been taking place slowly ever since. However, the popularity of the Salkantay/Santa Teresa route to Machu Picchu and the bridge across the Urubamba are bringing more people into the valley. Nonetheless, it remains a fairly plain settlement, with a smattering of basic hostel accommodation and cheap chicken restaurants, of little real interest to the casual visitor.

If you're staying overnight there are several cheap but reasonable places on Calixto Sanchez that advertise hot water and **wifi** (though it's best to check that they're both working before checking in), including *Hospedaje Laguna de Llaspay,* which charges s/20 per person. More atmospheric and classy, *Eco Quechua* (✉ www.ecoquechua.com, ☎ 630877 or ☎ 984 756855) is the smartest place in or, rather, just *outside* the town, by the bridge leading to La Hidroeléctrica, though their rooms are usually only for those who take a tour package with them. There are no banks or cashpoints, though at the top of Calixto Sanchez is a **moneychangers** that will change dollars. Nearby is *Yacumama*, with very acceptable pizzas (upwards of s/20), free wifi and a good atmosphere.

Some 4km (2½ miles) from Santa Teresa, the **Cocalmayo hot springs** (s/10) are a genuine attraction, with warm water pools and a café. Also popular is **Cola de Mono Canopy zipline** (✉ www.canopyperu.com; US$60), about 2km from Santa Teresa. Whisking people through the air above the Sacsara Valley, there are 2500m of cable in total over seven runs; the longest ride is 400m, the highest 150m and riders on the line reach speeds of 60kph (37mph).

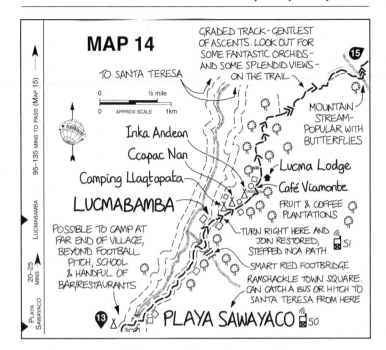

If you're on an organised tour, it is at Playa Sawayaco where you'll probably be picked up and **shuttled to the hot springs at Santa Teresa** (see box opposite). The next day many agencies now incorporate a morning's zip lining, before driving their clients to La Hidroeléctrica from where they must either catch the train or walk (3 hours approximately) to Aguas Calientes. Opt out of the zip-lining and you still have to get from Santa Teresa to La Hidroeléctrica, a dull 2½-hour trudge along a dusty road. In either case, you won't be able to complete the trail from Playa Sawayaco to Aguas Calientes on foot – a stage that includes the recently rediscovered and partially uncovered ruins of Llactapata (see box pp260-1). If this is important to you, make sure you negotiate with the agency beforehand and they should be able to arrange for you to walk this leg too.

PLAYA SAWAYACO TO LA HIDROELECTRICA
(FOR AGUAS CALIENTES)   [MAP 13, p257; MAP 14; MAP 15, p265]

Those who miss this **10.6km (6¾ miles; 3¼hrs to 4hrs 20 mins)** trek to Hidroeléctrica are, we think, missing some of the most pleasant walking on the trek. True, you don't reach the altitudes of the previous days; but the original Inca path up to the ruins at Llactapata is a joy and, given the altitude you gain, actually not too strenuous, such is the gentle nature of the incline. (cont'd on p262)

❏ Llactapata (Paltallacta)

Despite their proximity to Machu Picchu, the ruins of Llactapata (also known as Paltallacta) have been little investigated since they were initially uncovered by Hiram Bingham in 1912. The site, situated on and below a long ridge, lay untouched for more than 70 years after this discovery, until being 'rediscovered' in the early 1980s. Since then, studies have shown the site to be far larger and more significant than previously imagined.

The first account of the ruins was published by Bingham. An initial foray into the Aobamba Valley by Bingham's assistant had met with 'almost insuperable difficulty' as a result of the dense, impenetrable forest that clad the hillsides. Bingham himself explored the region 10 days later and recorded that he '... found some interesting ruins ... The end of that day found us on top of a ridge between the valleys of the Aobamba and the Salcantay.' The small collection of structures he then loosely described is part of Llactapata, which, owing to its strategic location overlooking Machu Picchu's western flank, and the clear and unrivalled view of the city from here, he decided was 'the ruins of an Inca castle'. He went on to attribute its construction to one of Manco Inca's captains.

In total, Bingham spent just five daylight hours at the site and failed to properly explore or map the ruins. His expedition was sorely handicapped by an unhelpful team of arrieros who had been press-ganged into service; his account of the trip in fact spends more time lamenting the deficiencies of his team than describing the ruins. The arrieros later abandoned him.

Unfortunately Bingham's imprecise notes regarding the location were too vague for anyone to be able to retrace his steps, and slowly the forest closed back over the ruins. In truth his descriptions of the ruins, published alongside news of the uncovering of Machu Picchu, Vitcos and Espíritu Pampa, failed to inspire people to follow in his footsteps. It wasn't until the early 1980s that Hugh Thomson rediscovered them, and not until the early part of the 21st century that any serious archaeological investigation was carried out, with extensive excavation and mapping undertaken by Thomson.

The site, whose name means 'High Town' in Quechua, is considerably larger than first thought, although it is still hard to tell where the ruins begin and the cloud forest ends. The complex faces Machu Picchu, which lies 5km (3 miles) to the east, on the far side of the Aobamba valley. The sacred peaks of Nevados Veronica and Salkantay are also visible from here.

The site consists of several interrelated high-status building groups including a feature thought to be a **sun temple**, which has uncanny similarities in terms of structure, size and alignment to the Coricancha (see pp151-2) in Cusco. There are also residential sectors here that might have served as high-status tambos, and agricultural areas thought to have been used to grow crops to supplement food production at Machu Picchu.

Although the stonework is generally less impressive than at Machu Picchu because of the metamorphic rocks available, the solid buildings, multiple niches, shaped corner stones and **double-jamb doorways** are indicative of a place of great importance. Evidence shows that the crude walls were in fact coated with light-coloured clay that would have concealed the rough stonework beneath a smooth, striking façade.

An Inca path uncovered by Hugh Thomson and Gary Ziegler leads from the site towards Vilcabamba and Vitcos, whilst the Inca path that starts at the Inca drawbridge behind Machu Picchu and runs across the head of the valley to Llactapata would have provided a suitably elaborate and spectacular entrance to the site. This would have allowed the Inca to visit the site for particular ceremonial occasions, such as the June solstice.

A unique feature is a 45m/145ft long **sunken corridor** set 1.8m/6ft into the earth and aligned so as to point directly at Machu Picchu. During the summer solstice, the sun rises over the Torreón in Machu Picchu, and falls directly along this channel. The building thought to be a sun temple and various viewing platforms throughout the site lend further weight to the ritual significance of Llactapata.

In his report on the site, Hugh Thomson suggests that the careful alignment (see p262) of the key buildings and features in relationship to Machu Picchu indicate that Llactapata was 'part of a carefully designed network of interrelated administrative and ceremonial sites supporting the regional administrative and ceremonial centre at Machu Picchu'.

Underlining the importance of the site and its ritual significance are the facts that a number of key buildings in Machu Picchu are set to look over the Aobamba valley towards Llactapata. The Intihuatana and the small structure at the summit of Huayna Picchu are both aligned to look west across the valley. The house on Huayna Picchu also contains a *huaca* that replicates the Llactapata ridge.

Much of the site is often off-limits to the public whilst investigations and excavations are carried out. Just a handful of buildings have been restored and since the pace of excavation is so slow, the forest has reclaimed some previously cleared areas, meaning that it takes no small amount of imagination to visualise the grandeur of the sprawling site and imagine the significance of the spectacular view of Machu Picchu spread out across the horizon to the east.

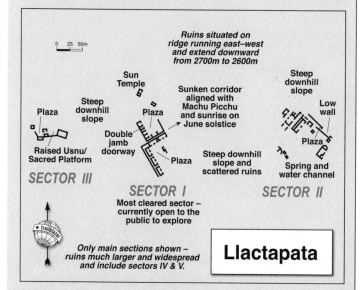

0 25 50m

Ruins situated on
ridge running east–west
and extend downward
from 2700m to 2600m

Sun
Temple

Sunken corridor
aligned with
Machu Picchu
and sunrise on
June solstice

Steep
downhill
slope

Plaza

Steep
downhill
slope

Plaza

Low
wall

Plaza

Double
jamb
doorway

Plaza

Steep downhill
slope and
scattered ruins

Spring and
water channel

Raised Usnu/
Sacred Platform

SECTOR III

SECTOR I

SECTOR II

Most cleared sector –
currently open to the
public to explore

trailblazer

Only main sections shown –
ruins much larger and widespread
and include sectors IV & V.

Llactapata

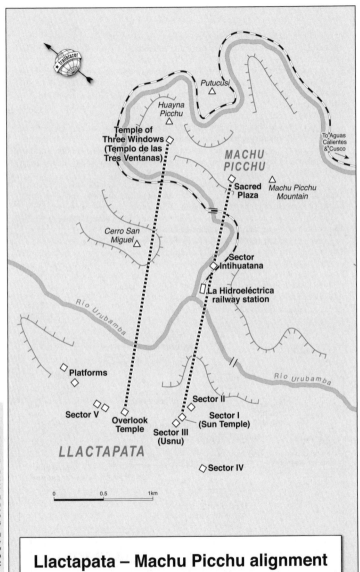

Llactapata – Machu Picchu alignment

(cont'd from p259) And the views from Llactapata across to Machu Picchu are the best sort of appetiser for the ruins. Having completed the very steep descent down to La Hidroeléctrica, even the additional **10.5km walk (6½ miles; 2½hrs)** along the train tracks to Aguas Calientes is rather fun (and, after a brief initial climb to cut through the switchbacks on the track, blissfully flat), with lush, enveloping nature providing a welcome distraction from the weariness you're probably feeling by now.

Having crossed the river that bisects Playa Sawayaco, continue along the road that runs above the river. After 3km (2 miles) there is a large **faded blue 'INC' sign** on the right-hand side (east) of the road, next to the small community of **Lucmabamba**. Turn right (east) here on to a grassy track and a short section of restored, broad Inca steps. There are a couple of lovely **campsites** here, *Camping Llaqtapata* and *Ccapac Nan*, where they sell drinks and snacks and, most importantly of all, insect repellent. The trail continues to climb past coffee **plantations**, houses with concrete slabs for drying coffee beans and plots of lemon and passion-fruit trees. Fifteen minutes from the junction, on the right-hand side of the track, stands the thatched, modern **Lucma Lodge**, another link in the Mountain Lodges of Peru chain (see p181).

Continue ascending for 80-120 minutes on a wide, even path, as plantations give way to scrub which in turn gives way to cloud forest that thickens as you climb around a series of spurs before entering dense, virgin forest; begonias (usually *Begonia bracteosa*) and the large purple orchid *Sobralia dichotoma* add a splash of colour to the path. Finally, go up a short section of steps and arrive at a **ridge pass** (2795m/9170ft).

Follow the narrow, muddy track branching left (north) along the ridge for a few minutes before it begins to descend into the Aobamba Valley. There are now tantalising glimpses of Machu Picchu sprawled across the ridgetop 5km (3 miles) ahead, shadowed by the unmistakable shape of Huayna Picchu.

The path runs down the hillside past the partially cleared ruins of **Llactapata** (see box pp260-1), the majority of which remains largely hidden under moss and leaves, all weighed down by a dense tangle of twisted tree roots.

Immediately below the ruins is a clearing boasting exceptional views of Machu Picchu sprawled across a ridge, where it is possible to *camp*. The next accommodation is in Aguas Calientes (though you may be able to ask the restaurants at La Hidroeléctrica if they have a space where you can sleep).

From the campsite, the descent begins in earnest for 40 minutes to an hour, plunging down a remorseless series of switchbacks to enter a **coffee plantation** and emerge at a **suspension bridge** across the Río Aobamba. On the far side of the river turn left (north) and follow the right-hand side (east) of the valley downstream towards the confluence of the Aobamba and Urubamba rivers. To your right and high on the cliff above, a huge stream of water spews from a hole in the cliff, part of the hydroelectric project.

Cut over a low hillock and enter the Urubamba valley. Join the broad gravel road running adjacent to the river and head upstream towards **La**

Hidroeléctrica and the small **railway station** next to it. Ignore the bridge over the Urubamba and instead stop at a **checkpoint** where you must show your passport. A minute or two further on is the station, the platform of which is lined with makeshift stalls and shabby cantinas selling drinks and snacks. The **ticket office** is on your left; it opens around 3pm and the train to Aguas Calientes departs around 4pm. Once on the train it takes almost an hour for it to trundle across the Urubamba, clatter past **Puente Ruinas** at the foot of Machu Picchu and squeal to a stop in Aguas Calientes (see pp206-9) at the old local railway station on Avenida Imperio de los Incas.

If you decide to walk the 10km (6 miles) to Aguas Calientes – you may have no choice, as the train usually gives priority to locals – and we recommend you do, the walk itself takes about 2-3 hours simply by following the train tracks.

Right at the start of the walk, there is a small but interesting **set of sculpted stones at Sector Intihuatana**, a short walk along the line. As Mark Adams writes in his book *Turn Right at Machu Picchu*:

> 'I followed him down a short path that led from the train tracks and through an arch-like opening in the flora. And I'll be damned if we didn't step out onto one of the most amazing pieces of stonework I'd yet seen in Peru. Carved out of a massive chunk of granite was a sculpture that wouldn't have been out of place at the Museum of Modern Art. Its wide platform top and thirty-foot-high face had been squared off and smoothed. Multiple niches and altars surrounded a set of steps that led up to a geometric base, like a gigantic trophy....'

Head down the tracks towards Machu Picchu and take the unmarked track *immediately* before the Restaurant Byon. Cross the railway line as it doubles back on itself and climb a further short slope into a patch of forest. Scattered here, surrounded by banana and avocado trees, is a series of terraces, walls, archways, fountains, scooped stones and carefully sculpted boulders, all within sight of Machu Picchu and the Inca drawbridge. The lack of signs and restoration here mean it is rarely visited. The site lies on the site line between Llactapata and Machu Picchu (see map p262); this suggests that the various ruins are interlinked and shared ceremonial roles, particularly during the summer and winter solstices.

Along the way there are several places where enterprising locals have set up stalls to sell soft drinks and snacks and you are treated to great views of the newly uncovered lower terraces at Machu Picchu. The train tracks are actually laid on an old mule track that was followed by Hiram Bingham back on his first expedition. As such, on the way you'll pass Mandor Pampa, where the innkeeper Melchor Arteaga promised to take Hiram Bingham to see some local ruins back in 1911 on a mountain called Machu Picchu – Quechua for 'Old Peak'. As you near Aguas Calientes, the tracks pass through two tunnels before arriving in the lower part of the town.

From **Aguas Calientes** you can catch a shuttle bus up to Machu Picchu, something you'll most likely want to do first thing the following morning to get a full day exploring the site. For details on moving on from Aguas Calientes to Machu Picchu see p319.

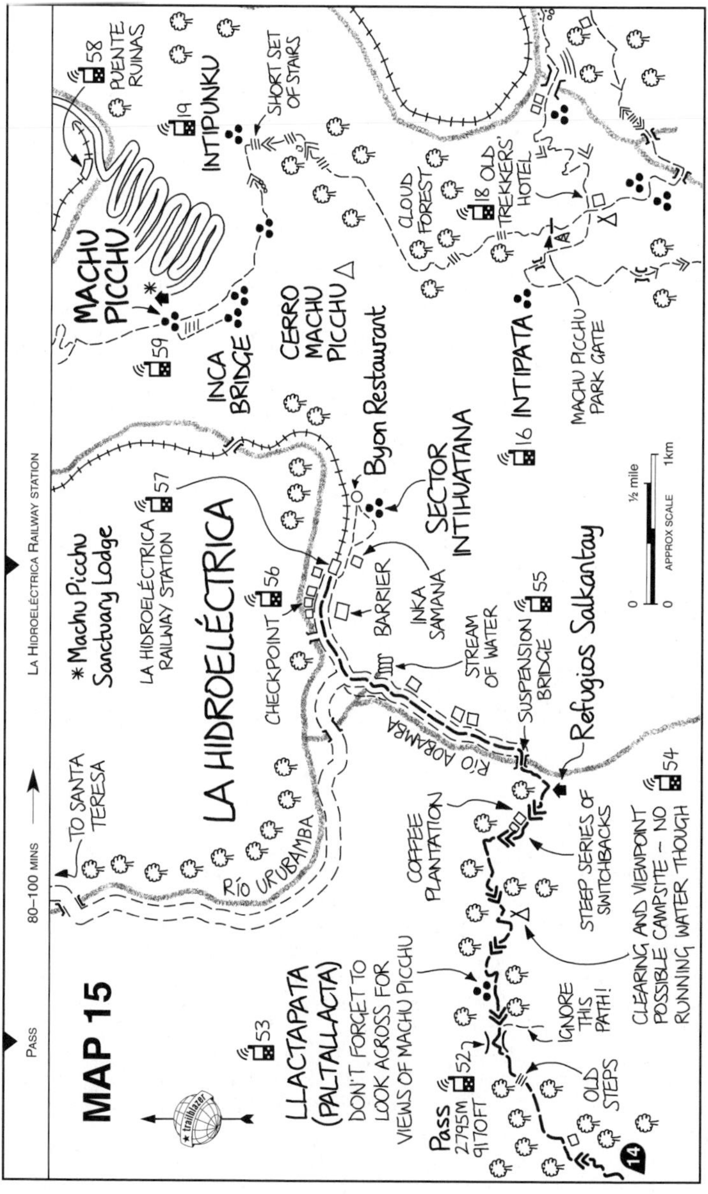

MAP 15

◄ PASS   80-100 MINS ──►   LA HIDROELÉCTRICA RAILWAY STATION ►

PUENTE RUINAS 📷58

INTIPUNKU 📷19

SHORT SET OF STAIRS

MACHU PICCHU

INCA BRIDGE

CLOUD FOREST

📷18 OLD TREKKERS' HOTEL

📷59

CERRO MACHU PICCHU △

Byon Restaurant

SECTOR INTIHUATANA

📷16 INTIPATA

MACHU PICCHU PARK GATE

*Machu Picchu Sanctuary Lodge

LA HIDROELÉCTRICA RAILWAY STATION 📷57

LA HIDROELÉCTRICA

CHECKPOINT 📷56

BARRIER

INKA SAMANA

STREAM OF WATER

SUSPENSION BRIDGE 📷55

Refugios Salkantay

RÍO ABOBAMBA

TO SANTA TERESA

RÍO URUBAMBA

COFFEE PLANTATION

📷54

STEEP SERIES OF SWITCHBACKS

LLACTAPATA (PALTALLACTA) 📷53

DON'T FORGET TO LOOK ACROSS FOR VIEWS OF MACHU PICCHU

Pass 2795M 📷52 9170FT

OLD STEPS

IGNORE THIS PATH!

CLEARING AND VIEWPOINT POSSIBLE CAMPSITE – NO RUNNING WATER THOUGH

14

0   ½ mile
0   APPROX SCALE   1km

The Lares Trek

Peru's Sacred Valley attracts hundreds of thousands of visitors every year. They come, of course, largely to visit the valley's spectacular Inca ruins, from the citadel at Pisac in the east to the royal estate of Pachacutec at Ollantaytambo in the west. Hundreds of hotels, restaurants, tour agencies and other tourist facilities have sprouted up over the decades as a result to cater for these visitors and throughout the year the valley reverberates to the noise of tourist buses making their way from one archeological site to the next.

Walk for just a minute north off the main road, however, and you enter a quite different world. One where the constant rumble of traffic is replaced by the gentle bubbling of streams and the delicate melodies of songbirds; where the buildings are still made in the traditional way, using stone and thatch, rather than with concrete; and where the hordes of noisy tourists that infest the Sacred Valley are replaced instead by ruminating herds of llama and alpaca – interspersed with the occasional intrepid trekker keen to explore this tranquil, traditional region.

It's become traditional to call any trek in this area a 'Lares trek' even though it's possible to trek through this region without visiting Lares itself. This is the region's largest settlement, with hotels, transport links, a restaurant or two and other facilities that you won't find anywhere else in the region. You'll even find a set of thermal baths, the one real visitor attraction in the region and a magnet for tourist buses. But walk five minutes up the hill from the baths and you're back in a serene tranquil rural idyll.

Sound attractive? Well it certainly is a lovely region for trekking, and provides visitors with the chance to see a rural way of life that's little changed over

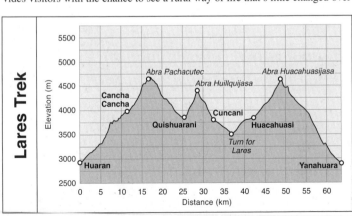

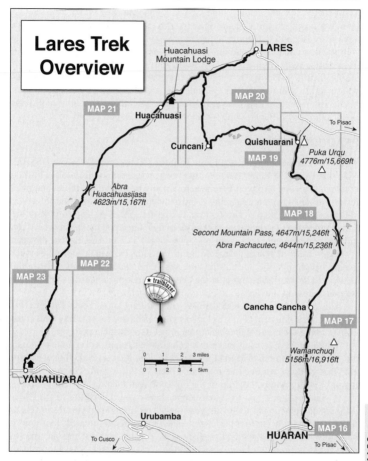

Lares Trek Overview

Huacahuasi Mountain Lodge

LARES

MAP 21

Huacahuasi

MAP 20

To Pisac

Cuncani

Quishuarani

MAP 19

Puka Urqu
4776m/15,669ft

Abra Huacahuasijasa
4623m/15,167ft

MAP 18

Second Mountain Pass, 4647m/15,246ft

Abra Pachacutec, 4644m/15,236ft

MAP 22

★ trailblazer

MAP 23

Cancha Cancha

MAP 17

0   1   2   3 miles

0 1 2 3 4 5km

Wamanchuqi
5156m/16,916ft

YANAHUARA

Urubamba

HUARAN

MAP 16

To Cusco

To Pisac

the centuries, without the need to travel all the way to Ausangate or further afield to do so. But before setting off you do need to heed the warnings. Firstly, **the walking in this region is tough**. Because many of the tour agencies advertise their Lares treks using such gentle-sounding sobriquets as 'The Weavers' Route', you may be misled into thinking that hiking in these parts is easy. It's not. Every day on the trek we describe here you'll be tackling at least one high mountain pass, which can be both exhausting and, on the jarring descent, excruciating.

Furthermore, the terrain underfoot is often horrible, with loose stones and rocks a menace to ankles. This means you may well spend most of your time on the trail looking where you're treading rather than admiring the scenery itself.

Surprisingly, it's not actually that easy finding your way either. And though there are people in the villages, once you're on the trail itself there's seldom anyone to ask; and if you *are* lucky enough to find someone to ask, they may well speak no Spanish – and almost certainly no English.

Finally, away from Lares town itself you won't find much in the way of tourist facilities. During research we came across one enterprising villager who'd set up a drinks stall at Quishuarani, and at one point we were able to hitch a lift back from Lares towards Huacahuasi, but there were no actual shops as such, nor any official public transport running between the villages.

PRACTICALITIES

Agents in Cusco can organise a Lares Trek for you beginning at about US$300. Note that we say '*a* Lares Trek', for the one we describe in this book is just the most popular (you still won't come across many people on the route, and even fewer – if any – who are tackling it independently) of a vast number of possible treks you can take in the region. Taking an agency-organised trek in the Lares region is not a bad idea; not only can they ferry you by minibus between villages and mountain passes etc, and thus cut out a lot of walking, but they can also open a lot of metaphorical doors in the villages, which will give you a greater insight into the lives of the villagers – and you may even get to see the weavers at work. Furthermore, at the end of the trek most agencies will organise your transport and entrance fees to Machu Picchu.

This particular trek is **63.8km (39¾ miles)** long and takes **3-5 days** – we recommend, if you can, taking as long as you can otherwise you may well come away cursing the name 'Lares' and wincing at its very mention.

While we have tried to make this guide and the maps as accurate as possible, it can't hurt to buy a second map as well. The IGN series is the most popular, though do be warned that it is rather poor for this region, with tracks missing or clumsily stamped on top of the topographical map.

If you're planning on trekking independently you'll need to bring all your camping equipment and food with you (outside of Lares town you'll struggle to find anywhere offering food). This trek is not to be underestimated, so if you're not going to sign up with an agency it is a good idea to hire an arriero. Unfortunately, finding one in Huaran at the start of the trek is tricky; instead, you may have to haul yourself up the hill for over 10 kilometres to Cancha Cancha to find one – it's probably your best bet.

But whether you hire an arriero or not, the basic advice is much the same: come prepared with a decent tent, enough food, warm clothes and a good pair of boots. And while on the trail be sure to take plenty of breaks, don't try to do too much each day – and keep this book close to hand to help you find your way.

GETTING TO THE TRAILHEAD

Minibuses and *colectivos* leave from Calle Puputi in Cusco to the start of the trail at **Huaran**, or **Huaran Fondo** as it's marked on some maps. Make sure you catch one that's going to Urubamba as this will take you all the way; if you get one that's going to Pisac only you'll need to catch further transport from there to take you the extra 30km.

Huaran itself looks pretty nondescript from the road and it's easy to drive through it without realising you've arrived; ask your fellow passengers or the driver to let you know when you need to alight.

The trek starts from a bus shelter, about 200m east of the turn-off for the *IFK Lodge Hotel & Nunay Restaurante* (🖥 www.ifk.pe/en, ☎ 974791456; room rates US$107-157). There is a **small store** behind the bus shelter where you can pick up last-minute supplies – but don't expect to be able to kit yourself out with much more than water and snacks.

HUARAN TO CANCHA CANCHA   [MAP 16, p270; MAP 17, p271]

It can be difficult deciding on where you should end this first day. Cancha Cancha is the first settlement you come to on the trail and while the route to get there is all uphill and can be a little steep in places, this **11.3km (7-mile)** hike should take you a little over three hours by our reckoning (**3hrs 10 mins to 3¾hrs**). The next village on the trail, however, Quishuarani, is five or six hours further on. Of course you could camp anywhere on the trail, and there is a lake beyond Cancha Cancha that seems to have been designed specifically by a higher power for the purpose of **wild camping**. But if you're looking to camp near some sort of human settlement, unless you're fit, fast and able to make a very early start from Huaran, we advise you to limit your ambitions and treat this first stage as just a leisurely ascent to Cancha Cancha; there is plenty of tough walking to come in the days ahead.

Route finding to Cancha Cancha is not tricky, save perhaps for the first couple of hundred metres as you worm your way through the houses of Huaran to the 4WD track you'll be taking. From the bus shelter cross the road and head north towards the church. Passing in front of the church's colourful façade, the trail passes between two high walls to reach a small memorial to Juan Velasco Alvarado, a left-wing Peruvian general who ruled Peru from 1968 to 1975 under the title 'President of the Revolutionary Government', having seized power in a bloodless coup. He's still revered by *campesinos* in Peru because of his efforts to help the country's poor.

Beyond lies the track you'll be following all day, its start marked by a sign in Spanish asking you to register before beginning your trek. Where exactly you are supposed to do this is not made clear, so if nobody stops you just walk on – there is a chance that you may be asked to pay further along the trail.

The gradient at the start of this track is pretty much the same gradient you'll be tackling all the way up to Cancha Cancha – a relatively gentle if relentless uphill. The route itself is easy to follow – just stick to the main trail, using the map on p271 whenever you have any doubts. Several attractive picnic sites present themselves along the way, though little black biting sandflies may persuade you not to linger too long in any one place; their bite can itch for several days afterwards, long after you've returned to Cusco at the end of the trek. *(cont'd on p272)*

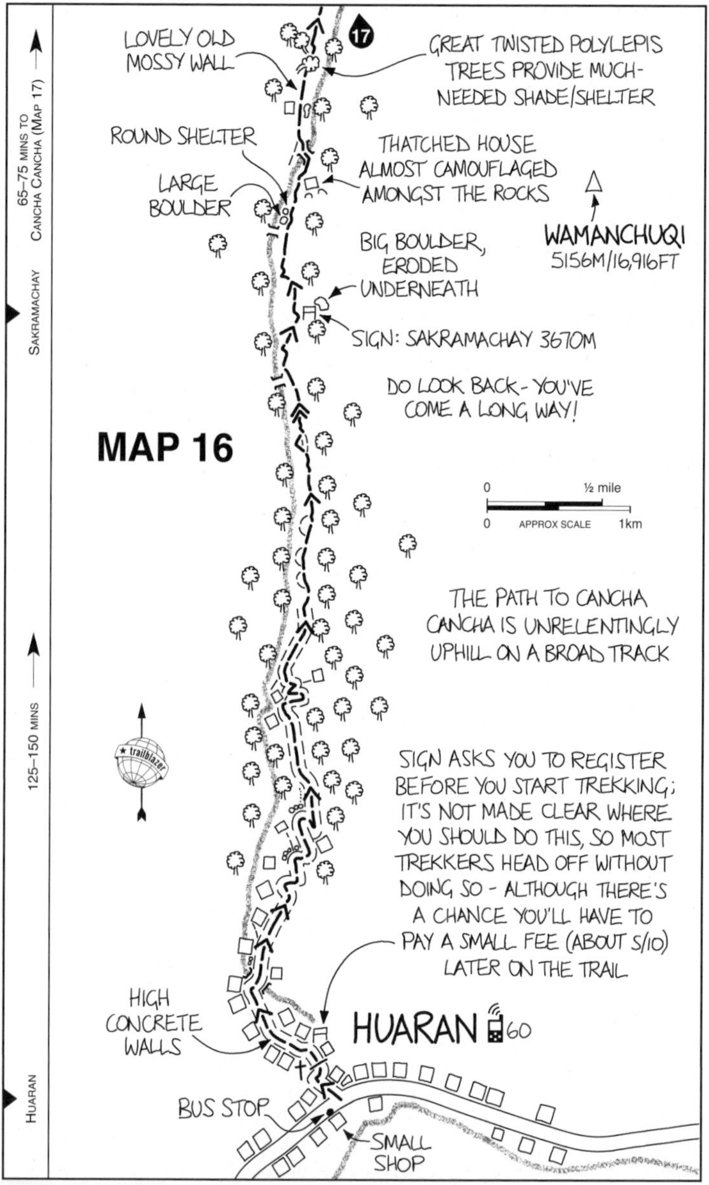

LOVELY OLD MOSSY WALL

GREAT TWISTED POLYLEPIS TREES PROVIDE MUCH-NEEDED SHADE/SHELTER

17

ROUND SHELTER

THATCHED HOUSE ALMOST CAMOUFLAGED AMONGST THE ROCKS

LARGE BOULDER

WAMANCHUQI
5156M/16,916FT

BIG BOULDER, ERODED UNDERNEATH

SIGN: SAKRAMACHAY 3670M

DO LOOK BACK - YOU'VE COME A LONG WAY!

MAP 16

0   ½ mile

0   APPROX SCALE   1km

THE PATH TO CANCHA CANCHA IS UNRELENTINGLY UPHILL ON A BROAD TRACK

★ trailblazer

SIGN ASKS YOU TO REGISTER BEFORE YOU START TREKKING; IT'S NOT MADE CLEAR WHERE YOU SHOULD DO THIS, SO MOST TREKKERS HEAD OFF WITHOUT DOING SO - ALTHOUGH THERE'S A CHANCE YOU'LL HAVE TO PAY A SMALL FEE (ABOUT S/10) LATER ON THE TRAIL

HIGH CONCRETE WALLS

HUARAN 📱60

BUS STOP

SMALL SHOP

65-75 MINS TO CANCHA CANCHA (MAP 17)

SAKRAMACHAY

125-150 MINS

HUARAN

ROUTE GUIDE AND MAPS

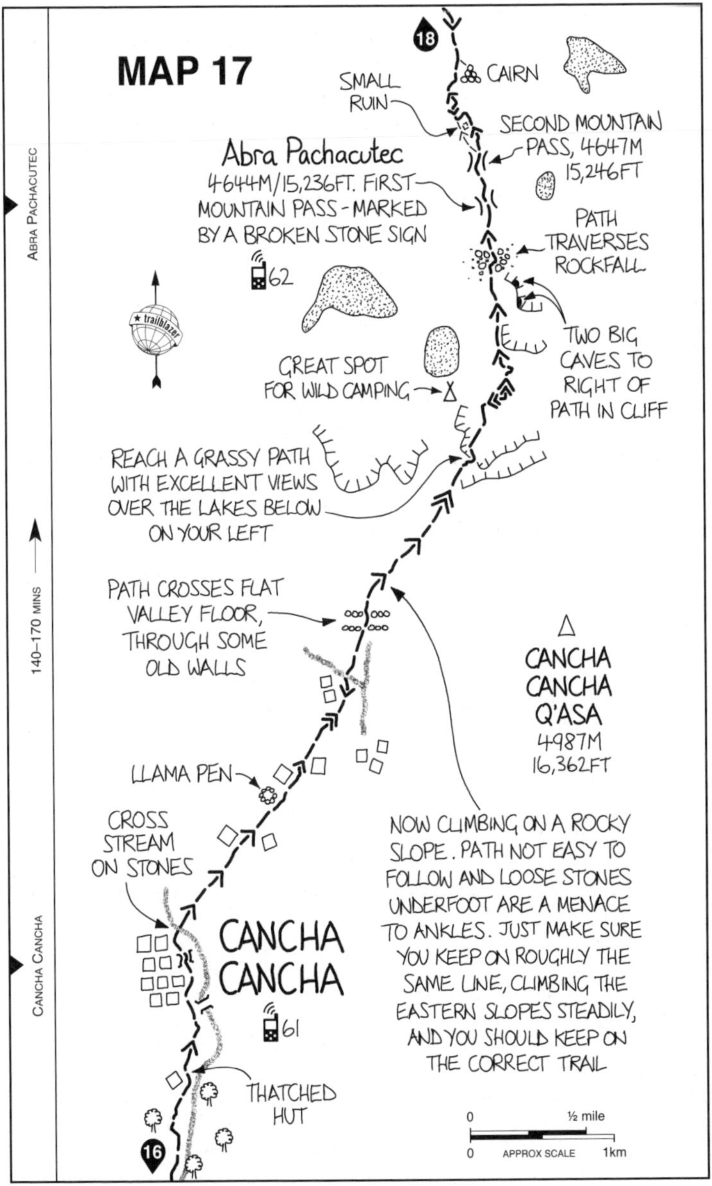

MAP 17

SMALL RUIN

CAIRN

(18)

SECOND MOUNTAIN PASS, 4647M
15,246FT

Abra Pachacutec
4644M/15,236FT. FIRST MOUNTAIN PASS - MARKED BY A BROKEN STONE SIGN

📱62

PATH TRAVERSES ROCKFALL

★ trailblazer

GREAT SPOT FOR WILD CAMPING → ✗

TWO BIG CAVES TO RIGHT OF PATH IN CLIFF

REACH A GRASSY PATH WITH EXCELLENT VIEWS OVER THE LAKES BELOW ON YOUR LEFT

140-170 MINS

PATH CROSSES FLAT VALLEY FLOOR, THROUGH SOME OLD WALLS

△
CANCHA CANCHA Q'ASA
4987M
16,362FT

LLAMA PEN →

CROSS STREAM ON STONES

NOW CLIMBING ON A ROCKY SLOPE. PATH NOT EASY TO FOLLOW AND LOOSE STONES UNDERFOOT ARE A MENACE TO ANKLES. JUST MAKE SURE YOU KEEP ON ROUGHLY THE SAME LINE, CLIMBING THE EASTERN SLOPES STEADILY, AND YOU SHOULD KEEP ON THE CORRECT TRAIL

CANCHA CANCHA

📱61

THATCHED HUT

(16)

ABRA PACHACUTEC

CANCHA CANCHA

0   ½ mile
0   APPROX SCALE   1km

ROUTE GUIDE AND MAPS

(cont'd from p269) Having passed the last of the houses above Huaran, the path enters into some pleasant forest, with hummingbirds and the wonderfully if suggestively named tit tyrants (a type of flycatcher) flitting between the branches and stands of bamboo that shade the trail, with the **Cancha Cancha River** gushing down the valley to the left of the trail. Don't forget to look back down the valley when the vegetation allows you to do so; it's a sweaty walk, no doubt, but you'll see that you've come a long way already.

There are a few landmarks along the trail, the first major one being **Sakramachay** (3655m/11,991ft), about two-thirds of the way to Cancha Cancha. There's little here save for a signpost, a large rock eroded from underneath that may, in an emergency, provide some sort of shelter, and, perhaps, a couple of ruminating cows, to differentiate this spot from any other you've already passed through; but hereafter there is the odd house and homestead to show that you're approaching Cancha Cancha, as well as some lovely little tracts of polylepis forest shading the trail once you cross to the western side of the river. Soon even these hardy trees give up trying to cling to survival, and you enter an area of grassland populated by grazing llamas. The narrow valley soon opens out onto an area of open pampas, and it's here you'll find **Cancha Cancha**, sitting at a lofty altitude of 3991m/13,094ft.

CANCHA CANCHA TO QUISHUARANI [MAP 17, p271; MAP 18]

The uphill nature of yesterday's stage is continued for the first half of today as you make your way towards the first of this trail's mountain passes. At just **13.9km (8¾ miles)** this stage can be completed in as little as **4 hours 50 minutes (up to 5hrs 55 mins)** and, as with the previous day's hike, it's very possible that you'll find it a little too short, even though it is also undoubtedly taxing. If this is the case, there are lakes and other spots on either side of the next pass that seem to be tailor-made for campers.

The path to the pass is fairly straightforward, the trail continuing in a north-easterly direction across the grassland, past several stone-walled farmsteads before eventually leaving the valley floor for the rocky eastern slopes. Here you may find the trail fading to nothing amongst the boulders and stones but fear not: just keep climbing in approximately the same direction and you'll soon pick up the trail again as it leaves the rockfall behind for something altogether grassier, with lovely views over the lakes below.

Thereafter the path to the pass is simple enough to follow, if not necessarily easy to complete, the altitude making every action onerous. **Abra Pachacutec** (4644m/15,236ft), lies around 2½ hours from Cancha Cancha and is marked by a simple broken stone sign. Curiously, this isn't actually the highest point of the climb. The trail continues to ascend to what feels like a second pass, just a few metres further on, where you get your first views of the valley beyond. From here the path divides: take either of the upper two paths, which continue to ascend the rocky slopes on your left before finally flattening out, having reached the lofty height of 4694m (15,400ft). Take your time to enjoy

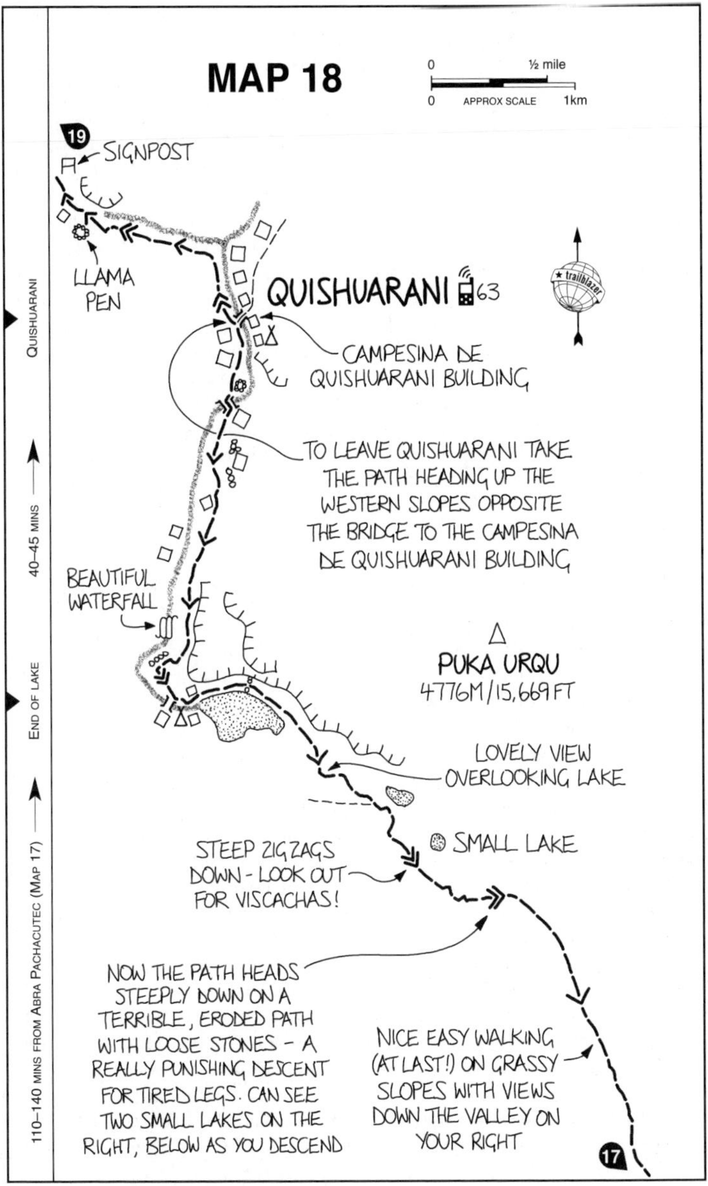

MAP 18

0 ½ mile
0 APPROX SCALE 1km

★ trailblazer

19 SIGNPOST

LLAMA PEN

QUISHUARANI 📱63

CAMPESINA DE QUISHUARANI BUILDING

TO LEAVE QUISHUARANI TAKE THE PATH HEADING UP THE WESTERN SLOPES OPPOSITE THE BRIDGE TO THE CAMPESINA DE QUISHUARANI BUILDING

BEAUTIFUL WATERFALL

△ PUKA URQU 4776M/15,669FT

LOVELY VIEW OVERLOOKING LAKE

STEEP ZIGZAGS DOWN - LOOK OUT FOR VISCACHAS!

◉ SMALL LAKE

NOW THE PATH HEADS STEEPLY DOWN ON A TERRIBLE, ERODED PATH WITH LOOSE STONES - A REALLY PUNISHING DESCENT FOR TIRED LEGS. CAN SEE TWO SMALL LAKES ON THE RIGHT, BELOW AS YOU DESCEND

NICE EASY WALKING (AT LAST!) ON GRASSY SLOPES WITH VIEWS DOWN THE VALLEY ON YOUR RIGHT

17

QUISHUARANI

40-45 MINS

END OF LAKE

110-140 MINS FROM ABRA PACHACUTEC (MAP 17)

ROUTE GUIDE AND MAPS

the views of the nearby glacier-topped mountains, with the peaks of Pitusiray (5432m/17,823ft) and Chicón (5530m/18,140ft) both visible.

Eventually, assuming you've stuck to the correct path, you'll be able to experience something that you've still yet to enjoy on this trail: a descent. Unfortunately, as much as you may be anticipating it with relish, the reality probably won't live up to your expectations, for this downhill section becomes very steep as it curves westwards to drop into the **Quishuarani Valley**. The trail itself is terrible too, with loose stones causing footsteps to falter and ankles to twist. Distract yourself from the pain by trying to spot viscachas scurrying amongst the rocks below, or the views of the two small lakes below you as well as the larger **Laguna Pachacutec** ahead.

The steepness of this descent finally relents as you reach the lake (camping is available at the far end of the lake; s/5), whereafter the path bends north to drop down the valley alongside the Río Quishuarani and past an impressive waterfall to the village of **Quishuarani** (3858m/12,657ft) itself. Centred on a garish pink-painted Comunidad Campesina de Quishuarani building (camping for groups only), this village feels more sophisticated than Cancha Cancha with its metal roofs and large concrete community hall; there's even a car parked here! But there's still little for the independent trekker, though you can camp nearby (s/5).

QUISHUARANI TO HUACAHUASI
[MAP 18, p273; MAP 19; MAP 20, p276]

Another day, another mountain pass to tackle. Yet the rewards on this **17km stage (10½-mile; 4hrs 55 mins to 6hrs)** are greater than on any other day on the trail. For one thing, once you've conquered the pass and stand at a lofty 4417m above sea level, the views down the other side over the several variegated lakes of the following valley is the best on the trail. And secondly, if you have the time and energy to tackle the straightforward 3.5km walk on the dusty 4WD track down to Lares, you can spend the rest of the day splashing around in the **thermal springs**, tending to tired tendons and soaking stressed-out soles and souls. (Though we should point out here that if you do decide to visit the baths, you will have to return back up the hill to continue on this trail.) And even if you decide to forego the baths, the hike to the next destination, Huacahuasi, is simple enough and the village itself is interesting, friendly and a nice place to relax for a night.

But first of all, you have to reach the pass, which lies at the top of a valley stretching west from Quishuarani. The route is generally uphill – of course! – though only as you approach the pass itself does it get properly steep. Before then, it's a fairly steady ascent with lovely **Laguna Queunacocha** on the way a perfect place to bolt down lunch, befriend a llama and gird your loins for the climb ahead.

Abra Huillquijasa (4417m/14,491ft) is a veritable knife-edge and provides little room for you to recuperate from your efforts. *(cont'd on p278)*

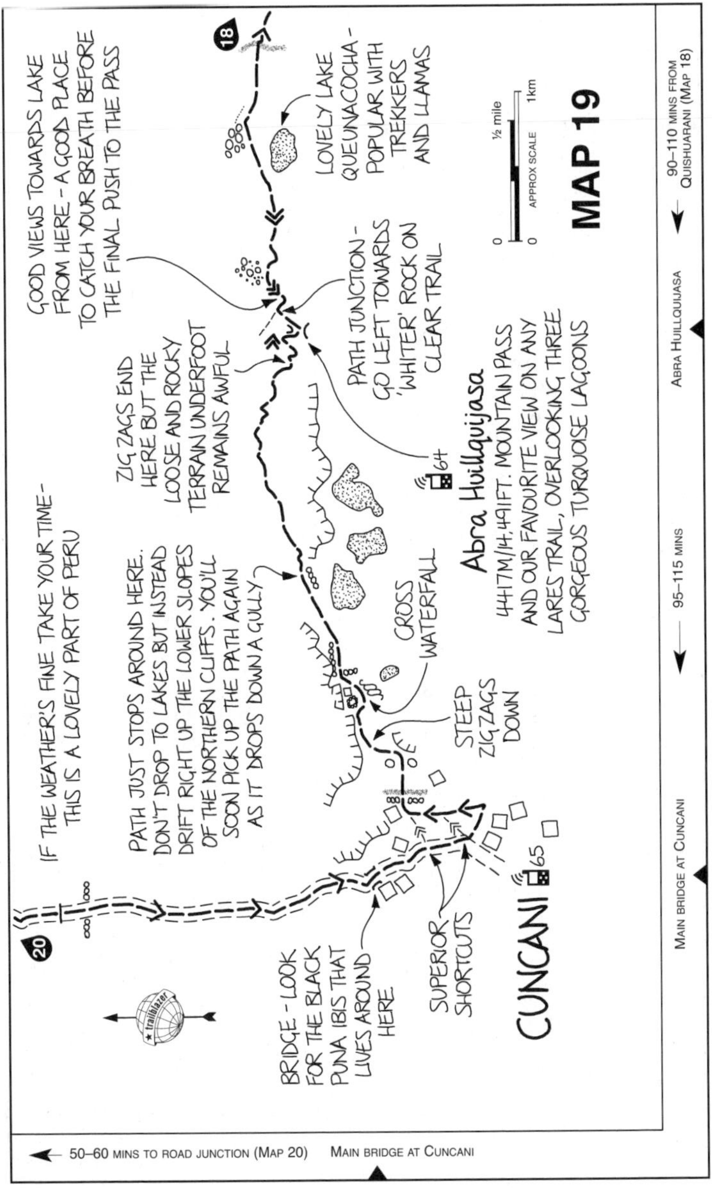

IF THE WEATHER'S FINE TAKE YOUR TIME – THIS IS A LOVELY PART OF PERU

GOOD VIEWS TOWARDS LAKE FROM HERE – A GOOD PLACE TO CATCH YOUR BREATH BEFORE THE FINAL PUSH TO THE PASS

LOVELY LAKE QUEUNACOCHA – POPULAR WITH TREKKERS AND LLAMAS

ZIG ZAGS END HERE BUT THE LOOSE AND ROCKY TERRAIN UNDERFOOT REMAINS AWFUL

PATH JUNCTION – GO LEFT TOWARDS 'WHITER' ROCK ON CLEAR TRAIL

PATH JUST STOPS AROUND HERE. DON'T DROP TO LAKES BUT INSTEAD DRIFT RIGHT UP THE LOWER SLOPES OF THE NORTHERN CLIFFS. YOU'LL SOON PICK UP THE PATH AGAIN AS IT DROPS DOWN A GULLY

CROSS WATERFALL

STEEP ZIGZAGS DOWN

Abra Huillquijasa
4417M/14,491FT. MOUNTAIN PASS AND OUR FAVOURITE VIEW ON ANY LARES TRAIL, OVERLOOKING THREE GORGEOUS TURQUOISE LAGOONS

BRIDGE – LOOK FOR THE BLACK PUNA IBIS THAT LIVES AROUND HERE

SUPERIOR SHORTCUTS

CUNCANI 🏠65

MAP 19

| 0 | ½ mile |
| 0 | 1km |
APPROX SCALE

← 50–60 MINS TO ROAD JUNCTION (MAP 20)   MAIN BRIDGE AT CUNCANI

MAIN BRIDGE AT CUNCANI ◄   95–115 MINS ◄   ABRA HUILLQUIJASA ◄   90–110 MINS FROM QUISHUARANI (MAP 18) ►

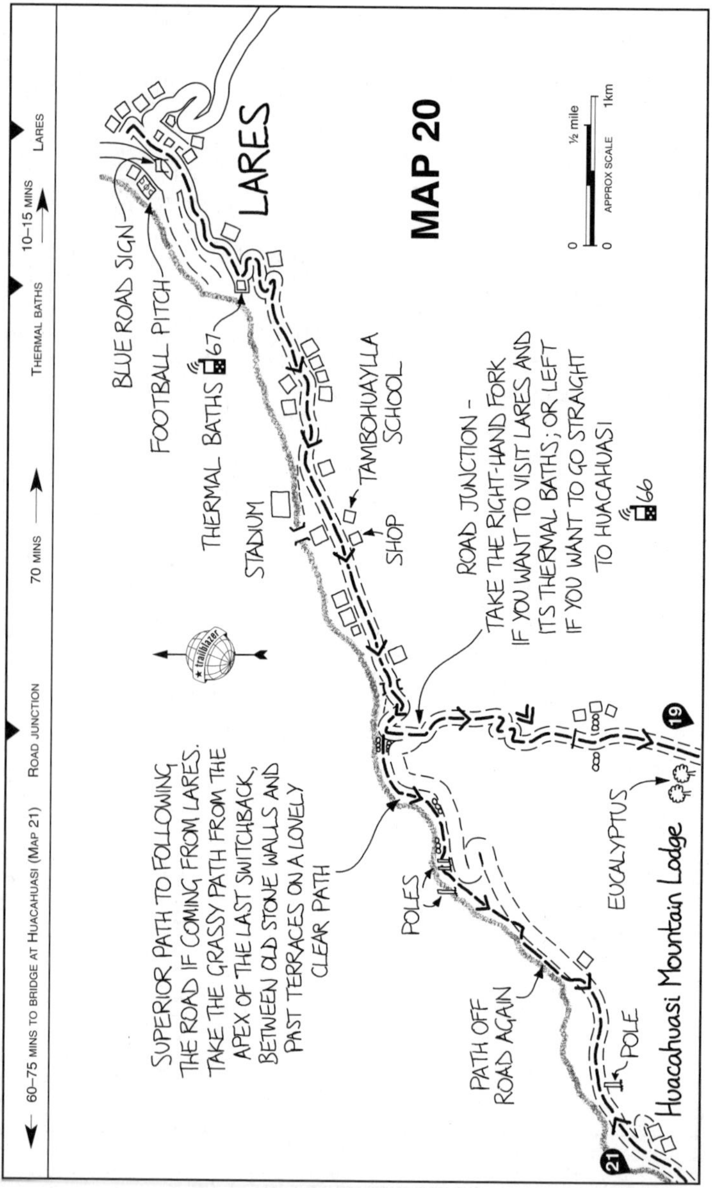

MAP 20

← 60–75 MINS TO BRIDGE AT HUACAHUASI (MAP 21)   ROAD JUNCTION   70 MINS →   THERMAL BATHS   10–15 MINS   LARES

LARES

BLUE ROAD SIGN

FOOTBALL PITCH

THERMAL BATHS 🏠67

STADIUM

TAMBOHUAYLLA SCHOOL

SHOP

ROAD JUNCTION –
TAKE THE RIGHT-HAND FORK
IF YOU WANT TO VISIT LARES AND
ITS THERMAL BATHS; OR LEFT
IF YOU WANT TO GO STRAIGHT
TO HUACAHUASI
🏠66

19

SUPERIOR PATH TO FOLLOWING
THE ROAD IF COMING FROM LARES.
TAKE THE GRASSY PATH FROM THE
APEX OF THE LAST SWITCHBACK,
BETWEEN OLD STONE WALLS AND
PAST TERRACES ON A LONELY
CLEAR PATH

POLES

EUCALYPTUS

PATH OFF
ROAD AGAIN

POLE

Huacahuasi Mountain Lodge 🏠

21

MAP 20

0   ½ mile
0   ½ km   1km
APPROX SCALE

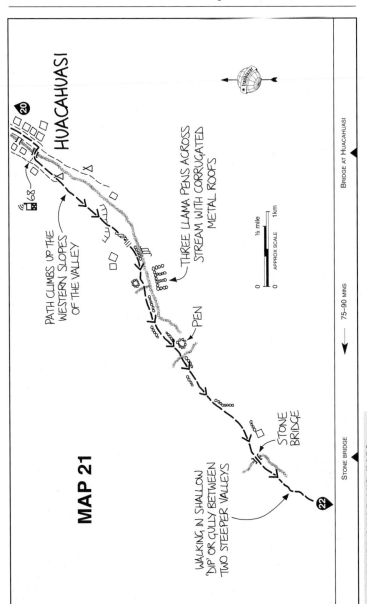

MAP 21

HUACAHUASI

PATH CLIMBS UP THE
WESTERN SLOPES
OF THE VALLEY

THREE LLAMA PENS ACROSS
STREAM WITH CORRUGATED
METAL ROOFS

PEN

STONE
BRIDGE

WALKING IN SHALLOW
'DIP' OR GULLY BETWEEN
TWO STEEPER VALLEYS

APPROX SCALE

0   ½ mile

0   1km

STONE BRIDGE   75–90 MINS   BRIDGE AT HUACAHUASI

(cont'd from p274) Nevertheless, you'll want to stay up here long enough to capture the beauty of the valley beyond with its idyllic turquoise lakes. The descent itself, steep at first, gradually flattens out, and the grassy terrain beckons you to sit awhile and enjoy the stillness. The occasional bird may chirp and the odd insect may buzz past but other than that the silence of this place is a rare thing indeed, and should be savoured.

Towards the valley floor the path becomes fainter and fainter until, near a few scattered buildings, it disappears altogether. It is at this point that you need to drift to the right (north), to pick up the trail again as it heads down a narrow gully, heading – more steeply now – to the village of **Cuncani** (3819m/12,529ft), where a 4WD track begins.

The rest of this stage is gentle, whether opting to visit the baths above Lares (see p276), or continuing on to the fairly sprawling village of **Huacahuasi** (3826m/12,552ft). You won't have to decide which option you prefer until the junction, about an hour north of Cuncani; with either option, the trail is along a road, easy to follow – and a bit of a relief after your exertions thus far.

HUACAHUASI TO YANAHUARA
[MAP 20, p276; MAP 21, p277; MAP 22; MAP 23, p280]

This may be the last day but the difficult nature of this trek does not relent. Once again on this final **21.6km (13½ miles; 6hrs to 7hrs 5 mins)** stage there's a 4600m-plus pass to tackle – followed by a lengthy descent, this time leading all the way down to the main road running through the Sacred Valley – and the end of the trail. If you're trekking with an agency the chances are you'll be collected at the trail's end and taken on to Ollantaytambo, from where you'll catch a train to Aguas Calientes and from there on to Machu Picchu. But for independent trekkers you'll just have to wait for a passing *colectivo* to run you westwards to Ollantaytambo, or east back to Cusco via Urubamba.

But first of all, you must get to the Sacred Valley, and that means crossing the final pass on this trek, **Abra Huacahuasijasa** (4623m/15,167ft). Lying just over 7km from Huacahuasi – and some 800m above it – the path to the pass starts off gently enough but the slope seems to increase exponentially, with switchbacks on the steeper parts both lessening the gradient while at the same time increasing the distance you are required to walk.

The reward for the effort to reach this pass is a condor's eye view of lovely **Laguna Aruraycocha**, to which you descend before continuing to the even more lovely **Laguna Millpo**, the banks of which provide an excellent venue for lunch. Thereafter the path – still a dreadful mixture of loose stones and rocks – continues down the eastern side of the valley above the Río Aruraycocha, joining up with a larger trail and crossing the river (to the western side) to reach the town of **Yanahuara**. A land of concrete and cars, the village plays host to several very smart hotels and spiritual retreats, all of which seem light years away from the life of those who live in the valleys above. It feels like the end of your Lares adventure, and it is, for at the foot of Yanahuara is the main road to Ollantaytambo and transport for your next destination.

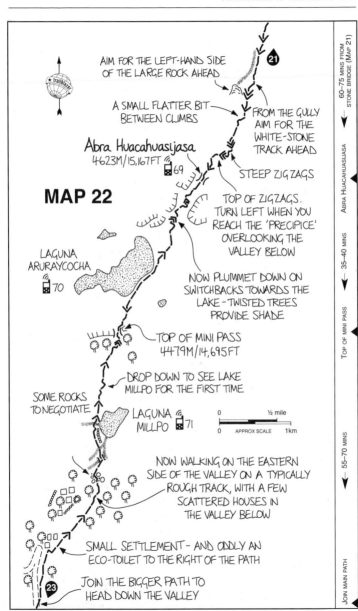

AIM FOR THE LEFT-HAND SIDE OF THE LARGE ROCK AHEAD

A SMALL FLATTER BIT BETWEEN CLIMBS

FROM THE GULLY AIM FOR THE WHITE-STONE TRACK AHEAD

Abra Huacahuasijasa
4623M/15,167FT
69

STEEP ZIG ZAGS

MAP 22

TOP OF ZIGZAGS. TURN LEFT WHEN YOU REACH THE 'PRECIPICE' OVERLOOKING THE VALLEY BELOW

LAGUNA ARURAYCOCHA
70

NOW PLUMMET DOWN ON SWITCHBACKS TOWARDS THE LAKE - TWISTED TREES PROVIDE SHADE

TOP OF MINI PASS
4479M/14,695FT

DROP DOWN TO SEE LAKE MILLPO FOR THE FIRST TIME

SOME ROCKS TO NEGOTIATE

LAGUNA MILLPO
71

0   ½ mile
0   APPROX SCALE   1km

NOW WALKING ON THE EASTERN SIDE OF THE VALLEY ON A TYPICALLY ROUGH TRACK, WITH A FEW SCATTERED HOUSES IN THE VALLEY BELOW

SMALL SETTLEMENT - AND ODDLY AN ECO-TOILET TO THE RIGHT OF THE PATH

JOIN THE BIGGER PATH TO HEAD DOWN THE VALLEY

60–75 MINS FROM STONE BRIDGE (MAP 21)

ABRA HUACAHUASIJASA

35–40 MINS

TOP OF MINI PASS

55–70 MINS

JOIN MAIN PATH

ROUTE GUIDE AND MAPS

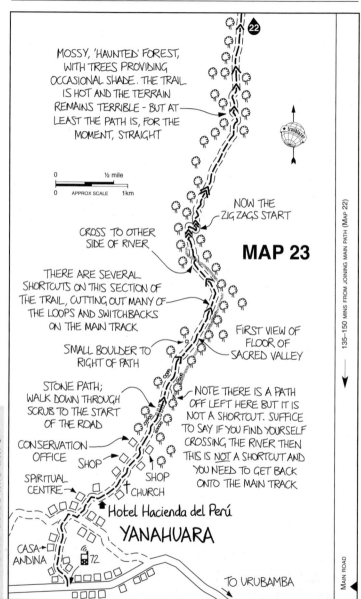

MOSSY, 'HAUNTED' FOREST, WITH TREES PROVIDING OCCASIONAL SHADE. THE TRAIL IS HOT AND THE TERRAIN REMAINS TERRIBLE – BUT AT LEAST THE PATH IS, FOR THE MOMENT, STRAIGHT

0 ½ mile
0 APPROX SCALE 1km

NOW THE ZIG ZAGS START

CROSS TO OTHER SIDE OF RIVER

MAP 23

THERE ARE SEVERAL SHORTCUTS ON THIS SECTION OF THE TRAIL, CUTTING OUT MANY OF THE LOOPS AND SWITCHBACKS ON THE MAIN TRACK

FIRST VIEW OF FLOOR OF SACRED VALLEY

SMALL BOULDER TO RIGHT OF PATH

STONE PATH; WALK DOWN THROUGH SCRUB TO THE START OF THE ROAD

NOTE THERE IS A PATH OFF LEFT HERE BUT IT IS NOT A SHORTCUT. SUFFICE TO SAY IF YOU FIND YOURSELF CROSSING THE RIVER THEN THIS IS NOT A SHORTCUT AND YOU NEED TO GET BACK ONTO THE MAIN TRACK

CONSERVATION OFFICE
SHOP
SHOP
SPIRITUAL CENTRE
† CHURCH

Hotel Hacienda del Perú
YANAHUARA

CASA ANDINA
72

TO URUBAMBA

ROUTE GUIDE AND MAPS

135–150 MINS FROM JOINING MAIN PATH (MAP 22)

MAIN ROAD

The Choquequirao Trek

"We would need the better part of two days to reach Choquequirao. John said that we were a little less than six miles as the crow flies from the ruins, but we had more than twenty miles to cover on foot. The map I consulted at breakfast made clear that this would be a very long and winding road; the trail zig-zagged like it had been based with an oscilloscope. And that was just the horizontal part – the easy part."

Mark Adams – *Turn Right at Machu Picchu*

Regarded by many as the original 'lost city' of the Incas, Choquequirao was the first fabled set of ruins to be uncovered. People had been aware of its existence from at least the 18th century but it was rarely visited and despite several acclaimed 'rediscoveries' over the years, it wasn't until Hiram Bingham arrived here in 1909 that it really came to people's attention. For Bingham it was the discovery of Choquequirao that fired his passion to uncover Machu Picchu and Espíritu Pampa.

Set in a remote part of wilderness, on a ridge spur around 1750m/5740ft above the Apurímac River against a backdrop of sheer, snow-capped peaks, it is an awe-inspiring destination that requires a degree of effort to reach. As archaeologists increasingly recognise the site's importance to the Incas, and awareness of the ruins grows, Choquequirao has gained in popularity as a trekking destination. A donation by the French government in 2003 (see p284) has also meant that further archaeological work at the site has been undertaken and further discoveries made that enhance the appeal of these ruins.

So is this **64.8km (40½-mile) trek** from Cachora to the ruins and back again a genuine alternative to the classic Inca Trail? Well, the ruins themselves are a pretty good substitute for Machu Picchu and the main features of both are

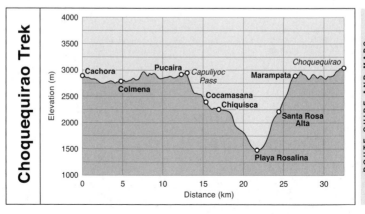

Choquequirao Trek

similar in many respects. Furthermore, even in the high season there's a good chance that there won't be more than half a dozen other trekkers visiting Choquequirao, all of whom have undergone the same privations as you to get there – which does add to a pleasant sense of camaraderie. Largely because of this absence of other visitors, we do find the place a whole lot more charming than Machu Picchu. The drama of the region's uncompromising wild landscape

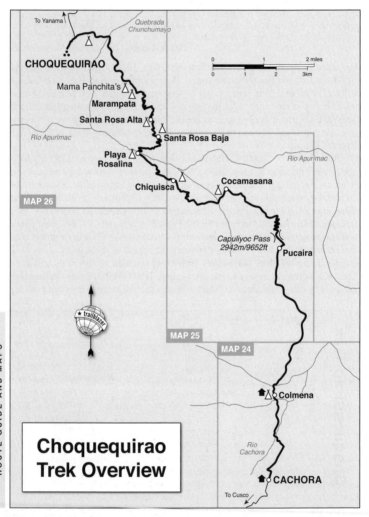

To Yanama

Quebrada
Chunchumayo

CHOQUEQUIRAO

Mama Panchita's

Marampata

Santa Rosa Alta

Rio Apurímac

Santa Rosa Baja

Playa
Rosalina

Chiquisca

Cocamasana

MAP 26

Rio Apurímac

Capuliyoc Pass
2942m/9652ft

Pucaira

★ trailblazer

MAP 25

MAP 24

Colmena

Rio
Cachora

**Choquequirao
Trek Overview**

CACHORA

To Cusco

is also thrilling and remains undiminished since Bingham's time; as such, his classic descriptions of the rigours and scenic attractions of the approach remain true to this day.

So what are the disadvantages? Well, the path itself has none of the ruins that you'll find along the classic Inca Trail. Furthermore, this trek is undoubtedly tougher than the route to Machu Picchu. Look at the altitude profile of this trek from Cachora to the ruins and back again and you'll wonder who the hell thought it was a good idea to build a trail that essentially spends the first day or so plummeting downhill – and the next one climbing up again! And in order to get back to civilisation, you have to do it all over again, only in reverse!

The answer to that question is, of course, Hiram Bingham himself, who blazed this trail back in the first decade of the 20th century; and while we can't argue that the walk is tough and, in places, a bit of a slog, it is also the easiest way to get to the ruins. For this reason, though the trek can easily be undertaken independently, you may want to consider hiring an arriero to help lighten your load.

BACKGROUND

Little is known about the origin of Choquequirao, not even its original Inca name. Its Quechua name translates as 'Cradle of Gold'. Only marginally more is known about those early explorers who uncovered the ruins, in search of the gold of its name, which they believed the Incas had buried there rather than allow it to fall into the hands of the grasping Spanish conquistadors.

The earliest report of the site is to be found in the writings of the prospector Juan Arias Díaz Topete who recorded the location of an uninhabited town, 'Chuquiquirao', during one of three expeditions to the region that he mounted in 1710. Over a century later, in 1834, the French explorer and treasure-seeker Eugène, Comte de Sartiges, approached the site. A village headman issued a warning to the Comte, declaring, 'Tell the white men that to get where we live, the roads are so bad that they will die on the journey, and that we have no chicken eggs to give them.' Undeterred, the Comte de Sartiges employed a team of porters to hack and burn their way across the mountains from Mollepata via an incredibly long and circuitous route. He endured great hardships on the expedition, lost a man and mules over a cliff and resorted to drinking rum all day to stave off the cold. He described the scenery as some of the finest in the Americas, but cursed the path and conditions, declaring 'I do not believe that man could ever live in this valley, however fertile it is, because of the voracious mosquitoes that have taken possession of it. It was impossible to breathe, drink or eat without absorbing large quantities of these insufferable creatures.'

Although he reached Choquequirao, the Comte de Sartiges' expedition produced neither detailed documentation of the site nor any gold. But this failed foray didn't deter the many treasure seekers that subsequently visited Choquequirao. However, none of them ever found any gold either.

The first-known drawings of the site were produced in 1847 by the French Consul in Peru, Léonce Angrand, although the originals of these maps languished in the vaults of the Bibliothèque Nationale in Paris until eventually being published in 1972. For a long time academics wrongly declared Choquequirao to be the site of Manco Inca's final capital, Vilcabamba.

Chief amongst those perpetuating this idea was the Peruvian naturalist and cartographer Antonio Raimondi, who spent the late 1860s scouring the upper Vilcabamba valley for the ruins of the capital. Upon finding nothing, Raimondi lent his prestige and academic weight to the theory that the site had already been found at Choquequirao, the only major Inca ruin known in the area at that time.

Hiram Bingham forged a path to the site in 1909 whilst travelling through Peru, an experience that inspired his search for Machu Picchu. Although largely uninterested in the accounts of the ruins hidden in the mountains – Bingham admitted that he 'had never heard of Choqquequirau' – he allowed himself to be persuaded by a local official, the prefect of Abancay, to mount an expedition to the site and there undertake some serious documentation of the ruins. Bingham pioneered a new and much more direct approach to the site from the south, which avoided the mountain ranges but did involve crossing the Apurímac river on an 80m-wide wire bridge: 'The bridge was less than 3 feet wide but 273 feet long. It swayed in the wind on its six strands of telegraph wire. To cross it seemed like tempting fate. So close to death did the narrow cat-walk of the bridge appear to be, and so high did the rapids throw the icy spray, that our Indian bearers crept across one at a time, on all fours and obviously wishing they had never been ordered by the prefect to carry our luggage... It must have seemed to them the height of folly for any one voluntarily to use this bridge' (*The Lost City of the Incas*).

His route reduced to a matter of days an approach that had previously taken weeks to accomplish and has been used as the way to Choquequirao ever since. To further simplify the trek, the authorities replaced the old cable bridge with a concrete and steel suspension bridge in 1994 and though a landslip destroyed this bridge in 2012, a new one was erected in 2015.

Despite developments, for much of the 20th century Choquequirao was overshadowed by Machu Picchu; it wasn't until the mid 1980s that the clearance and restoration of the ruins even began. Owing to its remoteness and lack of infrastructure, the site remained – and still remains! – off most people's radar. Ongoing exploration and excavation has resulted in the site being opened up though. In 2003 the French government donated €5 million (US$5.7 million) to Peru's government to fund the study of the ruins and the development of tourist facilities at the site. This coincided with a promotional push, designed to ease the pressure on the Inca Trail, ensuring that Peru's 'second Machu Picchu' came to greater prominence.

PRACTICALITIES

The trek to Choquequirao can be tackled for much of the year although it is **best during the dry season (May to September)**. Normally a hike just over 65 kilometres (40 miles) would make for a fairly decent 3-day stroll – 22km (13-14 miles) each day being a very reasonable target. But this ignores the fact that on this route not much of the path can be described as 'flat'. So while the fit, the fast and the just plain frantic can complete the trek in three days, it's far more sensible to take **five days**: two days from Cachora to Choquequirao and two days back again, plus there is more than enough of interest at Choquequirao to justify spending a day exploring the site. The route can also be incorporated into a longer, more arduous trek, one that links Choquequirao to Huancacalle and Vilcabamba. However, see box p34.

Although the trek to Choquequirao is harder than the classic Inca Trail – the steepness of the trek is enough to make your ears pop on occasion! – most aver-agely fit individuals with a degree of experience and a little preparation should be able to reach the ruins. Having said that, don't underestimate how exhaust-ing this trek can be, nor how hot it can get in the valley.

In terms of equipment, you'll need a **tent**. This trail tends not to be as cold as others in this book – the valley seems to keep the heat in and there are no mountain passes – so, tackling the trail in August, it is possible to get away with a **two-season sleeping bag**. Most campsites offer an evening meal though you'll still need **food** for breakfast and lunch, unless you plan to survive on the meagre snacks (chocolate bars etc) offered for sale at the campsites; there is nowhere else to buy any provisions after Pucaira (and there's not much there either). **Campsites** are shown on the maps.

You should make sure you have the **capacity to carry several litres of water** since the points at which you can refill bottles are far apart and you'll dehydrate very quickly once you begin to exert yourself. You should also carry sufficient **insect repellent**, since large sections of the track are plagued by sand-flies and mosquitoes.

The trek can be undertaken through an agency or done independently. If you undertake the trek independently you should **consider hiring an arriero** and mules to accompany you since climbing the sheer valley sides in the dry heat is tough enough without being laden down with equipment and food. An arriero can be hired in Cachora (see p287) or Colmena (see p288).

You won't need much in the way of **cash**: some money for transport to and from Cachora, plus camping fees on the trail (currently s/5 per night at most places), money for meals, snacks and drinks en route – and, if you decide to hire one, any fees and tips you've agreed with the arriero. (Even if you don't plan on hiring one, do bring money for this purpose just in case; the number of peo-ple who set out without an arriero but decide to get one once on the trail is unsurprisingly high!)

There's also a **fee** for visiting the ruins of s/57 per adult, which is collected at a little booth a few kilometres before the ruins themselves. If trekking with a guided group this entrance fee will probably be included in the price you pay your agency, and they should inform you of any extra payments you need to make on the trail.

As a final piece of preparation, **read** about the ruins in advance to get the most from your visit. Vincent Lee's excellent *Forgotten Vilcabamba* and Hugh Thomson's *The White Rock* are good places to start.

GETTING TO THE TRAILHEAD

To reach **Cachora**, catch an early morning bus (s/20) from Terminal Terrestre in Cusco (see p183) to Abancay and ask to be dropped off at the Cachora turn-off ('*cruce Cachora*'); Bredde are the most popular company and have several buses starting at 6am. Buses leave throughout the morning until around midday. Alternatively, and slightly cheaper, are the *colectivos* from Calle Arcopata in Cusco (s/15-20).

The drive takes 3½-4 hours and follows the Apurímac river through a spectacular, sheer-sided gorge. Two hours from Cusco the road crosses the Cunyac bridge over the Apurímac, the border between the departments of Cusco and Apurímac. The road climbs up and away from the river, passing Sayhuite (see box below) to arrive at the signposted junction for Cachora. There is a large sign for Choquequirao at the junction. Occasionally colectivos wait to ferry people (30-45 mins) along the winding dirt track to Cachora (s/5). Alternatively, it's a 75- to 90-minute walk downhill for 5.7km (3½ miles) through eucalyptus groves dotted with cacti, following a reasonably clear path that cuts across the bends in the road. From the junction, start by taking the road to Cachora. Behind the electricity substation, before the path bends left (and having just bent right), a clear track heads left off the road, descending gently and aiming for the cluster of houses you can see below. There are several places where the path forks or is slightly tricky to find, but there are usually people around to ask. All being

---

❏ Sayhuite (Saywite)

Opposite the junction for Cachora, some 45km (28 miles) east of Abancay and set back from the road, lies the community of Concachaca. In the midst of this hamlet, open to the elements, is the enigmatic Sayhuite (sometimes written as Saywite) monolith, one of several huacas scattered around this area. This sizeable, elaborately carved boulder is approximately 4m (13ft) in diameter and stands over 2m (6½ft) high. The delicate reliefs etched into the top surface represent aspects of Andean culture and appear to show a complex map of some kind: some rumours allege that it represents the construction plans for Tahuantinsuyo, the Inca Empire, and the author Hugh Thomson describes it in his book *Cochineal Red* as, 'a meteorite shot from the past containing the Inca world in capsule form'.

Elaborately carved buildings, terraces and geometrical patterns can be made out amidst the intricate sculpture, which has unfortunately been damaged by exposure to the elements and by souvenir hunters and vandals. There are also numerous figures including humans armed with arrows and a variety of llamas, vicuñas, pumas, snakes, monkeys and lizards. Channels on the stone hint at the rituals and ceremonies that may have been connected with it. The rim has notches around it, thought to once have held an elaborate textile or gold cladding. Stones such as Q'enko in the Sacred Valley have a similar sculpted surface. However, none is as elaborate as Sayhuite or as isolated within the landscape; nor does any have as intimate a relationship with their surroundings. It costs s/11 to visit this boulder. Close by are wells, canals and several large boulders that have been split in half, suggesting that Sayhuite stood at the heart of a larger religious complex. One such monolith, at the bottom of the hill, has steps that seemingly lead nowhere carefully cut into it.

well, after a little over an hour you'll hit the town cemetery in Cachora's south-eastern corner, from where it's a five-minute stroll west and north to the plaza, where the trek begins.

CACHORA [MAP 24]

Cachora sits in an idyllic spot cupped on three sides by steep sloping ridges at the head of the Cachora valley. It is a picturesque Andean town that enjoys fertile soils, a reliable water supply, reasonably temperate weather and stunning views north of the snow-capped peaks of the Vilcabamba range on the far side of the Apurímac river, including the imposing Padrayoc (5482m/17,985ft).

On the southern edge of the plaza is the **Comisaria PNP building**, where you should consider registering if trekking alone or without the backup of an agency (although it is not obligatory to do so). You can **hire arrieros** from around the central plaza and buy a small quantity of basic provisions from the handful of **small stores** on the way to the main street; the last one before the square itself is best.

Unfortunately, most people simply pass through the town, arriving early with their tour or trekking operator and hitting the trail immediately.

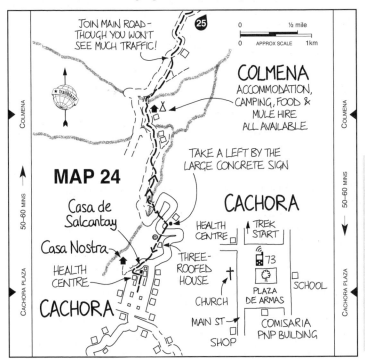

ROUTE GUIDE AND MAPS

Consequently Cachora hasn't benefitted from the influx of visitors and the infrastructure here remains very basic.

There are a few **hospedajes** (whose names frequently change), where families offer cheap double rooms, usually with a basic breakfast. The simplest just have mattresses on the floor, whilst the better ones also have hot water and may offer evening meals.

Also well worth considering is the small, friendly, family-run *Casa de Salcantay* (☎ 984 281171, 🖳 www.salcantay.com), situated just outside the main village. The house has hot water and wifi; evening meals are available too. The owner, a Dutchman with a wide knowledge of the area and experience of mountaineering in Peru, also organises horse rides, guided treks to Choquequirao and hires out mules and drivers to independent trekkers. Rates as advertised on the website are US$30 per person, though when we called in this had dropped to s/60 per person, including breakfast. Further down the lane, to the left across a river, is perhaps an even better choice: *Casa Nostra* (☎ 958 349 949; 🖳 www.choquequiraohotel.com) is run by an Italian and his Peruvian wife and is an absolute treat, a spotless hotel with excellent views, wifi and kind and generous hosts. Rates are s/80 for a double, s/110 for a triple room.

Around the town are a number of small, anonymous-looking hole-in-the-wall *cafés* that serve simple meals at very reasonable rates – look for one that's popular with the locals and stick your head round the door to see what's cooking. You can also pick up a small amount of fruit and vegetables from simple **shops** on the streets off the main plaza but don't expect to stock up for the full multi-day trek from here.

CACHORA TO CHIQUISCA [MAP 24, p287; MAP 25]

If you're going to lose your way anywhere on this trail, it's likely to be in the first 10 minutes of this **16.9km (10½ miles; 3hrs 50 mins to 4hrs 25 mins)** first day. In the north-western corner of the plaza a small road heads down the valley, directly towards the snow-capped peak of Padrayoc on the far side of the Apurímac valley. After passing the turn-off to Casa Nostra, branch left opposite virtually the last house in the village to follow a neat track as it descends for 5-10 minutes towards a multi-roofed house and an **'INC' waypost**. Turn left here and opposite a pond drop down, crossing road and channel, to a large red concrete Parque Arqueológico Choquequirao sign where you need to turn left. Follow the signs to the bridge, then climb gently through stands of eucalyptus to get up onto the left-hand side (west) of the valley.

Follow the wayposts and before long you'll arrive at **Colmena**, where several families live in ranch-style farmhouses. You can hire arrieros and horses from the last house here as well as **camp** (s/5), or sleep in the main house (s/50 for a double; s/20 per person for dinner). From Colmena, you can cross the Cachora river and climb up the western side of the valley to hit the main road heading north to **Pucaira**, 9.6km (just under 6 miles) from Cachora, where there's a small restaurant and a shack-cum-shop (Map 25).

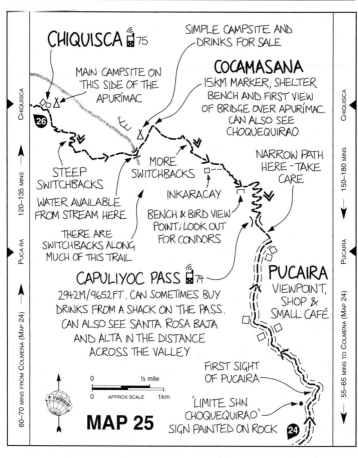

CHIQUISCA 🔋75

SIMPLE CAMPSITE AND DRINKS FOR SALE

COCAMASANA
15KM MARKER, SHELTER BENCH AND FIRST VIEW OF BRIDGE OVER APURÍMAC. CAN ALSO SEE CHOQUEQUIRAO

MAIN CAMPSITE ON THIS SIDE OF THE APURÍMAC

CHIQUISCA

26

CHIQUISCA

150–180 MINS

MORE SWITCHBACKS

NARROW PATH HERE – TAKE CARE

STEEP SWITCHBACKS

120–135 MINS

INKARACAY

WATER AVAILABLE FROM STREAM HERE

BENCH & BIRD VIEW POINT; LOOK OUT FOR CONDORS

PUCA RA

THERE ARE SWITCHBACKS ALONG MUCH OF THIS TRAIL

PUCAIRA

CAPULIYOC PASS 🔋74

2942M/9652FT. CAN SOMETIMES BUY DRINKS FROM A SHACK ON THE PASS. CAN ALSO SEE SANTA ROSA BAJA AND ALTA IN THE DISTANCE ACROSS THE VALLEY

PUCAIRA
VIEWPOINT, SHOP & SMALL CAFÉ

60–70 MINS FROM COLMENA (MAP 24)

55–65 MINS TO COLMENA (MAP 24)

0   ½ mile
0   APPROX SCALE   1km

★ trailblazer

MAP 25

FIRST SIGHT OF PUCAIRA

'LIMITE SHN CHOQUEQUIRAO' SIGN PAINTED ON ROCK

24

The track curves around a rocky promontory, which gives outstanding views of the surrounding valleys and ridges. An even better view – this time of the walk ahead – can be had just a few minutes away at the **Capuliyoc Pass** (2942m/9652ft), a narrow wind-beaten arête, whipped by clouds which frequently shroud the vertiginous cliffs and jagged peaks nearby. However, on clear days and with binoculars you can just make out the hazy outline of Choquequirao, perched high atop a forested ridge away to the north-west. Sometimes you can buy soft drinks and water at a shack up here.

The pass also marks the start of the lengthy, relentless drop down the Apurímac valley, one of the deepest ravines in the Americas. About 3.6km (2¼ miles) after the pass the path edges around a rocky prow and across a concrete ledge with handrail to a spectacular viewpoint at **Cocamasana**. From here you can make out the campsite at Chiquisca and, beyond that, the crossing point for the Apurímac river. Rather depressingly, you can also pick out the steep zigzags up the apparently sheer valley opposite – part of the route ahead. The roofs of Santa Rosa Baja and Alta can be seen glinting in the sun across the other side of the valley too. Just beyond the viewpoint, on a narrow terrace below a hill-side of blue agave cacti, is the Cocamasana *campsite*, which has a flimsy thatched shelter and room for a handful of tents that are treated to spectacular views straight down the valley. You'll also find a small bridge and stream here – the only place to get water (other than buying it from the campsites) between Capuliyoc and the Apurímac.

As the path descends for a further 5.2km (3¼ miles) down to the bridge you'll notice a change in vegetation, as trees festooned with bromeliads replace scrub and cacti; you'll also feel a rise in temperature. There are several landslip scars on the slopes here; rockfalls are frequent though rarely of sufficient magnitude to affect the route.

Before you get to the bridge, however, some steep and interminable switch-backs bring you to the largest campsite on this side of the river, **Chiquisca**, where a local family will let you *camp* beneath chirimoya, lemon and papaya trees in a clearing adjacent to their house or on a series of terraces behind the house. There's running water, toilets and even a cold shower; the family sells soft drinks and bottled water and can rustle up a cooked meal for a small charge.

CHIQUISCA TO CHOQUEQUIRAO   [MAP 25, p289; MAP 26]

An early start will give you the most of the shade and morning cool on this **15.5km (9¾ miles; 5hrs 5 mins to 6hrs 55 mins)** second day; the valley bottom becomes unbearably hot later and the ascent on the far side of the valley can be exhausting in direct sun.

❏ **The Apurímac**
'The sound of the Apurímac rises faintly from the gorge, like a murmur from outer space...
'Apurímac River! Apurímac River!' the Runa children repeat with tenderness and a touch of fear.'   **José María Arguedas**, *Los Ríos Profundos*

The Apurímac river rises near Arequipa and eventually flows into the Amazon as a raging torrent 75m (250ft) wide and 25m (80ft) deep. The rapids and churning water along its length led to its Quechua name, Apu-rimac, which literally translates as 'The God Who Speaks', or 'Great Speaker'.

During Inca times a famous rope bridge spanned the canyon where an Inca road crossed from one bank to the other. When threatened, the Incas simply cut the bridge, knowing the river was usually too violent to risk crossing any other way. Unfortunately, when the conquistadors marched on Cusco and the Incas cut the bridge, the invading Spanish were able to ford the river as the usually torrential Apurímac was particularly low.

Beyond Chiquisca the path descends steeply for around 45 minutes, often once again in a series of hairpin bends for 2km (1¼ miles) to the riverside and **Playa Rosalina** (Map 26), which used to have a lodge with dorm rooms and a restaurant standing amidst boulders and stubby trees. However, though the buildings still stand the place has been largely abandoned, the sand-flies having chased the inhabitants and campers away; indeed, the only permanent resident these days seems to be the poor official charged with registering the trekkers

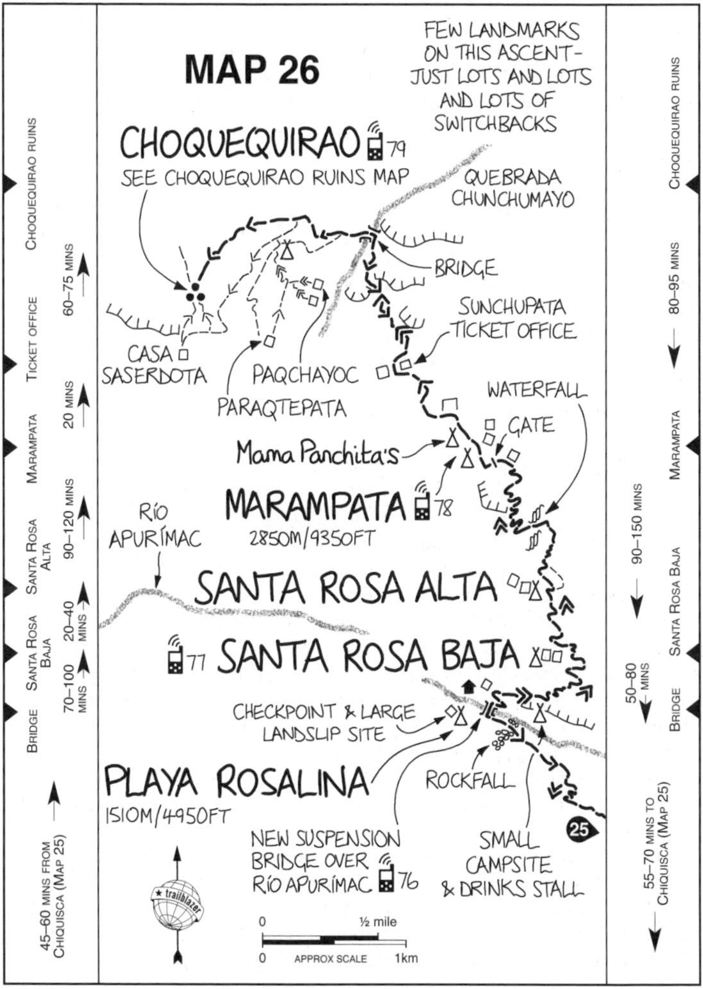
MAP 26
FEW LANDMARKS ON THIS ASCENT- JUST LOTS AND LOTS AND LOTS OF SWITCHBACKS
CHOQUEQUIRAO 79
SEE CHOQUEQUIRAO RUINS MAP
QUEBRADA CHUNCHUMAYO
BRIDGE
SUNCHUPATA TICKET OFFICE
CASA SASERDOTA
PAQCHAYOC
PARAQTEPATA
WATERFALL
GATE
Mama Panchita's
MARAMPATA 78
2850M/9350FT
RÍO APURÍMAC
SANTA ROSA ALTA
77 SANTA ROSA BAJA
CHECKPOINT & LARGE LANDSLIP SITE
PLAYA ROSALINA
1510M/4950FT
ROCKFALL
NEW SUSPENSION BRIDGE OVER RÍO APURÍMAC 76
SMALL CAMPSITE & DRINKS STALL
25
0 ½ mile
0 APPROX SCALE 1km
CHOQUEQUIRAO RUINS
60–75 MINS
TICKET OFFICE
20 MINS
MARAMPATA
90–120 MINS
SANTA ROSA ALTA
20–40 MINS
SANTA ROSA BAJA
70–100 MINS
BRIDGE
45–60 MINS FROM CHIQUISCA (MAP 25)
CHOQUEQUIRAO RUINS
80–95 MINS
MARAMPATA
90–150 MINS
SANTA ROSA BAJA
50–80 MINS
BRIDGE
55–70 MINS TO CHIQUISCA (MAP 25)

who pass across the new bridge. You may be able to buy a soft drink and snacks here too. The **Apurímac** is very strong, but you can get water and wash in the sheltered spots.

The crossing is the lowest point on the trek; once on the far, northern side you must begin the long climb to Choquequirao. The ascent begins gently before succumbing to a series of sweeping **switchbacks**. These become progressively shorter and tighter as they weave beneath a cliff and climb swiftly.

A little less than two hours beyond the bridge the path climbs to **Santa Rosa Baja**, a cleared area and settlement that overlooks the valley where they grow sugar cane, cultivated for the production of *cañazo*, the lethal spirit beloved by the local people. It is possible to *camp* here and there's a water source hosed in through the campsite's centre. Trekkers also rave about the food served here.

Separated by a stiff climb of about 20-40 minutes through yet more switchbacks is a second *campsite*, **Santa Rosa Alta**, next to a narrow stream, which boasts sumptuous views of the valley and the previous day's walk. At the farm here, you may be able to hire mules if you haven't already done so, but they are more expensive than at the trailhead and you'll probably be too exhausted to haggle. The long, strenuous climb continues, crosses a stream and zigzags up a forested ridge that rises ahead of you. This lengthy ascent can seem endless in the absence of landmarks or features by which to gauge your progress. After 1½-2 hours of toil from Santa Rosa Alta the path passes through a rustic gate and rounds a wooded prow to emerge at **Marampata** (2850m/9350ft), a village on a steep hillside. There are two **campsites** at the start of the village, including the well organised *Mama Panchita's*, where you can camp on the terraces for the usual s/5 and enjoy the exceptional, panoramic views. Once again dinner is available and the shop here is pretty well stocked given the remoteness of the location.

By now the valley is too steep to see the Apurímac at its foot; a series of hanging valleys block out each succeeding drop, hiding the true extent of the chasm. You can, however, see the outline of Choquequirao on an adjacent ridge top.

From Marampata the steepness of the path finally relents, the trail undulating westwards before turning into a subsidiary valley. Here you'll find the **Choquequirao checkpoint**, where you need to buy your ticket (s/57) – although it's still around 3.5km (over two miles) to the ruins' main plaza. The ruins themselves are clearly visible from this point across the gorge. The Upper and Lower Plaza straddle a ridge about 500m above a number of recently uncovered terraces that merge into thick forest; they seem to be clinging to a sheer slope that disappears into a bottomless ravine.

Skirt around the side-valley and at its head pick your way across the Chunchumayo River, which tumbles down in a series of giant shelves, on the boulders acting as giant stepping stones. After heavy rainfall this section can be very precarious and the river can rise significantly making the crossing complicated. Beyond the waterfall the path climbs briefly before dividing. The right-hand fork continues to climb through cloud forest to the ruins, whilst the left-hand branch descends gently for 800m to a pair of long, narrow terraces on which you can *camp*. There are toilets and cold showers here though, unlike

Marampata, you won't find anyone selling drinks or offering meals here. Use of the facilities is free.

From the junction the path climbs evenly through the thick forest for 20 minutes before emerging from the trees onto the north-eastern end of the long curved terraces beneath the Lower Plaza. A 2m-wide stone road runs along the base of these terraces to a rough path leading up to the Lower Plaza. There's a second path winding up from the campsite to the main plaza via the Pikiwasi ruins (see p296).

CHOQUEQUIRAO   [map p295]

Although only about a third of the site at Choquequirao has been cleared, there is still plenty to see. The site is potentially larger than Machu Picchu, but has fewer buildings. Despite the degree to which the area is still overgrown, or perhaps even because of it, the site is utterly spectacular and reinforces the belief that the Incas chose locations in part for their aesthetic value.

The terraces you could see on the way from Marampata are the lowest feature at the site. **Paqchayoc** lies about 350m below the Pikiwasi (Ridge Group) ruins, on a steep slope of between 35° and 45°. Ongoing restoration work here has revealed sweeping terraces over 450m wide and 250m high.

The tumbledown walls have been cleared and repaired and the single building at the heart of them restored. **Casa de la Caída de Agua** (House of the Waterfall) has several small rooms marked with niches and double-jamb door-

---

❏ So whose was it?

Unfortunately this enigmatic site is yet to give up all its secrets and until the material gathered by the current archaeologists is analysed fully there is no conclusive evidence suggesting who may have built Choquequirao or why. To further complicate things there appears to be no reference to the site in any of the Spanish chronicles.

The sweeping, stacked terraces are reminiscent of those at Huinay Huayna on the Inca Trail, whilst the site most closely resembles Inca country estates and ceremonial centres such as Pisac and, more pertinently, Machu Picchu. There are plenty of comparisons to be made between these two sites. Vincent Lee points to the ridge-top location and the way that the Apurímac relates to Choquequirao in the same way as the Urubamba does to Machu Picchu. He observes that although the setting of Choquequirao is probably more spectacular, being three times as far above the Apurímac as Machu Picchu is above the Urubamba, the latter remains the finer site by virtue of its superior architecture. Nonetheless, Choquequirao does exhibit high-status architecture designed for royal occupation, as evidenced by the large number of double-jamb doorways. Both places also exhibit the attributes of royal estates with watercourses and fountains, sacred outcrops and kallankas. In summary, Vincent Lee observed that, 'both sites evoke much the same feeling of reverence for and celebration of wild Nature and the splendours of the high mountain world.'

If, as is widely thought, Pachacutec built Machu Picchu, it's fair to surmise that Choquequirao was either also built during his reign or by someone powerful who admired his work. Based on the architectural style and the prevalence of double-jamb doorways, Lee himself concluded in his report into recent work at the site that Topa Inca, who succeeded Pachacutec, was 'the probable suspect' responsible for the site.

ways, leading archaeologists to suggest that it was connected in some way to religious ceremonies or the worship of water. There are superb views from here of the Chunchumayo River cascading down the head of the valley, and a broad, **smoothed ceremonial rock** just below the building. The terraces are well irrigated and it is likely that the Incas grew crops on them to support the main site.

Above the terraces and beyond a stretch of forest are the subtly **curved terraces** beneath the Lower Plaza where you first entered the site. A similarly gently curved **stone road**, known as the **Avenue of the Cedars**, runs the length of the 350m long terraces. The slight degree of curvature accommodates the contour of the slope and draws the eye left towards the Truncated Hilltop (Usnu), the focal point of the site, set to the south of the Lower Plaza.

Four sets of steps link the three broad, high terraces although there is no apparent stairway connecting either the stone road or the terraces to the **Lower Plaza**, where the majority of the high-status ceremonial and residential buildings are located. A great hall looking out over the Apurímac valley, a lesser hall and three double-sided two-storey buildings stand at the northern end of the plaza. High status is conveyed by the extensive use of double-jamb doorways on these principal buildings. The stonework is inferior to some of that found at Machu Picchu, something explorer Gary Ziegler attributes to the frangible metamorphic rock found at Choquequirao, which is an inferior building material to the granite and andesite of Machu Picchu.

An intricate **water channel** runs along the western edge of the ridge to a 'fountain', probably the site's water supply, on the Upper Plaza. From the Lower Plaza a rough path also climbs alongside the channel 50m north-west to the **Upper Plaza**. Rustic structures at the southern end of the plaza face an array of terraces and niched retaining walls. Their lesser stonework and the absence of any double-jamb doorways implies that they are less significant than those found around the Lower Plaza. On the western edge of the Upper Plaza stands an impressive retaining wall above a terrifying cliff-drop that plummets over 1600m/5250ft to the Apurímac river. At the south-western end of this group is the structure called the **Giant Stairway**. This peculiar set of eight small terraces is built around a large outcrop of bedrock and a number of big boulders. Like many of the features at Choquequirao its purpose remains unknown.

A path on the western edge of the Lower Plaza descends through the forested slope below the site to some of the most unusual discoveries at Choquequirao. A frighteningly steep Inca staircase drops off the plaza and plummets down the hillside to a set of terraces. Uniquely, these tall terraces are decorated with patterns. The first you encounter have white zigzags set amidst the dark stones, whilst a little lower down are the **llama terraces**. Images of 24 llamas, both adult and young, have been uncovered here, either singly or in pairs. They're mysterious, they're enigmatic – and they were discovered only in 2005.

Unusually, the terraces were built using vertical rather than horizontal stones, so that craftsmen were more easily able to insert shapes and patterns into them. The white rocks used for the patterns clearly stand out and the result, which is clearly visible from a distance, is a striking visual celebration of one

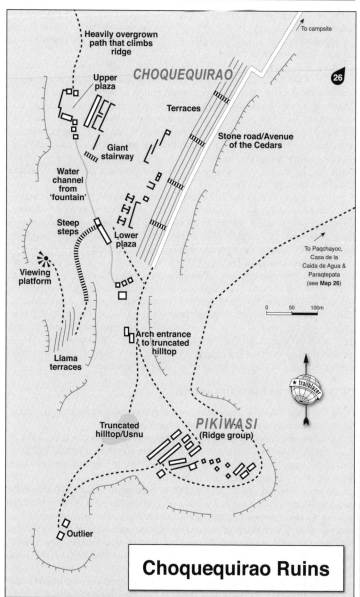

To campsite

CHOQUEQUIRAO

Heavily overgrown
path that climbs
ridge

Upper
plaza

Terraces

Stone road/Avenue
of the Cedars

Giant
stairway

Water
channel
from
'fountain'

Steep
steps

Lower
plaza

To Paqchayoc,
Casa de la
Caida de Agua &
Paraqtepata
(see **Map 26**)

0   50   100m

Viewing
platform

Arch entrance
to truncated
hilltop

Llama
terraces

★ trailblazer

Truncated
hilltop/Usnu

PIKIWASI
(Ridge group)

Outlier

Choquequirao Ruins

ROUTE GUIDE AND MAPS

of the Inca's most prized animals. Quite what the true purpose of this decoration was, no-one is entirely sure. A rough track leads from the far side of one of the upper terraces to a makeshift viewing platform that gives the best views of the uncovered stretch of hillside.

Back at the southern end of the Lower Plaza is a collection of what appears to be small shrines featuring double-jamb niches. Next to these is a sizeable double-jamb doorway through which a path climbs to the top of what Bingham described as the **Truncated Hilltop**. This ceremonial square, or *usnu*, was undoubtedly the focus of the site, as demonstrated by its elaborate entrance and the ring of stones around it. The platform, which would have required an enormous amount of effort to create, has stunning panoramic views of the surrounding ridges and peaks. Its use is unknown although people have speculated that it may have been a celestial observation platform or a place from which to communicate with other sites.

To the south-west of the Truncated Hilltop is a narrow ridge, above vertiginous drops on either side; a faint track leads along this ridge to the **Outlier**, where two well-crafted oblong buildings stand opposite each other across a small courtyard. The purpose of these buildings is also unknown, although the higher-quality stonework suggests that they were important.

Below the Truncated Hilltop, 50-100m to the south-east, is a large collection of buildings and terraces called **Pikiwasi (Ridge Group)**, signposted as *Sector IX administrativo*. This area was only explored and mapped in 1996 by Vincent Lee. Below here, and currently accessible only from **Paqchayoc**, is **Paraqtepata**, a further set of steep terraces poised above a sheer cliff. These terraces are the steepest on the site and have poor irrigation, suggesting that their main purpose may have been to reduce erosion. The surrounding slopes are still heavily forested but outlines of dilapidated structures and further terraces are clearly visible, hinting at what might lie beneath.

OPTIONS FROM CHOQUEQUIRAO

From Choquequirao you essentially have **three options** as well as one that at the time of writing was closed but may reopen one day.

The first and most common is to **retrace your steps to Cachora**. Back at the main road you can catch a bus or flag down a colectivo or taxi to Cusco, four hours away. These days most people travel first to Curahuasi, from where there are plenty of minibuses to Cusco.

Alternatively, you can extend your trek by **heading to Yanama, Huancacalle and Vilcabamba** following the trail described in the box on p32. It's a beautiful trek but it's also strenuous, isolated and should only be undertaken by more experienced trekkers after thorough preparation. You can also **walk to Machu Picchu** via Yanama, another tough walk. However, at the time of writing a road was being built near Yanama, which could well ruin the beauty and remoteness of this path. Do check on the latest situation before setting off.

There was once a fourth option, to **return to Cusco via San Ignacio and Abancay**. However, the **path was rendered impassable** and the San Ignacio bridge severely damaged by landslips in 2012, meaning that the route remains closed. The bridge is unlikely to be rebuilt anytime soon, given the remoteness of the crossing, and though the path is still there (it begins at the campsite at Choquequirao), and you can walk down the first 20 minutes or so, thereafter it remains closed.

The Ausangate Trek

Around 115km to the south-east of Cusco in the Andes' Vilcanota Range stands one enormous mountain. At 6372m, Ausangate is the highest peak in the department of Cusco. Despite its relative remoteness from their capital of Cusco, and the fact it lies in the opposite direction to the Sacred Valley, the mountain did have spiritual significance for the Incas – and it remains important for their descendants today. In particular, the Festival of Qoyllur Rit'i (Quechua for 'Star Snow', or Ice Festival) is celebrated on the slopes of Ausangate's near neighbour Qullqipunku (see p300). If you're in Peru at the time, we strongly recommend that you endeavour to make it to the festival – it's a colourful clash of celebrations and religions, with the non-Christian and Christian populations each uniting together to party through the night, even though their reasons for celebrating are poles apart.

But even if your visit doesn't coincide with the festival, we strongly urge you to pay a visit to the region – and to attempt this trail; **because we cannot emphasise enough just how delightful this trek is**. I used to say, when asked, that Nepal was my favourite country. This trek has gone a long way to tipping the balance towards Peru. It's that good.

This trek has been in guidebooks since the 1980s, which is quite heartening – to find a trek that's at least thirty years old but yet which is still so unspoilt.

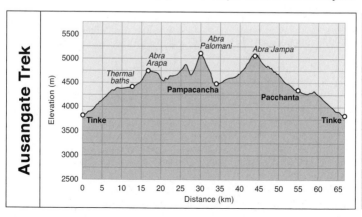

Indeed, the paths that you take on this **4- or 5-day, 66.7km trek (41½ miles)** are actually much older, having been used by the local llama and alpaca herders for many, many centuries before the Gore-Tex-clad tourists turned up. Yet, its venerable-age notwithstanding, you won't find any hotels or restaurants on the trail (until the last night at Pacchanta, at least); refreshingly, for the time being, at least, the locals have refrained from capitalising on the wondrous trek they have on their hands, and apart from a couple of places where you have to pay some sort of 'community fee', there isn't much evidence that this trek is being exploited.

Indeed, it'll come as quite a surprise to find the locals still dress in their rather spectacular traditional attire, with the women wearing large, fringed hats decorated with sequins, and multi-layered skirts. If you spent a few days in

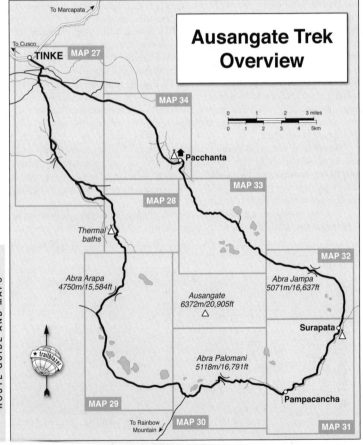

Cusco beforehand, you'll find it quite refreshing that they do so, not in the hope that a passing tourist will photograph them and they'll be rewarded financially as a result... but, well, because that's what they've always worn, and feel comfortable doing so. The litter on the trail, too, seems to be at a minimum, save for a little around the campsites; no amount of litter is acceptable, of course, but it's quite negligible here when compared to other well-known paths.

The unspoilt nature of the trail is in part because it isn't that easy, with **four passes over 4500m, including two over 5000m**. Such figures both limit the number of people who feel fit enough to undertake such a trek, and also tend to limit these to more experienced trekkers, who often look after the land through which they tread a little better. Furthermore, the season in which you can walk this trail comfortably is confined to the dry winter months of May to October. There are several boggy stretches that, while easy to cross when there's little water around, would be unpleasant – if not downright impossible – to cross when there's rain about. If I have one complaint it's that the trek described here, at just four or five days, is simply not long enough. Given the gorgeousness of the scenery it wouldn't be too far-fetched to say that it would be just as enjoyable at twice the length. But then it is easy to add days to this trek if you wish, and a walk of a week or more should be easy to build up given the many paths and passes around here.

And besides, if the main complaint about a trek is that we want more of it.... well that's not a bad fault to have, is it?

PRACTICALITIES

Given the extreme altitudes you'll be tackling it pays to be thoroughly acclimatised; we can't vouch for the medical expertise of the local alpaca population – who will in all likelihood be the only witnesses to your distress on the trail – but it pays to do all that you can to avoid getting into trouble in the first place. Packing Diamox, the locally available *soroche* pills or some other anti-altitude sickness preparation is only sensible.

Finding the route can be tricky in places so a map and compass, together with some knowledge of how to use them, is very useful. However, it is far from ideal, and inaccurate in some places. The most difficult bit of route-finding is actually on the first day; thereafter, though finding the way is more simple, the consequences of getting lost could be far more serious. The maps in this guide should be enough to help with any route finding, with the IGN map (J631/28t) as backup. Phone map apps such as MAPS.ME are also useful – see p214 for details.

As for packing, bring food, cooking utensils, torch, warm (very warm!) clothes, tent and camping equipment; in other words, all the usual stuff you'd take with you on any multi-day trek into the wilderness. Agencies in Cusco will sort all this out for you for around US$190 for a 4- or 5-day trek; or you can rent a man and horse in Tinke, at the start of the trek (see pp300-1). Remember, if you plan on hiring a horse, to bring a small daypack for yourself in addition to the larger bag that you'll be giving to him.

Or, of course, you can pack your rucksack high, pull the shoulders back, set your gaze towards the glacier, and set off by yourself – safe in the knowledge

ROUTE GUIDE AND MAPS

that the beauty you'll see, the glory of the landscape and the companionship of your fellow trekkers, will more than compensate for the aching muscles you'll inevitably suffer.

GETTING TO THE TRAILHEAD

Buses for the trailhead at Tinke (s/10) leave throughout the morning from Cusco's Tomasa Titto Condemayta, by the Coliseo Cerrado, and take just over three hours. If the skies are clear you should be able to see Ausangate 60-90 minutes before you reach Tinke, the peak first appearing as you climb to the top of Abra Uyuni, which, at 4185m, feels rather high at the time, though it's nothing compared to the altitudes you'll be reaching in a couple of days' time. The mountain pretty much dominates the landscape from then on, its main glacier tumbling down from the massif's centre – as if Ausangate had decided to dress up for your arrival by donning a rather natty white cravat. Tinke lies just 20 minutes beyond the large market town of Ocongate; alight when you see the slightly grotesque statue of a condor in front of Tinke's market square.

TINKE

For supplies, just up and across the road from the market is a very well-stocked **grocery store**, and next to it a small **pharmacy**. The most tourist friendly hotel

❏ Qoyllur Rit'i (The Festival of the Snow Star)

The **Andean bear**, known as *ukuku* in Quechua, is important in Andean folklore and plays a vital role in the Festival of the Snow Star, or Qoyllur Rit'i, held on the slopes of **Qullqipunku**, in the Sinakara Valley. Once a year, typically in early June on the full moon before Corpus Christi, thousands of pilgrims gather high in the mountains. Each group is accompanied by an *ukuku*, a dancer in a wool mask and shaggy tunic who represents the bear. The *ukuku* is thought to live on the edge of two worlds. He is portrayed as a mischievous clown and a trickster, but is also a savage, supremely strong guardian sent to guide the pilgrims across the glaciers and protect them from the souls of the damned that wander the ice. According to legend the bear earns his manhood by confronting and defeating one of these souls, and the role of the *ukuku* is now seen as a traditional rite of passage for young men.

The festival dates back to the days when Peruvians made pilgrimages to placate the spirits or *apus* of the mountains with sacrifices. Legend has it that there's always a death during the pilgrimage and the apu is satisfied. It is the responsibility of the *ukuku* to bring down the healing properties of the apu in the form of glacial ice.

The nature of the festival has, of course, altered since the arrival of the Spanish. In particular, part of the celebrations now have a distinctly Christian flavour. In their view, the celebration dates back only to 1780 when a young mestizo boy called Manuel miraculously transformed himself into a bush with a picture of Christ hanging from it. His friend who was with him, Mariano, died on the spot and was buried under a rock, on which an image of Christ was painted. The rock is known as the Lord of Quyllurit'i and remains the centrepiece of the Catholic festivities with processions and dances taking place around the rock. Despite this Christian adaptation, however, many of the indigenous population prefer to stick to the original format of the celebrations, falling to their knees in reverence at the rising of the sun on the Monday morning.

in town, *Hostal Ausangate* (☎ 950 359902/9/4 327538; s/22 per night), lies on the main road a few hundred metres down from the market back towards Ocongate. It's run by the local trekking expert Cayetano Crispin Gonzalo, the man who has done much to popularise treks in the area and who can help with your *arriero* arrangements. Count on paying s/40 per day for the arriero plus s/35 per animal. Alternatively, it's normally cheaper if you can arrange one yourself – there'll usually be one or two of the more enterprising arrieros waiting to greet tourists off the bus (you'll have a better chance of getting one if you arrive before midday). Expect to pay about s/25 per day for the horse plus s/25 per day for the arriero's guiding abilities; you need to make it clear from the outset whether you'll be feeding him too or whether you expect him to bring his own supplies.

As you leave Tinke on the trail, note that you'll be asked to pay a **s/10 community fee**; it may feel a bit like a scam but you will be issued with a ticket and apparently it's all legitimate. You'll be asked for another one on the next stage too.

TINKE TO THE THERMAL BATHS   [MAP 27, p302; MAP 28, p303]

Having just spent the previous pages eulogising about this Ausangate Circuit, we should now inform you that, actually, the trek's first day is, well, a little humdrum. Like a bland vegan starter before a main course of lobster or fillet steak, there's nothing bad about this first day; it just lacks the 'wow factor' of the rest of the trek. That said, this **12.7km (7¾ miles; 3hrs 5 mins to 3¾hrs)** stage is not without its charms as you make your way from the market square at Tinke to head up (and it is pretty much *all* up, for the first half of the day at least) towards the tiny hamlet of Upis and beyond, eventually arriving at the thermal baths preceding Abra Arapa, the trail's first mountain pass. Catch the early bus from Cusco and you may even be able to make it over the pass and on to Laguna Pucacocha – and pretty much our favourite landscape in the entire *country*. But for many, a later departure from Cusco or a delay in Tinke to sort out an arriero or buy supplies means that the lake will have to wait, and instead the thermal baths are a reasonable ambition for the first day; though whether you deserve a hot bath after just one day's walking is something you'll have to debate with your conscience.

Most of this first day is spent trudging uphill on a 4WD track past a smattering of shacks and houses, the trail seemingly making a direct beeline for the northern glacier of Ausangate. Which makes it all the more curious that this is also the day on which most people struggle to find the correct trail, thanks largely to several inviting tracks that lead off the correct route. Thankfully, there should be plenty of people around to ask the way (*¿Dónde están los baños termales por favor?* may not be the most detailed of Spanish sentences but it will see you through).

The trickiest section is after Upis, where some have trouble locating the correct road to take; and on the final push to the baths, where the trail – now, finally, a vehicle-free footpath – can occasionally be slightly difficult to find. Just keep your wits about you and follow the instructions given on maps 27 and 28 (p302 and p303) and you should be fine.

ROUTE GUIDE AND MAPS

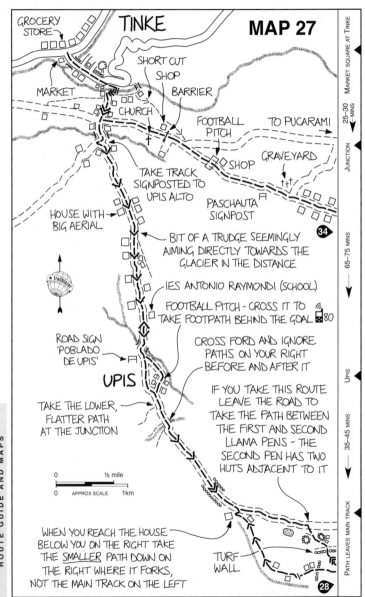

MAP 27

TINKE

GROCERY STORE

SHORT CUT

SHOP

BARRIER

MARKET

CHURCH

FOOTBALL PITCH

TO PUCARAMI

SHOP

GRAVEYARD

TAKE TRACK SIGNPOSTED TO UPIS ALTO

PASCHAUTA SIGNPOST

34

HOUSE WITH BIG AERIAL

BIT OF A TRUDGE SEEMINGLY AIMING DIRECTLY TOWARDS THE GLACIER IN THE DISTANCE

IES ANTONIO RAYMONDI (SCHOOL)

FOOTBALL PITCH - CROSS IT TO TAKE FOOTPATH BEHIND THE GOAL 80

ROAD SIGN 'POBLADO DE UPIS'

UPIS

CROSS FORD AND IGNORE PATHS ON YOUR RIGHT BEFORE AND AFTER IT

IF YOU TAKE THIS ROUTE LEAVE THE ROAD TO TAKE THE PATH BETWEEN THE FIRST AND SECOND LLAMA PENS - THE SECOND PEN HAS TWO HUTS ADJACENT TO IT

TAKE THE LOWER, FLATTER PATH AT THE JUNCTION

0   ½ mile
0   APPROX SCALE   1km

WHEN YOU REACH THE HOUSE BELOW YOU ON THE RIGHT TAKE THE SMALLER PATH DOWN ON THE RIGHT WHERE IT FORKS, NOT THE MAIN TRACK ON THE LEFT

TURF WALL

28

trailblazer

MARKET SQUARE AT TINKE

25–30 MINS

JUNCTION

65–75 MINS

UPIS

35–45 MINS

PATH LEAVES MAIN TRACK

ROUTE GUIDE AND MAPS

Once you've left Upis and the 4WD track behind the trail's upward gradient finally relents and you are able to enjoy a gentle stroll down to the valley floor, passing by (and through) several small homesteads and the remains of old stone-built llama pens. The **thermal baths** lie on the pampa towards the head of the valley. Called **Upis Basecamp** by some trekking agencies, at times this place can get very busy, with most guided tours pitching up here at the end of the first day. But most of the time you'll have the place – and the baths (s/5 per person) – if not to yourself, then to share with just one or two other intrepid and like-minded independent trekkers.

THERMAL BATHS TO PAMPACANCHA
[MAP 28; MAP 29, p304; MAP 30, p305; MAP 31, p306]

Having spent much of the previous day schlepping on a dusty 4WD track under a burning sun, you probably feel that you deserve a reward or two for your efforts (particularly if you decided against a bath at the end of the previous stage). Thankfully, today's **21.3km (13¼ miles; 6¼hrs to 7hrs 35 mins)** stage has treats aplenty. Gorgeous glacial lakes of varying hues, hilltops and mountaintops streaked in shades of red, orange, yellow and brown, vast herds of llamas and alpacas, hurrying vicuñas, scurrying viscachas – and views to still the tongue and make your jaw drop to the floor; this really is rather a special day of walking.

Such delights do not come easy, however, and there are also several parts that will get hearts pumping and calves screaming. In particular, there are three mountain passes to overcome, including one, Abra Palomani, towards the end of the stage, that tops the magical figure of 5000m. The first of these passes lies just a relatively steep hour from the thermal baths, past an isolated homestead where viscachas frolic amongst the old stone walls, and up through pampa where the black-and-white mountain caracara swoop and soar. The pass itself,

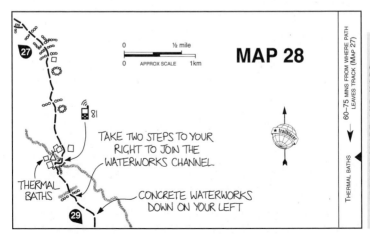

0 ——— ½ mile
0 ——— APPROX SCALE ——— 1km

MAP 28

☆ trailblazer

TAKE TWO STEPS TO YOUR
RIGHT TO JOIN THE
WATERWORKS CHANNEL

THERMAL
BATHS

CONCRETE WATERWORKS
DOWN ON YOUR LEFT

60–75 MINS FROM WHERE PATH
LEAVES TRACK (MAP 27)

THERMAL BATHS

ROUTE GUIDE AND MAPS

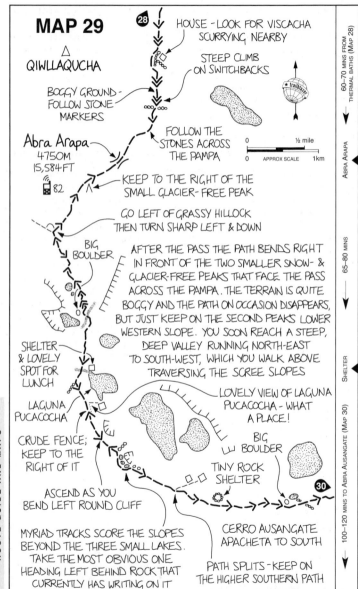

MAP 29

△ QIWLLAQUCHA

HOUSE – LOOK FOR VISCACHA SCURRYING NEARBY

STEEP CLIMB ON SWITCHBACKS

BOGGY GROUND – FOLLOW STONE MARKERS

★ trailblazer

Abra Arapa 4750M 15,584FT
📱 82

FOLLOW THE STONES ACROSS THE PAMPA

0   ½ mile
0   APPROX SCALE   1km

KEEP TO THE RIGHT OF THE SMALL GLACIER-FREE PEAK

GO LEFT OF GRASSY HILLOCK THEN TURN SHARP LEFT & DOWN

BIG BOULDER

AFTER THE PASS THE PATH BENDS RIGHT IN FRONT OF THE TWO SMALLER SNOW- & GLACIER-FREE PEAKS THAT FACE THE PASS ACROSS THE PAMPA. THE TERRAIN IS QUITE BOGGY AND THE PATH ON OCCASION DISAPPEARS, BUT JUST KEEP ON THE SECOND PEAKS LOWER WESTERN SLOPE. YOU SOON REACH A STEEP, DEEP VALLEY RUNNING NORTH-EAST TO SOUTH-WEST, WHICH YOU WALK ABOVE TRAVERSING THE SCREE SLOPES

SHELTER & LOVELY SPOT FOR LUNCH

LAGUNA PUCACOCHA

LOVELY VIEW OF LAGUNA PUCACOCHA – WHAT A PLACE!

BIG BOULDER

CRUDE FENCE; KEEP TO THE RIGHT OF IT

TINY ROCK SHELTER

ASCEND AS YOU BEND LEFT ROUND CLIFF

MYRIAD TRACKS SCORE THE SLOPES BEYOND THE THREE SMALL LAKES. TAKE THE MOST OBVIOUS ONE HEADING LEFT BEHIND ROCK THAT CURRENTLY HAS WRITING ON IT

CERRO AUSANGATE APACHETA TO SOUTH

PATH SPLITS – KEEP ON THE HIGHER SOUTHERN PATH

60–70 MINS FROM THERMAL BATHS (MAP 28)

ABRA ARAPA

65–80 MINS

SHELTER

100–120 MINS TO ABRA AUSANGATE (MAP 30)

ROUTE GUIDE AND MAPS

Abra Arapa, at 4750m/15,584ft, is not the most difficult to reach but the walk to it is certainly stiff enough to get the blood moving around the legs.

The pass also acts as a gateway of sorts – for after here the beauty of the scenery increases a notch or two, particularly once you descend to the picture-perfect **Laguna Pucacocha**. If the weather's right, this is a delightful spot, the still, silent lake glinting in the sun against a backdrop of grumbling, glistening glaciers, the silence broken only by the gentle tread of any camelids that happen to be grazing nearby, and the dull thud of jaws collectively dropping to the floor at the beauty of it all.

Further wonders follow as the path now bends east and climbs the valley's southern slopes above a smattering of isolated homesteads, the dazzling white of the ice on your left contrasting pleasingly with the dull, deep red of the opposite slopes. The walking is uphill but seldom strenuous and before the hour's up

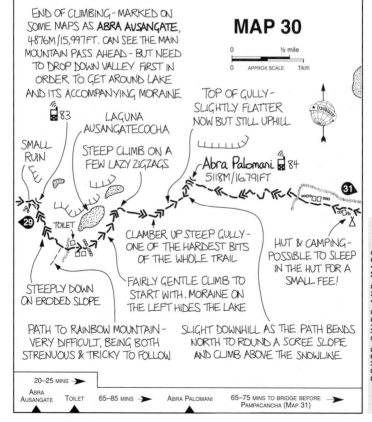

END OF CLIMBING - MARKED ON SOME MAPS AS **ABRA AUSANGATE**, 4876M/15,997FT. CAN SEE THE MAIN MOUNTAIN PASS AHEAD - BUT NEED TO DROP DOWN VALLEY FIRST IN ORDER TO GET AROUND LAKE AND ITS ACCOMPANYING MORAINE

MAP 30

0   ½ mile
0   APPROX SCALE   1km

★ trailblazer

📱 83

LAGUNA AUSANGATECOCHA

TOP OF GULLY - SLIGHTLY FLATTER NOW BUT STILL UPHILL

SMALL RUIN

STEEP CLIMB ON A FEW LAZY ZIGZAGS

Abra Palomani 📱 84
5118M/16,791FT

29

TOILET

31

CLAMBER UP STEEP GULLY - ONE OF THE HARDEST BITS OF THE WHOLE TRAIL

HUT & CAMPING - POSSIBLE TO SLEEP IN THE HUT FOR A SMALL FEE!

STEEPLY DOWN ON ERODED SLOPE

FAIRLY GENTLE CLIMB TO START WITH. MORAINE ON THE LEFT HIDES THE LAKE

PATH TO RAINBOW MOUNTAIN - VERY DIFFICULT, BEING BOTH STRENUOUS & TRICKY TO FOLLOW

SLIGHT DOWNHILL AS THE PATH BENDS NORTH TO ROUND A SCREE SLOPE AND CLIMB ABOVE THE SNOWLINE

20–25 MINS ➤

ABRA AUSANGATE

TOILET

65–85 MINS ➤

ABRA PALOMANI

65–75 MINS TO BRIDGE BEFORE PAMPACANCHA (MAP 31) ➤

ROUTE GUIDE AND MAPS

you'll find yourself at the stage's second pass, **Abra Ausangate** (4876m/15,997ft) with a lake silent below.

The third, final and highest pass on this stage, **Abra Palomani** (5118m/16,791ft), lies just a couple of kilometres further on as the condor flies; unfortunately, unlike condors, land-based creatures such as trekkers have to overcome the obstacles thrown up by the local topography, which in this instance means a steep drop down to the valley floor, followed by an equally stiff climb up the other side.

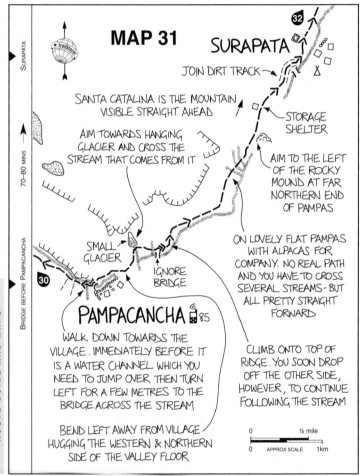

MAP 31

SURAPATA

JOIN DIRT TRACK

SANTA CATALINA IS THE MOUNTAIN VISIBLE STRAIGHT AHEAD

AIM TOWARDS HANGING GLACIER AND CROSS THE STREAM THAT COMES FROM IT

STORAGE SHELTER

AIM TO THE LEFT OF THE ROCKY MOUND AT FAR NORTHERN END OF PAMPAS

SMALL GLACIER

IGNORE BRIDGE

ON LOVELY FLAT PAMPAS WITH ALPACAS FOR COMPANY. NO REAL PATH AND YOU HAVE TO CROSS SEVERAL STREAMS - BUT ALL PRETTY STRAIGHT FORWARD

PAMPACANCHA 85

WALK DOWN TOWARDS THE VILLAGE. IMMEDIATELY BEFORE IT IS A WATER CHANNEL WHICH YOU NEED TO JUMP OVER THEN TURN LEFT FOR A FEW METRES TO THE BRIDGE ACROSS THE STREAM

CLIMB ONTO TOP OF RIDGE. YOU SOON DROP OFF THE OTHER SIDE, HOWEVER, TO CONTINUE FOLLOWING THE STREAM

BEND LEFT AWAY FROM VILLAGE HUGGING THE WESTERN & NORTHERN SIDE OF THE VALLEY FLOOR

0   ½ mile
0   APPROX SCALE   1km

SURAPATA

70–80 MINS

BRIDGE BEFORE PAMPACANCHA

32

30

At the foot of the descent, by a rather incongruous toilet block, you may well be approached by a little old lady who's probably been watching your progress since your silhouette first appeared at Abra Ausangate, and who'll doubtless ask you for a **s/10 community fee**. As on the previous stage, it is all above board and should be paid. The path up to the final pass starts close by the eastern edge of the lake, though the moraine ensures that you won't actually see the lake itself again until you've climbed above it. It's a relentless and tough climb, and rare are those who complete it without pausing on several occasions to catch their breath. No technical skills are required to reach the pass, just a certain amount of obstinacy and perseverance.

At the top you may feel that the all-encompassing views, including colourful striations of the slopes on your right, and the justifiable sense of achievement could *just* be sufficient reward for all your exertions getting here. Plus there's the knowledge that it's all downhill from now to the end of the stage, a fairly straightforward wander to the floor of one valley, which in turn leads to the floor of a second, with the village of **Pampacancha** lying at the junction of the two. Camp here for the night – your rest has been well-earned!

PAMPACANCHA TO PACCHANTA
[MAP 31; MAP 32; MAP 33, p308; MAP 34, p309]

The previous stage of the trek is undoubtedly a tough act to follow, but this **20.8km (13 miles; 5¼hrs to 6hrs 10 mins)** stage makes a really good fist of it. In many ways the two stages are similar, for today's stage also involves a 5000m-plus pass, many gorgeous lakes and enough sumptuous views to send the soul soaring; oh, and you'll be delighted to hear that there are more thermal baths at the end of this day too – and nobody can say that you don't deserve some time in these!

The start, however, is gentle enough, a simple limbering up along the floor of the Pampacancha valley which precedes a steady but increasingly steep foot-slog up via the settlement of **Surapata** to the 5070m-/16,637ft-high **Abra Jampa/Champa**. From Pampacancha to the pass takes about three hours in total and the majority of it is uphill; but it's pretty much the last uphill of the entire trek as from the pass you descend, gently at first, past numerous lakes – each vying with the next in the beauty stakes. The peaks of Pucapunta, Campa and, of course, Ausangate, watch your progress as you mosey on down to the next settlement on the path, **Acosere**. Life in this agricultural community, as everywhere else on this trail, is undoubtedly hard, and the people are poor; but when it comes to their surroundings, they are blessed, with 360 degrees of ter-rific scenery right on their doorstep.

The path to the day's final destination is a relatively gentle one, though **Pacchanta** itself comes as a bit of a shock, with cars and concrete present for pretty much the first time on the trail. Every other building here appears to

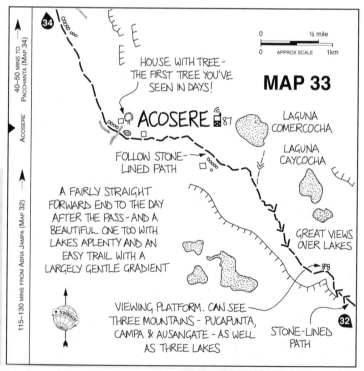

40–50 MINS TO PACCHANTA (MAP 34)

ACOSERE

115–130 MINS FROM ABRA JAMPA (MAP 32)

34

HOUSE WITH TREE - THE FIRST TREE YOU'VE SEEN IN DAYS!

MAP 33

ACOSERE 87

LAGUNA COMERCOCHA

LAGUNA CAYCOCHA

FOLLOW STONE-LINED PATH

A FAIRLY STRAIGHT FORWARD END TO THE DAY AFTER THE PASS - AND A BEAUTIFUL ONE TOO WITH LAKES APLENTY AND AN EASY TRAIL WITH A LARGELY GENTLE GRADIENT

GREAT VIEWS OVER LAKES

trailblazer

88

VIEWING PLATFORM. CAN SEE THREE MOUNTAINS - PUCAPUNTA, CAMPA & AUSANGATE - AS WELL AS THREE LAKES

STONE-LINED PATH

32

0   ½ mile
0   APPROX SCALE   1km

MAP 34

SIGN: POBLADO DE PACCHANTA

FOOTBALL PITCH

STREAM

WATER CHANNEL

HOSTEL

SHOP

THERMAL BATHS

SHOPS

PACCHANTA

0   ½ mile

0   APPROX SCALE   1km

◀— 135–150 MINS TO MARKET SQUARE AT TINKE (MAP 27)   PACCHANTA

advertise itself as either a mini-market (a beer is s/10) or a hostel, though for most people the main attraction are the thermal baths, where for s/5 you can sit, soak and watch the local population of black pampas ibis lazily drift across the village square.

PACCHANTA TO TINKE   [MAP 34; MAP 27, p302]

And so to the final day on the trail, a simple downward **11.9km (7½ miles; 2¼-2½hrs)** yomp on a dusty road, with evidence of civilisation increasing on all sides. As with the first day's path (which lies just a few kilometres to the west), it's all very straightforward if a little unspectacular, the only danger being the occasional vehicle on the road – which, after the past couple of days, may well be unfamiliar to you!

All being well you should be standing back in the centre of Tinke before lunch, allowing you to catch a bus to Cusco and be back in the bustle before dark. Your Ausangate odyssey is at an end – but undoubtedly the memories will stay with you for a long, long time.

MACHU PICCHU

In the variety of its charms and the power of its spell, I know of no place in the world which can compare with it. Not only has it great snow peaks looming above the clouds more than two miles overhead; gigantic precipices of many-colored granite rising sheer for thousands of feet above the foaming, glistening, roaring rapids; it has also, in striking contrast, orchids and tree ferns, the delectable beauty of luxurious vegetation, and the mysterious witchery of the jungle.
Hiram Bingham *Inca Land – Explorations in the Highlands of Peru* (1922)

Romance swirls about Machu Picchu like the mists that suddenly roll in from the mountains, bringing with it an equal degree of obfuscation. Why are these majestic ruins perched on a saddle ridge high above the Urubamba Valley? Who lived in them and what did they do? The briefest of visits to the site shows that the one thing everyone agrees on is that nobody knows for sure. That doesn't stop them having theories. From the most learned of academics to the youngest of guides, everybody has a hypothesis; just stop and listen to passing tours and you will hear the same place described in a dozen different ways. It adds greatly to the charm of the place – and it is unlikely that we will ever know the truth.

The fame that the 20th century brought to Machu Picchu has been a mixed blessing. It has fascinated the world since its rediscovery in 1911; tourism figures have risen steadily – to around 900,000 visitors a year – and are now supposedly capped at a 2500 maximum per day (though it's a figure that we think is being regularly breached). In 1983 it achieved international cultural status by joining the list of UNESCO World Heritage Sites. In 2007 it was chosen, by online public vote, as one of the world's 'New Seven Wonders'.

A dispute over the ownership of the land rumbles on. Two brothers, Edgar and Adolfo Abrill, are seeking compensation from the Peruvian government, claiming that the land was expropriated from their grandparents in 1935. Other issues include erosion of the Inca Trail and ruins from sheer numbers of enthusiastic visitors, and some controversial restoration programmes. However, a long-running dispute about the return of Machu Picchu artefacts from Yale University was settled in 2010 and the university has begun to return the 'goods, pieces and parts' that were taken from the ruins between 1911 and 1915 by Hiram Bingham and his team of archaeologists. Some of these are now displayed in Cusco (see p153 and p154).

But flawed beauty or not, whether it is your first time or your fifth, and whether you come by train, bus or on foot, you cannot fail to be amazed by the sheer, glorious improbability of Machu Picchu.

Historical background

Whoever they were, whatever name be finally assigned to this site by future historians, of this I feel sure – that few romances can ever surpass that of the granite citadel on top of the beetling precipices of Machu Picchu, the crown of Inca Land.
    Hiram Bingham *Inca Land – Explorations in the Highlands of Peru* (1922)

WHO BUILT MACHU PICCHU?

Myths aside, the Inca Empire evolved over a period of around 300 years (see pp90-102), from modest tribal beginnings in a village to the south of Cusco,

sometime early in the 12th century, to its demise at the hands of the conquistadors. When the ninth Inca, Pachacutec (Pachacuti Inca Yupanqui), took the throne in 1438, he began the great expansion of Inca territory. A 16th-century document found by the archaeologists Luis Miguel Glave, María Remy and John Howland Rowe seems to confirm that it was Pachacutec who rebuilt Cusco, in a manner befitting an imperial capital. He probably built Machu Picchu, as well, in the mid 15th century.

A CITY ABANDONED

Statue of Pachacutec
Aguas Calientes

Sometime early in the Spanish Conquest, however, it was abandoned for reasons we do not know. This did at least protect it from the Spanish who clearly knew nothing about it. This mysterious withdrawal from public life was probably caused by a combination of disease and vicious factional fighting amongst Inca clans. Whatever the reason, the collection of pale granite buildings on its ridge – a masterpiece in architecture and setting by any standards – was left to succumb to the encroaching foliage, much in the manner of Cambodia's Angkor Wat.

It is interesting that Machu Picchu's superbly constructed agricultural terraces, too good to abandon, were used for centuries by local farmers, who always knew about the ruins.

THE GREAT REDISCOVERY – 24TH JULY 1911

It was one of these farmers who in 1911 led the ambitious young explorer Hiram Bingham up the densely overgrown, snake- and insect-infested path to the ruins. Funded by Yale University, he was actually searching for Vilcabamba, or 'The Lost City of the Incas', which he believed had been built by the penultimate Inca after his defeat at the hands of the Spanish.

In *Inca Land – Explorations in the Highlands of Peru* (1922) he recounts the events of that historic day, 24th July 1911:

'We had camped at a place near the river, called Mandor Pampa. Melchor Arteaga, proprietor of the neighboring farm, had told us of ruins at Machu Picchu... The morning of July 24th dawned in a cold drizzle. Arteaga shivered and seemed inclined to stay in his hut. I offered to pay him well if he would show me the ruins. He demurred and said it was too hard a climb for such a wet day. When he found that we were willing to pay him a sol, three or four times the ordinary daily wage in this vicinity, he finally agreed to guide us to the ruins. No one supposed that they would be particularly interesting.'

Indeed, the other members of his team, naturalist Harry Foote and team doctor William Erving, declined to go. Foote set off to catch butterflies and Erving's excuse was that he had to 'wash his clothes'. Bingham left accompanied by the police sergeant who'd been allotted to them and the farmer, Melchor Arteaga. They followed the Urubamba upstream for 45 minutes and then crossed the 'foaming rapids' on some slender logs.

'Leaving the stream, we struggled up the bank through a dense jungle, and in a few minutes reached the bottom of a precipitous slope. For an hour and twenty minutes we had a hard climb. A good part of the distance we went on all fours, sometimes hanging on by the tips of our fingers. Here and there, a primitive ladder made from the roughly hewn trunk of a small tree was placed in such a way as to help one over what might otherwise have proved to be an impassable cliff. In another place the slope was covered with slippery grass where it was hard to find either handholds or footholds. The guide said that there were lots of snakes here. The humidity was great, the heat was excessive, and we were not in training.'

They reached a hut where 'two pleasant farmers, Richarte and Alvarez', gave them gourds of cool water. As they rested the farmers said they had come up here to use the old terraces and had been living here for about four years. They added that there were many more terraces and even some ruins nearby. Hot and exhausted by the climb Bingham was in no hurry to move on...

'Furthermore, the view was simply enchanting. Tremendous green precipices fell away to the white rapids of the Urubamba below. Immediately in front, on the north side of the valley, was a great granite cliff rising 2000 feet sheer. To the left was the solitary peak of Huayna Picchu, surrounded by seemingly inaccessible precipices. On all sides were rocky cliffs. Beyond them cloud-capped mountains rose thousands of feet above us.'

The farmers said that soon after they had come up here they had cleared some of the ruins and rethatched some of the houses to live in but they were too far from the water sources. The aqueduct which had brought water into the buildings was blocked with earth from the terraces so they had abandoned the Inca houses and built their own. They continued to farm the old terraces, growing maize, potatoes, sugar cane, beans, peppers, tree tomatoes and gooseberries. When Bingham finally left the cool of the hut to investigate further, he found that:

'Hardly had we rounded the promontory when the character of the stonework began to improve. A flight of beautifully constructed terraces, each two hundred yards long and ten feet high, had been recently rescued from the jungle by the Indians. A forest of large trees had been chopped down and burned over to make a clearing for agricultural purposes. Crossing these terraces, I entered the untouched forest beyond, and suddenly found myself in a maze of beautiful granite houses! They were covered with trees and moss and the growth of centuries, but in the dense shadow, hiding in bamboo thickets and tangled vines, could be seen, here and there, walls of white granite ashlars most carefully cut and exquisitely fitted together. Buildings with windows were frequent.'

Amazed at the quality of the masonry Bingham soon began to realise the significance of the ruins. Seeing the structures that became known as the Torreón and the Temple of Three Windows he wrote:

'To my astonishment I saw that this wall and its adjoining semicircular temple over the cave were as fine as the finest stonework in the far-famed Temple of the Sun in Cuzco. Surprise followed surprise in bewildering succession. I climbed a marvelous great stairway of large granite blocks, walked along a pampa where the Indians had a small vegetable garden, and came into a little clearing. Here were the ruins of two of the finest structures I have ever seen in Peru. Not only were they made of selected blocks of beautifully grained white granite; their walls contained ashlars of Cyclopean size, ten feet in length, and higher than a man. The sight held me spellbound.'

'It did not take an expert to realise, from the glimpse of Machu Picchu on that rainy day in July, 1911, when Sergeant Carrasco and I first saw it, that here were most extraordinary and interesting ruins. Although the ridge had been partly cleared by the Indians for their fields of maize, so much of it was still underneath a thick jungle growth – some walls were actually supporting trees ten and twelve inches in diameter – that it was impossible to determine just what would be found here.'

One of Hiram Bingham's photographs of Machu Picchu in 1911 before excavations began. (From *Inca Land – Explorations in the Highlands of Peru* (1922)

Bingham also discovered one other significant find in the Temple of Three Windows. Scrawled on one of the walls was the words 'Lizarraga 1902'- further proof that Bingham wasn't the first to 'discover' the ruins (though the fact that there were farmers living by the ruins and using the Inca terraces for their vegetable plots had already proved this; see box p314).

He returned to his university, Yale, raised funds and came back in 1912 with several projects in mind, including a more extensive investigation of Machu Picchu. He transported many of his finds – not gold, as is widely believed, but mainly potsherds and stone fragments – back to America, with the permission of the then government of Peru. It is now fashionable to disapprove of Bingham, who was one in a long line of post-colonial explorers discovering, or plundering, the world at the time – but nothing can take away from him what he must have seen that first time, peering beneath the undergrowth and realising the extent and quality of the ruins and their extraordinary position.

And it is Bingham who is responsible, for good or bad, for the second age of the Incas, the tourism age, which has brought so many people to Peru.

THE RE-BIRTH OF A LEGEND – BINGHAM'S THEORIES

Unfortunately he was also, often unwittingly, responsible for some of the myths and misunderstandings that have grown up around the site. He was, after all, not a trained archaeologist (though he was a history lecturer at Yale) but an explorer and treasure hunter, and one should not forget that he did go on to become a politician, elected as a US senator in 1922.

❏ Who really discovered Machu Picchu?

You'll hear various claims that it wasn't Hiram Bingham but a Peruvian landowner, an English missionary or a German entrepreneur who was the true discoverer of Machu Picchu.

Although the conquistadors certainly didn't get here, Bingham soon realised he wasn't the first outsider to see Machu Picchu. Amongst the ruins he found graffiti left by Peruvians Enrique Palma, Gabino Sánchez, and Agustín Lizárraga that they had made on their visit on 14th July 1902. Other visitors may have been Thomas Payne and Stuart McNairn, English missionaries whose descendants claim they visited the ruins in 1906, having been informed about them by an engineer named Franklin.

From the middle of the 19th century, as the South American rubber boom got under way, the whole area began to be opened up. Gold miners and prospectors also came searching this way. In the 1860s the land around Aguas Calientes was bought by Augusto Berns, originally from Germany, who set up a sawmill to make railway sleepers. Indeed, in 1911 Bingham noted this rusting machinery mistakenly identifying it as a press for sugar cane. It is claimed that in the 1880s Berns tried to get investors interested in an excavation business to search for gold and other treasures on Inca sites in the area. Although Machu Picchu isn't mentioned as one of them, 'Picchu' mountain is actually marked on a map dating from 1874. In the 1890s the Peruvian government pushed a road up the Urubamba right below Machu Picchu, bringing more people into the area. It was this road that Bingham followed in 1911.

So Bingham was not the first person to see Machu Picchu but what he did after seeing it was very different from what everyone else did: he recorded his visit scientifically and organised expeditions to study the site. As historian Daniel Buck says in an article published in *La República* (31 Aug 2008): 'There can be no doubt that Bingham is the site's "scientific discoverer," an honorific bestowed on the Yale professor by José Gabriel Cosío, a Cuzco academic and official delegate to Bingham's second expedition. It is also true that others had known of the ruins long before Bingham. One can make the case that Machu Picchu was never totally lost. It was periodically known and unknown, there and not there – visited, lived in, farmed, and even bought and sold – from the 16th century until Bingham permanently removed it from obscurity.'

As Bingham candidly admitted in a letter to a schoolmaster in Honolulu: 'I suppose that in the same sense of the word as it is used in the expression "Columbus discovered America" it is fair to say that I discovered Machu Picchu. The Norsemen and the French fisherman undoubtedly visited North America long before Columbus crossed the Atlantic. On the other hand it was Columbus who made America known to the civilised world. In the same sense of the word I "discovered" Machu Picchu – in that before my visit and report on it it was not known to the geographical and historical societies in Peru, nor to the Peruvian government.'

Detail of exterior of Temple of Three Windows. (Hiram Bingham, from *Inca Land – Explorations in the Highlands of Peru* (1922).

He was also a talented photographer, and when the National Geographic Society devoted an entire issue to the story it ignited world interest. It was sheer romance: the geographical setting, the sun worship, the mythical gold of the Incas, the brutal conquistadors. Reading the article you can quite see why it's said that the character *Indiana Jones* is based on Bingham:

'There was nothing for us but to run, and we did that, tearing through the jungle down hill in an effort to get around the side of the fire... the grass and soil under my feet let go, and I dropped. For about 20 feet there was a slope of about 70 degrees, and then a jump of about 200 feet, after which it would be bump and repeat down to the river. As I shot down the sloping surface I reached out and with my right hand grasped a mesquite bush that was growing in a crack about 5 feet above the jump-off.' *In the Wonderland of Peru* **Hiram Bingham**, **National Geographic Society** (April 1913).

He wrote several books about Machu Picchu and the Incas, the best known being *Inca Land – Explorations in the Highlands of Peru* (1922) and, in 1948, the best-selling *Lost City of the Incas* (he simply transferred the label from Vilcabamba; it was too good a title to lose). The three conclusions that he reaches in the first book and develops in the second are certainly sensational but have lost their credibility over the last hundred years. Bingham was most excited to find a fine building with windows at Machu Picchu, the building he called the Temple of Three Windows, as he considered that it fitted a description of the temple at Tampu-tocco, **the birthplace of the first Inca**, **Manco Capac**, who lived around 1200AD. There are, however, several other more likely contenders for the site of Tampu-tocco, Chokepukio near Cusco among them. Furthermore, in the historical description of the site it's difficult to separate myth from reality.

In his mind this was not just a lost city of the first Inca but *the* Lost City, the final refuge of the Incas who had fled in the path of the conquistadors. This was also **Vilcabamba**, the city of gold that the Spanish had been looking for. It was the position of Machu Picchu, on a promontory that afforded such good protection from attack and was easily defensible, that made him believe that it was their final stronghold. Actually Bingham did discover the true lost city when he found the ruins at Espíritu Pampa but the setting of Machu Picchu made it infinitely more romantic cast as a final refuge for this doomed civilisation. He ends the books with his most fanciful theory:

'In its last state it became the home and refuge of the Virgins of the Sun, priestesses of the most humane cult of aboriginal America. Here, concealed in a canyon of remarkable grandeur, protected by art and nature, these consecrated women gradually passed away, leaving no known descendants, nor any records other than the masonry walls and artifacts...'

Early excavations revealed that over 80% of the skeletons discovered in Machu

Picchu were female. The Incas dedicated their most beautiful daughters to the service of the Sun God and Bingham suggested that these skeletons might be **Virgins of the Sun**, the chosen women who had escaped from Cusco when the Spanish arrived. Disappointingly, more recent studies have shown that male and female remains were found in almost equal numbers.

SO WHY WAS MACHU PICCHU BUILT?

In the century that has elapsed since Bingham's rediscovery of Machu Picchu the body of knowledge about the Incas has grown considerably as this and other sites have been more thoroughly excavated, the study of archaeology has evolved and more credible theories have emerged.

It was clearly not a conventional city. Built between 1450 and 1470, during the reign of Pachacutec, it's thought that Machu Picchu would have accommodated only 750-1000 people so it was actually quite small. It was certainly at least agriculturally self-sufficient; the Incas had long since mastered the art of making a little land go a very long way and the ruins are skirted by steep terraces with stone holding walls and efficient drainage systems. In fact, the area occupied by terraces should have been able to produce a surplus of foodstuffs.

Bingham emphasised Machu Picchu's military characteristics, keen to make it fit as the last citadel of the Incas. He identified some of the buildings as barracks, but also recognised distinct areas that he labelled agricultural, spiritual or residential (for nobility or priests, and more humbly, for artisans, farmers or servants). Those divisions, loosely speaking, still hold today. It is certainly true that Machu Picchu's position on the promontory in a bend in the Urubamba would have made it easy to defend. It would have made an excellent lookout station but the quality of the buildings suggests it was very much more than this.

Near one of the trade routes out of the lowland forests to Cusco, could Machu Picchu have been an administrative centre? The Incas kept tabs on their sprawling empire by constant stock- and census-taking. The tallies were knotted into strings (*quipus*) and carried along the trails by swift-footed relay runners (*chasquis*). There could have been a way station here but the buildings seem too grand for it to have been an administrative centre. It's certainly not like any others the Incas built specifically for this purpose.

The setting is important: Machu Picchu is laid out on a north-south axis, which means that it gets the full benefit of sunrise on its main flank and a clear view both of significant peaks around it and the moon, stars and planets in the sky above. There is also the sacred river far below. For the Inca and his people, animists and Sun God worshippers, such a position would not have been a coincidence.

Machu Picchu as a spiritual centre?

To a Western eye, the ruins bring to mind a mediaeval monastic complex, combining spiritual, ceremonial and agricultural elements with a degree of fortification. Some of the most significant buildings are obviously for religious use.

In Machu Picchu: The Sacred Center, Johan Reinhard examines the sacred and symbolic aspects of the landscape archaeology of the region. The site is spread across a saddle between the two peaks, Machu Picchu and Huayna

(Wayna) Picchu. Huayna Picchu is the furthest point of a long spur running north from the snow-capped sacred mountain of Salkantay. In Reinhard's words: 'At Machu Picchu we find a unique combination of landscape and cosmological beliefs which together formed a powerful sacred center which united religion, economics and politics. These factors led to the construction of one of the most impressive ceremonial sites of the ancient world'. He suggests, furthermore, that Machu Picchu would have been an important place of pilgrimage.

While it's undeniable that the sacred buildings of Machu Picchu are carefully aligned and of a high quality suggesting their importance, surely a place of pilgrimage would not have been so quickly forgotten?

The most credible theory – a royal retreat

Imagine that you're standing on the top of Machu Picchu Mountain looking down on the view as shown in Hiram Bingham's photograph on p313, but that the overgrown terraces that can just be discerned in the picture do not exist. There's nothing here but virgin jungle and you have all the money in the world to build your dream retreat. Where's the perfect site? You wouldn't put it down in the deep dark valley but on that saddle between the two peaks, just where Machu Picchu is now. Richard L Burger and Lucy Salazar-Burger (just as Bingham, both from Yale) have put forward the theory that Machu Picchu was just that: a royal retreat and hunting lodge.

They noted that the site does not resemble any of the five main types of Inca settlement. It's far too small to have been a provincial capital; also too small and lacking the adequate proportion of types of building to have been an administrative centre; unlikely to have been built as a way station or *tambo* or rest stop along the Inca road network because of the fine religious buildings; not a government-established agricultural settlement and obviously not a non-Inca village that paid tribute to the empire. Within the 1% of other known Inca settlements is that of the royal estate, and some of the characteristics and features of these can also be found at Machu Picchu.

Royal estates were outside the state administrative system and owned and operated by *panacas* (royal corporations) for a particular Inca king and used by him as a country getaway for relaxing and entertaining.

The relatively small size of the settlement at Machu Picchu, the high quality of the stonework and the fact that its location and extent indicate it wasn't built for economic reasons together suggest that it probably was a royal estate. The archaeological evidence is backed up by a historical reference. In a document written in 1568, historian John Howland Rowe found a reference to a site named Picchu that was within Pachacutec's estate.

Examined as a royal retreat, the type and style of the buildings of Machu Picchu seem to make much more sense. There are groups of buildings obviously designed for high-status households and others which must have housed their retainers. The fact that there were fine religious buildings of particular significance here is not surprising since the royal retinue would have required rituals, sacrifices and astronomical observations needing numerous priests and attendants. The location is idyllic but also safe, defensible and very private – the perfect royal hideaway.

MACHU PICCHU GUIDE

Practical information

OPENING TIMES & TICKETS

The site is open daily from just before dawn (around 6am) until around 6pm but last entry is at 4pm. **Tickets must be purchased in advance as they cannot be bought at Machu Picchu**.

In July 2017, new regulations were announced allowing only half-day visits (*1er turno*: 6am-12 noon or *2do turno*: 12 noon to 5.30pm; both priced at **s/152/77** adults/students and children) and the stipulation that these visits must be made with a guide (available at the site). As we go to press (Sep 2017), however, reports are that readers are visiting without guides and that the morning visitors are not being made to leave after 12 noon – but things may change as the new system gets going. If you want to be absolutely sure to spend the whole day there you need to also buy an afternoon ticket. There's also a cheaper ticket that runs from 1pm (*Vespertino*, **s/100/50**), as well as the full price *2do turno* ticket that runs from 12 noon.

To ensure you are able to visit on the day you want, buy your ticket online (💻 www.machupicchu.gob.pe) well before arriving at the site; during the busiest times of year **consider buying it up to two weeks in advance**. However, if you also want to climb **Huayna Picchu** (see pp321-2) or **Machu Picchu Mountain** (Montaña, p323) you need to buy a combined Machu Picchu entrance and climbing ticket **(s/200/100** adults/students and children) and these sell out **several months in advance**. Tickets can also be purchased from the offices in Cusco (see p160) or Aguas Calientes (see p206); take your passport and cash (either soles or dollars), or a Visa or MasterCard. If you're booking online sometimes the English version of the website doesn't work for payments and you'll need to revert to the original Spanish-language site; only Visa credit cards are accepted.

The authorities are also bringing in defined circuits to be followed when viewing the ruins. **Circuit 1** is the longest and roughly follows the route set out in this guide, taking 2½-3 hours to complete; **Circuits 2** & **3** cover just the lower sectors.

If you're walking the Inca Trail your permit will include entry into the ruins. Note that if you want to also climb one of the peaks, since the ticket to climb either peak includes an entrance fee to the ruins, in effect you are paying two entrance fees to Machu Picchu (as it is already included in your Inca Trail permit fee). The authorities are said to be looking at this issue, though at the time of writing it still hadn't been resolved.

WHAT TO BRING

The site is exposed, so can get very hot when the sun is out. Conversely, if the cloud has rolled in, it can get very cold. It also rains unpredictably. You'll need clothes suitable for a variety of conditions including **waterproofs** and **sun-screen**. It's worth bringing **insect repellent**, and a **torch/flashlight**.

As no backpacks larger than 20 litres (a small daypack) are allowed into the ruins you must leave them at the **left luggage offices** inside the entrance. Also forbidden are food, disposable plastic drink bottles and walking sticks. You'll need a metal or durable plastic water bottle (not a disposable plastic bottle) so that you can have water with you as you look round.

GETTING THERE AND AWAY
On foot

On the **Inca Trail** trek you reach Machu Picchu via **Intipunku**, the Sun Gate. From here it's a walk of around 40 minutes, gently downhill. The first walkers from the last camp at Huinay Huayna tend to arrive in a rush in a bid to see

---

❏ **Top tips for making the most of your visit to Machu Picchu**

❶ **Try to visit on a Sunday** as many tour groups visit the Sacred Valley markets instead; Tuesday and Thursday are also typically a little quieter. Very early in the morning and late afternoon are the quietest times of day to be here.

❷ **Get here as early as possible, ideally when the site opens**. From Aguas Calientes, for the first buses people start queuing around 4am. Make sure you get your bus ticket (see p320) at least a day before. Rather than spending an hour or more in the bus queue, you may prefer to walk from Aguas Calientes although it's a strenuous climb – see 'Getting there and away' above – and note that because the gate at the bridge opens only at 5am there's no point in leaving Aguas Calientes earlier than 4.40am.

❸ **Climb Huayna Picchu** but if tickets for that have gone – they sell out months in advance – climb Machu Picchu Mountain (Montaña). The views are superb but you can only buy tickets for each ascent in advance (see opposite). The views are even better from Machu Picchu Mountain (it's 300m higher than Huayna Picchu) and the climb less steep (though longer), but there are no ruins to visit on the way.

❹ You're allowed to take only **a small 20-litre day-pack** into the ruins – see 'What to bring' above. Officially food isn't allowed but some people try to sneak in a snack for lunch, given the prices in the café and restaurant. You may be made to leave this in a locker at the entrance.

❺ **Spend as long as possible at the ruins** Ideally spend at least a full day exploring the site so that you can see it at different times of day, as the sun and light affect the atmosphere and appearance of the place. Stay as long as you can; it's busiest between 9am and 4pm, so is much more atmospheric before or after these times. Avoid the bus and walk back down to Aguas Calientes.

❻ **Visit the museum and botanical garden** See p206.

You can hire a guide at Machu Picchu. Visiting with a guide may soon be made compulsory. © H Stedman

sunrise. Walking up from **Aguas Calientes** takes 1¼-2 hours depending on your fitness. Turn right over the bridge and follow the road out of Aguas Calientes. The first 15 minutes are along the flat then it's over the bridge (**note this opens only at 5am**) and steeply uphill. When the road begins to zigzag up the hill, find the path that shortcuts straight up. Coming back down takes around 50 minutes.

By bus from Aguas Calientes
A large fleet of buses ferries day-trippers (adult/child one-way US$12/6, return US$24/12) up to the ruins. The first buses leave at around 5.30am or half an hour before dawn and then depart every 10-20 minutes. Queues stretch for hundreds of metres and if you want to be sure to get on the first buses you need to be there by around 4.15am.

The bus ticket office in Aguas Calientes opens 15 minutes before the first bus leaves but it's much better to buy your ticket the day before. Don't buy a return ticket unless you're positive you're going to take the bus back as it's a pleasant walk down along the trail through the trees.

WHERE TO STAY
The only accommodation here is at *Machu Picchu Sanctuary Lodge* (☎ 0845 0772 222, 🖳 www.belmond.com), scandalously close to the ruins. It's the kind of place which these days they'd never allow to be built in such an environmentally and archaeologically sensitive position. None of the rooms looks over the ruins themselves but you can see Huayna Picchu from some. Well equipped and comfortable, they cost upward of US$675 a night for B&B, with those looking out on the mountain costing US$850 and suites starting at US$1450. If you can afford to stay here you may as well go the whole way and book a wedding package – from US$2400 all in, including the services of a shaman to officiate as you take your vows before an undeniably spectacular backdrop.

Most people stay in **Aguas Calientes** (see pp206-9).

WHERE TO EAT
Food isn't allowed in the ruins and if the snack lunch in your daypack is discovered they'll probably make you leave it in a locker at the entrance.

Tampu Restaurant in Machu Picchu Sanctuary Lodge serves breakfast (5.30-9am), lunch (noon-3pm) and dinner (6.30-9.30pm). A buffet lunch (11am-3.30pm) is available in *Tinkuy Buffet Restaurant*.

There's also an overpriced *snack bar* by the entrance to the ruins. They sell hamburgers, hot dogs, pizzas, empanadas, sandwiches, beer, water, tea and coffee. A hamburguesa macchupicchu is about US$10. You're far better off bringing your own water and food though don't eat it within the ruins themselves.

MACHU PICCHU GUIDE

Above all, there is the fascination of finding here and there under the swaying vines, or perched on top of a beetling crag, the rugged masonry of a bygone race; and of trying to understand the bewildering romance of the ancient builders who ages ago sought refuge in a region which appears to have been expressly designed by Nature as a sanctuary for the oppressed, a place where they might fearlessly and patiently give expression to their passion for walls of enduring beauty.

Hiram Bingham *Inca Land – Explorations in the Highlands of Peru* (1922)

ORIENTATION

Machu Picchu is at 2430m/7970ft and most of the buildings are spread across a saddle between two mountains, Machu Picchu ('Old Peak', 3061m/10,040ft) and the soaring sugarloaf of Huayna/Wayna Picchu ('New Peak', 2700m/8860ft) – with the Urubamba river and Aguas Calientes far below at 2000m/6560ft. If you've bought tickets in advance you can climb either **Huayna Picchu** (see below) and visit the Temple of the Moon below it or **Machu Picchu Mountain** (see p323). Other excursions include the **Inca drawbridge** (20 minutes each way; see p334).

❑ **CLIMBING HUAYNA PICCHU (WAYNA PICCHU)**

[Tickets must be bought well in advance: see p318; limited to 400 people]

To sit on the 2700m/8860ft shaggy crest of Huayna Picchu on a clear morning, with the ruins laid out below you and the sun sliding up behind the mountains like a new *centavo*, is probably the most magnificent experience that Machu Picchu can offer. But it takes advance planning and shouldn't be attempted if you are unfit, struggling with the altitude or suffer from vertigo. Since only 400 tickets a day are available they sell out months in advance, so book early. Half this number are allowed to climb the peak between 7am and 8am and must be down by 10am; the second half are allowed to begin the ascent between 10am and 11am and must return by 1pm. A

certain amount of scrambling is involved and you'll need good shoes.

Huayna Picchu summit

The vertiginous walk up takes anything from 40 minutes to 1½ hours depending on how busy it is and your state of fitness. The path zig-zags relentlessly upwards; after 15-20 minutes there's a junction: **take the right path for the top**; the left path is the Gran Caverna Trail to the other side of the peak. Near the top and some narrow terraces, there's **another fork**: to the right leads up eventually through a short tunnel to the summit and to the left also leads to the summit but via terraces and some small ruins including an intact, though roofless, building which catches the morning sun on its impossibly steep crag. No doubt offerings to the Sun God would have been made from up here and the building may have been a **temple**. (*Cont'd overleaf*)

Huayna Picchu stairway. Slip here and you could land up in the Urubamba River.

❑ CLIMBING HUAYNA PICCHU (WAYNA PICCHU)

(Cont'd from p321) The **terraces** here are really too small for growing anything use-ful and it has been suggested that they may have been planted with bright flowers to provide a splash of colour that could be seen from the royal estate below. It's also likely that some royal guards would have been posted up here as it would make the perfect lookout station. This area is sometimes roped off, particularly after wet weath-er when the stairs are treacherous. The views from the **summit** are spectacular.

On the steep route from the summit of Huayna Picchu to the Temple of the Moon.

Temple of the Moon & Gran Caverna Trail

From the top you can take the fantastically steep trail, some parts of it by makeshift ladder, down the far side, amongst birds, butterflies and beetles. After a 30- to 40-minute descent to a point lower than Machu Picchu itself, you reach a clearing and a fine double wall of masonry appears, with alter-nating windows and niches. The cave behind con-tains the **Temple of the Moon**: a beautiful double-lintel door fits into the cave, along with walls, nich-es and a fine throne or platform of white granite. This is some of the finest Inca stonework in Machu Picchu; obviously an important ceremonial build-ing, it may have contained mummies. It's unlikely to have had anything specifically to do with obser-vation of the moon, but the star cluster known as the Pleiades, which had a special significance in Inca culture, would have been clearly visible from the cave. About 50m below is **another group** of caves and buildings. The stonework is less impressive and in places defaced with graffiti.

The Temple of the Moon

Lower buildings, Gran Caverna

To return, walk anti-clockwise along the **Gran Caverna Trail** around the mountain for 40-60 minutes to rejoin the trail at the junction 15-20 minutes from the entry kiosk. This can also be done in reverse but the climb up from the Temple of the Moon to the summit is very steep: it's easier to approach the summit the normal way.

Inkaraqay Archaeologists are currently clearing these ruins, lower down the steep north face of Huayna Picchu. Covering about 4500 square metres mainly of terraces, it appears that Inkaraqay was mainly agricultural in nature, supplying food for Machu Picchu. It is hoped that it will eventually be opened to visitors. A near-vertical, snake-infested trail leads from Inkaraqay to the summit of Huayna Picchu.

❑ CLIMBING MACHU PICCHU MOUNTAIN (MONTAÑA MACHU PICCHU)

[Tickets must be bought in advance: see p318; limited to 800 people]

As an alternative to Huaynu Picchu you can climb **Machu Picchu Mountain** (3061m/10,040ft), the peak opposite. As with Huaynu Picchu, there are timed entries: 7-8am and 9-10am. It's about a four hour trip: the climb takes up to two hours, it's an hour to walk down and you should allow an hour at the top. It's a steady climb, if not especially difficult, with only a couple of very steep sections and certainly nothing as vertiginous as the route up Huaynu Picchu.

Head up the path towards Intipunku, away from the main site. After 150m look for a signposted turning to the right and join a series of broad steps that ascend through trees and scrub to reach the entry gate where you need to sign in.

On the way up are viewing platforms and, close to the top, a long curved stone staircase. On the summit itself there are several interconnected terraces and the remains of a small building. Hiram Bingham decided that the mountain was a signalling station, given its elevation. While this may

On the stairs descending from the top of Machu Picchu Mountain.
On this walk you'll get that classic view of Machu Picchu with Huayna Picchu rising behind.

have been one of its functions and the 360 degree-views certainly make this the perfect lookout, the primary use for these terraces would have been religious, with offerings to the gods being made from here. This was also the mountain that provided the sacred water for the fountains in Machu Picchu – springs that flowed from its side were diverted into the city. For the Incas this was undoubtably a sacred mountain.

The views are spectacular, even better than from Huaynu Picchu, the summit of which is 300m lower than Machu Picchu Mountain's. From here you have a condor's eye view of Machu Picchu, 500m below. To the east are Putucusi and Nevado Veronica; the San Miguel range lies to the west whilst to the south is Nevado Salkantay.

If it's cloudy, it can get quite crowded on the summit as people wait for a clearer view of Machu Picchu but when it comes it's truly spectacular.

MACHU PICCHU

Inca Trail to Intipunku

Entry to Machu
Picchu Mountain

Machu Picchu
Viewed from Huayna Picchu

N

Start

Hotel &
Entrance

3

21

8

9

20

19

Eastern Terraces

Inca Trail to Drawbridge

1 Viewpoint & Guardhouse
2 Kallanka
3 Agricultural Sector
4 Dry Moat
5 City Gate
6 Quarry
7 Fountains Street
8 Temple of the Sun
9 Tomb of the Princess
10 Royal Quarter
11 Western Terraces
12 Principal Temple
13 Temple of Three Windows
14 Intihuatana
15 Central Plaza
16 Plant Collection
17 Sacred Rock
18 Group of Three Doorways
19 Industrial District
20 Temple of the Condor
21 Storage Huts

Entry to Huayna/Wayna Picchu hike

The sites below are keyed to the overview map on p324-5.

VIEWPOINT & GUARDHOUSE [1]

That first sight, so familiar from a thousand posters and brochures, of the whole of Machu Picchu spread out before you has all the more impact if you come upon it suddenly as you do when approaching on the Inca Trail. To get something of this effect if you've come up by bus from Aguas Calientes, after passing through the checkpoint and walking 100m, don't continue into the ruins but take the path to the left that climbs steeply through the trees and brings you out at the top of the agricultural zone by the guardhouse. You're rewarded with a magnificent view of the ruins, Huayna Picchu and the spinach-green peaks beyond. This is a good place to come to watch the sunrise or take that classic picture.

Guardhouse (aka Watchman's Post) with the kallanka at the back (right)

The Guardhouse [1] (*Recinto del guardian*) looks too grand to be a restored thatched sentry box, but its position overlooking the entire site suggests some sort of surveillance role. Above it is a low, carved boulder known as the **Funerary Rock**. Since human bones were found in this area Bingham assumed it was a cemetery. Perhaps the rock was a mortician's table for the evisceration of bodies during the process of mummification, or a sacrificial altar; the hole on the side of the rock could have been for tying up the llama that was waiting to be sacrificed.

Funerary Rock: a mortician's slab?

Across the open area here at the southernmost extent of Machu Picchu is a large unremarkable building (the largest building on the site) with eight openings in its walls. This is probably a **kallanka [2]**, a hall which provided lodgings for a large number of people. As it is right beside the Inca Trail which runs in here from Intipunku and out to the drawbridge it may also have been used as a rest stop.

Below the Guardhouse are the extensive terraces of the **agricultural sector [3]** (*zona agrícola*). These had to be very carefully constructed to allow adequate drainage given the very high rainfall in this region. Each terrace had a base layer

The Dry Moat divides the agricultural sector from the urban sector.

of stones followed by gravel, sand and then topsoil. Given the number of terraces at Machu Picchu, which is increasing as more are uncovered (recently at Inkaraqay, see p322), it's clear that they could have produced far more food than would have been needed by the city's population of about 750 people. It's been suggested that some of the terraces may have been given over to the cultivation of the sacred coca leaf, which flourishes in this climate and altitude. It would have been in high demand in Cusco.

At the northern side of the agricultural sector and across the **Dry Moat [4]** you reach the main buildings of the city. As well as providing an obstacle that could have provided some defence if Machu Picchu were under attack it also served as the main drain for the city's carefully constructed drainage network.

CITY GATE [5]

There's usually a bottleneck at this handsome trapezoid entryway, partly because people want to admire the fine stonework with its lintel of one hefty stone slab, and partly because it's instinctive to want to stop on stepping through and absorb the

City gate

view. Look back as you do so to see the stone eyelet that probably served as some sort of lock for a door hinged into the stone. The sturdy construction, widening towards the base, is classic Inca design; beautifully fitted stones, no mortar and a form that is said to weather earthquakes. Its size is interesting; this is a doorway, not a magnificent entry to a city – it appears deliberately discreet and low key.

QUARRY [6]

The source for Machu Picchu's stone is within the city itself: you pass the large area of boulders shortly after going through the city gate. To carve their building blocks without iron tools the Inca masons probably employed the labour-intensive neolithic technique known as flaking, using a hammer stone. They may have split stones using wooden wedges hammered into natural cracks. Bingham attempted to show that the Incas used boiling water to split stones but the experiment was unsuccessful. The whackiest suggestion is that the Incas cut the rocks using solar power reflected off large par-

Work in progress at the quarry.

abolic reflectors made of gold but it's certainly true that such objects were found by the conquistadors who promptly melted them down into ingots.

Some rocks have clearly been worked on but it's said that the one that's usually pointed out by the guides (photo above) was actually a modern experiment

Machu Picchu's water
supply still functions

by the archaeologist Manuel Chavez Ballón. This is a good place to come back to when you want to sit and rest; you'll find lots of viscachas (see p333, rabbit-like rodents) sunning themselves on the rocks.

FOUNTAINS STREET [7]

Follow the steps down Fountains Street (*Fuentes*), so named for the 16 watercourses (not actually fountains) that flow along it. Water from the main spring runs for 750m to feed into the topmost of these square cisterns, which descend the hill in a series, getting progressively less fancy as they go. The highest and grandest tank was no doubt reserved for the Inca himself so he would get the cleanest water. Near the bottom of the street is an open-fronted building, known as a *wayrana*, with its thatched roof restored so you can get an idea of how all the buildings would have looked. It shows how the stone pegs protruding at the top of many of the walls were used to secure the roof struts. This wayrana may have been the focus of ceremonial activities involving worship of the water that flowed past it.

Perfect stonework on the tower of the
Temple of the Sun

The Temple of the Sun, just after the
winter solstice

THE TEMPLE OF THE SUN [8]

This tower (*El Torreón*), which curves inwards like a snail shell and encloses a mysterious, tomb-like rock, is surely the most beautiful structure here. Currently roped off, you may only be able to view it from above or below. Bingham went into raptures when he first glimpsed it:

'Owing to the absence of mortar, there are no ugly spaces between the rocks. They might have grown together... The elusive beauty of this chaste, undecorated surface seems to me to be due to the fact that the wall was built under the eye of a master mason who knew not the straight edge, the plumb rule, or the square. He had no instruments of precision, so he had to depend on his eye. He had a good eye, an artistic eye, an eye for symmetry and beauty of form.'

Its stonework is darker and finer than that of the surrounding buildings, it has narrow windows towards the top of the wall and one larger window has holes drilled around the edges, though nobody can be sure of their exact function. It may have been that astronomical instruments were attached to them as this temple was used as an astronomical observatory. At the winter solstice (21st June), the rays of the sun as it rises align perfectly with the rock on the floor of the temple. Niches around the walls of the temple would have held offerings and idols. Animal sacrifices may have taken place on the carved central rock. Excavations nearby also discovered a tomb with excellent stone walls just outside the walls of the *Torreón*, leading some to speculate that this was the tomb of Pachacutec himself. Proponents of this theory also suggest that the Sun Temple had at its heart a gold statue of this, the greatest of the Incas, on top of the rock, which would dazzle in the sunlight on the midwinter sol-

Entrance gate to the Palace of the Princess and Temple of the Sun

stice. It's an appealing theory – though there is no evidence of any gold statue, nor that the tomb was royal – nor, even, that it was a tomb at all.

Stairs lead from the temple down to the fine two-storey building which Bingham fancifully misnamed the **Palace of the Princess** (*Ñusta*). Its position suggests that it was a kind of sacristy used by the high priest presiding over ceremonies in this temple.

The entrance to this area is through one of finest examples of an Inca gate.

THE TOMB OF THE PRINCESS [9]

Right underneath the Temple of the Sun is a striking triangular cave, formed by the hewn edge of the massive supporting boulder and carefully fitted masonry. Inside, a set of steps carved into the natural rock and markedly pale against the darkness, ascend to nowhere. This classic step symbol is often found at Inca sites. It's said to represent the three levels of the world: heaven, earth and the underworld. Again, the 'Princess' title is not based on fact and Bingham found no evidence of bodies buried here and probably didn't expect to as burial was only for the masses; nobles were mummified. It may, however, have been used

as a temporary mausoleum for the mummies of important ancestors of the Inca king, which he would have brought with him when he was staying here.

Guides often explain that the four sites above (the fountains, wayrana, the Temple of the Sun and this tomb), symbolise the four elements of water, air (the wayrana being open on one side), fire and earth. The Incas certainly worshipped the elements but whether they identified these particular four sites as a symbolic group is debatable.

Directly beneath the Temple of the Sun is the Tomb of the Princess

THE ROYAL QUARTER [10]

Apartments in the Royal Quarter

The Inca class system was clearly expressed in stone – the better the dressing, the grander you were – as well as in the distinct division between *hanan* (upper class) and *hurin* (lower class) districts. The fine ashlars used in these buildings, their size and finesse, show that they belonged to the elite. The Royal Apartments are laid out as a classic *kancha* (group of rooms for an extended family), with two large rooms and two wayranas around a central patio. One of the open-sided wayranas would have been used as a kitchen. Attached to one of the large rooms is an addition known as the 'Inca's bathroom' which has a drain in the corner.

WESTERN TERRACES [11]

Walk back up the hill, over and around the quarry, to peer over the back wall at the precipitous terraces. Recent research has shown that in Inca times more varieties of maize and potatoes could be cultivated at altitude than today. Whatever they grew, the engineering is impressive: few slopes are so steep that they have not been terraced. Along the top of the terraces runs the path leading to what was once an Inca bridge, probably made of timber and vines, which crossed a sickening drop and continued down the mountain.

THE PRINCIPAL TEMPLE AND SACRED PLAZA [12]

The small open patch of ground often referred to as the Sacred Plaza (*Sector de los Templos*) is surrounded by buildings which, from their elevated position and sophisticated stonework, obviously had religious significance. The **Principal Temple** is in the wayrana style (open on one side) and has an impressive row of niches all along the back wall. There's some evidence of subsidence here with a large gap opening up on the right-hand side of the temple back wall. In front is a huge block of stone, rising altar-like out of the ground; this may have been

The Sacred Plaza and the Principal Temple

a roof support. There is much speculation about the building; certainly the sun does enter during the winter solstice along an identifiable course and broken pottery remains have been found in the plaza, suggesting some sort of ritual involving the breaking of vessels. Just outside the temple, on the ground, is a kite-shaped rock which is said to be a representation of the stars of the Southern Cross, astronomically important to the Incas. It does, indeed, point south.

Behind the Principal Temple is a separate structure which may have had a priestly function – Bingham named it the **Sacristy** and it's also known as the Ornaments Chamber; it contains a famously elaborate stone, with 32 edges carved into the raw rock, to the left of the doorway. The one on the right has 28 corners.

Temple of Three Windows
(viewed from outside)

Next to the Principal Temple is the **Temple of Three Windows [13]** (*Templo de las Tres Ventanas*), with a wall of perfectly-finished masonry pierced by three trapezoid windows overlooking the ruins below. It was this building that convinced Bingham that he'd located Tampu-tocco, the birthplace of the first Inca, Manco Capac (see p315). The temple actually has five windows, two of which have been blocked up. Opposite the wall of windows and the remains of the roof pillar is a rock carved with the step symbol representing heaven, earth and the underworld.

INTIHUATANA – THE HITCHING POST OF THE SUN [14]

Steps lead up to this startling carved stone, carved in situ into a wide step and squared-off post aiming skywards, the focus of the highest and perhaps the most significant part of this religious section of Machu Picchu. Similar stones were found at many of the Inca ruins and early archaeologists called them *intihuatana* meaning 'place where the sun is tied'. In winter, believing the sun was drifting further from the Earth, the Incas felt compelled to ritually secure it to hitching posts such as this one lest the life-giving sun desert them permanently. The festival of Inti Raymi was (and still is) held at the winter solstice (21st June). Realising their importance to Inca culture, the Spanish settlers damaged every intihuatana they found by breaking off the post; this post was the sole complete survivor.

The archaeologist Johan Reinhard has shown that Machu Picchu was carefully aligned with sacred peaks, the intihuatana being at its very centre. The top of Huayna Picchu, for example, is due north. The position of the sun and stars was important to the Incas both for religious reasons and, more prosaically, in order to chart the progress of the seasons which was important to farmers so that seeds were planted at the right time to allow for the best harvest. At the equinoxes the sun rises behind the summit of Nevado Veronica. The careful alignment of the intihuatana means that it was probably used as an observatory. It has also been suggested that the stone was a

Rock in the shape of
The Southern Cross

sundial but this is unlikely as the Incas had no concept of time in terms of hours and minutes.

Reinhard has also done some fascinating work on structures built to replicate significant mountains. From the south of the stone, look north towards Huayna Picchu and the shape of the intihuatana does appear to be a conscious imitation of the mountain behind it. If ever there was a stone with presence, however, this is it – which only added to the national fury when it was damaged during a beer commercial shoot in 2000.

Visitors under the guidance of a local shaman offer prayers to the setting sun, beside the Intihuatana

THE CENTRAL PLAZA [15]

This huge rectangle of flat green grass is a welcome breathing space amongst all the steep steps and stones and is generally grazed by a llama or two. It must have been significant with so little space available and was probably used for commerce and wider ceremonial purposes. Anyone who has seen the (now colossal) Inti

Viscacha

Raymi celebrations in Cusco or at Tiahuanaco at the winter solstice can imagine a smaller version of the event happening here. It could also be the place where a young Che Guavara played soccer, as recounted in *The Motorcycle Diaries*.

In the south of this plaza, near the Temple of Three Windows, is a small collection of **plants [16]** that would have grown here in Inca times. As well as various orchids, *yuca* (the cassava root and foodstuff, not yucca the decorative plant), strawberries and moonflower there are coca plants, all helpfully labelled.

THE SACRED ROCK [17]

Beside the entry gate to Huayna Picchu this large rock faces a small open square with two thatched wayrana on opposite sides of it. The rock itself is a huge slab, again made significant by its enclosure by its neighbouring buildings and the plaza. Its very position shows it was an object of veneration and its surface may well originally have been polished like the sacred

The Sacred Rock

rocks found at Ollantaytambo. Its shape seems to mimic the mountains behind it.

(**Opposite**): The Intihuatana. This photo was taken before it was damaged during the filming of a Cusqueña beer commercial when a camera platform collapsed onto it.

GROUP OF THE THREE DOORWAYS [18]

You are now in the residential area to the north-east of the site that was probably occupied by less elevated inhabitants – perhaps the people who did the work, fed and looked after the nobility, maintained the terraces and harvested the crops. It is so called because there are three fine doorways to be seen. Below it is another cemetery area, east facing, and outside the Machu Picchu equivalent of the city limits.

EASTERN TERRACES

Covering an area of four hectares, this is the most extensive set of terraces at Machu Picchu. Not quite as steep as their western counterparts but impressive nonetheless, there are two sections: a smaller run set below the lower residential area and a whole hillside of them, facing due east below. The terraces were constructed between 1470 and 1530 and include ceremonial watercourses.

INDUSTRIAL OR MORTAR SECTOR [19]

Bingham quite understandably believed, when he saw that one of the buildings in this more crowded, commercial zone had mysterious, crater-like protrusions on the floor of its courtyard, that they were mortars for grinding corn. It is now

thought that the surfaces are too flat for the purpose. It is possible that they may have had some sort of astronomical function; water may have been poured into them, for example, and celestial events such as eclipses observed in reflection.

TEMPLE OF THE CONDOR [20]

This is one of most mysterious structures at Machu Picchu. On the ground is a piece of dark granite, unmistakably polished and wrought into the shape of a condor seen from above, with its distinctive head and white collar formed by a separate piece of stone. If you have a very vivid imagination you may be able to identify the swoops of natural rock behind as wings. The Incas worshipped the Apu Kuntur (Condor God) and even today some Andean villages such as Cotabambas celebrate the Yawar Fiesta. In this a captured condor, the spirit of the Incas, is tied to the back of a bull symbolising the Spanish Conquistadors.

Temple of the Condor
(red lines showing how the rocks behind may be seen as the wings)

The Jail

Surprisingly, the condor actually often overpowers the bull, lashing at it with its beak, drawing blood and gouging out the bull's eyes. If the fight goes to plan, the bull dies and the condor is released, the Inca god triumphing over the Spanish to bring good fortune to the village.

The rock beneath the natural rock has been hollowed into small vaults, sometimes referred to, with wistful relish, as 'jails'. This idea was first suggested by Bingham who referred to these buildings as the Prison Group. Some guides will tell you that prisoners may have been held here and in the buildings behind. In the so-called **jail** there are human-sized niches with holes in the stones halfway up each side to which the arms of the prisoners could have been bound. This is unlikely as it's believed that the Incas didn't have prisons; wrongdoers were dealt with immediately: either by being put to death or by losing their privileges.

STORAGE HUTS [21]

Cross the terraces of the agricultural sector again to return to the entrance. Bingham referred to these huts as barracks, but being located conveniently at the end of the agricultural terraces, it is likely that they functioned either as housing for farmers or storage huts for tools and supplies, or both. Some have been rethatched.

SIDE TRIPS

A considerable feat of Inca engineering, the **drawbridge** is a worthwhile (short) excursion. The main Inca Trail skirts through the southern end of the ruins via the guardhouse and the kallanka to reach the drawbridge. A stone wall was built against the cliff face with planks to cross the gap in the middle. These could have been withdrawn to close this entrance to the city. Since a visitor

Agricultural sector and storage huts

plunged to his death from the bridge the path has been closed a short distance before it but you can get a good view of the drawbridge from the viewpoint. It takes about 20 minutes each way from the guardhouse; the path climbs steeply for the first five minutes and then levels out, clinging to the cliff edge with superb views across the valley.

If you didn't reach Machu Picchu by following the main Inca Trail it's well worth walking up it to **Intipunku (The Sun Gate)**. The robust stone paving on the path is still intact after all these years. Allow 1-1½ hours to walk there and back, with some time at the gate to sit and enjoy the superb views back over the ruins.

Inca drawbridge

Overleaf: Machu Picchu © Henry Stedman

MACHU PICCHU

APPENDIX A: THE VILCABAMBA TRAIL:
a trek through the last stronghold of the Incas

For those whose thirst for Inca ruins remain unquenched, and who have found the other treks in this book a little, well, tame, there is the possibility of exploring the wild and remote Vilcabamba region and to visit the very last Inca capital. Following the Spanish conquest of Cusco in 1534, Manco Inca and his followers fled to this region, building (so it is believed) their first capital at Vitcos, near the modern-day town of Huancacalle, before heading even further into the forest to construct their final stronghold at a place we now call Espíritu Pampa.

The trek between these two capitals is an exceptional, strenuous and rarely tackled 3- to 4-day walk through the forest. The trail follows a route believed to be similar to that taken by Manco Inca as he fled the Spanish in 1537 and later taken by the conquistadors themselves in their two invasions of Vilcabamba in 1539 and 1572.

The ruins at Espíritu Pampa (Vilcabamba La Vieja), although substantial, do not bear close comparison with those on the Inca Trail or at Choquequirao. Nevertheless, these partially uncovered ruins, cloaked by tree roots, lianas and thick vegetation offer a glimpse of how early explorers and pioneers would have encountered them. In addition, the route, an original Inca trail that retains some of its distinctive giant paving slabs, is stunningly beautiful and takes you through almost every type of ecological zone in Peru, offering excellent opportunities to see flora and fauna not usually encountered elsewhere.

PRACTICALITIES

Until recently there were some issues over safety in the area, with reports of increased activity by narco-traffickers in parts of the jungle. As a result you should **check on the situation before setting out** and also hire an arriero to help carry your equipment and act as a guide. Experienced arrieros can be engaged in Huancacalle (see p341). Alternatively, there are a handful of agencies that run treks on this trail, who will supply guides and mules as part of the package (see pp177-82).

The trail is best tackled between May and October. Outside these months the trail can be very wet and muddy – at times the narrow, slippery paths are virtually impassable – and you will struggle to find a guide or arriero happy to take you. No permits are currently required; facilities en route are basic too, with no designated campsites or flush toilets. Bridges often get washed away by the swollen rivers during the rains and landslips loosened by the wet weather invariably obliterate the trail in places.

There's no accommodation or opportunity to resupply along the trail so a tent, camping equipment and food must be brought with you. No special equipment is required, although a machete might come in handy if the trail is overgrown: your arriero ought to have one of these. Make sure you have plenty of wet-weather gear and that your kit is stored in waterproof bags as there is a higher than usual chance of it getting soaked in this part of the region. Insect repellent is also essential as the trail can be plagued by mosquitoes, and you must have some sort of anti-malarial medication.

To get the most out of your trek and fully appreciate the history and significance of the region and the ruins, you should also read up about the Vilcabamba district (see p43).

(Opposite) Top: Hummingbird (see p113). **Bottom**: Eromboni Pampa (see p344) at Espíritu Pampa, (Vilcabamba La Vieja). The overgrown ruins here are still much as they were when Bingham saw them in 1914. (Photo © Henry Stedman).

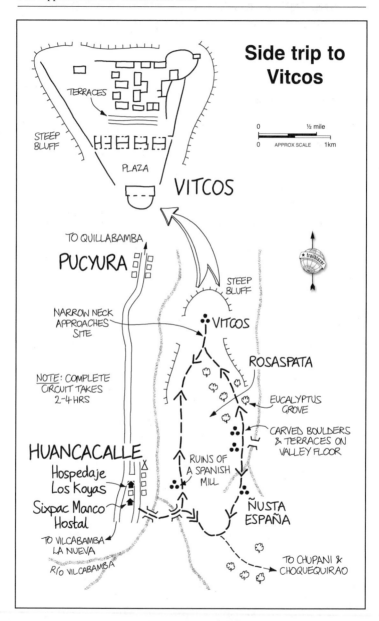

TERRACES

STEEP
BLUFF

PLAZA

VITCOS

Side trip to Vitcos

0   ½ mile

0   APPROX SCALE   1km

TO QUILLABAMBA

PUCYURA

STEEP
BLUFF

NARROW NECK
APPROACHES
SITE

VITCOS

ROSASPATA

NOTE: COMPLETE
CIRCUIT TAKES
2-4 HRS

EUCALYPTUS
GROVE

CARVED BOULDERS
& TERRACES ON
VALLEY FLOOR

HUANCACALLE

Hospedaje
Los Koyas

Sixpac Manco
Hostal

RUINS OF
A SPANISH
MILL

ÑUSTA
ESPAÑA

TO VILCABAMBA
LA NUEVA

RÍO VILCABAMBA

TO CHUPANI &
CHOQUEQUIRAO

GETTING TO THE TRAILHEAD

The trek begins in Huancacalle. To get there, take the bus from Cusco's Santiago Bus Terminal to Quillabamba (7 hours). In Quillabamba, the **bus stations** for Huancacalle and Cusco are several blocks south of Plaza Grau; minibuses depart for Huancacalle before noon (4-5 hours; s/10-15). After visiting the ruins most people continue on the trail to the village of Chaunquiri (see p342), which is occasionally served by public transport. To maximise your chances of picking up a bus aim to reach the village in time for the weekend markets, after which you should be able to find a ride. Bear in mind it takes a long time to travel to the Vilcabamba region and that you may want to spend a day in and around Huancacalle, exploring the nearby ruins and archaeological sites. So, you should allow at least a week for the entire trip and possibly as many as nine days.

Huancacalle is a simple, typical Andean town set in a very pleasant part of the Vilcabamba valley, and you can hire arrieros and guides and pick up a smattering of last-minute provisions here. The best **accommodation**, *Sixpac Manco Hostal* (☎ 812714), at the far end of the village, is run by the Cobos family. This family are also the best-known and most reliable guides in the region. There are few other facilities in town.

VISITING VITCOS

Before your Vilcabamba trek you can take a pleasant half-day side-trip from Huancacalle to Vitcos. Here, on the crest of the hill known as **Rosaspata**, are the ruins of Manco Inca's first capital following their retreat from Cusco in 1537. Discovered by Hiram Bingham in 1911, this was the centre of operations for the Incas whilst in exile. On the far side of the plaza stands a series of finely crafted ashlars and double-jamb entrances opening onto large rooms filled with niches. Look out, too, for a finely carved stone throne.

It is believed to be at Vitcos that Manco Inca met with his untimely end, stabbed to death after a game of quoits by Spanish renegades who had come to Vitcos to seek refuge after assassinating Francisco Pizarro. Manco's son, Titu Cusi, witnessed the attack and the assassins were burnt to death by Manco's supporters. Their severed heads were paraded at Vitcos and staked there for more than 20 years as a gruesome reminder of their fate. Titu Cusi went on to become Inca in his turn and later also died at Vitcos, following a severe illness.

A path heads south from Rosaspata via a number of **carved boulders** to the site known variously as **Ñusta España**, Yurac Rumi (White Stone), or Chuquipalta. Sculpted boulders, carved stone seats, water channels and baths surround an enormous carved granite boulder

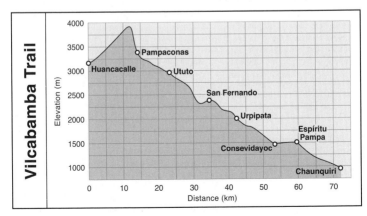

more than seven metres tall and fifteen metres wide. This giant *huaca* was the spiritual centre of the exiled Inca state. A Spanish priest, Antonio de la Calancha, recorded that a devil 'captain of a legion of devils' used to inhabit the rock. Such was the fear of this creature and the dislike of the Inca habit of worshipping natural objects such as stone that in 1570 two Augustinian friars exorcised the rock and had it burnt.

THE VILCABAMBA TRAIL – AN OVERVIEW

The trek begins by following the dirt road that snakes westwards from Huancacalle via the village of San Francisco de la Vitoria de Vilcabamba to the **Ccolpa Casa Pass** (3900m/12,792ft), which marks the boundary between the Andes and the Amazon basin, before descending and undulating across the puna to the crossroads at **Mollipunku**. Great slabs of Inca paving and original steps descend from here to the Río Chalca and the **Puente Antiguo**, from where the higher of two trails to Ututo takes you past **Pampaconas** (3340m/10,955ft) and the **remnants of an Inca plaza and platform** that were used by the Incas for ceremonial sun worship. Titu Cusi also gave permission for the first Christian cross in the region to be erected here.

Having camped at **Ututo**, on the second day most people choose as their destination the collection of scattered houses known as **Vista Alegre**, the trail leaving the fields and pasture behind in favour of virgin forest, passing the site of the Inca fort **Huayna Pucará** on the way. Continuing through ever-thickening forest on the third day, the path now leads you via **Urpipata** to **Consevidayoc**, thought by Vincent Lee to be the site of Marcanay, where Friar Diego Ortiz was martyred for failing to cure the Inca Titu Cusi with medicine he had given him. Climbing through plantations, the trail eventually ascends via a set of steps to the top of the hill and the remnants of a small Inca building thought to have been a **watchtower** which looks out over the broad, restored Inca steps that sweep down towards **Vilcabamba La Vieja**, with the ruins of **Espíritu Pampa** just 10 minutes away.

From the ruins, the trek's final stage to Chaunquiri is short but taxing, as the combination of exertion and heat can be debilitating. In **Chaunquiri** you can *camp* in the central square to await your bus back to **Kiteni**, two hours away. (It is possible to walk there, but this is a long, dry, full-day's trek.) From Kiteni you can pick up a bus or truck to **Quillabamba**, which is 7-9 hours away (s/15). If you are lucky you may even find a direct truck from Chaunquiri to Quillabamba.

THE RUINS OF ESPÍRITU PAMPA   [Map p344]

Some 400 ruins lie concealed by jungle and vegetation at Espíritu Pampa, which literally translates as the 'Plain of the Spirits'. Bingham gave a good indication of the thickness of the vegetation and the challenge in spotting, let alone uncovering, the ruins when he wrote that: 'Nothing gives a better idea of the density of the jungle than the fact that the savages themselves have been within five feet of these fine walls without being aware of their existence'. It also explains why he failed to uncover the extent of the city or recognise its true scale and importance. Even today only a handful of the most important structures have been uncovered, with very little reconstruction having taken place.

Although archaeologists have discovered that the Incas weren't the first culture to reside here, Espíritu Pampa was built according to an Inca template and the layout is reminiscent of other sites. The central section where you first arrive is the most carefully cleared and exposed part of the site. The trail to the impressively large central plaza passes several carefully carved **baths** and crosses a **bridge** over an Inca canal. In the **plaza** several giant kapok trees still stand; an indication of just how much vegetation subsumed the site. The plaza is backed by a long **kallanka** and **terraces** surround it. There are also lots of shards of imitation Spanish roof tiles, scattered around the site along with stone pegs and eye-bonders that would have been used to secure the thatched roofs. A sculpted stone phallus found at the site is also displayed in the main plaza, although where this would have

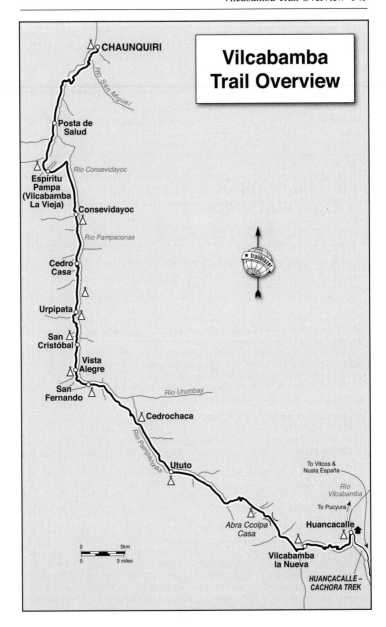

Vilcabamba
Trail Overview

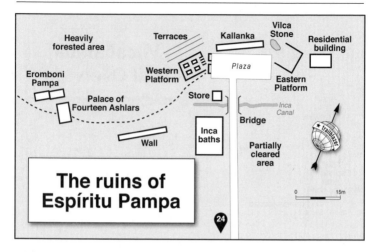

The ruins of Espíritu Pampa

Labels: Heavily forested area, Terraces, Kallanka, Vilca Stone, Residential building, Eromboni Pampa, Western Platform, Plaza, Eastern Platform, Palace of Fourteen Ashlars, Store, Inca Canal, Wall, Inca baths, Bridge, Partially cleared area, trailblazer, 0 15m, 24

originally been sited or what its purpose was, is unclear. Other features include a number of crumbling walls that have niches in them; another has three carved water spouts jutting from it, which would have created small fountains.

In the north-east corner of the plaza is a huaca; the **Vilca stone** is a giant, uncarved boulder leaning slightly on its side and described as looking 'like a great egg' by Gene Savoy. A couple of minutes to the south of the plaza is a lengthy striking stone wall now covered in moss. Beyond this lies the section originally uncovered by Bingham, called **Eromboni Pampa**, where the **Palace of Fourteen Ashlars** stands.

Beyond this, the outskirts of this considerable city are subsumed by the jungle, providing a fascinating 'before and after' feel to the site. The still-buried ruins await discovery by you; be careful moving vegetation though so as to not disturb any of the stones.

For a fuller picture of the site, check out Vincent Lee's book *Forgotten Vilcabamba*, which contains maps and drawings of the ruins.

So is this place really Manco's capital?
Though he was responsible for their discovery in 1914, Hiram Bingham in fact refused to believe that the small collection of buildings he found was the last capital of the Incas and got himself into all sorts of intellectual knots arguing that Machu Picchu must have been the last city of the Incas simply because it looked more suitable and majestic. In fact, it wasn't until 1964 that **Gene Savoy** realised the extent of the ruins and exposed the true scale of the site. Though it's true they are less spectacular than other major Inca sites, the distinctive layout, style of craftsmanship and stonework coupled with the features found at the site including canals, baths, ashlars and sacred rocks are all indicative of Inca architecture and conclusively prove that this place is of Inca origin.

Debate has raged as to whether the site constituted Manco's final capital, though. The giant sweeping staircase that descends to the site and the Vilca stone, positioned to dominate the plaza and eerily reminiscent of the celebrated *huaca* Ñusta España (see p341), lends weight to the theory that the site also had a special ceremonial significance. Furthermore the uncovering of a number of terracotta roof tiles, imitations of Spanish roof tiles, prove that the site must have been built after the arrival of the Spanish conquistadors. The type of structures built, allied to the date when they would most likely have been constructed, suggest that the site is indeed the last Inca capital, Vilcabamba.

There is, however, no absolute proof that this is the case and some doubts do still remain. Evidence to support descriptions in some of the chronicles of the time is inconclusive; although modern-day Pampaconas still bears the same name as that used by the conquistadors, Marcanay may or may not be the modern village of Consevidayoc; Huayna Pucará is more than likely the site of the Inca ambush that went horribly wrong, but Machu Pucará may or may not be the actual site of the Inca Old Fort. As John Hemming wrote in *Conquest of the Incas*, 'Unless someone can discover another ruin that so exactly fulfils the geographical and topographical details known about Vilcabamba, and that also contains imitation Spanish roofing tiles, the lost city of Vilcabamba has finally been located as Espíritu Pampa'.

APPENDIX B: QUECHA & SPANISH

Although Spanish is the main language of Peru, you will find that Quechua, also known as *Runasimi*, is widely spoken in the Andes. Although spoken by a number of Andean tribes prior to the spread of the Inca empire, the language was adopted by the Incas to unify their multilingual subjects and consolidate their empire.

After the Spanish Conquest, Quechua continued to be used largely as the general language and main means of communication between the Spanish and indigenous people, so continued to expand its range, but all administrative use of the language was banned in the late 18th century in the wake of the Túpac Amaru II revolution. Despite a brief revival post-independence the language has generally declined and is increasingly restricted to rural areas but it is still one of the most widespread indigenous languages in the Americas. It remains a largely oral language as there is a lack of written material. There is, though, a realisation of Quechua's value as a national symbol and vehicle for promoting native culture.

QUECHUA

Quechua is quite a guttural, 'throaty' language and sounds quite strange to those encountering it for the first time; indeed, one of the creatures in Star Wars is reported to have spoken Quechua, the makers rightly thinking that it sounded truly alien to most ears.

Quechua and Spanish have become intermixed over the years and there are lots of Spanish loan words in Quechua. There are also some Quechua loan words in English, via Spanish. These include ayahuasca, coca, condor, llama, puma, quinoa and vicuña.

Until the 20th century Quechua was written using Spanish spelling (eg Inca, huayna, collasuyu, quipu, condor), making it more familiar to Spanish speakers and also easier to use for borrowings into English. In 1975 the Peruvian government adopted a new orthography (eg Inka, wayna, Qollasuyu, khipu, kuntur). The different spellings are still highly controversial in Peru. The Spanish system, which is largely used in this book, is more readable, makes Quechua easier to learn and is how place names are usually depicted on maps. The newer form is, however, thought to be a better phonology of Quechua.

The only readily available book is *Quechua Phrasebook*, published by Lonely Planet.

SPANISH

The conquistadors brought their language with them to South America. Over time Castillian Spanish evolved into Latin American Spanish, an arbitrary name for the idiomatic and native expressions and specific vocabulary of Spanish spoken in Latin America. The version of the language spoken here is a dialect of Castillian Spanish as opposed to a distinct language, even though it contains various features that distinguish it from European

Spanish. The differences are akin to those between British English and US English. Apart from slang or extreme colloquialisms, the main differences are in pronunciation, rhythm, grammar and unique vocabulary.

Particular pitfalls are 'll', pronounced 'y', 'hu' pronounced 'w', 'q' pronounced 'k' and the 'c' in 'ce' or 'ci' pronounced 's' (rather than with the 'th' lisp) and 'v' as in English rather than as 'b'. Stress goes on the penultimate syllable unless there's an accent to indicate an alternative stress.

ENGLISH	QUECHUA	SPANISH
General words and phrases		
Hello / Good day	¡Napaikulyaiki!	¡Buenos días!
Goodbye	Hokhkootikama	Adiós
See you	Ratukama	Hasta luego
Mr / Sir	Tayta	Señor
Madam	Mama	Señora
How are you?	¿Allillanchu?	¿Cómo está usted?
What's your name?	¿Iman sutiyki?	¿Cómo se llama usted?
I'm ...	... -n sutiy	Me llamo ...
Please / Thank you	Allichu / Añáy	Por favor / Gracias
Excuse me	Munayniykimanta	Con permiso
Sorry (apologies)	Pampachayuay	Discúlpame
Where are you going?	¿Maytataq rishanki?	¿Adónde vas?
What's this called?	¿Imatataq kaypa sutin?	¿Qué es esto?
Can I stay here?	¿Puñupayukuykimanchu?	¿Puedo pasar la noche aquí?
Yes / No	Arí / Mana	Sí / No
impossible	mana atina	imposible
good / bad	allinmi / manan allinchu	bueno / malo
beautiful	añañá	bonito
hot / cold	ruphay / ch'ulli	calor / frío
rain / snow	para / rit'i	lluvia / nieve
wind	wayra	viento
Directions		
left / right	lloq'e / paña	izquierda / derecha
here / there	kaypi / chaypi	aquí / ahí, allá
over there	haqay	por ahí
up / down	wichay / uray	arriba / abajo
near	sispa	cerca
far (far off)	karu	lejos
straight ahead	dirichu	derecho
everywhere	maypipas	en todas partes
Where is a / the ...?	¿Maypin ...?	¿Dónde está ...?
... bus / truck / minibus	... omnibus / karro	... el bus / el camión / el minibus
... bus station	(N/A)	...la estacíon de autobuses
... hotel / hostel	... qorpa wasi	... el hotel / hostal
... house	... wasi	... la casa
... pass	... q'asa	... el abra
... path	... ñan	... el camino, el sendero
... railway station	... ferrocarril	... el estacón de ferrocarril
... river	... mayu	... el río
... toilet	... bañu	... los baños
... village	... llaqta, marka	... el pueblo
... water / ... food	...unu / ... mikuna	... agua / ... la comida

ENGLISH	QUECHUA	SPANISH

When?

When?	*¿Hayk'aq?*	*¿Cuándo?*
soon	*kunan*	*pronto*
right now	*kunallan, kunanpacha!*	*ahora mismo*
later	*qhepata*	*más tarde / luego*
never	*manan hayk'aqpas*	*nunca*
today	*kunanmi*	*hoy*
tomorrow	*qayantin*	*mañana*
yesterday	*qayna*	*ayer*

Help!

Help me!	*!Yanapaway!*	*¡Socorro!*
Take me to a hospital	*Uspitalman pusaway*	*Llévame al hospital*
It hurts	*Nanan*	*Me duele*
I'm cold	*Chiriwashan*	*Tengo frío*
I'm hungry	*Yarqawashan*	*Tengo hambre*
I'm thirsty	*Ch'akiwashan*	*Tengo sed*
I'm tired	*Sayk'usqa kan*	*Estoy cansado*
I'm hot	*Q'uñi*	*Tengo calor*
I've got a headache	*Umaimi nanawan*	*Tengo un dolor de cabeza*

Numerals

	Quechua	Spanish		Quechua	Spanish
1	*u'/ huk*	*uno*	18	*chunka pusaqniyuq*	*dieciocho*
2	*iskay*	*dos*	19	*chunka isqunniyuq*	*diecinueve*
3	*kinsa*	*tres*	20	*iskay chunka*	*veinte*
4	*tawa*	*cuatro*	21	*iskay chunka hukniyuq*	*veintiuno*
5	*pisqa*	*cinco*	30	*kinsa chunka*	*treinta*
6	*suqta*	*seis*	40	*tawa chunka*	*cuarenta*
7	*qanchis*	*siete*	50	*pisqa chunka*	*cincuenta*
8	*pusaq*	*ocho*	60	*suqta chunka*	*sesenta*
9	*iskun*	*nueve*	70	*qanchis chunka*	*setenta*
10	*chunka*	*diez*	80	*pusaq chunka*	*ochenta*
11	*chunka hukniyuq*	*once*	90	*iskun chunka*	*noventa*
12	*chunka iskayniyuq*	*doce*	100	*pachak*	*cien*
13	*chunka kinsayuq*	*trece*	101	*pachak hukniyuq*	*ciento uno*
14	*chunka tawayuq*	*catorce*	200	*iskay pachak*	*doscientos*
15	*chunka pisqayuq*	*quince*	1000	*waranqa*	*mil*
16	*chunka suqtayuq*	*dieciséis*	2000	*iskay waranqa*	*dos mil*
17	*chunka qanchisniyuq*	*diecisiete*	1,000,000	*hunu*	*un millón*

Money and costs

money	*qolqe*	*dinero / plata*
How much is ...?	*¿Maik'ata'g ...?*	*¿Cuánto cuesta ...?*
... that one	*... haqay, chay*	*... eso/a*
more / less	*aswan / aswan pisi*	*más / menos*
a little	*chika, pisi*	*un poco, poquito*
big, large	*hatun*	*grande*
small, little	*huch'uy*	*pequeño/a*

ENGLISH	**QUECHUA**	**SPANISH** *(cont'd from p347)*
How much does it cost to hire ...?	*¿Maik'ata'g ...?*	*¿Cuánto cuesta para...?*
... a guide	*... pusawasqaykimanta*	*... contratar un guía?*
... a horse	*... caballoykikunamanta*	*... alquilar un caballo?*
... a llama	*... llamaykikunamanta*	*... alquilar una llama?*
... for a week / day	*... sapa semanan / p'unchay*	*... por semana / día*
Do you sell ...?	*¿Icha ... ta bendiwankiman?*	*¿Me vende ...?*

Food and drink (see pp81-3)

beer	*sirwisa*	*cerveza*
bread	*t'anta*	*pan*
chicken	*wallpa*	*pollo*
coca	*kuka*	*coca*
egg	*runtu*	*huevo*
fish	*challwa*	*pescado*
fruit	*ruru, añawi*	*fruta*
maize (corn)	*choqllo (sara)*	*maíz (choclo)*
meat (dried)	*aycha (ch'arki)*	*carne (charqui)*
potato	*papa*	*papa*
soup	*chupi*	*sopa*
roast	*kanka*	*asado*
boil	*t'impuy*	*hervir*
fry	*theqtichiy*	*freír*
raw	*hanku*	*crudo*
cooked	*chayasqa*	*cocido*
fizzy drink / pop	*bebida gaseosa*	*bebida gaseosa*
hot (temperature)	*q'oñi*	*caliente*
spicy	*haya*	*picante*
cold food	*kharmu*	*comida fría*

Food and drink glossary

ají hot pepper from which a spicy sauce is made

ají de gallina shredded chicken stewed in a rich, gently spiced cream sauce

anticucho beef-heart kebabs cooked on a skewer over hot coals and served with a range of spicy sauces

bodega wine shop or bar that also serves snacks

butifarra pork and sweet onion salsa sandwich; the pork is cooked with pepper, garlic, cumin, achiote and oregano

cafecito small black coffee

cañazo strong alcoholic spirit distilled from sugar cane

cantina a bar room

causa / causa rellena a lightly spiced potato cake mixed with tuna, egg, shrimp, avocado or chicken

ceviche / cevichería (also *cebiche / cebichería*) raw fish marinated in citrus juice and spiced with chilli / restaurant that serves ceviche

chicha de jora Peru's famous fermented maize beer

chicha morada a drink made from purple maize (corn) and spices

chicharron(es) deep-fried pork & pork skin

chuño type of traditional freeze-dried potato

cuy guinea pig

huacatay an aromatic Andean herb

leche de tigre literally 'tiger's milk', a mixture of lime juice, salt and hot pepper used to 'cook' classic ceviche

llipta a mixture of lime or quinoa and potash taken with a plug of coca leaves and chewed together to release the active ingredients in the leaves

Food and drink glossary (cont'd)

lomo cordon bleu beef loin steak stuffed with cheese and ham

lomo milanesa beef loin beaten into a thin steak and fried in breadcrumbs

lomo a lo pobre beef loin fried with an egg on top

lomo saltado strips of beef stir-fried with onions, spicy orange peppers, tomatoes and soy sauce, served with rice and fried potatoes

mercado market

moraya freeze-dried potato

Novoandina style of fusion cuisine that combines modern techniques, traditional raw materials and both Peruvian and Asian culinary ideas

pachamanca traditional feast cooked in an earth oven beneath hot stones

parrillada BBQ/grill method of cooking, also a plate of grilled meat and a restaurant that serves this kind of meat

picantería a traditional local restaurant often serving spicy food

pisco sour drink made from pisco (Peruvian spirit), lemon and egg white

quinoa an Andean grain-like crop grown for its edible seeds

tamal(es) steamed or boiled dough stuffed with meat, veg, cheese or fruit.

APPENDIX C: GLOSSARY

AMS acute mountain sickness

abra high mountain pass

aclla a 'chosen woman' of the Inca, an Inca nun

acllahuasi convent or nunnery

alpaca type of domesticated camelid resembling a small llama, bred for its wool

altiplano an area of high-altitude plateau

amauta Inca oral historian who cultivated their myths and legends

andene broad agricultural terrace or set of terraces built on Andean slopes

andesite igneous volcanic rock common in mountains of North and South America, including the Andes, after which it is named

Antis collective term for tribes living in Antisuyu and the rainforest

Antisuyu the eastern part of the Inca empire, bordering the upper Amazon

apacheta cairn; pile of stones

apu / apus god(s) or spirit(s) of the mountains that protect local people in high areas

arpilleras appliqué pictures illustrating Peruvian life and traditions

arriero muleteer, wrangler of pack animals

ashlar sculpted square blocks of stone or any dressed stonework

audiencia a seat of government of Spanish South America; also type of court set up to administer royal justice

awaska type of cloth garment worn daily by ordinary people

ayllu Inca kinship group

Aymara ethnic group living to south and east of Lake Titicaca and their language

baño (when used archaeologically) a ceremonial bath

barranca/o ravine

cabildos town councils

cacique leader of indigenous tribe

calle street

cambista money-changer

cambio (bureau de change) place to exchange money

campesino Peruvian peasant or worker of the land

cancha small plot of land or block of houses in an Inca town

casona large house/mansion

caudillos the military leaders at the time of Peruvian independence *cejas de la selva* literally 'eyebrows of the jungle' (the eastern slopes of the Andes, fringed with forest)

ceques sacred lines radiating from the centre of the Sun Temple in Cusco and passing through a set of huacas or shrines

cerro mountain

ceviche / cevichería see box p81

chacos royal hunts

chasqui messenger or courier usually operating as part of a relay

Chinchaysuyu the northern quarter of the Inca Empire

chullo type of traditional woolly hat

chullpa tomb or burial chamber

ciudadela high-walled enclosure housing a series of storage rooms, a large platform cum burial place and a number of audiencias or audience rooms

coca plant used by Peruvians to ease altitude sickness and for stamina and health; the basic ingredient of cocaine

colectivo shared taxi that plies a set route (name is often used interchangeably with *micro* and *combi*)

Collasuyu south-eastern province of the Inca Empire

collpas clay licks ie areas of exposed clay where parakeets congregate to eat the soil in order to get salt

Condesuyu the south-western quarter of the Inca Empire

conquistadors Spanish explorer soldiers who conquered South America in the 15th and 16th centuries

Coricancha Inca Sun Temple

corregidor chief magistrate appointed by the king of Spain; local, administrative and judicial position

correos post office

costa coast

Coya the Inca's sister, his official wife and high priestess

Creole Peruvian-born person of European descent

Criolla Creole-style music and cooking predominately found along the coast

Curaca Inca name for local noble

double-jamb an entrance or doorway framed by two jambs (vertical columns) indicating an important access point

El Niño A weather phenomenon where a band of anomalously warm ocean water temperatures develops off the western coast of South America and causes climatic changes across the Pacific Ocean

encomendero name given to the owner of an encomienda

encomienda plot of land governed by a Spaniard whose native inhabitants paid tribute to an encomendero

eye-bonder archaeological term for the pierced stones found in Inca buildings, often round or protruding from walls or gables; probably used for securing thatched roofs and hanging doors

fuente fountain; source of water

garúa low level cloud formed on the coast during cooler months of the year

gnomon a carved vertical stone

guanaco type of wild camelid related to the llama and alpaca

guano sea bird excrement used as a fertiliser

HACE / HAPE rare conditions of high-altitude sickness caused by ascending too quickly, which can be fatal

Hanan Inca clan division, also a part of an Inca town, more powerful/prestigious than Hurin (see below)

hospedaje lodging, accommodation

huaca sacred spot, usually a sculpted stone or feature in the landscape

huaquero tomb-robber or treasure-hunter

huayna small or young, opposite of machu

huayno form of Peruvian Andean music with high-pitched vocals

Hurin Inca clan division, also a part of an Inca town, less powerful/prestigious than Hanan (see above)

INC Instituto Nacional de Cultura, the government department responsible for managing and preserving archaeological sites

Inca see Sapa Inca

Indios Indians

Indigenismo early 20th-century political movement

Inti the sun, and the name of the Sun God

Intihuatana ritual stone, literally the 'hitching post of the sun'

Inti Raymi Inca religious festival to observe the winter solstice and honour the god Inti; now recreated and a major tourist attraction

jirón (jr) street

kallanka Inca meeting hall

llama a South American camelid (relative of the camel) used in Andean countries as a pack and food animal

machay cave

machu old, big, opposite of huayna

mamacona mother superior in a convent that is dedicated to serving the Inca

mestizo person of mixed Indian and European blood

micro public transport minibus, also known as a *combi*; similar to a *colectivo*

mirador viewpoint

mit'a Inca tax, often paid in compulsory community labour

mitimaes Inca settlers transplanted to perform mit'a in another part of the country

mochadero common Indian word for their shrines

nevado mountain peak, usually covered in snow

orejones literally 'big-ears', slang term used to refer to Hispanics and by the Inca to refer to conquistadors

oroya traditional cable-car style river crossing using a cage attached to a zip line and manoeuvred over the river by a series of ropes

Pachamama goddess revered by Andean Indians, literally Earth Mother

pampa plain, or occasionally any small, flat area

panaca the tradition of preserving the estate of a dead person

peña a bar or club featuring live folkloric music

picka basic method of Inca construction

polylepis type of shrub/tree species endemic to the mid and high elevation areas of the Andes

posta de salud health station

pucará Inca fort

pueblos jóvenes shanty town or slum

puna high-altitude grassland, usually above the treeline

Punchao a sacred idol of the sun from Cusco's Sun Temple, looted by the conquistadors

Q'enko sacred sculpted stone near Cusco

qeros a drinking vessel, especially for chicha

quebrada deep, sheer-sided river valley

Quechua native South American language spoken primarily in the Andes and used by the Incas, also refers to the Incas' descendants currently living in Peru

quipus literally 'talking knots', a recording device of knotted strings used by the Incas; could only be read by skilled interpreters, the quipucamayos

qollqa Inca storehouse

qompi fine fabric woven for the Inca

raccay ruins

Runasimi the Quechua word for the language, literally 'people's speech'

Sapa Inca the Great Inca, the Inca emperor and ruler of Cusco and the empire, also known simply as 'the Inca'

sapo traditional Peruvian game

sierra highland region

selva jungle

sol(es) unit of Peruvian currency

soroche altitude sickness

suyua division of the Inca empire

Tahuantinsuyu name of the Inca empire

tambo an inn or rest-house

tarjeta telefónica telephone card

taxista taxi driver

Tiahuanaco a pre-Inca Peruvian culture

tumi a ceremonial Andean knife

urpu traditional fat-bellied pot with a curved base and long spout

usnu raised ceremonial square in an Inca city

vicuña undomesticated camelid living in high alpine areas of the Andes that is related to the llama and alpaca, with very fine wool

Valle Sagrado Sacred Valley of the Incas; lies along the Urubamba River, north of Cusco

Vilcanota alternative name for the upper Urubamba River

Villac Umu chief of the caste of priests in the Inca state religion

Viracocha the creator of the Incas and a key figure in Inca mythology, also the name of one of the early Incas

Wayrana style of building with one of its long sides open

APPENDIX D: RAIL INFORMATION

Traditionally, buses have been the cheapest and easiest way of getting around Peru, even if journeys take a long time and aren't always comfortable. However, there is no road access to Aguas Calientes, the gateway to Machu Picchu. Thus the only alternatives are to walk in or take the train. Not surprisingly, the train emerges as the only real option for many visitors. However, around the end of the 20th century the privatisation of the rail network saw the new owners, PeruRail, introduce restricted tourist services and much higher fares. Competition was finally introduced in the form of Inca Rail, though they have fewer services than PeruRail.

RAIL SERVICES

Timetables can change at short notice and occasionally there are enforced changes due to track damage or bad weather meaning that departure points, particularly from Cusco (Poroy) can also vary. In most instances, if the train can't run from a particular station, a replacement bus service will shuttle you to a new departure point. Before travelling, make sure to check operator timetables for up-to-date information and advice.

● **PeruRail** Currently PeruRail (💻 www.perurail.com) operates three services of their **blue-liveried tourist train** from the station at Poroy, 13km (8 miles) outside downtown Cusco (about a 20-minute drive; taxi s/30), through the Sacred Valley to Aguas Calientes. Sadly the trains no longer leave from the main station in Cusco meaning you miss out on the slow, scenic zigzag as the train ascends a series of switchbacks to leave the city. However, the majority of their services to Aguas Calientes operate from Ollantaytambo in the Sacred Valley. A taxi to Ollantaytambo from Cusco costs around s/80, bus s/10.

The 'budget' **Expedition service** (previously called the Backpacker) is the cheapest, see opposite. The **Vistadome service** has panoramic windows, complimentary drinks and snacks and takes slightly less time to complete the route but costs a little more.

The top-of-the-range ride is aboard the **Hiram Bingham**. The exorbitant fare (see opposite) entitles you to brunch and dinner in the opulent dining car, cocktails and live entertainment en route as well as guides; bus transfers from Aguas Calientes to Machu Picchu, entrance to the ruins and afternoon tea in the plush Machu Picchu Sanctuary Lodge. That's still a lot of money for a day trip, though. The Hiram Bingham service doesn't run on the last Sunday in each month.

Tickets can be bought from the main office at Portal de Carnes 214 on Plaza de Armas in Cusco, or from a subsidiary office at Calle Regocijo 202 on Plaza Regocijo; both are open daily 7am-10pm. PeruRail also has a stand at Cusco airport (6am-8pm) and in Lima at Jorge Chavez International Airport in the National Departures area on the 2nd Floor between gates 13 and 14 (daily 4am-8pm); there is also an office in Larcomar Mall on Malecon de la Reserva in Miraflores, Lima (daily 11am-10pm).

Tickets can also be bought at the stations in Poroy, Urubamba, Ollantaytambo and Aguas Calientes or **online** with a credit card. Print the e-voucher and take it along with your passport to the station at least an hour ahead of departure, where you can exchange it for a ticket. The e-voucher alone is not valid for travel.

PeruRail also run the train service that connects Aguas Calientes to La Hidroeléctrica. Tickets (from US$25 one way) can only be bought from the station in Aguas Calientes – though the service sometimes operates from the local railway station on Av Imperio de los Incas – or from the ticket office adjacent to the tracks at La Hidroeléctrica. **Note that we have had many reports of people being refused on this service – locals are usually given priority on this service rather than tourists.**

● **Inca Rail** (🖳 www.incarail.com) operates one service daily from Poroy via Ollantaytambo to Aguas Calientes and four others from Ollantaytambo to Aguas Calientes. **Tickets** can be bought from their office on Calle Portal de Panes 105 on Plaza de Armas in Cusco (☎ 581860) or from the station in Ollantaytambo (☎ 204211) and Poroy. You can also buy tickets online. They have four classes, Presidential, Executive, First and Premium economy; Presidential is only available on request.

TIMETABLES AND FARES

Bear in mind that the **timetables** below are subject to change at very short notice and are a guide rather than a rule. To get the most up-to-date information check locally at the railway stations or try visiting the respective company's website.

Unfortunately there aren't any ways of making these journeys cheaper. In real terms the **fares** are representative of what you might expect to pay for such a spectacular ride elsewhere in the world; they just seem hugely inflated by Peruvian standards.

1. PERURAIL

Cusco (Poroy) to Machu Picchu (Aguas Calientes)
Services are daily, except for the Hiram Bingham which does not run on the last Sunday of each month.

SERVICE NAME	TRAIN No	FARE (US$) ONE-WAY FROM	DEP CUSCO (POROY)	ARR MACHU PICCHU (AGUAS CALIENTES)
Vistadome	31	$95	06.40	09.54
Expedition	33	$80	07.35	10.52
Vistadome	203	$94	08.25	12.11
Hiram Bingham	11	$403	09.05	12.24

Machu Picchu (Aguas Calientes) to Cusco (Poroy)
Services are daily, except for the Hiram Bingham which does not run on the last Sunday of each month.

SERVICE NAME	TRAIN No	FARE (US$) ONE-WAY FROM	DEP MACHU PICCHU (AGUAS CALIENTES)	ARR CUSCO (POROY)
Vistadome	32	$84	15.20	19.05
Expedition	34	$85	16.43	20.23
Vistadome	604	$84	17.23	20.52
Hiram Bingham	12	$392	17.50	21.16

La Hidroeléctrica to Machu Picchu (Aguas Calientes)
Note: This service uses the local railway station in Aguas Calientes. Locals are usually given priority on this service rather than tourists – so it is very possible you won't be allowed to buy a ticket.

SERVICE NAME	TRAIN No	DEP LA HIDROELÉCTRICA	ARR MACHU PICCHU (AGUAS CALIENTES)
Expedition	72	07.53	08.35
Vistadome	504	15.00	15.42
Expedition	22	16.35	17.50

Machu Picchu (Aguas Calientes) to La Hidroeléctrica

Note: This service uses the local railway station in Aguas Calientes. Locals are usually given priority on this service rather than tourists – so it is very possible you won't be allowed to buy a ticket.

SERVICE NAME	TRAIN No	DEP MACHU PICCHU (AGUAS CALIENTES)	ARR LA HIDROELÉCTRICA
Expedition	71	06.44	07.20
Expedition	21	12.35	13.30
Vistadome	501	13.30	14.22

Ollantaytambo to Machu Picchu (Aguas Calientes)

Most train services operate from Ollantaytambo; trekking operators generally transfer clients from Cusco to Ollantaytambo by minibus if they're not already based in the Sacred Valley. PeruRail lays on occasional special trains between Ollantaytambo and Urubamba.

SERVICE NAME	TRAIN No	FARE (US$) ONE-WAY FROM	DEP OLLANTAYTAMBO	ARR MACHU PICCHU (AGUAS CALIENTES)
Expedition	71	$63	05.05	06.35
Expedition	81	$62	06.10	07.40
Vistadome	301	$81	07.05	08.27
Expedition	83	$68	07.45	09.15
Vistadome	601	$83	08.00	09.25
Vistadome	501	$83	08.53	10.29
Vistadome	203	$87	10.32	12.11
(fare plus buffet at the Sanctuary Lodge costs $114)				
Expedition	73	$61	12.55	14.25
Vistadome	303	$68	13.27	14.50
Vistadome	603	$65	15.37	17.02
Expedition	75	$64	19.04	20.45
Expedition	51	$58	21.00	22.45

Machu Picchu (Aguas Calientes) to Ollantaytambo

SERVICE NAME	TRAIN No	FARE (US$) ONE-WAY FROM	DEP MACHU PICCHU (AGUAS CALIENTES)	ARR OLLANTAYTAMBO
Expedition	50	$53	05.35	07.44
Expedition	72	$55	08.53	10.52
Vistadome	302	$72	10.55	12.32
Vistadome	204	$77	13.37	15.04
Expedition	74	$74	14.55	16.31
Vistadome	304	$93	15.48	17.29
Vistadome	504	$76	16.22	18.01
Vistadome	606	$76	18.10	19.51
Expedition	84	$66	18.20	20.05
Expedition	76	$60	21.50	23.35

Urubamba to Machu Picchu (Aguas Calientes)

Most train services operate from Ollantaytambo but there are a few from Urubamba.

SERVICE NAME	TRAIN No	FARE (US$) ONE-WAY FROM	DEP URUBAMBA	ARR MACHU PICCHU (AGUAS CALIENTES)
Vistadome	601	$94	06.50	09.24
Sacred Valley	91	$200	10.30	13.34

Machu Picchu (Aguas Calientes) to Urubamba

SERVICE NAME	TRAIN No	FARE (US$) ONE-WAY FROM	DEP MACHU PICCHU (AGUAS CALIENTES)	ARR URUBAMBA
Vistadome	304	$103	15.48	18.43
Sacred Valley	92	$200	19.30	22.37

Between Cusco and Puno (Lake Titicaca)

This is one of the highest passenger railway routes in the world: at its highest point, La Raya, the altitude is 4313m/14,146ft. The luxurious **Andean Explorer** train, decorated in the style of the Pullman trains of the 1920s, leaves Cusco for Puno from Huanchac Station on Monday, Wednesday and Saturday at 8am and gets to Puno at 6pm. During the high season (Apr-Oct) there is an additional departure on Friday.

Trains from Puno to Cusco also depart on Monday, Wednesday and Saturday at 8am and arrive in Cusco at 6.30pm. Again, during the high season there is an additional departure on Friday.

Tickets cost US$292 from Cusco to Puno and US$176 from Puno to Cusco and include a three-course lunch.

2. INCA RAIL

Ollantaytambo to Machu Picchu (Aguas Calientes)

CLASS	FARE (US$) ONE-WAY	DEP OLLANTAYTAMBO	ARR MACHU PICCHU (AGUAS CALIENTES)
Executive	$62	06.40	08.01
Premium Economy	$60	07.20	08.48
Executive	$57	11.15	12.45
/First	$135		
Premium Economy	$60	12.36	14.00
Executive	$61	16.36	18.09

Machu Picchu (Aguas Calientes) to Ollantaytambo

CLASS	FARE (US$) ONE-WAY	DEP MACHU PICCHU (AGUAS CALIENTES)	ARR OLLANTAYTAMBO
Executive	$51	08.30	10.10
Premium economy	$53	10.32	12.09
Executive	$63	14.30	16.04
Premium economy	$63	16.12	17.50
Executive	$62	19.00	20.32
/First	$135		

Poroy to Machu Picchu (Aguas Calientes)

CLASS	FARE (US$) ONE-WAY	DEP POROY	ARR MACHU PICCHU (AGUAS CALIENTES)
Premium Economy	$73	05.55	08.48

Machu Picchu (Aguas Calientes) to Poroy

CLASS	FARE (US$) ONE-WAY	DEP MACHU PICCHU (AGUAS CALIENTES)	ARR POROY
Premium Economy	$85	16.12	19.38

APPENDIX E: GPS WAYPOINTS

Each GPS waypoint below was taken on the route at the reference number marked on the map as below. This list of GPS waypoints is also available to download from the Trailblazer website – 🖳 www.trailblazer-guides.com.

See p214 for more information.

MAP	REF	LATITUDE	LONGITUDE	LOCATION
The classic Inca Trail and variations				
1	01	13° 13'34"S	72° 26'10"W	Km88 – disembark from the train and cross the bridge
	02	13° 13'53"S	72° 25'30"W	Patallacta
	03	13° 14'08"S	72° 25'24"W	Huillca Raccay
	04	13° 15'25"S	72° 26'34"W	Hatun Chaca
	05	13° 15'51"S	72° 26'49"W	Huayllabamba
2	06	13° 15'01"S	72° 28'18"W	Llulluchapampa campsite
	07	13° 14'32"S	72° 29'03"W	Abra de Huarmihuanusca (First Pass)
	08	13° 14'01"S	72° 29'53"W	Pacamayo campsite
	09	13° 13'42"S	72° 30'06"W	Runcu Raccay
3	10	13° 13'36"S	72° 30'18"W	Second Pass
	11	13° 13'41"S	72° 31'01"W	Sayac Marca
	12	13° 13'36"S	72° 30'57"W	Concha Marca
	13	13° 13'21"S	72° 31'10"W	Chaquicocha campsite
	14	13° 12'37"S	72° 31'38"W	Inca Tunnel
	15	13° 12'24"S	72° 31'56"W	Third Pass and Phuyu Pata Marca
4	16	13° 11'13"S	72° 32'28"W	Intipata
	17	13° 11'35"S	72° 32'10"W	Huinay Huayna
	18	13° 11'24"S	72° 32'13"W	Old Trekkers' Hotel
	19	13° 10'13"S	72° 32'06"W	Intipunku
	20	13° 09'57"S	72° 32'44"W	Machu Picchu
	21	13° 09'21"S	72° 32'45"W	Huayna Picchu
	22	13° 11'09"S	72° 30'30"W	Km104 – disembark from the train and cross the bridge
	23	13° 11'10"S	72° 30'37"W	Chachabamba
	24	13° 11'15"S	72° 31'51"W	Choquesuysuy
5	25	13° 12'57"S	72° 23'02"W	Km82 – disembark from the train or bus and cross the bridge
	26	13° 13'52"S	72° 24'18"W	Football pitch
	27	13° 14'08"S	72° 25'24"W	Huillca Raccay
	28	13° 13'53"S	72° 25'30"W	Patallacta
The High Inca Trail				
6	29	13° 30'32"S	72° 31'40"W	Mollepata Plaza de Armas
	30	13° 27'16"S	72° 32'21"W	Marcoccasa
7	31	13° 23'40"S	72° 34'28"W	Salkantay Lodge & Adventure Resort
8	32	13° 21'59"S	72° 33'35"W	Salkantay Pampa
	33	13° 21'26"S	72° 32'22"W	Inka Chiriasqa Pass
9	34	13° 19'55"S	72° 28'26"W	Pampa Cahuana
10	35	13° 16'49"S	72° 27'00"W	Paucarcancha
	36	13° 15'51"S	72° 26'49"W	Huayllabamba

MAP	REF	LATITUDE	LONGITUDE	LOCATION
The Salkantay Trek				
6	29	13° 30'32"S	72° 31'40"W	Mollepata Plaza de Armas
	30	13° 27'16"S	72° 32'21"W	Marcoccasa
7	31	13° 23'40"S	72° 34'28"W	Salkantay Lodge & Adventure Resort
8	32	13° 21'59"S	72° 33'35"W	Salkantay Pampa
11	37	13° 21' 43"S	72° 33'39"W	Top of Siete Culebras
	38	13° 21'28"S	72° 33'57"W	Soroyccocha campsite
	39	13° 20'58"S	72° 33'58"W	Salkantay Pass
	40	13° 20'58"S	72° 34'58"W	Pampa opens out after boulder field
12	41	13° 19'58"S	72° 36'12"W	Huayraqumachay campsite
	42	13° 18'50"S	72° 38'16"W	Rayampata
	43	13° 19'02"S	72° 38'47"W	Campsite on old terraces
	44	13° 19'51"S	72° 39'51"W	Chaullay and Colpa Lodge access
	45	13° 19'10"S	72° 40'14"W	Ccolpapampa
	46	13° 18'59"S	72° 40'10"W	Turn left onto dirt track from road
	47	13° 18'18"S	72° 39'31"W	Cross by waterfall
13	48	13° 17'50"S	72° 38'56"W	Winay Poccos
	49	13° 15'09"S	72° 38'16"W	Rest Place Shopping Centre
	50	13° 13'59"S	72° 37'56"W	Playa Sawayaco town square
14	51	13° 12'51"S	72° 37'04"W	Lucmabamba turn off track
15	52	13° 11'16"S	72° 35'36"W	Ridge top
	53	13° 11'14"S	72° 35'07"W	Llactapata
	54	13° 11'13"S	72° 34'58"W	Clearing, viewpoint and campsite
	55	13° 11'22"S	72° 34'32"W	Cross Río Aobamba on suspension bridge
	56	13° 10'24"S	72° 33'44"W	Checkpoint
	57	13° 10'28"S	72° 33'24"W	La Hidroeléctrica railway station
	58	13° 09'15"S	72° 31'36"W	Puente Ruinas railway station
	59	13° 09'57"S	72° 32'44"W	Machu Picchu
The Lares Trek				
16	60	13° 18'40"S	72° 01'35"W	Huaran
17	61	13° 13'50"S	72° 01'29"W	Cancha Cancha
	62	13° 12'12"S	72° 00'44"W	Abra Pachachutec
18	63	13° 09'37"S	72° 01'52"W	Quishuarani
19	64	13° 09'16"S	72° 03'18"W	Abra Huillquijasa
	65	13° 09'35"S	72° 04'49"W	Cuncani
20	66	13° 07'23"S	72° 04'52"W	Junction
	67	13° 06'36"S	72° 03'17"W	Thermal baths at Lares
21	68	13° 08'22"S	72° 06'30"W	Bridge at Huacahuasi
22	69	13° 10'45"S	72° 08'54"W	Abra Huascahuasijasa
	70	13° 11'03"S	72° 09'03"W	Laguna Aruraycocha
	71	13° 11'54"S	72° 09'26"W	Laguna Millpo
23	72	13° 16'40"S	72° 11'08"W	Main road at Yanahuara

MAP	REF	LATITUDE	LONGITUDE	LOCATION

The Choquequirao Trek

MAP	REF	LATITUDE	LONGITUDE	LOCATION
24	73	13° 30'43"S	72° 48'46"W	Cachora Plaza de Armas
25	74	13° 26'36"S	72° 48'38"W	Capuliyoc Pass
	75	13° 25'46"S	72° 50'29"W	Chiquisca campsite
26	76	13° 25'19"S	72° 51'12"W	Playa Rosalina campsite & river crossing point
	77	13° 24'49"S	72° 50'54"W	Santa Rosa Baja
	78	13° 23'59"S	72° 51'28"W	Marampata
	79	13° 23'35"S	72° 52'25"W	Choquequirao

The Ausangate Trek

MAP	REF	LATITUDE	LONGITUDE	LOCATION
27	80	13° 42'34"S	71° 18'22"W	Football pitch at Upis
28	81	13° 45'04"S	71° 16'27"W	Thermal baths
29	82	13° 46'34"S	71° 16'29"W	Abra Arapa
30	83	13° 49'10"S	71° 14'37"W	Abra Ausangate
	84	13° 49'00"S	71° 13'22"W	Abra Palomani
31	85	13° 49'32"S	71° 11'27"W	Pampacancha
32	86	13° 46'05"S	71° 10'34"W	Abra Jampa/Champa
33	87	13° 44'29"S	71° 13'54"W	Acosere village
34	88	13° 43'07"S	71° 14'31"W	Pacchanta

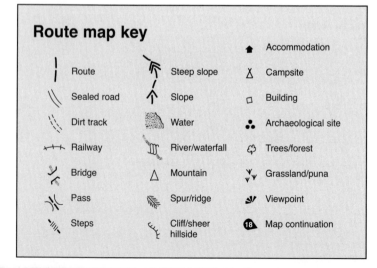

Route map key

Route	Steep slope	♠ Accommodation
Sealed road	Slope	Χ Campsite
Dirt track	Water	▢ Building
Railway	River/waterfall	⁘ Archaeological site
Bridge	Mountain	⌘ Trees/forest
Pass	Spur/ridge	Grassland/puna
Steps	Cliff/sheer hillside	Viewpoint
		Map continuation

INDEX

Page references in **bold** type refer to maps

The symbol used at the start of each section of this book is the *Chakana* or Inca Cross,
the Inca equivalent of the Tree of Life. The three steps on each side symbolise
Hana Pacha (the abode of the gods), *Kay Pacha* (the world of men) and
Ucu Pacha (the underworld or spirit world). The hole through the centre represents the
centre of the Inca empire: Cusco; it also stands for the Southern Cross constellation.

TRAILBLAZER TREKKING GUIDES

Europe
British Walking Guides – 17-title series
Scottish Highlands – The Hillwalking Guide
Tour du Mont Blanc
Walker's Haute Route: Mt Blanc – Matterhorn

South America
Inca Trail, Cusco & Machu Picchu
Peru's Cordilleras Blanca & Huayhuash

Africa
Kilimanjaro
Moroccan Atlas – The Trekking Guide

Asia
Nepal Trekking & The Great Himalaya Trail
Sinai – the trekking guide
Trekking in the Everest Region

Australasia
New Zealand – The Great Walks

Peru's Cordilleras Blanca & Huayhuash
The Hiking & Biking Guide
Neil & Harriet Pike, 1st edn, £15.99
ISBN 978-1-905864-63-8, 242pp, 50 maps, 40 colour photos
This region, in northern Peru, boasts some of the most spectacular scenery in the Andes, and most accessible high mountain trekking and biking in the world. This practical guide contains 60 detailed route maps and descriptions covering 20 hiking trails and more than 30 days of paved and dirt road cycling.

Kilimanjaro – the trekking guide
Henry Stedman, 5th edn, £14.99 – **new edn Jan 2018**
ISBN 978-1-905864-95-9, 368pp, 40 maps, 50 colour photos
At 5895m (19,340ft) Kilimanjaro is the world's tallest freestanding mountain and one of the most popular destinations for hikers visiting Africa. Route guides & maps – the 6 major routes. City guides – Nairobi, Dar-es-Salaam, Arusha, Moshi & Marangu.

Sinai – the trekking guide *Ben Hoffler,* 1st edn, £14.99
ISBN 978-1-905864-41-6, 288pp, 74 maps, 30 colour photos
Trek with the Bedouin and their camels and discover one of the most exciting new trekking destinations. The best routes in the High Mountain Region (St. Katherine), Wadi Feiran and the Muzeina deserts. Once you finish on the trail there are the nearby coastal resorts of Sharm el Sheikh, Dahab and Nuweiba to enjoy.

Moroccan Atlas – the trekking guide
Alan Palmer, 2nd edn, £14.99
ISBN 978-1-905864-59-1, 420pp, 86 maps, 40 colour photos
The High Atlas in central Morocco is the most dramatic and beautiful section of the entire Atlas range. Towering peaks, deep gorges and huddled Berber villages enchant all who visit. With 73 detailed trekking maps, 13 town and village guides including Marrakech.

Trekking in the Everest Region
Jamie McGuinness 6th edn, £14.99 – **new edn Oct 2017**
ISBN 978-1-905864-81-2, 320pp, 95 maps, 30 colour photos
Sixth edition of this popular guide to the world's most famous trekking region. Covers not only the classic treks but also the wild routes. Written by a Nepal-based trek and mountaineering leader. Includes: 27 detailed route maps and 52 village plans. Plus: Kathmandu city guide

TRAILBLAZER'S LONG-DISTANCE PATH (LDP) WALKING GUIDES

We've applied to destinations which are closer to home Trailblazer's proven formula for publishing definitive practical route guides for adventurous travellers. Britain's network of long-distance trails enables the walker to explore some of the finest landscapes in the country's best walking areas. These are guides that are user-friendly, practical, informative and environmentally sensitive.

● **Unique mapping features** In many walking guidebooks the reader has to read a route description then try to relate it to the map. Our guides are much easier to use because walking directions, tricky junctions, places to stay and eat, points of interest and walking times are all written onto the maps themselves in the places to which they apply. With their uncluttered clarity, these are not general-purpose maps but fully edited maps drawn by walkers for walkers.

● **Largest-scale walking maps** At a scale of just under 1:20,000 (8cm or 3^1/$_8$ inches to one mile) the maps in these guides are bigger than even the most detailed British walking maps currently available in the shops.

● **Not just a trail guide – includes where to stay, where to eat and public transport** Our guidebooks cover the complete walking experience, not just the route. Accommodation options for all budgets are provided (pubs, hotels, B&Bs, campsites, bunkhouses, hostels) as well as places to eat. Detailed public transport information for all access points to each trail means that there are itineraries for all walkers, for hiking the entire route as well as for day or weekend walks.

Coast to Coast *Henry Stedman*, 7th edition, £11.99
ISBN 978-1-905864-74-4, 268pp, 110 maps, 40 colour photos

Cornwall Coast Path (SW Coast Path Pt 2) *Stedman & Newton*, 5th edition, £11.99
ISBN 978-1-905864-71-3, 3526pp, 142 maps, 40 colour photos

Cotswold Way *Tricia & Bob Hayne* 3rd edition, £11.99
ISBN 978-1-905864-70-6, 204pp, 53 maps, 40 colour photos

Dales Way *Henry Stedman* 1st edition, £11.99
ISBN 978-1-905864-78-2, 176pp, 45 maps, 40 colour photos

Dorset & South Devon (SW Coast Path Pt 3) *Stedman & Newton*, £11.99
ISBN 978-1-905864-45-4, 336pp, 88 maps, 40 colour photos

Exmoor & North Devon (SW Coast Path Pt I) *Stedman & Newton*, 2nd edition, £11.99
ISBN 978-1-905864-86-7, 224pp, 68 maps, 40 colour photos

Great Glen Way *Jim Manthorpe*, 1st edition, £11.99
ISBN 978-1-905864-80-5, 192pp, 55 maps, 40 colour photos

Hadrian's Wall Path *Henry Stedman*, 4th edition, £11.99
ISBN 978-1-905864-58-4, 224pp, 60 maps, 40 colour photos

Offa's Dyke Path *Keith Carter*, 4th edition, £11.99
ISBN 978-1-905864-65-2, 240pp, 98 maps, 40 colour photos

Peddars Way & Norfolk Coast Path *Alexander Stewart*, £11.99
ISBN 978-1-905864-28-7, 192pp, 54 maps, 40 colour photos

Pembrokeshire Coast Path *Jim Manthorpe*, 4th edition, £11.99
ISBN 978-1-905864-51-5, 224pp, 96 maps, 40 colour photos

Pennine Way *Stuart Greig*, 4th edition, £11.99
ISBN 978-1-905864-61-4, 272pp, 138 maps, 40 colour photos

The Ridgeway *Nick Hill*, 4th edition, £11.99
ISBN 978-1-905864-79-9, 208pp, 53 maps, 40 colour photos

South Downs Way *Jim Manthorpe*, 5th edition, £11.99
ISBN 978-1-905864-66-9, 192pp, 60 maps, 40 colour photos

Thames Path *Joel Newton*, 1st edition, £11.99
ISBN 978-1-905864-64-5, 256pp, 99 maps, 40 colour photos

West Highland Way *Charlie Loram*, 6th edition, £11.99
ISBN 978-1-905864-76-8, 208pp, 60 maps, 40 colour photos

'The same attention to detail that distinguishes its other guides has been brought to bear here'.

THE
SUNDAY TIMES

IN PREPARATION
FOR PUBLICATION IN
2018
Cleveland Way
ISBN 978-1-905864-91-1

North Downs Way
ISBN 978-1-905864-90-4

TRAILBLAZER TITLE LIST

Adventure Cycle-Touring Handbook
Adventure Motorcycling Handbook
Australia by Rail
Cleveland Way (British Walking Guide) – due 2018
Coast to Coast (British Walking Guide)
Cornwall Coast Path (British Walking Guide)
Cotswold Way (British Walking Guide)
The Cyclist's Anthology
Dales Way (British Walking Guide)
Dorset & Sth Devon Coast Path (British Walking Gde)
Exmoor & Nth Devon Coast Path (British Walking Gde)
Great Glen Way (British Walking Guide)
Hadrian's Wall Path (British Walking Guide)
Himalaya by Bike – a route and planning guide
Inca Trail, Cusco & Machu Picchu
Japan by Rail
Kilimanjaro – the trekking guide (includes Mt Meru)
Moroccan Atlas – The Trekking Guide
Morocco Overland (4x4/motorcycle/mountainbike)
Nepal Trekking & The Great Himalaya Trail
New Zealand – The Great Walks
North Downs Way (British Walking Guide) – due 2018
Offa's Dyke Path (British Walking Guide)
Overlanders' Handbook – worldwide driving guide
Peddars Way & Norfolk Coast Path (British Walking Gde)
Pembrokeshire Coast Path (British Walking Guide)
Pennine Way (British Walking Guide)
Peru's Cordilleras Blanca & Huayhuash – Hiking/Biking
The Railway Anthology
The Ridgeway (British Walking Guide)
Sahara Overland – a route and planning guide
Scottish Highlands – Hillwalking Guide
Siberian BAM Guide – rail, rivers & road
The Silk Roads – a route and planning guide
Sinai – the trekking guide
South Downs Way (British Walking Guide)
Thames Path (British Walking Guide)
Tour du Mont Blanc
Trans-Canada Rail Guide
Trans-Siberian Handbook
Trekking in the Everest Region
The Walker's Anthology
The Walker's Anthology – further tales
The Walker's Haute Route – Mont Blanc to Matterhorn
West Highland Way (British Walking Guide)

For more information about Trailblazer and our
expanding range of guides, for guidebook updates or
for credit card mail order sales visit our website:

www.trailblazer-guides.com